Bible Interpretation and the African Culture

Bible Interpretation and the African Culture

Gospel Reception Among the Pökot People of Kenya

David J. Ndegwah

RESOURCE *Publications* • Eugene, Oregon

BIBLE INTERPRETATION AND THE AFRICAN CULTURE
Gospel Reception Among the Pökot People of Kenya

Copyright © 2020 David J. Ndegwah. All rights reserved. Except for brief quotations in critical publications or reviews, no part of this book may be reproduced in any manner without prior written permission from the publisher. Write: Permissions, Wipf and Stock Publishers, 199 W. 8th Ave., Suite 3, Eugene, OR 97401.

Resource Publications
An Imprint of Wipf and Stock Publishers
199 W. 8th Ave., Suite 3
Eugene, OR 97401

www.wipfandstock.com

PAPERBACK ISBN: 978-1-5326-1141-4
HARDCOVER ISBN: 978-1-5326-1143-8
EBOOK ISBN: 978-1-5326-1142-1

Manufactured in the U.S.A.   01/07/20

To my wife, Evelyne Cherotich Koech; daughters, Daisy Nyamburah Ndegwah and Kimberly Muthoni Ndegwah; and parents, Philomena Nyambura Ndegwa and Simon Ndegwa Gaitĩu. With gratitude and love.

CONTENTS

Preface | xiii
Acknowledgments | xvii
Abbreviations | xix

CHAPTER 1: GENERAL INTRODUCTION

1.1   Rationale and Motivation | 1
1.2   The *Status Questionis* and Our Objectives | 5
1.3   The Research Issue and Questions | 10
1.4   Definition of Key Concepts | 11
1.5   Strategies in this Research | 20
1.5.1   The Grounded Theory Approach | 21
1.5.2   The Qualitative Research Method | 22
1.6   The Social Situation | 23
1.6.1   The Place | 23
1.6.2   The Actors | 24
1.6.3   The Activities | 25
1.7   Methods and Sources | 28
1.7.1   Data Collection | 29
1.7.2   Data Analysis | 31
1.7.3   Literature Review and Theological Reflections | 33
1.8   Organization of the Study | 33

CHAPTER 2: THEORY AND PRACTICE OF INCULTURATION IN AFRICA

2.1   Introduction | 36
2.2   The Meaning and Purpose of Inculturation | 37
2.2.1   What Inculturation is not and How to Approach it | 39
2.2.2   The Extent and Scope of Inculturation | 42

2.2.3   Obstacles to Inculturation | 43
2.3   A Brief History of Inculturation in Kenya | 51
2.3.1   Suppression of the African Culture | 53
2.3.2   Why the Suppression of the African Culture? | 55
2.3.3   Emergence of Cultural Schizophrenia | 57
2.3.4   Appreciation of the African Culture | 59
2.4   The Use of the Bible in Africa | 61
2.4.1   Biblical Hermeneutics in Africa | 62
2.4.2   Development of an African Biblical Hermeneutics | 67
2.4.3   Characteristics and Requirements for an African Hermeneutics | 69
2.5   The Understanding of Culture Today | 72
2.5.1   Modern and Post-modern Understanding of Culture | 72
2.5.2   Organization of Diversity | 74
2.5.3   Culture, Evangelization and Mission | 77
2.6   Communitarianism in the African Culture | 78
2.6.1   Communitarianism in African Anthropology | 79
2.6.2   Communitarianism in African Philosophy | 80
2.6.3   Communitarianism in African Theology | 93
2.7   Conclusion | 100

CHAPTER 3: THE PEOPLE AND SOCIAL CONTEXT OF WEST PÖKOT

3.1   Introduction | 102
3.2   Literature on the Pökot People | 102
3.3   Location and Topography | 105
3.3.1   Rainfall Distribution, Relief and Drainage | 106
3.3.2   Socio-Economic Development | 108
3.4   Description of the Pökot Lifestyle | 109
3.4.1   Unity and Identity of the Pökot People | 113
3.4.2   The *Shared* Elements Among the Pökot | 113
3.4.3   The Future of Pastoralism and Threat of 'Civilization' | 115
3.5   The Pökot Concept of Ownership | 117
3.5.1   The Pökot *Tilya* System (Economic Relationship) | 118
3.5.2   The Kinds of *Tilya* | 120
3.6   Political Governance and Social Life | 123
3.6.1   Social Divisions and Classifications | 125

3.6.2   The Age-Set System | 129
3.7   The Pökot Astronomy | 131
3.8   *Chi* (The Pökot Concept of a Person) | 132
3.9   The Pökot Belief System and Religious Practice | 135
3.10   The Pökot Cultural Values | 138
3.10.1 *Tany* (The Cow) | 138
3.10.2 Relationship Between Cows and Women | 140
3.11   Side Effects of Pökot Cultural Values | 141
3.12   The Pökot Social Wisdom | 146
3.13   The Rites of Passage | 147
3.14   *Pöghisyö* (Harmony) as the Goal of Life | 149
3.15   Moral Uprightness in the Pökot Community | 150
3.15.1 *Poyon Nyole Pöghïn* (A Good Man) | 151
3.15.2 *Korka Nyole Tingän* (An Industrious Woman) | 151
3.16   Ritual Purity and Appeal to the Supernatural | 152
3.17   Evil and Uncleanness | 153
3.18   Immorality in the Pökot Community | 156
3.19   Pökot Culture and the Challenge of Modernity | 157
3.19.1 Respect | 158
3.19.2 Education, Religion and Social Demeanor | 159
3.19.3 The Rites of Passage and Economy | 160
3.20   Conclusion | 161

CHAPTER 4: THE PÖKOT UNDERSTANDING OF JOHN 10:1–16

4.1   Introduction | 164
4.2   Communitarianism in the Pökot Worldview | 166
4.2.1   Analysis of Verbal Sources | 166
4.2.2   Analysis of Material Sources | 171
4.2.3   Analysis of Behavioral Sources | 171
4.3   Individualism in the Pökot Worldview | 183
4.3.1   Analysis of Verbal Sources | 183
4.3.2   Analysis of Material Sources | 187
4.3.3   Analysis of Behavioral Sources | 189
4.4   Interpretation of John 10:1–16 in the SCCs | 193
4.5   Individualistic Influence of the Lumko Method | 197
4.5.1   Cultural Traits in the Pericope | 197

4.5.2 Inculturation of the Pericope | 199
4.5.3 The Understanding of the Concept "Shepherd" | 201
4.5.4 The Relevance of John 10:1–16 to the Life of a Pöchon | 203
4.5.5 The Role of a Shepherd in the Pökot Community | 204
4.5.6 The Place of a Shepherd in the Pökot Community | 206
4.6 Conclusion | 209

CHAPTER 5: PASTORS' INTERPRETATION OF JOHN 10:1–16

5.1 Introduction | 211
5.2 A Brief Historical Overview of Evangelization in West Pökot | 212
5.2.1 Challenges to Evangelization | 213
5.2.2 The Mission of the Protestant Churches in West Pökot | 217
5.3 Analysis of the Homilies | 220
5.3.1 Word Count | 221
5.3.2 The Understanding of the Concept "Shepherd" | 222
5.3.3 The Problem of Translation | 223
5.3.4 Relevance of John 10:1–16 to a Pastor's Life | 225
5.3.5 The Place of a Shepherd Among the Pastors | 226
5.3.6 The Role of a Shepherd Among the Pastors | 227
5.3.7 Cultural Traits in the Pericope | 228
5.3.8 Inculturation of the Pericope | 229
5.4 Analysis of Commentaries | 230
5.4.1 Commentaries on the Good Shepherd | 231
5.4.2 The Understanding of the Concept "Shepherd" | 232
5.4.3 Cultural Traits in the Pericope | 233
5.4.4 Inculturation of the Pericope | 234
5.5 Religious Practice Among the Pastors in West Pökot | 235
5.5.1 The Know-it-all Attitude | 236
5.5.2 A Segregatory Exclusivist Attitude | 238
5.5.3 Manifestation of Power and Control | 240
5.5.4 General Observation on Preaching Practices | 241
5.6 Pastors' Interpretation of John 10:1–16 | 242
5.6.1 Individual Nature of Sin | 242
5.6.2 Individual Accomplishments of the Shepherd | 243
5.6.3 Preaching to Christians Individually | 245
5.6.4 Pastors as the Good Shepherd | 245

5.6.3   Abstract Conceptualization in Preaching | 246
5.6.6   Individual Reward-centered Preaching | 247
5.6.7   Individualistic Appeal of the Christian Faith | 248
5.6.8   Matters of Faith and Social Life | 248
5.6.9   Communitarian and Individualistic Interpretation | 249
5.7   Training in Seminaries and Catechetical Institutes | 250
5.7.1   Seminary Formation | 251
5.7.2   Fear and Despondency | 253
5.7.3   Catechetical Training | 256
5.8   Tension Between People's and their Pastors' Religious Practices | 257
5.8.1   Sunday Celebration of the Liturgy | 257
5.8.2   The Method of Preaching | 257
5.8.3   Conceptual and Cultural Conflicts | 258
5.9   Conclusion | 263

CHAPTER 6: TOWARD A COMMUNITARIAN HERMENEUTICS

6.1   Introduction | 264
6.2   Tension Between Two Worldviews | 265
6.3   Theology of Reconstruction | 270
6.4   The Concept of Deconstruction | 274
6.5   Communitarianism Among the Pökot | 281
6.5.1   The Strength of Communitarianism | 284
6.5.2   The Weakness of Communitarianism | 286
6.6   Inculturation Among the Pökot People | 289
6.6.1   Communitarianism and *Lük* (Cattle Rustling) | 290
6.6.2   Communitarianism and *Kokwö* (Council of Elders) | 297
6.7   Communitarianism and Intercultural Hermeneutics | 301
6.8   Conclusion | 303

General Conclusion | 305

Glossary | 311
Appendices | 319
Bibliography | 333
Index | 353

PREFACE

The resolve to take up the challenge of this research was prompted by something that occurred by chance. In 1999, we were asked to teach the course on Bible, in an acting capacity, at Christ the Teacher Institute for Education (in Tangaza College, a constituent college of the Catholic University of Eastern Africa—CUEA), in Langata—Nairobi (Kenya). Our interaction with the students, most of whom were religious brothers and sisters, revealed one startling thing. For them, the Bible was just a piece of foreign literature that did not have much relevance to their real life. This contention was vividly manifested in the term papers that they had to write every semester, which showed total inability for them to contextualize and interpret various bible passages within their own life situations. This was shocking, considering who they were—part of the religious leadership in Africa (since they comprised students from East, Central and West Africa).

Of immediate concern was the future of the Church in Africa and its seemingly doomed prospects, and the urge for a suitable answer could not go away. After two years of mind-boggling reflections, it became clear that the answer lay in the way they read and interpreted the scriptures—and with it biblical hermeneutics became the obvious culprit and the way forward at the same time. When people encounter new ideas, events, people and texts, including biblical texts, they perceive and conceptualize them in accordance with their worldview, which is in turn shaped by their culture that is modelled to suit various geographical locations; even as geography shapes it. Thus, culture, more than geographical locations, has played and continues to play an important role in the way the Bible is read and interpreted in Africa. This is why when we got a scholarship to study theology at the newly started Graduate School of Theology, Radboud University Nijmegen—The Netherlands, the topic of biblical hermeneutics became a natural choice.

In this research, the work has been divided into small manageable bits that ended up as five chapters. The first chapter is conceptual in nature, and dwells on the philosophical-theological debate in Africa, particularly the issues of inculturation, culture and the question of communitarianism in relation to the development of an African hermeneutics. It, therefore, deals with a short history of theology and philosophy in Africa, where it is shown that Christianity was introduced in many parts of Kenya and in West Pökot (in north-western Kenya) in particular, at the same time with the colonial occupation, sending mixed signals to the indigenous inhabitants.

Just as colonialism uprooted the people and disrupted their social order, so did Christianity interfere and demonize their cultural and religious order. The end result was a double religious allegiance, which has been referred to as cultural schizophrenia, because it was based on obedience to the African culture on the one hand, and allegiance to the Christian culture on the other hand. This topic was not pursued in greater details as to the nitty-gritty of what needs to be done, but the need for a different kind of approach to bible interpretation was highlighted, and later termed as communitarian hermeneutics. The dominant feeling was that the Pökot worldview is a communitarian one, and yet the Pökot were introduced to individualistic hermeneutics, which is at loggerheads with their communal aspirations.

Then there was a brief mention of the relationship between the two biblical sciences, of exegesis and hermeneutics, and the fact of their interdependence. On the one hand, exegesis focuses on the production of a biblical text—authorship, when and where it was written, its meaning at the time, its audience and reason(s) for writing it. Hermeneutics, on the other hand, focuses on its reception—how the reader understands an ancient text today and the factors that influence this understanding.

Under examination also, was the role of biblical hermeneutics in the dissemination of the Word of God by the church in Africa and the need to develop a distinctly African biblical hermeneutics. The research did not, however, dwell on the exact boundaries of the relationship between hermeneutics and exegesis because its main interest is hermeneutics, which was further distinguishable as a practice—'hermeneusis' and as a theory—'hermeneutics'. As a practice, the interest was how the people of West Pökot read and interpret the Bible, using a particular bible text of John 10:1–16, an effort that was meant to develop a relevant and effective theory.

The second chapter serves as the hinge of this research and it is descriptive in nature because its purpose is transforming the reader's thoughts from academic hermeneutical debate to the situation on the ground. It does this by introducing the reader to the location of West Pökot, in Kenya, and the general life style of the people there. This includes their traditional values, the nature of their society and in particular their religious practices, which enables the reader to look at the people from a bird's eye view and compare their cultural and religious practices with those of Christianity. Of particular importance to be mentioned was the geographical location, the concept of ownership, the rites of passage and the concept of evil in relation to ritual purity, believed to emanate from community's ability to maintain a balance between natural and supernatural forces.

Chapters three and four are anthropological in nature and they form the backbone of this field research. They dwell on the method of ethnography that helped the researcher to understand the Pökot community and the way people interpret the scripture vis-à-vis the interpretation methods of their pastors. The third chapter analyzed and described the results of our fieldwork that was carried out in West Pökot for a period of six months, between March and August 2002. We presented the aforementioned text from the Bible (Jn 10: 1–16) and listened as the Pökot people shared their understanding and its application to their daily lives. Here, insights from Spradley's method of social analysis and the Kwalitan computer program, were used in order to know how much cultural traits have (or have not) penetrated into their interpretation of the Bible.

The major lesson we learned here was that the Pökot community is not purely communitarian as we previously had presumed. There was, therefore, a need to deconstruct our own mode of thinking where we underwent a personal 'fusion of horizons' (*Horizontverschmelzung*), in the sense of Gadamer's new prejudgment (*Vorverständnis*). This led to a new predisposition toward the nature of the Pökot community by realizing that the situation on the ground is more complex than many scholars would admit. Although the Pökot communitarianism is dotted with several traits of individualism, the overall contention is that the Pökot are more communitarian than individualistic. It was, however, observed that people have not managed to internalize the Gospel and to make it part of their daily life. They still see it as a foreign imposition into their otherwise blissful social decorum. Hence, we treated this as a confirmation of our earlier observation that there is a need to adopt a different method of evangelization that would make the Gospel 'feel at home' among the people of West Pökot in particular and among Africans in general.

Chapter four is a report of the results of the same bible text, which was presented to the pastors in the same region and their sharing recorded, mainly during Sunday sermons. They were then interviewed in private with regard to these sermons and generally their lifestyle vis-à-vis that of their flock was observed. There were a number of differences between the people and their pastors, notwithstanding the fact that some pastors do really try to be part and parcel of their flock and present the Gospel from the vantage point of the local people. Many, however, do not succeed in doing this, particularly to incorporate themselves into the Pökot culture. Among the many reasons that contribute to this state of affairs is the attitude that Christians do not know anything in theology and as such cannot be looked upon to offer any insight in the understanding of the Gospel.

Then it was discovered that the general way of interpreting the Gospel among the pastors is predominantly individualistic. This is in direct opposition to the predominantly communitarian way of bible interpretation among the Christians. One of the difficulties that the pastors face is that most of them have not managed to master the Pökot language and to interpret the Bible from a communitarian perspective. Most of them cannot say Mass in the Pökot language, let alone preach and communicate with the people they call their parishioners in their mother tongue. This causes many cultural tensions that find their way into the very nature of faith as practiced here.

Chapter five is a correlational interplay between the conceptual chapter one and the empirical chapters three and four. The chapter starts by analyzing the tension between the people's way of interpreting the Bible and that of their pastors. Also, to be noted is the fact that the situation is more fluid than had been imagined, and as such one could not simply make general statements about individualism and communitarianism. But since the communitarian inclination of the people, has been established a suggestion is made to develop a communitarian hermeneutics based on the concept of communitarianism. This kind of hermeneutics has not actually been developed but only necessary conditions for such an endeavor have been laid down, key of which is the deconstruction of all hitherto acquired attitudes toward evangelization and culture. That means that communitarian hermeneutics has to be built on the deconstructed cultural values and two concrete examples of *lük* (cattle rustling) and *kokwö* (the council of elders) have been enumerated.

Then it has been said that the effort of developing a communitarian hermeneutics is not aimed at creating a ghetto hermeneutics that helps to cut off the Pökot people from the rest of humanity. To the contrary, communitarian hermeneutics is but a prelude to the wider field of intercultural hermeneutics. In conclusion, there is an acknowledgment of the fact that this suggestion is not a once-for-all panacea to the problems of evangelization, but rather it is a small contribution to the already existing efforts to make the Gospel 'feel at home' in Africa. It is but a beginning of a long and difficult, but worthwhile, path for the scholars and faith communities (here referred to as SCCs) to make the Gospel of Jesus Christ reach all nations (Mt. 28: 19).

When all is said, and done, this work can be summarized in one sentence: that culture plays a determinant role in the way people perceive, interpret, understand and respond to new reality—ideas, events, people and literature, including sacred literature. In this case the people that were investigated are the Pökot of Kenya; the new reality is the arrival of Christianity among them, bringing new ideas about God, inter-human and inter-ethnic relationship. The events and people are the presence of foreign missions and missionaries, who brought the sacred literature as the Word of God, necessarily creating an intercultural encounter. But culture is diverse and complex, which makes the quest for inculturation a more difficult and challenging job than had previously been envisaged. In the age of globalization it is almost impossible to determine the cultural orientations that need to be inculturated.

ACKNOWLEDGMENTS

This book is the work of many hands, without which it could not have been achieved. We, therefore, wish to sincerely thank our informants who diligently, selflessly and assiduously labored to provide us with all the information we needed in the field in order to make our research a success. More so, we thank all those who gave us operational bases (mainly though not exclusively the catholic parishes) from where we carried out the field research with ease. Since we cannot afford to say "Goodbye", we say, *sörö nyo wow nyo man wechara, a kiperurok Tororöt*. We also wish to thank the students of Christ the Teacher Institute for Education (CTIE), Tangaza University College (a constituent college of the Catholic University of Eastern Africa) who made us aware, for the first time, of the existing discrepancy between the written word of the Scriptures and the actual practice of the people on the ground. We would like to thank Aylward Shorter (former principal of Tangaza), Fritz Stenger (field supervisor) and Ronald Roggenback (former director of CTIE).

We sincerely thank the theological faculty of the Radboud University Nijmegen, particularly the Graduate School of Theology for making this study possible through the award of a four-year study scholarship. We say a big thank you to the scholarship committee for considering us for this unique opportunity. We also wish to thank the entire teaching and non-teaching staff in the faculty for the kind assistance they offered us when we first arrived as new comers and had to be literally led to where we could get the required facilities. They could always say *loop met me*— walk with me—because they realized that it was futile to try and tell us where such facilities were available. And when things were not clear, even to themselves, they would urge patience and tell us, *even kijken*—let's see. In particular, to be thanked is the student community because, they introduced us to the way of studies in Netherlands and helped us with the much-needed adjustment—a process that is still going on.

Last but not least, we thank our supervisors in a very distinguished way for walking with us, step-by-step (*stap voor stap*) from the start of this study to its conclusion. It has been a long and tedious, and sometimes unpleasant walk, but all in all worth the effort we have all put to it. For this we would like to thank Frans Wijsen,

ACKNOWLEDGMENTS

Johannes Jacobus Visser, Patrick Chatelion-Counet and Pim Valkenberg. Johannes van der Ven (the immediate former dean of the faculty of theology) and Peter Nissen (a former dean). Rogier van Rossum (former rector, Nijmegen College) deserves to be mentioned in a special way because he was the person to welcome us in this country and gave us a room to rest our tired bodies and minds. He also slowly and painfully introduced us to life in the Netherlands and many are the times he even did shopping for us, when we bought wrong items due to language barrier! Special thanks go to members of the Manuscript Commission, Georg Essen, Robert Schreiter and Victor Zinkuratire for the approval of this work. Others that deserve to be mentioned are Ad Mommers, Aart Verburg, Bettineke van der Werf, Bianca Roelofs, Elly Meijer, Evert Jan van der Werf, Fritz Stenger, Hans Stoks, Hans de Wit, Hans Schilderman, Henk Wissink, Jan Jongeneel, Joe Kahiga, Martha Frederiks, Mary Getui, Niek Henckmann, Richard Roelofs, Renée Nachenius, Stans Elders, Ton Dietz, Vincent Simonis, Völker Küster, Wim Haas, Wim Verschuren, and all others we have failed to mention by name. Thanks to all of you and God bless. *Asanteni sana na Mungu awabariki. Nĩ ngatho mũno na Ngai amũrathime. Hartelijk dank en God zegene u.*

ABBREVIATIONS

AACC	All-Africa Conference of Churches
AAS	*Acta Apostolicae Sedis*
AGC	African Gospel Church
AFER	*African Ecclesial Review*
AIDS	Acquired Immune Deficiency Syndrome
AIM	African Inland Mission
AMECEA	Association Member Episcopal Conference of Eastern Africa
API	AMECEA Pastoral Institute
BC	Before Christ
BCE	Before the Common Era
BCMS	Bible Churchmen's Missionary Society
BFBS	British and Foreign Bible Society
BICAM	Biblical Institute for Africa and Madagascar
BSK	Bible Society of Kenya
CBF	Catholic Biblical Federation
CCC	*Catechism of the Catholic Church*. Translated by the United States Catholic Conference, Liberian Editrice Vaticana. Malwa, New Jersey: Paulist, 1994.
CE	Common Era
CTIE	Christ the Teacher Institute of Education
CMS	Church Missionary Society
CSM	Church of Scotland Mission
DB	Deutsche Bibelgesellschaft
DC	District Commissioner (a government officer in Kenya in charge of a district)

ABBREVIATIONS

DDC	District Development Committee
DELTA	Development Education for Leadership Training in Action
DO	District Officer (a government officer in Kenya below the rank of a District Commissioner)
DV	*Dei Verbum Divinus*
EATWOT	Ecumenical Association of Third World Theologians
ELCK	Evangelical Lutheran Church of Kenya
FAO	Food and Agriculture Organization
FGM	Female Genital Mutilation
GS	*Gaudium et Spes*
GTA	Grounded Theory Approach
KEC	Kenya Episcopal Conference.
LG	Lumen *Gentium*
MP	Member of Parliament
NCCK	National Council of the Churches of Kenya
NGO	Non-Government Organization
NGOs	Non-Government Organizations
RCEA	Reformed Church of East Africa
SOS	Save Our Souls (an international code for a distress call)
SACBC	Southern African Catholic Bishops' Conference
SCC	Small Christian Community
SCCs	Small Christian Communities
SDA	The Seventh Day Adventist
SECAM	Symposium of the Episcopal Conferences of Africa and Madagascar
UBS	United Bible Society
UK	United Kingdom
UNEP	United Nations Environment Program
UNESCO	United Nations Education, Scientific and Culture Organization
WCC	World Council of Churches.
WCFBA	World Catholic Biblical Federation for the Biblical Apostolate

CHAPTER 1

GENERAL INTRODUCTION

Rationale and Motivation

AS WE START THE third millennium of Christian evangelization, inculturation has become the pet subject among many pastoral workers, particularly in developing countries. This preoccupation has seemingly deflected the mission of the church from other equally important aspects like liberation, reconciliation, option for the poor,[1] environment,[2] and discipleship.[3] But we postulate that all these issues are addressed and taken care of in the whole question of inculturation, which "has to do with identities, that of Jesus Christ and those of you and me and every person and people. It has to do with the whole human project itself."[4] To this end there is an ongoing debate among African theologians from which various theological themes or trends, that are regarded as the principles, or starting points, of inculturation have emerged.[5] They can

---

1. Donal Dorr (2000). *Mission in Today's World.* Maryknoll, New York: Orbis Books.109, 128, 144.

2. Mary Getui (2000). Mission of the Church and Concern for the Environment. In A. Nasimiyu-Wasike and D.W. Waruta (eds). *Mission in African Christianity: Critical Essays* in *Missiology.* Nairobi: Acton Publishers, 40–58.

3. Anthony Bellagamba (1992). *Mission and Ministry in the Global Church.* Maryknoll, New York: Orbis Books, 66.

4. Simon E. Smith (2002). Forward. In Fabien E. Bougala (2002). *Chritianity Without Fetishes: An African Critique and Recapture of Christianity.* Hamburg, London: Lit Verlag Münster, x.

5. John Mary Waliggo (1986). Making a Church that is Truly African. In *Inculturation: Its Meaning and Urgency.* Nairobi: St. Paul Publications—Africa, 20–21.

be classified as Bible,[6] incarnation, or Christology[7] church history,[8] pastoral reality[9] spirituality[10] and liturgy.[11] This study is in line with the tradition that sees the Bible as the starting point of inculturation, not merely as a book or a piece of literature, but more fundamentally, as the Living Word of God. In this trend, there are two paths, one traditional, the other more recent. The traditional path is biblical exegesis, which lays emphasis on the scientific methods used to analyze and interpret bible texts.

The more recent path is biblical hermeneutics, which is a reflection on these methods and their usefulness to the African reader, here and now (*hic et nunc*), in his or her reading of the Bible as a post-colonial encounter.[12] That means, re-examining the relevance of the Bible in its current African social context, following the regaining of the independence of African states from the European colonial powers.[13] This 'regaining' can only be realized through the struggle and determination to contest

6. Justin S. Ukpong (1995). Rereading the Bible with African eyes: Inculturation and Hermeneutics. In *Journal of Theology for Southern Africa,* 91, 3–14; Gerald O. West (1997). On the eve of an African Biblical Studies: Trajectories and Trends. In Journal *of Theology for Southern Africa,* 99, 99–115, Louis (2001). Towards a "communal" Approach for Reading the Bible in Africa. In Mary N. Getui et al (eds). In *Interpreting Old estament in Africa.* Nairobi: Acton Publishers, 77–88; Victor Zinkuratire (2001). Morphological and Syntactical Correspondences Between Hebrew and Bantu Languages. In Mary N. Getui et al (eds). In *Interpreting Old Testament in Africa.* Nairobi: Acton Publishers, 217–226, Emmanuel Adow Obeng (1997). The use of Biblical Critical Methods in Rooting the Scriptures in Africa. In Hannah W. Kinoti and John M. Waliggo (eds). *The Bible in African Christianity.* Nairobi: Acton Publishers, 8–24.

7. Joseph Blomjous (1980). Development in Mission Thinking and Practice 1959–1980: Inculturation and Interculturation. In *AFER, Vol.* 22, No. 6. Eldoret. GABA Publications, 393–398; Charles Nyamiti (1989). African Christologies Today. In J.N.K. Mugambi and Laurenti Magesa (eds) *Jesus in African Christianity: Experimentation and Diversity in African Christology.* Nairobi: Initiatives Ltd, 17–39; Simeon Onyewueke Eboh (2004). *African Communalism: The Way to Social Harmony and Peaceful Co-Existence.* Frankfurt: IKO-Verlag für Interkulturelle Kommunikation, 144; Francoise Kabasele Lumbala (1994). Africans Celebrate Jesus Christ. In Rosino Gibellini (ed.). *Paths of African Theology.* Maryknoll, New York: Orbis Books,78–94.

8. John Baur (1994). *Two Thousand Years of Christianity in Africa: An African History 62–1992.* Nairobi: Paulines Publications Africa,226ff.

9. Bénézet Bujo (1998). *The Ethical Dimension of Community: The African Model and the Dialogue Between North and South.* Nairobi: Paulines Publications, 93–208; Peter Wassa Mpagi (2002). *African Christian Theology: In the contemporary context.* Kisubi: Marianum Publishing Company Limited,110–155: Waliggo (1986) op. cit., 12; Aylward Shorter (1987). New Attitudes to African Culture and African Religions. In *Towards African Christian Maturity.* Nairobi: St. Paul Publications–Africa, 17.

10. Patrick A. Kalilombe (1994). Spirituality in the African Perspective. In Rosino Gibellini (ed). *Paths of African Theology.* Maryknoll, New York: Orbis Books, 115–135; Patrick A. Kalilombe (1999). *Doing Theology at the Grassroots: Theological Essays from Malawi.* Gweru: Mambo Press, 212–235.

11. Elochukwu E. Uzukwu (1994). Inculturation and the Liturgy (Eucharist). In Rosino Gibellini (ed). *Paths of African Theology.* Maryknoll, New York: Orbis Books, 95–114.

12. Fernando F. Segovia (2000a). *Decolonizing Biblical Studies: A View from the Margins.* Maryknoll, New York: Orbis Books 119–142; Musa W. Dube (2002). Rereading the Bible: Biblical Hermeneutics and Social Justice. In Emmanuel Katongole (ed). *African Theology Today.* Scranton: The University of Scranton Press, 57–68.

13. Kwame Gyekye (1997). *Tradition and Modernity: Philosophical Reflections on the African Experience.* New York: Oxford University Press, 158.

subordination, repression and social exploitation by reclaiming the continent's history, even as this history is being made. Serequeberhan paraphrases.

> In view of all of the above, then, and beyond the initial moment of counter-violence, the African liberation struggle is an originative process through which the historicity of the colonized is reclaimed and appropriated anew. . . . this will be our hermeneutical response to the question: what are the people of Africa trying to free themselves from and what are they trying to establish?[14]

The post-colonial context calls for a conscious and critical agenda to reflect on the Bible and its impact on the colonized people. That is, an agenda

> . . .to engage and subvert texts of doubtable ethos, exposing their imperialist/colonialist ideologies. As representations of reality, texts have mimetically engendered agendas that have condemned peoples to subjugation in matters of socio-political import, or have worked to legitimize processes that have deprived (people) of their rights, their lands, their human dignities, or have otherwise interfered with their essentially inalienable freedoms.[15]

Croatto explains the dynamics between the text and context in various societies or worldviews, in what he calls 'the production of meaning'.

> Indeed, any reading is the *production* of discourse, and thus of a meaning, from a point of departure in a text. We do not read a meaning but a text, an account, actualizing its *competency*, competency which is analyzed by semiotics. In this way, a text is open to various patterns. The structural analysis of an account or discourse is not endowed with the precision one finds in mathematics; results vary according to different combinations of elements. The structure of an *account* is analyzed in terms of its "narrative program"—the actantial figures in the text; the "functions" of the text. The structure of a *discourse* is analyzed in terms of semantic axes, semiotic framework, verification, and so on, as the piecing together of *one* among many possible meanings of words or themes within a given society or worldview.[16]

The post-colonial period is characterized by two, almost simultaneous happenings: an end to forcible dictation and imposition of foreign values and institutions, and a period of autonomous self-expression, self-assertion and reflection on values and goals of a hitherto subjugated people of Africa. The latter helps accelerate the

---

14. Tsenay Serequeberhan (1994). *The Hermeneutics of African Philosophy: Horizon and Discourse.* New York: Routledge, 85.

15. Gosbert T. M. Byamungu (2002). Scripture, Tradition(s) and the Church(es): An Ecumenical Quo Vadis. In Hg. von Silja Joneleit-Oesch and Miriam Neubert (eds). *Interkulturelle Hermeneutik und Lectura Popular: Neuere Konzepte in Theorie un Praxis.* Frankfurt an Main: Verlag Otto Lembeck, 141— footnote 6.

16. Severino J. Croatto (1987). *Biblical Hermeneutics: Towards a Theory of Reading as the Production of Meaning.* Trans by Robert R. Barr. Maryknoll, New York: Orbis Books, 21.

gradual weaning away from the self-flagellating aspects of the colonial mentality acquired through decades of colonial subjugation, and in the restoration of people's dignity and identity.[17]

There are traditional ways of studying and reading the Bible (classical methods of exegesis) and modern ones (e.g., feminist-liberation-ecological). All these methods are subject to philosophical scrutiny and there is a need for them to be drawn into the hermeneutical debate.[18] Various authors agree that the traditional methods of bible interpretation were not very helpful for the project of inculturation in Africa, but that there seems to be a beacon of hope in the more modern methods of bible interpretation.[19] Our guiding question thus is this: how can the newer biblical methods play a more effective role in the inculturation of the Gospel in Africa? We are going to concentrate on the analysis of how the Pökot people read, understand, interpret and apply the Bible in their social context. This, as we will show later, is the second main aspect of hermeneutics. We hope that our work will enrich the efforts for inculturation, through biblical hermeneutics, because of its proximity to the people and the central role it plays in the general understanding and response to the Word of God by those who hear it for the first time.

We have chosen the topic, *Biblical Hermeneutics as a Tool for Inculturation in Africa: a Case Study of the Pökot People of Kenya*, because of the conviction that the Bible is not just another principle or mere starting point of inculturation but the very foundation or bedrock of inculturation. As the goal of this study, we are interested in suggesting a way forward towards developing an African hermeneutic theory that can be fruitfully used to achieve this important goal of inculturation. We suppose that a home grown biblical hermeneutics is the most effective tool with which to stimulate a relevant process of inculturation that can deliver the Word of God home in a meaningful and fruitful way. Hence there is need to develop a hermeneutic theory based on the practical way of bible interpretation among the Pökot. When working with the different classes and categories of people, therefore, it is not helpful to try and call them back to where they were or call them to where one is, but such an effort requires the rare "courage to go with them to a place that neither you nor they have ever been before."[20] "The goal of biblical hermeneutics" then, as has observed, "is to bring about

17. Gyekye (1997). Op. cit., 158; Serequeberhan (1994). Op. cit., 85.

18. Manfred Oeming (1998). *Biblische Hermeneutik: Eine Einführung*. Darmstadt: Wissenschaftliche Buchgesell-schaft.

19. Teresa Okure (1993). Feminist Interpretations in Africa. In E. S Fiorenza (ed) *Searching the Scriptures: A Feminist Introduction*. New York: Crossroad, 76–85; Justin S. Ukpong (1999). Developments in Biblical Interpretation in Modern Africa. In *Missionalia*, 27(3) (November), 313–329; Victor Zinkuratire (2004a). Inculturation the Biblical Message in Africa: Current Trends. In *African Christian Studies*, Vol. 20, No. 1. Nairobi: CUEA Publications, 41–70; Gerald O. West (2005). African Biblical Hermeneutics and Bible Translation. In Jean-Claude Loba-Mkole and Ernst R. Wendland (eds). *Interacting with Scriptures in Africa*. Nairobi: Acton Publishers.

20. Vincent J. Donovan (2004). *Christianity Rediscovered: Twenty-Fifth Anniversary Edition*, Reprint. Maryknoll, New York: Orbis Books, xiii.

an active and meaningful engagement between the interpreter and the text, in such a way that the interpreter's own horizon is re-shaped and enlarged."[21]

Where there is proper and relevant hermeneutics, one that directly addresses people's needs, fears and aspiration, the Word of God is likely to take root and become part and parcel of the day-to-day undertakings of those who receive it. Thus, it tends to be 'more effective' in the mission of evangelization.[22] On the same token, biased hermeneutics[23] can easily brainwash people through manipulation or, worse, destroy the very faith it is meant to nurture. A case in history is what happened in the apartheid South Africa and the oppressive Latin American situation, as well as in many other developing nations.[24] Here the Bible was used to justify the position of the oppressors, to intimidate or even silence those who questioned the *status quo*[25] A direct consequence of this is inhibited resentment and silent opposition (or at times, outright rebellion) that has, in some cases, ended up in schisms.

The *Status Questionis* and Our Objectives

Our guiding question, as mentioned in chapter one, section one above, will be answered and goal hopefully achieved for a specific group of people in a region—the Pökot of northwestern Kenya. About the state of the question and our objectives, two things can be factually noticed. To begin with, a whole century has passed by since the Word of God was first preached in this part of Kenya (by the BCMS). This notwithstanding, the population still sees the Christian faith as an alien concept that has no place in the social structures of the Pökot community. Moreover, many pastors in West Pökot have once and again expressed an opinion that the Pökot are a difficult lot that has no regard for religion, unless adherence to it brings about some

---

21. Anthony C. Thiselton (1993). *The Two Horizons: New Testament Hermeneutics and Philosophical Description*. Carlisle: Grand Rapids, xix.

22. Itumeleng J. Mosala (1989). *Biblical Hermeneutics and Black Theology of Liberation in South Africa*. Grand Rapids, Michigan: Eerdmans.

23. We use this term to refer to that kind of hermeneutics that stems from the sectarian whims, emotional prejudice and worldview of an individual or a group, rather than addressing the needs, aims and goals of the whole community. It is usually not properly thought out or tested in the field to prove its scientific worth in relation to the reality it claims to represent. And yet it is accepted and used as though its existential import and validity are not disputable.

24. Baur, op. cit., 191–192; Dwight N. Hopkins (1999). *Introducing Black Theology of Liberation*. Maryknoll, New York: Orbis Books, 167–172.

25. B. Tihagale and I. Mosala (eds) (1986); Justin S. Ukpong (2004). Contextual Hermeneutics: Challenges and Possibilities. In J. N. K. Mugambi and Johannes A. Smit (eds). *Text and Context in New Testament Hermeneutics*. Nairobi: Acton Publishers, 29–30). *Hammering Swords into Plough Shares: Essays in Honor of Desmond Tutu*. Johannesburg: Skotaville Publishers, 185. It has to be clarified that the Bible was not the cause of the said situations, which were used as political tools of oppression. It was used to give credence and justify the existing oppressive systems and structures. Thus, Bible interpreters used the existing ideologies and ethos to interpret the Bible.

tangible material benefits that would have otherwise not been attained within their traditional social set-up.

But as Verstraelen observes, "The gospel was inherently culture-conditioned from the beginning by virtue of the Incarnation and of the cultural matrix and the languages in which the Scriptures are expressed."[26] Then one is bound to ask him/herself, why was the gospel not sufficiently inculturated in West Pökot? This creates an interest to know the right approach that pastors need to employ in the contextualization of the Gospel, that is, how they can permeate the rich Pökot cultural heritage with the gospel teaching, without compromising the gospel value, or alienating the people from their culture. We think these are hermeneutical questions, and we will argue that it would be a lot more beneficial if the pastors could adopt a form of hermeneutics that has some resonance to, and seriously takes into consideration, the actual lifestyle and daily practice of the people of West Pökot.

In the light of this conviction then, the objective of our research is to find out the condition(s) through which biblical hermeneutics can be used as an effective tool for the inculturation of the Gospel, in Africa in general, but particularly among the people of West Pökot.[27] Then we can be in a position to make recommendations on the use of the Bible at the grass roots level and suggest the condition(s) necessary for developing an African hermeneutic theory: one that makes an explicit effort to create a stronger rapport between the people and their pastors in what we regard as a communitarian hermeneutic model, that is community-centered in the sense of being both community-based and community-oriented. That means that it has the community as its starting point (*status a quo*) or origin, as well as its final point (*status ad quem*) or finality, one that truly embraces inculturation in a critical but sympathetic way.

Many hermeneutic theories have emerged ever since *general* hermeneutics[28] acquired the status of a serious academic field of inquiry, with the work of Schleiermacher in which he attempted to clearly define the principles of valid interpretation. "Before him [Schleiermacher]," says Ricoeur, "there was on one hand a philology of classical texts, principally those of Greco-Latin antiquity, and on the other hand an exegesis of sacred texts, of the Old and New Testaments. In each of those two domains, the work of interpretation varies with the diversity of the texts."[29] So, it was Schleiermacher and

---

26. Frans J. Verstraelen (1976). *Tradition and Reconstruction in Mission: A Report of IAMS Conference at San José, Cost Rica*. Leiden: Interuniversity Institute for Missiological and Ecumenical Research (IIME), 33.

27. David Ndegwah (2006). Understanding the Nomads: The Role of Culture in Evangelisation In Francesco Pierli et al (eds). *The Pastoralists: A Challenge to Churches, State, Civil Society*. Nairobi: Paulines Publications Africa, 8.

28. March C. Taylor (1982). *Deconstructing Theology*. New York: The Crossroad Publishing Company and Scholars Press, 81, note 1) distinguishes Schleiermacher's *general* hermeneutics from the previous theories of interpretation which were, by contrast, *regional* in the sense that instead of trying to identify general rules of interpretation that could be applicable to any text, analysts focused on a particular field of inquiry, such as classical, juridical, or theological studies.

29. Paul Ricoeur (1983). *Hermeneutics and the Human Sciences*. Cambridge: Cambridge University

other scholars after him who heralded the birth of hermeneutics as we know it today by raising exegesis and philology to the level of 'technology' (*kunstlehre*), "which is not restricted to a mere collection of unconnected operations."[30] But in doing this, scholars used their own reflections coupled with personal experience to determine which theories fit particular communities. Consequently, says Thiselton, "Reflection on the interpretation of texts then, has led on to a hermeneutics of lived experience,"[31] but this has mostly been done by individual scholars rather than communities of the faithful. Even those who root for a reader-response type of hermeneutics, which is said to be community-centered, usually do so as a matter of inference or deduction.[32] This is because, as a form of criticism, this kind of hermeneutics " . . . focuses on the reader (as an individual)[33] and the reading process, trying to establish the role actual readers play in the determination of literary meaning."[34] Then there are those who are ordinarily referred to as 'community of interpreters'.[35]

They, too, do not represent a 'community' in the African sense of the word. These are usually small groups of intellectuals that generally do not even share a common neighborhood (except in certain circumstances), and sometimes live far apart in completely different circumstances. In most cases the common denominator of the members in these communities is their academic pursuit rather than a shared, common, and organic communal life. Hence their communality is the convergence of their thoughts and the influence they exert on each other stems from individuals' free association, not the other way around. The individual is seen as the prime mover that starts the relationship and it is in his/her interpretation that the said 'community' is reflected.[36]

In contrast to this individual-centered kind of interpretation, we espouse a communitarian hermeneutics, one that is community-centered, with the community as its starting point (community-based) as well as its finality (community-oriented). This is similar to what Magesa calls 'popular hermeneutics',[37] one that is not born behind a desk or in the library, by an individual and then presented to the community as a

---

Press, 45.

30. Ibid., 45.

31. Anthony C. Thiselton (1996). *Interpreting God and the Postmodern Self: On Meaning, Manipulation and Promise*. Edinburgh: T&T Clark Ltd, 47.

32. West (2005) Op. cit., 11.

33. Brackets are our addition.

34. Armando J. Levoratti (1998). How to Interpret the Bible. In William R. Farmer et al (eds). *The International Bible Commentary*. Collegeville, Minnesota: The Liturgical Press, 28.

35. Thiselton (1996). Op. cit., 48; Stanley Fish (1970). Literature in the Reader: Affective Stylistics. In J.P. Tompkins (ed). *Reader-Response Criticism*. London: Baltimore, 70–100.

36. Patrick Chatelion-Counet (2000). *John, A Postmodern Gospel: Introduction to Deconstructive Exegesis Applied to the Fourth Gospel*. Leiden: Koninklijke Brill NV, 40.

37. Laurenti Magesa (1997). From Private to Popular Biblical Hermeneutics. In Hannah W. Kinoti and John M. Waliggo (eds). *The Bible in African Christianity*. Nairobi: Acton Publishers, 24–39.

ready-made package. We would like to suggest a hermeneutic theory born in the field with the community of the 'ordinary Christians'[38] as the obstetricians for their own spiritual edification, and break a new ground as to what really happens when Christians read the Bible in a community setting.[39] Clearest is the classification of Boff and Boff, who identify three levels of doing theology as popular, pastoral and professional.[40] We look at hermeneutics from the same perspective and make a similar division, where we divide it into popular, pastoral and scientific or academic hermeneutics. Our concern is the interplay between popular and pastoral hermeneutics and we aim at identifying the weakness inherent in both, through a philosophical interrogation of the two, in a deconstructive way.[41]

Then we suggest a scientific theory that makes this interplay possible and fruitful in a form of hermeneutics that is inclusive of pastoral concerns as well as popular cultural heritage. "What we do know since Heidegger, Gadamer, Ricoeur and the contextual hermeneutics is that situation, culture and 'horizon' determine the interpretation of bible texts to a large extent; how this 'contextual bible reading' is done exactly and which factors are operative is still unknown (and, we add, sufficiently *unexplored*) territory."[42] We suggest a return to the more practical arrangement for African theology "interpreting legends, fables, and oral traditions as 'texts' and 'documents', which with the help of archaeological data could contribute to the foundation" of an ethnographic fieldwork.[43]

This suggestion follows the footsteps of anthropologists like J. Vansina, Y. Person and G. Balandier, who had dealt with African history from an anthropological perspective,[44] with Vansina suggesting 'ethno-history' as a discipline that combines

---

38. The term 'ordinary people' or 'ordinary Christians' is used in the same sense as that used by Manus, which "refers to a social class that does not belong to the elite group. Most of them are simple Christians who live their lives by the worldview provided by their traditional customs. Generally, they live poor and are on the periphery of the society" Chris Ukachukwu Manus (2003). *Intercultural Hermeneutics in Africa: Methods and Approaches.* Nairobi: Acton Publishers, 35).

39. Hans De Wit (2003). Through the Eyes of Another: Towards Intercultural Reading of the Bible. In Hg. von Silja Joneleit-Oesch and Miriam Neubert (eds). *Interkulturelle Hermeneutik und lectura popular: Neuere Konzepte in Theorie und Praxis.* Frankfurt am Main: Verlag Otto Lembeck, 23–24; Joseph G. Healey (1981). *A Fifth Gospel: the Experience of Black Christian Values.* Maryknoll, New York: Orbis Books, 124; Justin S. Ukpong (2001). Bible Reading with a Community of Ordinary Readers. In Mary Getui et al (eds). *Interpreting the New Testament in Africa.* Nairobi: Acton Publishers, 190; Néstor Míguez (2004). Reading John 4 in the Interface Between Ordinary and Scholarly Interpretation. In Hans de Wit et al (eds). *Through the Eyes of Another: Intercultural Reading of the Bible.* Amsterdam: Institute of Mennonite Studies, 344.

40. Leonardo Boff and Clodovis Boff (1996). *Introducing Liberation Theology,* ninth printing. Maryknoll, New York: Orbis Books, 12–14.

41. Maciern Towa (1971). *Essai sur la problematique philosophique dans l'Afrique actuelle.* Yaounde: Editions CLE., 30.

42. De Wit (2003). Op. cit., 25.

43. V. Y. Mudimbe (1988). *The Invention of Africa: Gnosis, Philosophy, and the Order of Knowledge.* Bloomington and Indianapolis: Indiana University Press, 166.

44. Ibid., 166.

history and anthropology.[45] In this line of thought, Mudimbe sees anthropology as the best sign for the existence of an African *gnosis* (secret knowledge), but admits that this should be considered as both a challenge and a promise. "Perhaps this *gnosis* makes more sense if seen as a result of two processes: first, a permanent reevaluation of the limits of anthropology as knowledge in order to transform it into a more credible *anthropou-logos*, that is a discourse on a human being; and, second, an examination of its own historicity."[46] And Éla seems to support a return to anthropology when he expresses his dream:

> I dream of "a theology under the tree," which would be worked out as brothers and sisters sit side by side wherever Christians share the lot of peasant people who seek to take responsibility for their own future and for transforming their living conditions. In order for that to happen, people must leave the libraries and give up the comfort of air-conditioned offices; they must accept the conditions of life in the insecurity of study in poor areas where the people have their feet in water or in mud and can neither read nor write.[47]

With Mudimbe's inspiration we opted to carry out a field research, using an empirical approach, and supplement it with philosophical as well as theological reflections, based on the concept of deconstruction. The empirical aspect is designed to guide this project to the popular, spontaneous, reading of the faithful; who approach the text with an 'existential attitude'.[48] We, therefore, opted to go and learn from a specific people, the Pökot, living in a particular localized situation, West Pökot, in Kenya. We hoped to do this first, by listening to the people's interpretation of a bible text[49] and then, by listening to their recommendations on what they consider to be fruitful and relevant hermeneutics in their midst. In this way, we hoped to come up with an ethnography that would help reduce the gap between the professed and the practiced faith, between the hierarchical church's interpretation of the Gospel and that of the 'ordinary Christians' at the grassroots. "Ordinary believers," says Cochrane, "in their original experiences of faith and their practical reflection on daily life, however, unsophisticated or flawed their theology, confront us with issues and challenges too seldom incorporated into the formal theological work of the Christian community."[50]

In this down to earth and concrete way, we look forward to making some contribution towards the realization of what Nthamburi and Waruta regard as 'an African

---

45. J. Vansina (1961). *De la Tradition Orale. Essai de Méthode Historique.* Tervuren: Musée Royal de l'Afrique Centrale.

46. Mudimbe (1988). Op. cit., 186.

47. Jean-Marc Éla (2001). *My Faith as an African.* Nairobi: Acton Publishers, 180.

48. Paul Ricoeur (1970). Qu' est-ce qu'un texte? Expliquer et Comprendre. In R. Bubner et al (eds). *Hermeneutik und Dialektik.* Tübingen: Mohr, 181–200.

49. Jn. 10:1–16.

50. James R. Cochrane (1999). *Circles of Dignity: Community Wisdom and Theological Reflection.* Minneapolis: Fortress Press, xvii.

Hermeneutic,[51] one that embraces "a more existential and reflective approach which has made the Bible the basis of the African Christian expression at the individual and community level." This then, is an attempt to crash the pillars of " . . . those traditions that have often led to a separation of the theologian from the experience of living communities."[52] Indeed "It grounds and vindicates a particular kind of voice, not so much against other voices, but against their silencing effects wherever they overwhelm or simply ignore the marginalized or subjugated voice."[53]

We chose the Pökot people because their community presents a good cultural scene for the current study. Although cultural globalization is unstoppable, the assumption here was that it also brings with it an acute sense of self-awareness that culminates in identity reconstruction of individuals or communities. Consequently, various communities remain distinct and unique because the elements that form the core of their identity continue to influence them, in spite of the many cultural orientations that come into play in an intercultural setting.[54] These are their 'root paradigms'[55] or the unquestioned assumptions about the fundamental nature of the world and humanity that underlie social actions within specific cultural contexts.

The Research Issue and Questions

The research objective mentioned above hinges around one key missionary issue that has triggered the undertaking of this research. This, as already mentioned above, is the desire to know if there is a hermeneutic theory that can stimulate a symbiosis between biblical values and the Pökot culture (or any other, for that matter) without compromising or watering down either of the two.[56] To address this concern, we formulated four sub-questions that will guide our research activities, both in the library and in the field. These questions will be in our minds during bible sharing sessions, discussions and interviews with the people and their pastors; and during private readings, as well as during philosophical and theological reflections. They are as follows:

1. Why is it that the Gospel did not take root in West Pökot?

---

51. Zablon Nthamburi and Douglas Waruta (1997). Biblical Hermeneutics in African Instituted Churches. In Hannah W. Kinoti and John M. Waliggo (eds). *The Bible in African Christianity.* Nairobi: Acton Publishers, 51.

52. Robert J. Schreiter (1985). *Constructing Local Theologies.* Maryknoll, New York: Orbis Books. 18.

53. Cochrane (1999). op. cit., 2.

54. David Ndegwah (2004). The Pökoot: Christianity and Cultural Heritage. In Kwame Bediako et al (eds). *A New Day Dawning: African Christians Living the Gospel.* Zoetermeer: Uitgeverij Boekencentrum, 83.

55. Victor W. Turner (1974). *Dramas, Fields and Metaphors.* Ithaca, 33–42.

56. A. De Groot (1995). One Bible and Many Interpretive Contexts: Hermeneutics in Missiology. In F.J. Verstraelen et al (eds). *Missiology: An Ecumenical Introduction: Texts and Contexts of Global Christianity.* Grand Rapids, Mich.: Eerdmans.

2. To what extent do the Pökot people interpret the Gospel in an African (communitarian) way?

3. To what extent do their pastors interpret the Gospel in a non-African (individualistic) way?

4. How can the interplay between popular and pastoral hermeneutics be facilitated?

Definition of Key Concepts

Although there are many concepts at play in this project the central ones are eleven and they need to be defined in order to give the reader a bird's eye view of this work. These are communitarianism, contextualization, culture, deconstruction, evangelization, hermeneutics, inculturation, individualism, missiology, mission, and worldview.

Communitarianism

As it will be shown later, the main concepts to be deconstructed in view of inculturation are 'individualism' and 'communitarianism'. By 'communitarianism' we mean 'community-centeredness', the spirit of living together as an organic group, both as starting point (community-based) and normative reference (community-oriented) of people's activities.[57] We prefer the word 'communitarian'[58] over other commonly used words like communalism,[59] because it captures the ontological reality of closeness and proximity to the community, among Africans, in a better way than merely doing things together or communally. This dedication to the community even takes on a moral character to the extent that "What is good and just for the individual is defined by the community to which they belong."[60]

The word community is used in different and varied senses. There are political communities, like the East African Community; economic communities, like the European Economic Community; academic communities, like what Kuhn calls 'scientific community'.[61] In the internet world, there are virtual communities, that create

---

57. Eboh (2004). Op. cit.

58. Kwame Gyekye (1992). Person and Community in African Thought. In Kwasi Wiredu and Kwame Gyekye (eds). *Person and Community: Ghanaian Philosophical Studies, I.* Washington D.C.: The Council for Research in Values and Philosophy, 101; Remy Beller (2001). *Life, Person and Community in Africa: A Way Towards Inculturation With the Spirituality of the Focolare.* Nairobi: Paulines Publications Africa.

59. B. J. Van der Walt (1997). *Afrocentric or Eurocentric? Our Task in a Multicultural South Africa.* Potchefstroom: Potchefstroom University of Christian Higher Education.

60. Nicholas Bunnin and E. P. Tsui-James (eds) (2003). *The Blackwell Companion to Philosophy*, 2nd edit. Oxford: Blackwell Publishers Ltd, 271.

61. Thomas S. Kuhn (1970). *The Structure of Scientific Revolution.* 2nd ed. Chicago: The University of Chicago Press, 18–19.

new forms of social life, and communities of hackers that create technology,[62] more often in the negative sense of the word. Then there are religious communities, like the Small Christian Communities in the Catholic Church; social communities, like friends who choose to live together for a purpose and so on. All the above constitute what Rahner calls a 'willed community'.[63]

It is widely believed that communities in this traditional sense no longer exist, at least in the Western world, and that today they only exist as 'networks of individuals and the networks of groups'.[64] The debate on whether such communities do exist in fact dates back to the beginning of the twentieth century; and many argue in the negative. Worth of mention in this regard is Tonnies (1935), who came up with two terms to reflect the communal evolution. *Gemeinschaft*, according to him, refers to the community, as it existed in the pre-modern times while *Gesellschaft* refers to the current state of affairs, which translates to 'society'.[65]

In the African setting, two conceptual kinds of communitarianism can be envisaged, referred to as *structural* and *functional* communitarianism. The former refers to the blood relations, that is, social and natural structures that an individual finds him or herself in and therefore goes on to act and behave in a particular way as dictated by the community (i.e., behaving in a communitarian way), with or without personal conviction. In this case, the community functions as the custodian of the individual in his or her ideas and actions. Thus, as Gyekye has observed, "The sense of community that characterizes social relations among individuals is a direct consequence of the communitarian social arrangements." [66]

The latter is a willed phenomenon, in which a group of people comes together in order to fight a common enemy or achieve a common goal in a voluntary association, or a network. And once the goal has been achieved or the threat is over, everyone goes his or her way; or chooses to remain together to ward off any such need in future. This, according to political philosophers, is precisely how our modern states came into being. From this perspective, we see that structural communitarians can form functional communities, whereas functional communitarians cannot form structural

---

62. Manuel Castells (2001). *The Internet Gallaxy: Reflections on the Internet, Business, and Society.* Oxford: Oxford University Press; Gordon Graham (1999). *The Internet: A Philosophical Inquiry.* London and New York: Routledge.

63. Karl Rahner (1986). *Encyclopedia of Theology: A Concise Sacramentum Mundi,* reprint. London: burns & Oats.

64. Johannes A. Van der Ven (1993). *Practical Theology.* Kampen: Kok Pharos Publishing House, 246ff. In sociology, this term 'network of individuals' is sometimes used in contrast to the term 'community'. In our understanding though, there can be networks of individuals within a community. Thus, our usage of the term above is that individuals or groups choose to work together without necessarily being under the umbrella of the community.

65. F. Tonnies (1935). *Gemeinschaft und Gesellschaft.* Leipzig: Buske.

66. Kwame Gyekye (1992). Person and Community in African Thought. In Kwasi Wiredu and Kwame Gyekye (eds). *Person and Community: Ghanaian Philosophical Studies, I.* Washington D.C.: The Council for Research in Values and Philosophy, 102.

communities. This is because structural communities are not formed. One finds them there, and the most one can do is to secede or rebel from one of them and join another because, there is no life outside the community and if there is, it is not worth living.

Contextualization

The term 'inculturation' is often seen as equivalent to 'contextualization'. We understand contextualization as the various processes by which a local church integrates the Gospel—the text—with its local culture—the context.[67] This effort has been referred to in many names, among them adaptation, acculturation, incarnation and more recently, inculturation. Our study centers on the latter and how the Bible can be used in an effective way in the process of inculturation. The primary concern for contextualization is the integration of the message of Christ with the local church to which it is preached. Emphasizing the importance of contextualization Droogers says the following: "The need for contextualization is one of the *raisons d'être* of the discipline of missiology."[68]

Culture

When we speak about 'inculturation' we have to clarify what we mean by 'culture'. The word 'culture' comes from the Latin word '*cultura*', which is, in turn, related to the word *colere*. These can be translated into English as cultivating, care, tending or cultivation. Its (old) French equivalent, *couture*, translates to husbandry, tilling (of the land or cultivation of soil), worship, and training of the mind, the body, faculties, and manners.[69] In this study, we envisage two understandings of culture, one modern, and the other postmodern. In the modern sense, culture is understood to mean " . . . the integrated system of learned behavior patterns which are characteristic of the members of a society and which are not the result of biological inheritance."[70] Gritti, "who tried to strike a balance between the many emerging conceptions of the term," regards culture as a constituent of two aspects, which he calls 'practical' and 'symbolic'.[71] According to Spradley, these two aspects are so intertwined with human life that culture could be looked at in terms

---

67. Louis J. Luzbetak (1998). *The Church and Cultures: New Perspectives in Missiological Anthropology*, eighth print. Maryknoll, New York: Orbis Books.

68. André F. Droogers (2003). Changing Culture and The Missiological Mission. In Inus Daneel et al (eds). *Fullness of Life for All: Challenges for Mission in Early 21st Century.* Amsterdam/New York: Rodopi, 59.

69. A. L. Kroeber and C. Kluckhohn (1952). *Culture: A Critical Review of Concepts and Definitions.* New York: Vintage Books.

70. Adamson E. Hoebel (1972). *Anthropology: The Study of Man*, 4th ed. New York: McGraw-Hill, 6.

71. J. Gritti (1975). *L'expression de la foi dans les cultures humaines.* Paris: Centurion, 13.

of the rules guiding our lives.⁷² Thus, culture is said to be "*the acquired knowledge people use to interpret experience and generate behavior.*"⁷³

According to Hannerz, culture ". . .is the meanings which people create, and which create people, as members of societies. Culture is in some way collective." Accordingly, "culture has two kinds of loci and the cultural process takes place in their ongoing interactions."⁷⁴ He classifies these loci as overt and covert loci. According to him the overt locus consists of what he calls 'public meaningful forms', i.e., what can be heard and whatever else that can be known through external realities. The covert locus is the human mind, which contains instruments that interpret these public forms and give them meaning.⁷⁵

The difference between modern and post-modern understanding of culture can be pinned down on the presuppositions of these two. The former presupposes harmony within a community, while the latter presupposes chaos, and hence culture is a unifying principle. Aware of the diverse meanings of the word culture that straddle between its modern and post-modern understanding, we are not going to make preference between either of the two because, as we will show later, one does not exclude the other. Most of the aspects mentioned in the former understanding of culture are not discarded in the latter. They are just "decentered or re-inscribed within a more primary attention to historical process . . . Some aspects of the modern are substantially revised; the functions of most of these remain, however, much the same."⁷⁶

Deconstruction

In this study, we try to understand the condition(s) necessary for developing a sound African hermeneutic theory as a deconstructive enterprise. By explicitly using the word 'deconstruction' we simply seek to name what has been going on over the years. As Segovia has pointed out: "The process of deconstruction is going on in the Third World theologies without using the term . . . "⁷⁷ It has been going on " . . . by bringing into question the European texts and traditions so forcefully imposed on the colonized" by questioning their relevance and existential value here and now. This, we believe, is the task of philosophy, " . . . to carefully deconstruct these texts and traditions,

---

72. James M. Spradley (1972). Foundations of Cultural Knowledge. In: J. M. Spradley, *Culture and Cognition*. New York: Chandler Publishing Company, 18–24.

73. James P. Spradley (1980). *Participant Observation*. New York: Holt, Rinehart and Winston, Inc, 6 (Italics are in the original text).

74. Ulf Hannerz (1992). *Cultural Complexity: Studies in the Social Organization of Meaning*. New York: Columbia University Press, 3.

75. Ibid., 4.

76. Kathryn Tanner (1997). *Theories of Culture: A New Agenda for Theology*. Minneapolis: Fortress Press, 56–57.

77. Fernando F. Segovia (2000b). Deconstruction. In Virginia Fabella and R. S. Sugirtharajah (eds). *Dictionary of Third World Theologies*. Maryknoll, New York: Orbis Books, 67.

critically rejecting the mind-set steeped in European categories"[78] as well other rigid categories based on such traditions.

Deconstruction is a term that was coined by Jacques Derrida but it has since turned into a movement that enjoys the support of philosophers and theologians. However, its meaning remains unclear and shrouded in controversy, a fact that makes it highly resistant to any formal definition (6.4). According to Derrida, deconstruction is not 'an analysis, a critique, a method, an act, or an operation'.[79] Hence, there is a great deal of confusion as to what exactly deconstruction can be said to be—a school of thought, a method of reading, or merely a 'textual event'. Part of the difficulty in defining *deconstruction* arises from the fact that the act of defining *deconstruction* in the language of Western metaphysics requires one to accept the very metaphysical ideas that are the subject of deconstruction.

The central concern of deconstruction is a radical critique of the enlightenment project and of metaphysics, including the founding texts by such philosophers as Plato, Rousseau and Husserl but also other sorts of texts in literature within the Western philosophical tradition. It is aimed at the 'metaphysics of presence' (also known as logocentrism or sometimes phallogo-centrism), which holds that speech-thought (the *logos*) is a privileged, ideal, and self-present entity, through which all discourse and meaning are derived. Deconstruction has important and far reaching consequences in many fields and our fields of interest, religious and cultural studies.

While directing our attention to critical problems that merit serious consideration, deconstruction also identifies questions that contemporary theology and philosophy can no longer avoid.[80] Deconstructive reading in these disciplines tries to show that texts are not univocal. That they are not innocent, and so they cannot simply be read as works by individual authors communicating distinct and clear messages. Instead, they must be read as sites of conflict within a given localized culture or worldview. Because of deconstruction, texts reveal a multitude of many conflictual, if not contradictory, viewpoints existing side by side.

Evangelization

This study deals with inculturation as a method of evangelization. The word 'evangelization' is a noun that is etymologically derived from the Greek word, εὐαγγέλιον (*evangelion*), meaning 'that which is proper to the εὐάγγελος—the messenger of ancient Greece who was sent from the battle field by ship or by horse. This allowed a

---

78. Samuel Oluoch Imbo (1998). *An Introduction to African Philosophy*. Lanham: Rowman & Littlefield Publishers, Inc, 30.

79. Jacques Derrida (1985). Letter to A Japanese Friend. In David Wood & Robert Bernasconi (eds). *Derrida and Différance*. Warwick: Parousia Press, 3.

80. March C. Taylor (1982). *Deconstructing Theology*. New York: The Crossroad Publishing Company and Scholars Press, xix.

two-fold use in the antiquity of both reward/offering for tiding and the tidings themselves.[81] Paul used the word to cover 'the whole range of evangelistic and teaching ministry', that is, the good (eu) news (εὐαγγελιον) itself.[82] We think it is with this latter meaning that Pope Paul VI understood evangelization when he said " . . . it means bringing the Good News into all the strata of humanity, and through its influence transforming humanity from within and making it new."[83] In this study, we understand evangelization as the basic mission of the church, as Dorr puts it,[84] and successful evangelization as bringing the good news to people in their own language, hence expressing it in their mental categories and imageries.

Hermeneutics

The attempt to link a "text" (Gospel) to a given "context" (culture) is also known as "hermeneutics".[85] Etymologically, the word 'hermeneutics' comes from the Greek word ἑρμηνεία (*hermēneia*), which is, in turn, related to the verb ἑρμηνεύω (*hermēneuō*) that has many equivalents in English. It can mean to interpret, assert, translate, or even, mediate. The word is further related to Ἑρμής (*Hermes*), one of the twelve gods of Olympus in the ancient Greece. The ancient Greeks regarded him as the messenger god; who carried messages from gods to human beings and is, therefore, said to have taught humans how to speak. Being the bearer of messages from other gods and being himself the god of speech with which he communicated these messages to the people; it was said that he could use language, either to clarify the message, distort, or even to hide its intended meaning. In such circumstances then the Greeks had ". . .to face up to the bad news . . . to the fact that Hermes is also a well-known trickster and liar."[86] Consequently, he was the most revered god and people always sought to get favors from him in the form of good messages from other gods. Hermeneutics is, therefore, distinguishable *as a practice—hermeneusis* and as a theory *hermeneutics*.

The hermeneutic thought "rose to prominence historically as part of the Romantic reaction to the Enlightenment."[87] As a practice, though, hermeneutics is as old as human intelligence, when human beings started to interpret and understand reality

---

81. John P. Dickson (2005). Gospel as News: εὐαγγελ - from Aristophanes to the Apostle Paul. In *New Testament Studies,* vol. 51, no. 2 April, 212–213.

82. P. T. O'Brian (1995). *Gospel and Mission in the Writings of Paul: An Exegetical and Theological Analysis.* Grand Rapids, MI: Baker Books, 62.

83. Pope Paul VI (1977). *Evangelii Nuntiandi (On Evangelization in the Modern World).* New York: Liturgical Press, no. 18.

84. Dorr, op. cit., 76.

85. De Groot, op. cit., 151–156.

86. John D. Caputo (1987). *Radical Hermeneutics: Repetition, Deconstruction and the Hermeneutics Project.* Indianapolis: Indiana University Press, 6.

87. Nicolas H. Smith (1997). *Strong Hermeneutics: Contingency and Moral Identity.* London: Routledge, 4.

around them. As a theory, hermeneutics was born in the works of Schleiermacher, who attempted to clearly define the principles of valid interpretation.[88] Then Dilthey saw the necessity of incorporating the regional problem of the interpretation of texts into the broader field of historical knowledge.[89] Later on, Bultmann adopted the existential hermeneutics of Heidegger to 'demythologize' the New Testament.[90] It became formalized as an academic discipline, concerned with general interpretation of texts, as well as reality, in the works of philosophers like, Heidegger, Gadamer, Habermas and Ricoeur.[91] The historical development of hermeneutics can generally be divided into two: *general* hermeneutics, on the one hand, and *regional* hermeneutics[92] on the other; under which Biblical hermeneutics falls.

In the twentieth century, the hermeneutic theory has undergone a major transformation with respect to both the scope and methodology. It has, for instance, become the basis for a philosophical approach in the analysis of human understanding and behavior.[93] It is no longer confined to the spoken word or written texts, but also extends to reality in general, where it "...enquires into what conditions pertain for the understanding of 'what is other'; that is, of what lies beyond 'my' world of immediate concerns."[94] In the biblical sphere, too, hermeneutics can be understood both as a theory and a practice of interpreting the Bible. As a theory, it is the "...study of the general principles of biblical interpretation."[95] This is a purely academic function in which it analyses methods of biblical interpretations, as well as the way biblical writings are read, understood and applied in various social contexts outside academic circles.[96] On the practical realm, hermeneutics is the actual way in which people read and interpret the Holy Scriptures, a practice for which the term 'hermeneusis' would be more adequate, as we said above.[97]

---

88. F. D. E. Schleiermacher (1977). *Hermeneutics: The Handwritten Manuscripts*. Ed. by H. Kimmerle. Missoula, MT: Scholars Press.

89. Wilhelm Dilthey (1976). *Selected Writings*. Ed. by H. P. Rickman. Cambridge: Cambridge University Press.

90. Rudolf Bultmann (1961). *Kerygma and Myth: A Theological Debate*. New York: Harper & Row.

91. Martin Heidegger (1962). *Being and Time*. Trans by John Macquarrie and Edward Robinson. London: SCM Press LTD; Hans-Georg Gadamer (1975). *Truth and Method*. London: Sheed & Ward; Jürgen Habermas (1981). *The Theory of Communicative Action: The Critique of Functionalist Reason*. Cambridge: Polity Press; Paul Ricoeur (1983). Op. cit.

92. Taylor (1982), op. cit., 81, note 1.

93. see http://www.canisius.edu/~gallaghr/her.html

94. Anthony C. Thiselton (2002). *A Concise Encyclopedia of the Philosophy of Religion*. Oxford: Oneworld Publications, 129.

95. Philip W. Goetz (1989). Hermeneutics. In *Encyclopaedia Britannica* (Micropaedia) vol. 8: 15th ed. Chicago. Encyclopaedia Britannica Inc., 874.

96. Oeming, op. cit., 1.

97. Hans De Wit (2004). Through the Eyes of Another: Objectives and Back-grounds. In Hans de Wit et al (eds). *Through the Eyes of Another: Intercultural Reading of the Bible*. Amsterdam: Institute of Mennonite Studies.

Inculturation

This study focuses on the inculturational orientation of missiology, with interest in examining its practical application. In this study, the word 'inculturation' is used in the meaning given to it by John Mary Waliggo who defines it as an "honest and serious attempt to make Christ and his message of salvation evermore understood by people of every culture, locality and time"[98] in an effort to make the Gospel 'feel at home'.[99] Since the approach in this study is biblical, the presupposition is that the entire Bible is to be read in the light of Christ and his message, which then constitutes the Gospel. Thus, we postulate that the attempt 'to make the Gospel feel at home'[100] can best be realized by engaging the Bible in a meaningful dialogue with the *culture*(s) that surround(s) it. An engagement that is free from the fundamental instability that characterizes dialogue between unequal and unfamiliar partners.[101] Inculturation thus, is a method of evangelization which is, in turn, an aim of the mission.

Individualism

In this research the word 'individualism' is used to refer to the "social theory favoring freedom of action for individuals over collective or state control."[102] Individualism is a moral principle that forms the theoretical foundation of the supremacy of the 'I'. That is, "the recognition of the autonomy and the absolute rights of the individual in society."[103] Van der Walt has described this kind of individualism as a 'liberalistic' one, which places emphasis on being "free from and not necessarily freedom *towards* something. . . .Self-fulfilment and self-realization are of cardinal importance."[104] Hence, we contrast it with the community-oriented goals that, in the African context, sometimes even go against an individual's interests and wishes, for the benefit of the whole community.

---

98. Waliggo (1986). Op. cit., 12.

99. F. B. Welbourn, and B. A. Ogot (1966). *A Place to Feel at Home: A Study of Two Independent Churches in Western Kenya*. London: OUP.

100. Welbourn and Ogot, op. cit.

101. Cochrane, op. cit, xvii.

102. Judy Pearsall (ed.). (1999). *Concise Oxford Dictionary*, 10th ed. New York: Oxford University Press, Inc., 722.

103. Murad Saifulin and Richard R. Dixon (1984). *Dictionary of Philosophy*. New York: International Publishers, 194.

104. Van der Walt, op. cit., 44.

Missiology

The Greek word λόγος (*logos*) means 'study, word or discourse'. Thus, combined with the Latin word, *missio,* missiology means the study of the sending forth of missionaries.[105] As an academic discipline missiology arose as a form of critical reflection within the missionary movement that proceeded from European and North American Christianity to the rest of the world. New forms of Christianity in parts of the world where Western Christianity is no longer viewed as the norm have made missiologists aware of a legitimate pluralism and have gradually replaced the paradigm of expansion with that of communication.[106] Missiology, therefore, studies "the movement of Christianity in the midst of cultures, religions, socioeconomic systems and political institutions". It is particularly concerned with "the problems of communicating the gospel to the peoples of 'all nations' and with examining critically the theological concepts by means of which this faith interest is kept alive."[107] Missiology is not able to deal with its theological concerns without the aid of a variety of other disciplines, hence it is "multidisciplinary in character and holistic in approach."[108] In its long historical development, missiology has realized various models with different emphases. Luzbetak classifies them into three "major categories depending on whether the dominant trait of the model reveals (1) an ethnocentric, (2) an accommodational, or (3) a contextual orientation."[109] Within the contextual model, he distinguishes between incarnational and *inculturational* orientations.[110]

Mission

The Latin word *missio* means "a sending forth with a special message to bring or with a special task to perform."[111] Theologically speaking, 'mission' stands for the dynamic relation between God and the world. God *sends* his Son and the Spirit to fulfil his redemptive work. And those who feel called to become actively involved in this redemptive work understand themselves as missionaries, *sent* individuals and groups.[112] The word 'mission' has many components of meaning: mission as evangelization, inculturation, struggle for liberation, reconciliation, option for the poor and Power from the Spirit, to mention but a few.[113] But, as Pope John Paul II says: "It is not right to

---

105. Luzbetak op. cit., 12.
106. Frans J. Verstraelen et al (eds). (1995). *Missiology: An Ecumenical Introduction. Texts and Contexts of Global Christianity.* Grand Rapids, Michigan: William B. Eerdman Publishing Company, 1.
107. Ibid., 7.
108. Luzbetak, op. cit., 14.
109. Ibid., 64.
110. Ibid., 69.
111. Ibid., 12.
112. Verstraelen (1995). Op. cit., 4.
113. Dorr, op. cit., 76–186.

give an incomplete picture of missionary activity, as if it consisted principally in helping the poor, contributing to liberation of the oppressed, promoting development or defending human rights. The missionary Church is certainly involved on these fronts but her primary task lies elsewhere... Missionary activity must first of all bear witness to and proclaim salvation in Christ".[114] Here we use the word mission as it is used in the scriptures with the meaning of 'being sent to proclaim the Gospel'.[115] According to Pope John Paul II,[116] the first and basic form of mission is evangelization, while inculturation is but one way for evangelization.

Worldview

The words 'individualism' and 'communitarianism' (discussed above) are ambiguous because they can refer to both a social structure, and a social theory or 'worldview'.[117] Although the word 'worldview' is widely used and its meaning often taken for granted, its definition is as elusive as its comprehension. Sihna and Jansen López capture this difficulty when they refer to "the notorious difficulty of defining the notion of 'world view.'"[118] We would, however, like to borrow the understanding of Palmer for whom "the term refers to the fundamental cognitive orientation of a society, a subgroup, or even an individual."[119] We think this 'cognitive orientation' is shaped by culture and it determines the way people perceive, interpret, understand, and therefore, respond to new ideas, events, people and even texts, including biblical texts. A worldview thus, is that lasting impression that lies behind a people's meaning system that dictates their daily operations in any cultural scene. In any given community, a worldview is manifested in what Spradley calls 'cultural themes'.[120]

Strategies in this Research

This study is focusing on inculturation as a method of evangelization which, in turn, is understood as the basic mission of the church.[121] Evangelisation and inculturation will be looked at from a missiological perspective. Since its very beginning, missiology has had an interdisciplinary approach; it comprises the philosophy, science and

---

114. Pope John Paul II (1991). *Redemptoris Missio.* Nairobi: Paulines Publications Africa, no. 83.

115. Mathew 16: 15.

116. John Paul II (1991). Op. cit., no. 42.

117. Gyekye (1997). Op. cit., 149.

118. C. Sihna and Jansen K. de López (2000). Language, Culture and the Embodiment of Spatial Cognition. In *Cognitive Linguistics* 11 (1/2), 27.

119. G. B. Palmer (1996). *Towards a Theory of Cultural Linguistics.* Austin: University of Texas Press, 113–114.

120. Spradley (1980). Op. cit., 141.

121. Dorr, op cit., 76.

theology of mission.[122] This study is also interdisciplinary because it uses insights and instruments of three disciplines: philosophy, anthropology and theology. The epistemological notion of 'constructivism' (which is philosophical) serves as a link between anthropology and theology (1.8, 2.7, 6.3). Within theology it uses insights from systematic theology (because it is focuses on the principles of hermeneutics), practical theology (because it studies the dialectical relationship between the actual practice of inculturation and what it should be), and literary theology (because it seeks to use the passage of the Good Shepherd—Jn. 10: 1–18 to present its case). The bulk part of this project will be based on literature review, whereby we will examine the philosophical-theological debate going on in Africa and the hermeneutic theories being used, and then make personal reflections on them. But the most important part of the work, in which lies the originality of our contribution, is an ethnographic field research. We will follow Spradley's research method in the hope that it will help us come up with practical suggestions for a form of hermeneutics that may contribute in reducing the gap between the real and the ideal in the process of inculturation.

The Grounded Theory Approach

Spradley's approach is directed toward the development of theories grounded on empirical data of cultural description, what Glaser and Strauss have called 'Grounded Theory'.[123] A Ground Theory Approach works with sensitizing concepts. As a starting point, we tend to think that the Pökot people have a communitarian worldview, yet the form of hermeneutics they have so far been exposed to is born of a Western thought-pattern, which tends to be individualistic. The extent to which this is the case is included in the research questions. Thus, there is a gap between the people's and their pastors' mental frameworks. As a result, the Word of God has not sufficiently taken root in West Pökot due to the inadequacy of this kind of approach. We, therefore, think that this situation calls for a kind of hermeneutics that is developed from a Pökot perspective, worldview and social set-up. Hence our research objective to investigate the conditions necessary for the development of a hermeneutics that will adequately address the Pökot people's needs and aspirations.[124]

To develop these sensitizing concepts into a credible hypothesis, we are going to use a bottom-up investigative process in the field approach, as opposed to the current top-down approaches. In such practices, a person uses personal experience and education from books to develop various theories of hermeneutics. On the contrary, we are going to investigate how ordinary people on the ground actually interpret the Bible (*hermeneusis*) and then look for a way forward in developing a credible hermeneutic

---

122. Jan A.B. Jongeneel and P. Lang (1995). *Philosophy, Science and Theology of Mission in the 19th and 20th Centuries. A Missiological Encyclopedia. Part I and II.* Frankfurt am Main: Lang.

123. Spradley (1980). Op. cit., 15.

124. Ndegwah (2006). Op. cit., 84.

theory (*hermeneutics*). It is these people we intend to make the target of our investigations and learn how they apply the Bible in their day-to-day life. What we are suggesting here is not new, since individuals (like Cochrane) and organizations (like EATWOT) have already done the same, "in a bid to understand the significance of religious insights drawn from daily struggles in a local community."[125] The Ecumenical Association of Third World Theologians (EATWOT) had adopted the approach since its inception in 1976, when the participants chose to 'reject as irrelevant' what they perceived as Western "academic type of theology that is divorced from action".[126] In its place, they pledged "a radical break in epistemology which makes commitment to the first act of theology and engages in critical reflection on the reality of the Third World".[127] A notable example in this regard is the work of Kalilombe, where he tried, as De Groot puts it, to 'localize' the missionary reading of the Bible, to suit the local situation and people's aspirations.[128] What is new is the fact that we are going to involve 'ordinary Christians' at the grass root level, within the set-up of the small Christian communities (henceforth referred to as SCCs), in all the stages of understanding the bible text of our choice. Then we build on their experiences to recommend a hermeneutic model that we think befits their social situation.

The Qualitative Research Method

We have chosen to use a qualitative method and carry out ethnographic interviews, as participant observers among the Pökot people. The choice of the qualitative method for our research is not based on a bias that it is better than other research methods, or that it is more desirable than the rest. There are two reasons for this. First, the current researcher has worked with the Maryknoll Institute of African Studies of St. Mary's University of Minnesota and Tangaza College, Nairobi, for four years (1997–2000) as a research assistant, where the qualitative research method is used. Due to this past training, we thought it is wise to carry on and use the same method as the basic frame of reference in our fieldwork. The second and most important reason is that, the qualitative method has distinct characteristics that clearly fit the intentions of the researcher.

We are interested in understanding the meaning system the Pökot people use to interpret their experience and to generate their behavior. According to Spradley, parts of meaning systems are tacit and cannot, therefore, be observed directly.[129] They

---

125. Cochrane, op. cit., xvi.

126. S. Torres and V. Fabella (1976). *The Emergent Gospel: Theology From the Underside of History. Papers From the Ecumenical Dialogue of Third World Theologians*. Maryknoll, New York: Orbis Books, 269.

127. Ibid., 269.

128. Kalilombe (1999). Op. cit., 167–195; De Groot, A., (1995). One Bible and Many Interpretive Contexts: Hermeneutics in Missiology. In Frans F.J. Verstraelen et al (eds). *Missiology: An Ecumenical Introduction: Texts and Contexts of Global Christianity*. Grand Rapids, Mich.: Eerdmans, 147–149.

129. Spradey (1980). Op. cit., 5.

are only inferred from what people do in their daily lives, what they say within their culture and from the things they make: thus, he talks of *cultural behavior*, *cultural speech*[130], and *cultural artifacts*. These, as Spradley has shown, are the elements that guide an ethnographic research. In our case the element 'speech' is the most important one, since what people know about the Gospel is of ultimate importance in determining whether, and to what extent they appropriate the Word of God into their lives. We are also going to use behavior and artefacts to see how people go about reading the text, and whether this has a reference to their culture or not. This, we will do in two ways, participant observation and ethnographic interviews.

The Social Situation

Spradley understands a social situation as any place (e.g., a street corner, a village, a town and a city) where a researcher participates in people's activities through observation. When people begin attaching a meaning to the social system, then he refers to this as a cultural scene, when its meaning system is shared. Accordingly, a social situation is identified by three primary elements of the place, actors and activities.[131] As a participant observer, this researcher located himself in a place and watches actors of some sort and becomes involved with them. He also observed and participated in activities that went on in this social situation.

The Place

We carried out the field research for a period of six months (March—August 2002), in nine small Christian communities, one in each of the nine Catholic parishes within the West Pökot County in the North-western part of Kenya (Appendix 1: map 1). Since the inhabitants of this county, the Pökot, are not a homogeneously regimented society, we will subdivide the county, rather than the land they occupy[132] into five smaller regions following the various physical and social-cultural features that have dominated their lives. The first three regions are the most densely populated, characterized by low-lying flat, dry plains and evergreen highlands that are dotted with hills, mountains and escarpments. The first region generally covers the locations of Mnagei, Kapenguria,

---

130. Although Spradley uses the word *cultural knowledge*, we think the word *cultural speech* is better because it is consistent with his own subsequent references to his method of participant observation whereby the former can only be inferred from the latter. Therefore, what people know (knowledge) is inferred from what they say (speech). Moreover, equating speech with knowledge would be to assume too much in the sense that sometimes one is not able to express thought in speech or only does so partially.

131. Spradley (1980). Op. cit., 39.

132. Note that the Pökot people occupy more than the administrative county of West Pökot and 'spill' into Trans Nzoia County on the south, Baringo and Elgeyo-Marakwet Counties to the east, Turkana County to the north and into the Pökot County in the neighboring Republic of Uganda.

Kipkomo and Batei (see Appendix 1: map 2), which are in the ecclesiastical jurisdiction of Tartar, Bendera, Chepareria and parts of Ortum Catholic parishes. It also has the advantage of a tarmac road passing through it and is more susceptible to influence from the outside world. The inhabitants have a different mannerism because they are no longer rigid in following the traditional ways of life and even their diction in spoken Pökot is heavily influenced by English and Kiswahili.

The second region comprises Lelan, Cheptulel, Mwino and Lomut locations, situated in Kabichbich and parts of Sigor (traditionally written as Psikor) Parishes. These are mainly highlands and the inhabitants are basically agriculturists, growing crops like pyrethrum, keeping exotic cows and rearing merino sheep for wool export. Here the neighboring Marakwet language influences the spoken Pökot and culture cannot be said to be sacrosanct. The third region covers the locations of Masol, Weiwei, Sekerr and Sook within parts of Sigor Parish and Chepnyal Parish. The inhabitants are thought to speak the 'pure' Pökot since they have less contact with outsiders and their culture is regarded as still intact. The last two regions are in the purely pastoral Pökot area known as Karapökot, a low-lying, dry and arid area that spots few hills here and there, with green vegetation only seen near the rivers and water points. It is roughly divided into two parts—the northern and southern region. The fourth region covers the locations of Riwa, Suam and Kapchok in Kacheliba Parish, with the spoken Pökot bearing influence from the Sebei and Karimojong languages of Uganda. The fifth region consists of three locations; these are Kasei, Chemerongit and Alale, all of which are in Amakuriat Parish. Here the spoken Pökot bears a lot of linguistic marks from their northern neighbors, the Turkana (of Kenya) and Karimojong (of Uganda) from the west. From each of these regions we randomly selected two SCCs for cross checking the results. Geographical location and socio-cultural influence then came out as the main criteria of choosing which SCCs to participate in this research.

The Actors

The actors in our field of operation are the Pökot people of North-western Kenya (in East Africa) and their pastors. In a nutshell, the Pökot are, broadly speaking, divided into two groups, the purely pastoral Pökot who live in the arid, sparsely populated low-lying plains and those who live in the mountainous regions. The former are known as 'the people of cows—*pipö tich*' while the latter are known as 'the people of grains—*pipö pagh*', because they mix pastoralism with farming.[133] The Pökot are part of the Kalenjin speaking communities in Kenya and Uganda, and they speak their

---

133. The variant spellings by Fedders and Salvadori (1998), in their book, *Peoples and Cultures of Kenya,* reprint. Nairobi: Trans Africa Press, 67, may be a result of two factors: one, they may not have had the knowledge of the Pökot language grammar and so depended on listening to the way the people sounded when talking about these groups of people. Two, there were no text books written in the Pökot language at the time of their research and so it was difficult for them to get the exact wording of the two expressions.

own language, called *ngala Pökot*, which has not been in writing until only about 40 years ago. This is manifested by the fact that there are not many people who can fluently read the few available Pökot text books: namely the New Testament, a book on proverbs, sayings and idiomatic expressions, and the first Pökot class text book. The pastors consist of catechists (most of whom are Pökot), the sisters in charge of pastoral work (who are very few and most of them are missionaries, except in Tartar where we have a diocesan congregation) and the priests. The latter group consists of missionaries (from two religious congregations—the Kiltegans and Combonis) and diocesan priests, all of whom are non-Pökot, as the only Pökot priest works outside the county. More about the Pökot will be said in chapter two where we deal with the people and social context of West Pökot, whereas more about their pastors will be said in chapter four, where we deal with the way they interpret the Bible and give their historical involvement in the county.

The Activities

The daily activities of the people depend very much on their geographical location which we will deal with later in chapter two. It is in this context that 'ordinary' Pökot Christians live and practice their faith, part of which is to attend the church service (or Mass) on Sundays and weekly attendance of the SCC prayers, which is the focal point of our field research. The meetings are arranged on a rotational basis and the organizers see to it that every Christian's home is visited before the start of another round. The SCCs in West Pökot use the 'Seven Step' Lumko method of Bible Meditation in the SCC setting. It was developed for neighborhood gospel groups by the Lumko Institute, in the Catholic Diocese of Johannesburg, South Africa. From there, it has spread into many African countries and has been well-received in other countries as well. It deals with a method of communal, prayerful approach to Sacred Scriptures which may help the readers to encounter God and one another and help them open their eyes to the presence and to the working of God in their everyday life. The method provides the opportunity for: allowing the Bible to speak to oneself first and, out of this perplexity, to share with one another (rather than just 'talk about' the Bible). The process consists of seven steps as follows:

> FIRST STEP: We invite the Lord
>
> Once the group settles down, the facilitator asks someone to volunteer "to invite the Lord". The belief in the living presence of the Risen Christ in our midst is the presupposition and basis of our meditation. We want to meet the Word who became flesh and dwells among us. We remember Jesus' promise: "Where two or three are gathered in my name, I shall be there with them."[134]

---

134. Mathew 18: 20.

SECOND STEP: We read the text

The facilitator announces the chosen text. First the book, then the chapter. He/she waits until everyone has found the chapter and only then does he/she announce the verse. When everyone has found the passage, the facilitator invites someone to volunteer to read the text. A moment of silence follows.

THIRD STEP: We dwell on the text

The facilitator continues: "We dwell on the text. Which words strike you in a special way?" In doing so, almost the entire text is listened to again. The participants spontaneously read aloud the word or words that have impressed them. Whole verses are not read, only short phrases or individual words. The participants are encouraged to repeat those words silently to themselves three or four times. It is extremely important that a moment of silence be kept after each person has spoken, allowing the message to "soak in". As a result of this step, "simple" words often take on new meaning.

FOURTH STEP: We are quiet

After spending time on the individual word, the entire passage is read again slowly. Then the facilitator announces a time of silence, giving the exact length of time, for example, three minutes. We advise the people to spend this time in silence before God. "We are open to God." "We allow ourselves to be loved by him." "We let God look at us." A helpful practice during this silence is to repeat a specific word. Meditation: Simply to be open to God, to wait for him, to be with him, "in fact he is not far from any of us."[135]

FIFTH STEP: We share what we have heard in our hearts

After the time of quiet, the facilitator announces the next step: "We share with each other what we have heard in our hearts." We do this to share with one another our faith experience and to help each other to grow in the faith. The entire Sacred Scripture is nothing less than a God experience which the People of Israel and Jesus "share" with us. It is somewhat strange that we can talk to friends about almost every aspect of our life yet when it comes to sharing with others our experience with God, we become shy. In this Bible meditation method, however, anyone can learn "to risk" this sharing in a very natural and unpressured way.

SIXTH STEP: We search together

The facilitator announces: "We search together." Now the time has come for the participants to examine their lives in the light of the Gospel. At this stage, a basic community might discuss everyday problems such as the following:

Someone needs help in the neighborhood . . .

---

135. Acts 17: 27.

Children need instruction in the faith . . .

Who will lead the Service of the Word next Sunday, since the priest will not be there? . . .

How can we settle a discord that has arisen? . . .

What can we do about getting the street lamp repaired? . . .

None of these problems need to have a direct connection to the Bible passage which had been read and shared. However, they emerge and can be resolved because of the mutual confidence that now exists in an atmosphere of the presence of God. Things look different when God is allowed to be present.

SEVENTH STEP: We pray together

The facilitator now invites everyone to pray. The words of Scripture, the various experiences of God's Word, the daily problems—these all become fuel for prayer. Some find this form of sharing in prayer the easiest way to communicate with others. The participants are encouraged to incorporate in their personal prayer whatever has been of special importance to them during the meditation. Only at the end is a formal prayer known to everyone recited.

In ordinary circumstances, this seven-step prayer session lasts between one and two hours, with steps four and six taking the lion's share of the total time schedule. These prayer sessions are conducted weekly in the homes of every Christian and the animator is usually the person in who's home the prayer session is conducted. There is, however, a trained catechist in charge of coordinating all SCC prayers in the whole parish, whose work is to ensure that Christians know what to do during the prayer sessions. It must be clarified that the Lumko method of bible sharing is not a research method, but it provided a suitable occasion for us to record the Christians' (who in this case are our informants) bible sharing.

The activities of the pastors range from the administration of their parishes to the dispensation of sacraments. The administrative duties include building of new churches, workshop centers and other mundane activities like organizing food-for-work programs, paying the catechists, and other parish workers, their monthly salaries and so on. Spiritual duties include visiting the sick, at home and in hospitals, preparing the catechumens for baptism, confirmation, marriage and so on, dispensing sacraments like saying Mass and administering extreme Unction to the sick. The parish priest shares these duties with his catechists (and sometimes with the sister-in-charge of pastoral work, where such provision exists, and/or with the assistant priest, where there is one) in meetings arranged every month (or fortnight). Here duties are shared out and everyone is expected to stick to his or her specific duty until the next meeting, where evaluation is done to determine success and failure, followed by a discussion to make things clearer. Of the three cadres of pastoral workers, catechists are the more active in the SCCs.

Methods and Sources

Our research methods were three—fieldwork, literature review and theological as well as philosophical reflections that correlate the fieldwork and the literature review. In the fieldwork part our sources were the people of West Pökot and their pastors, while for literature review we used the literature we could find about the Pökot people and in the discipline of hermeneutics. For the fieldwork, we used the methods of participant observation and ethnographic interviews. We observed and interviewed the people and their pastors, within the SCCs prayers sessions, and outside the prayer setting in their day-to-day life situation. As participant observers we presented the pericope of the Good Shepherd[136] to eight small Christian communities (one from every parish) in West Pökot and tape-recorded the proceedings of a spontaneous bible sharing session by the people and their pastors. Then, we interviewed the community members later in their own homes about their bible sharing experience and then used ethno-semantic analysis to determine the relevance of the text to the people's lives as they go about their daily business. We also made field notes as we interacted with the people and participated in their life activities in their homes.

Then we repeated the whole process with the pastors: that is, we recorded their Sunday sermons and interviewed them, in the same way we had done with the people and then observed their daily routine and made more field notes. Next, we compared the results of people's lifestyle, and their interpretation of the parable of the Good Shepherd to that of their pastors and what the commentaries say, which made the basis of our final suggestion in the last chapter of our research. In this case, the correlation between what the people say and what their pastors say was the determining factor of what we said, earlier on, about the hermeneutic approach that is relevant to the Pökot social situation and people's mental disposition. The choice of the parable of the Good Shepherd was influenced by, but not limited to, the fact that the Pökot people are pastoralists and so the term shepherd is likely to evoke many cultural themes,[137] and points of density which can easily be identified by the lay[138] people in the event that these have found their way into their religious lives.

The choice of a single text has been preferred in order to limit the frame of reference in our discussions and also to control its scope, due to the time factor (which was only six months of field research). We need to clarify that any other text could have been used with similar, if not the same, results given sufficient time and without the undue worry of beating specific deadlines in terms of travelling, both inside and outside the country and compilation of the findings. Then finally we went through the available literature about the Pökot people and the discipline of hermeneutics and

136. John 10: 1–18.
137. Spradley (1980). Op. cit., 140.
138. Unless otherwise stated, the word 'lay' is used, throughout this study in the traditional ecclesiastical sense of those members of the church that are not ordained into the clerical hierarchy, irrespective of whether they are theologically trained or not.

tried to synthesize it with our findings in the field, before incorporating it into our work as chapters two, three and four.

Data Collection

The first phase of our fieldwork was data collection in which we had two sources—the Pökot informants and their pastors on the one hand, and the available literature on the Pökot people and on the discipline of hermeneutics, on the other hand. We took on the role of participant observers and just watched what goes on in community life among the Pökot and listened to their stream of consciousness as they shared the bible passage.

Through immersion in the Pökot lifestyle, the researcher hoped to discover the cultural themes, as expressed in folk terms, cultural domains and other points of density, which serve as the Pökot frame of reference as they try to understand new situations, people, events and ideas. Together with participant observation were ethnographic interviews through which we hoped to discover the religious themes and existential values that characterize the Pökot culture and how they influence their belief in God, as preached by Christianity. We did this by mainly asking *descriptive*, *structural* or *contrast*[139] questions; and these were supplemented with other kinds of questions like the third-party, personal and story questions, as the need arose. This, we believe, is an effective way to give Christians a chance to freely express their thoughts, feelings, opinions and, more importantly, their perspective on bible teachings; and how these are passed on to them. The words of Denzin are as true today as they were when he wrote them: "While the interviewer is the expert in asking the questions, the respondent is the expert as far as answers are concerned."[140]

Firstly, we paid special attention to the use of personal pronouns like 'I', 'my' and 'me', on the one hand, and 'we', and 'our', and 'us', on the other hand, by the Pökot Christians in the SCC prayer sessions (such analysis of personal pronouns has been supported by other African scholars like Kenyatta and Gyekye.[141] We regarded the

---

139. These three kinds of questions form the backbone of any qualitative research and so we think they merit a short explanation. Descriptive questions simply ask the respondent(s) to describe a particular kind of situation or form of behavior. For instance, can you tell me something about cattle rustling among the Pökot? Structural questions seek to understand the structure(s) behind a certain form of behavior or protocol. For instance, what is the structure of the Pökot clan system? Finally, contrast questions have something to do with comparing one situation with another. For instance, what is the difference between a person married to one wife and another married to many wives among the Pökot? The first kind of questions lead to domain analysis, the second one leads to taxonomic analysis, while the last kind of questions leads to componential analysis. This latter analysis finally leads to the discovering of cultural themes.

140. Norman K. Denzin (1970). *The Research Act in Sociology*. London: Butterworth, 142.

141. Jomo Kenyatta (1999). *Facing Mount Kenya*, reprint. Nairobi: Kenway Publications; Kwame Gyekye (1997). *Tradition and Modernity: Philosophical Reflections on the African Experience*. New York: Oxford University Press, 166.

dominant usage of the latter as an indicator of communitarianism; whereas the use of the former challenged our assumption. Secondly, we observed people's sitting arrangement in the SCCs, whether a speaker in the sharing session addressed other members in general or only the chairperson; and whether the social atmosphere projected the aims of a coherent group work. Thirdly, we observed their artefacts. We tried to see if there were special ornaments or cultural tools attributed only to shepherds and whether the people were willing to identify them with Jesus as a Good Shepherd. About the extent to which cultural thinking influences bible interpretation, this was determined by the extent to which people drew practical examples from their own cultures to illustrate certain points in the Bible. To achieve this, we made a domain analysis of the most predominant cultural points of density and then made a componential analysis of those domains, through which we hoped to discover the Pökot cultural themes in relation to the parable of the Good Shepherd.[142]

It is, however, not lost on us that the mere use of collective personal pronouns, like 'us' and 'we', is not in itself a clear proof of communitarianism among the Pökot. We, therefore, needed to go back to the people after the prayer session and carry out an in-depth interview to come out with a detailed and precise meaning of the most recurrent terms. In the recitation of Our Lord's Prayer, for instance, the words '. . .give us this day our daily bread. . .' are used, but the main question is whether they mean the same thing in all parts of the world. In the Pökot case, we wanted to know the kind of 'ownership' they had in mind when they talk of 'our daily bread'. We had to find out if they were thinking of a communal ownership, where this bread belongs to all members of the society in a collective way; or to every member of the community individually.

The second part of our research method was the Sunday sermons and interviews with the pastors (catechists, sisters and priests). We started by attending, listening to and recording Sunday sermons by priests and catechists in various churches and homes within West Pökot. In general, we asked the priests (or catechists), within the area where we were conducting our research, to preach on this pericope the Sunday after our interviews: that is, just before we moved on to a different area. The indicators we were looking for were the usage of individual pronouns like 'I', singular 'you', 'me' etc., as opposed to the more inclusive pronouns like, 'we', 'us' etc. We also examined the sources of the materials used to prepare sermons and tried to identify their relevance to the Pökot situation. Then we interviewed the pastors in West Pökot and training institutions to see how they realize their goals of evangelization among the Pökot. Finally, we consulted the available literature about the Pökot and the discipline of hermeneutics to give us a more focused view of the people and their way of life.

---

142. Spradley (1980). Op. cit., 140-144.

Data Analysis

Once the data collection phase was complete, we started the second phase, which is data analysis. For this, we used two methods that supplemented each other. The first one is the Kwalitan[143] computer program, which supplements Spradley's method by helping to break down the raw data from the field into short analyzable sentences according to the respondents or personal field notes. We divided the raw data into two files (one of the Christians and one of their pastors) with 110 segments, (according to the number of informants) each of which was divided into two fragments (bible sharing and interview). Next, we subdivided the segments into six codes in accordance with the key field research questions that we had formulated at the onset of the research (5.1). Then we used Kwalitan to identify all key categories within the created codes and finally we made a tree structure that gave us a bird's eye view of how these categories are related to the codes and segments. Other important activities of Kwalitan in data analysis were word-counting, word-search and word-context, which helped to identify not only how many times a word was used but also the context and number of people that had used it. Division into files, segments and codes are aimed at organizing the raw field data to ease its analysis, word-count, word context and word search are to identify predominant cultural domains.

We used Kwalitan as an effective supplement to the insights from the method developed by James Spradley on practicing ethnography, componential analysis and the discovering of cultural themes. Spradley was trained in the early sixties and a lot of criticism has been levelled against his method and new insights developed into his structural method of doing research. We, therefore, tried to update his knowledge (and our own) with the use of more recent scholars in qualitative research like, Denzin[144] and current ones like Silverman.[145] The goal of doing ethnography is to "...grasp the native's point of view, his relation to life, to realize his vision of his world,"[146] so this research aimed at discovering how these elements affect the Pökot people's interpretation of the Gospel. In this analysis, our aim was to find the Pökot cultural themes that may have found their way into the bible sharing; a fact that helped us in determining if they have succeeded in inculturating the Word into their lifestyle or they had failed to do so.

Spradley describes ethnographic analysis as the search for the parts of a culture and their relationships as conceptualized by informants.[147] This is done through the discovery and analysis of cultural domains, taxonomies and their related components

---

143. Kwalitan is a qualitative computer program that has been developed in the Radboud University Nijmegen by Prof. Vincent Peters and his colleagues.

144. Denzin (1970). Op. cit.

145. David Silverman (2000). *Interpreting Qualitative Data: Methods for Analysing Talk, Text and Interaction*, 2nd ed. London: SAGE Publications.

146. Malinowski, Bronislaw (1922). *Argonauts of the Western Pacific.* London: Routledge, 25.

147. Spradley (1980). Op. cit., 85.

and has successfully been done at the doctoral level by Frans Wijsen, Joan Burke and Caleb Chul-Soo Kim.[148] Domain analysis involves a search for the larger units of cultural knowledge called domain. A domain is any symbolic category that includes other categories in which all members share, at least, one feature of meaning (Spradley 1980: 88). Among the Pökot tribe of the larger Kalenjin ethnic group in Kenya, for instance, the category 'friend' (*konget*) includes eight other categories of a ritual friend, close friend, casual friend, opponent, follower, ally, neutral and personal enemy (*punyon*). Including personal enemies (*püng*) in the domain of friends is meaningful in the Pökot culture because, they can be transformed into ritual friends through a special reconciliation ceremony called *parpara*.[149] Taxonomic analysis involves a search for the internal structure of the domain, and leads to identifying contrast sets.[150] A folk taxonomy is a set of categories organized based on a single semantic relationship. For example, to buy a newsmagazine, say, Time, one goes to a magazine rack, but leaves out all other *kinds* of magazines and concentrate on the section of newsmagazines. A taxonomy differs from a domain in one respect; it shows the relationship among all folk terms within a domain.

Componential analysis is a search for the attributes that signal differences among symbols in a domain. Whenever a researcher discovers contrasts among members of a category, they are best thought of in terms of attributes or components of meaning for any term.[151] Among the young people in Nairobi, for instance, the terms *kuhata* and *kulenga* belong to the domain of failure, but they have different attributes that are not revealed by their similarity. The former has an attribute of an individual who fails to do something due to weakness or ignorance, whereas the latter has an attribute of one who intentionally fails to do something. Theme analysis searches for the relationships among domains and how they are linked to culture. A theme is "a postulate or position, declared or implied, and usually controlling behaviour or stimulating activity, which is tacitly approved or openly promoted in a society."[152]

---

148. Frans Wijsen (1993). *There is Only One God.* Ph.D. Dissertation. Kampen: Uitgeverij Kok; Joan F. Burke (2001). *These Catholic Sisters are all Mamas! Towards the Inculturation of the Sisterhood in Africa, an Ethnographic Study.* Leiden: Koninklijke Brill NV; and Caleb Chul-Soo Kim (2004). *Islam among the Swahili in East Africa.* Nairobi: Acton Publications.

149. James Spradley (1980: 88) has reported a similar observation among the Tausug people of the Philippines, and Lucy Mair (1965). *An Introduction to Social Anthropology.* Oxford: Clarendon Press) observed the same trend among the Nuer people of South Sudan.

150. Spradley (1980). Op. cit., 94.

151. Ibid., 131.

152. Morris E. Opler (1945). Themes as Dynamic Forces in Culture. In *American Journal of Sociology,* No. 53, 198.

GENERAL INTRODUCTION

Literature Review and Theological Reflections

Once data analysis was finished we entered the third phase of correlating the field data with what the available literature says about the Pökot people and the discipline of hermeneutics, before incorporating the results of our fieldwork, about the Christians in West Pökot and their pastors, into the other chapters of our dissertation. We hoped that the discovery of cultural themes among the Christians would help us come to grips with why the Pökot people interpret the scriptures the way they do. We then compared this with the way the Bible was brought and continues to be preached to them by both the missionaries and local preachers; trained in a Western model of interpreting the Bible. Then we tried to look at how they have managed to live with their own worldview vis-à-vis this new biblical worldview of interpreting and understanding the world—a sort of double-faceted worldview. We presumed that understanding the dialectical relationship between the two worldviews, its pros and cons, would help us make a meaningful contribution in the field of African biblical hermeneutics. One that has made informed recommendations on the necessary steps that can lead to relevant, culture-friendly hermeneutics, necessary for the inculturation of the Gospel in West Pökot.

Organization of the Study

This dissertation consists of an introduction, five chapters and a summary, with the following structure. Chapter one is primarily theological-philosophical in nature. It revisits the inculturation debate going on in Africa, by looking at the general contribution of both philosophy and theology. It, therefore, starts with definition, and a brief historical survey of the development of the term 'inculturation'. It then looks at the use of the Bible in Africa and the efforts by African theologians to develop an authentically African biblical hermeneutics, based on African cultural values. The suggestion made here is that there is need for a communitarian hermeneutics that is community-centered, both as its starting point and as its final point. Such hermeneutics necessarily seeks to liberate people, from all kinds of oppression in both sacred and secular spheres, as a community rather than as individuals. It also tries to show the relationship between hermeneutics and culture and posits that the latter influences the former. There follows a sketchy analysis of the current understanding of culture and an effort to link it to the understanding of the African culture, with its main characteristic of communitarianism versus individualism. Next, it briefly mentions the main trends in African philosophy and their failure to adequately address the issue of communitarianism in Africa and ends with the call for deconstruction by hermeneutical philosophy in Africa. It also looks at the growth and development of theology in Africa, which has culminated in various theological trends. At the close of this chapter it looks at the conceptual model of the Church-as-Family and shows the problems that bedevil it in the face of the rapidly changing values in Africa.

Chapter two is a contextual bridge between chapter one and chapters three and four. It contextualizes the debate in the first chapter by taking a look at the geographical and social realities of West Pökot, by enumerating people's cultural values and their social structure, in order to help the reader to capture their worldview, by understanding their cultural meaning system. This helps one appreciate the Pökot conceptualization of issues and how they interpret new realities, ideas and texts around them. Chapters three and four are anthropological in nature, based on fieldwork among the 'ordinary' Christians in West Pökot and their pastors. Chapter three starts by examining the Pökot way of life, through domain analysis, of their verbal sources (language), material sources (artefact) and behavioral sources (behavior), particularly their ritual system. This is followed by the outcome of the bible sharing sessions on the parable of the Good Shepherd[153] and the interviews we made as we partook in people's lives as participant observers.

Chapter four is a presentation of the outcome of the same bible text, the parable of the Good Shepherd,[154] that we presented to the pastors, then observed and listened to their interpretation so as to compare it with that of the 'ordinary Christians'. We had also taken part in their everyday life, to the extent that they allowed us, as participant observers, and carried out interviews with them on the nature of their work. It starts off with the brief history of evangelization in West Pökot, which only dates back fifty years ago, then it examines the methods the missionaries used to bring the Word of God to the people and their reaction to it. It particularly highlights the problems faced by the missionaries, like translation and communication. The chapter ends by pointing out the underlying tension between the people's worldview and that of their pastors.

In chapter five we revisit this tension and suggest a way forward—an adoption of a communitarian hermeneutics. We thus make a link between the theological-philosophical debates in chapter one and the results of our anthropological findings in chapters three and four. This gives our project an interdisciplinary as well as practical-theological approach. We try to show how the two perspectives—the abstract and the practical—can be bridged, through the change of approach to the very idea of inculturation, as a method of evangelization; geared towards the good of the mission of the church. We hope to have added a new dimension to the study on biblical hermeneutics by showing cause why we think that a hermeneutics, based on the key concept of communitarianism, is better placed to bridge the gap between the worldview of the people and that of their pastors.

This requires a form of flexibility on the part of the Christians and their pastors to abandon their old ways of looking at the notion of evangelization and adopt a dynamic approach that brings the two parties together to meet midway from either

153. John 10: 1–16.
154. Ibid.

of the extreme positions. Hence we employ Derrida's concept of deconstruction to understand the nature of communitarianism among the Pökot. In conclusion, we make a general survey of our work and point out the successes and limitations of our achievements. We also give the reason(s) for this and make suggestions on what could be done to ward off such failures in the future as well as how the already gained success can be enhanced.

CHAPTER 2

THEORY AND PRACTICE OF INCULTURATION IN AFRICA

Introduction

IN THIS CHAPTER, WE are going to situate the debate on inculturation in its historical context in the fields of philosophy and theology within the African continent. It explores the general development of hermeneutics in Africa, and the subsequent need for authentically African hermeneutics, built on African categories of thought. The chapter starts by examining the beginning and development of the word 'inculturation' because this study is primarily concerned with seeking an effective way to inculturate the Gospel in the African context. We go through the historical process of evangelization, which reached the Pökot people at the same time with colonialism and as such they could not distinguish between these two enterprises. These historical events witnessed the suppression of the African culture by both the colonizers and the missionaries—the former for the purpose of uprooting the Pökot from their ancestral land and the latter for the purpose of salvation (which the missionaries regarded as incompatible with the Pökot culture)—with the resultant situation of what we call 'cultural schizophrenia'[1] in which people paid allegiance to two, often incompatible cultures, in the sense that one was officially condemned. Then we look at the reactions of both philosophers and theologians concerning this scenario and what they regard as the distinct African feature in the two fields. It is important to, though, to point out that philosophers have extensively dealt with other major issues, in Africa, but not many of them have addressed the issue of communitarianism versus individualism.

Theologians have addressed the issue of communitarianism, particularly with the use of the family model for the African Church and have made an effort to construct a distinctively African hermeneutics, but we think that more still needs to be done. Hence the need for an adequate hermeneutical approach in Africa, based on, but not limited to the African concept of communitarianism.

---

1. Ndegwah (2004). Op. cit., 87.

The Meaning and Purpose of Inculturation

The word 'inculturation' is the corollary of assiduous efforts on the road to what has come to be known as contextual theologies, which started in the early 1940s when Placide Tempels made an attempt to understand the Baluba people (of the then Belgian Congo) and preach the Gospel to them using their own cultural imageries and mental categories. Due to the various prevailing political situations and theologians' responses it developed into various forms of contextual theologies like, Liberation Theology, Black Theology, Feminist Theology, Theology of Inculturation, Theology of African Renaissance and Theology of Reconstruction.[2] At the moment we are interested in the development of the theology of inculturation, which we see as part of the wider contextual theology that was born in the African soil as a direct challenge of the prevailing social situations. The introduction of the term 'inculturation' in the Catholic Church is credited to the members of the Society of Jesus, beginning with Joseph Masson of the Gregorian University. He probably used it for the first time in 1962, but it was only discussed at length at the 32nd Congregation of the Society in Rome (December 1974–April 1975), more than a decade later.

As Bujo notes, the first African theologians used terms like 'adaptation', 'Africanization' and 'indigenization', "which gave the impression that all that was required was a kind of *aggiornamento*."[3] Others used the term 'incarnation', while still others used 'interculturation' as a companion to inculturation.[4] These terms were said to fall short of clearly expressing the reality of the interaction between the Gospel and culture, and as such some theologians dedicated their energy towards an all-inclusive resolution. Shorter's book on whether we are talking about adaptation or incarnation is a manifest example of this lack of clarity that has so far refused to melt away.[5] A year after Shorter's book, the term 'inculturation' became popular following the publication of a letter by the Jesuit Superior General, Pedro Arrupe, in which it was defined and explained. The actual breakthrough came with the Extraordinary Synod of bishops on catechesis in 1979, which explicitly spoke in favor of 'inculturation'.[6] Then Arbuckle wrote his decisive article on the change of name, from 'adaptation' to 'inculturation'.[7]

---

2. These six are, according to us, the essence of African Theology and can be seen as making certain demands; both from the international community and our national leaders. Their demands are political liberation, gender equality, cultural recognition and the right for theologians to participate in development matters without undue restraints from politicians.

3. Bénézet Bujo (1992). *African Theology: In Its Social Context.* Trans by John O'Donohue. Nairobi: St. Paul Publications - Africa, 59.

4. Blomjous, op. cit., 393–396.

5. Aylward Shorter (1977). *African Christian Theology: Adaptation or Incarnation?* Maryknoll, New York: Orbis Books.

6. Pedro Arrupe (1978). Letter to the Whole Society on Inculturation. In *Studies in the International Apostolate of Jesuits*, 7 (June).

7. Gerald A. Arbuckle (1988). Inculturation not Adaptation: Time to Change Terminology. In

To many people, inculturation means nothing more than a translation of symbols; just finding some suitable symbols or rituals from a given culture and use them to express the Christian message. We are, however, of the opinion that this is only the starting point and not the process itself. Left at this juncture, it will finally develop social, if not cultural problems, as it will ultimately try to evolve some sort of a national liturgical rite, as Okure has pointed out, and encouraged uniformity rather than unity. A case in point is Nigeria, which is made up of some three hundred and fifty ethnic groups "each with its own distinct language and other cultural values." Indeed, as she says, "The very impossibility of evolving a liturgy that would be truly expressive of such composite cultures, and hence acceptable to all, would discourage anyone from even embarking upon such a venture."[8] Inculturation is firmly rooted on culture with all its dynamism and should not be separated from people's daily lives. Okot p'Bitek rejects the "view of culture as something separate and distinguishable from the way of life of a people, something which can be put into books and museums and art galleries, something which can be. . .enjoyed during leisure time in theatres and cinema halls is entirely alien to African thought."[9]

Culture is not a static structural reality out there that dictates what people are to accept or discard. It is a much more fluid reality that abhors clear-cut mental categories like black and white, short and tall and so on. It is a continuously evolving ". . .concept of the world intentionally formed by a pattern of univocal and linear symbols which a people conceives to order, express and unify the constellation of its own physical, social, historical, political and religious world."[10] As part of cultural reality, inculturation cannot be limited to the altar—the vestments, vessels or be left to Sundays and other days of obligation.[11] It necessarily has to encompass our entire life set-up and be discouraged from acting as mere reminiscence of the past. For this reason, theologians in Africa have come up with an all-inclusive definition and meaning of inculturation, which has been articulated by John Mary Waliggo as follows:

> Inculturation means the honest and serious attempt to make Christ and his message of salvation evermore understood by peoples of every culture, locality and time. It means the reformulation of christian life and doctrine into the very thought-patterns of each people. It is the conviction that Christ and his Good News are ever dynamic and challenging to all times and cultures as they become

---

Reprint, no. 369. Eldoret: GABA Publications, 511.

8. Teresa Okure (1990). Inculturation: Biblical/Theological Bases. In Teresa Okure, Paul van Tiel et al (eds). *Inculturation of Christianity in Africa* (Spearhead, 111–114). Eldoret: Gaba Publications, 57.

9. Okot p'Bitek (1983). On Culture, Man and Freedom. In H. Odera Oruka and D. A. Masolo (eds). *Philosophy and Culture.* Nairobi: Bookwise Ltd, 106–107.

10. Théoneste Nkéramihigo (1986). Inculturation and the Specificity of the Christian Faith. In *Inculturation: Its Meaning and Urgency.* Nairobi: St. Paul Publications—Africa, 69.

11. Smith (2002). Op. cit., x.

better understood and lived by each people. It is the continuous endeavour to make Christianity truly "feel at home" in the cultures of each people.[12]

Inculturation entails two essential things—dialogue and assimilation, which will help our people, become truly Christians and authentically Africans as demanded by Pope John Paul II. "*You wish to become fully christians and fully Africans.* The Holy Spirit asks us to believe, in fact, that the leaven of the Gospel in its authenticity has the power to bring forth Christians in the different cultures, with all the riches of their heritage, purified and transfigured."[13] This authenticity is not a nostalgic fantasizing about lost cultural practices, but rather a pragmatic, dynamic and critical effort to reclaim lost values and incorporate them to the spread of the Gospel, even if they are foreign to our traditional practices. This is the cradle of evangelization and the guarantee that Christianity is here to stay. Waliggo quotes John Wijngaards as showing a distinction between the essentials of Christianity from the non-essentials as seen in the form of social amenities of the church in Africa when he wrote thus:

> The durability of Christian faith in Africa will not depend on its network of schools and parishes, hospitals and other institutions. Economic strength and even political support will not guarantee its future. The permanence of Christianity will stand or fall on the question whether it has become truly African: whether Africans have made Christian ideas part of their own thinking, whether Africans feel that the Christian vision of life fulfils their own needs, whether the Christian world view has become part of truly African aspirations.[14]

What Inculturation is not and How to Approach it

Inculturation is neither a cultural struggle nor a global rejection or demolition of non-African values, *in toto*. It is also not a mere implantation of Christian values into the African culture, which ends in a juxtaposition of events, or a kind of syncretistic Christianity. It is a rejection of the cultural elements that have uncritically been passed on to Africa that virtually make Christ subservient, in the sense that one must accept them, no matter how foreign they may be, to become a Christian.[15] Owing to the long rapport between Christianity and the Jewish culture and later the Graeco-Roman culture, it becomes very difficult to distinguish between the essentials and the superficial aspects of the Gospel. This calls for a careful and competent scrutiny of what must be rejected and what must be retained. Inculturation is not a superficial activity like

---

12. Waliggo (1986). Op. cit., 12.

13. Pope John Paul II (1980). The Gospel and African Cultures. In *Africa Ecclesial Review* 22 (4). Eldoret. GABA Publications, 222.

14. Ibid., 12.

15. Dieudonné Ngona (2003). Inculturation as a Face of African Theology Today. In Patrick Ryan (ed). Faces of African Theology. Nairobi: CUEA Publications, 140.

"merely sprinkling holy water on every facet of life. It also involves excising anything that is sinful, redeeming and raising up what is humanly good. . ."[16] Rather, it is a serious " . . . movement which aims at making Christianity permanent in Africa by making it a people's religion and a way of life which no enemy or hostility can ever succeed in supplanting or weakening."[17]

Inculturation, therefore, should integrate the Christian experience of a local church into the culture of its people. This way, it can express itself in elements of this culture and also become a force that animates, orientates and innovates this culture. That way it would help create a unity and communion, not just within the culture in question but also within the universal Church.[18] We do not pretend to say that this is an easy task that can be achieved overnight. It requires time, cultural expertise and dedication because, as we have seen above, it involves discerning what is Christian from what is merely cultural from the West. It is a possible goal when all of us get down to it and work at it tirelessly and diligently. The Vatican II document on the church in the modern world (*Gaudium et Spes* or GS) recognizes this fact when it expressly states the following:

> Although the Church has contributed largely to the progress of culture, it is the lesson of experience that there have been difficulties in the way of harmonizing culture with Christian thought arising out of contingent factors. These difficulties do not necessarily harm the life of faith but can rather stimulate a more precise and deeper understanding of that faith.[19]

In fact, as Ngona has observed, "Inculturation is also not a nostalgic exhumation of the folklore and ancestral customs for archeological purposes."[20] Recourse to the past needs to have a sound existential justification, rather than just digging up African traditions merely because they are African. This would amount to romanticism or recourse to an imaginary lost glory of some nebulous or even non-existent 'Golden Age' in the past. There are many practices in the African religion that are in direct conflict with the official interpretation of the gospel teaching—witchcraft, throwing away or killing of twins, communal marriages, polygamy and, in the Pökot case, cattle rustling. Consequently, any reclaim of our lost values needs to have a direct bearing on improving our lives today as Africans and Christians. This calls for the rejection of any cultural practices that did not promote our well-being as persons and those that are simply anachronistic. This issue is contentious, as it can be construed as a rejection or attack on culture, but we cannot just sit and hope that the tension is going

---

16. Patrick C. Chibuko (1996). Inculturation as a Method of Evangelization in the Light of the African Synod. In *Journal of Inculturation Theology*, Vol. 3 no. 1, 33.

17. Waliggo, op. cit., 13.

18. Chibuko, op. cit., 34.

19. Austin Flannery (ed). (1975). *Vatican II Council*. Northport, New York: Costello Publishing Company, 966.

20. Ngona, op. cit., 141.

to disappear on its own or merely take a reactive position, of only responding when things go wrong. We need to take a proactive position of initiating dialogue with the aim of building on and improving what we already have. What is needed is to bring the Gospel into dialogue with culture with the express aim of harmonizing the two.[21] On the one hand, we should Christianize all our positive cultural values and change or do away with what has outlived its usefulness. On the other hand, we need to make the Gospel relevant to peoples at specific times, using our diverse cultures. Otherwise the Christian message remains abstract, without appeal to the people's needs here and now and so risks becoming irrelevant or simply obsolete. This, as Bellagamba declares, is the true process of inculturation.

> In fact, inculturation is a process by which the gospel enters into a culture, takes from the culture all that is already *gospelled*, and is enriched by it. And so does the culture. In addition to this, the gospel challenges the culture in those aspects that are *ungospelled*, and the culture challenges the gospel in those aspects that are *western*, and both are purified and universalized. So the dynamics between culture and gospel are such that the one enriches and is challenged by the other. There is a call and a response; there is a challenge and an enrichment; and there is also a rejection of elements of the culture which are contrary to the pure gospel, and of elements of the gospel which are not the genuine gospel, but is westernized interpretation. Inculturation is a response to culturalism; and mission, with all its activities, should be influenced by it. If it is not, and remains alien to culture, it will be at best irrelevant to the people, or, at worst, be rejected altogether.[22]

Moreover, inculturation is not a rejection of ecclesiastical authority in the guise of local traditions but rather a search for the strengthening and enriching of our catholic communion, in the bond of unity rather than uniformity. It addresses the issues that concern the very basic worldviews, the basic human values and the very question of sharing the ecclesiastical power.[23] Once this has been realized, the result is something new, a new creation[24] what the Bible refers to as 'what no eye has seen, no ear has heard'.[25] The difficulty with this path is superficiality and as such, Appiah warns of the underlying danger to the quest for inculturation in Africa. That there are many and complex sets of meaning that determine the approaches a person takes in applying the concept of inculturation to the concrete religious experience of the people. Yet these

21. With 'harmony' here we mean both mutuality and confrontation, which involves both agreements and agreeing to disagree on certain issues but respecting each other's position and agreeing to carry on.

22. Anthony Bellagamba (1991). The Role of Cross-Cultural Ministers in Mission and their Formation. In *African Christian Studies,* vol. 7, no. 1, 3.

23. Smith (2002). Op. cit., x.

24. Peter K. Sarpong (2002). *Peoples Differ: An Approach to Inculturation in Evangelisation.* Accra: Sub-Saharan Publishers, 21.

25. 1 Corinthians 2: 9a.

sets of meanings are taken for granted so that "we become inattentive to the divergent points of departure for doing inculturation theology. The danger involved in this lack of attentiveness is the possibility of developing a theory-praxis of inculturation based on a fictive consensus of meaning."[26]

On the fear of change, people are normally afraid of things they cannot predict. They generally want what they already know or can comfortably manage without the fear of being caught off-guard. But inculturation is a resolute decision to move to the future, to go to the unknown and happily accept whatever comes by with humility and gratitude, as churches world-wide make the marks of their identity felt in the universal church. Pope Paul VI pegged the effectiveness of evangelization on language:

> The individual churches, intimately built up not only of people but also of aspirations, of riches and limitations, of ways of praying, of loving, of looking at life and work which distinguish this or that human gathering, have the task of assimilating the essence of the Gospel message and of transposing it, without the slightest betrayal of its essential truth, into the language that these particular people understand, then of proclaiming it in this language.[27]

This, we think, is the proper approach to inculturation, and with it we agree with Wachege on its effects. "A proper approach to *Inculturation* will enable African Christians to overcome the crisis of having a double identity; living a dichotomized life as Africans and as Christians. Instead, they will be exposed to a deeper understanding of *Salvation* within their own life experiences."[28]

The Extent and Scope of Inculturation

"Do two people walk together unless they have agreed?" asks prophet Amos.[29] We can reframe this bible quotation in the context of inculturation and ask, 'Can two cultures work together unless they have agreed to do so'? This can certainly not happen. The scope of inculturation is both intensive and extensive, particularly in places like West Pökot, and it should ideally be done by the people themselves, under the guidance of an interested evangelizer who could be a priest or any other trained theologian. This is what Burke has called 'inculturation from the bottom up,'[30] whereby the people produce cultural raw material, while the theologian produces doctrinal raw material. The rich, age-old, traditions, which so many people still practice, should not be tampered

---

26. Simon K. Appiah (2000). *Africanness Inculturation Ethics: In Search of the Subject of an Inculturated Christian Ethics*. Frankfurt: Peterlang, 36.

27. Pope Paul VI (1969b). Closing Discourse to All-Africa Symposium. In *Gaba Pastoral Paper, 7*. Kampala: Gaba Pastoral Institute, no. 20.

28. Patrick N. Wachege (2001). Inculturation and Salvation Within the African Context. In *AFER, Vol.* 43 Nos.1&3. Eldoret: Gaba Publications, 33–34.

29. Amos 3: 3.

30. Burke, op. cit., 193.

with or be allowed to fade away, in the name of modernity. These outward signs and symbols are essential tools on the road to inculturation, but they are not enough, by themselves. Inculturation of the Christian worship, for instance, cannot be confined to mere external signs like Sunday liturgy and traditional melodies. There must be an inner change of heart and openness to the whole set up of the Christian living. This, in our view, can be achieved if we transform Christian Scriptures into Pökot Scriptures; something akin to what Healey has called 'a fifth gospel'.[31] This is the kind of Scriptures that both respect and match the Pökot social structures with their lifestyle. This is how far we must go if inculturation is to be a reality in Africa. Christianity has, of necessity, to approach culture as an equal partner in the dialogue to map out concrete ways to bring the Word of God home.

The benefits of such healthy dialogue are immense but one that stands out as the most important of them is double faceted, due to its effects of universality and particularity at the same time. On the universal plane, the Christian faith liberates culture from undue parochial considerations that are only centered on a given community or locality. However, the particularity of culture helps to concretize the otherwise abstract ideals of the Christian faith, lest they remain nice but dry concepts that have no meaning in the real life of the people. It is with this spirit of inculturation in mind that Christians are called upon to survey the numerous fields of pastoral theology with the diligence and urgency they deserve, in view of realizing their potentials to inculturation, as "a global Christian method of evangelization."[32] And this includes tackling the sharp edges or uncomfortable zones of inculturation without fear or favor.

Obstacles to Inculturation

We have tried, in the preceding pages, to show that inculturation is an important and desirable endeavor in evangelization, its conceptual problems notwithstanding. Now we need to discuss some of the concrete obstacles that stand on the way to the realization of this noble goal. The actual obstacles and barriers to inculturation are many and varied, depending on the people and place in question, but three of them, i.e., fundamentalism, mediocrity and syncretism, come out as the most common. Let us briefly see how these hamper inculturation and what can be done about the situation.

Fundamentalism

". . .Fundamentalists maintain that the Bible is inspired by God and thus each word in the Scriptures is without error; so, they take every word in the Bible at its face

---

31. Joseph G. Healey (1981).

32. Jean-Claude Loba-Mkole (2004). Bible Translation and Inculturation Hermeneutics. In Ernst R. Wenland and Jean-Claude Loba-Mkole (eds). *Biblical Texts & African Audiences.* Nairobi: Acton Publishers, 42.

value and reject any attempt to apply human skills and scholarship to analyze a bible text. This leads to literary interpretation of the Bible."[33] The word 'fundamentalism' refers to "a form of Protestan Christianity which upholds the belief in the strict and literal interpretation of the bible (in opposition to more modern interpretations)."[34] In the religious circles, though, the term fundamentalism is used as "a description of those who return to what they believe to be the fundamental truths and practices of a religion."[35] In Africa, Christian fundamentalists also tend to adopt a magical view of the Bible, that is, "an attempt to make God conform to human problems by the performance of certain ecstatic acts or incantations."[36] The term fundamentalism arose in the United States of America, among the theologically conservative Protestants, who insisted on 'holding on the great fundamentals of their faith',[37] but theologians have widened the word beyond Christianity, to cover all religions that exhibit fundamentalist traits. Marty and Appleby see them in what have come to be popularly regarded as the 'religions of the book'. "Fundamentalists," they say, "are usually found among the religions of the book; where there is an easily accessible canon which can serve as an authority."[38] Here we will concentrate on its effects on inculturation by the Catholic Church in West Pökot.

We observed fundamentalist tendencies among the 'ordinary Christians' who can be divided into two: the ecumenical members of the Catholic Church, who regularly co-operate with members of other churches and the 'saved ones' (these are members of the Charismatic Catholic Renewal Movement), who emphasize the works of the Holy Spirit. The only thing they have in common is the way they compartmentalize certain bible passages and use them to justify their cause, over and against those perceived to be outsiders, or uninitiated. This falls into place with the observations of Perera who noted that: "Fundamentalism abstracts a set of strict rules from scripture in order to elaborate a narrow and exclusive religious system."[39] The third group is that of the traditionalists, who have never become Christians in their lifetime and deserters who decided to abandon the Catholic faith 'upon realizing it had nothing new to offer'.[40]

---

33. SECAM, (2005). *The Bible: Source of Christian Life and Vocation.* Takoradi: St. Francis Press Ltd, no. 12.

34. Pearsall, op. cit., 573.

35 John Bowker (ed) (1997). *The Oxford Dictionary of World Religions.* Oxford: Oxford University Press, 694.

36. SECAM, op. cit., no. 13.

37. Andrew Rippin (1993). *Muslims: Their Religious Beliefs and Practices.* London and New York. Routledge, 37.

38. Martin E. Marty and R. Scott Appleby (1992). *The Glory and the Power: The Fundamentalist Challenge to the Modern World.* Boston: Beacon Press, 3.

39. Rienzie Perera (2000). Fundamentalism. In Virginia Fabella and R. S. Sugirtharajah (eds) *Dictionary of Third World Theologies.* Maryknoll, New York: Orbis Books, 90.

40. Ibid., 90.

The two most common elements of fundamentalism witnessed in Africa today are: the feeling of being a chosen people, who have a somewhat direct communication with God and, so they tend to disregard the Church protocol and a total denial of their own culture with constant attempts to use the scripture as a justification. Then there is contempt for modernity and with it, young people, who are often seen by old and middle-aged persons as the incarnation of evil itself. We believe these Christians lack scientific and in-depth knowledge of the Bible and interpret it as though it were a bibliographical entry for some contemporary piece of literature. Indeed, it is a common thing, in Kenya, to notice among Christians what Rippin calls 'Protestant Fundamentalism' of ". . .inerrancy of the Bible, a stance which is a defence of basic religious ideals—the seriousness of sin, the need for redemption and the idea that Jesus has granted that redemption."[41] Literal interpretation of the Bible, such as this one, lacks the ability to contextualize bible passages in their *Siztim-Leben* (life situation) and cannot, therefore, apply them meaningfully to our own life situations (*aggiornamento*), and herein lays the difficulty to inculturation: hence the need for trained bible scholars to engage even more vigorously in this important project of the church in Africa.

Mediocrity

In religious terms the word mediocrity means a situation in which one is neither a committed Christian nor a serious traditionalist. The religious connect-ions of such people depend on momentary convenience. If one is in the company of traditionalists then such a person is a staunch traditionalist, but when among Christians, one takes up Christian mentality and speaks all sorts of good things about Christianity. Mediocrity in inculturation can be attributed to two main causes: one, the lack of general guidance on the question of inculturation, its scope and extent, and two the fear, on the part of church leaders, to break new ground, lest one is victimized by the institutional Church. This is the case since "in the life of the Church, the phenomenon of inculturation is not universally welcomed."[42] The onus, then to face this challenge in a special way lies on the shoulders of bishops, since they are the "official heirs and custodians of the responsibility for evangelisation as understood and practiced since Christianity was introduced in Africa."[43] But lack of a positive tradition towards the African culture keeps them preoccupied with the risk of syncretism, so much so that it is an odious task, on their part, to determine with ease what is acceptable and what is not.

---

41. Rippin, op. cit., 37–38.

42. Ngona, op. cit., 163.

43. Patrick A. Kalilombe (2004). Praxis and Methods of Inculturation in Africa. In Patrick Ryan (ed). *Theology of Inculturation in Africa Today: Methods, Praxis and Mission*. Nairobi: CUEA Publications, 39.

Were the doctrine of collegiality to be upheld and allowed to grow, it would go a long way in providing the basis for "pluralism of theological viewpoints and local initiatives. It would compel the centralised authority of Rome to be more responsive to local needs as understood in the more than 2000 dioceses globally."[44] Henceforth the church would show that it is indeed world's bishops themselves who are real successors of the apostles, who shared authority with Peter. Thus, they would act in communion, rather than unity with the bishop of Rome, since the latter has nearly always been taken to mean, or at least treated as, uniformity.

In the absence of clear guidance from the church hierarchy on inculturation, the lay people have been doing their own inculturation in line with what they perceive to be of interest to them here and now. "Just as they have been engaging in their own culture change, so also, as they were confronted with the preaching of the Gospel of Jesus Christ, they have been struggling with their own past and present in order to decide what their future should be."[45] Here the tension is that the people did not bother to let their evangelizers know what has been going on because of the latter's conviction that "the reality was what they themselves expected, what they themselves had set out to achieve."[46]

This tension sets the stage for a silent confrontation with the evangelizers insisting on what, in the eyes of the people, is irrelevant. One such example is giving priority to material expression of worship in the form of singing, dancing, drumming and so on, which seems like a nostalgic return to the past; and hence retrogressive. "If we wanted to retain forms of the past," suggests Kalilombe, "it should be as a way of stressing values that are positive and forward looking, like revalorisation of past achievements of power, unity, joy, discipline, etc., values which can be identified as relevant because they can be re-employed in the modern setting for a forward looking utility."[47] It would, thus be helpful if evangelizers would consult with the people on the exact fields of their lives they would like inculturated. People seem to be more attached to the area of more basic ideas, attitudes and customs that are linked up with their worldview.[48]

Éla is even more forceful on this as he narrates the woes that beset the Africans. "Today Africa is subject to conditionings far more effective than the values of tradition. Urbanization, contemporary economic constraints, the phenomenal increase in school enrolment, the growth of unemployment, drought, and famine are phenomena

---

44. Patrick Ryan (2003). Seven Theses on Inculturation: A Response to "Inculturation as a Face of African Theology Today. In Patrick Ryan (ed). *Faces of African Theology.* Nairobi: CUEA Publications, 177.

45. Kalilombe (2004). Op. cit., 43–44.

46. Ibid., 43.

47. Ibid., 44.

48. Ibid., 45.

completely upsetting human conditions in black Africa."[49] He, therefore, calls for more autonomy in the Christian communities to map out their road map to inculturation and avoid what he brands 'clerical imperialism'.

> Christian communities in Africa have no future unless they can trust their own internal dynamics, their ongoing ability to respond to challenges, and their on-going capacity to face their crises and make full use of community resources and potential. Ecclesiastical institutions within these communities must undergo radical changes. They are still branded by a form of clerical imperialism that has inhibited their ability to innovate and stunted the growth of the laity.[50]

Finally, Ngona calls upon all members of the church to work as a team, under their bishops to realize this goal. "When the realisation of the process of inculturation is envisaged, it has to be said right from the beginning that the task of inculturation is not the task of theologians alone. It is a task that must involve the whole Church: Bishops, priests, religious and laity."[51]

Syncretism

The word syncretism is a tricky term. "Its main difficulty is that it is used with both an objective and a subjective meaning. The basic objective meaning refers neutrally and descriptively to the mixing of religions. The subjective meaning includes an evaluation of such intermingling from the point of view of one of the religions involved."[52] Rahner defines syncretism as ". . .an eclectic mixture of philosophical and theological doctrines, which ends up in a fusion of different godheads, cults or religions."[53] Both in the history of its usage and the contemporary times, the word 'syncretism' has attained negative as well as positive meanings.

> Originally it was applied to political alliances in ancient Greece. Then it described the way the Old Testament assimilated elements from surrounding cultures. In the age of the Reformation it pointed to the links between Christianity and humanism, and to the need for the Protestant and Catholic churches to come together. Today it retains many of these varied meanings, with either negative or positive connotation.[54]

49. Éla, op. cit., 171.
50. Ibid., 60.
51. Ngona, op. cit., 154.
52. Droogers, André F., (1989). Syncretism: The Problem of Definition, the Definition of the Problem. In Jerald Gort et al (eds). *Dialogue and Syncretism: An Interdisciplinary Approach.* Grand Rapids, Michigan: William B. Eerdmans Publishing Company, 7.
53 Karl Rahner (ed). (1986). Op. cit., 657–658.
54. Peter Schineller (1992). Inculturation and the Issue of Syncretism: What is the Real Issue? In Justin S. Ukpong et al (eds). *Evangelization in Africa in the Third Millenium: Challenges and Prospects.*

In this case, we use it as the "...the process of integrating the gospel into cultural codes," as has been seen by some people, but in the negative light of "... 'amalgamating' two or more incompatible religions."[55] We, therefore, distance it from a healthy process of dialogue between the Gospel and culture, which leads to inculturation where the two can live in a happy symbiosis. We understand syncretism as the merging or fusion of two or more incompatible doctrines between religions. People who are not theologically trained always do this either unconsciously or secretly. In the former case, they are influenced by things like culture, habit and so on, while in the latter case they are out to find answers, where they perceive Christianity to have failed them. It is noteworthy that people always carried out their own modes of inculturation even without understanding it. Magesa found out that the concept is too much of a technical term for them and even where translations into local languages were provided no one knew its meaning, especially when applied to the life of the church.[56] Syncretism is still a reality that cannot be denied, even as *Ecclesia in Africa* warns against the danger.

> Considering the rapid changes in the cultural, social, economic and political domains, our local churches must be involved in the process of inculturation in an ongoing manner, respecting the two following criteria: compatibility with the Christian message and communion with the universal church . . . In all cases, care must be taken to avoid syncretism.[57]

Syncretism is the very opposite of dialogue for it merely juxtaposes events or practices. As opposed to inculturation or symbiosis, syncretism takes place without any thought being given to it; it is not systematic and has no direction. What we need is not syncretism (though it has always happened) but a conscientious and happy symbiosis. It is helpful to marry acceptable practices in African Religion to Christianity, and then do away with all unacceptable elements in both religions. Arinze has called for objectivity in a research to such an undertaking. "The study should be an objective and factual work so that the heralds of the Gospel will see more clearly the positive and the negative in the religious and cultural situation of the people to whom the Gospel is being brought."[58] One such seemingly healthy Christian practice that is unacceptable to the African people in general, and the

---

Port Harcourt: CIWA Press, 52.

55. Christopher Duraisingh (2000). Syncretism. In V. Fabella and R.S. Sugirtharajah (eds). *Dictionary of Third World Theologies.* Maryknoll, New York: Orbis Books. 193.

56. Laurenti Magesa (2004b). *Anatomy of Inculturation: Transforming the Church in Africa.* Nairobi: Paulines Publications Africa, 24.

57. Pope John Paul II (1995). *Ecclesia in Africa.* Nairobi: Paulines Publications Africa, no. 62.

58. Cardinal Francis Arinze (1988). *Pastoral Attention to African Traditional Religion: Letter from the Pontifical Council for Interreligious Dialogue, Vatican City, to the Presidents of the Episcopal Conferences of Africa and of Madagascar,* Rome, 25 March, 2.

Pökot in particular, is the formula in the matrimonial ritual, which limits marriage to death "...until death do us part..."[59]

Among many Africans, marriage is never dissolved by death since the wife does not belong to an individual but rather to the whole community in general and to a clan in particular. Traditionally, then, such a marriage can only be dissolved if the whole clan has been exterminated, which so far has not happened in the known history of African ethnic groups. Magesa quotes a young person who is enraged by this Christian notion of love and marriage.

> The Christian concept of love is too abstract for most African Christians. We believed in love that is expressed in symbolic exchange of gifts, ritual visits and exchange of vows or agreements between the clan members of the betrothed before marriage. In this regard, marriage was a matter between relatives of the bride and the groom. After marriage the two groups were held responsible for the outcome [of the relationship] of the newly wedded couples. This has been watered down by the Christian concept of marriage, which is highly influenced by western, Euro-American values. Marriages are becoming more individualistic, secularist and hence the knot tied on the wedding day is loose and weak. No wonder divorce cases are prevalent.[60]

We are not out to romanticize the African Religion, or in any way wish to idealize it, as Arinze has warned. "There should be no attempt to romanticize ATR or culture or to defend every practice in them. Therefore the research should also spell out the negative elements that may be found in ATR and culture, such as inadequate ideas on the objects of worship, objectionable moral practices, degrading rites, polygamy, discrimination against women, human sacrifice and rejection of twins (where these are practiced), etc."[61] Just like in Christianity, many traditional African practices need to be reviewed or be done away with altogether, in the light of the rapidly changing situations and cultural dispositions. Once this has been done, the result is something new; referred to in the Bible as 'what no eye has seen, no ear has heard'.[62] The main difficulty to this path is that people are normally afraid of change, afraid of things they cannot predict or control; and yet this seems to be the only sure way forward.

People generally want what they already know or can comfortably manage without the fear of being caught off-guard. But inculturation is a resolute decision to move to the future, to delve into the unknown and happily accept whatever comes by with humility and gratitude. This, we think, is the proper approach to inculturation, and so we agree with Wachege. "A proper approach to *Inculturation* will enable African

---

59. Catholic Church (1998). Rite of Marriage During Mass, in *The Roman Missal*. Rome: Libreria Editrice Vaticana, 5087.

60. Laurenti Magesa (2004a). Reconstructing the African Family. In Andrew A. Kyomo and Sahaya G. Selvan (eds). *Marriage and Family in African Christianity*. Nairobi: Acton Publishers, 24.

61. Arinze, op. cit., 3.

62 1 Corintians 2: 9a.

Christians to overcome the crisis of having a double identity; living a dichotomized life as Africans and as Christians. Instead, they will be exposed to a deeper understanding of *Salvation* within their own life experiences."[63]

One thing that badly cripples the process of inculturation in West Pökot is that it is a one-way affair, which starts from top downwards and the people, particularly the catechists, are not happy with the trend, because they feel sidelined. This, we think, is a wrong starting point because what happens then is that there is a lot of talking and a lot of writing without corresponding concrete actions on the ground. If we are to experience, real, tangible results in inculturation then, this trend must change. And as Arbuckle says this, while quoting the scriptures (1 Cor 3:5–9); "Earthing the Gospel is a team effort—evangelizers, those being evangelized and the Lord himself: 'After all, what is Apollos and what is Paul? . . .We are fellow workers with God.'"[64] But, how are we going to make inculturation an all–inclusive affair, in the light of the above problems that we have already cited? The answer, like Plato averred long ago, lies on education, which he equated to philosophy.

> . . .the human race will have no respite from evils until those who are really and truly philosophers acquire political power or until, through some divine dispensation, those who rule and have political authority in cities become real philosophers.[65]

And the preferred forum to effectively utilize this education is the SCCs, as a good number of theologians have stated. "Small Christian Communities are seen as privileged contexts for promoting an integral, balanced and effective inculturation. They constitute the milieu in which the Christian life is to take roots. They constitute the environment in which the actual life experiences of the Christian faithful take place."[66] There is an urgent need to re-evangelize those with fundamentalist ideas, to re-activate the lukewarm and the mediocre, and finally, to re-train the syncretistic. These will, hopefully, create conducive atmosphere that meets the requirements for inculturation.[67] That is, appreciation of traditions and respect for other people's culture, cultural self-awareness, an attitude of openness and acceptance of prophetic criticism. This can lead to ". . .an encounter between the Gospel, the Church and Christian life and a local culture, traditional systems of thought, values and religiosity-which are already the fruit of human efforts under divine inspiration."[68]

63. Wachege (2001). Op. cit., 33–34.

64. Gerald A. Arbuckle (1991). *Earthing the Gospel: An Inculturation Handbook for Pastoral Worker*. London: Geoffrey Chapman, 3.

65. Plato (1992). *Republic*. Trans by G.M.A. Grube. Indianapolis: Hacket Publishing Company, Inc., 324b–326b.

66. Ngona, op. cit., 164–165.

67. E. Mutabazi (2004). Le management des équipes multiculturelles: l'expérience des équipes afro-occidentales, *Management International, vol. 8, n° 3,* 63–65.

68. Waliggo (1986). Op. cit., 22–23.

A Brief History of Inculturation in Kenya

The history of inculturation, in Kenya, dates back to " . . . the Portuguese presence that was marked by the death of the Mombasa martyrs in 1631."[69] That is, to say that evangelization, more or less, reached the African continent at the same time with colonization. But because the faith was not made part and parcel of the people's culture, when the Portuguese left Mombasa in 1729, the whole region fell into firm Islamic control. Even the 19th century Christian mission (notably by the CMS, Methodists and Holy Ghost Fathers) faced problems in Mombasa, not only due to a strong Islamic presence, but also due to its interference with the local cultures.[70] The situation was made worse by the ensuing colonial enterprise that followed into the hinterland, from when "Western . . . political hegemony went, hand in hand with religious hegemony . . . "[71] wreaking havoc to the people and places of Africa.[72]

Magesa characterizes the history of evangelization in Kenya, as far as the people are concerned, as "ambivalent: a blessing and a drawback, good news and bad news. In many, if not in most cases," he continues, "both of these aspects of the church's presence have been so intertwined that, though conscious of their existence, it has been hard for the people to unravel them." Evangelisation can, nonetheless, still be regarded as Good News because the church was more tolerant and less discriminating that her colonial counterpart; that way, though still a 'foreign institution', "she strove to provide a relative haven, amid the social and psychological alienation of colonialism."[73]

The church also helped to pacify the hitherto warring ethnic groups through the unifying, albeit challenging message that we are sons and daughters of the one true God.[74] The other most important thing done by the church was to introduce modern medicine and education to the Kenyan population, which improved their health as well as enhancing their sense of self-worth and dignity.[75] Evangelisation in Kenya was also bad news to the people due to the attitudes and actions that portrayed missionaries negatively, with many resultant damaging effects. "The most comprehensively damaging impact of these attitudes was the missionaries' indiscriminate discouragement, rejection and sometimes destruction of African customs and cultural values, as being complete contradiction to the will of God, and thus, to being Christian."[76]

---

69. Baur, op. cit., 474.

70. Baur, op. cit., 228.

71. Johannes A. Van der Ven et al (2004). *Is there a God of Human Rights? The Complex Relationship Between Human Rights and Religion: A South African Case.* Leiden. Boston: Brill, xviii.

72. Cochrane, op. cit., xvi.

73. Laurenti Magesa (1990). Overview of 100 years of Catholicism in Kenya. In *AFER*, Vol. 32, No. 1. Eldoret: GABA Publications, 43.

74. Ibid., 24–43.

75. Ibid., 45.

76. Ibid., 47.

It generally happened something like this: a (native) government chief was appointed, and then a (settler) District Officer (DO) or a District Commissioner (DC) was brought to the area. Head Tax was introduced and natives were required to carry a Passbook with them. Then missionaries came around and built churches, dispensaries and schools. Other times, the opposite was the case. Missionaries came and asked the village elders for a piece of land to build a church, which they gave generously, sometimes as much as 3000 acres.[77] A church was built and better still a dispensary and a school were added. Then a police station (or post) was built, a chief[78] was appointed, and then a DO or DC was posted to the area.

This latter group built their administration offices on the same parcel of land, originally dedicated to the church or forced people to donate more land for this purpose. In the meantime, should the priest's car breakdown he went to the local administrator to ask for assistance and vice-versa. Due to this intimacy, the church inherited "a judicial type of ecclesiology rather than a Eucharistic or sacramental one."[79] Moreover, the church's teaching seemed to echo and affirm colonialists' technological achievements. Mazrui gives a pure example of the parallelism between the gunfire and theology of hell.

> In time the fear of hell-fire accompanied this dreaded gunfire. The fear of hell-fire was in part a ritualization of terror. The use of supernatural symbols under European Christianity consolidated the readiness to submit which had been exacted by the new military technology. The God of Christianity was not really the God of the Old Testament full of revenge and the capacity to use power. Nevertheless the control of the church in many African countries used the incentives of salvation and the dissenting ones of damnation. In the case of the Catholic Church—and African Catholics outnumbered African Protestants south of the Sahara—the threat of excommunication was an additional invocation of hell-fire as an accompaniment to gunfire.[80]

This mutual relationship left no doubt in the minds of the natives concerning the unity of purpose between the missionaries and the colonizers. Among the Gĩkũyũ people of Kenya this intimacy was alluded to in a rather derogatory way by the infamous

---

77. Baur, op. cit., 477.

78. It must be clarified that the new colonial chiefs did not have the same mandate and authority from the people, as was the case with the traditional chiefs or members of the council of elders. These were used as mere pawns by the colonial regime to foster the colonial interests and those who opposed this role were simply sacked. Bujo (1992). Op. cit., 41) gives Blukwa the traditional Chief, of the Bahema people, as a concrete example: "The colonialists found him uncomfortable because he was not prepared to be a simple yes-man, and he was therefore sent into exile." And he sadly adds, "The contempt for traditional authority, and its virtual destruction by the colonialists, produced alienation in African society."

79. Adrian Hastings (1967). *Church and Mission in Modern Africa.* London: Burns & Oats, 20.

80. Ali A. Mazrui (1977). *Africa's International Relations: The Diplomacy of Dependency and Change.* Boulder, Colorado: Westview Press, 94.

expression *Gũtirĩ mũthũngũ na mũbia*—there is no difference between a European [settler] and a priest [missionary].[81] It was later to be used by leaders of the independence struggle as a weapon to fight the white man, who had oppressed the black man, both politically (the colonialist) and religiously (the missionary). Kenyatta is quoted to have expressed it as a land question and said thus: "When the missionaries came we had the land and they had the Bible in their hands. They told us to pray, closing our eyes. When we looked up again, we had the bible and they had—the land."[82]

Suppression of the African Culture

The other major factor that did not augur well for evangelization in Africa was the fact that the missionaries, in conjunction with their colonial counterparts, systematically destroyed the entire social fabric of the African culture condemning it as 'heathen'. Africans were to abandon their cultural and religious heritage and adopt European and American norms to be regarded as good Christians.[83]

> The practical objective was to turn the prospective converts into replicas of the missionary. Thus, on scale of conversion, the foreign missionary gave himself 100% while the prospective convert was supposed to start at zero. On such a scale the missionary could measure his progress in terms of the degree to which his converts imitated him.[84]

In many parts of the continent, early missionaries destroyed people's cultural institutions in cohort with their colonial hosts who came to their assistance when they failed to achieve their goal(s).

> The colonial endeavour had three arms: government, mission, commerce and all had to work together. Government officials had a keen sense of their obligations towards missionaries, and were punctilious, for example, in visiting mission schools.
>
> The co-operation of the church and state extended also to the strictly religious field.... In Zaïre (Now DRC—Democratic Republic of Congo),[85] church and state were very severe on ancestor-cults. A document issued in September

---

81. Baur, op. cit., 479.

82. Baur, op. cit., 477. This, however, is not a rejection of the entire corpus of the colonial heritage because, as Gyekye (1997). Op. cit., 158) observes, there are many features and elements that Africans have considered worthwhile and conducive to their cultural and intellectual development. One such element is literacy that helped put down their cultural heritage in writing; something that was previously being done through oral history only. Writing makes a people's heritage permanent and consistent, as opposed to orality, which is susceptible to distortion and exaggeration due to memory lapse.

83. Jesse N. K. Mugambi (1995). *From Liberation to Reconstruction: African Christian Theology After the Cold War.* Nairobi: East African Educational Publishers Ltd., 42.

84. Jesse N. K. Mugambi (2002). *Christianity and African Culture.* Nairobi: Acton Publishers, 8.

85. Parentheses are our addition.

1923, in Stanleyville, now Kisangani, by the Superiors of the Belgian Congo Mission lists customs considered harmful to public order, and requests the colonial government to take action against them. The customs included: offerings to spirits and ancestors; . . . dancing and hunting ceremonies; magical or religious rites on the occasion of a birth. . . or circumcision, or a girl's puberty, or marriage, or illness.[86]

However, their efforts did not succeed, to a large extent, as the resilience of African religion and cultural practices have shown, or the constancy of what Mazrui calls the 'indigenous'[87] component; which is not to say that the damage had not been done. Indeed, as Wiredu notes " . . . colonial racism had succeeded in alienating many Africans from their own culture."[88] Most missionaries (even though without intentional or deliberate malice) ignored any possibility for a dialogue and demonized the African culture because they regarded everything the African did or thought as evil.[89]

Consequently, they embarked on a project " . . . to rescue the depraved souls of the Africans from the 'eternal fire'; they set out to uproot the African, body and soul, from his customs and beliefs, put him in a class by himself, with all his tribal traditions shattered and his institutions trampled upon."[90] Shorter gives testimony to this supplanting of the African culture with the foreign 'gospelled' ones. A missionary showed them the slides of a new church he had built in Malawi with all Canadian religious relics and then remarked with 'a naughty twinkle in the eye', "As you can see, we have tried to create here a little Canada."[91]

He further observes that even though this man had dedicated his life to preach the Gospel in Africa, he "did not feel it necessary to make a distinction between the Christianity he preached and his own home culture. He had certainly not considered giving an African cultural expression to the Christian faith when building his church."[92] This happened in 1959, notwithstanding the fact that exactly three hundred years earlier (1659), the Congregation for the Evangelization of Peoples (then known as Propaganda Fide)[93] had warned missionaries against exporting their cultures to China. "Can anyone think of anything more absurd than to transport France, Italy, or Spain or some other European country to China? Bring them your faith, not your country."[94]

86. Bujo (1992). Op. cit., 44.

87. Ali A. Mazrui (1986). *The Africans: A Triple Heritage*. London: BBC Publications, 64.

88. Kwasi Wiredu (1992). Problems in Africa's Self-Definition n the Contemporary World. In Kwasi Wiredu and Kwame Gyekye (eds). *Person and Community: Ghanaian Philosophical Studies I*, Washington D.C.: The Council for Research in Value and Philosophy, 59–60.

89. Ndegwah (2006). Op. cit., 83.

90. Kenyatta, op. cit., 269–270.

91. Shorter (1987). Op. cit., 17.

92. Ibid., 17.

93. Propaganda Fide (1907). *Collectanea S. Congregationis de Propaganda Fide seu Decreta, instructiones, rescripta, pro apostolicis missionibus*. Romae: Ex Typographia Polyglotta, 130–141.

94. Ndegwah (2004). Op. cit., 76.

This warning notwithstanding, some young converts in mission lands turned their backs on their own culture and looked up to the missionaries for role-models to emulate; for moral, social and cultural instructions. They scoffed at anything traditional as evil, including their own African names, and as such destined to hell.

Why the Suppression of the African Culture?

The immediate question that comes to mind is why the early missionaries chose to destroy a people's heritage, something that had been built for as long as they could remember. Although many reasons, like the now revised theology of 'outside the Church there is not salvation—*extra ecclesiam nulla salus*'[95] can be advanced as the cause for this attitude, we think that three things triggered this cultural bias—colonialism, propaganda and lack of adequate training. To begin with, colonization was a politico-economic enterprise and its justification, by the powers that be, lay in personal gain and ostentation.

> There were at the time rather respectable theoreticians who considered the right to colonize as a natural right. According to this doctrine, it was up to the most advanced humans to intervene in the "sleeping regions" of Africa and to exploit the wealth meant by God for all humanity. Through his presence and his policies, the colonizer was intended to awaken "lethargic peoples" and introduce them to civilization and true religion. . . Thus, the right to colonize was duplicated by a natural duty and a spiritual mission.[96]

The second element was intellectual or theoretical in nature and was founded in the unfavorable comments made against Africans by European philosophers like Rousseau, Hume, Hegel and others. It seems that the missionaries forgot, or simply did not realize, that the views of such philosophers were culture and context-bound.[97] A quotation from the latter that classifies 'the Negro' as wanting in humanity will suffice:

> In Negro life the characteristic point is that consciousness has not yet attained the realisation of any substantial objective existence in which the interest of man's volition is involved and in which he realises his own being. . .so that knowledge of another and a Higher than his individual self, is entirely wanting. The Negro. . .exhibits the natural man in his completely wild and untamed state and we must lay aside all thought of reverence and morality. . .there is nothing harmonious with humanity to be found in this type of character.[98]

---

95. Oliver A. Onwubiko (2000). *The Church as the Family of God (Ujamaa): In the Light of Ecclesia in Africa*. Nsukka: Fulladu Publishing Company, 23.

96. Mudimbe (1988). Op. cit., 137.

97. M. T. Speckman (2001). *The Bible and Human Development in Africa*. Nairobi: Acton Publishers, 54.

98. Georg W. F. Hegel (1956). *The Philosophy of History*. New York: Dover Publications, Inc., 93.

This view was later endorsed, either directly or at least indirectly, by anthropologists like Evans-Pritchard, Westermann and Lévy-Bruhl. The latter was particularly notorious in this regard with his provoking titles like: "*Les Fonctions mentales dans les sociétés inférieures* (1910), *La Mentalité primitive* (1922), *L'Ame primitive* (1927), *Le Surnaturel et la Nature dans la mentalité primitive* (1931), and *L'Expérience mystique et les symboles chez les primitifs* (1938)."[99] This bias did not stop in anthropology but inevitably encroached into the religious circles as depicted by the many articles written in two Montfortian periodicals by Muris, a missiology lecturer in Montfortians' Missionary Seminary. He portrays the same kind of anthropological contempt towards the African; which greatly influenced the young seminarians that were paradoxically being trained to go and work in Africa—among the same Africans.

> In this connection the many names Muris gives to Africans in general and to those of Malawi in particular are revealing. In those, Western superiority, racial differences, and the inferiority of the Africans are forcefully and humiliatingly expressed. He calls them variously "negro", "uncivilised negro", "nigger", "black-belly", "blackie", "painted offspring of Abraham", "frizzy head", "wild man", "primitives", "native", "man of nature", "lump of nature", "child of nature", and "big child."[100]

It is highly unlikely that a professor with such attitude could instill anything better in the minds of the young missionaries, who look up to their seniors for religious and character formation.

A provincial superior of the Spiritan Dutch Province has no kinder words on the African culture. Indeed, he blames it for the slow pace of the growth of Christianity in Africa. "The reason that Christianity has still not fully taken root is the Africans' attachment to their old pagan customs and usage. They do not yet know the genuine virtue of love, of dedication, and of self-sacrifice." Some of these 'pagan customs', he says, "include certain immoral dances and especially initiation rites for girls."[101] Today the situation in Tanzania remains pretty much the same among the Sukuma people and scholars are calling for a change in missionary approach within the Catholic Church.

> It is our contention that the Catholic Church could have a decisive impact on the future of Usukuma, if it appreciated and accepted to a significant degree the depth and extent of this everyday religion of the people and was able to overcome the gap between official and popular Catholicism. It is this gap,

---

99. Mudimbe (1988). op. cit., 135). Towards the end of his life, though, Lévy-Bruhl repudiated his demeaning theory of 'primitive mentality' as noted in his posthumously published *Carnets* or notebooks (J. Cazeneuve (1972). *Lucien Lévy-Bruhl*. New York: Harper).

100. Albert De Jong (2000). *Mission and Politics in Eastern Africa: Dutch Missionaries and African Nationalism in Kenya, Tanzania and Malawi 1945–1965*. Nairobi: Paulines Publications Africa, 27.

101. De Jong (2000). Op. cit., 27.

according to us, that is the main problem facing the Catholic Church in Sukumaland at the moment.¹⁰²

The third element that bedeviled the missionaries' (of course and other personnel in the colonies) work was lack of adequate training,¹⁰³ as this was considered unnecessary. As a result, most of them had quite vague ideas about the exact nature of Christian love and brotherhood of humankind. Daniel Thwaite elaborates this in a more candid way:

> It was deemed unnecessary for white men to have any special training before dealing with and being put in charge of natives. It was a common assumption that work on the colonies required men of less education than work at home, so the colonies became a sort of clearing-house for failures and worse. This unfortunately applied equally to the missionary as to other callings, and until recently it was the prevalent opinion that the Gospel could be better preached and interpreted to ignorant and degraded savages by less intellectual and less educated men.¹⁰⁴

Emergence of Cultural Schizophrenia

With due respect to the work done by missionaries (of all religious denominations), particularly that of evangelization, and their good intentions notwithstanding, their wanton destruction of the African culture only helped to further alienate the African Christian in Kenya and make him or her feel a stranger to him or herself.¹⁰⁵ Hence this attitude proved to be counterproductive and divided Kenyans into three groups: the first group rejected Christianity, as a white man's religion and stuck to their traditional religion, the second one 'backtracked' into schism and formed independent churches like *Akūrinū*¹⁰⁶ and *Dini ya Msambwa*.¹⁰⁷ The third group accepted Christianity, sometimes through the signing of an official declaration to turn away from their 'heathen practices'¹⁰⁸ but they started living in two cultural realities—that of Christianity and that of their traditions—even where the two were considered to be diametrically opposed to each other.

Lo Liyong observed this situation, in his native Sudan, in a tripartite syncretism between Christianity, Islam and Traditional Religion.

---

102. Frans Wijsen and Ralph Tanner (2000). *Seeking a Good Life*. Nairobi: Paulines Publications Africa, 12.

103. Donovan, op. cit., 21.

104. Quoted in Kenyatta (1999). Op. cit., 270.

105. Magesa (1990). Op. cit., 46.

106. Nahashon Ndung'u (1997). The Bible in an African Independent Church. In Hannah W. Kinoti and John M. Waliggo (eds). *The Bible in African Christianity*. Nairobi: Acton Publishers, 58–60.

107. Johannes Jacobus Visser (1989). *Pökoot Religion*. Oegstgeest: Hendrik Kraemer Instituut, 39.

108. Baur op. cit., 477; Ndung'u, op. cit., 60.

> Christmas is coming. And everybody is going to buy presents. There will be Christmas shoes, clothes, cards, sweets, goats and sheep as well as beer, Sharia Law or no Sharia Law. Meanwhile, should anybody fall sick, they will run to the nearest traditional medicine man if they want to reach Christmas alive.[109]

Instead of uprooting the African from his 'heathen' ways of life, and 'bringing him to the light', as per their intention, it created what we have termed as 'cultural schizophrenia'.[110] Cultural development of the self was curtailed because "the way to African self-identification was closed at one end leaving only the Western-Christian outlet."[111] On the one hand, the African was expected to discard all his/her cultural practices and ". . .follow the white man's religion without questioning whether it was suited for his condition of life or not."[112]

On the other hand, Africans did not want to abandon their age-old traditions to blindly follow the white man's way of worship. Many accepted the new religion but also continued with their cultural practices unabated. This created double-personalities among religious adherents and did not augur so well for evangelization in Africa. Instead of bringing forth a united Christian body of committed men and women, it divided the people into two opposing groups. The first one consisted of the subtle, albeit neurotic, members of the congregation, who were dogged by many religious and cultural aberrations. Using the findings of Gray and Luke, Waliggo expresses the situation of this group of Christians as follows:

> They find themselves divided into two personalities, one African and the other christian. During the times of joy and peace they may be able to live as true christians, but when crises come, whether of illness, suffering misfortune, death, barrenness and so on, they easily, move back to their African personality and engage in ceremonies, rites, and world view that have been constantly condemned by the church. This tension spares very few people.[113]

---

109. Taban Lo Liyong (1991). *Culture is Rutan*. Nairobi: Longman Kenya, 30.

110. Ndegwah (2004). Op. cit., 87. Mark R. J. Faulkner (2006. *Overtly Muslim, Covertly Boni: Competing Calls of Religious Allegiance on the Kenya Coast.* Leiden, Boston: Brill) has carried out an extensive research on this issue on the Kenyan coast on the spread of Islam among the Awer (or Boni) people, where he found out that they are overtly Muslims but covertly remain Boni, culturally and religiously. Other scholars use different, though not exactly equivalent, terms like 'dual religious systems' (Robert J. Schreiter (1985). Op. cti., 148, 155), 'dualism' (Waliggo (1986). Op. cit., 22), 'double identity' (Wachege (2001). Op. cit., 33–34) and 'cultural depersonalization' (Kwasi Wiredu (2005). African Philosophy, Anglophone. In Edward Craig (ed). *The Shorter Routledge Encyclopedia of Philosophy*. London and New York: Routledge, 9). Mazrui (1986). Op. cit.) calls it a double-faceted 'triple heritage', one modern, the other ancient. The former consists of 'the indigenous-Arabic- Western polarity, while the latter consists of the indigenous-Semitic-Graeco-Roman polarity.

111. Mazrui (1986). Op. cit., 83.

112. Kenyatta (1999). Op. cit., 270.

113. John Mary Walliggo ((1986). Making a Church that is Truly African, 22, quoting R. Gray and F. Luke (1978). *Christianity in Independent Africa*. London: OUP, 606–613.

The second group consisted of those who could not suppress their feelings and openly rebelled to start their own churches; which they felt could adequately meet their religious needs. Again, this is manifested in what came to be known as the 'circumcision controversy' among the Gĩkũyũ people of Central Kenya; resulting to a schism with political overtones.

> Two Scottish doctors disapproved of female circumcision chiefly on medical grounds, and an inter-church conference (CSM, CMS, AIM) in 1929 prohibited it. Unfortunately Dr Arthur forced the issue by demanding a thumb-print promise of the parents not to circumcise their daughters. On their side the Kikuyu Central Association joined the controversy and protested against this "demoralization of the ancestral tribal customs". They warned that the thumb-print would imply the signing-away of one's land. An emotional campaign started with abusive songs against the missionaries. The result was not apostasy but schism. Dr Arthur was blamed and the well-founded slogan coined: "*There is no eleventh commandment*", [that says "Thou shall not circumcise"]. His Presbyterian congregations lost the vast majority of their members.[114]

Appreciation of the African Culture

Due to this disturbing phenomenon theologians started asking questions with regard to the resilience of African traditional practices within Christianity and other foreign religions. One could find no better answer than that offered by Tempels, albeit derogatorily. "It is because the pagan founds his life upon the traditional groundwork of his theodicy and his ontology (which include his whole mental life in their purview) and supply him with a complete solution to the problem of living."[115] Convinced of the necessity for change, missionaries started to take a fresh look at the method(s) of evangelization. With the coming of African theologians on the scene (in the 1950s), the situation changed and they started lobbying for the recognition and acceptance by the mainstream church(es) of positive elements in the African culture. This request necessarily presupposed the recognition of African traditional religious practices, for these two are not separable. The declaration to the effect that African culture has something to offer to Christianity was made by the first General Assembly of the All-Africa Conference of Churches when it met in Kampala. In a well-balanced statement, it said the following: "Traditional African culture was not all bad; neither was everything good."[116]

In the Catholic Church, the seeds for the acceptance of this quest were sown slightly later by the Vatican II Council; when, in 1964, it dedicated a whole document (*Lumen Gentium*—LG) to the possibility of the Word of God finding a home in the

---

114. Baur, op. cit., 479.
115. Placide Tempels (1969). *Bantu Philosophy*. Paris: Presence Africaine, 26.
116. Ndegwah (2004). Op. cit., 86.

local cultures where it is being preached, and affirmed it a year later by dedicating yet another, more forceful document (GS—*Gaudium et Spes*) to the question of culture. The document starts by examining the situation of man in the modern world[117] and finally addresses itself to the theme of culture in general, and then its specific relationship with faith. It lays emphasis on *reformulation* as the important principle in this regard.[118] However, the papal approval and blessing came much later, with the publication of the encyclical *Evangelii Nuntiandi (On Evangelization in the Modern World)*, which explicitly recognized the importance of culture in evangelization. "Evangelisation loses much of its force and effectiveness if it does not take into consideration the actual people to whom it is addressed, if it does not use their language, their signs, their symbols, if it does not answer the questions they ask, and if it does have an impact on their concrete life."[119]

On the African continent though, the climax of this trend of thought came much later, with the address of Pope Paul VI to the African bishops in Uganda in 1969, when he said thus: ". . .by now you Africans are missionaries to yourselves. . .you Africans must now continue, upon this continent, the building up of the church."[120] Elsewhere, he talked of the relationship between faith and culture and had this to say:

> The expression, that is, the language and mode of manifesting this one Faith may be manifold, hence it may be original, suited to the tongue, the style, the character, the genius and the culture of the one who professes this one Faith. From this point of view, a certain pluralism is not only legitimate, but desirable. An adaptation of the Christian life in the fields of pastoral, ritual, didactic and spiritual activities is not only possible, it is even favoured by the Church. The liturgical renewal is a living example of this. And in this sense, you may, and you must have an African Christianity. Indeed you possess human values and characteristic forms of culture which can rise up to perfection so as to find in Christianity, and for Christianity, a true superior fullness and prove to be capable of a richness of expression all in its own, and genuinely African.[121]

Pope John Paul II went on in the footsteps of Paul VI and tirelessly pursued this goal as he openly declared: ". . .there is an organic and constitutive link between Christianity and culture," and that, "the synthesis between culture and faith is not just a demand of culture but also of faith. *A faith which does not become culture*," he continues, "*is a faith which has not been fully received, not thoroughly thought through, not fully lived out.*"[122]

---

117. Flannery, op. cit., nos. 4–10.

118. Ibid., nos 53–62.

119. Pope Paul VI (1977). Op. cit., no. 63.

120. Pope Paul VI (1969a). To the Inaugural 1969 SECAM, Kampala. In Teresa Okure, Paul van Tiel et al (eds). *Inculturation of Christianity in Africa* (Spearhead, 111–114). Eldoret: Gaba Publications, 33–34.

121. Paul VI (1969b). Op. cit., 50–51.

122. Pope John Paul II (1982). Letter to Cardinal Agostino Casaroli, Secretary of State, 20th, May.

This official embrace of inculturation opened the doors and windows for the ingenuity and authenticity into the African Church; and theologians immediately went to work. Leading the list in the African soil are systematic theologians, particularly in the field of Christology, where they adopted a comparative method and tried to express Christ in familiar African terms like 'ancestor', 'chief', 'king', 'conqueror' and 'healer'.[123] Nyamiti who had long held this position declared it publicly while delivering a paper titled 'African Christologies'. He wrote: "There is no doubt that Christology is the subject which has been most developed in today's African theology. This is so true that already at the present moment an adequate survey of that subject would need a much broader essay than is not possible within the confines of this paper."[124] But 'Why Christology?' perhaps one may ask. It must be noted that the core of Christian evangelization centers on the person of Christ and his message of salvation to the community of the faithful. Hence Christology determines ecclesiology in both its mode of being (*modus essendi*), i.e., the way of being church in particular social situations, and mode of operation (*modus operandi*), i.e., the way the church carries out and expresses the message of salvation. It is no wonder then, that incarnation has been accepted as one of the basic principles of inculturation.

The Use of the Bible in Africa

The reflection on the use of the Bible in Africa is a result of the struggle, by many people—both scholars and non-scholars—of rereading it as a post-colonial subject.[125] The paradox of this struggle lies in the fact that "African Christians accept the Bible as an affirmation of their humanity, while in most cases the missionary enterprise has presented the Bible as a negation of African culture. This paradox has resulted in a discrepancy between missionary and African reading of the Bible."[126] The central issue, concerning the use of the Bible in Africa, has been put together by a group of academicians in the form of a question. "Does the Christian church claim that its Bible, which originated in a particular time and context, possess an exclusive and universally normative value for people living in quite different contexts and times with their own sacred traditions?"[127] We think that the answer to this question is in the negative, hence

---

In *L'Osservatore Romano*, June 28, 7–8.

123. Zinkuratire (2004a). Op, cit., 48.

124. Nyamiti (1989). Op. cit., 17.

125. Dube (2002). Op. cit., 57; Segovia (2000a). Op. cit., 119–142.

126. Jesse N. K. Mugambi (2003). *Christian Theology and Social Reconstruction*. Nairobi: Acton Publishers, 122.

127. Isabel Mukonyora et al (eds) (1993). Introduction. In I. Mukonyora et al (eds). *"Rewriting" the Bible: The Real Issues*. Gweru: Mambo Press, xi.

the need to distinguish the Word of God[128] from the culture in which it reached us, and then redress it in our own cultural practices and idiomatic expressions.

Some people have called for the rejection of the Bible because it is a Jewish piece of literature, while others have called for a total 'overhaul' in the form of re-writing it. According to Banana, this exercise "...would include revision and editing to what is already there, but would also involve adding that which is not included."[129] He further argues that a re-written Bible will be experienced worldwide by peoples of many traditions and faiths, a fact that will more adequately enable them to fulfil their responsibility as a people of God.[130] He then goes on to explore the history of canonicity and finally calls for a repeat of the same (averring that we need a newer and updated canon).[131] The one thing he failed to address adequately was the Canonical Controversy that has haunted Christian unity to this day. Giving in to his demand would not only rekindle this war but is likely to arouse skepticism and divisions, among Christians, which are likely to go on *ad infinitum*. We, therefore, agree with those who have banked on both exegesis and hermeneutics as the sure foundation of making the Bible relevant to the peoples of all races and cultures.

> Sound Biblical and Religious studies, by applying exegetical and hermeneutical methods, reveal the core of the biblical message as an announcement of salvation and liberation for all while duly respecting human freedom and the value of other non-Christian faith-experiences. This essential biblical message recognises, therefore, that God cannot be held captive by any created construct, including Christianity and its Bible.[132]

Biblical Hermeneutics in Africa

The growth and development of biblical hermeneutics in Africa is based on the desire by theologians, pastors and the church hierarchy to present the Word of God in terms and categories relevant to the lifestyle of their people. Thus, they are struggling to

---

128. Here a distinction is made between the bible as the Word of God and the bible as Scriptures or sacred literature (Letty M. Russell (1985). *Feminist Interpretation of the Bible*. Oxford: Basil Blackwell, 17). The former is universal and encompasses all cultures as God has always revealed Himself to all peoples of the world in His own mysterious ways. But as the latter, the bible is conditioned to cultures, social demeanors and talents of its writers and it can always be improved or localized by using cultural imageries or literary prowess of the people reading the bible in different parts of the world.

129. Canaan S. Banana (1993). The Case for a New Bible. In I. Mukonyora et al (eds). *"Rewriting" the Bible: The Real Issues*. Gweru: Mambo Press, 30.

130. Ibid., 30–31.

131. Joseph G. Healey (1981. Op. cit) has expressed the same opinion and said that every community must (metaphorically speaking) re-write the four gospels in order to come up with one, relevant, gospel of life that suits their local situations. This new gospel he calls 'a fifth gospel'.

132. Frans J. Verstraelen (1993). The Real Issues Regarding the Bible: Summary, Findings and Conclusions. In I. Mukonyora et al (eds). *"Rewriting" the Bible the Real Issues*. Gweru: Mambo Press, 289.

"develop their own methods of reading and interpreting the Bible that are based on their culture and in conformity with their world-view in order to make its message more easily understood and assimilated."[133]

In line with these efforts the Pontifical Biblical Commission has finally urged churches to put the bible teaching in their own culture, because missionaries have failed to do it for them. "Missionaries, in fact, cannot help [but] bring the Word of God in the form in which it has been inculturated in their country of origin. New local churches have to make every effort to convert this foreign form of biblical inculturation into another form more closely corresponding to the culture of their own land. Thus, dedication to inculturation is the driving force to this noble endeavour."[134] Locheng identifies biblical pastoral ministry and biblical hermeneutics as some of the key areas of inculturation, if the Word of God is to 'feel at home'[135] in Africa.

> Possibilities have further to be explored by African theologians for a real African hermeneutics that is based on African cultural values and forms, in view of making the word more intelligible and to unleash its power and vitality (Heb 4:12) to African men and women. Besides African biblical hermeneutics, the process of inculturation requires a) working out the significance of the story of Jesus in his times; b) bringing out the story of Jesus for the African Christian communities; c) drawing out the significance of the story of Jesus in relation to traditions of people of different faiths.[136]

Towards this end individuals and organizations have started various projects to try and bring the Gospel home in Africa. These efforts are well-documented in the work of West and Dube where they have co-edited essays of thirty contributors and made an extensive bibliography "of all known works of biblical interpretation produced by Africans, for Africa, or about African interpretation."[137] Among the individuals we can mention Ukpong, Dickson, Okure, Oduyoye, Bediako and Uzukwu in West Africa, Jonker and West in South Africa, Zinkuratire, Magesa, Nasimiyu, Waruta, Getui, Nthamburi and Mugambi in East Africa, and Holter from Norway. Among the organizations, we have AMECEA Pastoral Institute (API), BICAM, EATWOT, and the LUMKO Institute in South Africa leading the way. Here we will briefly discuss them except EATWOT, which is an association of theologians rather an institution.

---

133. Zinkuratire (2004a). op. cit., 42.

134. Pontifical Biblical Commission (1993). *The Interpretation of the Bible in the Church.* Rome: Libreria Editrice Vaticana, 119.

135. Welbourn and Ogot, op. cit.

136. Callisto Locheng (2004). Praxis and Methods of Inculturation in Africa: A Response. In Patrick Ryan (ed). *Theology of Inculturation in Africa Today: Methods, Praxis and Mission.* Nairobi: CUEA Publications, 70.

137. Gerald O. West and Musa W. Dube (2000). *The Bible in Africa: Transactions, Trajections and Trends.* Leiden: Brill, 633.

The AMECEA Pastoral Institute (API), situated in Eldoret—Kenya, is an institute of AMECEA[138] that has the strengthening of SCCs as its pastoral policy. It was founded in December 1967, at Ggaba—Kampala (Uganda) from where it was forced to move to Eldoret (Kenya) in 1976 due to the unfavorable political climate. It, however, retained its name, Gaba, albeit with different spellings. Through organizing short courses, seminars and conferences, API provides ongoing formation and pastoral renewal in a supportive setting enriched by dialogue among lay persons, religious men, women and the clergy. The vision is to have creative, effective, prophetic, humane, up-to-date, and open-minded pastoral agents who are committed to deeper evangelization through the training of others and the building of the Church as the Family of God, within the reality of globalization, technological advancement and the rapidly changing African context.

The API offers a nine-month residential on-going formation program that starts from mid-January to mid-October. The focus of the program is on pastoral, spiritual, theological and development studies. The program is offered in two distinct but related parts: comprising core courses and workshops in specific ministries. The course on Scripture seeks to bring the Bible closer to the people, through the training of the Christian community leaders. It also promotes the use of the Bible through subsidies that provide for cheaper copies and holding sub-regional seminars on the training on the use of the Bible.

BICAM stands for Biblical Centre for Africa and Madagascar and its headquarters are in Accra—Ghana. The aim of BICAM is to stimulate, encourage, plan and coordinate the biblical pastoral ministry in Africa and Madagascar, according to the policies and guidelines of SECAM (Symposium of the Episcopal Conferences of Africa and Madagascar). The following are the tasks of BICAM:

- Stimulate, encourage, plan and coordinate the biblical pastoral ministry in Africa and Madagascar, according to the policies and guidelines of SECAM.
- Promote and undertake studies in exegesis which is necessary for the incarnation of the bible message in local Churches within Africa and Madagascar.
- Promote bible translations into local languages.
- Promote the production, publication and propagation of biblical material concerning the Biblical Apostolate.
- Promote Biblical formation of the Christian faithful at all levels.
- Highlight the biblical foundations of the Church's evangelizing mission.
- Promote Biblical associations and Bible Study Groups at different levels.

---

138. This is an acronym for "Association of Member Episcopal Conferences in Eastern Africa". It is a service organization for the National Episcopal Conferences of the eight countries of Eastern Africa, namely Eritrea (1993), Ethiopia (1979), Kenya (1961), Malawi (1961), Sudan (1973), Tanzania (1961), Uganda (1961) and Zambia (1961). Djibouti (2002) and Somalia (1995) are Affiliate members.

- Foster Biblical Spirituality among adults, youth and students in primary and secondary Schools, Colleges and Universities.[139]

One of the key achievements of BICAM, in bible translation, is the publication of the African Bible, one that interprets bible pericopes in the light of the African situation and experience. Another achievement is of the establishment in Africa, of the worldwide Biblical Apostolate Movement, which has now established branches in virtually all dioceses in Africa. BICAM nourishes it by providing expertise and material help to the association through regular regional seminars on how to use the Bible.

The Lumko Pastoral Institute belongs to The Southern African Catholic Bishops' Conference (SACBC), which is comprised of the bishops of Botswana, South Africa and Swaziland; serving in the ecclesiastical Provinces of Cape Town, Durban, Pretoria and Bloemfontein. The institute's purpose is pastoral and mission research, training through workshops seminars and courses; production of audio-visual and printed materials.[140] Its most important contribution towards the use of the Bible is the seven-steps that are followed during the SCC bible sharing sessions. But, although much has been achieved by the endeavors of the above institutions and individuals, there are feelings, among many scholars that much still needs to be done, particularly in the quest for inculturation.[141]

The development of biblical hermeneutics took place against the background of a negative attitude, from the early missionaries, against whatever was perceived to be African. "From its beginning it resisted the colonial readings/interpretations of the Bible that began by dismissing all aspects of African culture as pagan, exotic, evil, savage, ungodly, or childish."[142] It was in response to this negative attitude that some Africans started doing research in comparative religion with the aim of legitimizing African religious and cultural traditions.[143] Following this lack of appreciation for the African culture and ways of religious conceptualization, Western methods of bible interpretation were introduced in African theological colleges and seminaries. These methods have, however, proved inadequate for the needs of African Christians, hence necessitating a search for a specifically African way for reading and interpreting the Bible.[144]

Historically, exegesis has gone through three stages: "in the first stage, interest was more on the author and the production of the text. In the second stage, interest shifted to the text and its message. In the third stage, there is a shift towards the impact of the text on the reader . . . "[145] Thus, classical exegesis (which is basi-

---

139. http://www.sceam-secam.org/english/documents/bicam.rtf

140. http://www.smom-za.org/cidsa.htm

141. P.K. Sarpong (1975). Christianity Should be Africanized not Africa Christianized. In *AFER* 20. Eldoret: AMECEA Gaba Publications, 325.

142. Dube (2002). Op. cit., 58.

143. Zinkuratire (2004a). Op. cit., 48.

144. Ibid., 42.

145. Speckman, op. cit., 37.

cally diachronic) focuses its attention on issues like the dates of a text or a book in the Bible, its author, his (or her?) intention, and audience and so on. Among such methods are source criticism and historical criticism. Modern methods of exegesis, which are more synchronic, focus on the reader of this text here and now: how best to get the hidden meaning of the text and the interplay between the reader and the text. Among these we can mention post structural criticism (or deconstruction) and reader-focused (or reader-response) criticism.

The three stages can be expressed in a linear diagram that moves from the author through the text to the reader as follows:

Author (hermeneutics of production)	Text (hermeneutics of 'Sache')	Reader (hermeneutics of reception)

Contemporary methods, considered to be synchronic (because they focus on how a word or text is used) are different in their approach and are varied in their emphasis. Structuralist methods are text-centered and so look at the text itself for an answer. With the use of semiotics and other linguistic analysis tools, they try to analyze the surface structure of words in a text in order to get to their deeper meaning.

The reader-focused exegesis does not reject the role of the text and the fact that the reader has manipulated it, but also looks at how the text has manipulated the reader, in order to reach at his/her current understanding. Thus, it is centered on the rapport between the text and the reader, almost relegating the author to the background.

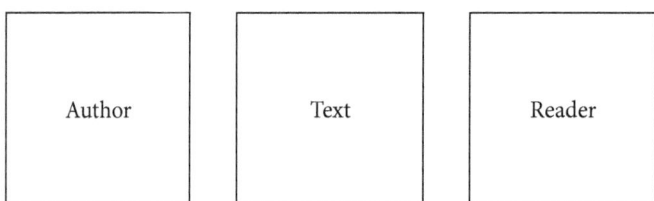

Poststructuralism, especially deconstruction, moves a step further and tries to 'discover' how this meaning has been distorted by looking at the missed points of weakness and how the reader 'violently' portrays his/her power by manipulating the text to suit his (or her) own aims. Deconstruction denies an existing center of meaning or an original meaning of a text. All elements (author, text and reader, even the 'object' of reference) are seen as textual situations. One speaks of 'the linguistic turn'.

Derrida uses the concept 'écriture' for this situation. Deconstruction is not text-oriented, author, or even reader-oriented. It is concerned with how the 'écriture' operates as a meaning producing force in accordance with an elusive process of differentiations.

Hence the meaning is neither found in the interplay between the author and the text nor in the interplay between the text and the reader only. According to Derrida, meaning is 'sous rature'—under deletion and this can be illustrated as follows:

"These methodologies, though scientific to the core were not easily actualisable in the African situation. The overriding question is: Did such approaches help bring the message of the Bible down-to-earth in a way for the Africans to comprehend? Or did they help to promote evangelization and the establishment of a virile church growth in the African soil?" [146]

According to Manus, these methods failed to address the African situation since they are developed outside and simply transported to the continent. It has to be clarified, as Zinkuratire does, that "the problem was not with the methods themselves. The problem was that those who used them stopped precisely at the point where the interpretation of the text should have started, according to the specific meaning of the term 'hermeneutics' as the application of a text's original meaning to a contemporary situation."[147] Therefore, African biblical scholarship has endeavored to develop a distinctively African way of reflecting on the above methods of bible interpretation, and how to relate them to the African situation.

Development of an African Biblical Hermeneutics

As pointed out, biblical hermeneutics in Africa is still in its formative stage.[148] It is, therefore, not one thing and it is still in the process of being defined, but the aim is the same: to read bible texts ". . .from the perspective of the ordinary Africans or read and interpret the text bearing in mind the African context as the target of one's hermeneutic deliverance."[149] In his widely-researched article on the evolution of bible interpretation in Africa, has distinguished three phases of development, which correspond and fit neatly with the development of the secular history in the

---

146. Chris Ukachukwu Manus (2002). Methodological Approaches in Contemporary African Biblical Scholarship: The Case of West Africa. In Emmanuel Katongole (ed). *African Theology Today.* Scranton: The University of Scranton Press, 4.

147. Zinkuratire (2004a). Op. cit., 48.

148. West (2005). Op. cit., 3.

149. Chris Ukachukwu Manus (2003). *Intercultural Hermeneutics in Africa: Methods and Approaches.* Nairobi: Acton Publishers, 35.

continent.¹⁵⁰ He says that phase one, which ranges from the 1930s to the 1970s, was: "Reactive and apologetic; focused on legitimizing African religion and culture; dominated by the comparative method". This was the period of the colonial yoke, in which the value of African culture was questioned and the African religious experience was dismissed as riddled with superstition.

The comparative method was based in central, western and eastern Africa, where the main concern was the defense of the cultural heritage. Hence the method "tried to point out the common elements and similarities, but also differences, between African cultural and religious traditions and those of the bible, particularly the Old Testament."¹⁵¹ This phase can be said to have applied the hermeneutics of suspicion, because it questions those interpretations that denied anything good among the African and seems to suggest that anything western was good for the continent.¹⁵² Among the key proponents of this phase, are John Mbiti, Kwesi Dickson and Justin Ukpong.¹⁵³

Although the comparative method lacked clear hermeneutic principles as its foundation, it cannot be dismissed as useless. Its aim was "to salvage Africa's good cultural traditions and values and make use of them in the theological task of contextualizing the Gospel message and making it relevant to the everyday life of the people"¹⁵⁴ According to Ukpong, the second phase ranges from the 1970s to the 1990s and, he says, it was 'reactive-proactive'.¹⁵⁵

This phase was characterized by the " . . . use of African context as resource for biblical interpretation; dominated by Africa-in-the-Bible approach, inculturation-evaluative method and liberation hermeneutics . . . "¹⁵⁶ The earlier apologetic approach of trying to justify African religion and culture gave way to more confident approaches that took the values of African traditions for granted and used them in their interaction with the Bible. During this time, African countries had attained independence and were confronted by the disillusionment of new dictatorial regimes, corruption and many other social ills. The desire to fight these evils saw the rise of liberation hermeneutics, black theology and feminist hermeneutics.¹⁵⁷

The Africa-in-the-Bible approach tried to investigate the place of Africa and Africans in the Bible and their contribution to the biblical history of salvation.¹⁵⁸ The evalu-

---

150. Ukpong (1999). Op. cit., 313–329.

151. Zinkuratire (2004a). Op. cit., 63.

152. Gerald O. West (2002). Negotiating With the "White Man's Book": Early Foundations for Liberation Hermeneutics in Southern Africa. In Emmanuel Katongole (ed). *African Theology Today*. Scranton: The University of Scranton Press, 28.

153. Zinkuratire (2004a). Op. cit., 49.

154. Ibid., 49.

155. Ukpong (1999). Op. cit., 314.

156. Zinkuratire (2004a). Op. cit., 49.

157. Ibid.

158. J. N. K. Mugambi (2001) Foundations for an African Approach to Biblical Hermeneutics. In: Mary Getui et al (eds). *Interpreting the New Testament in Africa*. Nairobi: Acton Publishers, 9–29.

ative method tries to "relate the biblical text to the African context in a variety of ways in order to make the biblical message address Africans in their concrete life situation."[159] The liberation hermeneutics is an interpretive approach that uses the Bible in its struggle against any form of oppression, on the presupposition that the message of the Bible, that is Good News, is essentially a message of liberation.[160]

Feminist hermeneutics resists the oppression of women by men using the Bible as a justification. Its equivalent is Black theology in South Africa, which resisted the attempt by the Boers to justify racial discrimination using the Bible.[161] African women theologians try, in this kind of hermeneutics, to read the Bible from the perspective of their cultural experience where many oppressive practices are sanctioned by the society. Phase three ranges from the 1990s onwards, which he says is proactive. It is characterized by the ". . .recognition of the ordinary reader; African context as subject of biblical interpretation; dominated by liberation and holistic inculturation methodologies."[162]

He, however, cautions that the above divisions are not meant to compartmentalize bible interpretation in Africa; since, ". . .the seeds of one phase are sown in the previous phase, and that the emergence of a new phase does not mean the disappearance of the former"[163] He further clarifies that in this stage, the effort is based on trying to merge the two distinctively diverse models of inculturation and liberation hermeneutics, in what he calls Inculturation Biblical Hermeneutics.[164]

Characteristics and Requirements for an African Hermeneutics

The development of a single, unified and methodical biblical hermeneutics in Africa is a welcome idea. But it appears that more needs to be done for it to take cognizance of the fact that many of the concepts it employs are still not clear and in need of further analysis and streamlining in the face of changing socio-cultural situations. Zinkuratire has exemplified some characteristics of the inculturation hermeneutics as contextual interpretation, committed interpretation, engaging the whole community and deliberately being based on African frame of reference or worldview.[165] As West says, "it might be argued that in certain important aspects ordinary African 'readers' of the Bible partially constitute African biblical scholarship."[166]

159. Zinkuratire (2004a). Op. cit., 50.
160. Ibid., 52.
161. West (2005). Op. cit., 3.
162. Ukpong (1999). Op. cit., 314.
163. Ibid., 314.
164. Ukpong (1995). Op. cit., 3-14.
165. Zinkuratire (2004a). Op. cit., 55-58.
166. Wiredu (2005). Op. cit., 12.

On the role of the 'ordinary' readers of the Bible, Zinkuratire concurs and adds: "It is mostly from them that the African contextual frame of reference will come. They will in fact be better equipped than most westernized African biblical scholars and theologians to read the Bible from within the African world-view."[167] Zinkuratire adds that its exegetical procedure involves four elements that work together as follows: a) the text, b) the context of the text, c) the reading community and d) the context of the reading community.[168]

> So the meaning of a text is produced in the process of a community within their social-cultural context, reading the biblical text against its social-historical context. This requires a careful analysis of both the contemporary social-cultural context of the readers, on the one hand, and the social-historical context of the biblical text on the other. This is done so that a meaningful relationship between the two contexts may be established.

To the above characteristics of the African hermeneutics we would like to add four requirements. These are bible translation, orality, a more focused under-standing of culture and the need to embrace deconstruction as an ongoing activity. Zinkuratire lauds bible translation efforts as an important contribution towards the contextualization of the Bible in the process of interpretation. "I am personally also convinced," he confesses, "that a truly contextualised reading of the Bible can best be done from a vernacular translation of the Bible rather than from a European language."[169]

Whereas we agree with the importance of bible translation, if the Bible is to become a book of the people, we also think that there is an urgent importance of training all bible translators in the original languages of the Bible; otherwise they keep on reproducing translations of other translations. This carries the risk of losing the advantage Zinkuratire envisages of a vernacular Bible, making it easier "to visualise biblical events taking place in one's village instead of Palestine."[170] Although various bible translation projects have been going on, West bluntly puts the point of their limitations across: "African biblical translation is often not hermeneutical enough...it does not partake of and draw from the rich array of resources currently available to biblical hermeneutics generally."[171] Hence "African biblical translation must engage more fully with African biblical hermeneutics."[172]

Then there is the oral dimension of an African hermeneutics as an intrinsic part of the African cultural way of life and as a path to knowledge. Goody distinguishes two different paths to knowledge: "In oral culture," he says, "the bulk of knowledge is

---

167. Zinkuratire (2004a). Op. cit., 61.
168. Ibid., 62.
169. Ibid., 61.
170. Ibid., 61.
171. West (2005). Op. cit., 17.
172. Ibid., 3.

passed on orally, in face-to-face contact among members of the family, clan and village. In written culture knowledge comes from an outside, impersonal source (book) or is acquired in an extra-familial institution, such as a school."[173] Healey and Sybertz point at the place of orality in the theology of inculturation more succinctly. "Oral literature and traditions are an important source, a 'living stream' of an African narrative theology of inculturation. Oral literature covers very broad and complex genres as seen by its many equivalent names and descriptions: fold literature, folklore, fold media, oral art, oral civilization, oral communication, oral culture. . ."[174]

As Okure has rightly observed, traditional Africans were 'a people of the word, not people of the book'[175] so the Bible is, first and foremost, interpreted as an oral text. And even today, with the advent of literacy, many people, who participate in bible sharing, both at home and in the SCC context, still do not know how to read and write. "Most of their information about the Bible comes from socialisation in the churches themselves as they listen to prayers and sermons."[176] Theirs is an oral culture that infuses into the bible sharing what West calls 'kinetic orality'[177] that Dononvan has expressed in the following words: "The art of conversation in Africa is delicate, developed, complex, and beautiful."[178] They add this complexity and beauty to the Scriptures by the way they listen to the bible stories, memories and recite them, talk about the Word of God, dramatize it, sing, and dance it: manifestly living its power and vitality.[179] Thus, in the African context, ordinary bible interpreters work more with their memories by remembering bible texts than by reading them.

To understand the divergent ways non-literate Africans have interpreted the Bible, scholars " . . . cannot simply rely on the historical-critical method, literary criticism, and reader-response criticism, because these methods give primacy to the written text of the Bible," argues Pui-lan. "Such methods fail to provide tools to analyze the negotiation of meaning in discursive contexts, the retelling of stories to meet the particular needs of an audience, or the thought process that lie behind oral transmission."[180] While comparing the written and oral traditions Lord observes the tremendous differences, and in particular the huge hiatus, between these two (written

---

173. John R. Goody (2000). *The Power of Written Tradition.* Washington, DC: Smithsonian Institution Press, 164.

174. Joseph Healey and Donald Sybertz (1997). *Towards an African Narrative Theology.* Nairobi: Paulines Publications Africa, 34.

175. Okure (1993). Op. cit., 83.

176. Itumeleng J. Mosala (1996). Race, Class, and Gender as Hermeneutical Factors in the African Independent Churches' Appropriation of the Bible, *Semeia*, 73, 43.

177. Cornel West (1988). *Prophetic Fragments.* Grand Rapids, Mich.: William B. Eerdmans, 5.

178. Donovan, op. cit., 134.

179. Hebrews 4:12.

180. Kwok Pui-lan (1999). Hearing and Talking: Oral Hermeneutics of Asian Women. In James A. Scherer and Stephen B. Bevans (eds). *New Directions in Mission and Evangelization.* Maryknoll, New York: Orbis Books, 82.

and oral) cultures and warns against the domination of the latter by the former.[181] "Once the oral technique is lost, it is never regained. The written technique, on the other hand, is not compatible with the oral technique, and the two could not possibly combine, to form another, a third, a 'transitional' technique."[182] The rich cultural heritage and oral techniques in the African culture can well augment the interpretation, understanding and application of the Bible in the African soil.

Then there is necessity for a sound understanding of culture. Much of the literature we have gone through in this section point to a good understanding of culture as a pre-requisite for an effective and fruitful inculturation. Droogers is more explicit, "Missiologists cannot exercise their tasks without paying attention to culture," he asserts, "and the Christian religion has its own cultural roots."[183] This calls for an examination of the current understanding of culture in order to see how it can be used for inculturation in the African context. Hence the need for deconstruction as an ongoing activity in order to understand and appreciate the distortions made to the Africa concepts and properly appropriate them in the face of the changing world.

The Understanding of Culture Today

In the recent past, the word culture has been taken to be above all a matter of meaning.[184] To understand culture then, one must " . . . study ideas, experiences, feelings, as well as the external forms that such internalities take as they are made public, available to the senses and thus truly social. . . .For culture, in the anthropological view, is the meanings which people create, and which create people, as members of societies."[185] According to Hannerz, culture has two loci (grounds), which can be classified, as overt and covert loci. The overt locus consists of what he calls 'public meaningful forms', i.e., what can be heard and whatever else that can be known through external realities. The covert locus is what he refers to as the human mind's instruments that interpret the overt human activities and give them meaning.

Modern and post-modern understanding of culture

The current understanding of culture can be classified into two schools of thought: one modern, the other post-modern.[186] Kroeber and Kluckhohn have summarized the modern understanding of culture as follows:

181. Albert B. Lord (1964). *The Singer of Tales*. Cambridge: Harvard University Press, 124–138.
182. Ibid.,129.
183. Droogers (2003). Op. cit., 59.
184. Ulf Hannerz (1992). *Cultural Complexity: Studies in the Social Organization of Meaning*. New York: Columbia University Press, 3.
185. Ibid., 3.
186. Tanner (1997). Op. cit., 25–58.

> Culture consists of patterns, explicit and implicit, of and for behavior acquired and transmitted by symbols, constituting the distinctive achievement of human groups, including their embodiments in artifacts; the essential core of culture consists of traditional (i.e. historically derived and selected) ideas and especially their attached values; culture systems may, on the one hand, be considered as products of actions, on the other hand as conditioning elements of further action.[187]

The modern understanding of culture seems to perceive it as a system 'out there',[188] with rules and structures of its own. All that one needs to do, therefore, is just to learn these rules and one would understand and classify certain systems as culture and reject others. According to this view culture is group-specific and it can be confined to certain groups of people and even geographical places. "If cultures are group-specific, then cultural differences must fall between such groups and not within them."[189] Thus, culture is considered as "the specific pattern of behaviours which distinguishes any society from others."[190]

Hence the definite and clear-cut talk about the Javanese culture, the Ndembu culture, the Kikuyu culture, and so on. Tanner has identified nine basic elements in the modern understanding of culture as follows: 1) culture is understood as a human universal, 2) it highlights human diversity, 3) culture varies with social group, 4) culture tends to be conceived as a people's entire way of life, 5) cultures are associated with social consensus, 6) culture is understood to constitute or construct human nature, 7) although human beings are made by culture, they also construct culture, in the sense that cultures are human conventions, 8) human cultures are contingent and 9) culture suggests social determinism.[191] Several theories of culture have arisen in the modern period, which include evolutionism (Tylor, Morgan and Frazer), diffusionism (William Perry, Grafton Elliot Smith, Wilhelm Schmidt and Wilhelm Koppers), historicism (Franz Boas), functionalism (Radcliffe-Browne and Bronislaw Malinowski), structuralism (Claude Levi-Strauss), essentialism (John Gray), relativism (Richard A. Shweder) and constructivism (Lev Vygotsky).

Although these theories understand and interpret culture in different ways, they have one thing in common; they see culture as an entity on its own that can be studied and understood in its own right. In the post-modern view of culture though, "It seems less plausible to presume that cultures are unified wholes of beliefs and values simply transmitted to every member of their respective groups as principles

---

187. A. L. Kroeber and C. Kluckhohn (1952). *Culture: A Critical Review of Concepts and Definitions*. New York: Vintage Books, 359.
188. David Ndegwah (2004). Op. cit., 87.
189. Tanner (1997). op. cit., 27.
190. John Bennet and Melvin Tumin (1948). *Social Life*. New York: Alfred A. Knopf, 209.
191. Tanner (1997). Op. cit., 25–29.

of social order."[192] Post-modern position stresses the following elements: the interactive process, negotiation, indeterminacy, fragmentation, conflict and porosity, which accordingly, form a new basis for reinterpretation of culture.[193] It acknowledges the complexity of culture in an increasingly mobile world, where different people are constantly interacting and dealing with each other. In its extreme form, post-modernism even denies the very existence of culture, claiming that it is no more than a plurality of intersecting 'cultural orientations'.[194]

This has made anthropologists to focus more on the difference within cultures rather than between cultures, as has been the practice. Although the post-modern view has retained the self-critical function of the modern notion, it has made the internal diversity of cultures as much the object of self-criticism as any criticism of external cultural 'others'.[195] An example of such a shift is the different starting points espoused by modern anthropologists and their post-modern counterparts. Spradley defines culture as a 'shared meaning-system' presupposing the existence of a consensus as a cultural *product*,[196] whereas Hannerz defines culture as an 'organization of diversity'.[197]

His presupposition is the existence of diversity, while culture is a *process* of consensus building. These are but two ways of looking at the same reality and one does not exclude the other. One can still consider culture as an essentially consensus building feature of group living. That consensus, however, becomes very minimalist, since it forms the basis for conflict or diversity as much as it forms the basis for shared beliefs and sentiments. Whether or not culture is a common focus of agreement, it binds people together as a common focus for engagement.[198]

Organization of Diversity

Hannerz points out that studying the distributive dimension of culture is a matter of engaging in the difficult issue of the 'relationship between culture and social structure'. There already exist ways of dealing with each one of them separately, but not of dealing with the relationship between them. Anthropologists, for instance, have been criticized in their cultural analysis because all anthropological trends evince a weak sense of social structure; and yet culture does not exist in a vacuum. Sociologists, on the other hand, carry out their studies of the social life as if culture does not matter.

---

192. Ibid., 38.
193. Ibid., 38.
194. Wim Van Binsbergen (1999a). 'Cultures do not exist': Exploding Self-evidences in the Investigation Interculturality. In Wim van Binsbergen (2003). *Intercultural Encounters: African and Anthropological Lessons. Towards a Philosophy of Interculturality.* Münster: Lit Verlag, 61.
195. Tanner (1997). Op. cit., 58.
196. Spradley (1980). Op. cit.
197. Hannerz, op. cit., 1992.
198. Tanner (1997). Op. cit., 57.

He, however, observes that there exist different ways of dealing with the linkage between the two: one of which is the theory that, "...meanings and symbolic forms are predominantly generated in, or shaped by, particular types of social relationships..."[199] This, in his words, is a matter of confronting a customary commitment, to particular understanding of culture as collective, socially organized meaning—the idea of culture as something *shared*, in the sense of homogeneously being distributed in society. Although this premise of cultural sharing is not accepted by all and sundry in the field of anthropology, it has its ardent proponents, who agree that study of culture must incorporate sociology of knowledge, showing meanings as distributed and controlled. In this regard, Tanner understands culture as a 'consensus building', characterized by 'agreement' and 'engagement'.

> The Postmodern anthropologist can still consider culture as an essentially consensus-building feature of group living. That consensus becomes, however, extremely minimalistic, it forms the basis for conflict as much as it forms the basis for shared common beliefs and sentiments. Whether or not culture is a common focus of agreement, culture binds people together as a common focus for engagement . . . all parties at least agree on the importance of the cultural items that they struggle to define and connect up with one another. Participants are bound together by a common attachment to investment in such cultural items, and not necessarily by any common reference points for making sense of social action, but they need not produce a genuinely common understanding of what is happening.[200]

There exists a strong and mutual interdependence between the social and the cultural since " . . . the social structure of persons and relationships channels the cultural flow at the same time as it is being, in part, culturally produced."[201] This means that a distribution of cultural items within a population is a matter of cultural structure. That people have understandings of that distribution which makes a difference in their life. These are meanings in their own right, and they affect the ways in which people think, deal with ideas and produce meaningful external forms. The major implication of a distributive understanding of culture is that people must deal with other people's meaning.

This, in turn, means that there are meanings and meaningful forms on which other individuals, categories, or groups in one's environment have a prior claim, but one is yet to respond to. And yet this response can only be done within the set-up of a social structure. The most challenging thing in trying to understand the relationship between culture and social structure is that the latter, to which understandings of the distribution of culture is hinged, exists in the borderlands between culture and

---

199. Hannerz, op. cit., 11.
200. Tanner (1997). Op. cit., 57.
201. Ibid., 57.

non-culture. Apart from the distinctions that people make in attaching meanings to themselves, to others and relationships; the social structure also involves the demographic distribution of power and material resources.[202]

In brief, the idea of the relationship between culture and social structure that results here is quite old, complex and dynamic. On the one hand, culture is distributed and includes understandings of distributions. On the other hand, the social structure is based, in part, on cultural distinctions and in part on distributions of other characteristics; which are drawn into culture by being meaningful, but at the same time standing outside it insofar as the meaning is not wholly arbitrary. And the distinctions and the attributions of meaning on which social structure draws also entail distribution.

There is an intimate interplay between existing practices of the people, which shape their worldview, and whatever they perceive as foreign and in need of being interpreted in the light of their cultural heritage. The post-modern view of culture thus, rests on the thesis that culture cannot be confined in a geographical place, or be pegged to a given language or even be confined to a particular race. What exist are mixtures of various 'cultural orientations' that depend on individual social encounters.[203] An academician is likely to have cultural orientations from other scholars world-wide, while a businessman (or woman) is likely to have cultural orientations from other business people outside his (or her) community, and so would a member of a religious community.[204] The post-modern criticism of the modern notion of culture is a movement away from the view of culture as closed and static, to viewing it as open and flexible. It is not only a result of growing academic insight but also a consequence of changes in the world society that cannot be overlooked.[205]

In general, the globalized situation of the world has made it necessary for people to achieve a greater awareness of their cultures as well as being critical of the historical processes that have distorted the same.[206] How then, could we approach the notion of culture in the African context? It is important to note that most of the aspects mentioned in the modern understanding of culture are actually not discarded, but only "decentered or reinscribed within a more primary attention to historical process . . .Some aspects of the modern are substantially revised; the functions of most of these remain, however, much the same."[207] For example, as we have argued above, one may still consider cultures as wholes but focus more on the difference within rather than the

---

202. Hannerz, op. cit., 14.

203. Wim Van Binsbergen (1999b). Some Philosophical Aspects of Cultural Globalisation: With Special Reference to Mall's Intercultural Hermeneutics. In Wim van Binsbergen (2003). *Intercultural Encounters: African and Anthropological Lessons Towards a Philosophy of Interculturality*. Münster: Lit Verlag, 476.

204. Ibid., 492.

205. Droogers (2003). Op. cit., 61.

206. Byamungu (2002). Op. cit., 149.

207. Tanner (1997). Op. cit., 56–57.

difference between cultures, one can consider them as contradictory and internally fissured wholes. Spradley had shown inkling to this approach, when he talked of 'cultural contradiction'[208] while referring to the tension between what communities portray their cultures to be and what actually happens. In the light of these analyses, particularly the complexity and fluidity of culture, our approach to the process of inculturation in Africa needs to be more cautious and focused. Cautious in making blanket statements about 'the Africans' and focused in pointing out cultural overlaps.

Culture, Evangelization and Mission

We already said that evangelization is the basic mission of the church, and that inculturation is a method of evangelization. We would like to add that the understanding of culture determines the way we approach mission and so the way we evangelize. If we try to evangelize a people without incorporating their culture into the mission, we would be forgetting ". . .that 'Christianity as such' does not exist. It exists when people believe; and it becomes deeply rooted when it touches people and their lives where and as they are."[209] Moreover, evangelization has to do not just with handing on a body of beliefs, or promotion of those values that affect people as individuals and as communities; it is also concerned with human culture and society in general—the patterns which mold our thinking, our feeling, our behavior and how we experience life. "It is not just a question of replacing or transforming each human culture so that all become identical. The gospel is compatible with many different cultures. It respects cultures. It is enriched by them. And it also poses a challenge to each one of the cultures with which it comes into contact."[210]

Even those who have accepted Christianity without any prior conditions still " . . . desire to see their cultural values, traditions, way of life mirrored in their religious experiences and in the life of the church."[211] In this regard, we cannot afford any longer to sit and continue blaming the past, i.e., the colonialists and early missionaries. We, of necessity should, as the Chinese would put it, stop blaming the darkness and light a candle. What we need to do is to try and clothe the Gospel in our own cultural garb. Then we will start talking, rather than pontificating to our people, and they in turn will start listening to, rather than dismissing, us. A move that can help Christianity to become more proactive than reactive and, like a river, to naturally finds its own way to 'feel at home'[212] in every locality of the universal church.

208. Spradley, op. cit., 152.

209. Cecil McGarry (1986). Preface. In *Inculturation: Its Meaning and Urgency*. Nairobi: St. Paul Publications—Africa.

210. Dorr, op. cit., 94.

211. Bellagamba (1992). Op. cit., 76.

212. Welbourn and Ogot, op. cit.

Doing mission in this way is the core of inculturation in the modern world,[213] which parts ways with the traditional understanding of the same when mission was understood simply as taking the church and Christianity to the people who have never heard the Good News. Pope Paul VI is clear about the lack of depth and seriousness in the day-to-day life of a faith that is not inculcated into the societal structure of a people. The consequence of this is a profession of a peripheral faith, because its incarnation remains wanting. Against this danger, the pope has warned for the umpteenth time, in his oft-quoted blue print of evangelization.

> ... evangelization loses much of its force and effectiveness if it does not take into consideration the people to whom it is addressed, if it does not use their language, their signs and symbols, if it does not answer the questions they ask, and if it does not have an impact on their concrete life. But on the other hand evangelization risks losing its power and disappearing altogether if one empties or adulterates its content under the pretext of translating it ... [214]

As if to echo Pope Paul's word, John Paul II insists that, there is an organic and constitutive link existing between Christianity and culture. To his secretary of State, Cardinal Agostino Casaroli, he wrote, "A faith which does not become culture is a faith which has not been fully received, not thoroughly thought through, not fully lived out."[215] We do not endeavor to 'culturalise' Christianity, and neither are we out to 'Christianize' our culture, as p'Bitek[216] and Mazrui[217] have argued. The important thing, as already stated, is to reach out for a genuine dialogue which, in essence, calls for a frank discussion between the Gospel and culture. And this is only possible if Christianity recognizes and accepts African Religion as an equal negotiating partner. This kind of dialogue sees to it that the Gospel sifts culture of any traits unacceptable to the Christian faith, while culture helps to concretize the otherwise abstract faith in particular localities, making it relevant and meaningful to the people.

Communitarianism in the African Culture

Many authors[218] hold the view that an effective African hermeneutics needs to take place within the parameters of a community because Africans are more inclined to a communitarian rather than individualistic lifestyle.[219] Indeed, to some communi-

---

213. Dorr, op cit., 91–108.
214. Paul VI (1977). Op. cit., no. 63.
215. Pope John Paul II (1982). Op. cit, 7–8.
216. Okot p'Bitek (1970). *African Religions in Western Scholarship.* Kampala: East African Literature Bureau.
217. Ali A. Mazrui (1980). *The African Condition: A Political Diagnosis.* London: Heinemann
218. Ukpong (1999). Op. cit., 313–329; Dieudonné Ngona (2003). Op. cit; Zinkuratire (2004a). Op. cit., 41–70.
219. Ifeanyi A. Menkiti (1984). Person and Community in African Traditional Thought. In Richard

tarianism is what defines Africanness and is, as such, one of the key elements of the African culture that must be taken seriously.[220] According to Van der Walt, therefore, "...communalism is the key to understand—both traditional and contemporary African culture."[221] We will, therefore, look at the notion of communitarianism in the African culture and the extent to which African thinking is, in fact, community-centered. The main interest is the way communitarianism has been addressed in anthropology, philosophy and theology, the three disciplines we rely on in this study.

Communitarianism in African Anthropology

The question whether and to what extent Africans are indeed communitarian has been raised once and again due to the many unpleasant things that happen within the continent. But while contrasting the African worldview to that of the Westerners, Sundermeier, summed it up as a matter of priority in life:

> For the Westerner, life means individuality. We know each other as individuals; the development of life is understood as enhancing individuality. Community, being with others, is secondary. For Africans, it is the other way round. Individuals only exist because of the community. "Because we exist, I exist", as John Mbiti puts it. The community is the given condition of life. It extends in time beyond the bounds of the present era, backward to the ancestors and forward to the future generations.[222]

Although our earlier discussions on culture indicate that the quotation above portrays a simplistic dichotomy of Africa and the West it, nonetheless, says that the community plays a major role in the everyday life of an average person in a rural African village. Taylor captures his amazement at the quality of human relationship that he witnessed in Africa.

> It is an unfailing wonder and delight, this tranquility of human relationship in Africa. Whether it be child or adult makes no difference; one can enjoy the other's presence without fuss or pressure, in conversation or in silence as the mood dictates. Whether the task in hand may be continued or must be left depends upon a score of fine distinctions which the stranger must slowly learn; but one thing is certain—a visitor is never an interruption.[223]

A. Wright (ed). *African Philosophy, An Introduction*. Lanham, Md.: University Press of Americas, 171–180; Joseph Nyasani, (1991). The Ontological Significance of 'I' and 'We' in African Philosophy. In *African Christian Studies* 7 (1). Nairobi: C.H.I.E.A., 52–62; Kwame Gyekye (1997). Op. cit.

220. Kwesi A. Dickson (1977). *Aspects of Religion and Life in Africa*. Accra: Ghana Academy of Arts and Sciences.

221. Van der Walt (1997). Op. cit.

222. Theo Sundermeier (1998). *The Individual and Community in African Traditional Religions*. Hamburg: LIT., 17.

223. John V. Taylor (1963). *The Primal Vision: Christian Presence Amid African Religion*. London:

In traditional African languages, however, the word 'community' does not exist; people just live a communal life. So, the word 'community' is an essentially alien concept. Wijsen and Tanner say that the Sukuma did not have regular communal rituals and yet in the same breath admit that "Communal tendencies may have occurred periodically in order to cope with wide ranging crises, such as extreme drought or Masai raids."[224] The Sukuma appear to have a social system midway between the very individual cattle keeping Maasai to the east with occasional semi-centralized ceremonies related to age-set changes and the centralized inter-lacustrine chiefdoms of the Haya and the Ganda to the west and the north with highly developed rituals focusing on their chiefs.[225]

From an anthropological point of view, then, communitarianism in Africa seems to differ with people, time and place. The Nyakyusa, for instance, seem to be a much more communitarian people than the rest,[226] whereas others, like the Ik, appear to be a lot more individualistic.[227] The main question is whether the difference between these two realities is not that of *degree* rather than of a *kind*. Communitarianism in the traditional sense tends to be more structural and rigidly controlled based on the idea of kinship, whereas in the modern sense it tends to be more flexible and based on the idea of free association. Since our main concern is the traditional African community, the word communitarian(ism), in this study, is used to mean structural communitarianism, unless explicitly stated.[228]

Communitarianism in African Philosophy

Up until now the majority of African philosophers have largely concerned themselves with what we see as an apologetic philosophy—either proving that Africans have a philosophy of their own or grappling with the foundations and identity of this philosophy. However, we think that the central problem of African philosophy is whether the African society is individual or community-centered. And the onset of this debate was set by Senghor with his Négritude Movement, when he claimed thus: "Negro African society puts more stress on the group than on the individual, more on solidarity than on the activity and needs of the individual, more on the communion of persons than on their autonomy."[229] So far five trends, which can be regarded as characteristics

---

SCM Press Ltd., 17.

224. Wijsen and Tanner (2000). Op. cit., 74.

225. Ibid.,74

226. Monica Wilson (1951). *Good Company: A study of Nyakyusa Age-Villager*. London, New York, Toronto: Oxford University Press.

227. Colin Turnbull (1972). *The Mountain People*. London: Pimlico, Random House.

228. Van der Walt, op. cit., 46.

229. Leopold S. Senghor (1964). *On African Socialism*. Trans. Mercer Cook. New York: Praeger, 93–94.

of African philosophy, have emerged, taking two diametrically opposed positions of communitarianism versus individualism.

Oruka classifies these trends into four as follows: professional philosophy (Hountondji, Masolo, Wiredu, Wambari, Wanjiru, and Kiruki), nationalist-ideological philosophy (Nkurumah, Kenyatta, Nyerere, and Kaunda), ethnophilosophy (Tempels, Kagame, and Mbiti) and Sage Philosophy (Oruka, Ochieng'-Odhiambo and others).[230] Nationalist-ideological philosophy and ethnophilosophy hold that communitarianism permeates the African thought system from the societal to the national level, but professional philosophy and sage philosophy espouse the notion that individualistic tendencies run through both levels. But although the tentacles of communitarianism versus individualism keep recurring here and there, the actual discussion between philosophers hardly addresses these two central issues. It, instead, concentrates on issues like "...whether an African philosophy exists, how it is to be defined, what distinguishes it from Western philosophy, whether it is oral or written, and whether it can be accessible to non-Africans or is so unique that only Africans can understand it."[231]

We classify the debate on African philosophy in two levels, one ontological, the other epistemological. On the ontological level lies the question of African identity, is it communal or is it individual? In ethnophilosophy African identity is considered to be communal and as such, the individual only recognizes himself in the community. "Only in terms of other people does the individual become conscious of his own being, his own duties, his privileges..."[232] says Mbiti. Nationalist-ideological philosophy picks up from this presumption and comes in with national philosophies like *ujamaa*, *harambee*, consciencism, and humanism that are supposedly a reflection of the national identities of the citizens of various countries.

Professional philosophers have accused these leaders of being the source of oppressive regimes in Africa, characterized by the violation of individual freedom in the name of state security. On the other hand, is sage philosophy and professional philosophy. The former holds that individuals, even in the traditional societies, still maintained their identity and gives examples of those sages, who sought to explain issues from their own individual perspectives, rather than from the commonly held views. At the epistemological level, the two sides disagree on whether wisdom in Africa is regarded as an individual or communal enterprise. While ethno-philosophy and nationalist-ideological philosophy insist on the latter, professional philosophy insists on the former, with sage philosophy taking a middle ground in what it regards as popular and didactic wisdom.

---

230. Henry Odera Oruka (1991). *Sage Philosophy: Indigenous Thinkers and Modern Debate on African Philosophy.* Leiden: E. J. Brill. 27–28.

231. Imbo (1998). Op. cit., xi.

232. John S. Mbiti (1995). *African Religions and Philosophy,* reprint. Nairobi: East African Educational Publishers, 108.

Ethnophilosophy

In their quest to prove that traditional Africans indeed had a philosophy in its own right, Placide Tempels, Alexis Kagame and John S. Mbiti (among others) put together worldviews of several ethnic groups and presented them, first as a Bantu Philosophy, then as a symbiosis between African philosophy and Religions. A concrete example of this are the two widely read books by Placide Tempels and John S. Mbiti, titled *Bantu Philosophy* and *African Philosophy and Religions*, respectively. Tempels wrote (presumably against the racially prejudiced philosophers and anthropologists) and showed the inconsistency of a hard-liner's position with reality. ". . .to declare on *a priori* grounds that primitive people have no ideas on the nature of being, that they have no logic, is simply to turn one's back on reality" [233]

The question that calls for an answer is this: what is ethnophilosophy is? We have not yet come across a clear and precise definition of this kind of philosophy, but Ochieng'-Odhiambo shows that the African, both the traditional and modern one, is capable of philosophizing. That Africa is not a place devoid of philosophy. Ethnophilosophy is the very first scholarly attempt to grant philosophical status to African thought patterns and worldview.[234] According to Tempels, as Ochieng puts it; "African philosophy is made up of the basic principles that underlie their behavior, belief and customs."[235]

Inspired by Senghor's 'group orientation, over and above the individual', the starting point of ethnophilosophy is Mbiti's famous expression,[236] 'I am, because we are; and since we are, therefore I am'. Thus, relationship between the individual and the community, in the traditional society, is such that the former only exists under the umbrella of the latter.

> In traditional life, the individual does not and cannot exist alone except corporately. He owes his existence to other people, including those of past generations and his contemporaries. He is simply part of the whole. The community must therefore make, create or produce the individual; for the individual depends on the corporate group.[237]

In this regard Mbiti explains the necessity to incorporate and integrate the individual into the community, in order to make him or her, a social being. This is what Eboh refers to as 'the communitarian dimension of initiation'[238] which requires that the individual must go through the rites of passage, which begin at birth (or at conception

---

233. Tempels, op. cit., 22.
234. Francis Ochieng'-Odhiambo (1997). *African Philosophy: An Introduction,* 2nd edit. Nairobi: Consolata Institute of Philosophy, 43–44.
235. Ibid., 46.
236. Mbiti (1995). Op. cit. 108–109.
237. Ibid., 108–109.
238. Eboh (2004). Op. cit., 76.

in some communities) and goes on until one's deathbed or 'death mat'. Nkemnkia gives the intricate interplay that exists between the 'I' and the 'We'.

> ...the meaning of an individual's life is found in and through his relationship with the Other or Others. In fact it is meaningless to ask oneself "who am I" without having a complete knowledge of the Other, from whom, in the final analysis, one expects the answer. When we say "I," in reality one means "You," that is the Other. By saying "We" one is essentially saying "man." If this is how things stand, then each "I" is always mediated by "the Other," who is none other than "oneself." In this dialectic each one of us contains exclusively the Other, in such a way that, if one wants to do good to the Other, all that needs to be done is to consider the other as a "self."[239]

The above interplay between an individual and the community was considered to be so vital that a person was not expected to survive outside a community environment. For that reason, African communities provided room for one to be 'born' (in some communities, by slaughtering a sheep, cow or a goat, but in others by simply being smeared with honey and then being washed with milk) into another community (which was more often a different ethnic group) in cases where one has been rejected by (or just migrated from) his own community.

The main criticisms on ethnophilosophy come from professionally trained philosophers, who accuse its proponents of denying African philosophy a critical, individual analysis: and for addressing themselves primarily to Europeans, rather than to Africans. It seems to claim that, "African philosophy is a lived communal philosophy, a *Weltanschauung*, and is therefore not identifiable with any individual in particular. It is at best exercised as a collective wisdom of the people, shared by every individual in the society."[240] Sage philosophy also rejects this view because it seeks to identify individual sages within the traditional African society, who tried to explain or question the commonly accepted beliefs, without recourse to tradition.

Nationalist-ideological Philosophy

The Nationalist-ideological Philosophy finds a place in the annals of philosophy only if we widen the philosophical enterprise into two categories of '*having* a philosophy' and '*doing* philosophy' or philosophizing. While the former is characteristic of any level-headed human being with a vision, the latter is strictly a technical enterprise in which only the initiated can venture. Therefore, we talk of the philosophy of life, nationalistic philosophy, social philosophy and so on. Its proponents are actually politicians, who led their countries out of the colonial yoke. The genesis of this trend of philosophy

---

239. M. Nkemnkia (1999). *African Vitalogy. A Step Forward in African Thinking.* Nairobi: Paulines Publications, 111–112.

240. Ochieng'-Odhiamb, op. cit., 65.

was the European colonization of Africa, associated with a form of racism that was, according to Wiredu, "not just a state of mind, but an active program which sought to change the African's supposedly inferior way of life to conform to European models in some important areas of human existence, such as education, religion, economics, politics, etc. It was therefore natural," he argues, "that the anti-colonial struggle should take the form of both a cultural and a political nationalism."[241]

This philosophical trend was, therefore, based on the latter aspect of the struggle against colonialism. Some of the proponents of the trend include Kenneth Kaunda of Zambia (He based his political philosophy on African Humanism),[242] Jomo Kenyatta of Kenya (*Harambee*—pulling together), Julius Nyerere of Tanzania (*Ujamaa*—familyhood) and Kwame Nkrumah of Ghana (Consciencism). Their philosophies, had one thing in common—the political liberation (Independence), as the pre-requisite to all other forms of liberation. Their vision is summed up in the famous slogan by Kwame Nkrumah, 'Seek ye first the political kingdom and all these things shall be added unto you'; which is an echo of the biblical words attributed to Jesus on the fundamental importance of the kingdom of heaven.[243]

In line with this motivation their political thoughts were inspired, either by the communistic Eastern Bloc (headed by the former Soviet Union) or the Capitalistic Western Bloc (headed by the United States of America). The resultant military coups, wars and other atrocities in Africa can be interpreted in the wider frame-work of the war between the East and the West. And as the old adage goes, where two bulls are fighting the grass is the sufferer; it is the African peoples who bore the brunt of it all. This catastrophic development in the African political arena notwithstanding, Whitaker remained cautiously optimistic.

> The cry of *uhuru* (freedom) which is heard everywhere in these territories today is a call for political independence. It is the cry of people who want to develop themselves, using the means whereby men in the West have managed to get as far as they have. . . . If political freedom is to have any real meaning. . .it is most important that these countries should enable their citizens to develop themselves in their own particular way, which will be different from the development of people in any other country.[244]

The national philosophies, espoused a kind of communitarianism that Gyekye considers to be 'radical, excessive, and unrestricted'.[245] They do not appear to have

---

241. Kwasi Wiredu (1992). Problems in Africa's Self-Definition n the Contemporary World. In Kwasi Wiredu and Kwame Gyekye (eds). *Person and Community: Ghanaian Philosophical Studies I*, Washington D.C.: The Council for Research in Value and Philosophy, 59–70.

242. Kenneth Kaunda (1966). *A Humanist in Africa*. New York and London: Nashville.

243. Matthew 6:33.

244. Philip Whitaker (1964). *Political Theory and East African Problems*. London: Oxford University Press, 4.

245. Gyekye Kwame (1992). Op. cit., 104.

allowed room for individual freedom and hence their view of communitarianism is, to that effect, unsupportable. The leaders of these philosophies presumed that all people would identify themselves with their slogans and that they reflected the general knowledge and will of their citizenry. For this reason, dissent was not tolerated, as it was seen as a direct challenge and threat to the president. These leaders sought to control every aspect of people's lives and individual opinions were never accepted, especially where they went against the official policy or philosophy. In Tanzania, for instance, people were forced to live an imagined African communal life, in the spirit of *ujamaa*, even where it did not exist, or was not practical, like in Sukumaland. Wijsen and Tanner explain.

> Thus what the one-party government wanted, the elected one-party assembly passed into law. The essential parts of what they passed was based on ideological preconceptions about socialism as the only way guaranteeing overall progress rather than being developed from local and national realities. Overall trading monopolies were given to inefficient cooperatives and the enforced concentration of the population into villages where the environment in Usukuma dictated a spread out pattern of homesteads and cultivation.[246]

Like all other Nationalist-ideological philosophers, among them Nkurumah and Senghor, Nyerere cherished the doctrine of the good old days and a kind of return to the past, nostalgic desire that was re-incarnate in his *ujamaa* policy in Tanzania. According to him traditional African society comprised of what he regards as African socialism. It was based on mutual respect, common property ownership and an obligation to work. All basic commodities were held in common, there was mutual concern and farmers used to help each other in their fields.[247] Thus, in his philosophical justification of the political theory of *ujamaa* (familyhood), Nyerere reverted to the norms and values of the African culture. According to him, "The foundation and the objective of African socialism is the extended family."[248] Hence, the development of modern African society, within the boundaries of a modern nation (Tanzania) was to be based on the traditional African community spirit, *ujamaa*.

This amounted to what Ryle calls a 'category-mistake', which consists of "presenting the facts of mental life as if they belonged to one logical type or category (or range of types of categories), when they actually belong to another."[249] Thus, the differences

---

246. Wijsen and Tanner (2000). Op. cit., 98.
247. Julius K. Nyerere (1967). *Freedom and Unity*. Dar es Salaam: Oxford University Press.
248. Julius K. Nyerere (1968). *Freedom and Socialism*. Dar es Salaam: Oxford University Press. 11.
249. Gilbert Ryle (1955). *The Concept of Mind*, reprint. London: Hutchinson & Co (Publishers) Ltd., 16) had attacked what he regarded as Descartes' 'official doctrine' of a ghost-in-the-machine concerning the relationship between the body and the mind, in which he had applied mechanistic operations (of the body) to a spiritual entity (the mind). Thus, he accused him of making a category-mistake of "presenting the facts of mental life as if they belonged to one logical type or category (or range of types of categories), when they actually belong to another."

between the physical and the mental were represented as differences inside the common framework of the categories of 'things', 'stuff', 'attribute', 'state', 'process', 'change', 'cause', and 'effect'.[250]

In like manner, Nyerere confused traditional socio-ethical values of a community with a modern politico-economic reality of capital, production, market and profit, without paying due regard to the differences and/or incompatibility of the meanings of these two sets of categories, leading to a 'culture shock of villagization'.[251] It is no wonder then that professional philosophers disagree with Nyerere's vision of a blanket return to the past. According to Gyekye, for instance, the idea that African traditional societies were harmonious and egalitarian, with a worldview shared by all members of the group, is "overstated and somewhat misleading."[252] His assessment of "the Socialist Interlude" is harsh. In a response to Nyerere's *ujamaa* political policy he argues thus: "it may be pointed out that a hierarchical social arrangement, such as the traditional African system undoubtedly was—and still is—but it would not be devoid of exploitation of some sort." [253]

The administrative failure to consult the people and respond to their needs led to a situation of despair that translated into resentment and passive resistance. "The high hopes of the era of political independence seemed to have faded into a chimera of development projects."[254] In many countries, the passive resistance exploded into a full-blown rebellion in the form of military coups that in some cases only helped to start a spiral of *coups d'état* that went out of control, as in Nigeria.

In Kenya people were forced to give contributions for projects they did not approve of and which ended benefiting only a few, in the name of *harambee*, or pulling together. Today these leaders are praised or condemned depending on the performance of their respective countries in terms of economy and political stability, which comes closer to the issue of communal identity. Individual failure or success is attributed, first, to their ethnic groups, and then to their countries as a whole. Consequently, they are basically blamed for the sorry state of affairs that African nations find themselves in. Most (if not all) of them are seen as brutal constitutional dictators, who, by adopting a one-party rule, did not allow natural political growth of their citizens hence suppressing any form of political dissent. "All (African countries) but a few had, at independence opted for one-party rule, arguing—often correctly—that their level of technical and intellectual development could not withstand political frivolity and differing for differing's sake."[255]

---

250. Ibid., 19.

251. Frans Wijsen and Ralph Tanner (2002). *'I am Just a Sukuma': Globalization and Identity Reconstruction in Northwest Tanzania.* Amsterdam: Editions Rodopi, B.V., 127–132.

252. Kwame Gyekye (1997). Op. cit., 37.

253. Ibid, 151.

254 Wijsen and Tanner (2002). Op. cit., 99.

255. The Nation Media Group (2000). Editorial: Lessons Kenya Can Learn from Ghana. *Daily*

This did not augur well for the countries concerned, and eventually "It led to a situation where intellectual midgets holed themselves up in political stockades, perpetuated themselves in power, divorced themselves from the people, held their countries at ransom, stunted their economies and stultified intellectual growth."[256] Most of them are considered as corrupt in two basic ways: one, stealing state money to bank it in secret accounts in foreign countries, like Switzerland and Liechtenstein, which are thought to be politically stable. A group of disenfranchised Kenyan intellectuals, who did not want to be identified for fear of political repression once, wrote a stinging critique of the trend to divert the country's resources to private pockets in the name of the community. They complain:

> We can no longer afford to be naive. The intervening decades have demonstrated that 'independence' can in fact point the way to a deepening state of economic, political, and spiritual dependence. 'Independence' in Kenya has led to the looting and squandering of our resources, and the virtual silencing of our people. It has led to increasing misery and impoverishment for the many. Aspirations for better lives under *uhuru* have been betrayed by predatory politicians who talk of 'nation-building' while fattening on the nation's wealth and people's labour. The system which our so-called 'leaders' have created is used to deny us our basic democratic rights and keep us perpetually subordinate. We are informed that criticism will be treated as subversion, and that we have nothing to do but to obey and follow where they lead. They lead us further along the path of dependence, debt and national decline.[257]

The second mode of corruption is the promotion of mediocrity, nepotism, sycophancy and tribalism in government structures, resulting in ruthless repression of the masses, or outright civil war, as has already been witnessed in several African countries.

> Since the end of colonialism, many African societies have been dismayed by their experience of anomalies between the promises of independence and the actual accomplishments of the post-colonial state. In many ways, the ideals of justice, liberty, democracy and economic prosperity that inspired independence struggles in many African countries have not materialised. Wars of liberation were quickly succeeded by vicious civil wars or bitter strife between various factions of former independence movements. Where there has not been civil wars, societies have been plagued by brutal repression, corruption, obsession with personal power, nepotism and tribalism.[258]

Nation, 8 December. Nairobi: The Nation Media Group, 4.
  256. Ibid., 4.
  257. Journal of African Marxists (1982). *Independent Kenya.* London: Zed Press, xi.
  258. Hezekias Assefa and George Wachira (1996). *Peacemaking and Democratisation in Africa: Theoretical Perspectives and Church Initiatives.* Nairobi: East African Educational Publishers, 1.

The latter has become so entrenched in most African countries that many see it as a cancer that eats away the continent's social fabric slowly, but surely.

> The word 'tribalist' has come to acquire an all-encompassing meaning in official usage. Anything that is anti-establishment or remotely suspicious automatically becomes tribal, with the sinister attributes that are tied to the term . . .
>
> Curious, some Kenyans have come to confuse this reckless tweaking of ethnic loyalties with high political art. It is not. . . . That this phenomenon of politics has intensified since the 1980s is no accident. And as they say, *siasa mbaya, maisha m(a) baya*—bad politics, bad life.[259]

Finally, most leaders are seen as selfish and narrow-minded with regard to expounding long-term goals for their respective countries. It has been argued that they, generally speaking, left their countries worse off than they found them. The prevalence of political myopia in Africa has left many political analysts wondering whether it was not time to accord church leaders a greater say in political decisions. "In Benin, South Africa, Mozambique and at least a half dozen other countries, the church, in different ways and at different times, had chosen to take up the people's struggle for peaceful change. Perhaps the church, with its moral authority in a political environment distinctly lacking in trust and goodwill, had something to offer that should be investigated in depth."[260]

As a way of consolation to our founding fathers of the independent Africa, not all of them are judged harshly by history. Few of them stand out to be counted, either for their leadership qualities, or simply for accepting defeat when they could not deliver. One such leader is Nyerere. "So towering was his intellect and such was his moral fiber that he admitted publicly that his attempt to re-establish ujamaa (the African extended family system) was a signal failure. Therefore, said he, he was calling it a day so another person could give it a shot."[261] Other African leaders that received this kind of praise and recognition include Leopold Sedar Senghor (Senegal), Ahmed Ahidjo (Cameroon), Quett Masire (Botswana) and Nelson Mandela (South Africa). And these, out of a continent with more than fifty independent states!

Professional Philosophy

Professional philosophers have so divergent views that we can only put together those whose views are slightly related. They also deal with virtually all issues affecting the African continent, and as such we cannot talk about them all here. For these reasons,

---

259. Gitau Warigi (2000). Kenya: Tribalism Is Not High Art, It Is Bad Politics, *Daily Nation*, 24 December. Nairobi: The Nation Media Group, 4.

260. Ibid., vii.

261. Daily Nation (2000). 8 December, op. cit., 4.

we will concentrate on those philosophers who have expressly addressed the twin issues of communitarianism versus individualism.

Kwame Gyekye has addressed the communitarian problem and demonstrated a re-evaluation of African (and the Akan people in particularly) cultural elements that he considers negative or outdated in building a modern community.[262] The main negative features he handles include: 1) African culture's negative attitude towards science, 2) ethnicity over and above humanity, such as its communitarian inheritance patterns and patronage practices, 3) apathy towards public service and 4) primacy of the community over the individual. According to him, African culture seems to be satisfied with the *status quo* since it portrays no (or only a few) instances of sustained probing or pursuit of scientific knowledge for its own sake. And yet technology, serving as a purely practical matter—with uncritical application and little attempt at understanding or improving the technology—is basically related to this.

Secondly African culture, according to Gyekye, portrays fierce ethnic loyalty that serves to justify inhumane acts against persons from other ethnic groups. Thirdly, he decries African people's 'unnecessarily excessive and incessant attention to their ancestors' and superstitious practices related to this. He further contends that these negative features could be improved, or at least reduced, through comparison with modernity's answers to such issues. An emphasis on educational and training programs in science and technology, for instance, can go a long way to help and turn around cultural attitudes; whereas a substitution of the negative factors related to extreme communitarianism with a stronger focus on individual responsibility and equality could obtain some form of credible dialogue with modernity.

Gyekye is not opposed to communitarianism *per se*; indeed, his warning emanates from the fact that he regards some of the communitarian values in the African culture as precisely its positive features that can be blended with modern development. Key among these is Africa's 'relationalism' with its humanistic and social conception of morality. Nyasani praises the spirit of what he calls 'philosophy of sociality' in spite of its shortcomings in the following words:

> Whatever negative aspects that this curious philosophy of sociality might evince, it has certainly succeeded in keeping generations of Africans in a genuine state of cohesion, mutual dependence and humanistically healthy. The world could look to Africa for the principles of social harmony and interdependence especially now that there is a worldwide movement to return to the roots of humanity and humanism.[263]

However, this does not mean that individualism is to be abandoned, because both the individual and the community are to receive equal moral consideration and standing. Thus, an individual does not, for instance, cease to take responsibility for his or her

---

262. Gyekye (1997). Op. cit., 297.
263. Nyasani (1991). Op. cit., 60.

own misdeeds, but rather assumes responsibility, not as a detached element from the whole but as an element within the whole Processes of modernity such as urbanization, industrialization and 'technologisation' must be analyzed not only on account of their impact on the community, but also on the individual as well. Gyekye calls this 'moderate communitarianism' which he contrasts with normative communitarian-ism that gives precedence to the community over and above the individual.[264]

He understands moderate communitarianism as rather descriptive of the fact that healthy individual action implies a supportive community while the individual remains normative in his or her decisions. In this regard, humanism surfaces as the key feature and this could be Africa's contribution to her own modernity. Gyekye mentions many other positive African cultural features like the normativity of economic practices and ownership, the importance of kinship and family values, Africa's 'communal democracy' of limited government and civic responsibility to local (and thus decentralized) leadership, and Africa's practical wisdom. However, as Museveni says, these values are in danger of extinction, in the face of the onslaught by modernity. He comments on the problem and gives cues on the strategy for survival.

> Societies that do not master science and technology will either be slaves, surviving at the mercy and sufferance of others, or will perish altogether. Indeed, a futurist cartographer's map of the world of 2025 AD recently appeared in *The Economist*; in that map, only bits of Northern and Southern Africa appeared on that map (sic). In only a short 31 years, most of Africa will economically disappear. The only way we can prevent this tragedy is to begin our scientific and technological revolution now and in an organized and systematic manner.[265]

The above description does not, in any way, give a full account of Gyekye's stimulating discussion on an 'African modernity'. It is intended to demonstrate how the process of dialectical change within and between traditions may occur, in an attempt to develop a relevant form of hermeneutical approach that both recognizes African traditional values and at the same time updates them to suit the current situation. In such a process, it is not only the ancient African tradition that undergoes a transformation, but also the modern tradition, which may be influenced to take on some of the humanistic features of the African culture.

Sage Philosophy or Philosophic Sagacity

Oruka and Ochieng'-Odhiambo have one preoccupation in Sage Philosophy—to retrieve individual philosophic trends in the traditional African belief system and

---

264. Gyekye (1997). Op. cit. 41.

265. Yoweri K. Museveni (1996). Science and Technology as a Solution to Africa's Underdevelopment. In T. Abdul-Raheem (ed). *Pan Africanism: Politics, Economy and Social Change in the Twenty-First Century.* London: Pluto Press. 193–197.

thought patterns. Hence it has come to be known as sage philosophy or philosophic sagacity. Oruka gives an insight into what he considers to constitute, and hence define Sage Philosophy:

> ... the expressed thoughts of wise men and women in any given community and it is a way of thinking and explaining the world that fluctuates between *popular wisdom* (well-known communal maxims, aphorisms and general common sense truths) and *didactic wisdom,* an expounded wisdom and rational thought of some given individuals within community. While the popular wisdom is often conformist, didactic wisdom is at times critical of the communal set-up and the popular wisdom.[266]

According to the proponents of this school of thought, philosophic sagacity is the true representative of the African philosophy, because it encompasses both popular and didactic wisdom in the African culture. Oruka thus, distinguishes between three kinds of sages: "(1) those wise in service of their stomachs, (2) those wise for having learnt from the wisdom of the wise, and (3) those wise because they were born wise."[267] He dismisses the first as pseudo-sages, and accepts the last two, ending up with two kinds of sages.

> There are, therefore, two interesting types of sagacity: First, is sagacity as *popular wisdom*. This consists of maxims, aphorisms, and wise sayings associated with no particular persons, yet they are popularly known and generally employed in the oral literature of the community. And secondly, there is sagacity as *didactic wisdom*, i.e. an expounded and well-reasoned thought of some individuals in a given culture.[268]

It is for this reason, that he set the criterion according to which one must qualify to be regarded as a sage: "A person is a sage in the philosophic sense only to the extent that he is consistently concerned with the fundamental ethical and empirical issues and questions relevant to the society and his ability to offer insightful solution to some of those issues."[269] Although professional philosophers found misgivings with ethnophilosophy and disqualified it as a philosophy at all, they too have come under another form of criticism from sage philosophers, who also happen to be professionally trained. "The professional African philosophers having been schooled, colleged and universitied in the Western tradition are often accused of illegally using the western techniques and methods in African philosophy, largely because of their training in Western philosophy."[270] It is thus, argued that "They use *Western spectacles* to see

---

266. Oruka, op. cit., 28.
267. Ibid., 53.
268. Ibid., 53.
269. Ibid., XVII.
270. Ochieng'-Odhiambo, op. cit., 98.

African philosophy, hence what they conceive is not African philosophy as it is in itself. It is at this juncture that philosophic sagacity comes in handy."[271]

Ochieng goes on to argue that this approach seeks to identify African philosophy in the technical sense as seen through *African spectacles*, or as portrayed by those Africans that have had little Western influence. He does not, however, say when one is said to have a lot of Western influence or how to determine that one has little Western influence. But going by his description of the failure by professional philosophers to produce an authentically African philosophy, it appears that formal education is the only criterion; which does not seem to be very convincing.

Major criticisms to this way of doing philosophy have been voiced by Keita, Bodunrin and Masolo, just to mention a few professional philosophers. Their main contention is with the efficacy of its methodology employed by Sage Philosophers; hence the question whether its results are indeed philosophical. In sharp scrutiny is the method of 'going out quite literally into the market place' or 'chasing *wazee* (old men) around', as some have pejoratively regarded the practice. The proponents of sagacity have tried to answer their critics, but a preview of the merits or demerits of the debate is outside the scope of this section, which is to explore the sensitizing concepts of communitarianism in African philosophy.

Hermeneutical Philosophy

One other trend in African philosophy, that Oruka does not mention is what Imbo calls hermeneutical orientations.[272] The main proponents of this tradition are Tsenay Serequeberhan, Maciern Towa and Okonda Okolo. "These philosophers take African traditions as their starting point. Rooting themselves in what is traditional to Africa, they seek to escape an enslavement to the past by using that past to open up the future."[273] Hence, they deviate from ". . .ethnological considerations and universalist abstraction and call into question the real relations of power in Africa."[274] Thus, Serequeberhan links the discourse of African philosophy, directly or indirectly, to the demise of European hegemony That is, colonialism and neo-colonialism, and he argues that it is aimed at fulfilling or completing it.

> It is a reflective and critical effort to rethink the African situation beyond the confines of Eurocentric concepts and categories. In this indigenized context, furthermore, questions of "class struggle" (the "universal concern of Marxist theory!) and the empowerment of the oppressed can fruitfully be posed and engaged.[275]

271. Ibid., 98.
272. Imbo (1998). Op. cit., 27.
273. Ibid., 27.
274. Ibid., 27.
275. Tsenay Serequeberhan (ed). (1991). *African Philosophy: The Essential Readings*. New York:

As well as insisting on the need to disentangle African philosophy from the European canons, horizons and worldview, Serequeberhan also suggests a historical re-appropriation of the Africans through a "direct confrontation between the colonizer and the colonized . . . "[276] The key way to do this is by deconstructing the texts and traditions that are steeped in European categories rejecting those that are irrelevant and modifying those that are anachronistic.[277] Accordingly, hermeneutical philosophy sees Africans fighting for their recognition, not as individuals, but as a people or, in other words, as a community of the oppressed. Thus, the question of 'power relations' lies behind the core problem of communitarianism versus individualism, as manifested in the nationalistic-ideological philosophy struggle for the political liberation of the Africans.[278]

Communitarianism in African Theology

The birth of theology on the African soil came as a response to a crisis, and so we regard it as 'remedial'. It came forth to address various pertinent issues that were a source of disquiet among the African people in their religious disposition. The symptoms of this were many and varied: there was, on the one hand, a mushrooming of indigenous churches as a result of dissatisfaction with the mainstream churches. On the other hand, there was a double-faceted problem in which there existed serious tension between the core beliefs of the African adherents of these churches and their actual lifestyle. There was also a growing resentment against Western religious paternalism that subordinated African religious aspirations. Hence the emergence of African theology was a rebellion against Western theology as Appiah-Kubi and Torres say:

> We believe that African theology must be understood in the context of African life and culture, and the creative attempt of African peoples to shape a new future: that is different from the colonial past and the neo-colonial present. The African situation requires a new theological methodology, that is different from the approaches of the dominant theologies of the West. African theology must reject, therefore, the prefabricated ideas of North Atlantic theology: by defining itself according to the struggles of people, in their resistance against the structures of domination. Our task, as theologians, is to create a theology, that arises from, and is accountable to the African peoples.[279]

Paragon House, 22–23.

276. Ibid., 78.
277. Imbo, op. cit., 30.
278. Serequeberhan (1994). Op. cit., 85.
279. K. Appiah-Kubi and S. Torres (eds) (1979). *African Theology En Route*. Maryknoll, New York: Orbis Books, 193.

BIBLE INTERPRETATION AND THE AFRICAN CULTURE

The Meaning of Community Life in African Theology

The meaning of community life, among the Africans, was captured by Menkiti when he accorded it a metaphysical dimension of ontological primacy over and above the individual. He says that "as far as Africans are concerned, the reality of the communal world takes precedence over the reality of the individual life histories, whatever these may be."[280] Onwubiko borrows Nyerere's word *ujamaa*, and says it befits the African sense of community in theology, because, "it forges an extended family relationship that, in concept and reality, goes beyond the tribe, a particular community and even beyond a nation."[281] Eboh also makes 'African Communalism' central to his theology which, in his view, is the way to social harmony and peaceful co-existence.[282] Our main concern is theological response to this phenomenon of community life taking precedence over and above the life of an individual. And we find it in the newly launched, church as family-of-God, theological paradigm. We are going to briefly survey it and look at the strong points and challenges that face theologians as they try to incorporate it into African theology.

The Church as Family-of-God Model

During the African Synod, held in Rome in 1994, Pope John Paul II appealed to the bishops in the following words: "It is earnestly to be hoped that theologians in Africa will work out the theology of the Church as family with all the riches contained in this concept, showing its complementarity with other images of the church."[283] Although the concept of Church-as-Family was not a unique conception of the synod, its Fathers certainly brought it to fruition. The model is based on images like 'Mystical Body', 'People of God', 'Temple of the Holy Spirit', 'Flock' and 'Sheepfold', as presented by the Vatican II Council in the Dogmatic Constitution *Lumen Gentium* Its onset was, however, marred in a controversy as to why an African Synod was being held outside the African continent. The church went on and held this synod in Rome, which came to be derogatorily referred to, by some, as the 'Roman Synod for Africa', rather than 'African Synod'.[284]

But what is the meaning of Church-as-Family? The answer is provided by the Pope in his summary to the Synodal activities: it means, "care for others, solidarity, warmth in human relationships, acceptance, dialogue, and trust." Hence the Synod adopted "the

---

280. Menkiti, op. cit., 171.

281. Onwubiko, op. cit., 14.

282. Eboh (2004). Op. cit., 219.

283. Pope John Paul II (1996). "Post-Synodal Apostolic Exhortation" in Africa Faith and Justice Network. In *The African Synod: Documents, Reflections, Perspectives*. Maryknoll, New York: Orbis Books, 251.

284. John Paul II (1995). Op. cit., 48.

Church as God's Family as its guiding idea for evangelization in Africa."[285] But why should we have yet another model of the church in Africa? "The rationale for this choice stemmed from the understanding that 'church-as-family' expresses both the nature and mission of the church in a way which is particularly appropriate for Africa."[286] Healey and Sybertz have made the following observations in that regard:

> . . . Church-as-Family is a new theological category which can deepen the present understanding of the 'church'. This theme developed from and built on the image of the People of God of the Second Vatican Council. The synod portrayed this dominant model of church as family through such terms as Church-as-Brotherhood, Church as the Family of God and Church-Family. The vision of the Church as God's family has a natural appeal to African people. This ecclesiology of Church-as-Family emphasizes the warmth of love among widely extended relationships and an authority that finds its proper context in service. The bishops emphasized the great value in the Church's social teaching that every person belongs to the family of God.[287]

While elaborating the reason for the choice of this model of the church, Waliggo states the following:

> The bishops could have chosen the Vatican II concept of Church as Communion or as People of God. They purposely chose Church as Family; they wanted to use the African family as the model for being and living church. The family model includes everyone, baptized and non-baptized, involving every member. It serves well the emphasis on Small Christian Communities.[288]

As opposed to the physical and human families, this new family is rooted not in biological kinship but in the Trinity. Human families and all types of church communities are, therefore, invited to take the Trinity as their role model. This means that every Christian community is understood, at least in some way, to reflect the Trinitarian communion, who is its source and ecclesial communion, which is its sign. With regard to the synod documentation, the Church as the Family of God is described in the following terms:

> The African sense of family solidarity affords a valuable base on which to build an ecclesiology of the church as the 'Family of God' on earth. In this ecclesiology, Living Christian Communities [SCCs] form cells within which love of

---

285. Ibid., no. 63.

286. A. E Orobator (2000). *The Church as Family: African Ecclesiology in Its Social Context.* Nairobi: Paulines Publications Africa, 11.

287. Healey and Sybertz (1997). Op. cit., 145–146.

288. John Mary Waliggo (1994). The Church as Family of God and Small Christian Communities. In *AMECEA Documentation Service*, No. 429, 1 December, 1.

God is inseparable from love of neighbour, and in which the tendencies to disunity—egoism, tribalism, etc.—are discerned and overcome.[289]

The synod's specific message to the Christian family stated the following:

The vitality of the Church-as-Family, which the synod wishes to highlight, can only be effective insofar as all our Christian families become authentic domestic churches ... The extended African family is the sacred place where all the riches of our tradition converge. It is therefore the task of you Christian families to bring to the heart of this extended family a witness which transforms from the inside our vision of the world.[290]

On the face of it, this model is interesting, and also a scripture-based image of the church. The New Testament is particularly replete with instances that depict the Early Church and 'Pauline Churches' more as families or small Christian communities.[291] There are many advantages of this model to the African situation, among them the communitarian nature of the African lifestyle, which can conveniently be based on the Last Supper, instituted by our Lord, just before his departure.[292] However, while building the African church on the family image, it is important to be alive to the fact that the modern family has undergone many changes, and still has many challenges to overcome, and the African family is no exception.

It is important, then, to ask ourselves what we can make of a church built on this fluid, and thus unstable model. Magesa poses several questions in this regard, among them the following two: "But what kind of family is being referred to in these passages? Does such family exist in the concrete situation of Africa, or were the bishops and the Pope painting a desirable image of family, as they would have wished it to be in the continent?"[293] The traditional African under-standing of family is subject to multiple and constant changes because of, among other factors, the invasion of modern cultural Euro-American or Western, as well as Asian influences. Thus, it is apparent that there are many challenges to this fluid model of the church.

Challenges Facing the Family Model in Africa Today

The challenge of globalization to the traditional African structures and its consequent 'disruptions' cannot be ignored; and the family set-up is the most hit natural institution by this phenomenon. Onwubiko admits the fact that there are 'dangerous changes' that threaten this model, like the tendency to individualism, "sometimes

---

289. Healey and Sybertz, op. cit., 146.
290. Ibid., 146.
291. Acts 9:31, 5:11; 1 Corinthians 10:32, 1:1–2; 1 Timothy 3:15; 1 Thessalonians 1:1.
292. Luke 22: 20.
293. Magesa (2004a). Op. cit., 9.

induced by the new lifestyles that have resulted in a complex interplay of modern societal forces. . ."[294] like the complex relationship between European education, culture and Christianity. Although there are many points of contention in this regard, three of them take the center stage in trying to conceive of the church as a family in the African context. To begin with, it is not clear anymore what can be legitimately and representatively regarded as the 'African Family'.[295]

The African situation is so varied and diverse that it is safe to talk of many Africas, sociologically speaking, that exist side by side in the common geographical Africa, and yet their demarcation is not clear-cut. Some Africans have adopted the European Christian concept of family, of the so-called nuclear family under Christ as the head; while others have settled for a modern secular Euro-American sense of a family, associated with modernity and liberation from the 'enslaving' religious and cultural stuff. But even this one is no less controversial today, in the face of globalization, than it was in the sixties when Goode argued against the existence of a nuclear family system; if by this is meant a system in which most families maintain few or no relations at all with their extended kin.[296] Where the existence of such a family system is taken for granted (or at least accepted) its weaknesses and disadvantages are too obvious to be neglected; and they seriously challenge the system as a model for the church.

> Generally nuclear family members exhibit close emotional ties and economic stability, and place more emphasis on the marital bond. However they are viewed as being distant, and unstable since they rely heavily on the marital bond. Divorce easily leads to the disintegration of the family unit. Members of the family are also exposed to limited role models and the socialization process may be limited.[297]

Then there is what Zani refers to as 'quasi families or single parent families' that consist of "single male or female adults with their children only."[298] They, too, are a serious challenge to the Christian concept of marriage as they also cause problems to other people's marriages.[299] The men tend to have love affairs with other people's wives, whereas the women tend to get children with married men. Then there is a type of families where spouses live together apart, out of choice or due to economic

---

294. Oliver A. Onwubiko (2000). *The Church as the Family of God (Ujamaa): In the Light of Ecclesia in Africa.* Nsukka: Fulladu Publishing Company, 82.

295. Magesa (2004a). Op. cit., 5–28.

296. W. Goode (1964). *The Family.* Englewood Cliffs: Prentice Hall.

297. Agnes P. Zani (1997). The Family in its African Socio-Cultural Context. In Patrick Ryan (ed). *The Model of "Church-as-Family": Meeting the African Challenge.* Nairobi: The Catholic University of Eastern Africa, 49.

298. Ibid., 50.

299. Auli Vähäkangas (2004). The Crisis of Christian Marriage. In Andrew A. Kyomo and Sahaya G. Selvan (eds). *Marriage and Family in African Christianity.* Nairobi: Acton Publishers, 39.

consideration, where the husband has to stay away from home for long spells of time, with serious consequences.

Wachege notes the complaints of a woman victim of this situation: "I did not marry to eat alone, stay alone, for in my home I had plenty of good drinks and cloths. Sure, you give me nice food, but I get tired of eating alone."[300] The other aspect connected to this kind of 'separation' is the rise of polygamy and concubinage, as Bahemuka explains. "Due to social change, sequential polygyny is on the increase, and the custom of concubines and mistresses is widely practiced in urban centres."[301] Then there is the question of caring for the widows, like, for instance, in leviratic union and what is commonly referred to as 'widow inheritance'. Kirwen shows the complexity of the matter and the failure of many church leaders to understand the custom by classifying it as adultery or fornication.

> In discussing the marital relationship of the widow with the brother-in-law in the leviratic union (a major issue of contention with the Catholic ethic), it is clear that the sexual union cannot be equated with any lawful or unlawful sexual unions practiced in the Western world. It cannot be classified as adultery or fornication, plural marriage or monogamy, or even cohabitation.[302]

How these will be incorporated in the Church-As-Family model, owing to the narrow definition of a family in the Catholic Church remains a matter of conjecture. Finally, there is the traditional concept of an African family, which is basically patriarchal and polygynous (at least in East Africa); features that are dominant in both patrilineal and matrilineal communities. In these communities, there is a general cultural practice that favors and also privileges the father and the sons at the expense of mother and her daughters. Such a sanctioned favoritism presents an inadequate picture of the family of God model in Africa, assuming that this is what the synod Fathers had in mind. Waliggo has, already cautioned against the first ill. The family of God in Africa should not be a patriarchal structure in which bishops, priests and religious are the parents and the laity are children. He argues that it has to be redesigned in order to give the laity—and especially lay women—their rightful responsibility. "The theology of Church-as-Family is a two-edged sword. It can be profitably used but may also lead to benign paternalism. Before it is applied, the image of the family

---

300. P. N. Wachege (1992). *African Women Liberation: A Man's Perspective*. Nairobi: Industrial Printing Works Ltd., 61.

301. Judith Mbula Bahemuka (1995). Social Changes and Women's Attitudes Towards Marriage in East Africa. In M. A. Oduyoye and M. Kanyoro (eds). *The Will to Arise: Women, Tradition, and the Church in Africa*. New York: Orbis Books, 132.

302. Michael C. Kirwen (1979). *African Widows: An Empirical Study of the Problems of Adapting Western Christian Teachings on Marriage to the Leviratic Custom for the Care of Widows in Four Rural African Societies*. Maryknoll, New York: Orbis Books 59.

must be fully liberated. We should not once again end up with a pyramid structure of the church but rather a circular one of communion."[303]

That the Church-as-Family concept needs liberation is not in doubt, but that is only part of the story; when talking about 'liberation' there is the negative sense of being liberated from certain oppressive forces. But there is also a positive sense in which we get liberated for something and to be able to do something; which Waliggo does not address. Then there is the more urgent issue that calls for an immediate dialogue, if only to keep it going, this is the issue of polygyny; and since he does not talk about it we can only assume that it too needs to be liberated. And yet the ways and means of doing this remain a matter of speculation. Last, but not least, is the question of the many forms of African families accepted for the purpose of fecundity.[304]

In this regard, the African family still faces a lot of uncertainty in the future, due to the current disaffection and complaints that surround its setting. Many theologians feel that not much has been done to address the worries and concerns mentioned by Waliggo. The family structure is, for instance, still dominated and determined by patriarchy: "Patriarchal definitions of family," says Oduyoye, "yield paradigms like monogamy (one man with one wife) or polygyny (polygamy in which there is one man with more than one wife concurrently) living in one house or in dispersed domiciles."[305] Many forms of oppression are still being meted upon the female members in the form of taboos that deny women their rightful place as members of the human family, a situation that is portrayed as ordained by God and enforced by nature.[306]

Even the challenges posed by women's movements are yet to succeed in changing this face of family and give it a neutral face that embraces both sexes and treats them equally. This, and other pending issues, shows that changing models (good as this may be in itself) is not the solution to African problems but rather, adopting an appropriate form of hermeneutics is. Perhaps it is in this light that many scholars, including Waliggo himself, had advocated the African clan system as the true model of the church in Africa prior to the African synod. It is this quest for a 'true model of the African Church' that calls for hermeneutics that interprets the Bible as a communal rather than individual perspective.[307]

---

303. John Mary Waliggo (1997). From Private to Popular Biblical Hermeneutics. In Hannah W. Kinoti and John Mary Waliggo (eds). *The Bible in African Christianity*. Nairobi: Acton Publishers, 1.

304. So many theologians in Africa have discussed this issue that only limited key references can be given to the interested reader. See Laurenti Magesa (1998). *African Religion: The Moral Traditions of Abundant Life*. Nairobi: Paulines Publications Africa, 128–133), Eugene Hillman (1975). *Polygamy Reconsidered: African Plural Marriages and the Christian Churches*. Maryknoll, New York: Orbis Books and John Njenga (1974). Customary African Marriage. In *AFFER*, Vol. XVI, Nos. 1&2. Eldoret: GABA Publications, 117ff.

305. Mercy A. Oduyoye (1998). Family: An African Perspective. In William R. Farmer et al (eds). *The International Bible Commentary*. Collegeville, Minnesota: The Liturgical Press, 289–292.

306. Olivia Nasaka (1996). Women and Taboo: A Case Study in Buganda. In R. A. Musimbi et al (eds). *Groaning in Faith: African Women in the Household of God*. Nairobi: Acton Publisher, 163–167.

307. John Mary Waliggo (1990). The African Clan as the True Model of the African Church. In J.

Conclusion

In this chapter, we have situated the debate on inculturation in its historical context in Africa, by giving a short exposé on its beginning and development. Then we have gone through the historical process of evangelization, which, reached the Kenyan people at the same time with colonialism and thus they could not make a distinction between the two enterprises. We have shown that these two historical events witnessed the suppression of the African culture, leading to what we have called 'cultural schizophrenia'. This has been followed by the reactions of both philosophers and theologians, with the former concentrating on issues other than what we consider to be the central question of African thinking and personality—communitarianism.

We have then looked at the use of the Bible in Africa and the questions that arise among scholars and non-scholars, leading to the desire for some authentically African hermeneutics. We have, therefore, surveyed the development of an African hermeneutics which, up until now, is still evolving and pointed out the need for it to become interdisciplinary: the need to make a serious study of the meaning of culture in Africa, incorporate orality as a part of its development and the need to embrace deconstruction as an ongoing activity.

Of key importance in the study of culture is its seemingly conflicting modern and post-modern understanding. In this we have concluded that we do not need to favor one and discard the other but to incorporate both understandings and approach culture more cautiously, by focusing not only on the difference between cultures but also on the difference within cultures. On the notion of communitarianism in the African culture, we have postulated that the key issue in African philosophy is communitarianism versus individualism, although it seems not to take cognizance of this fact. Then we looked at communitarianism in African theology as a direct response to the then prevailing situation that called for a theology that is based on African mental categories.

We have more specifically focused on the Church-As-Family model. We have also established the challenges facing the very concept of family in Africa, in the face of rapid changes and external influence, calling for a relevant and adequate hermeneutical approach. Then we have said that an adequate response to these challenges calls for a community-centered form of hermeneutics that is based on, but not limited to, the African concept of a community. In conclusion then, we can hypothesize that lack of inculturation was responsible for what we earlier referred to as cultural schizophrenia, which negates the very message of Christianity as Good News. Thus, there can be no authentic African Christianity without inculturation. Concerning the debate on the African culture, we conclude that it is a result of the interaction with the European culture, through missionaries and colonial settlers.

N. K. Mugambi and Laurenti Magesa (eds). *The Church in African Christianity: Innovative Essays in Ecclesiology.* Nairobi: Initiative Printers, 117.

Those who were uprooted from their own cultural roots were (and still are) not accepted as equals by the Europeans. This sense of being excluded led them to lean back to their cultural heritage, and to use it to create a culture that could supposedly compete with the Euro-American culture. Hence the people involved in this debate (both religious and laity) are those who went through the schooling system that is based on foreign systems of education, which consequently estranged them from their culture. They, therefore, nostalgically painted a rosy picture of some imaginary qualities of the African culture, like communitarianism, as if to appeal for some lost paradise; hence the need to re-examine, and possibly nuance, such a picture. We now move on to the second chapter and introduce the reader to the people and social context of West Pökot, in order to understand the factors that influence their reading of the Bible.[308]

---

308. John S. Mbiti (1986). Theological Impotence and the Universality of the Church. In G. Anderson and T. Stransky (eds). *Third World Theologies. Mission Trends,* No.3. New York, Grand Rapids: Paulist Press, 6–18.

CHAPTER 3

THE PEOPLE AND SOCIAL CONTEXT OF WEST PÖKOT

Introduction

THE LAST CHAPTER HAS ended with an appeal to re-examine, and possibly nuance, the notion of communitarianism in Africa. In this chapter, we introduce the reader to the Pökot social and cultural context, before embarking (in chapter four) on the actual hermeneutic practice (*hermeneusis*) of the people. This immersion to the cultural context will help us envisage how well to relate the (Christian) text to its (Pökot) context. The chapter is descriptive in nature, with some theoretical explorations and critical evaluations. In it, we are going to describe the Pökot people, their general lifestyle (economic, political, cultural and religious) and the geographical realities of their land.

This includes weather conditions, rainfall distribution and the terrain. Then we will examine their social life in general: how they spend their recreation time, what kind of food they eat and their economic enterprise. Next, we will look at the important aspects in their culture and life in general. Then we will zero in on a few cultural values that impact more forcefully on the way the Pökot people relate to outsiders and look at the influence of modernity to these values. This has two advantages: one, it will help us understand the set-up in which the Word of God is interpreted, understood and applied. Two, it will help us, in the following chapter (three), to know if and to what extent cultural values are reflected in people's bible sharing sessions.

Literature on the Pökot People

The major handicap in gathering information about the Pökot people is that there is not much literature about them and certainly no authoritative work on the Pökot language and culture, except Beech and Baroja,[1] although they admit not to have said the last word about the Pökot. Much of what exists is in the form of articles and dissertations in

---

1. Tomás Herreros Baroja et. al. (1991). *Inside the Beehive of Life: A Descriptive Work of the Most Peculiar Traditions of the Pökot People.* Unpublished work.

various fields like anthropology,[2] religion and geography that normally treat only one or two aspects of the Pökot lifestyle, or treat the Pökot people as a small part of their research. However, three books that have been dedicated fully to the Pökot people need to be mentioned because we have extensively relied on them.

These are: *District Atlas West Pokot* by Hubert Hendrix and others,[3] *Pökoot Religion* by J.J. Visser and *Pastoralists in Dire Straits: Survival Strategies and External Interventions in a Semi-arid Region at the Kenya/Uganda Border:*[4] *Western Pokot, 1900–1986* by Ton Dietz (these last two are PhD dissertations) and an MA thesis, *Secret Sweet:*[5] *Female Genital Mutilation in West Pökot, Kenya* by Lilian Plapan.[6] Towards the end of our study, we came across a PhD dissertation titled *A Missiological Analysis of Traditional Religion Among the Pokot People of East Africa* by E. van Sanders. It was defended at the Southwestern Baptist Theological Seminary, Fort Worth, Texas.[7]

It is to the latter that we would like to dedicate a few lines in a short analysis of its approach to the Pökot religion for one key reason. We share a lot in common, particularly in terms of approach, which is religious-anthropological, and the theme of his study. He explains: "This dissertation takes as its thesis that the worldview and culture of the Pokot provide points of contact that can serve as bridges for cross-cultural evangelism and enable missionaries to present the gospel to the Pokot in both a theologically and culturally appropriate manner."[8] We regard the thesis as an important religious-anthropological contribution to the available literature on the Pökot people. We will start our review of his dissertation with a look at the aim of the work, the approach that the author employed and then his conclusion.

Sanders starts his work by introducing the thesis of his work in which he declares that "The gospel of Jesus Christ must be communicated in a manner that addresses the non-Christian's daily life. Such gospel communication is a process of translation."[9] He, therefore, emphasizes that, "Cross-cultural missionaries must communicate the gospel in a manner that leads to understanding and assimilation into appropriate cultural dress. As a corollary to this commitment, on the part of part of the cross-cultural missionaries, "Their ultimate goal is to effect worldview transformation and establish

---

2. Mervyn W. H. Beech (1969). *The Suk: their Language and Folklore,* reprint. New York: Negro University Press.

3. Hubert Hendrix et. al. (1985). *District Atlas West Pokot.* Kapenguria: Arid and Semi Arid Lands Development Programme (ASAL).

4. Visser (1989). Op. cit.

5. Ton Dietz (1987). *Pastoralists in Dire Straits: Survival Strategies and External Interventions in a Semi-arid Region at the Kenya/Uganda Border: Western Pokot, 1900–1986.*

6. Lilian J. C. Plapan (2000). *Secret Sweet: Female Genital Mutilation in West Pökot, Kenya.* MA Thesis. London: University of Reading.

7. E. Van Sanders (2001). *A Missiological Analysis of Traditional Religion Among the Pokot People of East Africa.* PhD Dissertation. Fort Worth: Southwestern Baptist Theological Seminary.

8. Ibid., 2.

9. Ibid., 2.

an indigenous Christianity."[10] After stating his thesis as the 'communication of the gospel', which he says is a 'translation', he does not address the problems that hamper such a translation, particularly the difficulties involved in the translation of concepts from the Pökot to the Christian worldview.

How, for instance, do we translate the Pökot worldview on polygyny to the Christian worldview on monogamy? Or, how do we translate the Pökot notion of witchcraft and cattle rustling into the Christian tenet of the love of God and neighbor? All we are saying here is that things on the ground are more complicated than Sanders seems to tell the 'cross-cultural missionaries', as we will show in chapters three and four. In fact, we think that the starting point of a receptor-oriented evangelization is missionaries' translation of their own worldview to that of the Pökot people, not the other way around. Then they can work from an insider's perspective to accommodate the Gospel.

Owing to the lack in his work of concrete issues that need to be tackled by the cross-cultural missionaries working in West Pökot, his 'receptor-oriented' approach to the above thesis appears to us to be both individualistic and abstract. Individualistic because he simply appears to read what others have said about the Pökot people and then goes ahead to make recommendations on the cultural points of contact, in spite of having worked with the Pökot from 1991 to 1997. Nowhere, in his dissertation, does he make direct references of the Pökot people to hear their views, for instance on the missionaries, before making the recommendation. It is also abstract because he starts with principles and only presents theories on how 'points of contact' can be used to realize his preferred thesis, but hardly does he present the difficulties posed by the actual situation on the ground. The difference between the ideal and the real, between mental categories and actual human life is so astronomical that bridging them requires a quantum leap. Our own experience with the Pökot people suggests that the opposite approach, which we perceive to be both communitarian and concrete, could be more fruitful.[11]

The abstract aspect of Sander's approach leads to several mistakes, which are both grammatical and conceptual. One such conceptual mistake is on the issue of theism among the Pökot. It is very easy for an outsider to claim that they believe in the existence of three gods—*Tororöt, Asis,* and *Ilat*, and that all these gods influence Pökot life.[12] But Christians too, are aware of the notional mistake made by non-Christians who claim that they are polytheists because they believe in the holy trinity. Today many people who have known the Pökot way of life, including the educated Pökot would hesitate to make such a claim, or associate the Pökot religion with animism, even as a descriptive term. "The Pokot traditional belief system," says Sanders, "is

---

10. Ibid., 2.
11. Ibid., 2.
12. Ibid., 79.

animistic because it focuses on using and manipulating the power of the spirit world for personal well-being."[13]

The conclusion that follows Sanders' approach seems to be far removed from the social reality in which the people of West Pökot live; a fact that makes it appear to be both peripheral and ephemeral. Peripheral because it seems to lack the inside knowledge of the working and dynamics of the Pökot culture and as such it is extremely difficult, if not impossible, to forge a working relationship between strangers. Ephemeral because no lasting symbiosis can be attained in a relationship where one partner regards the other as inferior; and yet Sander's dissertation seems to imply that this is indeed the relationship between Christianity and the Pökot religion. He seems to relegate the Pökot culture to 'preparatio evangelica' when, for instance, he makes the following claim: "The Pokot, in response to general revelation, have a well-developed concept of a High god, *Tororot*. *Tororot* is not the God of the Bible. Therefore, when the Pokot speak of *Tororot* they are not speaking of the true God revealed in the Bible. However, the Pokot concept of *Tororot* as the high god is the beginning point of God's progressive revelation of himself to them."[14]

Location and Topography

West Pökot County[15] is situated along the Kenya-Uganda border, in the northwestern part of the then Rift Valley Province, in the northwestern part of the country. From North to South, the county stretches from 2°40'N to 1°7'N. From west to east, it is located between 34°37'E and 35°49'E. The total area covered by this county is about 9100 km2 or five per cent of the Rift Valley Province. The distance from Kapenguria (which is the county headquarters of West Pökot) to Kitale (the headquarters of the neighboring, Trans Nzoia County) is approximately 42 km. The distance from Kapenguria to Nakuru, the provincial headquarters, is 250 km, while from Kapenguria to Nairobi, the capital city of Kenya, is 435 km by road. West Pökot County varies in both topography and climate, from low-lying hot and dry plains to cold and wet high grasslands. Thus, it has a great variety of topographical features and a remarkable geographical diversity.

The south-eastern part of the county is situated in the Cherangani Hills (which the Pökot claim should be called Pökot Hills), with altitudes over 3000 meters above the sea level. The northern and northeastern part of the county, on the other hand, stretches towards the hot, dry plains of Turkana at altitudes less than 900 meters above sea level,

---

13. Ibid., 78.

14. Ibid., 89.

15. For the purposes of update, it is important to add that the administrative and governance structure in Kenya has drastically changed since the promulgation of the new constitution (in 2010). The eight provinces that formed administrative units have been abolished and replaced with forty-seven counties. Then the Provincial Administration has been restructured in line with the new realities. Hence the then West Pökot District has now become a county, which has further been subdivided into three districts (Pökot Central, Kacheliba and Pökot North).

excluding Mtelo and Kadam, the highest and second highest mountains in West Pökot, respectively. As a result of this diversity, there are magnificent landscapes associated with this large variety of altitudes within West Pökot boundaries; including spectacular escarpments of more than 700 meters. Among them are Cheptoch cliff, in Sook location, and the Kamatira escarpment on the Kapenguria-Lodwar Road.[16]

West Pökot is one of the two counties that constitute the Catholic Diocese of Kitale, in the hierarchy of the Roman Catholic Church. It borders Trans Nzoia County in the southeast, Elgeyo-Marakwet County (which is part of Eldoret Catholic Diocese) and Baringo County (which is part of Nakuru Catholic Diocese) in the East. Turkana County (which also forms the Catholic Diocese of Lodwar) is in the North and on the Western side, West Pökot County borders the country of Uganda. West Pökot County is a deanery of its own comprising twelve parishes as follows: Amakuriat, Chepareria, Chepnyal, Kabichbich, Kacheliba, Kapenguria, Makutano, Ortum, Sigor, Sinar and Tartar. However, Sinar and Makutano Parishes were treated as parts of Kabichbich and Bendera Parishes since they had not been created at the time of our research. Other Christian denominations and their religious activities are briefly mentioned in chapter four because they are not the subjects of our research.

West Pökot is among the most difficult places to evangelize, in Kenya, due to the harsh climatic conditions, which plague the evangelizer's life. It is one of those counties regarded as 'hardship areas', because of its remoteness.[17] The region is mostly semi-arid with little or sometimes no rain at all. Except for some parts, the ground is mainly sandy with small thorn bushes and is generally not suitable for farming, thus the inhabitants are mainly pastoralists. This brings into light the cause of the ever-increasing cases of cattle rustling between the Pökot, the Turkana, and their cousins the Karimojong and Sebei (also called Kupsapiny) of Uganda, not to mention the sporadic cases of livestock theft in other neighboring counties of Trans Nzoia, Elgeyo-Marakwet, and Baringo. This way of life has left an indelible mark of mutual distrust and perpetual suspicion between these neighboring communities.

Rainfall Distribution, Relief and Drainage

Annual rainfall in West Pökot County varies from less than 400 mm per year in the lowest areas to more than 1500 mm per year in the highest areas. The possible deviation from yearly and monthly means can be considerable, particularly in the lower and drier areas of the county. Total rainfall per year can deviate more than 40% from the long-term average. In some years, rain in April can be as little as 10 mm or less, while in other years, rain in the same month can be as high as 120 mm or more. Apart from insufficient total rainfall, shortage of water during critical periods of growth occurs regularly. An important factor that influences the distribution of rain needed

---

16. Hendrix, op. cit., 5.
17. Ndegwah (2004). Op. cit, 86.

for plant growth is potential evaporation, which in turn depends on temperature. Optimal yields of crops can be expected if rainfall in the wet season is more than two thirds of potential evaporation.[18]

In West Pökot, there exists a distinction of several landscapes, which can suit three major divisions as follows:

- High altitude areas: these areas are more than 1800 meters. These are the mountainous and hilly areas, such as Cherangani Hills, Sekerr Mountains and Chemerongit Range.
- Medium altitude: this range between 1500 and 2100 meters. They are the places from rolling to the hilly areas.
- Low altitude: these are the areas below 1500 meters. They are the flat plains along the rivers and undulating open plains.

Ninety-five per cent of the catchment areas in the county are part of the main Turkwel catchment. Rivers Turkwel (also called Suam) and Kerio (also called Weiwei) are perennial streams that drain into Lake Turkana, while River Muruny drains in the Kerio River, while all other major and minor tributaries are seasonal. Nearly two thirds of the Alale and Suam catchment areas contribute water only in the wet season, mainly because the infiltration capacities and the retention by vegetation are low. This results in a high run-off and a low water storage capacity. The North-western part of the Muruny catchment area is also responsible for the flash floods, again due to run-off and low storage capacity, and as such it hardly contains water in the dry season. The South-eastern part of this catchment area and the Weiwei catchment, situated in the Cherangani Hills, supply continuous flow, good vegetation cover and causes high retention and a good soil structure that result in good infiltration.[19]

Only about one third of the huge West Pökot County is good for agricultural practice, while the rest is either arid or semi-arid. This, according to Dietz, makes life for the people, the majority of whom are pastoralists, very difficult because the land is prone to major climatic disasters, casting doubts on the very future of pastoralism. He explains further: "There is considerable evidence of a major crisis of pastoralism in Africa. Droughts are sometimes selected as primary causes, but population growth, ecological deterioration—or 'desertification'—and an adverse political and economic environment are also often mentioned. Societies of largely autonomous mobile livestock herders seem to be doomed."[20]

---

18. Hendrix, op. cit., 21.
19. Ibid.,14.
20. Dietz (1987). Op. cit., 13.

Socio-Economic Development

Social and economic development in West Pökot started later than most parts of the country and so far, this county has one of the lowest rankings in almost all its economic variables. For instance, school attendance at the time of writing this dissertation was only 24% in comparison to the average 62% in Kenya. While the percentage of people having attended school in the county in 1979 was a miserable 18% compared to 49% in the rest of the country, the percentage of labor force population was a paltry 5% compared to 16% in the whole country.[21] The rate of annual population growth in the county is 3.5%, raising the Pökot population to an approximate 337,870 inhabitants, according to the 1989 census report, and only about 10% of them are Christians. The estimate figures of livestock given in 1995 for the county are 209,000 heads of cattle and 392,000 goats and sheep, with 225,000 Stock Units (SU) and 0.8 SU/ca. The ragged topography of the county (see map 3) has made access to many of its resources difficult.

There are no major towns in this county, no large-scale farming and no industries except the recently built Turkwel Hydro-electric dam. However, minor roads are penetrating a few of the formerly inaccessible areas, although many places remain untouched. Schools are rapidly increasing, only that attendance register of the pupils is very poor, mainly in primary schools. Food production is also increasing at a fast pace and the money economy is quickly replacing subsistence and barter economy. But this is not to say that West Pökot is comparable to many other counties in Kenya, not even to its southern neighbor, Trans Nzoia. As we have already mentioned, farming activities are confined to only a quarter of the county, since the rest 76% is either arid or semiarid. Where applicable, farming is hampered by input and marketing constraints; a fact that, from an outsider's perspective, makes the people really poor.[22]

However, the people have different views about poverty as respondent X, who opted to remain anonymous, put it forward. "We are not poor! We have cows, sheep, goats, strength, time, goodwill and a fountain of ideas," she asserted. "We feel the government has neglected us for leaving our fate to the Churches and non-governmental organizations (NGOs) which have, in turn, reduced us to paupers through relief food and charity-dependency. What we need is not relief aid but concrete, well thought out development projects that take our views seriously."[23] Schneider endorses this position when he designates 'livestock as food and money'[24] and seems to contradict

---

21. DDC (1997). *West Pökot: District Development Plan 1997–2001*. Nairobi: Office of the Vice-President and Ministry of Planning and National Development of the Republic of Kenya, 37.

22. Dietz (1987). Op. cit., 13.

23. This respondent is only referred to as X for fear of reprisals from vengeful government officials, since it is not an ordinary thing to openly criticize the government for its failure, whether real or apparent.

24. Harold K. Schneider (1981). Livestock as Food and Money. In John G. Galaty et al (eds). *The Future of Pastoral Peoples: Proceedings of a Conference held in Nairobi, Kenya, 4–8 August 1980*. Ottawa:

Dietz' view that pastoralists are "...starvation-prone, without assets other than their own bodies..."[25] This protest gives a cue to the church and the government to change tack and treat the Pökot people 'as subjects rather than objects'[26] by consulting them before starting development projects.

Description of the Pökot Lifestyle

Majority of the inhabitants of West Pökot County (almost 95%) are Pökot (singular, Pöchon), the most northern branch of the Southern Nilotic people. This is one of the communities within the Kalenjin speaking ethnic group, to which also belong the Keiyo, Kipsigis, Marakwet, Nandi, Tugen and Sabaot, who extend into the neighboring country, the Republic of Uganda, where they are known as Sebei (Kupsapiny). In fact, many of the Sabaot tribesmen in Kenya have blood relatives, in-laws or other homes in Uganda and the same applies to the Pökot who live on the Kenya-Uganda border. The only difference is that even in Uganda the latter are referred to as Pökot. It must not be forgotten that apart from other Kalenjin speaking people, who live in the interior parts of Kenya, the Sabaot live along the slopes of Mount Elgon (Kony) at the border between Kenya and Uganda.

There exist many theories concerning the origin of the Pökot people and as such it is not easy to ascertain which of them is false or true. According to Dietz,[27] the Pökot trace their origin to a 'Proto-Kalenjin' group of pastoralists that came from an area near the Sudan-Ethiopia border to settle in the surroundings of Mount Elgon around AD 1000. He reports Hubert Hendrix (and his co-authors) as postulating that they probably formed around 2000 years ago in the area to the north and the west of Lake Turkana (formerly Lake Rudolf) and gradually moved south towards their present location.

He further argues that migration to other areas took place due to reasons like shortage of land, epidemics and livestock wars with neighboring groups.[28] According to Visser, though, the Pökot are an amalgamation of different tribes that eventually came together. An argument he supports with the diversity of their physical features. Thus, the formation of the Pökot, as a people, can be traced to the migration patterns of small groups of people from their neighbors. These, then, came together in order to ward off attacks from other pastoralists and formed the various clans, which still owe allegiance to their places of origin. Examples of this include

---

International Development Research Centre, 210.

25. Dietz (1987). Op. cit. 13.

26. John G. Galaty and Dan R. Aronson (1981). Research Priorities and Pastoralist Development: What needs to be Done? In John G. Galaty et al (eds). *The Future of Pastoral Peoples: Proceedings of a Conference held in Nairobi, Kenya, 4–8 August 1980*. Ottawa: International Development Research Centre, 20.

27. Dietz (1987). Op. cit., 26–27.

28. Ibid., 32.

the Terik and Ptuyin who came from Mount Elgon, and the Söchoy, who came from Eldoret, to mention but three.[29]

The Pökot language (*ngala Pökot*) is classified as Kalenjin but distinguishes itself within that group as a separate branch. The Kalenjin languages are characterized by a richness of inflectional forms in their declension and conjugation. It is thought, by some, that the 'closed' nature of the Pökot people has contributed to its special position within the Kalenjin group. Its present vocabulary however, shows some lexicographic influences, particularly from Marakwet and from the Eastern Nilotic languages Karimojong and Turkana. The Pökot language has, since the early 1970s been put down to writing and now with the publication of a class textbook,[30] it is being taught in primary schools and adult literacy classes. These efforts have, however, not as yet solved the problem that most people, including the Pökot themselves, have great difficulties reading the language fluently.

This is blamed on the fact that many people are still illiterate and the influence of modernity, whereby young educated people prefer to read English or Swahili, rather than their own mother tongue.[31] If this trend continues unchecked, then it is likely that the pökot language will die a natural death. "The death of a language," says Mayor, "is a loss for all of us since it is often the final act in the disappearance of a way of life, a culture and particular view of the world for which it was the main vehicle."[32] Deliberately allowing a language to perish, we insist, is suicidal, because with it "is the freedom and dignity of a community that perishes Mayor."[33]

Together with the evolution of Pökot language is the identity of the people. During the colonial era, the Pökot were known as 'Suk'[34] a corruption of the Pökot word 'mïsik', which means 'a stump'. It is said that the Pökot did not want to reveal their identity to the colonialists and so when they asked for the head tax and wanted to record down people's names everybody said their name was 'mïsik', which made it difficult to distinguish those who paid the tax from those who did not. In the ears of the colonialists the word (*mïsik*) sounded like 'suk' and so they started referring to them as such.

In order to know who had paid the tax and who had not they had to arrest all men and depend on their good will by asking in Swahili if they had paid (that is, *Umelipa?*), hence the name Kacheliba (lit. the home of payment), for the then colonial center for taxation. However, according to Beech, 'Suk' was given to the Pökot people by another

29. Visser (1989). Op. cit., 4.

30. James P. W. Kapello (1985). *Keneta Kegh Ngala Pökot*. Nairobi: The Regal Press Kenya Limited.

31. Jan P. Sterk and Margaret J. Muthwi (2004). The Publishing of Christian Scriptures in Africa: Sociolinguistic Challenges. In Ernst R. Wenland and Jean-Claude Loba-Mkole (eds). *Biblical Texts & African Audiences*. Nairobi: Acton Publishers, 157.

32. F. Mayor (2001). *The World Ahead: Our Future in the Making*. London: Zed Books, 343.

33. Ibid., 343.

34. Juxton Barton (1921). Notes on the Suk Tribe of the Kenya Colony. In *The Journal of the Royal Anthropological Institute*. Tome LI, 82–89.

nomadic group—the Masai. "It has been conjectured," he argues, "that they were so called owing to the small short sword worn by the hill tribes and called *chuk* or *chôk*."[35] When the first anthropologists started doing research in this area, notably Schneider and Beech the people did not like to be referred to as 'Suk' and identified themselves as Pökot which, to them, sounded like 'Pôkwut' or 'Pakot'.

Then later anthropologists used varied spellings, depending on their conviction. Meyerhoff used the Swahili version of the word (Pokot), Visser started off with the Swahili spellings but later changed and tried to come closer to the sound made when the word is pronounced (Pökoot). We have, however, adopted the spelling found in the current standard school textbook, which is approved by the Ministry of Education in Kenya. The etymology of the word 'Pökot' is not clear and as such various myths exist with regard to its actual meaning. Some people think it is a shortened form of the possessive case of the word house (*kö*) and so it means 'people of the house' (*pö-kot*) or belonging to the house. Others think it is derived from the association of the Pökot people with the calabash (*mïkö*) by their neighbors, who called them *kïmïkony*.

It is said that the Pökot people carried calabashes with them wherever they went and then other people started referring to them as 'people of the calabash' (*pipö mïkö*). Still others think that it is derived from the Pökot word for injury (*kot*) and that it means 'the injured people' (*pich chole koot*), who are also survivors (*pö-koot*) because their neighbors have hurt them (the Pökot) for long. The final explanation is that it is a corruption of the expression of the Pökot as 'the house of the rock' (*köpö-kogh*), since the Pökot are said to be strong and firm like the rock.

The actual land inhabited by the Pökot can be divided into three major regions, first, the proper western part of the Pökotland (the region to the north and west of Suam River, which until 1970 was being administered, from Uganda). It has for a long time now been referred to as *Kenya Mpya*—New Kenya, due to this factor, otherwise called Karapökot (the Pökotland), whose inhabitants are two distinct Pökot groups known as Kasauria and Kacheripkö. The former is named after the famous cattle watering point called Sauriria, because men spend much of them time around it, while the latter are said to spend much of their time in the house, which they are said to watch over (*ripkö*). This region extends to the Amudat District of the eastern Karamoja Region, in the Republic of Uganda.

Then there is the central region, the area extending from Kapenguria down to Sigor and Lomut via Chepareria and Kabichbich; which can be referred to as Central Pökot. Finally, there is Tiaty, the eastern part of the Pökotland, which extends to the northern part of Baringo County. Karapökot and Central Pökot form the current administrative region known as West Pökot, where we carried out our field research. The Pökot can be said to be the least sedentary among all Kalenjin speaking people in Kenya because they are goat, cattle, sheep, and, to a small extent, camel-herding people, who also practice some agriculture. They live a nomadic lifestyle in different

---

35. Beech (1969). Op. cit., 1.

degrees, depending on the number of the livestock they possess and the fertility of their land.[36] An estimated sixty to seventy per cent are pure pastoralists, who depend solely on animals, hence they are known as people of cattle (*pipö tich*), who live in homesteads *(kaneston)* and their huts are different from their counterparts. These live in the lower parts of the county (Karapökot), which are very dry with little or, at times, no rainfall at all. For this reason, their way of life involves a lot of movement with their herds (sometimes across the border into the Republic of Uganda) in search of water and pasture.

The other section of the Pökot people settled in the high-altitude areas like Cherangani Hills, Sekerr Hills and the highlands around Kapenguria and Lelan. Apart from keeping animals, they also got down to farming and are now identified with crops; hence the term *pipö pagh* (the people of grains). This is because they mix pastoralism with agriculture.[37] Later on they moved down hill and occupied the lowlands of Cheptulel, Lomut and Sigor, where they started practicing channel irrigation, most likely with influence from their Marakwet neighbors who are known for this method of farming.

Although 'the people of grains' (the agriculturist Pökot) have adopted the growing of modern crops like cassava, vegetables, fruit and maize (corn); the traditional crops (finger millet—*matay* and sorghum—*mosong*) remain the most valued ones, even among the pastoralists. From these two crops the traditional food (*pan*) and the all-important traditional beer (*kumïn*), without which no ceremony can take place, are made. They lead a more permanent life and do a lot of farming in the rich soiled highlands but a cow remains basically important in their lives. Indeed, for the Pökot in general, attachment to the cow acquires a religious dimension whereby they see it as their unique gift from God.[38] Visser describes three categories of the Pökot as follows: those who keep animals, those who are pure farmers and those who practice mixed economy, that is, they keep animals and also carry out some farming.

> The Pokot belong to the Kalenjin cluster of the Southern Sudan Nilotes. Some are pastoralists, who herd their cattle, sheep and goats in the low lying vast plains of the semi-arid and arid areas of the district. Others practise subsistence farming, especially on the slopes of the mountains, which rise to over 3000 metres and so attract far more rain. Still others have a mixed economy, keeping some animals and having small *shambas* (cultivated fields) of millet and maize.[39]

36. Harold K. Schneider (1955). The Moral System of the Pakot. In Vergilius Ferm (ed). *Encyclopedia of Morals*. New York: Philosophical Library, 403.

37. It has to be clarified that the people of grains do not mix pastoralism with agriculture in a proportional way and the degree of mixing ranges from light to balanced, depending on the fertility of the land and reliability of the rain for the production of subsistence and cash crops.

38. Schneider (1955). Op. cit., 404.

39. Johannes Jacobus Visser (1983). We Follow Someone Who Speaks the Truth. In Wout van den Bor (ed). *The Art of the Beginning: First Experiences and Problems of Western Expatriates in Developing*

However, our research did not reveal the second group as a classification of the Pökot. Although there could be some people without cattle, this could be a temporary result of pestilence, cattle raiding or some other misfortune, but not an approved way of life, because for them, 'a Pöchon without cattle is a dead one'.[40]

Unity and Identity of the Pökot People

The Pökot identify themselves as a people, distinct from other Kalenjin communities, culturally speaking, and as a political entity, socially speaking. Their identity is not founded on some philosophical conceptions like the principles of essence and existence. Rather, it is based on the practicality of their life, various relational aspects of day-to-day survival that tie people together and the word of mouth from the elders. Meyerhoff sees this unity in terms of responsibility and interdependence towards each other as manifested in the reconciliation ritual *(parpara)*.[41] However, our efforts to find out the essence of the Pökot identity did not yield much in terms of abstraction.

Our research showed that Pökot identity is a matter of historical construction, based on common social practices and folklores, which are difficult to verify for the lack of written sources, as it is the case with many other communities.[42] We did not come up with anything we could point our fingers at and say, yes, this is the *Pökotness*, or essence of the Pökot people. All that we came up with are some shared elements in the form of cultural practices, at the functional level of the community. These have become their cultural identity, at once creating a sense of belonging (among themselves) as well as distinction (against others). Thus, they give them a feeling of 'us' against 'them', just as Wijsen and Tanner have observed elsewhere, acting as a cultural divide with neighboring communities.[43]

The *Shared* Elements Among the Pökot

In the Pökot social situation, we managed to come up with four practically *shared* elements that are said to distinguish the Pökot from other people as follows: genealogy, language, relationship and culture. In terms of genealogy, a person is considered to be a true Pöchon if he or she is born of a Pöchon father and Pöchon mother. If a person is born of a Pöchon father and a non-Pöchon mother he/she is accepted but is always regarded as half-Pöchon unless his/her mother was a victim of cattle raid, where they

---

Countries with Special Emphasis on Rural Development and Rural Education. Wageningen: PUDOC, 13.

40. Johannes Jacobus Visser (1989). *Pökoot Religion*. Oegstgeest: Hendrik Kraemer Instituut, 15.

41. Elizabeth L. Meyerhoff (1982). The Threatened Way of Kenya's Pokot People. In *National Geographic*, Vol. 161, No 1, 120.

42. Wijsen and Tanner (2002). Op. cit., 26–28.

43. Ibid., 19–22.

'carried home' not only their cows, but also their wives. If, however, a person is born of a Pöchon girl who is married to a man from another community that person is never at any time regarded as a Pöchon unless he/she was born outside wedlock. Thus, in a bid to prove one's authenticity as a Pöchon, a person will always try to name one's ancestors up to the tenth generation and the exact location where they lived.

The Pökot people share one language called *ngala Pökot* (literally, Pökot words), which is their first spoken language and all second languages are nearly always colored with the Pökot syntactic and syllabic pronunciations, popularly referred to as mother tongue interference. Some Pökot, therefore, try their level best to speak the Pökot language as perfectly and as accurately as they can, taking into account diction, intonation and pronunciation; need-less to mention the scramble for a rich vocabulary. So, during cattle raiding expeditions one way the raiders are able to identify their enemies is through the language, mainly if they have an accent that is not known in Pökotland and the use of a secret language (*ngotinyön*) learned in seclusion, only known to the initiated.[44]

The Pökot people have a network of social interaction that can easily be referred to as a paradox of relationship, based on blood and clan. A person is not allowed to marry his/her relative or someone from one's clan and yet all Pökot are said to be related by the virtue of all clans coming from the same progenitor. When a Pöchon marries from another clan, the two clans become related by virtue of this affinity: the relationship is real and permanent, but in order to allow another member of the same clan to get married to another person of either clan, the children, properly speaking, belong to the father's clan and the influence of their mother's clan is minimal.

Consequently, they can go and marry a girl from their own mother's clan without a problem, but only after two generations. From this perspective, the Pökot are seen as a web of a people related either by affinity or consanguinity. The Pökot share the cultural values and social practices, as mentioned above, which are conventionally agreed to be part and parcel of what distinguishes them from other people who they, therefore, see as outsiders. Apart from the said cultural values that are typically Pökot, another popular mark that cattle raiders use to identify and flush out the enemy from their midst is to see if one has extracted the two lower front teeth; which is done during a rite of passage called *keghot kelat*. This, according to *Mzee* Ibrahim Kotit,[45] is despite the fact that it has nothing to do with culture because it is purely done for medical reasons and is, therefore, a traditional hallmark of many other Kenyan peoples (e.g. the Kikuyu, of Central Kenya, who traditionally also extract their lower teeth): a thing that makes it quite difficult, if not impossible, to determine with certainty what is actually Pökot and what is not. For this reason, all non-Pökot who wish to become Pökot must undergo a special rite called *rwakat* that incorporates them into the Pökot

---

44. Visser (1989). Op. cit., 177.

45. Interview with Ibrahim Kotit, a 78-year-old resident of Chepareria Division, retired catechist and teacher.

family. This means that they share common cultural values, belief system and embrace the Pökot way of life and worldview as their own.

The Future of Pastoralism and Threat of 'Civilization'

Questions have been raised with regard to the possible endurance of the Pökot culture in the face of the serious onslaught by modernity and globalization. Due to their lifestyle and heavy dependence on animals, the Pökot are classified as pastoral nomads and many people have raised questions concerning the future of the nomadic lifestyle, arguing that it is soon going to die out. With the dawn of what has been regarded by many as 'civilization' from the West, much of African traditional ways of life have been despised or forgotten altogether. However, many pastoralist groups, including the Pökot, seem to have resisted this onslaught; and for that reason, they are under threat from all sides to relinquish their mode of existence in favor of modernity, which basically translates to adopting a sedentary and a seemingly European way of life.

> Once called 'the lords of the plains' roaming around with their large herds on extensive pastures the nomadic pastoral future now seems to have turned bleak. The processes of structural impoverishment and acute major crises of hunger and starvation of man and of animals, although not new phenomena, have seemed to become more frequent in recent times.[46]

In this regard, Jahnke uses the expression 'pastoralism under pressure', especially when one compares the lives of the pastoralists today to the hitherto lifestyle of a traditional pastoralist, which was characterized by a "free-ranging husbandry man with an abundance of livestock and land resources at his disposal."[47] Consequently, Meyerhoff sees pastoralists as 'a threatened people',[48] while Dietz sees them as 'pastoralists in dire straits'.[49] Schwartz and Schwartz indict pastoralism and nomadism on account of food insecurity, because these two "show a decreasing self-reliance in terms of food production."[50] Hence, as Hjort observes that growing scores of nomads are being pushed out of the pastoralist economy.[51] As a result of this situation Dietz wonders aloud whether pastoralism has any chance of survival. He explains:

---

46. Marinus M. E. M. Rutten (1992). *Selling Wealth to Buy Poverty: The Process of the Individualization of Landownership Among the Maasai Pastoralists of Kajiado District, Kenya, 1890–1990*. Saarbrücken-Fort Lauderdale: Verlag Breitenbach Publishers, 3.

47. H. E. Jahnke (1982). *Livestock Production Systems and Livestock Development in Tropical Africa*. Vauk: Kieler Wissenschaftsverlag, 82.

48. Meyerhoff (1982). Op. cit.

49. Dietz (1987). Op. cit.

50. S. Schwartz & H. J. Schwartz (1985). Nomadic Pastoralism in Kenya—Still a Viable System of Production? In *Quarterly Journal of International Agriculture*, Vol. 24, and No.1, 5.

51. A. Hjort (1982). A Critique of 'ecological' Models of Pastoral Land Use. In: *Nomadic Peoples*, No. 10, 24.

There is considerable evidence of a major crisis of pastoralism in Africa. Droughts are sometimes selected as primary causes, but population growth, ecological deterioration or 'desertification'—and an adverse political and economic environment are also often mentioned. Societies of largely autonomous mobile livestock herders seem to be doomed.[52]

However, none of the above authors has been more categorical about the demise of pastoralism than Neville and Rada Dyson-Hudson who had predicted its death by the turn of the 20th century: "The collective future of traditional pastoralists is . . . at risk in East Africa. By the end of the century they may belong merely to memory, as traditional African hunter-gatherer populations already do."[53] Indeed, for others, it is not merely that pastoralism is at stake, but the pastoralists themselves are on the road to extinction. Thus, Campbell & Axinn courageously asked whether pastoralists are not 'obsolete societies en route to extinction'.[54] As early as 1910 H. and S. Hinde published their book 'The Last of the Masai'. "In the early 1930s a medical survey among the Maasai of Kenya's Kajiado District revealed that the birth rate among the Maasai was not high enough to maintain the population as a result of gonorrhoeal infections."[55] These predictions of doom notwithstanding, the century came to an end and yet pastoralists today number more than ever before. This is in agreement with Sandford's position that pastoralism is indeed not dying out. He, however, points out that many pastoralists are leaving pastoralism in favor of agriculture and further says that pastoralism is proportionally less important in the economy today than it was 50 years ago.[56] But he also concurs that "most of the areas which are pastoral at present will continue to be so in future and many millions of people will continue to be pastoralists."[57]

In fact, there are several cases where traditional pastoralism has gained ground in structural importance within a group's economy. Experience has shown that the keeping of animals has, in the recent past, become a preferred mode of living in counties like Nakuru and Laikipia, Kitui, Machakos and Nyeri in Kenya, due to increasing rain patterns that are not favorable to crop production.[58] Holy has also reported increased importance of nomadic pastoralism within the mixed economy

---

52. Dietz (1987). Op. cit., 13.

53. N. Dyson-Hudson & R. Dyson-Hudson (1982). The Structure of East African Herds and the Future of East African Herders. In: *Development and Change*, Vol. 13, 213.

54. D. J. Campbell and G. H. Axinn (1980). *Pastoralism in Kenya: Obsolete Societies en route to Extinction, or Appropriate Technologies for a Fragile Environment?* Hannover: Field Staff Reports no. 30. American Universities.

55. Rutten, op. cit., 3.

56. Ndegwah (2006). Op. cit., 67.

57. S. Sandford (1983). *Management of Pastoral Development in the Third World.* London: John Wiley & Sons, Overseas Development Institute, 2–3.

58. Ndegwah (2006). Op. cit., 67.

of the Berti people living in northern Darfur Province in the Sudan;[59] while Haaland reports a similar observation among the neighboring Fur.[60] Finally, a joint survey carried out by UNESCO, UNEP and FAO, in 1979, also indicated that the Fulani groups of Niger and Nigeria changed from agriculture to nomadic pastoralism, just before the drought of the1970s.[61]

Cissé, however, gives a different picture whereby he classifies the two lifestyles as complementary, leading to what he calls 'agropastoralism'.[62] He argues that both systems are losing or gaining ground, depending on the prevailing weather situations as is the case in Mali. He says: "Two apparently contradictory trends characterize the rural society in this part of Mali: the transformation of nomadic herders into cultivators and the tendency for cultivators to become herder-farmers."[63] This happens to be the case among the Pökot people, whereby the purely pastoralist people also practice a little bit of farming and vice versa.

In the light of the discussion above, we can comfortably say that pastoralism has endured many years of historical test. It is here with us to stay and it will go on for a long time to come, if not to the end of time. Understandably, pastoralists, like all other traditional groups of people, have been affected by modernity, post modernity and globalization in particular. Hence, today's pastoralists are not the same as those of yesteryears; just as today's sedentary people are different from their forefathers in style and mannerism. But this is way far from the postulate of extinction that is seemingly designed to make us indifferent, in response, or generally ambivalent to the cause of the nomadic lifestyle.[64]

The Pökot Concept of Ownership

Among the Pökot the concept of ownership is only loosely appropriated to individuals but properly bestowed on the community; either as a whole or at the clan level. All important things belong to the community, i.e., children, land and cows. All children (*moning*) belong to the community and as such any adult community member has a right to discipline them when they misbehave and a duty to assist

---

59. L. Holy (1987). Property Differentiation and Pastoralism in an Agricultural Society: the Berti. In: Baxter P.T.W & R. Hogg (eds), *Property, Poverty and People: Changing Rights in Property and Problems of Pastoral Development*. Manchester: University of Manchester, 210.

60. G. Haaland (1972). Nomadism as an Economic Career Among the Sedentaries in the Sudan Savannah Belt. In: Cunnison I & W. James (eds), *Essays in Sudan Ethnography: Presented to Sir Edward Evans-Pritchard*. London: C. Hurst, 149–172.

61. Ndegwah (2006). Op. cit., 68.

62. Salmane Cissé (1981). Sedentarization of nomadic pastoralists and "pastoralization" of cultivators in Mali. In John G. Galaty et al (eds). *The Future of Pastoral Peoples: Proceedings of a Conference held in Nairobi, Kenya, 4–8 August 1980*. Ottawa: International Development Research Centre, 321.

63. Cissé, op. cit., 321.

64. Ndegwah (2006). Op cit., 68.

them whenever in need. Hence if you asked a Pöchon, 'how many children do you have - *itïngönyi monïng ata?* What comes to his or her mind is the entire number of children in his or her home, irrespective of whether they are his biological children or not. In return, children are supposed to respect all adult Pökot as though they were their own (biological) parents (*yiyï*).

The land (*kor*) question is a very sensitive one in West Pökot and ideally, it cannot be raised for discussion anywhere else except in the special council of elders meeting called *kokwö*. Traditionally, land could neither be sold nor be bought by any individual. It strictly belongs to the community at the level of the clans (*ortïn*) and not even a single homestead can claim it. Every clan has what it regards as its ancestral land and no individual member can claim its ownership as an individual. Even among the agriculturalist Pökot, nobody could cultivate the land without a special permission from the elders, which they only gave after certain ritual, called *sintagh,* which marked the beginning of the year, had been performed. The purpose was to determine the future and possible weather condition. The *sintagh* ritual was performed in a meeting of elders (*kokwö*), which was normally called to identify the new land and how to organize the labor. Before the day of the meeting they had to ascertain that all was well for cultivation by listening to a voice of a bird, in a process known as *kipir tarit.* This was done in the dawn before any other sound. If the first sound indicates peace, then they will proceed for a meeting.

Homesteads were built collectively and people lived as a community, animal grazing was done communally and as such the issue of an individual asking for a personal piece of land did not arise. In some places (like Kapenguria, Lelan, Chepareria, Sook) the government has introduced land title deeds for individual land appropriation. This has generated so much heat, in a good number of cases, that land demarcation has finally been left to individual clans and the councils of elders to decide how to accommodate the new development. It is, however, slowly gaining ground in some parts, but even then, litigation on land matters rests with the local chiefs and land committees, that have been elected with government approval, to replace the traditional council of elders. These, however, remain largely symbolic leaders since people only go to them when the traditional way of solving issues has failed. Indeed, in another pastoralist setting, subject to the same trend, Rutten sees the practice as selling wealth to buy poverty.[65]

The Pökot *Tilya* System (Economic Relationship)

As for cattle ownership, they essentially belong to the community, and as such individuals only own them in stewardship. They can be exchanged from one person to another and then to another without much ado, so much so that every person in a given

---

65. Rutten, op. cit.

locality can claim ownership to every other person's cattle with sufficient justification, hence the expression, *tupa Pökot* (Pökot cattle). If a person, for instance, has a celebration that requires the slaughter-ring of an ox, he can easily go to a neighbor and ask for one in exchange for a heifer or even a calf. When grown up the cow will provide milk to the one who received it, but the original owner still has a claim to its offspring which are known as *tupa tilya* (relationship cattle) as opposed to *tupa Pökot* (sing. *tepa Pökot*). Once it has had three steers, the new owner can 'cut the linkage' (*mutat*) by giving back an ox and six goats or so, depending on the practice in a particular area, and the original owner will give away the ox in exchange for another calf, which will create a new cattle lineage.

As pointed out earlier on, the concept of relationship is of prime importance in the Pökot community. It is not only limited to biological and social events like consanguinity and affinity; it is not even limited to the cultural level. It is extended to the very concept of ownership in an economic relationship called *tilya*. The word 'tilya' in itself means 'a blood relative' and its plural is *tilyay*, i.e., relatives. This relationship normally comes about through biologically and it is restricted to the people of one's own lineage. However, anyone who shares your wealth in a close relationship is also, in an analogical way, regarded as an 'economic relative' (literally, cow relative—*tilyantan* or *tilya tany*). In some places of West Pökot (like Sook, Krich, Alale and Kacheliba), you cannot even marry from the home of such a person, and neither can you allow it between your children since, as they put it, 'you have eaten the same wealth'. Perhaps this is why Meyerhoff defined *tilya* as a "stock association system, transcending the one of kinship."[66]

Where marriage between *tilyay* takes place (like Kapenguria, Chepareria and Lelan) the question of bride price is nearly always problematic since they must first count the property they owe each other in order to settle it. If the girl's father owes the boy's father more than is demanded in marriage, then he must return the rest of the animals, since the *tilya* system does not work between in-laws. The reason for this is that the two categories of cattle have different classifications as explained above—*tupa tilya* and *tupa koyugh*; which is, in turn, different from the general classification of the cattle that belong to all Pökot (*tupa Pökot*). This economic system has a number of advantages: first, it helps in maintaining a closer tie between neighbors or clans, since everyone is a debtor to everyone else. Secondly, in case of an epidemic and cows in a given location die, the people have recourse to their other debtors in the places that were not affected by the epidemic. The same logic applies in the case of cattle raiding. When all animals have been stolen, people are never completely impoverished as they can always go to their debtors in other places and get 'something to start life with' again. Plapan further clarifies the origin of this system of economic relationship:

---

66. Elizabeth L. Meyerhoff (1981). *The Socio-Economic and Ritual Roles of a Pokot Woman*. Cambridge: Lucy Cavendish College.

> The economic relationship arises out of one lending a cow not for sale but to enable one solve a problem, may be one has a ritual and does not have the prescribed colour, visitors, or does not have a bull in his herd or in a case where all the cattle dry and the family has small children who need milk. In these situations, one goes to his friend and discusses the problem. The culture demands that if one has the cow, he should give. He will then give the cow or bull to the person. He will not ask when the cow will be returned but will wait even for five years. Should the cow die, the person who had been given the cow, dries the skin and keeps or takes to the owner to prove that the animal really died.[67]

In case the cow was stolen then, of course, there is no need or possibility to take the skin of the animal but, still the custodian of the cow must make sure that the owner gets the information as soon as possible. Other times it is not possible to take the skin when such a cow dies because the owner lives far away or is unavailable at the moment. What the custodian does in such cases is to slaughter the animal and invite his neighbors to eat the meat so that they act as witnesses, should the owner eventually cause problems, say, by alleging foul play or fraud.

The penetration of this concept of relationship into their economic system is so deep that even the purely social or professional services delivered for a fee are converted into an everlasting relationship. If you go to a shop or market to buy a dress or a banana, among the Pökot, this is not a purely economic transaction, where money just changes hands. It is also a socio-communal event in which the shopkeeper or seller wants to know how the buyer is doing at home and the problem(s) he or she might be facing, and even offer to suggest some solutions. This gives rise to an interest-free credit system where people just come and collect what they need for consumption at home only to pay 'at the end of the month', which actually means 'when funds get available'. The point here is that people carrying out business transactions are generally related, in one way or another. They may belong to one family, sub-clan, a clan or simply neighbors. Even the social functions like midwifery in the community carry their permanent relationship as well. If a midwife helps a woman to deliver successfully she develops a special attachment to the child until it grows up, just as its biological mother does. Should the child do well in life, the midwife will visit him or her and demand presents for helping the mother into a safe delivery.[68]

The Kinds of *Tilya*

Tilyantan (or *tilya tany*) is an economic arrangement designed to help a needy person gain the acceptable social status in the community or simply solve his economic woes. It can arise out of anything, at anytime, anywhere and for a variety of reasons.

---

67. Plapan, op. cit., IV.
68. Ibid., IV.

Consequently, there are so many kinds of *tilya* but six of them are more common than the rest and such merit to be briefly discussed here. The first kind of *tilya* arises when a person needs to undergo the rite of passage called *sapana*, so we call it ritualistic *tilya*. The second one arises when a needy person borrows a cow from his friend purely to get milk for his children, so we call it goodwill *tilya*. The third kind of *tilya*, code-named treasure *tilya*, arises from sheer poverty and a person goes around looking for a number of animals from well-wishers. The fourth kind arises from the need to perform a sacrifice and whoever offers the sacrificial animal enters into a kind of economic relationship with the leader of this sacrifice, hence we called it sacrificial *tilya*. The fifth one arises from simple leisure or convenience. So, we called it conventional *tilya*. Then lastly, there is a kind of economic relationship that results from marriage, and we accordingly named it marital *tilya*.

Ritualistic *tilya* comes about when a person needs to undergo a traditional ritual that requires the slaughtering of an ox (*eghin*). If the initiate does not have an ox he can go to a neighbor or a friend and ask for one in exchange for a heifer (*mösör*) or even a calf (*mogh*) in the name of *tilya*. Though given out, the calf essentially still belongs to the original owner because, the slaughtered ox has come to an end yet the calf still has the potential to bring forth many more oxen (*egh*). For this reason, once the calf has grown into a big cow and calved three times, the new owner is culturally obliged to give one ox to the original owner plus some twelve goats to 'cover its legs'. This is done in a social ceremony designed to cut the economic linkage, lest the original owner claims all offspring of his heifer; something that ordinarily only happens when the two *tilyay* quarrel before cutting the linkage.

Sometimes it happens that a person finds himself in severe shortage of milk, either because all his cows are dry or for any other reason. Such a person can decide to ask for assistance from his friends. They normally would give him a cow that has just calved and has enough milk for the family. This marks the beginning of goodwill *tilya*. According to the Pökot cultural norms, the borrower cannot benefit from anything else apart from the milk he gets for his kids no matter how long he keeps this cow and its calf, even if they multiply into many cows. Otherwise, it will be said that he squandered the goodwill and, as a result, a curse will befall him. However, if he takes good care of the cows and he stays with them for too long, then the owner is obliged to say 'thank you' by surrendering some of the cows to the borrower.

This way they become economic relatives and their mutual respect can even go on to their children. But should the borrower, in the meantime, get into problems that require to be solved by giving out or slaughtering a cow he can use these cows even if they are not his, only that he is obliged to tell the real owner during the filing of returns. The confession goes like this: "These are all the cows that I have been herding for you except that there is one (or two) I have kept (for you) on the crotch of a tree (*kakachan sokotun pö ket*)."[69] This means that I was in need and used your cow without your

---

69. Wilikoi Lokelima, a 55-year-old old man who has been working as a research informant for

express permission since the matter was urgent. But I knew you could not refuse me its use (because cows generally belong to all Pökot) and should you get into a problem in future you can always come to me for assistance without hindrance.

Due to the persistence of insecurity, West Pökot is a county with a lot of peculiarities. A person can wake up one morning to find that all his cattle gone, either as a result of theft or epidemic. Since it is not possible for a person to survive without cattle, then he has a right to ask for a donation of cows from relatives, friends and neighbors. If their animals have survived the onslaught, they just cannot refuse him. However, these donations are not without strings attached since all those who make the contribution have a right to occasionally come and ask for a heifer, an ox, a cow and so forth. They, as it were, make a treasury *tilya* with the person who borrowed the cows. This relationship can go on for many years until they decide to cut it off and remain just good friends. The advantage with this kind of *tilya* is that no one can suffer want when others have wealth, while the disadvantage is that although a person may appear to have a lot of cows they are basically not his; 'they belong to the Pökot people' (*tupa Pökot*).

The fourth kind of *tilya* is what we dubbed sacrificial *tilya*. When the local seer has predicted an impending catastrophe and ordered that a cow of a given color, mainly an ox, be slaughtered. If you are the only one with that kind of an ox the council of elders will plan and send one of their own to request you to surrender it. He, in turn, gives you a calf and thereby becomes your *tilya* on behalf of the community. This means that from then on, you are going to treat this person as an economic relative, even though this relationship is only held in trust.

When the weather is not quite favorable and there is not much food, the elders might decide they want to 'spear (kill) an ox'. The one who provides the animal to be 'roasted' a euphemism for slaughtering, enters into a conventional *tilya* with whoever is suggested by the elders to go and get the animal from him. Alternatively, it might be that they want to discuss a certain important matter pertaining to the community and they might wish to relax with a piece of meat each during the discussion. In either case, they will require a big ox for the purpose so they identify the person with such an ox and send one of their own to go and ask for it.

The person goes and asks for the ox and he is the one to spear it just above the front leg (*karas*), then he provides a heifer (*mösör*) or a calf (*mogh*) to the owner and by that fact they become *tilyay* (plural of *tilya*). The last kind of *tilya* results from marriage. In the Pökot culture, marriage is not an individual affair; rather it is a family, indeed a clan affair that borders on creating social alliances. So, if a person marries off his daughter, nearly all his close relatives have a share of their cows, at least one each. Once the obligatory shares (which are known as *tupa koyugh* (cows for marriage) or *kantin* (cows for a bride) are over and there are more cows remaining then it is wise to distribute them to friends and neighbors in the name of *tilya*. You give them out for

---

several years now. He lives near Kacheliba Center and is mainly a livestock farmer.

the purpose of security that should raiders come to your home on the incentive of the bride price,[70] they will not find much of these cows.

Although the *tilya* economic system works very well for the Pökot, this is not to say that it does not present some problems to the community. People, being what they are, might want to reap where they did not sow and hide other people's cows, especially if they have stayed for long. Plapan further explains what happens if a person tries to cheat another out of this system. "If the borrower tries to hide or cheats the owner, a controversy that affects the whole clan arises involving 'oath' ritual that is believed that one dies."[71] She, therefore, warns would-be cattle buyers in West Pökot of the thing to watch out for. "If one goes to ones home to purchase a cow, one has to ascertain whether it is market or tilya. If it is tilya, the person will sell at lower price but will still follow one for economic relationship."[72]

Political Governance and Social Life

The people of West Pökot have a full traditional juridical structure, which is also the administration system that governs their day-to-day lives, settles their disputes and solves all domestic problems. It comprised—and still does—of *kokwö* (a council of elders) headed by the elders as a group and they solved all social issues through a decision-making process (*kirwok*) that was arrived at by consensus and laid down traditional beliefs and customs.[73] Hence, as Dietz contends, 'the Pökot leadership was neither authoritarian nor hierarchic'.[74]

However, there nearly always emerged an individual whose words held sway of what was to be adopted by the council as its final decision. This may have been a famous person (*chi nyo oror*), who was revered due to his riches, raiding skills, brilliant contributions leading to sound judgements or simply a good composer of songs. Such a person was referred to as the 'cutter of words' (*mutinto ngal*), but this did not mean that he was *ipso facto* the official leader of the council. He could, at best, be regarded as a moral or informal leader.

---

70. The word 'bride price', gives a negative connotation when translated into the Pökot language, whereby it sounds like paying for a wife (*tar*), or selling (*kealta*) a girl in the same way one would buy a dress, but our informants seemed to agree that this 'buying' is different from the ordinary buying of stuff in the market.

71. Plapan, op. cit., IV.

72. Ibid., IV.

73. Visser (1989). Op. cit., 78; Harold K. Schneider (1959). The Moral System of the Pakot. In Vergilius Ferm (ed). *Encyclopedia of Morals.* New York: Philosophical Library, 167.

74. Dietz (1987). Op.cit., 179. It is important, however, to note that the lack of authoritarianism, in the Pökot leadership, was only to an extent, because it excluded the opinions of women and children. And although the *mutinto ngal*, spoke after all other elders had spoken, the decision, once arrived at, was never questioned or challenged.

The *kokwö*, which functioned both as leader and judge of the Pökot was (and still is) divided into two, the clan council of elders, who addressed clan-related issues and the community supreme council of elders, who concerned themselves with matters affecting the whole community. It is, however, important to note that not every village or ridge had (or has) its own *kokwö* and that not every male was accepted in it. Men had to fulfil all social regulations before they could be accepted as members.

Since the Pökot leadership style was neither authoritarian nor hierarchical there were no chiefs, no legal succession and no designation of office. The present-day term *kirwokïn* is based on the government concept of leadership, which constitutes a chain of individual leaders, going down all the way to the chiefs at the grassroots. The colonial government introduced the position of the chiefs but these remained hated as traitors, who collaborated with the white to manipulate the people by collecting taxes and sometimes introducing forced labor. With the coming of independence, the situation has changed and the chieftain has generally been accepted but only as government representative. Chiefs, therefore, do not in any way supplant the traditional leaders like litigators, diviners and prophets.

Religion, among the Pökot, is understood as part and parcel of social life and so is prayer and worship. They pray to God (*Tororöt*), whose abode is believed to be in the sky (*yim*) and he comes to Mtelo (the highest mountain in Pökotland) to reveal his will to the people. The *kokwö* was (and again in many cases still is) responsible for the religious welfare of the people, and as such, when there is a serious catastrophe that requires offering(s) to be made to Tororöt, elders gather together overlooking mount Mtelo and sit in a semicircle (*kirket*) with the oldest man sitting in the middle, while the youngest ones sit at both ends of the crescent.[75] The Pökot generally practice the rites of passage, which run from birth to death. One such rite is clitoridectomy (for girls) and circumcision (for boys), simply referred to as *mutat* (cut) or *tum* (song or dance).

This is an important stage in the life of a Pöchon and it consists of several other steps and rituals. Clitoridectomy, for instance, consists of four main stages with a slight difference between the pastoralists and the agriculturalists. Among the pastoralists the stages are *ptengöwo* (a vigil dancing session that precedes the actual operation), *mutat* (the cut itself), *löpow*[76] (a cleansing ritual carried out a few days after the cut) and *lapan* (the final ceremony that declares the initiates (*chemeri*) fully healed and ready for marriage). Among the agriculturalists, they start with *ptengöwo*, followed by *mutat*, then *lapan* or *lopow* and finally *kipunö* (which, among the agriculturalists replaces *lapan*, as the final ceremony that declares the initiates (*chemeri*) fully healed and ready for marriage). It is during these rites that the initiates undergo instructions on the values of the Pökot as a people and what is expected of them as adults and responsible members of the community.

---

75. Visser (1989). Op. cit., 116.
76. This cleansing ritual is also carried out a few days after a woman has given birth.

As for the food, the pastoral Pökot lived mainly on blood and milk (*kison nko chö*)[77] while the agriculturists lived mainly on food prepared from finger millet (*panta mataiywö*), as the main dish, with either fresh milk (*kegha*) or sour milk (*lölön* or *chë chö lölöte*) as a side dish. When there is no milk they used traditional vegetables like *ptanya*, *kïsoyö* or *sokoria*, to mention but a few. The latter is picked from a common deciduous tree called *tuyunwo* in Pökot, whose botanical name is *balanite aegyptica*.

As modern changes penetrate the community, there is more and more dependence between these two groups in what can be loosely termed as a barter trade. Even the eating habits have changed as the pastoralists also adopt a bit of agricultural foodstuff and the agriculturists too retain blood and milk, at least for their ceremonies. During the dry spells, for instance, people from Karapökot traverse the mountains of Lelan in search of grains from their fellow Pökot, which they get either through cash exchange or by giving honey, butter, or livestock in return. Similarly, when the people in Lelan are invaded by their erstwhile enemies, the Marakwet, they send an SOS message to their well-armed brothers in the plains (of Karapökot), who come and fight off the invaders at no cost save for the loot they take from the enemy (*punyon*).

For recreation, the old and young men together with male children sit around the evening bonfire and listen to riddles (*tyankoy*) and stories (*lökoy*) about their heroes and the majesty of the Pökot as a people, while women and girls are in the kitchen preparing food for the day. Other forms of recreation are characterized by games and singing in times of celebration (e.g., *sapana*), initiations (e.g., *ptengöwo*) and reconciliation (e.g., *parpara*). For girls and young women there are some forms of dances like *kedonga* and *chepelaleyo* that defy seasons and are held as often as possible.

Social Divisions and Classifications

The social arrangement of the Pökot community and its inherent values are manifested in the way a Pöchon introduces himself to a fellow Pöchon. If you meet a Pöchon for the first time, he will first tell you his name, then the name of his father, then his village (mountains, ridges or plains), his age grade and most importantly, he will elaborately describe his clan—going into what an outsider would see as unnecessary and trivial details of—its origin, its dos and don'ts and so forth. Our inquiry into this kind of self-introduction showed that the stranger wants to prove that he is a true Pöchon and as such subject to all duties and obligations that befall an adult male among the Pökot and also an object of all privileges that being a Pöchon bequeaths him.

---

77. These days, exclusive use of blood and milk has been left to warriors (*mrën*) who move with their herds in search of pasture during the dry season and live in a community of men only called *keporiak*. Those who remain at home (mainly old men, women and children) have, together with the people of grains (*pipö pagh*), resorted to using maize (also known as corn) to prepare food (*pan*) and as such millet and sorghum are only rarely used.

Clans play a very important role in the community life of the Pökot because it is these that help to identify true Pökot from tricksters. Every clan is well known in the Pökotland,[78] all ancestral founders of clans are known and all clan totems are a household talk. It is, however, not easy to establish the exact number of clans due to lack of consensus because of cultural differences between the people who live in East Pökot, those who live in West Pökot and those who live in the republic of Uganda, on the distinction between full clans and sub-clans. Visser's list of clans and sub-clans that was gathered in Amolem is, for instance, disputed in places like Kapenguria, Tiatiy, Lomut, Sook, Amudat and Amakuriat,[79] while many elders regard that of Plapan as unrepresentative of the Pökot clans and sub-clans.[80]

What further compounds the matter even more is the fact that elders have a right to disband some sub-clans if, for instance, their members are involved in too many accidents or catastrophes. It is thought that the ancestors are either not happy with the birth of the sub-clans, or some of their important members have indulged in some unacceptable social behavior. Thus, this disbandment only affects the particular sub-clan that has not prospered in the recent times and its members resort to their original mother clan as Plapan has explained.

> Clans have split but when met with calamity, the Council of elders of that clan sit down and examine why the new clan developed from the main clan. The decision may be taken to disband the later developed clan. For example, recently the silokot clan, whose totem is sirere or hawk, had a sub clans (sic)[81] called Chemakew, Chepochkok and the main Kapsokom. The elders discussed and resolved to disband all the other clans and use only the Kapsokom.[82]

For this reason, we only put down what seems to be agreeable to the people in all parts of the Pökotland. Each clan has a specific cattle ear mark and just by looking at a particular ear mark of any given cow one would tell to what clan it cows belongs. It is, however, common to see cows with different ear marks in a home, meaning that they belong to economic relatives (*tilyay*) from different clans. The other importance of the clan is to distinguish who can marry whom among the Pökot in order to avoid consanguinity, or so we think, since our informers only said it is a taboo for members of one clan to get married. Firstly, the members of the same clan cannot marry, since they are regarded as related in the sense that they have a common founder. Secondly, a boy or girl cannot marry from the clan of his or her mother up to the fourth generation.[83]

78. Due to population increase many sub-clans have developed and in such a case one is asked to name the mother clan and in some cases the grandmother clan together with their totems.

79. Visser (1989). Op. cit., 250–255.

80. Plapan, op. cit., 23–24.

81. Parentheses not in the original text.

82. Plapan, op. cit., 22.

83. F. P. Conant (1965). A Variable Unit of Social Space Among the Pokot of East Africa. In *American Anthropologist* (67:2), 318.

The third, and perhaps the most important, role of the clan is that once a girl comes out of seclusion (*ko pö chemeri*) she graduates in a special ceremony called *kïpuno*; then she abandons her old childhood (or maiden) name (also called 'medicine name') and gets a new clan name. If she is a first-born in the home she will be called *kaporet*, if second, she will be called *seretow* and if third born she will be called *cheperow*. If she is from a distant village and only 'jumped' into the ceremony she will be called *chesortum*. If, however, she was afraid of the knife she gets a derogatory name that is rather unpalatable to hear, that is, *chepta*.[84] Below is a table of clans, sub-clans, totems, ear marks and origins, arranged in an alphabetical order.

Table 1. Clans, Sub-clans, Totems, Cattle Ear Marks and Origins

NO	CLAN (OR)	SUB-CLAN	TOTEM (LILÖ)	EAR MARK	ORIGIN
11.	Kapilyon	Chepöcherïs, Chepörelo, Chepönyoryö	Dog (*Kukïy*)	Half of the ear is cut	Marich
22.	Kösom	Chepotintar, Chemitiny, Chepotïrim, Chepotiskaya, Chepokamolet	Bees (*Kösomyon*)	Square cuts at the edges of both ears	Tiyatiy (Baringo)
33.	Lëkenï	Chepurai, Chepökïpay, Chepönyonkï, Chemoyo, Chepöcherikïyech	Frog (*Pnyakaw*)	Cut on the point of one ear	Tugen
44.	Moyoi/ Rong	Cheposera, Cheposiya, Cheptangat, Chepökana, Chepochesundu, Chepocheptinti	Dove (*Kapan*)	Two cuts near the apex of the ear	Iten
55.	Oröyin	Cheplege, Chemusö, ChepongeremwaCheparsich, Chepeitum	Monitor (*Maratas*)	One cut on each ear	Keiyo
66.	Ptingo	Chepöchonkïl, Cheman, Chepöchepkataw	Snake (*Moröy*)	Three cuts near the apex of each ear	Kölköl
77.	Ptuyin	Chepösekerr, Chemichich, Chemirkew	Donkey (*Sikiryö*)	One broad cut	Mount Elgon

84. Another word that is closely related to *chepta* but is not restricted to clitoridectomy or circumcision is *chemnyokoria,* which refers to any coward in general, whether male or female.

NO	CLAN (OR)	SUB-CLAN	TOTEM (LILÖ)	EAR MARK	ORIGIN
88.	Riiy	Chepoyong, Chemoley, Chepokakiy, Chepsanak, Cheparchok, Chepöyong	Hyrax (*Kaner*)	Cut series on the edges of both ears	Tiatiy Hills
9.	Sanyökin	Chemanang, Chepötuyany, Chepökosöm, Chepsepa	Red-Ants (*Pirech*)	The ear is cut off at the root	Mösop
110.	Siköwo	Cheptakar, Chepösopön, Chepachikwa, Chepartïl	Bees (*Sakam*)	Four broad cuts on both ears	Karapökot
111.	Sïlökot	Chepökapsoköm, Chemakew, Cheparaw, Chepöcheptamus, Cheptoiton, Chengalit, Chepochompus, Chepöchpnyatïl	Hawk (*Sirörö*)	Half of the ear is cut off	Mwino
112.	Sïpan/ Kasopon	Chepötula, Chepoteltel, Chepökerieng, Cheptanï, Chepuryo, Cheptures	Elephant (*Pelyon*)	Three cuts near the apex of the ear	Tiatiy Hills (Baringo)
113.	Söchony	Cheptöyö, Cheparayï, Chepöchemuma, Cheparsich, Chemöset, Chemket	Lion (*Ngötïny*)	Small cuts from the points to the end of the ear	Moïpen (Eldoret)
114.	Sötöt	Cheplomin, Cheporwala, Chepotumewo, Chepokamuk, Chepokrel	Sun (*Asis*)	A narrow cut on both ears	Kanyierpit
115.	Talay	Chemingëny, Chepörït, Chepömurkü, Chepöchechentö	Baboon (*Mayos*)	Half of the ear is cut off	Marakwet
116.	Terik	Chepochepkai, Chepatet Chepatet, Cheparter, Chepösotim	Thunder (*Ilät*)	One broad cut	Mount Elgon
117.	Tinchön	Chepögh, Chepayös, Chepochepkok, Chepocheminyar	Hyena (*Kawagh*)	Both ears are cut in half	Tugen (Baringo)

NO	CLAN (OR)	SUB-CLAN	TOTEM (LILÖ)	EAR MARK	ORIGIN
116.	Toyoi	Chemirkakew, Chemirkwan, Cheposangiy, Chepöchepköntör	Bufallo (Sö)	Points of both ears are cut	Mösop
119.	Tul	Chepöyonto, Chepoghe, Chemining, Chepökatul, Chepöcheptïrök	Jackal (Chepkonö)	Both ears are cut in half	Marakwet

The Age-Set System

The social division among the Pökot is, among other things, characterized by the age-set system (pïn), which is exclusively male based and consists of men who were circumcised and initiated at the same time irrespective of one's background–family, clan or social status. They act as one body on all tribal (and sometimes family) matters and develop a strong bond of brotherhood among themselves, since they are 'age mates' (pïnwöy). Thus, in every generation, the Pökot community is stabilized by the activities of various age-sets (pïnwöy) that act together in harmony for a common goal, in all spheres of the community life. It was not clear from our informants whether age-sets have any specific role in cattle rustling or defense of the community in case of an attack from enemy communities. The main role of the age-set system seems to be presiding over rituals and to make political decisions during their tenure of community leaders-hip. However, a reigning age-set can, on certain occasions consult with an older age-set, though not necessarily the immediately preceding one.

There are twelve age sets sets among the Pökot people, consisting of nine major and three minor ones, plus a totem, which is referred to as an ornamental design. The minor age-sets are strategically placed in-between the major ones as if to separate them. The major age-sets are divided into three levels: there are senior members, middle and third level members and all share a common ornamental design. Then there is an age-set change, with each age-set lasting four years. This means that the nine, main age-sets take thirty-six years of alteration between them, before they can start from the first. Below is a list of the age-sets, their divisions and their ornamental designs arranged in an alphabetical order.

Table 2. Age Grade Levels, Years and Ornamental Designs

MAIN AGE GRADE	THREE LEVELS	YEARS	ORNAMENTAL DESIGN
1. Chumwö	Chonokopr	1st year	
	Kamashiap	2nd year	Zebra (*Ngetei*)
	Kapsaks	3rd year	
		4th year	
2. Kaplelach	Chonokopr	1st year	
	Kamashiap	2nd year	Monkey (*Monges*)
	Kapasaks	3rd year	
		4th year	
3. Koronkoro	Chonokopr	1st year	
	Kamashiap	2nd year	Warthog (*Mulunchö*)
	Kapsaks	3rd year	
		4th year	
4. Mayna	Chonokopr	1st year	
	Kamashiap	2nd year	Zebra (*Ngetei*)
	Kapsaks	3rd year	
		4th year	
5. Mürkutwo	Chonokopr	1st year	
	Kamashiap	2nd year	Guinea-fowl (*Mangarach*)
	Kapsaks	3rd year	
		4th year	
6. Nyonki	Chonokopr	1st year	
	Kamashiap	2nd year	Zebra (*Ngetei*)
	Kapsaks	3rd year	
		4th year	
7. Siroy	Chonokopr	1st year	
	Kamashiap	2nd year	Dikdik (*Siran*)
	Kapsaks	3rd year	
		4th year	
8. Sowö	Chonokopr	1st year	
	Kamashiap	2nd year	Impala (*Chemil*)
	Kapsaks	3rd year	

MAIN AGE GRADE	THREE LEVELS	YEARS	ORNAMENTAL DESIGN
		4th year	
9. Sumpay (Pköymot)	Chonokopr	1st year	
	Kamashiap	2nd year	Bees (*Sakam*)
	Kapsaks	3rd year	
		4th year	

The Pökot Astronomy

When talking about the Pökot astronomy, it would be wrong to think of it in the modern understanding of the science of heavenly bodies and the outer space. Theirs is just a study of the position of the stars (*kokel*), their constellation (*ara tipïn*), the Milky Way (*ara psör*), the Pleiades (*sïta*), the Orion (*koretaran*) the moon (*arawa*) and the sun (*asis*) in relation to the events happening here on earth (*yete nguny*). The Pökot astronomy was (and in many cases, still is) used to determine their secular, day-to-day events as well as for religious purposes. In the secular domain the sense of time, like counting of days or dates and seasons, is based on the position of the moon and the stars, particularly the Pleiades and the Orion. The moon, for instance, determines the twelve months of the Pökot year (*Mu*—January, *Tirtïr*—February, *Pokokwö*—March, *Rïkïsa*—April, *Pöröwö*—May, *Melwon*—June, *Sukukï*—July, *Mkeyon*— August, *Tapach*—September, *Kïpsit*—October, *Kokelyan*—November and *Kwöghe*—December) and its four seasons (*kömöy*—dry season, *sangartat*—beginning of wet season, *pengat*—wet season and *kïtokot*—beginning of dry season).

When making an appointment a Pöchon will, for instance, say: 'I will come when the moon is (or the Pleiades are) in such and such position'. Other events determined by the position of the moon and the stars include the timing of initiation ceremonies, the rites of passage, migration of livestock to any given areas for grazing and cattle raiding. In the sacred domain these heavenly bodies helped the seers and diviners to predict and to ward off the danger by determining the necessary steps that needed to be taken so as to avert catastrophes. Among the things they foretold were: pending invasions from other tribes, approaching droughts and epidemics, to mention but a few. Meyerhoff has recorded a personal interview with a Pökot elder in this regard and she reports thus: "By the position of the morning star, P'katieny told me, his people could predict if their small children would stay healthy or when it would rain."[85]

In order to predict when the rainfall will come, for example, the Pökot looked at the position of *töpogh*, that is, the positions of the Morning Star and the Evening Star (the planets Mars and planet Venus, respectively) vis-à-vis each other. When the

---

85. Meyerhoff (1982). Op. cit., 121.

latter (which they say is a female) is ahead or 'on top' of the former (which they say is a male) then there is no rain, but when the opposite is the case, then the rains would come. The positions of the stars guided all their actions and if something happened that they did not expect, they always consulted a diviner or a seer (*werkoyon*).[86] Then he/she would trace it to some sin of commission or omission and then recommend some kind of offering to the ancestors, who were said to be displeased.

Chi (The Pökot Concept of a Person)

The Pökot believe that *Tororöt* (God)[87] created human beings (referring only to the Pökot people but not their enemies—*püng*) out of the clay from an anthill (*tulwö*)[88] and put them on earth. He blessed them with land (*kor*), livestock (*kyak*), especially cows (*tich*), and children (*monïng*). But also, when there is drought, God sends his deities to provide for the people, even if with agricultural products.[89] Being a creation of God the almighty, a person then is supposed to endure in life and stand like an unshaken rock (*kögh*) or mountain (*kutïng*); and as such death is the worst enemy to humankind. Indeed, when elders or parents are blessing their children and wish them prosperity, one of the most commonly used phrases is, "stand like this or that mountain."[90] People avoid talking about death and funeral rites are carried out in complete silence, mainly at night. In this regard, the Pökot culture has a very big problem with the Christian Easter celebrations, and in particular the Easter triduum that starts on Holy Thursday through Saturday; because they see God as glorifying the death of his own Son. The ideal life, among them, is somehow materialistic. It comprises of an elderly man who has gone through all rites of passage, and is surrounded by plenty of cows and children. Thus, when Mbiti says that 'Africans are notoriously religious', this should not be understood to exclude the material aspect of religiosity; because the African views a person holistically, without compartmentalizing between the various human faculties.[91]

---

86. There seems to be no difference in name (and at times in functions) between a seer and a diviner among the Pökot. A seer who predicts a major disaster to the community is called *werkoyon* and when they go to a diviner to learn what the position of the stars portends, they again say that they are going to consult a *werkoyon*.

87. The word *Tororöt* is derived from the word *oror*, which means 'the famous one'; hence God is the most famous or the highest One, over and above everyone else. Their knowledge about God, as manifested in God's attributes, is only through inference, that is, the denial of what is negative in human beings and pre-eminence of what is positive.

88. The doctrine of *creatio ex nihilo* (creation out of nothing) sounds nonsensical to the Pökot, because for them, it is a simple postulate that either something comes out of something, or nothing at all comes out of nothing (this thinking is in line with the Latin expression, *ex nihilo nihil fit* . . . out of nothing comes nothing).

89. Visser (1989). Op. cit., 11–12.

90. Ibid., 103.

91. Mbiti (1995). Op. cit., 1.

Eschatology among the Pökot is both vague and anthropomorphic, as nobody knows, for sure, what happens to a person after death.[92] Only one thing is clear: the person is gone for good, he/she is finished, at least in the physical sense. However, it is also expected that the deceased joins the ancestors and continues leading a life just like our own with a lot of (good or bad) influence on the people on earth. If one died as a good person, he/she is expected to continue being good out there and vice-versa. If one died rich it is expected that he will continue with his wealth and so should one's wealth disperse after his death, the generally accepted expression is that 'his wealth has followed him' (presumably because he needs it out there). Thus, there is no concept of resurrection among the Pökot; what they have is remembrance and as such reference to life after death is only limited to the Christian circles. This brings with it the difficulty of the Christian doctrine on the miracle of Jesus being stronger than death as it lacks an indigenous conceptual correspondence in the Pökot language.

Pökot anthropology regards the heart, the head and the shadow of a person as the most important parts of the body.[93] The head registers all things from outside the person, while the heart is credited with feelings, encouragement and refusal. These two are thought to form the center of one's personality and are thus evoked in the moments of crisis, say, like when one must take an oath (*muma*). Indeed, all evil desires and even curses (but also blessings as well) are thought to originate from these parts of the body. The will of a human being is understood to reside in the chest, particularly the lungs; while it is agreed that emotions dwell in the stomach and especially the belly. Thus, people considered to be good or kind are referred to as 'people with good stomachs'. When a person has an inclination towards something one makes reference to his or her stomach: 'my stomach tells me/wants/desires. . . (*meranin/mochanin/mokanin mu. . .*)'.

The shadow of a person is also very significant and there exists three words for it, *rurwö*, *kïtontögh* and *kïmïr*. The Pökot distinguish between the human shadow that is also projected by an inanimate object, which is static (*rurwö*), the shadow that cannot be grasped or touched, which moves with a person and it is believed to leave the body at the time of death (*kïtontögh*). This is the shadow that connects the body to the outside world.[94] Hence the Pökot believe that a dead body has no shadow, and if it has, then it is simply the object shadow. Then there is a lighter,

---

92. Based on this vagueness there developed a historical phenomenon in the early 1950s whereby a religion from the neighboring Luhya land (*Dini ya Msambwa*, also called *Mafuta ya Roho*, *msango* or *masankwï* in the Pökot language), led by one, Elijah Masinde, promised its followers free material things here on earth and ultimately to take them to Zion at the end of times. One of its prominent Pökot leaders was Lukas Pkech, but it was finally suppressed by the colonial government (Visser 1989: 39–48), only to reappear after independence and it still has a sizeable following in mountainous regions of Pökotland.

93. Visser (1989). Op. cit., 104.

94. Ibid., 104.

faster more vague shadow that only the spiritual beings or the extraordinary people can communicate with (*kïmïr*).[95]

Finally, the Pökot measure an individual's worth as a person to the extent that he works, or fails to work in conjunction with others, always in reference to the community norms and tenets. This means upholding community's standards, morals and social demeanor and to subscribe to all that is dear to the community. Outside the community, one is considered to be perverted and so having lost one's humanity, as is the case with witches and other social misfits, who are normally condemned to death by the society. A young man who has never gone to school summed up this notion when he told us that he couldn't grow as a person outside the community. "I am a person, yes, but I can only grow into maturity and later become an ancestor within the community. Otherwise I remain like a stump (*mïsik*) or a rock (*kögh*) that neither grows nor develops."[96]

The human soul (*mïkulow*) is believed to be in constant interaction with the ancestors who bestow some supernatural powers to those they deem fit. These are regarded as extra-ordinary people and as such they have special roles in the community. Some of them (like witches—*ponü*, and sorcerers—*mutin*) are thought to cause misfortune and others (like medicine women—*chepsakitis*, diviners—*chemowos* and seers—*werkoy*) are thought to promote the well-being of the land, animals and the community in general. A confrontation or collision with the former group of people is avoided as much as possible while the latter group officiates in rituals of purification (e.g. *parpara*). They also pronounce collective blessings done in the name of the community. In this context, the understanding of a person is that of a relationship, as has Nkemnkia has summarized it:

> The Other is another Self. The I is lost in the You; the You and the I is lost in the We. We are the living beings. Every time we talk about man, we should not think of a concept, but of humankind in its real and substantial unity. Through the category of relation each one places himself in front of the other and considers himself as the Other of the Other. In this hierarchy of values no one is better than the other and no one can be his very self outside the relation with the others. No other law, except the one of living together can constrain anyone to work for the common good. Everyone knows how to belong to a

---

95. In this regard, the Pökot concept of a person was found to be closely related to the biblical understanding of the same in which the Hebrews used tangible body organs such as the heart, kidneys, throat and breath (Lawrence Boadt (1984). *Reading the Old Testament: An Introduction*. New York: Paulist Press, 247). Indeed, the basic quality of human life is denoted by the word *nephesh* (נֶפֶשׁ), which is equivalent to the Pökot word *mïkulöw*, both of which are translated as soul or wind. In general, the Old Testament uses various words, all of which refer to a human being, that is, a person in his or her integral unity. Among them is the soul (*nephesh*—נֶפֶשׁ), denoting the act of being alive and dynamic, the spirit (*ruah*—רוּחַ, in Pökot, *yomöt*), denoting human will and determination, and the flesh (*basar*—בָּשָׂר, in Pökot, *por*), to denote human weakness (Genesis 2: 7; Psalms 51: 10).

96. Pkemoi wero Kapelinyang is a 22-year-old man from Kewawa, married and has two children.

community which takes care of each member. All acts by individuals or the community are motivated by love, by solidarity with everyone.[97]

The Pökot Belief System and Religious Practice

The Pökot have their own indigenous belief system and religious practice, variously referred to as Pökoot religion,[98] Pakot moral system[99] or Pakot religious life,[100] which encompasses their entire life and is characterized by a sense of mystery and awe. For this reason, there is no word for 'religion' and also no distinct religious practices set aside from the rest of individual or community life. For the indigenous Pökot believer, the river is as holy as the mountain and so is the traditional shrine; a trait also manifested among the Pökot Christians, who do not regard the church to be any holier than the mountain or the cave. When it rains heavily and the lightning and thunderstorm strike, that is holy because the rain Spirit, *Ilat,* it passing on a message to the people.

When the drought persists, the elders have to go to the sacred mountain and sacrifice an animal in a salient moment of prayer. And that, too, is holy. Indeed, for the Christian Pöchon, the same reverence accorded to the church or the tabernacle is also accorded to the traditional medicine woman (*chepsakitian*), because both of them heal, albeit in different ways. When the agricultural Pökot are going to break new grounds for cultivation, they do it ceremoniously in order to appease the spirits of the forest lest they get angry and destroy their crops, and that is religious. Once they have reaped the first harvest from the land, they do it in a special thanksgiving ritual, and that too is religious. Indeed, religion permeates the very fabric of the Pökot society; making good Mbiti's famous dictum that Africans are notoriously religious.[101]

However, the same lack of distinction between the sacred and the secular can be advanced to argue that Africans are notoriously secular, or negatively put, Africans are not, after all, notoriously religious. Platvoet and van Rinsum have advanced such an argument, claiming that "…it is a masterful counter-invention against the numerous European 'inventions of Africa', from classical times till now."[102] And that it is in particular, those 'inventions' that were a dismissal of religiosity among Africans. Here,

97. Nkemnkia, op. cit., 201–202.
98. Visser (1989). Op. cit.
99. Schneider (1955). Op. cit.
100. Schneider (1959). Op. cit.

101. Although scholars have criticized this statement more than once on the ground that it is too general, it is our opinion that more often than not this has been out of the context. Traditionally speaking, no Pökot is irreligious; every community member is an automatic adherent of the Pökot Religion into which he or she is born, but when it comes to Christianity (or any other 'exotic' faith for that matter) that is a different matter. The Pökot need a more convincing argument (not just a simple explanation) as to why they should abandon their old faith (*kighanat nyo pö köny*), which has served them so well, for the new faith (*kighanat nyo rel*).

102. Jan Platvoet & Van Rinsum (2003). Is African Incurably Religious? Confessing and Contesting an Invention. In *Exchange* Vol 32:2, April, 123.

again, lies the very real danger of falling prey to Ryle's 'category-mistake' by using a modern concept of religiosity or secularization to deny a traditional concept of the same, without paying due attention to the differences or incompatibility in the meanings of these two sets of categories.[103] On his part, p'Bitek warns against such misuse of concepts concerning the idea of God in Africa. "The interpretation of African deities in terms of the Christian God does not help us understand the nature of the African deities as Africans conceive them."[104]

Thus, it is logically perfect to argue that the Pökot are both notoriously religious and notoriously irreligious. The two statements are neither mutually exclusive nor contradictory. They are a simple contrariety that poses no logical dilemma. On matters religious, every Pöchon is extremely religious; it is not even possible for anyone to think of not being religious; say, by not partaking in communal religious activities. Then on matters secular, every Pöchon is equally extremely secular and they fully enjoy all earthly goodies that come with that secularity without any reservation or fuss.

The Pökot traditional faith is grounded on the cosmology that sees the universe as made of the world, heaven and God's abode, which is above the sky (*yim*). There seems to be no concept of the 'underworld' where the evil spirits live because the Pökot hold that evil people go to Mount Kadam (near the border with Uganda) once they die, whereas all the righteous and upright ones go to Mount Mtelo. This belief system seems to contradict Schneider's assertion that, ". . .the Pakot, like most Nilotics, lack a systematic verbalized cosmology, although under the surface there seems to be a complex system of beliefs about the nature of the universe."[105] The Pökot teaching about nature, man and heaven is a result of the teachings imparted by the elders to their young people in their day-to-day life experiences and particularly during the seclusion period after circumcision.

The indigenous Pökot religion is a strictly monotheistic one although many writers have mistaken it for pantheism or animism, because the Pökot believe that God has given a unifying spirit (*onyöt*)[106] to all people, animals, plants, and inanimate objects, and even to the heavenly bodies. One of our informants had this to say:

> We, the Pökot, believe in God (*Tororöt*), whose abode is in the sky (*Yim*) beyond the stars, moon, the sun and all other heavenly bodies. We see His wonderful work in the many things He has given us free of charge— good land, animals and children. We see His Majesty in the mountains (*kutingkot*), rivers (*lalwatin*), and in lightning (*kirial*) and thunder (*tilet*) as controlled by

---

103. Ryle's (1955). Op. cit., 16–18.
104. p'Bitek (1970). Op. cit., 59.
105. Schneider (1959). Op cit., 157.

106. There was no agreement among our informers on the correct Pökot translation of the word 'spirit': some regarded it as *onyöt*, others as *mikulöw* (heart) while still others considered it as *yomöt* (wind). We settled for the former because it does not seem to have another meaning besides that of spirit.

Ilat, which is the guardian of life and death. Through it, God punishes the evil ones and warns the errant. *Ilat* is, therefore, regarded as a lifesaver because God is in it and in water generally, without which no one could be alive. This should not be construed to mean that *ilat* is a sort of a god or an independent deity, but rather that God manifests himself in a more special way in it than he does in other natural phenomena like the sun (*asis*), moon (*arawa*) and the stars (*kokel*).[107]

Upon further inquiry with regard to this being, *Ilat*, he explained that it only acts on behalf of Tororöt, particularly as a guardian against blasphemy. *Ilat* is a kind of a super being or semi-deity that controls the flow and effects of the rain, the lightning and thunder and keeps them from harming innocent people. Some Pökot (especially from the central part of Pökotland) hold that the sickness brought forth by thunder (called *yomöt*) is accidental and one does not have to be a sinner to fall victim. For others (particularly the *Kasauria*) though, *yomöt* does not just get a person; one must have gone astray in one way or another in order to fall victim. These believe that *Ilat* punishes the errant, say, by sending sickness like paralysis or any other seemingly incurable disease to the sinner and for full recovery to take place one must confess one's mistakes.

The Pökot people are, however, in agreement that *yomöt* cannot be treated by modern medicine and so going to the hospital is a waste of time. When a person has tried all known medication without success then, he/she goes to a medicine woman (*chepsakitian*) who identifies the effects of *ilat* (called *tiompö lalwa* or *tiompö yim*) and sends the person for traditional treatment (*kilokat*) where they find out the color of the *tilet* (thunder) that struck the patient and then it is appeased by slaughtering a goat of the same colour and through incantations she sends off these bad effects of *Ilat*, and the person gets well. Although our informants could not explain the cultural reasons behind it, they observed that *yomöt* treatment is only carried out by women while other treatments, like reversing a curse, are done by men only.[108]

Communal worship among the Pökot is not an everyday happening. This is a special occasion that may be prompted either by a certain calamity (e.g., drought) or a thanksgiving ceremony after a year's bumper harvest. A diviner says what will be offered to *Tororöt*, the colour of the sacrificial animal and how the offering should be made: the place of offering and the time. The elders then sit in a semicircle (*kirket*) and the 'priests' proceed to slaughter the animal. They utter prayers to *Tororöt* while the rest of the men reply in the affirmative. Those present eat part of the meat and leave the rest of the meat for *Tororöt* and the good or bad ancestors to eat, depending on the nature of the sacrifice.[109]

107. Interview with Ibrahim Kotit.
108. Visser (1989). Op. cit., 33.
109. It appeared to us that blessing has a binary value because it always went hand in hand with curse. The Elders would pray to *Tororöt* to grant blessings to the Pökot people (that they get all good

The ordinary form of prayer among the Pökot, at home, has been individual and was said by the head of the family, early in the morning. The man wakes up before sunrise, raises his hands up towards the sky, spits towards the rising sun and utters some prayer as follows, *Sörö Tororöt*[110] *ompö kingarakatengu nyopö asna* (or *amna*) *ntakwit ye* (Thank you God for your help last evening (or last night) up to this time): thus, blessing *Tororöt* and offering himself and his family to *Tororöt*. By doing that, the head of the family will have 'consecrated' himself and all his wealth (i.e., cattle, sheep, goats, children and wives) to *Tororöt* and asked his guidance throughout the day. In the evening, too, the head of the family will again thank *Tororöt* for a good day and for protecting him and his wealth from all harm. Other forms of prayers are said when a person is sick, particularly when the sickness has persisted for a long time.

When normal herbal medication would not work it required a witchdoctor (*chepsakeyon*) to come and offer special treatment to the patient and say prayers to appease the evil spirits (*oy*), since it was believed that they were responsible for any misfortune that befell the family. Even today, another 'latent' form of prayer manifests itself whenever elders meet to drink their local brew. A bit of it is poured down for the ancestors to drink, and this also happens when an animal is slaughtered: a little blood has to be shed in their honor.

The Pökot Cultural Values

There are many cultural values among the people of West Pökot, but due to space and the scope of this research, we will only mention the most important ones and those that are relevant to our study. Thus, we will only talk about the cow (*tany*), its cultural relationship with women, and the rites of passage. Then we will look at how these values impact on the life of the Pökot people in general.

Tany (A Cow)

The most valued thing among the Pökot is a cow (*tany* whose plural is *tich*). A cow is, practically speaking, the lifeline of the pastoral Pökot. It is from a cow that they get their food (i.e., milk, blood and meat); from a cow, they get the household items like drinking 'cups' (the horns are used by many for this purpose) and other valuables in the household. A cow is also used to pay the bride price for their wives, to pay fines and also to be given out as a present. For all these reasons, a person's wealth is

---

things in life, like rain, cattle, children and health) and in the same breath curse their enemies (that they get all bad things in life, like pestilence, drought and hunger).

110. It is important to note here that the Pökot hardly mentioned this name, unless there was a ritual offering to *Tororöt* but when the missionaries translated their God into *Tororöt* and started using it with ease and indiscriminately; Pökot Christians followed suit and eventually influenced the rest of the people. But even today, elderly men and women (most of whom are not Christians) hardly mention the name *Tororöt*, if at all.

measured in accordance with the number of the cows he has. "*Tera monechu*" (listen children), an informant told us, "*anyïn tany aki sopon*" (a cow is sweet and (it is) life (itself). [111] A cow for a Pöchon then is everything for his/her very existence. Against this background, a Pökot child is taught; from the very tender age not only to respect and love a cow, but also to cling to it even if it means death.

Thus, the Pökot believe that all cows in the world (the entire limits of their environment) belong to them. Just like the Maasai,[112] the Pökot went (and many still go) for cattle raiding expeditions, also called cattle rustling—*lük*[113] with the understanding that they are proving their bravery as warriors by 'bringing' back home what rightfully belongs to them. Lopsikur explains the reason for these cattle raiding missions:

> A young man is considered to be a real warrior if he brought home a herd of his own cattle. Then women will surround him and sing his praises for coming back, from such a dangerous but worthwhile mission in peace; with girls beseeching him to marry them, while asking other young men to emulate his courageous action. This brings about wealth, prestige to the individual and high status within the community. It is against this background that every young Pöchon struggles to see to it that he has brought home a herd of misplaced cattle from our *püng* (enemies). Since it is only in this way that one proves himself to be a crafty warrior, capable not only of defending a home but also attacking an enemy and bringing back our cattle home—*ronghu tuacha kaw*. Cattle rustling, then, is seen more like traditional war games or war dances and show of strength, in which combatants try to outwit each other, rather than theft.[114]

On the question of what would happen if a warrior was killed in cattle raiding expedition, he had this to say: "If a young man died during a raid mission, he would have died for a just cause and that brings fame, wealth and status to his people. He becomes a hero, just as it would have been the case if we were attacked by enemies and people die while protecting our property."[115] From this, one apparently sees that cattle rustling among the Pökot—just as it is the case with other pastoralists, like the Maasai—is not regarded as theft. In fact, stealing (especially a cow) is regarded as an abominable crime. If a person stole a cow belonging to a fellow Pöchon, the fine meted out against him is to pay four-fold (because they count the legs of the stolen cows).

---

111. Clement Lopsikur is a 70-year-old, respected elder in his community, within Chepareria Division, and has been a church leader for a long time. He is also an authority on traditional matters among the Pökot.

112 See the work of Donovan, op. cit., 15.

113. We use the term cattle rustling in general, as the expression of the Pökot term *lük*, but cattle raiding as an expression of specific incidents of cattle rustling, which is normally inter-ethnic.

114. Interview with Clement Lopsikur.

115. Idem.

Since a cow occupies a central position in the life the Pökot, most of their wisdom and day-to-day life experiences are expressed within the context of a cow.

They, therefore, have numerous proverbs and sayings that use a cow as a symbol of learning and indeed the major contributory factor in their very existence. An oft quoted example of these is the most celebrated idiomatic expression that goes like this: *anyin tany aki ngwan*—a cow is sweet and it is also sour. This is to say that in life everything, no matter how good it may be, has its goodness and badness too; or rather, nothing is perfectly good or wholly bad. This proverb is used to warn people against irrational euphoria over victory or complete pessimism over failure. That there is always a second chance of grace in which one can do better.

Among the sayings that relate their teachings to a cow is one that has to do with happiness or pleasure: *Anyin la chepö roryon*—as sweet as colostrum, i.e., the milk of a cow that has just calved (especially for the first time). This expression is used to refer to something that has brought a lot of blessings to a person or to the family. It is also another way of saying that one has enjoyed something (say), like eating particular food. In a nutshell, the value of a cow among the Pökot is summarized by Visser as follows:

> Their life centres around the cattle. The ideal of every Pökot is to keep animals. A man without animal is looked upon as dead. Cattle are in the first place a means of subsistence. Blood is taken from them every month; cows are milked; oxen give meat. The Pökot make clothes, blankets, and shoes from the skins. The animals play a role in social relations, notably marriage, which is not only a union of individuals but also of families. They also have great ritual value, for one needs the skin or chime for the rituals or ceremonies. At a certain age every boy is given an ox, called a 'prize-ox', about which he composes his songs and after which he is named; one is known by his ox name, which is shouted in war when one is spearing the enemy. Cattle are the objects of raids on the neighbouring tribes. They are a form of legal tender and considered a mobile bank. They give a man prestige and wealth. They give him meat and clothes. They are the means for blessing and purification.[116]

Relationship Between Cows and Women

The Pökot lifestyle is basically centered on relationships between people and between people and animals (both domestic and wild). For instance, there is a strong relationship between the Pökot as a community and wild animals in the totem system, where a certain clan, or age-set, is said to be related to a given kind of wild animal and the sanctions are that you cannot kill this animal and have to treat it in the same way you would treat your human relatives. The intention of this section, however, is to examine the existing relationship between the cow and the Pökot women. During our fieldwork we

---

116. Visser (1983). Op. cit., 15.

discovered a deep rooted and interesting relationship between women and the cows. For example, we noted that it is the women who milk the cows; it is they who prepare the calabashes to store the milk and indeed to treat it so that it does not go bad and can last for up to six months. They even use the cow dung to smear both the walls and floor of their houses so that finally in the homestead you are surrounded by everything that has something to do with the cow.

As mentioned above, a cow is the bloodline of life among the Pökot; but more than that, a woman is the natural carrier of this life. This means that the two are partners in the struggle to ensure the survival and continuation of the Pökot, as a race and a people. The pivotal role played by these two is seen in the way they are treated within the social arrangement. It is a basic requirement for every Pökot man to get married and raise a family; yet it is only the cow that can see you through into this marital status, that is, you use a cow to get a woman who, in turn, bears children for you. Moreover, once a woman gets married, she is given a number of cows to help her nurture the life she will bring forth in her new home. It is a big disappointment then, if she fails to give birth since, as it were, there is nothing to nurture. In this regard a woman has special tasks towards that which enabled her to 'get a house' (as the Pökot refer to getting married) and nurture her children's life, i.e., the cow. These tasks include feeding the calves, watering the cows, and, in a particular way, milking (*pöghisyö*).

Hence, the latter is regarded as work (*pöghisyö*) *per excellence*, since it brings the labor of a shepherd into fruition, when the whole family has milk to feed on; hence creating harmony (*pöghisyö*) not only in the family but also in whole community. As we can see above, the Pökot use the same word to refer to milking (which is done by women), work (which only has meaning when it feeds the family—in this case milking) and harmony (which is the goal of life in the Pökot community), indicating that the three enjoy a special relationship. In this light, beautiful women in particular and good people in general are said to have 'a heart like that of a cow' (*lenye mikulow nyopö tany*), which means that they are as admirable as the cows are. And yet a cow still seems to enjoy special status because it is commonly said that it is better for a person to walk with a cow than with a woman (*kaykay küweste chi nko tany kïtil nko korka*)!

Side Effects

With regard to the amount of dedication that the Pökot have to the cow, Schneider has observed and commented that, "The amount of attention devoted to cattle seems to be the chief cause for lack of elaboration in other aspects of life—religious, political, aesthetic and so forth—for which there is little time or inclination."[117] Although we are hesitant to take Schneider's words literally, the point is already made that the Pökot

---

117. Schneider (1955). Op. cit., 404.

have a special dedication to cattle that seem to be lacking towards all other things. A memorable incident took place in one of these pastoralists' areas whereby a child was killed during cattle raiding; people instinctively forgot about the dead child and followed the stolen animals. It is even said that should the father of a home return from a journey, his questions dwell mostly on how his livestock (and especially the cattle), rather than his wife (or wives) and children, have been fairing during his absence. The discussion is said to proceed something like this:

Pöghisyö monechi—how are you children?

Mi kyak lapay (koroti kyak lapay)—are all animals safe?

Kirany gham (püng) tuka (aköroti mösöwonte)—have the enemies attacked the cattle?

Whether this is actually true or not, the very existence of such stories has led some scholars into think that the Pökot value cattle more than children. While we did not find any evidence on the ground, to corroborate such an attitude, there are several practices among men that can easily be interpreted and generalized as the official Pökot attitude on the importance of children vis-à-vis the value of a cow.

Lük (Cattle Rustling)

Lük, variously referred to as cattle raiding or cattle rustling, is an age-old practice between the Pökot and their neighbors that pervades their entire lifestyle, irrespective of whether they are Christians or not. It has to be noted that the Pökot in the Karapökot area stopped circumcising their boys because of armed raids from their Karimojong and Turkana neighbors who do not practice it.[118] Cattle raiding is a culturally sanctioned practice that even has a religious connotation. It is a communal affair that all members of the community (men, women, children and the ancestors) have a mandatory obligation to partake in. Women are, specifically charged with the responsibility of protecting their sons by always wearing a belt of beads, called *lökötyö* during the entire cattle raiding expedition.

Girls have a duty to welcome the warriors back home and sing their praises after a successful raid, while it is incumbent on the boys to care for the loot as the raiders bask in the glory of their achievement. The warriors and elders carefully plan the so-called official raids, which involve tens or even hundreds of young men. They send spies to the enemy tribe who will go and locate the position of the cows, the number of the people minding them and the kind of weaponry they have. Then the seer (*werkoyon*) must be consulted to predict the success of the raid and if he advises against it then it is postponed. Once he gives a go ahead, then the warriors undergo a cleansing ceremony, called *kölölyon*, so that should they die during the raid then they

---

118. Ndegwah (2004). Op. cit., 87.

are accepted in the community of the ancestors as heroes. It is during this time that the seer spells out the rules of engagement and says what the raiders should do and what they should not do, the route they should take and whether the enemy warriors are to be killed when captured, which, however, is not the tradition.

If, during the raid, a warrior kills an enemy and, say, captures his wife or children (who are never killed because they are only regarded as the 'belongings' of the enemy—*punyon*), he becomes a *de facto* leader of future cattle raiding expeditions. He is not allowed to rejoin the community until he is officially reconciled in the ritual of *parpara*, and then honored by special incision marks, on the right-hand side of the body, or on the arm. This is because, as one informant, told us: "Killing a person, even an enemy, turns your blood bad and the victim can easily possess the killer if not cleansed."[119] The special ritual distinguishes the hero from the rest of the warriors, since he becomes a *kölölyon* and receives special healing powers over the weak people in the community—mainly pregnant mothers and small children.

Sickness

Should a child fall sick and it happens that there is no money to take him/her to the hospital; the father does not seem to care much as this is considered to be the mother's business. If she asks for medication money, the father will only give if he has some extra money. If, for instance, there is no money and, say, he has to sell his prized ox, then he would rather the child heals naturally or dies because, he is capable of begetting another one, yet he cannot get another prize ox (*kamar*).

Keporiak (Cattle Camping)

During the dry season, all able-bodied men travel hundreds of kilometers in search for pasture (even if it means going as far afield as the Republic of Uganda) and they can live there for one, two, or three months (and in some rare cases even up to six months) in 'men only communities' called *keporiak*. All this time the men do not exactly know what is happening to their families and seemingly, this does not matter much as long as the animals are safe and eat well.

Bride Price

Marriage is one of the most prized social happenings in the Pökot community and an unmarried person cannot command any respect culturally. Although there is nothing inherently wrong with this, some parents tend to value the animals they get

---

119. Interview with Nicholas Tukei, a former catechist and successful livestock and agricultural farmer.

when they marry off their daughters more than their general welfare. Thus, it is not uncommon to see that many parents have no regard to the opinion of their daughters on the question of who they would like to marry. They just marry them off to people they do not even love, or very old people who sometimes treat them like objects, just to get rich. It is seemingly never a problem with them whether these girls are happy in their married life or not.

Human Sacrifice

Traditionally, the Pökot practiced what Nathanson would call an 'immoral'[120] and perhaps atavistic culture of sacrificing a human being in the face of extreme danger that threatened the whole community. During famine they tried very much to see what they could do in order to stabilize the situation, which was normally seen as an imbalance between natural and supernatural forces. This could have been a revenge act from some angry ancestor(s) or simply a punishment from *Tororöt* (God) resulting from people's iniquities. Should the situation have deteriorated to the extent that cattle started dying, then they went to a soothsayer, who at times recommended human sacrifice if a catastrophe of all cattle, and subsequently all people dying, was to be averted.

Although, in principle, the Pökot value human life over anything else, they value it, not in isolation but within the parameters of the community. Hence, they regarded it proper to do away with one person's life in order to save the entire community from extinction. They took the most beautiful and well-behaved virgin and offered her to God as 'a living sacrifice'. However, an elderly woman was never sacrificed, not even an elderly man or a young warrior. The reason given to us in this regard is that offering a virgin was a sign of both purity and innocence and that *Tororöt* is a male, hence the reasonableness of giving Him a girl for a wife.[121]

Although this practice is generally no longer in force and we did not come across any person that had actually witnessed it, the elders, particularly in Karapökot, agreed that they at one time or another heard about it and that it could be still be going on secretly. One such story is told of a girl (Chesinon) who was given out to the god of rain (*Ilat*), after a very severe drought. Her boyfriend went and rescued her, with the help of the lady who told him the secret of *Ilat's* power, and so he speared him when he produced green lightning. At least one person said that as recently as 1980 a man advised his own sister to go to school so that she could be far away from the community, otherwise she was likely to be sacrificed in case of any catastrophe in the community.

---

120. Stephen Nathanson (2001). *An Eye for An Eye? The Immorality of Punishing by Death.* 2nd ed. New York: Rowman & Littlefied Publishers, Inc.

121. This explanation can be regarded as wanting for two reasons: one, we only heard it in one part of the Pökotland and two; we did not come across anybody who had a personal experience with this offering of girls to *Ilat,* or even to *Tororöt* (both of whom are said to be male). However, it is worth noting that terrible as such an incident maybe it is still in people's consciousness.

One can easily think that human beings were being sacrificed in order to save the life of animals. Our numerous discussions with elderly people over this issue, coupled with the emphasis that the Pökot do value animals over children, made us form an opinion that this has something to do with the unuttered cultural theme that the latter are not yet fully human until they reach the circumcision age and have graduated from the ritual. Then they can get married and start their own families as adults. However, this instance of humanity still has the potentiality to be enhanced and strengthened by subsequent rites of passage until one reaches full maturity at death and hence gracefully passes on to 'ancestorhood'. For us, here lies the answer to the question why the warriors going for cattle raids have to undergo a special cleansing ceremony in order to be accepted to this community (of ancestors) in case they died in battle. Otherwise they would be banished from the community having died without undergoing the necessary rites of passage that qualify them as worthy members of the spiritual community.

Lack of Education

With the country's economy changing, some Pökot people have resorted to education as the only guarantee for a better (economic) future. However, most of them do not as yet see the need for education and so they let their children stay at home taking care of their large herds of cattle. Another question that could be raised is that of the relevance of the current market-oriented education system to the Pökot (or in general, pastoralist) way of life. Most educated young men and women become alienated from their own homes and villages, where they were born and brought up. They disappear and take up paid jobs in cities and only rarely come home; thus, hardening the hearts of the elders against education. "Pakot arguments against schooling are clear," says Schneider, "First, small boys assist in herding small stock, and putting them in school makes this impossible. Second, they see no value in learning reading, writing, or arithmetic; they do not envy the European ways and have no desire to emulate them."[122] When all is said and done, the question still remains, do the Pökot value animals more than children? We put this question to one old man who nearly ran amok with surprise.

> *Ooch wech wena, ne kite nya eh* (what man, what is wrong with you)? We Pökot know all too well that a cow is terribly important for our survival, dignity and all that is good within our social situation, but an animal cannot be more important than a child. An animal remains just that, an animal. Children are our heirs and when we are no more they take over the continuation of the race and keep our traditions alive. No cow, no matter how much prized can do that. We want to have many and healthy cows for the good of our children—to get

---

122. Schneider (1959). Op. cit., 159.

them wives, take them through the rites of passage and help them live a life full of harmony, which is *pöghisyö*.[123]

The Pökot Social Wisdom

With regard to the passing on of the Pökot cultural wisdom, riddles, proverbs, idiomatic expressions and sayings are used. While the last three are strictly used for teaching, riddles (*tyankoy*) have a dual purpose. They are used partly to teach and partly to entertain young people in the evening. They are normally in the form of a dual contest, the one setting the riddle says, '*tyankoy*', then the opponent answers '*tyo*' or '*cheptongu*'. A few examples of these will suffice: *Chemurio manyigh pögh*—Chemurio never gets enough water, *Nyelnyel mokilany*—Always struggling but never climbs and *Kewer meril kata kamas*—A leopard has (just) passed beside the house. When the opponent is unable to answer he/she is asked to figuratively give out something, say a cow, a town or so.

Then the person who set the riddle gives the answer and then gives his/her opponent a chance to set his/her own riddle and the process continues until at the end they see who has accumulated more imaginary gifts. Answers to the above riddles are: *tulwö* (anthill), *sirmyon* (neck chain) and *aryon* (ash) respectively. Although riddles and stories (*lökoy*) are used for education purposes, they are mainly for entertainment and for passing time mainly around the fireplace in the evening and after supper before going to bed. It has to be remembered that these are normally told to children because young men and girls go for night dances in the evenings. Among the very popular stories are those of Amiriat, Merkit and his father, Lopeymakal, who were seers (*werkoy*) and used to lead the Pökot very well due to their bravery and foresight: encouraging children to be as brave as their great leaders. The latter is known to have had a lot of problems with the British colonialists because of predicting their downfall and urging the Pökot to keep on resisting the colonial rule.

Another cultural value among the Pökot is old age, which is considered to come with wisdom and knowledge about the secrets of life and survival tactics of the community. Elders (*poy*) handle all social matters, within the Pökot community unlike in other communities where professionals and experts deal with various issues that affect the community. When it comes to the question of age, even the contentious issue of women being regarded as children is reconsidered. A young man cannot, for instance, refer to his mother or any woman of her age, as a child (*moning*). This would be regarded as a gross misconduct and lack of respect, not only to the woman in question but also to the community at large.

---

123. Interview with Simeon Lomerkoru, a 40-year-old man who has worked as a catechist and a church elder for about 10 years. The interview was carried out in Tamugh within Sook Location of in West Pökot.

However, it is an accepted norm for a man to refer to his wives, sisters and all other women younger than him, as children. It, therefore, emerges that, the older a person becomes the more respect and recognition he/she gets in the Pökot community. This is also manifested when there are great social activities taking place like ceremonies and sacrifices: it is the very old people that are chosen as the community representatives. It, therefore, was (and in many cases, still is) a great achievement for a young person to be respected by the elders. Moreover, it was an exceptional privilege for a young man to partake in the affairs of the elders, as the saying puts it, *atakuwun karachinin morïn kwomisiyi nko poy*—if a young man has washed his hands (clean), he can eat with the elders. This means that, if a person shows outstanding characters, he/she is loved and accepted by all (especially elders) his/her age or status notwithstanding.

The Rites of Passage

After a person and a cow and its relationship with women, the third most important value in the life of a Pöchon is the rites of passage; which span from the very time of conception, throughout life, up to the time of death. "From the beginning of his/her existence till the end of it the life of a Pökot is full of rites. They start even before birth. The main characteristics of these rites is that they are not real celebrations, they are surrounded by a mist of sadness because they are trying to patch up some kind of deficiency people find themselves in their living."[124] The entire life of a Pöchon is, therefore, a transition from one stage to the other and this is always marked with jubilation and pomp, except the occasion of death when nobody visited the family apart from the close relatives.

The rites of passage give to the initiates the power to stand up in the face of the harsh realities of life by incorporating them into the community. It is, therefore, only proper to say that the Pökot celebrate life and sincerely thank God for this gift and all other material benefits they have. A song popularly sung during celebrations by Christians goes like this: *Kikonecha Tororöt tïkuk lapoy, kighanecha*—God has given us all things; let us believe (in him). Among the Pökot, there are six major steps in life that one must undergo. These are: *Parpara* (a reconciliation ceremony for safe delivery), *malal* or *riwoy* as the case may be.[125]

Then the 'knocking out of teeth' (*keghöt kelat*), which goes hand in hand with body decorations (*sorïm*) follows this stage.[126] Then there follows the major rite of

124. Baroja et. al. Op. cit., 27.

125. This is a naming ceremony for one child, two children or a child born 'abnormally', that is, with the feet coming out first or a child who was conceived before the mother resumed her menstrual cycle since the previous birth.

126. These two rites, *keghot kelat* and *sorïm*, are basically for beauty but the former has a medicinal value. A person suffering from tetanus or any other disease that causes locked jaws is fed through that gap.

circumcision or clitoridectomy (variously referred to as *tum*—song, celebration or dance, *kepa rotwö*—going (to face) the knife or simply as *mutat*—the cut). Ordinarily the rite is immediately followed by another one for men called *sapana*.

However, among the agricultural Pökot, there is an allowance for it to be done after the greatest of all rites of passage—marriage (*kensyö*), on condition that the wife is sent back to her parents during this ceremony (*sapana*). Finally, there is the rite performed after a person has died. Although the dead person is not an active participant (and unlike in birth rites of *parpara* and *malal/riwoy*, he or she is no more), he/she has to undergo the full traditional set of rituals to cleanse the deceased, and those who have survived him/her, of death (*meghat*). Otherwise his or her spirit (*onyöt*) will come back and torment the living.[127]

The reason for these rites of passage is a metaphysical fear of evil befalling an individual or the entire community. They, therefore, said to help everybody realize the full potential of his or her life and also maintain a balance between the natural and supernatural forces. Apart from warding off possible misfortunes, the rites of passage are also a moment of great joy and celebration because they are moments to show their communality in which everybody must participate. During these moments, their lives are strengthened, healed and enriched, whoever fails to take part then is ostracized as anti-social and anti-life. In short, the moments of ritual transition mark the very understanding of the term community among the Pökot just as it is the case with other Africans.[128]

Thus, the rites of passage serve both the purpose of transition, from one stage of life to another, and integration into the community. This means that failure to undergo the rites of passage excludes a person from the day-to-day activities of his or her age mates, and whoever has not been initiated through these rites remains an outsider, *ipso facto*. The rites of passage also have other purposes. Marriage and the knocking out of teeth are meant to bring about some form ritual purity, while the other four are also meant to bring about some form of blessings.

Sapana, for example, is meant to bring about good luck, like the begetting of boys as well as freedom from social misfortunes. It is also meant to promote a junior elder into the status of being able to sit with elders, like in *kokwö*, and serve them during ceremonies. Although marriage is not intrinsically impure, there is a trace of suspicion as to the cleanliness of the bride and her bridegroom, including all the members of their clans. For this reason, there is reconciliation or blessing ceremony when the woman becomes pregnant for the first time, in order to ensure a happy and trouble-free marriage for the two.

---

127. Ndegwah (2004). Op. cit., 92.
128. Sundermeier, op. cit., 20.

Pöghisyö (Harmony) as the Goal of Life

The goal of life among the people of West Pökot is only one—harmony, which is translated as *pöghisyö*. Indeed, it is the only word that defies the strict grammatical rules of male-female relationship and as such also serves as a general greeting for everyone at every time. This harmonious life is realized only when three major observations are realized in the social setting. One, every adult member of the Pökot community is expected to get married and raise children for the defense of the community in case of external aggression and for the continuation of the race. Two, it is the desire of every male Pöchon to try and acquire as many animals as possible because, as Visser observes, "A man without cattle is looked upon as dead."[129]

Finally, the Pökot must keep in touch with the strict and rigid traditions of their ancestors as prescribed by the elders, who are their spokesmen. Once this internal harmony has been realized and there is no external aggression, only then do the Pökot say there is peace (*kalya*) in the land. Practically all our informants attributed the concept, *kalya*, to the absence of war and misfortunes, rather than seeing it as part of the ingredients that make a good life.

In his analysis of the word *pöghisyö*, Van Steenbergen,[130] has put forth nine elements that form the basis of what constitutes a good life in the Pökot social context. These contexts give some clues to understanding the meaning of *pöghisyö*:

1. The (extended) family is living peacefully in the homestead. There are no "bad words" that disturb the relationships.

2. There is harmony between human beings and nature. No wild animals are disturbing people. No "bad birds" are singing in the homestead, no snakes are entering the home. A good tree provides enough shade during hot days.

3. Nobody is sick or feeling uncomfortable, but everybody is in good health. Also the cattle, goats and sheep are in good condition.

4. There is peace in the land. Cattle raiders from neighbouring groups (especially the Turkana) have not been around for some time. In fact the conditions are becoming ideal for going out on a cattle raid to bring "home" the cattle from the other groups.

5. God (*Töröröt*) is not angry with the people. He is looking down upon them in favor from Mount Mtelö, the highest mountain in Pökoot.

6. Many children, calves, lambs and goats are being born and all in good health.

---

129. Johannes Jacobus Visser (1983). We Follow Someone Who Speaks the Truth. In Wout van den Bor (ed). *The Art of the Beginning: First Experiences and Problems of Western Expatriates in Developing Countries with Special Emphasis on Rural Development and Rural Education*. Wageningen: PUDOC. 15.

130. Gerrit Van Steenbergen (1999). Translating "Sin" in Pökoot. In *The Bible Translator*. Vol. 42, No. 4, 433.

7. People are standing firm in life like Mount Mtelö.

8. There is, or has been, enough rainfall to make the grass grow for the animals and to grow sufficient crops. There is prosperity in the land.

9. People don't do anything wrong to one another. There is no stealing, fighting, adultery, witchcraft, bad words and the like.

The Pökot are slow in accepting the Catholic teaching about celibacy and so are not willing to give their children, especially the firstborns, to become priests, sisters or brothers, because the action will kill the 'fire' of their genealogy. Indeed, up to the time of writing this work, there was not a single Pökot priest, in Kenya (since Fr. George Rotino Pororwo left the priesthood), while in Uganda there was also just one (Fr. Peter Loduk Loribo) who died a few years ago. With regard to the livestock, the cattle are the source of both wealth and prestige, which enable them to have a harmonious and socially recognized life.[131] Since for the Pökot cows are the basic means of subsistence; they cement relationships and are the major source of all ritual elements. They give access to the vitality of life: acquisition of wives through bride price and with it the meeting of their sexual and procreation needs as well as domestic assistance. In this sense, cows give identity to the Pökot as a people and as individuals.

As for keeping their tradition, the homestead is the center for the life of a Pöchon. Everyone has a task to perform as dictated by the head of the homestead (usually the oldest man). He also performs the rituals that guarantee peace and stability, not just at home but in the entire community. The ability to stand against the harsh environmental conditions is of paramount importance to the Pökot. Life hazards and natural catastrophes are countered with ceremonies and rituals, which are protecting and purifying since they stimulate the positive elements of life. These rituals safeguard the Pökot by enhancing the forces that bring life, while at the same time warding off those that provoke harm. Consequently, these ceremonies and rituals are believed to augment a relationship of control, supplication, respect and a sense of awe in the search for equilibrium with the supernatural powers.[132] Any upset of the social or supernatural equilibrium is regarded as a misnomer that calls for redress in the form of cleansing ceremonies or rituals.

Moral Uprightness in the Pökot Community

The word 'morality' does not exist in the Pökot language, all that we could establish are expressions like a generous man (*pöghin*) or hardworking woman (*tïngän*), who in effect leads a life of ritual cleanness or sweetness (*anyïn*). For them, leading a moral

---

131. David Patterson (1969). The Pökot of Western Kenya 1910–1963: The Response of a Conservative People to a Colonial Rule. In *Syracuse Occasional Paper*, 53.

132. Johannes Jacobus Visser (1982). *Towards a Missionary Approach Among the Pökot*. Zaandijk: The Netherlands, 16ff.

life means two distinct things: a life of ritual cleanness and conformity to the laws of God and community. Accord xing to the Pökot, most of the evil that occurs in life can be avoided if people conform to the good life. "God's wrath, uncleanness and its accompanying contamination of others, and even the revenge by angry ancestral and other spirits are avoided by following the moral life."[133]

Their moral system follows strict and legalistic moral codes and sanctions. If, for instance, I intentionally killed a Pöchon, there is a fixed fine of sixty heads of cattle, if the victim is a young person and has not left any offspring. If the young person has some children, then the penalty is forty-five heads of cows and for an elderly person, the penalty is thirty heads of cows, paid in a process known as *lapay*.[134] If the family did not have enough cows to pay the fine, then the clan comes in to settle the debt. The collective goal of the community is for everyone to try and lead a good life, devoid of misfortunes and death, which are direct results of evil. That is, to live in accordance with the socially accepted community norms.

Poyon Nyole Pöghïn (A Good Man)

The basic quality of a good man in the eyes of a Pöchon is one who values the current and future life of the Pökot people, not just as individuals but as a community. That means he must be married (preferably to more than one wife, especially for a leader) and have children; a fact that ensures the continuation of the race. This important requirement presupposes that the man has duly gone through the preceding rites of circumcision and initiation into adulthood. "Beyond these basic requirements he is conceived of as one who is fair in dividing food among his wife or wives and children, who deals fairly with his kin and helps them, who shares his beer with his neighbors and is obliging in slaughtering a steer for a feast for them when they desire it"[135] Such a person is not expected to pick unnecessary quarrels with his neighbors, to be boastful, proud or least of all wish them evil, say, by casting evil spells on them. Such a person is said to have a sweet life (*anyïn sopon*), he is highly respected in the community and his opinions are always taken seriously by his age mates. Thus, the Pökot regard him as a generous man (*poyon nyole pöghïn*).

Korka Nyole Tingän (An Industrious Woman)

Traditionally the most important qualification of a good woman, among the Pökot is that she should be industrious or hardworking and generous in several things. Firstly, she must be able to take care of her home, that is, her husband, children and their

---

133. Schneider (1955). Op. cit., 405.

134. Although this is the traditionally set standard, nowadays people have become more flexible and increasingly, the number of animals to be paid depends on the region and wealth of the assailant.

135 Ibid., 405.

property. Hence barrenness is seen as a real marital tragedy and families can do anything to avoid its embarrassment. Secondly, she must be one who does not keep visitors hungry or let them go away with their stomachs empty. Thirdly, she must be one who maintains a good relationship with her co-wives and neighbors, one who does not bring shame to her husband through daily quarrels. A Pöchon lady is expected to get married soon after the 'passing out' ceremony (*kipunö*), which marks the end of the transition period for a girl from childhood to adulthood through clitoridectomy; otherwise she will still be regarded as a *sorïn*[136] or derogatorily referred to as clitoris (*chawïr*) and no one will ever respect her.[137]

Among the agricultural Pökot, a good woman is expected to herd the cattle and cultivate the crops for the food security of her family. Among the pastoralists, she is expected to follow the men as they graze the animals in order to draw water from the wells for them, build the house for herself and her husband and finally take care of all domestic needs except security. And when age starts catching up, she gets a younger, more energetic, woman (or women) to take care of these chores and look after her husband. Such a woman is admirable and is said to be hardworking (*korka nyole tingän*).

Ritual Purity and Appeal to the Supernatural

The appeal to the supernatural, which Schneider calls 'magic',[138] seems to be part and parcel of the Pökot way of life including their belief system which, as we have noted earlier on, encompasses their entire lifestyle. Schneider distinguishes two kinds of magic: the first one has to do with the perception of ritual purity and uncleanness. "Life is pictured as a state of balance, or ritual 'cleanness' or 'sweetness' (*anyin*), any trespass of which, whether accidental, premeditated or circumstantial, automatically renders the person who has been involved 'unclean' (*kölölyon*)."[139]

The second kind of magic "…is the belief that there is an automatic supernatural mechanism that can be activated by anyone for either good or evil purposes. Thus, for example, the community may place a spell upon an evildoer, or an evil person may inflict ill on an enemy (sorcery)."[140] Schneider sees this as 'probably the most effective means of social control'. It may be used by individuals in authority and by the

---

136. The male equivalent of *sorïn*, i.e., an uncircumcised boy, is *somchon*.

137. This situation is increasingly changing with more people (especially those who are educated, though not all of them) refusing to have their daughters go through this initiation rite, variously referred to as going (to face) the knife—*kepa rotwo*, 'a cut'—*mutat* or just dance—*tum* (4.6, 4.12). More than education, though, geographical location is the strongest determining factor towards this direction or otherwise.

138. Schneider (1955). Op. cit., 405.

139. Ibid., 405.

140. Ibid., 405.

community as a whole to achieve their ends or by those who have been insulted or injured against who have offended them."[141]

Our interest was drawn to the issue of how 'the community punishes unknown criminals' and the response was basically the same everywhere we went. If a person, say, steals a neighbor's cow but remains incognito, the owner presents this case to the council of elders who give an ultimatum and warn the culprit to come out in the open or face their wrath. If by the end of the grace period he/she has not surrendered they perform a certain traditional curse ritual called *mutat* (i.e., being cut off from the community), which is designed to bring the anonymous offender to the open.

The exact cursing words differ from one place to another, depending on the gravity of the offence, actual idiomatic expressions of the local people, their diction and external influence. Around Mnagei, for instance, the actual words used are: '*iraite nko asis*—may you sink with the sun', in Sekerr they say, '*inyorï takat*—may you get chest pain',[142] while in Mwino they say '*inyorï sarti pat*—get thorns in yourself'. Whatever the case may be, these traditionally sharp words of cursing, are thought to have some power that goes beyond human ability to resist and they actually make the culprit own up and confess his guilt— '*ani nyay kyacheng tany wechara*—it is me who took the cow'. After this ritual is performed, the guilty person comes out in the open, just as the elders had predicted that he/she would.

When there has been drought for a long time, elders gather under a tree or at the foot of a mountain and perform their traditional prayers and that same day it rains cats and dogs. In the private sphere a number of people are said to practice magic for private ends, some for the good of other people, others for their own selfish ends. These are sometimes feared, other times hated or both and should they harm many people they are condemned to death by the community. All magic is accepted as part and parcel of the Pökot lifestyle, no one seemingly knows its origin or how it actually works, and yet there is a clear hesitancy to attribute it directly to God. Sorcery (*wutin*) seems to be an accepted part of the Pökot religion as the above suggests. In fact, the place of God in these two types of magic is never made clear. No one would, for instance, agree that God helps the sorcerer (*mutin*) to obtain his/her ends, but it is sometimes suggested that the activating force in the magical processes of uncleanness and socially acceptable magic is God himself. Even a witch (*ponïn*) prays to God for the paraphernalia to be effective in its operations.

Evil and Uncleanness

The Pökot cosmology brings into play the physical and the metaphysical in one unit that operate under various forces. One such force is vitality (the force of life), which is

---

141. Schneider (1959). Op. cit., 158.

142. The same word is used for Tuberculosis, a disease that is characterised by coughing mucus and sputum, fever, weight loss, and chest pain.

occasioned, not only by the sexual act of the two parents but also by the preponderant Will of the Creator (*Ighin*). Life is, therefore, sustained and controlled by both the physical forces (like food and shelter) on the one hand, and the balancing of the metaphysical forces with the earthly forces on the other hand. Any upsetting of this order of things is seen as a disorder or uncleanness and the cause of all evils that befall an individual or the community at large. A person is, therefore, considered to be ritually clean only and only if no evil deeds surround his/her life. An evil deed, in this case, is regarded as anything that causes disharmony in a person's social relations with others, or whatever disorientates the normal orderliness of the community. The effect of evil, then, is destabilization of the entire community, which works against its very well-being; eventually destroying communal harmony or *pöghisyö*.

This can be expressed in many forms. If a person kills someone, even killing an enemy (an action considered to be heroic in itself), he or she has upset the metaphysical force of being alive (since only God has the power to take away life), a fact that endangers the social equilibrium of things. The person is unclean in the eyes of the community and has, of necessity, to undergo the ritual purification, in order to be accepted back into the community. The situation is worse if the victim is a fellow Pöchon because the assailant has to pay a heavy penalty that ranges from sixty heads of cattle, for a man, to thirty, for a woman (as the traditional standard), in the accepted local practice of *lapay*. The general rule, therefore, is that all consequences of evil deeds (no matter how grave) can be redressed through corresponding rituals of purification.[143]

Evil, mistakes, uncleanness and social impurity destabilize the community since they oppose the well-being *(pöghisyö)* of all its members. The Pökot distinguish six kinds of evil, which differ in degree and intensity. These are *sirrïp, ptakal, ngokï, lelut, sulputyon* and *chipöt*. *Sirrïp* is a result of any kind of a quarrel. It is a word pronounced in anger; thrown, as it were, like and arrow towards someone at fault and it is said to produce bad effects. *Ptakal* is any extraordinary sin, resulting from unnatural acts like homosexuality, incest, or bestiality. *Ngokï* refers to sin in general. It is the effect produced by the transgression of society's codes and entails inevitable destructive consequences within a person. If not countered, it becomes an independent force of consuming evil within the community. *Lelut* is an unintentional mistake that requires an apology lest it provokes harm in one's own lineage. *Sulputyon* is the same as selfishness or general lack of self-respect but it is mostly in connection with failure to observe dietary regulations. If a man, for instance, took a milk gourd (*mkö*) and drank directly from it, this is *sulputyon*.

Chipöt is the most serious of all evils in the Pökot community, it is ordinarily carried out by the whole society against any person considered to be a pervert and the only remedy is to reverse the cursing ceremony before it takes effect. Once the effects have taken root, or once some of the people that took part in the cursing ceremony are dead, then it is not possible to reverse it. In the Pökot tradition, these five kinds of evil

---

143. Baroja, et. al. Op. cit., 27.

can be classified in two categories—first-degree (or grave) evil and second-degree (or light) evil, both of which render a person unclean (literally, blue or *orus*).

Actions that constitute the serious evil differ in degree but belong to the same category because they upset both social and metaphysical equilibrium, whereas the second-degree evil only upsets the social order. The seriousness of an evil act determines the severity of the penalty to be meted out and also the 'strength' of the cleansing ritual. Consequently, the remedy for *lelut* is simple forgiveness upon confession (*lastagh*). The remedy for *ptakal* is *tusöt*, the one for *sulputyon* is mere chastisement, while for *sirrip* is *pitet*, *lyakat* or *kikatat*, depending on the severity of the sharp words thrown at the victim.

Although this did not come directly from the people's mouths, our research suggests that *orus* (uncleanness) is a wider concept that engulfs not only the negative deeds a person has done but anything out of the ordinary (even if it is good in itself) thus understood to cause ritual impurity. Two examples in this regard would suffice. When, as we have mentioned above, a warrior kills an enemy during a cattle raid (a heroic deed in itself), he remains unclean and cannot visit his family until after a cleansing ceremony and decorations that mark him as a hero (*kölölyon*). The second example is the state an initiate finds him/herself in during the major transitional periods of life, in the rites of passage (a situation one finds oneself in without any personal fault). Ritual impurity merely means that it upsets the social equilibrium in that it occasions a special time when everything else is suspended and the daily flow of life is tampered with, in the sense that the initiate is neither here nor there.

At birth, ritual impurity is in both the mother and the child/children; during circumcision it is in the initiates while at death impurity is in the surviving relatives of the deceased. However, during the ceremonies of marriage (*kensyö*) and *sapana*, the concept of ritual uncleanness does not come out so strongly, although it is not lacking. Perhaps this is because the former makes one have the fullness of life (*chi nyo kiloko sorngonyon*) in the Pökot culture, whereas the latter is only an adoption from the Karimojong (of Uganda) and the Turkana (of Kenya).

Although *sapana* is no longer a *conditio sine qua non* (a necessary condition), in the Pökot life-cycle, it is still seen as a sign of prestige and is at times carried out to ward off an evil spell. This happens particularly when a person (especially if that person is the only boy in the family) is prone to accidents or other misfortunes in life. The community pleads with *Tororöt* on his behalf during the ceremony so that he may be blessed with more boys to perpetuate his clan.

Apart from this kind of uncleanness, which is a 'transitional social state', the other uncleanness (*orus*) *per se* which emanates from pure malice or wickedness can, in the Christian sense, be termed as sin and it requires a 'stronger' cleansing ritual. Specialized people in the community rather than any elder normally carry out such rituals. From the explanation, above, we see that rites of passage and other rituals, be they remedial, reconciliatory or thanksgiving, are not identical but also not detached from each other. All of them serve the same purpose of harmonizing the community life, which the Pökot people sum up as *pöghisyö*.

As a rule, then, all people considered to be ritually unclean are isolated from the rest of the community members lest they 'infect' them also and a serious calamity befalls the entire community. These remain excluded from others until they are cleansed through appropriate ritual ceremonies: such as sprinkling them with the blood or washing them with the entrails (*egyam*) of an animal, say, a goat or an ox. Schneider explains the nature of uncleanness and purpose of cleansing ceremonies in the following words:

> Uncleanness is clearly a transitional social state, a period of change of status which is a period of tension precisely because some shifting of the normal equilibrium of the group is in the process. The cleansing ceremony is a device for smoothing that transition. The net result of the system is to encourage equilibrium and to alert the group to special precaution to preserve it during those times when is most liable to disturbance.[144]

Immorality in the Pökot Community

Immorality, in the traditional Pökot community, was very uncommon because there were many social structures in existence to guard and militate against it; and even today, the vestiges of this high standard of morality can still be witnessed in some Pökot regions. Due to the strict moral code and the belief that deviation from traditional practices spells doom for the com-munity, immorality is severely punished for two reasons: one, to ward off any disaster that was likely to befall the family of the offending woman and two, to prevent a future recurrence of the same. "Social morality is rather rigid" says Tescaroli. "It is rare that a married woman betrays her husband. In case she is caught, she is beaten by her husband as well as by her parents."[145] On top of this, the offending man has to pay a fine equivalent to the bride price paid for the woman during her wedding.[146] Then the sinful partners, plus the woman's children have to be cleansed in a ceremony called *mwata*, where they have to posture their very act of adultery as everybody else watches and the leader of the ceremony recites some incantations to ward off the spirits (*onyötey*, whose singular is *onyöt*, as opposed to the evil spirits that are always in the plural form—*oy*) of immorality.

In spite of these severe, rigid, almost legalistic penalties to immorality, immoral practices were not unheard of in the traditional Pökot community. Thus, even today, immorality is classified in two categories: "1) acts which are against the law and custom and are punishable or deprecated, and 2) acts which make a person ritually

---

144 Schneider (1959). Op. cit., 158.

145. Cirillo Tescaroli (1979). The Karapokot, A Waiting People. In *Worldvision*, Vol. 30. No. 3. 81.

146. Tescaroli seems to dispute Schneider's (1955: 407) position on this issue who makes the following claim: "But so many people indulge in it (adultery) that its moral status is in dispute . . . "

unclean. Sometimes these conditions are contiguous, sometimes not. There is, however, a considerable correspondence between the two." [147]

The first category of immorality consists of the acts that are termed as illegal and the simplest punishment is flogging (for example when a person refused to co-operate with the rest of the community for apparently no known reason). If the act is more serious the offender is fined one or two cows, depending on the severity of the crime, as the council of elders may deem fit. Other crimes include theft and lying, condemned because they can cause harm to an innocent person.

The second category of immorality consists of evil deeds, which not only make a person culpable but also morally unclean. They are said to be wickedness *per se* or malevolence (*cheptughmu*—literally, a person with a black stomach). While the first category of immorality can, in the Christian terms, be regarded as the equivalent of *venial* sins, this second category can be equated to *mortal* sins. These constitute acts like murder, incest, bestiality and sorcery, to name but a few. Punishments for such acts are truly heavy as they involve brutal reprisals like impoverishment of the culprit (as it happens during *lapay*), magical cursing or expulsion from the community, or outright death sentence in which the culprit's relatives must play a leading role. But should the verdict be on the latter nobody will carry out the actual killing, the culprit is forced to climb a particular tree and commit suicide by jumping to his/her death.

Pökot Culture and the Challenge of Modernity

Although most Pökot cherished the traditional community lifestyle, modernity is on the rampage and it is taking its toll in West Pökot, just as it is the case with other parts of Africa, as Bujo has observed. "Sub-Saharan Africa is in a process of change. Modern technology has influenced the African people to an extent that seems to make the breakdown of traditional values obvious." [148] This change seems to have been catalyzed by what young people perceive as repugnant cultural practices that do not promote life and those that hinder personal freedom. A few examples of these practices would suffice: twins were traditionally killed because they were thought to be a bad omen, young virgins were sacrificed to *Tororöt* in case of misfortunes and what is more, the communitarian nature of the community did not allow personal initiatives and self-actualization.

Due to this fact, change has been sweeping the Pökotland in a hitherto unprecedented way that made Meyerhoff to hope (aloud) against hope that it will spare the 'Pökot beliefs and values'. "The Pökot are under pressure to assume a more active, participatory role in modern Kenya." She observes, "New roads cut through their home land, from both east and west. . . . I only hope that modernization will be carried

---

147. Schneider (1955). Op. cit., 406.
148. Bujo (1998). Op. cit., 15.

through with an understanding of, and sensitivity to, Pökot beliefs and values."[149] There are many pertinent issues that directly challenge the traditional way of life and the entire societal structure.

Among these are the modern social amenities like schools, health centers, development projects like the Nasukuta Sheep, Goat and Camel Multiplication and Demonstration Centre and the Turkwel Hydro-electric Power Station, which bring with them a change of attitude in the community. For the purposes of this study, we will only look at the issues of respect, education, religion, social demeanor and mannerism, rites of passage, and economy. Then we will try to see how these aspects impact on the community and its response in trying to cope.

Respect

Within the parameters of their own society and cultural practices, the Pökot are a very respectful people, but judged by modern criteria, this respect can be said to be wanting. In the traditional Pökot community women and children were (and in some cases, even today) not held in high regard and were obviously discriminated against. They were, sort of, relegated to second-class members of the community; their views were never sought and nobody seemed to care very much of what they thought. This is one of the areas where modern education has seriously clashed with the otherwise tranquil and serene traditional way of life. The government, churches and non-governmental organizations (NGOs) have vigorously launched a campaign to have all children go to school and to initiate many other development projects. Among them are reproductive and general health projects, clean water, animal husbandry, and soil erosion control projects.

Although most of these are received and accepted by many people, more still have their doubts with regard to the ultimate aim and the logic of some changes that come with the projects. In the name of equality and respect, for instance, women have risen against the traditional maxim held by all and sundry that 'women are children'; indeed, many of them told us without a wink in the eyes *chicha moning* (we are children). There is, however, an NGO called SETAT Women Group that tries to empower women in conjunction with another NGO called Sentinelles from Switzerland. It has started by helping girls who run away from clitoridectomy, which they regard as FGM (Female Genital Mutilation), and forced marriages. They do this in the name of human rights and particularly the rights of the girl child and women affirmative action that demand equality for both men and women.

Although the government supports such initiatives, the Pökot are themselves evenly divided on whether to accept the new developments or not, with the older generation, in particular pouring scorn on this turn of events. A frustrated elder complained

---

149. Meyerhoff (1982). Op. cit., 120.

to us: "Our daughters no longer face the knife (*rotwö*), they no longer adorn themselves and neither do they help their mothers at home. Instead they run away to school, then the government asks us to pay for this education and finally your daughter simply runs away with anybody, including our enemies (*püng*). It is a total loss!"[150]

This state of affairs is compounded by the fact that an uncircumcised girl is not allowed to get married and if she does, her parents-in-law cannot eat from her house and she cannot socialize with other young women because she is 'not yet a woman'. Come the time of delivery and she can easily die because it is a taboo for the traditional birth attendant to help her out, since she cannot look at the genitals of an uncircumcised girl. Thus, it is not just a question of cutting off an organ of the body, but a socio-cultural issue.

Education, Religion and Social Demeanor

Education is an aspect of development that the government has stressed in this area, but its prospects do not augur well with the people. The modern concept of education has nothing to do with the traditional Pökot understanding of the word. Education was carried out after the initiation of young people during the liminal stage [151], when they are regarded as *chemeri* (for girls) and *tyos* (for boys). The education was about marriage, how to take care of their spouses and livestock, and how to uphold the values and secrets of the community. A good girl, explained one, is the one who is initiated and then gets married to raise a family in order to pay the debt (of the fact that she was also born) and for the continuation of the Pökot race. Modern education disrupts all that and then creates a phenomenon of single mothers and mistresses, who lead a life of concubinage. Educated girls stay too long in school so that by the time they are through no one is willing to marry them as first wives, and yet they are not ready to settle down as second or third wives.

Then married men keep them as mistresses and now people are afraid that they may be a source of promiscuity and the spread of venereal diseases, particularly AIDS. A litany of the sins of omission and commission by educated girls included pride, on account of their financial independence, refusal to help in household chores, lack of respect towards elders and arrogance. They, for instance, want to show their mothers how to cook the 'white man's (*musunchon*) food' and want to have a say on who to marry and when they should be married off; and do not even shy off from eloping with the traditional Pökot enemies (*püng*). We asked one university educated girl, who is working as a secondary school teacher, about these accusations and she denied most of them. "It is all a question of perspectives and worldview," she told us, "an educated woman cannot

---

150. Kapelinyang is an 80-year-old respected man in Sook, who many younger people turn to for advice on a range of social and cultural issues.

151. Victor W. Turner (1969). *The Ritual Process, Structure and Anti-Structure*. Chicago: Chicago University Press, 170.

look at and interpret reality in the same way as one who did not go to school, or only has elementary education."[152] On the issue of missing husbands of their own and so opting to co-habit with other women's husbands, she was honest and candid.

> That is true. This is a developing and worrying scenario that needs to be addressed by all. There are not too many educated men in West Pökot at this point in time, and yet the few we have, are afraid of marrying someone equally qualified as them. Our university-educated men go for women from tertiary colleges, while those from colleges go for secondary school leavers. Then women from university are left hanging either to look for men from outside the county or remain as concubines that nobody wants to marry. If a woman does not 'fish' a husband in the college, she is doomed because those who will show interest in her once she goes back home are married men who are only interested in a causal relationship and then dumb you as soon they are done.[153]

The Pökot understand boys to be useful when they can take care of animals at home and finally go on to bring more from their enemies. Moreover, young men who have gone to school are also accused of eroding the Pökot culture and arrogance against the elders. First, they do not go raiding for they claim to be Christians or civilized; instead they want to advice their parents on various issues like modern agricultural techniques of farming or how to keep grade cattle for more production of milk and so on. For the old people, this is unbearable and they accuse the young of breaking the age-old traditions, lack of respect and humility.

Although education and religion are not directly related, most schools belong to Christian missions and by the time a child is through with secondary education, he (or she) is inevitably a Christian and does not subscribe to most traditional practices anymore. This is a factor that worries the elders because they think that their God (*Tororöt*) might bring a catastrophe to the community because they have allowed their children to go after a foreign god from Europe. What is more, educated men are reluctant to officially take a second or third wife, leaving a big number of girls without husbands. The men ignore their families and secretly cohabit with these girls, something that encourages immorality in the community.

The Rites of Passage and Economy

The rites of passage are a pre-requisite for acceptance, in the Pökot community, if one is to be regarded as an adult, capable of assuming leadership responsibility. However, they do not come about without the use of an animal, mostly a cow. This, coupled with the environmental factor that only supports the rearing of animals makes a cow the only

---

152. Irene Cheptoo is 35 years old, and among the very few women in Pökotland so far that have attained a Masters degree. She works as the secretary to the West Pökot County Service Board.

153. Idem.

source of survival and livelihood. This notwithstanding, education is trivializing the traditional way of life, boys cannot be circumcised in accordance with the traditional calendar because they need to be in school and then after school they do not want to undergo the remaining rites of passage, which, as it were, would make them full members of the community. Then there is the issue of economic development. Educated young men are trying to introduce the rearing of exotic animals that require medical care, like human beings. But not many elderly people have an idea of what to do with that kind of animals and as such left to their care the animals will all die.

The final problem is a change in the direction of economic activities in West Pökot, which includes gold prospecting, farming and paid government jobs.[154] This affects people's communitarian way of life in which everybody depends on everybody else for protection and defense from their enemies. But with a paid job one starts to have a feeling that he/she does not need other people and one starts development projects single-handedly. Educated people are even supporting the government idea of sub-dividing the land so that everyone can have a personal plot to which one can claim absolute proprietorship.

The advantage of this, they are told, is that with a land title deed one can get a loan from the government, "but what they are not being told," according to an informant, "is that in the event that one fails to repay the money, the same piece of land can be auctioned and disenfranchise the same person the loan was supposed to assist."[155] Indeed, they do not as yet know that even an individual can sell his portion of land to whoever he wishes, including outsiders, who are seen as enemies. Today two judicial systems are operational in the Pökotland, one by the law courts in Kapenguria (County Headquarters) and another by the *kokwö* (council of elders) yet in most cases these are at loggerheads, leaving the people confused. The effects of modernity are felt everywhere in the Pökotland and the most hit are the elderly people who feel robbed of their traditional power, and helplessly watch their society 'disintegrating' due to detribalizing effects of migration and development, which has, according to government officials, left them 1000 years 'behind'.[156]

Conclusion

As promised in the introduction, this chapter has been descriptive in nature. It has examined the available literature about the Pökot people, much of which is not comprehensive since it is only in the forms of articles and PhD dissertations. Of particular interest was the recently published dissertation by Van Sanders, since it deals with the same topic of evangelization, albeit using a different approach than our own. We

---

154. Visser, op. cit., 50.

155. Interview with Patrick Kadokot, a 48-year-old former catechist, from Ywalateke, within Chepareria Division.

156. Visser (1983). Op. cit., 20.

disapproved his approach because its results do not seem to tally with the actual life of the Pökot people on the ground. Then we have described the topography of West Pökot, which we have found to be varied between very high and very low, thus allowing a wide difference in climate and vegetation. We have also looked at the lifestyle of the Pökot people, their unity and identity, and their shared elements of language, relationship, culture and genealogy. Among all these, as we have observed, it is finally genealogy that distinguishes a Pöchon from an outsider.

We have also looked at the Pökot concept of ownership, particularly the *tilya* economic relationship, which acts as their livestock insurance against, calamities such as pestilence and theft. Then we have looked at their system of political governance, religion and the divisions of their social life and how they relate to all their cultural values: all of which help to tightly knit their community together. We have, for instance, shown that age-set is tied to circumcision, which is, in turn, tied to the cultural lessons learned during the seclusion period. More importantly is the Pökot understanding of communitarianism as unity with one's neighbors and their ancestors who passed down their culture.

We have looked at the Pökot astronomy and shown how it controls much of their ritual activities because of the belief that they directly communicate with the heavenly bodies, which give them directions. Then we looked at the concept of a person, which is mainly based on relationship. Here an implicit or tacit cultural theme is that the dignity and relevance of a person is pegged on the quality of his or her relationship with other members of the community. Then we looked at the Pökot belief system and religious practices, which are part and parcel of their social life. Next, we looked at their cultural values, at the top of which are the cow, the social wisdom, the rites of passage and the quest for harmony or *pöghisyö* as their goal of life.

We also looked at the Pökot moral system, the nature of immorality and the concept of moral purity, and how these relate to the supernatural in the light of ritual uncleanness. We showed that an everyday thinking about ritual purity is to maintain a good relationship between the physical and the metaphysical forces and between the people themselves. The presupposition is that they will prosper on earth and achieve social harmony (*pöghisyö*) unless there is an imbalance between the natural and supernatural forces. This, according to the Pökot, is caused by malevolent spirits (*oy*) or simple human failure to maintain the cultural code of conduct, leading to ritual uncleanness (*orus*).

The activities of malevolent spirits and human mistakes (intentional or unintentional), which result in failure, pave the way for evil forces to interfere with the peace in the community, by way of misfortunes, pestilence or other catastrophes, like epidemic and unexplainable or sudden deaths of otherwise healthy people. But should evil befall the land, the Pökot elders offer prayers and perform rituals in order to neutralize or ward off the forces of evil, by mollifying the deities and appeasing the spirits in order to restore the balance between the natural and the supernatural forces. We have concluded the chapter by looking at the Pökot cultural shortcomings and how these are exploited by young people to challenge the relevance of their own culture in the face of modernity.

In a word, we can say that a cow and the community life (divided into various strata) are the basic cultural motifs of the Pökot people, even the agricultural ones. The life of a Pöchon starts with the community and ends with the community. At birth a child is surrounded by a group of women, including a midwife (or even midwives), grows up with other children in a homestead and goes through all initiation rites while being surrounded by members of his/her clan, relatives and neighbors; learns from them how to acquire and take care of cattle and to raise the family of his or her own (that is, learns to be human), and this education goes on till death. It is important, then, for evangelizers to take cognizance of these facts, if they are to meaningfully inculturate the Gospel and make it feel at home among the Pökot. We now move on, to chapter 4, and see how the Pökot people respond to evangelization, especially, in the pericope of the Good Shepherd.

CHAPTER 4

THE PÖKOT UNDERSTANDING OF JOHN 10:1–16

Introduction

As explained earlier in the general introduction this chapter, and the next one, consist of an analysis of the field data gathered in a period of six months, between March and August 2002. Spradley distinguishes three sources of information: cultural behavior, artefact and language.[1] This distinction, as we have already said, acted as the organizing principle in this analysis, while Kwalitan was a tool for efficiency and accuracy in analyzing the field data. We treated the three sources of information as the fundamental aspects of the Pökot social experience and, there-ore, observed how they related to the religious experience of the people.[2]

Earlier on in chapters one, we identified culture as something shared, though not evenly, and argued that these shared elements constitute a whole range of cultural orientations that are found in people's social dealings among themselves and with others. In this light, we observed what the Pökot people and their pastors do (cultural behavior), the things they make and use (cultural artefacts) and we listened to what they said (speech messages).

The latter was mainly, but not only, done within the context of SCCs, whereby (81) members held bible sharing sessions and discussed the text of John 10:1–16 within the West Pökot County. We also recorded interviews, proverbs and Sunday sermons by the pastors. Whereas the informants for the next chapter (4) consisted of the pastors (10 priests and 19 catechists), for this chapter they consisted of 'ordinary' Christians of all ages, both sexes and different classifications in life. There were elderly people, most of whom do not know how to read and write, middle aged people, some of whom have had limited education, mainly to the primary school level. Then there were young adults, who have mostly finished high school and have had at least two years of training in tertiary institutions.

---

1. Spradley (1980). Op. cit., 10.
2. Ibid., 5.

We presented the above text and listened to their spontaneous sharing, which was later followed by interviews for the purpose of clarification or additional information. The length and nature of the interviews differed from one informant to another, depending on what was lacking in his or her earlier contribution in the SCC. We, therefore, became students of the local people—churchgoers, farmers and shepherds, who acted as able teachers in our effort to discover 'the insider's view',[3] of the Pökot community.

The aims of doing this were two: firstly, to find out whether and, if yes, to what extent the Pökot meaning system is a communitarian one. Secondly, to find out whether, and if yes, to what extent the Pökot use their meaning system to interpret the above-mentioned bible text. This was to be determined by the way and the extent to which the people referred to their cultural imagery during their sharing of the text in question. We did not, in this chapter, intend to engage ourselves in the exegetical-hermeneutical debate, but simply 'to get the native's point of view'[4] on bible interpretation.

This was meant to help us determine if the people in the place of our research have managed to make the Bible their own, by integrating its teaching with their culture. This, we did with the help of insights from Spradley's social research method, through which we analyzed the three aspects of the Pökot cultural pattern as mentioned above. In these three sources of information, we were looking for the elements of communitarianism, in the Pökot culture, through the analysis of the verbal sources, material sources and behavioral sources. Then, as a control measure to our findings, we also looked for the elements of individualism, again through the analysis of the verbal sources, material sources and behavioral sources.

As we have already said in chapter one, the objective of our field investigations was to find out the condition(s) through which biblical hermeneutics can be used as an effective tool for the inculturation of the Gospel among the people of West Pökot. We formulated six questions that remained in our minds during all our field research activities, as follows:

1. What is the Pökot understanding of the term shepherd (*mösöwoon*)?
2. What is their concept of the term community (*kokwö, kapor, poris, kaporiak, kor*)?
3. What is the role of a shepherd in the Pökot community?
4. As a shepherd, does Jesus have a place in the Pökot community?
5. When the people of West Pökot read/hear Jesus Christ referring to himself as a 'Good Shepherd' (*Mösöwoon nyo Karam*), what picture comes into their mind?
6. What is the relevance (if any) of the parable of the Good Shepherd in the social and Christian life of an ordinary Pöchon (man or woman)?

3. Ibid., 4.
4. Malinowski, op. cit., 25; Spradley (1980). Op. cit. 3.

Communitarianism in the Pökot Worldview

As mentioned in the introduction to this chapter, one aim of this section was to find out whether and, if yes, the extent to which the Pökot meaning system is a communitarian one. The quest started with the verbal sources, where the use of the language was analyzed. In the analysis of the material sources, the interest was in finding out if there were any artefacts meant for common or community use. In the analysis of behavioral sources, the interest was in the way people worship; how they show solidarity with one another and how they go about their daily businesses in relation to each other. This was aimed at helping us get a glimpse of the Pökot worldview.

Analysis of the Verbal Sources

In this section, we analyzed the domains that came up during our inter-views with the people and also analyzed their use of language. In doing this we used the Kwalitan computer program, not just for word-counting, but also for checking the context in which a domain was used, by whom and from which geographical region. While we found the domains helpful in understanding the Pökot predisposition in life, the analysis of the language helped in expressing their thoughts with regard to communitarianism or individualism. The Pökot people can be classified into three categories, two geographical and one social, as follows: 1) those that live in the mainly agricultural area; 2) those who live in the purely pastoral area; 3) the elderly people, most of whom are not literate; middle-aged people, a mixture of literate and illiterate people, and young people, many of whom are literate.

While the first group, in the geographical category had more cultural domains that are related to animals, crops and money, the second group had a lot to do with animals, particularly the cow. In the social category, elderly people had more domains to do with cultural and religious matters; the young people had more to do with education, development and politics, with the middle-aged people traversing between the two.

Whereas elderly people and those from the purely pastoral areas were more in favor of a strong community lifestyle, those from the mainly agricultural areas and the young were more interested in strengthening their own individual family lives over and above a strong community life. This is a general classification that takes consideration of all communities in quest-ion. It is, however, not to say that division between various groups in individual communities was as neat and clear-cut as mentioned here, there were few cases when common interests would overlap. In some cases, young people are interested in cultural issues and value community life over individual family life, while in others, people from the predominantly agricultural areas showed interest in livestock and so on.

Domain Analysis

During our period of stay in West Pökot we identified many points of density that can further be classified into two large categories: the socio-economic and cultural-religious. This is in spite (not because) of the fact that there is no clear-cut distinction, in ordinary daily talks, between secular themes of the state of economy and the current political situation in the country to the nostalgic glorify-cation of their culture as punctuated by their invariable religious beliefs. Spradley says that folk terms are the basic units for analyzing a domain,[5] which he defines as a "category of cultural meaning that includes other smaller categories."[6] He explains the nature of cultural domains as follows: "Any description of cultural domains always involves the use of language. Cover terms, included terms, and semantic relationships are all words and phrases that define and give meaning to the objects, events, and activities you observe."[7]

He identifies three kinds of domains, that is, folk domains (when all terms come from the language used by people in a social situation), mixed domains (when the researcher is interested in some domains for which there are only a few folk terms and so he/she is forced to select some analytic terms to complete the domains) and analytic terms (when cultural meanings remain tacit and the researcher must infer them from what the people do, say and their artefacts.[8]

Here we limited ourselves to the first kind of domains. To find and analyze these domains, we used Kwalitan—a computer-based social sciences method that helps break down field notes into short analyzable sentences according to the respondents. Then we carried out a word-search in all 110 interviews (Christians and their pastors) for the recurrent categories linked to the given words that we identified using the Kwalitan 'word in context' search package. After that, we coded them and formed a category tree structure that helped us see exactly how many times a particular folk term had been used (to determine its scope) and by how many respondents (to determine its extension).

Our general overview of the Pökot people indicates that although they are deeply aware of their God (*Tororöt*) and strictly adhere to their religious beliefs and practices, these do not form the most common aspect of their daily talks. More common, hence more important to the people, are the mundane or secular socio-economic activities that define their identity like age-sets (*pïnwöy*), natural groups, such as family or home (*kaw*)—which is also regarded as a house (*kö*)— neighborhood (*pororis*), village (*möngot*), clan (*ortïn),* the community, referred to as people of the land (*piko kore*) and family life (*otöp po keston*) in reference to social status in terms of wealth (*sikonöt*) and prestige. These are followed by climatical conditions

---

5. Spradley, op. cit., 87.
6. Ibid., 88.
7. Ibid., 89.
8. Ibid., 90–91.

like the dry season (*kömöy*), wet season (*pengat*) and how these affect their crops, but more especially, their *kyak* (livestock), that is, *tich* (cows), *ngaror/nekö* (goats), *kechir* (sheep), *sikiröy* (donkeys), *tamasin* (camels).

During the dry season, for instance, it is a common practice after greetings a person to hear expressions like *ata rop* (no rain) and *ata popolos* (no food). Other common points of density, like the meals and kinds of food *(omisyei)*, are *panta mataiywa* (food made of finger-millet flour, but eaten with vegetables), *nguiyon* (vegetables) especially *sokoria, chö* (milk)—*kegha* (fresh) and *lölote* (sour). Others are *peny* (meat), *kison* (blood) *musar* (porridge) and *kumïn* (beer) and recreational activities (like *kedonga, chepelaleyo* and *nyalat*). When a person visits a homestead, one usually alerts his/her hosts by asking for food from a distance—*weei, weei, anyi toon, ale pan!*

Then there is *semeut* (disease) that affects both people and animals, *ngal chopö kasiren* (health care) and *sakit* (medicine); *chirerie* (education), *otöptin* (customs), *osïl* (manners), *telenganen* (traditions), and *oghighyö nyopo söpon* (hardships of life), referring to the slump in economy and the fact that essential commodities have become too expensive (*ngwan*) bringing the means of living (*ighisyö*) beyond the reach of many people. Next are other cultural points of density proper to people's geographical areas and conditions of life. In rural areas, the main concerns are about *ngorisyö* (cultivation), *katkata* (planting), *keel* (harvesting), *keyakuy kyak* (herding of animals) and *lük* (cattle rustling). In towns people talk of *ighisyö kimar* (doing business) and *kepal koldin nko rupin* (gold and rubies prospecting).

The cultural-religious domains follow the socio-economic ones. With respect to *pöghisyö keston* (the situation in various homes) people talk about *keyi monïng* (begetting children) and the rites of passage, particularly *kensyö* (marriage), *ketarta kyak* (paying the dowry, also known as *(koyugh)*, and *noghsyö* (wedding). Others include *linyogh* (restoring broken relationships) between *pororis nko kapor* (neighbors and relatives), which includes *tilyay tich* (economic relatives) by the use of animals, through *parpara* (reconciliation), *tisö* (appeasing angry or unsatisfied ancestors (*kukötin nko kokötin*) and *ore po pikokwa* (genealogy). Outside the home environment they talk about *kanasyan* (homestead), *kongotin* (friends), *pororis* (neighbors), *kintoghoghï* (community leaders), that include, *kokwö* (the council of elders), *kirwok* (the process of judgement), *kirwokïn* (the chief) and *mutinto ngal* (the judge).

These are followed by the extraordinary people or people with *wunyote* (hidden (or mysterious) powers), like *chemowos* (diviners), *werkoy* (seers), magicians (*kapulokyontin*), herbalists (*chepsakitis*), priests (*padritin*) and *konetin* (catechists), *ponü* (witches) and *mutin* (sorcerers). Then there is the *wutot* (evil eye) and *kapolok* (the remote control phenomenon in which you treat someone like a zombie or robot and make him or her do what you like, or simply overlook your own weakness or machinations to exploit him or her). Apart from the extra-ordinary people, there is the concept of evil that manifests itself as cultural taboos. Breaking them results in one of the already mentioned (3.16) five classifications of evil—*ngokï* (sin), *ptakal* (serious mistakes) *lelut* (unintentional mistakes), *sïrrip* (quarrel), *morï* (past (unknown or unremembered) mistakes) and *orus* (uncleanness).

These go hand in hand with the accompanying rituals to remedy them as follows: *kilokat, amat, artakarerat, moy, eghpadia, kartapögh, karera, kityoghin, kitunga, kötkotka, kipunö, lapan, löpow, lyokat, parpara,* and *kikatat*. All these are associated with the supernatural realities that cannot be ascertained *(ngal cho memokisot kesat)*, except by the extra-ordinary people. They include *Tororöt* (God), *asis, ilat, arawa,* and *kokel* (deities), and *oy* (spirits in general—whether good or bad), *kukötin nko kokötin* (ancestors), *mïkulow* (soul or spirit), *kitontögh* and *kïmïr* (shadows).

Communitarian Usage of the Pökot Language

After domain analysis (as shown in the preceding section), we tried to discover whether the Pökot language carries elements of communitarianism by looking at a few domains, which, as Spradley says, include three elements—cover term, included terms and a single semantic relationship.[9] In order to get the most recurrent folk terms that indicate a communitarian theme, we carried out a word-counting exercise using the aforementioned Kwalitan computer program. The most compelling indicator of communitarianism that we discovered was the use of language to express or define 'human relationship'. For instance, the cover term 'relative' is inclusive. Thus, one talks of 'our relationship to him or her' rather than 'my relationship to him or her', which points towards communitarianism.

The Pökot do not, for instance, use expressions that portray individual ownership, like 'my God' (*Tororötönyan*). What they use are pluralistic expressions like 'our God' (*Tororötönyo* not *Tororötöncha*). They hardly use expressions like 'my father' (*paponyan*), 'my mother' (*yonyan*), 'my brother' (*werïnyan*) or 'my sister' (*cheptönyan*). Here the semantic relationship is the strict inclusion: X is a kind of Y.[10] The suffix *–nyan* unites all such terms in a single relational category. This means that a 'father' is a *kind* of a relative, and so is a 'mother', a 'brother' and a 'sister'; which are all included terms under the cover term 'relative'. The expressions stand in contrast to the ordinarily preferred terms that end with the suffix *–ncha* like 'our father' (*paponcha* or *paponyo*), 'our mother' (*yoncha* or *yonyo*), 'our brother' (*werïncha* or *werinyo*) and 'our sister' (*cheptöncha* or *cheptonyo*) as shown below.

---

9. Ibid., 89.
10. Ibid., 102.

Table 3. A Domain Analysis

RELATIVE (Tilya)

		is a kind of		
Father	Brother	Husband	Uncle	Grandfather
Mother	Sister	Wife	Aunt	Grand Mother
Son/Daughter	Cousin	Child	Nephew/Niece	Grandchild

A taxonomic analysis can also be done to show a deeper relationship between the cover term 'relative' and the other included terms we discovered above (table 3), but here we only use one term (*papo*—father). Spradley defines a taxonomy as a "set of categories organized on the basis of a single semantic relationship."[11] In table 4 below, we use the domain *papo* as a cover term. We show the included terms and their semantic relationship. The term like *papotinencha* (our fathers) means that a person cannot have only one father (*papo*), since there are several *kinds* of fathers: there is one's biological father, stepfather(s), brothers and cousins to one's own father (who are in English regarded as paternal uncles), all members of the age-set to which one's biological father belongs (*pïnwöy*), all his age-mates (even if they do not necessarily belong to his age-set), one's step-father and any elderly male Pöchon. They are all included under the term *papo* and each of them is treated as *a kind* of *papo*.

Table 4. Taxonomic Analysis

RELATIVE (tilya)

Blood Relative					
Father		Mother	Brother	Sister	Economic relative
Strict sense	Loose sense				
Stepfather	His age-mate(s)				
Biological father	His age-set				
His brother(s)	Any elderly man				
His cousin(s)					

The Pökot communitarian spirit also extends to the level of identity. A person is not identified on his or her own right but in relation to his/her parents, land and more importantly, tribe or ethnic group to which he or she belongs. If you want to know the identity of a stranger, for instance, the Pökot do not ask, 'who are you'? Rather they

11. Ibid., 112.

ask a series of relational questions as follows: 'Where do you come from' (*Ingwinonyi onö*)? 'Whose son/daughter are you' (*Ichinyi mombo ngo*)? Or, 'what tribe are you' (*Ichinyi kut nee*)? Similarly, the Pökot always talk about their home, putting the possessive pronoun in the plural. For example, 'let us go to our home' (*kepe katancha*) and 'where is your (pl) home' (*katankwa onö*)? And when a foreigner goes back to his or her country, they say 'he/she went back to their home' (*kimla katangwa*).

Analysis of Material Sources

Spradley also points out that observing a people's artefacts helps a researcher to notice their cultural points of density.[12] We, therefore, tried to look at the Pökot artefacts (both feminine and masculine) to see if there were any indicators of communitarianism. Once again, we found a lot of them that are meant for common use and ought not to be used individually. For instance, *ateker* is a traditional artefact curved from a tree trunk into a huge basin. It is used by a group of young men during their passing out ceremony as warriors to drink a mixture of blood and milk from the container. Then there is a smaller one called *otüpo* used for drinking milk, again not by individuals but by groups of warriors out in the grazing field.

On the feminine artefacts, *köipa pagh*, a common grinding stone, is used by women to grind maize (*pagh*), or millet (*matai*), to make a particular kind of food called *pan*, or home brew (*kumïn*). This giant grinding stone is specially designed by women to serve as a meeting point where they gather from the entire neighborhood, to do the grinding and also some gossiping—to catch up with the local news and know how their neighbors are faring on. Each woman has a personal grinding stone at home (*pagha koghin*), which is only used when one is caught up and has no time to join others, or when one is unclean (like during menstruation or when one has just given birth), and as such not fit to join any public gathering. When it comes to the exploitation of the supernatural powers, there exist communal amulets (*akimistin*) that are put in the roof of the house or at the gate of the home-stead to protect those who enter it against all forms of evil.

Analysis of Behavioral Sources

Spradley also says that by observing what people do, or their cultural behavior, the researcher can gain an insight into their cultural pattern by extracting some cultural domains from the social situation.[13] We, therefore, observed the social behavior of the Pökot and there were several indicators of communitarianism. When a woman gets married to a given man, she regards each of his brothers and age-set members as

---

12. Ibid., 85.
13. Ibid., 85.

her own husbands, and she is supposed to treat them as such by addressing them as 'my husband' (*santenyan*). This means that the same respect she accords her husband is accorded these people and in case the husband is away for a long time or has died, any of them can beget children with her on his behalf.

For this reason, marriage is more between families or clans rather than between individuals and as such should anything happen to this marriage the whole community is involved. The opportune example we witnessed was in Sook location where a man wanted to divorce his wife allegedly because of unfaithfulness. The man called all his relatives and clan members and so did the woman. Each side chose a spokesman to lead the litigation and after every side had spoken it was time for the clan representatives and then family representatives and finally there had to be representatives for the neighbors, for the two spouses and for their biological parents.

To open the floor was an elder spokesman for the council of elders who invited the man to put forth his allegations and then the woman was given a chance to respond. This particular woman accepted some of the accusations that her husband had alleged and asked for forgiveness (*lastagh*) but rejected others as his own fantasies. Then a spokesman from each of the two sides, after digesting the accusations, gave their recommendations. These were followed by other speakers, all of whom made it clear that their desire was to see them continue living as husband and wife in the spirit of reconciliation. When the man was given a chance to speak, he did not heed the elders' desire for reconciliation but insisted on getting a divorce.

At this juncture, the brother of the woman started speaking, and rather harshly when the husband tried to interject in his speech. Things nearly got out of control were it not for the elders who calmed the two men down. He summarized by saying that his sister was not up for sale and if the man had decided to divorce her in spite of her admission of guilt and request for forgiveness in front of all the people present, then they had to follow the traditionally laid down procedure.

The traditional demands are that the man provides for the woman and her children, which he agreed to, and that the children must stay with their mother since the man was likely to remarry. Moreover, once a woman has given birth, the bride price is never returned, because she has, as it were, 'been utilized'. Here things started getting tough for the man because he could not imagine 'losing' his children and wealth, and the prospects of having to start all over again. Then there is the special 'offering' to be made to the elders for taking all their time and refusing to heed their advice. We did not know how they ended up but those who were present made it clear to us that marriage, among the Pökot, is a family as well as clan, rather than an individual, affair.

Apart from the rites of passage, which are communal social activities for both men and women, there are many other things done communally by the two sexes separately. Men, for instance, go out grazing on their own, during the dry spells they travel far and wide in search of water and pasture, and they can live out there for one, two or even three months as a 'community of men' (*keporiak*). Here there are no women to help with cooking or to draw water and as such they feed on blood, milk and meat. They do not slaughter an ox when they want to eat meat; instead they just spear and just roast it with the skin still intact. Moreover, it is the duty of every man to provide such an ox for 'roasting'.

Women, too, carry out many of their activities communally. Apart from the common grinding place spoken of earlier, there are other meeting places like watering points, rivers or drifts where they go for water, during which time they also share a word or two, to release tension and pressure in their respective homes. Forests also serve as a suitable rendezvous for women to seek advice from their friends about issues that might be disturbing them, share frustrations and encourage one another, while fetching firewood. Since farming is considered to be the work of women, they generally do it communally and even build their barns together close to their pieces of land. The woman who wants to ask other women for assistance simply prepares some food and home brew, then sends a child to the home of all her neighbors and gives them a date, which they do not dispute or reject. If any one of the neighbors is not available, they send their daughters to assist on their behalf.

Communitarian Way of Worship

One of the most remarkable things about the Pökot is that they communally celebrate life in all its aspects, and at every stage. All rites of passage, from conception to death are, indeed, celebrations in the form of a series of graduations from one stage of life to the next. The entire life of a Pöchon starts within the parameters of the community and ends in the same ambience. As we have already seen in the last chapter, a Pökot child is born surrounded by a group of women, including a midwife (or even midwives), grows up with other children in a homestead without even distinguishing its biological mother from its other mothers till he/she attains the age of reason. The child goes through all initiation rites while being surrounded by members of his/her clan, relatives and neighbors, and in some cases, people from far away ridges.

Finally, he or she dies peacefully, again, while being surrounded by members of his or her family, because death (*meghat*) is seen as the last rite of passage, as explained in chapter three. Since religion is not dichotomized from the rest of the activities in life, it too is part of the great celebration. This cultural theme is manifested in a number of things found in their way of worship. To begin with, they thank God for his greatness, which is manifested in the many good things he has given them. "*Kikwolecha Tororöt ompö kingaratenyi*" (Let us praise God for his help), one informant told us. And we came across one Christian song that goes like this: "*Kikonecha Tororöt tikuk lapay kighanecha*" (God has given us all things, let us believe in him). Even as the solemn Christian way of worship takes root in some people's lives the celebratory and vibrant traits of traditional songs like *nyalat*, *chepelaleyö* and *adonga* (Appendix 3: picture 11) are still evident in the way they sing. Then there is the whole ritual-like way in which they behave towards each other and carry out their Sunday worship in general.

For example, the Pökot prefer to sing 'the Glory' while standing so that women can wave their hands with joyous ululation, as men join in with their deep voices as if to acknowledge women's *liliey* (waving of hands). For them Sunday worship has a double meaning: it is a day they share the Eucharistic meal, which is a foretaste of the great Eucharistic banquet in heaven; but it is also a reminder of their traditional meals held in different festivities that helped to cement people's relationships and heal the wounds of division in times of trouble.

More than attending to religious matters, Sunday is a special day to meet friends, relatives and neighbors, after a whole working week and know how they are doing. People come early to the church and before the commencement of the Mass or Service they stand in jolly groups chatting the time away; obviously enjoying themselves as they crack a joke or two. Prayer sessions take an average of two hours, but it is not uncommon for them to take up to three hours, as long as the priest is available. And yet all people seem to be at home with this, except for the young who complain of boredom, not really with regard to time, but the content of the sermons issued or their relevance.

After the service, people do not just walk away: they remain behind finalizing their unfinished businesses for almost the same period as that used in the prayer session, if not longer. People do not just want to pray; they want to pray with others and after the prayers they want to know how their neighbors are doing in their prayer life and also how they are faring in all other aspects of life. It is, therefore, not uncommon for people to pass by their neighbors' homes to accompany them on their way to the church. Should a Christian fail to come to the church twice or thrice, neighbors feel obliged to make an impromptu visit, in order to know what is holding him/her back. Finally, we noticed that people have their own criterion of what constitutes a 'good' sermon. It has to touch on the current state of their lives (farming, livestock keeping, the rising cost of living and joblessness, for the young). It should also try to show how culture can be practically integrated with Christianity, since, as some of them say, it is not helpful to mention the problems without a solution.

The SCCs, though not very strong in West Pökot, are another way that fosters the communitarian aspect of prayer life in the church. It mainly brings together Christians who live in the same neighborhood. They share the Word of God and relate it to the actual problems facing them, either collectively or individually. And they do not just pray; they also discuss how to help those among them that are in need.

A case in point is an old man suffering from cancer, which had completely eaten away one of his cheeks. After the prayers, members were taken to see the man and offer sympathy together with any material help they could afford. Here they visit their sick and comfort them as neighbors and also prepare their members for the receiving of various sacraments in the church. The principle is that nobody should struggle to go to heaven alone. "You know," a middle-aged woman, who wanted to remain anonymous, said to us, "if you go to heaven alone God will ask you one question at the gate, the same question he asked Cain: where is your brother?" Indeed, they sometimes invite their priest to come and celebrate Mass with them and dispense the sacraments in their presence. Most importantly their sharing of the Gospel seems to be more effective because they know their local situation better, as one of them elaborated.

> You know from time to time in the church on Sunday when they explain the readings; it is difficult to understand the priest's explanations. However, when we are in the Small Christian Community and reflect on the Word together, everybody understands better than in the church since each one of us has a chance to contribute the way he or she is touched. I think the Small Christian Community enables us to understand the Word, since it is the reading, which was read in the church the previous Sunday. You know when a person explains a reading in the church you can understand it in a different perspective but when we are out, different people contribute and quote different experiences and we get encouraged to share one or two words and apply them in our lives.[14]

Solidarity within the Community

From a very tender age, Pökot children are taught the importance of community life and its primacy over personal or individual life, interests and desire. Thus, as already mentioned above, a person's entire life revolves around the community and its demands, and individuals are always striving to achieve what the community members approve in solidarity with their leaders. This 'solidarity' rests in the hands of the elders (*poy*) who are considered to be wise and also regarded as intermediaries between the community and the ancestors in virtue of their age, which is closer to the latter than anybody else still alive.

What elders decide, for whatever reason, is then unquestionably passed on to the next generation and the next; finally becoming a tradition that no one dares to question or challenge. Principal among these demands is the defense of the community, owing to the insecurity that results from incessant practice of cattle rustling. The defense of the community is every member's task, although it is primarily the work of men; women (particularly girls) too have a role to play, should the need arise. Like in the biblical story of Samson and Delilah, the Pökot give away their girls for 'marriage' to their enemies in the pretext of peace pacts, only for these girls to go and steal their enemy's' secrets and pass them on to their relatives. This mainly happens after a woman has settled in her new home. Pökot young men disguised as 'relatives' come to spy on the enemy community in the name of 'knowing' the new home of their 'daughter'.

---

14. Teresa Nekesa is a 51-year-old leader of the SCC in Kacheliba Parish and also works as a cook to the Sisters in their convent.

Treachery within the community is an evil that fetches a very heavy fine, particularly if it involves a man. However, it is another matter if one betrays a member of the Pökot community to its enemies because one is effectively cut off from the community. Consequently, a Pöchon would rather risk his life, or even die, while defending his or her people against any aggressor(s). This point came into the fore when the government tried to disarm the community, in 1979, due to rampant acts of insecurity in the borders of West Pökot and other counties (i.e., Trans Nzoia, Elgeyo-Marakwet, Baringo and Turkana). Many people, including an ex-chief in Masol Location, chose to die rather than betray their kinsmen who owned guns. Even though about one thousand guns seem to have been recovered during the operation,[15] and the then Kapenguria MP jailed for previously unheard-of charges of promoting war-like activities, cattle rustling went on unabated.

The Pökot Worldview

At the beginning of our research we presumed that the Pökot worldview is a communitarian one, and it can be contrasted with the Western worldview, which we considered to be individualistic. With worldview, here we mean the perspective of reality (the world, God and humankind) that people have acquired, as a result of their survival strategies in a given locality.

> Cultures pattern perceptions of reality into conceptualisations of what reality can or should be, what is to be regarded as actual, probable, possible, and impossible. These conceptualisations form what is termed the "worldview" of the culture. The worldview is the central systematisation of conceptions of reality to which the members of the culture assent (largely unconsciously) and from which stems their value system. The worldview lies at the very heart of culture, touching, interacting with, and strongly influencing every other aspect of the culture.[16]

These strategies bring forth a meaning system, which they use as the criteria to interpret reality surrounding them and to generate their social behavior. Based on this, they lay a permanent frame of reference, which they use to judge all new events, ideas, people and texts, including biblical texts. Kraft further explains the interaction between culture and worldview.

> With respect to the organization or patterning of the culture, the worldview may be seen as the organizer of the conceptual system taught to and employed by the members of that culture/subculture. With respect to the behavior or performance of the participants in the culture/subculture, the worldview may

---

15. Visser (1989). Op. cit., 51.
16. Charles H. Kraft (1979). *Christianity in Culture: A Study in Dynamic Biblical Theologizing in Cross-Cultural Perspective*. Maryknoll, New York: Orbis Books, 53.

be thought of as that which governs the application of the culture's conceptualisations of their relationships to reality.[17]

Shorter shows that there is a relationship between a cultural meaning system and a worldview. Using concentric circles, he draws various levels of culture, with the outermost circle (level 1) consisting of industrial technical and the second one (level 2) consisting of domestic technical. The third circle (level 3) consists of values, while in the innermost circle (level 4) stands the worldview.[18] On his part, Luzbetak categorizes the items that occur in most worldviews into three: super nature, nature, human beings and time. He also says that a worldview has three dimensions: a cognitive dimension, an emotional and motivational dimension.[19]

The cognitive dimension tells the community what to think and how it is to think about life and the world. The emotional dimension of the worldview tells the community how it is to feel about, evaluate and react to the world and all reality. Then the motivational dimension of the worldview determines community's basic priorities, purposes, concerns, ideals, desires, hopes, goals, and drives corresponding to its understanding of the universe.[20]

We see no contradiction between a meaning system and a worldview because the latter is at the core of the former. In general, the Pökot under-standing of the world is not 'my world', but 'our world' and their basic question in life is not 'what is good for me', but 'what is good for us as a family, a house, a clan (door), as a community—as a people. This amounts to a communitarian worldview, which so permeates the societal fabric to the extent that banishment from the community life is the severest punishment, after the death penalty that can be meted out on an errant member. The unquestioned assumption here is that outside the community there is no life, and if there is, then it is not worth living. Thus, it is only fit for the perverts who have renounced their own humanity and therefore they do not deserve to live in communion with normal people.

Spradley has classified the characteristics of cultural themes into three: tacit (as when nobody mentions them but still everybody acts according to them), explicit (like in the case of proverbs, sayings and idiomatic expressions) and as relationships.[21] These are the cognitive principles that determine people's social behavior and dictate what is acceptable to them and what is not. The above cognitive principle with regard to life outside the community kept recurring in all cultural discussions on the Pökot life through many forms of expressions that militate against individualism.

---

17. Ibid., 53.

18. Aylward Shorter (1998). *African Culture: An Overview.* Nairobi: Paulines Publications Africa, 25.

19. Louis J. Luzbetak (1998). *The Church and Cultures: New Perspectives in Missiological Anthropology*, eighth print. Maryknoll, New York: Orbis Books, 252.

20 Ibid., 55.

21. Spradley., op. cit., 143.

Here we can only mention a few of them as follows: solidarity (in the form of age-sets, house, clan and so on), ownership (of animals, children, land and so forth), economy (declining wealth, lack of rain, high prices of basic goods and so on), taboos and rituals (both transitory and remedial). We are going to do an analysis of the remedial rituals due to time and space because transitory rituals are so detailed and elaborate.

Our interaction and extensive discussions with the Pökot always revolved around strengthening the natural and supernatural life within the community and trying to avoid whatever can upset this order. When, for instance, contra-sting the different kinds of evil, the Pökot always gauge the seriousness of a particular evil act by the degree that it disrupts life in the community. Even the whole concept of ritual rotates around community reconciliation—either by appeasing the spirits on behalf of the community or bringing back an errant member into the community life, lest the evil-doer is cut off forever. The following is a componential analysis to show how rituals are linked to the above-mentioned cognitive principle.

Analysis of the Pökot Ritual System

The Pökot do not have the word 'ritual' and instead they use a variety of words, like custom (*otöp*) and tradition (*telengan*). For them, rituals are but part of life, which cannot be conceived without them because it is these that make it complete and safe. By asking contrast questions we were able to come up with attributes of meaning under a mixed domain, which we called 'taboo and rituals'. The reason for the inclusion of the former is that among the Pökot rituals are understood as remedies for some broken taboo or as a fulfilment of some cultural requirements, failure to implement which amounts to a taboo. It is, thus, not possible to talk of one without the other. The members of this contrast set (of rituals) are *ngokï, lelut, sirrïp, ptakal, mori* and *orus, kilokat, amat, artakarerat, moy, eghpadia, kartapögh, karera, kityoghin, kitunga, kötkotka, kipunö, sapana, lapan, löpow, lyokat, parpara,* and *kikatat*.

Pökot rituals are very many, and they could be classified into many more groupings, depending on the researcher's point of departure. Firstly, they can be classified into two groups, those that are strictly remedial (e.g. *lapay* and *rïwoy*) and secondly, those that act as an assurance of a good life (e.g., all rites of passage, like *parpara* and *sapana*). Then we made a third classification of all taboos and tried to cross-relate them with the remedial rituals that the offenders are subjected to. Remedial rituals could be classifiable into three groups: rituals done on behalf of individuals, those done on behalf of specific groups and those that are done on behalf of the whole community.

This classification, as shown in the table below, further indicates the complexity of the Pökot culture, whereby it gives room for, and seems to acknowledge (if not directly encourage), the aspects of communitarianism as well as those of individualism in the community life. The first group consists of *tisö* (appeasement and purification), *parpara* (reconciliation) *rurwö* (retaliation and cleansing), *karatapögh* (untying), *kikatat* (untying) *moy* (appeasement) and *kilokat* (appeasement). The second group consists of *pöghisyö* (restoration and protection of a homestead), *amat* (reconciliation of age-sets), *lapay* (reconciliation of clans), *muma* (tying people together) and *mis* (ensuring peace).

The third group consists of *mutat* (cutting off evil), *karera* (fighting crop diseases), *oy* (appeasement), *amoros* (divination or sacrifice), *putyon* (protection, rain, fertility or blessing), *munyan* (protection rain or fertility), *muntin* (empowering). But this classification has a problem; some rituals no longer maintain a single value but have acquired a binary or even tertiary value. *Parpara* can, for instance, be done on behalf of an individual or on behalf of a group, while *amoros* and *muma* can be done on behalf of an individual, a group or even the whole com-munity depending on the circumstances.

Then there is another problem. It is not enough to classify a ritual as merely reconciliatory, because there is the question of the nature of reconciliation and to whom it is directed. Once again, we use the example of *parpara*, which is a reconciliation ritual performed by an individual (*parparin*), either to reconcile two quarrelling individuals or simply to wish a woman safe delivery during her first pregnancy. And yet *amat* is also a reconciliation ritual in which one age-set (*pïn*) is reconciled with another after a quarrel. The actors are the offended age-set, which is usually the senior age-set, out to reconcile with a junior (often perceived as the guilty) one. Although both of them are reconciliation rituals, they are directed to different beneficiaries and also conducted by different actors—sometimes, groups; other times, individuals, while still other times it is both of them. Below is a table of componential analysis for the remedial rituals only.

Table 5. A Componential Analysis

DIMENSIONS OF CONTRAST

DOMAIN	Purpose	Actors	Animal	Address	Comm[22]	Individ[23]	Group	Day	Night
Amat	reconciliation	age-set	no	age-set	no	no	yes	yes	yes
Amoros	sacrifice	elders	yes	spirits	yes	yes	yes	yes	yes
Karat[24]	untying	elders	no	people	no	yes	no	yes	no
Karera	diseases	women	no	worms	yes	no	no	yes	no
Kilokat	appease	family	yes	Ilat	no	yes	no	no	yes
Kikatat	untying	elders	yes	people	no	yes	no	yes	no
Lapay	punish	offend	no	offender	no	yes	no	yes	no
Mis	peace	elders	yes	people	yes	no	yes	yes	yes
Moy	appease	ngbs[25]	yes	spirits	no	yes	no	no	yes
Muma	binding	elders	yes	people	yes	yes	yes	yes	yes
Muntin	power	all	no	enemy	yes	no	no	yes	yes
Munyan	protect	werkoy	no	enemy	yes	no	no	yes	no
Oy	appease	elders	no	worms	yes	no	no	no	yes
Parpara	reconcile	anyone	no	spirits	no	yes	yes	no	yes
Pöghisyö	restore	father	no	anyone	no	no	yes	yes	yes
Putyon	protect	elders	yes	enemy	yes	no	no	yes	yes
Tisö	appease	anyone	yes	spirits	no	yes	no	yes	yes

In the table, above, we observe that cultural complexity takes a prominent place, whereby it becomes even harder to say with any degree of certainty whether the Pökot are actually a communitarian, or an individualistic people, or whether they are an amorphous mixture of the two. Here we can pinpoint several dimensions of contrast. Starting with the third column we see that individuals perform some rituals (*lapay, parpara, tisö*), while others are performed by particular groups of people (*amat, karatapögh, karera, kilokat, moy*), and still the entire community performs others (*munyan*).

22. Community.
23. Individual.
24. Karatapögh.
25. Neighbours.

In the fifth column, we can observe a similar phenomenon, whereby some rituals are addressed to particular groups (*amat, amoros, karera*), others to individuals (*lapay, kilokat, pöghsyö*), and still others to the entire community (*mis, muma, kikatat, karatapögh*). *Lapay* is a punishment ritual against someone who has killed a fellow Pöchon and it is addressed specifically to the offender. *Amat*, already mentioned above, is addressed to the offending age-set, which is normally the junior one. *Munyan* is a protection ritual that is conducted by a seer (*werkoyon*), designed to keep the enemy, who is usually a neighboring comm.-unity, away when there is fear of an imminent attack.

In the sixth, seventh and eighth columns we observe that some rituals are done on behalf of the entire community (*karera, muntin, munyan, oy, putyon*), others on behalf of individuals (*karatapögh, kilokat, lapay, moy, tisö*), while others are done on behalf of particular groups (*amat, pöghisyö*). There are those rituals that are done both on behalf of the community and a particular group (*mis*), those done on behalf of individuals and particular groups (*parpara*) and those done on behalf of the community, individuals and groups (*amoros, muma*). Significantly, there are no rituals carried out on behalf of the community as well as individuals. Then there are those rituals that are carried out only during the day (*karatapögh, karera, kikatat, lapay, munyan*), those carried out only at night (*kilokat, moy, oy*) and those that are carried out both during the day and at night (*amat, amoros, mis, muma, muntin, pöghisyö, putyon, tisö*).

Further analysis of rituals (both transitional—which are not included in the table above—and remedial) shows that irrespective of the target group, rituals can be classified into three other categories as follows: transitory (*parpara, kiporcha asis, malal or riwoy, keghot kelat, sorïm, tum* or *rotwo, kensyö sapana* and *meghat*), reconciliatory (*kikatat, karatapögh, pöghisyö, amat, muma, mis, mutat, lapay*) and appeasing (*tisö, moy, kilokat, karera, oy, amoros, putyon, munyan muntin*).

The remedial rituals are carried out at night for the moon and the stars to witness, assurance rituals are carried out during the day for the sun, which is the custodian of life, to witness and appeasing rituals could be carried out at night or during the day depending on its nature. The same problem recurs with this classification because transitory rituals also tend to be assurance rituals, with the exception of those rituals that double as both assurance and remedial, hence they also go on throughout night and day.

Efforts to find components of meaning in this set revealed that only two terms of 'taboo' category are used in the Christian context. These are *ngokï* (sin) and *lelut* (mistake) while the other four (*sirrïp, ptakal, orus* and *mori*) are not. *Ngokï* is used to signify the general nature of human 'fallenness' and inclination to sin, while *lelut* signifies our individual frailty and mistakes. Like in the 'Our Father' prayer they say: "forgive us our failures (or trespasses) . . . (*ilostowech lelutkocho*. . .)." Hence *ngokï* is used as a cover term to the other five terms. However, in the traditional sense, *orus* seems to be the cover term for all of them, including *ngokï* since it is the general state in which any breaking of taboo leaves the offender. These terms are specific to particular failings and clearly define what needs to be done when a specific cultural code has been broken. Abnormal actions related to animals, like bestiality, are classified as *ptakal*: both between humans and animals and also between animals themselves.

So, if a young bull mounts a heifer from the front, that is regarded as *ptakal* and when a rooster crows at odd times (like 10.00pm), it is also *ptakal*. We are sure that if the summer phenomenon where the sun is still shining after 8.00pm was to be experienced in West Pökot it would be considered as *ptakal* and would require the slaughtering of an animal to cleanse the earth of some unknown kind of blasphemy.[26] Although these terms are different, specific and distinguished from each other, it is still easy to show that they are connected; as in the expression '*ptakalian* are abominable sins' (*ptakalian kï ngokï cho orusech*).

With regard to the transition rites, it is believed that they are necessary if the child is to be accepted in the community, survive the tribulations of life and grow to his/her full human potential. The tying of *lökötyö* (a traditional belt made of skin hide from a cow) by the mother immediately after birth manifests the necessity for this, which ties the child to the Pökot way of life; given that she had, on behalf of the child undergone the ritual of *parpara* that signaled a safe delivery. Transition rituals are contrasted with other rituals because they do not involve any personal guilt and, as such the partakers are basically passive participants.

And yet it is unanimously agreed that the partakers are in the state of uncleanness (*orus*) until certain cleansing ceremonies have been carried out, to make them worthy members of the community. Emphasizing the importance of the role played by the community, one informant pointed to us that all acts of taboos and rituals are either initiated by the community or by individuals on behalf, or in the name of the community, within which they feel safe and through which they have acquired their life and status.

All our informants agreed that the Pökot form of communitarianism, which permeates all aspects of their lifestyle and the entire societal fabric, is sustained by two aspects, one positive and the other negative. One, there is the desire for every member to be regarded as a generous person (*pöghïn*), concerned with the well-being of their kin and kith; and two, there is fear of being regarded as an unworthy member of the community, or worse, being thrown out of the community life altogether. Michael Dillon explains the extent of the Pökot sense of communitarianism in a better way:

> The Pökot see themselves as a people rather than individuals. This has so many implications in the relationship to the people around, property and their animals. There is this community awareness and the consciousness that the world

---

26. We met two people from West Pökot (Albino Katomei and Rachel Andiema) in Amsterdam and asked them what they thought of this phenomenon and they tied it to the land question. It was okay for the sun to set at whatever time it wished, they said, as long as this did not happen in the Pökotland!

belongs to us rather than to me, and this has a bearing on the way they live and act. I am struck by this that in trying to teach them the Gospel they too teach me how to perceive and live it with my neighbours, since they will receive the Gospel according to the vision that they have of the world and of the other, not as another but as the self. And yet this is the hardest thing to accept for many of us in the West.[27]

Individualism in the Pökot Worldview

Although the Pökot worldview heavily leans towards communitarianism, as shown above, there are far too many elements of individualism that cannot be wished away or swept under the carpet, and hence need to be addressed. This is because there is a discrepancy between the claims of communitarianism, as many scholars have made, and what actually goes on the ground. In analyzing the elements of individualism, we follow the same procedure that we followed when analyzing the elements of communitarianism within the Pökot culture in the same order. We analyzed their *cultural* behavior, their *cultural* artefacts and their *cultural* speech.[28]

Analysis of Verbal Sources

In this sub-section, we used the Kwalitan word-count and the proverb analysis, which, together with sayings, Spradley links to cultural themes.[29] Although there are many definitions of a cultural theme, here we stick to James Spradley's definition.[30] After we carried out a word-count exercise we noticed that although the number of plural articles was higher the difference was actually not big. So, individual expressions cannot be wished away as exceptions, indeed at one particular instance (them/they versus him/her) singular articles outnumbered the plural ones.

Word-count

The word 'we' was used 608 times against the word 'I' which was used 555 times (a difference of 53 times), the word 'us' was used 279 times as opposed to the word 'me' which was used 157 times (a difference of 122 times). The word 'our' was used 215 times against the word, 'my' which was used 140 times (a difference of 75 times). The word 'they' appeared 614 times whereas the words 'he' and 'she' appeared 416

---

27. Oral interview with Michael Dillon, a 72-year-old Kiltegan missionary who has worked in West Pökot for forty-three years. He is currently the parish priest of Chepnyal Catholic Parish in Sook location. The interview was carried out on 16/06/2002.
28. Spradley (1980). Op. cit., 85.
29. Ibid., 142.
30. Spradley (1980). Op. cit., 141.

and 103 times respectively (a difference of 95 times). The word 'them' appeared 244 times whereas the words 'him' and 'her' were used 126 and 85 times (a difference of 33 times). The words 'you'/yourselves were used 433 times in contrast to the singular forms of 'you' and 'yourself', which were used 322 times. For the purpose of strengthening our case, we also counted other related words and the number of times they were used as follows: 'mine' (1), 'your' in its plural form (66), 'yours' in its singular form (1), 'his'/ 'hers'/ 'its' (213) and 'their'/'theirs' (214).

Table 6. Pronoun Articles

Plural	Frequency	Singular	Frequency	Difference
We (*acha*)	608	I (*ani, ante*)	555	55
Us (*acha*)	279	Me (*ani, ante*)	157	122
Our(s) (*chicha*)	215	My/mine (*nyinyan*)	141	174
You/yourselves (*akwa/akwane*)	433	You/your-self (*nyi*)	322	111
Their(s) (*nyingwa*)	314	His/hers/its (*nyenyi*)	192/1/20	101
Them/they (*chane*)	244	Him/her (*nyinte*)	120/85/60	27[31]
Your(s) (*nyinkwa/chikwa*)	66	Your(s) (*nyengu / cheku*)	1	65

Ngotinyö (Proverbs)

The other aspect we investigated concerning individualism is the proverbs which, in the Pökot community, act as a means of communication and are embodied in the teaching about morality, history, admonition and advice. "Proverbs are a mirror in which a community can look at itself and a stage on which it exposes itself to others. They ascribe its values, aspirations, pre-occupations and the particular angles from which it sees and appreciates realities and behavior. What we call mentality or way of life is best pictured in them."[32]

In this light then, we argue that proverbs too encompass and reflect the entire worldview of the Pökot people. Although most proverbs exhort the value of community life and urge people to be keepers of their brothers we found that there exists some that call upon the people to strive for success individually, rather than depend on the community, clan or one's family. We found a booklet that has compiled most of the Pökot proverbs, but since it is not sufficiently detailed in its explanation, we

---

31. This is the only calibration that singular articles outnumbered plural ones among the Christians.
32. Patrick A. Kalilombe (1969). Preface. In *Bantu Wisdom: A Collection of Proverbs*. Kachebere: Privately Printed, 3.

discussed them, one by one, with the elders in order to gain their hidden meaning. Since we cannot review all of them here, we will only mention and explain a few.

1. *Asyara kolyong ompö chö* (Remove flies from the milk)—*anateghena pich cho ghach otöp ompö kwenu pich.*[33]

   The Pökot people believe that it is better to remove unwanted people (flies) from the midst of good people (milk) otherwise they too, will get spoiled. This proverb is used to justify the acts like the one stated above of killing the witches and other undesired elements in the community, like notorious thieves.

2. *Awira mïsïköy* (Knock out the stumps)—*anateghena pich cho ghach otöp ompö kwenu pich.*[34]

   Like the first proverb, this one too urges the community to rid itself of unwanted people in its midst, here referred to as 'stumps' (*mïsïköy*). They need to be put down or be removed completely; otherwise they will cause more harm to the whole community.

3. *Okwölö per* (Remove the bark of a tree)—*apara pich cho le pung ompö kwenu pich.*[35]

   The proverb states the same as the earlier two, only that here the enemy that needs to be removed from the midst of the people (community) is referred to as the 'bark of a tree', a clever way to disguise the original meaning in case the enemy knows the first two.

4. *Mi sikonöt morin* (Wealth is in the hands)—*mi sikonöt kokay ato tökïsööy chi.*

   If someone wants to get plenty of wealth, or riches, one is encouraged to work hard for it (with the hands). In spite of any calamity that may befall an individual or society in general, one need not worry because wealth is in the hands as long as one is alive.

5. *Metöngönye rurwö wop akonga osis* (The shade of a tree does not always fall in the same direction)—*mekolö kegh tïkwïn ompö wolo wonyot.*[36]

   This is a warning to lucky people who boast over their fortune. The saying reminds them that luck may not be theirs forever. Just like the shade of a tree moves with the movement of the sun, so does fortune.

6. *Meteptepöy kegh le mïrara syapïk* (Do not boast like the bridegroom of syapïk)—*kisusöt/kinyïlitat.*[37]

---

33. Daniel P. Angele (1993). *Pokot Proverbs, Sayings and Idiomatic Expressions.* Kapenguria: Arid and Semi Arid Lands Development Programme, 3.
34. Ibid., 4.
35. Ibid., 19.
36. Ibid., 15.
37. Ibid., 34.

This proverb takes a direct hit at the proud people and tells them to the face, not to show off! The point here is that by showing off they try to say that they are better than the rest of the community, which goes against the Pökot practice of the primacy of the community, over and above the individual.

7. *Owetan onuchöy kwentenyu* (I am going to extinguish my firewood)—*owetan omisïyi*.

This proverb simply means 'I am going to eat'. The firewood it is talking about is the burning sensation of the stomach when one is hungry, and so the person is going to put it out by eating. Again, here we see that the individual person is encouraged to do what he or she has to do because there is no one in the community to do the eating for him or her.

8. *Owetan orötöy kwantinyu* (I am going to tie my bow)—*owetan omisïyi*.

The proverb means 'I am going to eat'. The bow here refers to the stomach.

9. *Owetan oghoghöy yitïnyu* (I am going to boil my ear)—*owetan oriwoy*.[38]

It means I am going to sleep. Once again, this is an appeal to the individual to do what he or she has to do without fear of what others in the community say or think of him or her. It can be interpreted as a way of remedying the concept that one should always do what the community approves of, or always look up to the community to do everything for him or her.

10. *Tenyorï imel tököghögh* (If you get it you will lick your elbow)—*memukonye, menyorunenyinye kokay*.[39]

This proverb is used to warn a person when is thought that he/she cannot get something then he/she is told it is impossible to get it, just as it is impossible to lick the elbow. Our informants gave this as a good example of individual-ism because the warning is directed to the individual as an individual, rather than as a member of the community.

Unlike prose and poetry, proverbs contain a lot more than appears on the surface and only native (though not all) speakers of a particular language, within which a proverb is used, can explain this deeper meaning. Spradley suggests that the way to go about this problem is theme analysis through which the outsider, after domain analysis, taxonomic and componential analyses, tries to discover the cultural themes by examining various components of culture, how they relate to each other and to the whole cultural scene.[40] Only then can one be able to discover the underlying cultural themes, most of which are tacit and are implied in people's conversation. The above quoted proverbs and sayings may, for instance, seem to be innocently urging people

---

38. Ibid., 20.
39. Ibid., 21.
40. Spradley (1980). Op. cit., 85.

to be aware of themselves and their bodies, an appeal that apparently has nothing to do with the communitarian-ism versus individualism divide.

They can even be said to be in support of communitarianism rather than individualism because some of them, for instance, speak out against evil individuals for the good of the community. But the underlying message, according to an elderly informant, is to act as an individual rather than just sit and depend on the community for all your needs and aspirations. Going by the understanding of a community within the African context, where all the rules are decided and deter-mined by the community, it is out of the ordinary to urge the same people to go against these rules and make independent decisions as individuals.

There are many other proverbs, sayings and idiomatic expressions that lay emphasis on individuality within the Pökot community, but these are put forth to show that individualism has always existed side by side with communitarianism. This co-existence cannot be fully comprehended or exhaustively explained because there is no time that one ever threatened or subsumed the other. And yet the two have peacefully co-existed since time immemorial. Once again one is faced with the notion of the complexity as well as contradiction of culture.[41]

So, complex and contradictory is the Pökot culture that many questions about life are not answered verbally. They are only lived and experienced. We say experienced because there seems to be no enough or exact words to explain the actual nature of the reality on the ground to an outsider. It means that unless one lives and takes part in the daily life activities as a participant observer, one cannot simply get to *know* the Pökot and their culture. The furthest one can go is only to know *about* them, conceptualize and theorize *about* their culture. But experiencing the human warmth of their community life leaves you trapped and you do not want to leave, as Dillon, Staples and Visser have attested.

Analysis of Material Sources

There are many indicators of individualism in the Pökot traditional community that were pointed out to us during our encounter with the people, as opposed to those brought about by the influence of modernity. Once again, we cannot name them all here but we are only going to enumerate two that are most common in people's lifestyle: one used by men, one used by women.

Kaideke or Ngachar (The Stool)

One of the cultural artefacts among the Pökot is *kaideke* (see the cover page), a strictly personal stool given to an elder after the initiation ceremony of *sapana* and no other

---

[41] Hannerz, Op. cit., 8; Spradley (1980). Op. cit., 152.

person is supposed to sit on it irrespective of whether the owner is using it or not. It is also immaterial whether the one who would like to use it has another chair to sit on or not. The only person who is exempted from this rule is one's age mate (*pïn*) if he has come from very far for a visit, and he has undergone the ritual of *sapana*. Then the host would slaughter a goat or an ox for him and could also give him one of his wives for the night. This is the apex of generosity that one can show his age mate in accordance with the Pökot tradition.

As opposed to other, ordinary, chairs, *kaideke* has three common uses. Even though it is very small, it can be used as a chair, and indeed it is very comfortable to sit on. It can also be used as a pillow to rest one's head during a nap outside the house to avoid insects entering into one's ears and nostrils. Finally, it can be used as a shield. During minor disagreements, the Pökot people ordinarily fight using sticks (*lëkiip*), which they also use for walking. In major departure, they traditionally used ordinary bows and arrows, which they made themselves, but when fighting an intruding enemy they used poisoned arrows, although these days they also use guns.

Kaideke is an excellent cover for the zooming sticks to land on rather than on one's body. Now it would be easy to argue against this point and say that the possession of private property is not in itself individualistic, which is true as it stands. But viewed from the communitarianism versus individualism axis, this can be seen to be the case, going by the principles that govern such ownership. In Individualistic communities, private ownership bestows absolute proprietorship rights to an individual, on the property in question, to the exclusion of anybody else, unless expressly allowed by the individual owner. In communitarian communities, however, ownership is in trust. Although a person may own something, other members have a right to claim it by virtue of their membership.

Pagha Koghin (The Grinding Stone)

Traditionally (and even today in many places) the Pökot people did not have grinding mills to grind their millet and sorghum, in order to make food (*omisyö*) or beer (*kumïn*). It is the job of women to think of what to do in order to prepare something for their husbands and children. So, they use two stones to grind the grains (*pagh*), a small one (called *ngisya*) and a big one called *pagha koghin*. The big one is normally used in common, ordinarily near the river or watering point, so that they can make flour and from the same place carry water home. Then there are small grinding stones that belong to each woman individually and are usually not given away, unless under very strenuous circumstances.

Analysis of the Behavioral Sources

Apart from artefactual indicators, there is a host of behavioral indicators of individualism in the traditional Pökot lifestyle. Once again space cannot allow us to enumerate all of them here but we are going to name the three most common aspects of this phenomenon.

Ghakta (The Payment of a Fine or Penalty)

Earlier on we said that the Pökot cattle (and by extension all other animals) are owned communally and that individuals only own them in trust. They are, therefore, referred to as Pökot cows (*tupa Pökot*). But this remains a general rule with so many concrete exceptions that one wonders, in this case, if the rule itself is not the exception. If, for instance, a person's cow is stolen and the thief is found, the payment that is meted out on him is paid to the owner of the stolen animal, not to the community, even though it is the community that has fixed the penalty. Moreover, the initiative to look for the lost animal and to mobilize the community into action lies purely on the individual owner, not the community. So, if he does not take the initiative to summon the *kokwö* (council of elders) and pay for their sitting expenses, then no one is going to do this on his behalf. Moreover, when the case is on trial the two individuals are not allowed to be present and the judgement is made on individual basis.

Witchcraft and witch hunting has been part and parcel of the Pökot social life for as long as anyone can remember. The witches (*ponü*) are classified among the extraordinary people with power to manipulate the supernatural powers for their own selfish ends that usually go against the common weal. Due to this fact, a witch (*ponïn*) is regarded as a perverted individual and does not, therefore, deserve to live in the community, since his or her perversion is not seen as an extension of the community. Instead of working for communal harmony (*pöghisyö*), he/she works to destroy life and negate all that is dear to the comm.-unity. Once a person was identified, as a witch, the community or his relatives did not shoulder the burden of his/her sins, it is him/she that was killed by being forced to publicly hang him/herself on a designated tree. Nobody would kill him/her for the fear of becoming ritually unclean or being haunted by his/her spirit *(onyöt)*.

Although this practice is still going on in the entire West Pökot County, we did not witness any person being forced to take his/her own life. We already mentioned that we visited one catechist whose father was forced to hang himself in December 2001 on the charge that he was a witch. He narrated this sad story to us and showed us the tree on which his father died in the presence of the area assistant chief and the councilor. His accusers elaborated on how he had bewitched three people, all of whom had died, and they brought forth the paraphernalia he was using for the job. Tied to the accusation of witchcraft was another issue of land, making the matter even more complex, so we asked him why he did not seek legal protection since his own brother is a prisons officer.

He said it is very difficult to mix the two legal systems for two main reasons. Firstly, the civil legal system is expensive and yet it is not necessarily just. Secondly, where there is a conflict of interest between civil and traditional legal systems, the latter always wins. Consequently, he thought it was pointless to seek any legal redress from the courts. So, he lost his father, as per the decision of the council of elders, and also surrendered a huge chunk of his father's land (which he showed us) to those same people who accused him of witchcraft. No doubt again, Nathanson would condemn the elders involved in the whole decision-making process, in the strongest possible terms.[42] An informant explained the co-existence between the traditional and civil legal systems in Sook location:

> These two legal systems are evident here in Chepnyal. Every Thursday the local *wazee* (elders) meet to judge the community cases or problems that have arisen—disputes between individuals or the problems of land. The local community hears the evidence brought forward and then the council of elders gives its verdict. The community handles most cases. We have no jails to lock people but elders penalise people according to their faults and they give stiff penalties in the form of money or property in compensation for the fault. The other system is the civil legal system where someone is taken to court in Kapenguria and the offender is individually dealt with according to the laws of this country. But in the traditional legal system, an offence like murder will make the whole clan to be penalised; therefore, clans try to ensure that their members are not involved in such offences. This is the contrast between the legal system and the traditional system.[43]

Saghtaghin nko Akimistin (Rituals and Amulets)

Another aspect, in the Pökot social behavior that manifested a sense of individualism is rituals. With the help of Visser's work,[44] we have established that individualistic rituals do exist among the Pökot. These include, but not limited to *kikatat* (to ward off individual misfortune and disease), *karatapögh* (meant to treat barrenness), *moy* (to remedy abnormalities), *kilokat* (to treat the disease of *ilat*) and *tisö* (to cater for an individual's instant needs). Visser has further explained how these rituals are carried out and how they differ from group as well as community rituals.[45] Many of these rituals go together with individual amulets (*akimistin*), which are not transferable to

---

42. Nathanson (2001). Op. cit.

43. Benedict Ywalaita is a school teacher and has served the Catholic Church in various capacities, particularly in Chepnyal Parish, where he hails from.

44. Visser (1989). Op. cit., 14.

45. Ibid., 115.

any other person and, in some cases, they could be harmful to the second person they are transferred to, if it ever happened. Thus, the effect of these amulets is destined for a given, particular individual only, as opposed to communal benefit or impact.

Lük (Cattle Rustling)

Although cattle rustling remains an acceptable practice within the Pökot community, some Christians see it as a way to satisfy individual greed rather than a community need. The raid is planned communally; with the permission of the elders and more crucially, that of both the seer (*werkoyon*) and the medicine man (*kapulokyon*), as Visser has observed:

> The youngsters take the initiative in showing off those virtues valued by society. When they have gathered sufficient information through reconnaissance parties, they invite the elders to a meal of meat and wine. The *werkoyon*, the foreteller . . . is among these elders as is the *kapulokyon* or magician. . . The youngster's request is put in the secret language which they learned during their circumcision period. . . . The foreteller's advice is essential since he or she has 'seen' and can give exact directions as to the route to follow and about which things to do or to leave. It is for him to say whether or not enemies need to be killed. He might even choose the party's leader. Neglect of all this advice will bring disaster as many stories testify.[46]

Once the raid has been successful, the stolen animals will not just be brought to the community and be mixed with other animals. The raiders, celebrate their victory, by killing an ox, and a ceremony has is carried out, particularly for those who have killed the enemy. During this period, some of the warriors, either individually or collectively, conspire to snatch the animals from the rest of the group, especially when the loot is regarded as too little to satisfy everybody. So, as people are busy eating the meat or undergoing the cleansing rituals some of them just go and snatch (*sarap*) as many animals as possible and quickly mix them with their own herds, after which no one can reclaim them.

The existence and seeming communal approval of such a practice, then, casts a serious doubt as to the homogeneity of an exclusive communitarian claim among the Pökot. To conclude this part that addresses our first aim, we would like to say that the Pökot are not a purely communitarian people, because there are many traits of individualism in their cultural heritage. We would, however, want to point out that they are more communitarian than individualistic. And this is mainly due to the nature of their existence, which is dictated by their economic and geographical dispensation. First, they are a pastoralist community (though in varying degrees), largely

---

46. Ibid., 22.

surrounded by other pastoral communities. Animals and cows in particular, are their livelihood and the same applies to their neighbors.

This creates a situation for an exceeding demand for the cow, portraying "...the Pokot as possessors of what M. J. Herskovits has called the 'cattle complex.'"[47] This common demand, for the cow, has created an atmosphere of mutual suspicion and as such each group has to cling together in order to keep its enemies at bay; just in case of an attack. Communitarianism, then, can be regarded here, as a purely survival strategy that has evolved into a social structure, in the face of which there exists no viable option. Secondly, much of the land is either arid or semi-arid, and as such unsuitable for other economic activities like farming or business. For this reason, they resort, once more, to the cow, with crops serving as only secondary to animal husbandry.

Another geographical factor that exacerbates the local situation is that there are by far too many diseases that claim lots of animals, needless to mention the serious droughts that are a common feature; hence the need to increase their cows by taking from their neighbors on a regular basis, for the purpose of restocking. This perpetuates the state of insecurity on the one hand and cements the sense of community on the other. But as we have shown above, the Pökot are not homogeneously communitarian; there are several traditional traits of individualism. Visserreminds us about this social phenomenon in the Pökot social structure of "...how the individual is part of several social units (e.g. homestead, clan and age group) but that he is not absorbed by these structures...He is an entity on his own. Whenever an individual is struck by misfortune, or attacked by disease, a ritual is performed by people of the local community within the cluster of neighbourhood."[48]

This, according to one young informant, explains the ease with which young educated people abandon the communitarian lifestyle in favor of the modern, more individualistic way of life. To end this analysis, we can say that there exists a difference between the African worldview and non-African or Western worldview for that matter, but the difference is that of *degree* rather than of a *kind*. It is just a matter of emphasis rather than opposition, distinction rather than dichotomy.

Our original presupposition was that, the Pökot are a communitarian people and we contrasted their worldview to the Western, individualistic, one. One of our sub-questions was, on the extent to which this is true. The situation on the ground suggests that communitarianism in West Pökot is more complex than we had presupposed at the beginning of this study. While the Pökot people are predominantly communitarian in their meaning system, which they use to interpret reality and generate their social behavior there are, nonetheless, many traits of individualism that can be traced to the very roots of their traditions. This discovery made us realize the extent of "cultural complexity" as well as "cultural contradictions" among the

---

47. Schneider (1955). Op. cit., 404.
48. Visser (1989). Op. cit., 114.

Pökot people.⁴⁹ Hence, we discovered that cultural issues cannot be put in black and white, like logical or mathematical issues, since they are more fluid with a lot of grey areas. Perthaps this can be explained by the understanding that the former issues are emotional whereas the latter are abstract.

Hence, it is presuming too much to do what we had done by making a clear dichotomy between the West (which we regarded as individualistic) and Africa (regarded by many people as communitarian). There is always a grey line of tolerance that needs to be constantly examined and perfected or updated; which is the essence of dynamism in culture. In short, we can authoritatively say that although communitarianism is the dominant Pökot worldview (as evidenced by their meaning system) there nonetheless, exists individualism in their community. We will now move on to the second aim and see if, and to what extent, the Pökot use their meaning system to interpret the Gospel.

Interpretation of John 10:1–16 in the SCCs

As mentioned earlier we presented the Pökot version of the parable of the Good Shepherd (John 10: 1-16) to the Christian weekly prayer meetings in the SCCs and recorded their spontaneous contributions, and then later carried out personal interviews as the need arose. The total number of the people that gave their contributions or agreed to be interviewed is 110. These agreed to have their contributions taped and consequently used for the research project, although some gave the condition of anonymity. We interviewed 50 other people (49 women and 1 man) but they shied away from the tape and categorically refused to have their response to our questions used in this research. At the end of the day we recorded 110 contributions and/or interviews from 64 (including 29 pastors—10 priests and 19 catechists) men and 46 women. This is an interesting turn of events owing to the fact that ordinarily the majority (90%) of those who attend the SCC prayers are normally women.

From this scenario, we derived two major points. One, the large number of women who shied away from facing the tape recorder can be attributed to the inferior status of women, particularly in front of male participants. Two, the huge number of men that appeared in the SCCs was only attracted by the mere fact of the research project, since they felt that it is they (rather than women) who ought to contribute to this event, a feeling we attributed to the prevailing traditional attitude of male superiority over women within the Pökot community, just as Healey had,⁵⁰ observed among other pastoralist communities. We repro-duce that bible text below, with an equivalent English translation.

---

49. Spradley (1980). Op. cit., 100, 152; Hannerz (1992). Op. cit.
50. Healey (1981). Op. cit., 124.

Körkeyïn pö mösöwonto kechiir
The Parable of the Sheepfold

1. "*Omwowokwa nyoman, lö, chii anka tïkwïl nyo mölïtönye kwegho kechiir kuweröy kukat, wölo kïwechï kïlït kweghonay ompö are anka, kï chorin chichoni akimosin. Wölo chii nyo lïtöy kuweröy kukat kï mösönto kechiir nyinte.*

   "Truly, truly, I say to you, he who does not enter the sheepfold by the door but climbs in by another, that man is a thief and a robber; but he who enters by the door is the shepherd of the sheep.

2. *Yotini nyinte chii nyo rïpöy oor, akïlïmöy kechirye kutinyi, akïkuröy nyinte kainötutko kechiryechi, akïyat akuntöghoghchï chane.*

   To him the gatekeeper opens; the sheep hear his voice, and he calls his own sheep by name and leads them out.

3. *Nyini kayat kechiryechay kïpka sany, kuntötoghoghchï, kïpechï kechiryechay kïrïp nyinte, ompöwölo nkït kutinyi.*

   When he has brought out all his own, he goes before them, and the sheep follow him, for they know his voice.

4. *Mörïpöcha chii nyole toon, nyinö kötörïpöy, kupertegho nyinte, ompöwölo menkïtcha chane kutïwa too."*

   A stranger they will not follow, but they will flee from him, for they do not know the voice of strangers."

5. *Kïmwochï Yesu chane körkeyïnoni, wölo kïmöpköchïcha ngölyontononi kïmöröy nyinte kïmwochini chane.*

   This figures Jesus used with them, but they did not understand what he was saying to them.

Yesu nyole mösöwoon nyo karam
Jesus the Good Shepherd

6. *Kïlenyona kïlenchï Yesu chane ngat, "Omowokwa nyopo nyoman lö ochan kuka kechiir.*

   So Jesus again said to them, "Truly, truly, I say to you, I am the door of the sheep.

7. *Piich löwïr cho kipka tawunyan kï chorï akï mosï akïmölïmchïcha kechirye chane ngalekwa.*

   All who came before me are thieves and robbers; but the sheep did not heed them.

8. *Ochan kukat. Chii anka tïkwïl nyo lïtu wölo omitan kesöru; akïlïtu kot ori, akïwetöy sany, akïnyorï omisyö.*

    I am the door; if anyone enters by me, he will be saved, and will go in and out and find pasture.

9. *Ngwïnöy chorin paat atökumï kïchoor akïtïgh, akuwuur. Kangwïnan atökïsïch piich söpoon, akïsïch nyoni kuwayta.*

    The thief comes only to steal and kill and destroy; I came that they may have life, and have it abundantly.

10. "*Ochan mösöwoon nyo karam. Chömtoy mösöwontö nyo karam söpontanyi ompö kechiryechi.*

    I am the good shepherd. The good shepherd lays down his life for the sheep.

11. *Ato sïwa chii nyo melö mösöwoon, amelö chechi kyaki, suyoon kungwïnöy kïpïstooy kechiryechay akuperta. Kungwïn nyu suyontonay kïnam akutoyö kechiryechay.*

    He who is a hireling and not a shepherd, whose own the sheep are not, sees the wolf coming and leaves the sheep and flees; and the wolf snatches them and scatters them.

12. *Sughöy söpontanyi chii nyo kikiröy ompöwölo kakikiir nyinte paat möyongönye kechiir.*

    He flees because he is a hireling and cares nothing for the sheep.

13. *Ochan mösöwoon nyo karam; ankïtön pikachu, akunkïtanïn chane.*

    I am the good shepherd; I know my own and my own know me,

14. *Kïle wölini nkïtanïn Paponyan ankïtön Paponyu, onkïtön lenyoni kechiryechu, akunkïtanïn chane. Amitan kïpsach ameey ompö chane.*

    as the Father knows me and I know the Father; and I lay down my life for the sheep.

15. *Mitoni kechirye walaka chole chichan cho mömichay kweghonetenyï! Mïchinanïn orongwan chane lapoy. Lïmöy kechiryechoni kutinyan, atökumï kïlïkï okwot akonga nko mösöwoon akonga.*[51]

    And I have other sheep that are not of this fold; I must bring them also, and they will heed my voice. So there shall be one flock, one shepherd.[52]

---

51. Bible Society of Kenya (1988). *Lökoy cho Karamach cho pö Piich Lapoy.* Nairobi: Bible Society of Kenya.

52. United Bible Societies (1989). *The New Testament in Today's Greek Version.* Athens: United Bible Societies.

Our general observation concerning the way the Pökot people read and interpret this passage is that it is more than just a bible story for them because it is informed by their social and cultural context, as well as their lifestyle. They start with their own life situation and then move to try and locate themselves within the bible story. Thus, when interpreting the passage of the Good Shepherd, "they are more preoccupied with the search for resonance rather than a quest for dissonance."[53] Their concern in the Bible is based on their 'life interests', that is, "those concerns and commitments that drive or motivate the interpreter to come to the text." [54]

These life interests, as we have mentioned earlier on manifest themselves in the most recurring points of density. They range from socio-cultural to politico-economic issues, depending on who is speaking, where he or she comes from and their most dominant social problems and concerns. People tend to see themselves as involved in the gospel story and try to see what they can learn from it; thus, they keep on quoting their own life experiences and comparing them with the story in question. The parable of our choice was generally very well received since it is about shepherding and so affirmed their dignity as pastoralists.

Our first observation, before the prayers started, was the seating arrangement; members sat in circles similar to the ones they sit during their traditional ceremonies. When, for instance, people are taking the traditional brew, they normally sit in a circle and use long straws to drink from the same pot. When there is a problem and elders have to meet and sort it out, they sit in a circle so that they can 'feel the sense of equality'. At the same time, we inquired why people sat in a circle during the SCC prayers and they replied that it was to give every member a sense of equality. "You know," explained the chairman of the meeting, "all of us in the SCC are leaders and followers at the same time, we are all learning something from each other and also teaching one another. This is why we must sit in a circle with Christ, who is our uniting force in the middle. Even in our traditional way of life, we sat in a circle with our ancestors in the middle, but now Christ has become our Great Ancestor."[55]

During the sharing of the Word of God, it was evident that every member was addressing all other members as a group, rather than the chairperson. Hence the usage of expressions like *tupchenichu* (brethren), *wechara* (dear colleagues) and *wakristu chole chaman* (beloved Christians). The prayer meetings are also carried out in such a way that members meet in the home of a fellow member every other week until they have visited all of them and then they start all over. Apart from the general expressions used by the Christians in the SCCs we also observed that the seating arrangement was such that the participants sit in a circle, even when the house is not circular in its architecture, so that everyone can have a clear view of the other and the speakers can

---

53. Mugambi (2003). Op. cit., 118.
54. West (2005). Op. cit., 7.
55. Simeon Lokeliman, is a teacher at Empokech Primary School and also the chairman of the Parish Council in Chepnyal Parish, within Sook Location.

address the whole group rather than just the leader. Then we went ahead to look for the various themes that formed the backbone of our research questions.

Individualistic Influence of the Lumko Method

Apart from the traditional aspects of individualism, we also realized that Christianity has contributed to the individualistic way of understanding and interpreting the Scriptures in West Pökot. It was obvious to us that "the manner in which they read the Bible does not reflect 'innocence' but the influence of those who have trained them. In other words, they read within a specific doctrinal framework."[56]

Here we only discuss the effects of the Lumko method that is used by the Christians in the SCCs. Although the Lumko Institute in South Africa aims at going back to the roots of the church at its infancy and share the Gospel and the general life of Christian living as the early converts did, its method in the SCCs has had different effects in West Pökot. We noticed that the prayer formula for bible sharing in the SCCs exerts some influence on the members towards an individualistic interpretation of a bible text. This method was already explained in the general introduction but it is good to reiterate that the entire method consists of seven steps, the fourth of which starts on a personal note (in both Kiswahili and Pökot t) as follows: "This is how the passage has touched me... (*Mimi nimeguswa hivi*... (*ochan sungwate lo*)."

Although some Christians are perfectly at home with this kind of individualistic sharing, many more are not and they quickly switch to the more communitarian way of sharing their understanding of bible passages as soon as they are done with the formulaic part of introducing the sharing session. So, it was common for us to hear people start the formula and then shift as follows: "*Mimi nimeguswa na mstari... Sasa tunaona ya kwamba*—I have been touched by the verse (*ochan sungwate ompo mstari*)... Now we see that (*ye nyu, suwecha lo*)..." Another point worth mentioning is that community leaders seem to be doing the sharing all the time and hardly give other members a chance, and when they do, only the same people tend to speak. Even the reading of the Gospel passage was done by the same people, just as Healey had observed elsewhere. Most of them had serious difficulties reading the text in the Pökot language—their mother tongue![57]

Cultural Traits in the Pericope

We were also eager to know how much the people interpreted the pericope of the Good Shepherd from their cultural perspective, that is, by quoting examples from their cultures while explaining their understanding of the pericope. To use Spradley's

---

56. Speckman, op. cit., 51.
57. Healey (1981). Op. cit., 124.

language, we were looking for the cultural themes and how often they surfaced in people's contributions. We found out that 50 people (mainly women) did this, while 60 did not. A classic example came from Albino Kotomei who expressed the close relationship between the Christians and Jesus using the traditional way in which a shepherd communicates with his lost livestock.[58]

When a cow is lost, a shepherd uses a special language as follows: *Buuu . . . cho-cho-cho*. When a goat is lost, the language changes as follows: *Ym . . . be-e-e-e-ya*. When a sheep is lost, the language is again different as follows: *Re-e-e-e-e . . .* And finally when a donkey gets lost the call goes like this: *He-e-he, he-e-he. . .* Individual shepherds would add their own words of praise to the lost animal like the following: *He-sakate, he-lowanye sebu*, and so forth. When, however, the animals are being called for water or salt, the language is the same for all of them, and it goes like this: *Prrrp-prrrp-prrrp*. A shepherd keeps repeating these standard words for as long as necessary. In the same way, Jesus uses a special language of grace to summons us back to him when we get lost in sin and he is ready to wait for us for as long as it takes so that we may come back to him.

We tried to find out the reason why some people did not use explicit cultural themes in their bible sharing and the explanation given was that it is not appropriate to mix the Gospel issues with cultural ones. They further said that they acted in the cultural ways when they were still in the dark but now that they have seen the light, they cannot go back to the old ways. Their justification was the famous quotation of the old wineskin and new wine expression by Jesus.[59] This was properly the case for the elderly people that we talked to, but the same also applied to some educated young people, though with a completely different explanation.

They regarded the Pökot culture as both backward and atavistic. They further said that Jesus Christ is the light of the world and that Christianity had delivered them not only from the primitive Pökot culture but also from eternal damnation in the fires of hell. Although we still detected a sense of communitarianism, these people gave a slightly different meaning to the concept, since they only regarded as members of their 'eschatological' community only those Pökot who have accepted Christ and have become saved. Situations like this one, coupled with the influence of modernity have bred a young generation of people so prejudiced against their culture that Meyerhoff[60] thought the phenomenon is, in many ways, a threat to the traditional Pökot way of life.

---

58. Albino Kotomei is a 56-year-old resident of Kacheliba and active Church member. He is also involved in various research projects with different foundations from the Netherlands.

59. Matthew 9: 14–17, Mark 2: 18–22.

60. Meyerhoff (1982). Op. cit.

Inculturation of the Pericope

In our effort to know what comes to the mind of a Pöchon upon hearing that Jesus is the Good Shepherd, we tried to examine how often they appealed to their cultural imageries. Then how they related them to the whole phenomenon of shepherding and to see how they would apply it to Jesus. In this regard, we captured and counted the most commonly used folk terms in relation to the parable and the results were exciting as we discovered various tacit cultural themes in the Pökot culture.

The term *lük* ('cattle rustling' or 'cattle raiding') was used 6 times by 4 out of 110 people, in spite of the fact that it is a very rampant practice in this community. The word chorin ('thief') was used 39 times, by 20 people, even though Jesus himself used it or its synonyms (like robbers or brigands) five times, *chorï* (thieves) three times and *mosï* (robbers) two times, and in a way, indicted those responsible. Other related words are *chelosëy* (brigand), *chelolosion* (bandit) and *mïrön* (warrior). When they themselves are going to raid cattle from a neighboring community, then the latter term is used, but when others (also regarded as warriors by their own people) come to get cattle from the Pökot, then any of the former terms are used. Moreover, we noticed that Christians were somehow ashamed of this traditional practice and yet they tried to explain it away because whenever they used either of them they were both apologetic and defensive.

This discrepancy, or 'cultural contradiction'[61] between what people say about theft and cattle rustling, and what actually happens on the ground helped us to discover that it is one of the many tacit Pökot cultural themes that people would hardly (if ever) talk about, but impacts negatively on their Christian life. Words like *otöptin* (customs), *telenganen* (traditions), *möngot* (lifestyle), all indicating 'culture' (since there is no single word for it in the Pökot language) were used 87 times by 26 people, with the majority explaining that it connotes the old days when they used to live in darkness, but now they have seen the light in Jesus Christ.

The word *kukat* (door) was used 7 times by 6 people in spite of Jesus referring to himself as the 'door' (of the sheepfold). Upon investigations, the people said that the idea just did not strike them, but we made further inquiries only to find out that traditionally there was no door to the sheep's pen, since they lived together with people in the same house. Hence, culturally speaking, the idea of a door to the sheepfold simply made no sense to them and as such most people 'conveniently' avoided using it. But little did they know that the situation was pretty much the same in the New Testament world and that in the periscope it is the shepherd who literally stands for the door.

The word *aran* (goat) was used 83 times by 40 people and for the second time the gender cultural divide became evident. Men did not consider a goat to be important enough to deserve prominence in bible interpretation. It is almost exclusively women who used the term in their sharing sessions, presumably because goats and chicken

---

61. Spradley (1980). Op. cit., 152.

nearly always help them solve the small problems at home by selling or exchanging them with what they needed. These are the only things they can sell at home without asking for permission from their husbands and if they did, it is only out of courtesy.

The word 'sheep' was used by 21 people and for the first time the geographical difference in the interpretation of the text came to the fore. The answers we got from those who did not use the term varied from a cow being more important to a sheep not being commonly used in the community. However, we are of the opinion that this is due to environmental influence. Those people who live in the cold high lands of Cherangani and Sondany hills can only rear sheep as their major source of income and as such it is easier for them to associate it with the Gospel reading than those in the low dry plains of Karapökot. Then 16 people (from Karapökot region) used the word *pögh* (water), and yet much of the land is dry, hence, it is part of the vital 'components' that support life here.

Finally, the word *tany* (cow) was used 209 times by 49 people and yet a cow is, as it were, the bloodline of the Pökot lifestyle. The importance of the cow and the special role it plays in the daily life of a Pöchon cannot be gainsaid. One lady put it more succinctly:

> A cow is like our mother or our land. We get a lot of things from a cow: milk, blood, cooking fat, and hides. We use the hide of a cow for sleeping and drying out things in the sun. We use the horn of a cow to put oil inside and other foodstuff like ants. Also, a cow helps us in digging, and carrying heavy loads like firewood and water especially when we have to fetch it from far. The *Wazungu* (white men) have their jeeps, Land Rover and tractors; but for us, a cow is all these and more, because we also drink of its milk, then drink its blood and finally it offers its very life for the sake of the survival of the Pökot community. So, you see, a cow is important to us in life and also in death, because as I have already said, after it dies we use parts of its body for other things that are still necessary in our daily lives.[62]

In general, we concluded that people's cultural reality has definitely had some impact (sometimes positive, but other times negative) on the way they understood and responded to the Word of God and made it part of their social and environmental reality. This notwithstanding, the people were not able to use their local imageries, like that of a cow, in their bible sharing adequately. So, we tried to inquire why they made such a great omission, but the interviewees simply said that the image of a cow was not used in the pericope and that they were more at home talking about the sheep, even if they are not equally important in the eyes of their culture.

"We are a new race, you know." One member of the charismatic group who did not want to be identified told us. "We now belong to only one clan, that of Jesus Christ

---

62. Anna Teko is a 54-year-old chairperson of the Parish Council at Kacheliba, who is basically a livestock farmer and only works part time as a catechist.

in whose blood we have been washed. The traditional clan system, age-sets and other practices belong to the past; now we look forward to the coming of the Son of Man." Using Spradley's terminology this can be regarded as another case of 'cultural contradiction' in which both Christianity and the cow are considered to be an important part of the people's meaning system and yet the two are treated as incompatible. This, we think, is because the importance of the former is seen to be on the individual plane while that of the latter is regarded as a communal enterprise.

The Understanding of the Concept 'Shepherd'

We had a particular interest in knowing what the Pökot people understand with the term *mösöwoon* (shepherd) or how they conceptualize it. Out of 110 people 14 made an attempt to define the term or give it some conceptual analysis and came out with some socially acceptable definition. This is in spite of the fact that the Pökot have four different terms used to refer (although sometimes loosely) to a shepherd as follows: *mösöwoon, kyakuyin, ripin* and *mötworin*, all of which are wider than their English equivalents.

Mösöwoon means a person who takes care of his own animals; he is dedicated to their well-being and he has no other engagements. *Kyakuyin* is a person who happens to relieve the *mösöwoon*, for a certain period of time, for whatever reason. He/she takes up the duties for only a short while and later goes back to his/her work when the owner of the job returns. We can say he or she is a temporary *mösöwoon*. The word *ripin* means one who watches over both the animals and the entire homestead and its English equivalent is 'watchman'. Then there is one more term (*ngorokö*) that we only heard in the Karapökot region, among the purely pastoral Pökot, which refers to the heavily armed youth, who protect those minding the animals as well as the shepherds; we thought that the English equivalent for this is 'sentry'.

For the second time we noticed the geographical difference in bible interpretation between the purely pastoral Pökot and those who mix pastoralism with agriculture. The former not only had more terms for the shepherd than the latter, but the word had more significance to them. This, we later learned, was due to the diminishing importance of a shepherd in the agricultural areas of West Pökot. The people did not think that our concern was of any value because what matters to them is the image the term invokes in the community and how the person it represents relates to the community.

Any other thing like trying to give etymological definitions of some words used in the Bible or conceptual analysis of terms and concepts mostly passes unnoticed. We asked one informant what he thinks about the difference in terminology between the two languages, but he said this posed no problem to him.

> When Jesus talks about the Good Shepherd it is very close to the lifestyle of our people. I see no problem with the difference between the English term

'shepherd', on the one hand, and the Pökot terms *mösöwoon, rïpin, kyakuyin* and *mötworin,* on the other hand. All of them, whether general or specific, refer to all those caring for animals. When we speak of the Good Shepherd we might be talking about minding the sheep. Here in Pökot the sheep are not that important, the goats would be more important and the cow a lot more important: but I see no problem since all of them are about caring for the animals, and that is what we do. In the Gospel Jesus talks about being the gateway to the fold. This will not have much significance to our people because the fold is for the individual family and the animals are not mixed up. If we talk in a general way about caring for animals, we find that it is similar. Since we have leopards across the hills that like nice fat goats. The other wild animals also take the smaller animals like sheep and lambs. So the shepherd has to be watchful and keep the danger away. These aspects would be very common with Jesus talking about the shepherd because it is relevant to the Pökot context.[63]

When the word 'shepherd' (*mösöwoon*)[64] is treated as a cover term, the words *mösöwoon, rïpin, kyakuyin, ngorokö* and *mötworin* as included terms, whereby they are linked to each other by a single semantic relationship of strict inclusion, each one of them is a kind of a shepherd. Once again, their semantic relation is by strict inclusion, "X is a kind of Y".[65] Our componential analysis revealed that the relationship of these terms is so close and vital in the Pökot cultural scene that sometimes they are used synonymously; and yet there are deep-rooted contrasts, which did not come up during the bible sharing.

Upon investigating the cause of this discrepancy, it occurred to us that people did not see the direct connection between the pericope of Jesus as a shepherd and their daily lives as shepherds. We came to know that the traditional socialization of the Pökot people has taught them to be mainly concerned with concrete things that have practical and tangible results, not just for (but also not excluding) me as an individual but with a direct bearing on the community. This, for them, contrasts with abstract analyses that most of the times have no connection with social reality and they blame it on the method of evangelization that focuses on abstract exegetical analysis of the Bible. People think that this is not useful to them unless it is transformed into communally based conceptual imageries that appeal to their day-to-day life experience, as one member of the SCC observed.

> Our culture is quite different from that of the white people, you might find a person from abroad analysing the Gospel and yet it does not apply to our

---

63. Jacob Samali is a 32-year-old, successful educated farmer and businessman in Chepareria Division. He is one of the few committed Christian and regular churchgoers in this division.

64. The Pökot word *mösöwoon* appears both as a cover term and as part of the included terms because it has two meanings. One reflects the general shepherd and the other reflects the situation where the owner of animals personally takes care of them, as opposed to employing someone else.

65. Spradley (1980). Op. cit., 93.

traditions. So if it is a person who knows how we live while explaining, he will pick examples from here that will touch us. There are many such examples but one that really annoys people very much is the one to do with family life. When people come from abroad while explaining the Gospel in relation to how fathers and mothers behave, the examples they quote do not apply. They should come and study our way of life and quote what the Bible says, while giving examples, which are familiar to our lifestyle.[66]

Relevance of Jn. 10:1–16 to the Life of a Pöchon

To gauge whether, and to what extent the parable of the Good Shepherd was relevant to the Christian life of the people in West Pökot, we counted how many of them gave concrete steps that they needed to take in order to experience conversion and how many used personal examples in this regard. We found out that 9 people had internalized the reading by citing examples from their daily lives in which they identified themselves with the Good Shepherd, but never with the sheep; 36 internalized it in a general way and 65 had not internalized the gospel reading, in the sense that they never gave any concrete or general example.

They gave such vague and impersonal contributions that basically amounted to mere repetition of the exact wording of the parable of the Good Shepherd, while focusing the attention on themselves as individuals and their personal accomplishments. We used a sample of one such sharing in which a member only identified herself with the shepherd rather than the sheep.

> Let us praise the Lord. My name is Felistus Kirwa. I am touched by the verse that says, ' . . . a Good Shepherd calls his sheep by name and they hear his voice. . . . It is like what happens at school, when teachers call a register. Especially like the very small, standard one children that I take care of. They are so used to me because I am always calling them; they know me and I know them, and when I call them they respond. But when they are outside and another person, who is not their teacher, calls them, those children are not likely to come to that teacher, they only want their own teacher. So this reading has touched and made me realise that if I hear the voice of the one calling me I would also realise who I belong to. . . . I should act towards Christ just as those children act towards me, I call them by name and they listen to me and they love me because I am their teacher, and in that sense their shepherd.[67]

---

66. Imelda Chebet is a 33-year-old nurse at Kacheliba Health Centre and a committed leader in her SCC.

67. Felistus Kirwa (not her real name) is a 35-year-old member of one of the SCCs regarded as very progressive in West Pökot.

The Role of a Shepherd in the Pökot Community

Our choice of the parable of the Good Shepherd[68] was mainly influenced by the fact that the Pökot are a predominantly pastoralist that have a special relationship with animals, a fact that amazes every visitor, even those who have lived there for long. A non-Pökot member, who has lived in West Pökot, most of his life expresses his own dismay at the quality of that relationship in a way that leaves no doubt of his attraction to it:

> I have been impressed by the way the Pökot handle their animals. I remember especially at one time I was out in Sebit, we were having a *baraza* (meeting) I heard goats coming down the hill and they were with an old man. He wanted to get them across the river and the goats were very many yet he was alone. There was a very close relationship between the animals and him. The animals knew him as a Good Shepherd. He would put out his stick and control the animals to go in a particular way. I was attending a *baraza* (meeting) but I was also looking at him. I was especially impressed by the relationship that existed between him and the animals. They understood one another and responded to the *mzee* (old man) according to the way he was directing them although goats were very stubborn.[69]

Indeed, we were overwhelmed by the closeness of a shepherd to his animals in the grazing field. When you find someone in the actual act of shepherding, the almost rhetorical question you ask him suggests that he (or she) is part of the animals. '*Mite ne nya achey*?' Or, '*Mite ne nyi tich*?' These questions can literally be translated to mean something like this: 'what is in herding (that keeps you so preoccupied)? Or, are you (in fact, part of the) cattle? With these and many other examples in mind, we thought the Christians would not have much difficulty relating the concepts and imagery in the parable to their own lifestyle and culture. However, when it came to bible sharing, the results were not as we had envisaged. Out of 110 people 48 of them talked of the traditional role of a shepherd and compared it to the role of Jesus in the Christian setting.

We also observed that this omission was, in fact, higher in the purely pastoral Pökot areas than in the agricultural areas (33 out of 62), of the people who did not give the role of a shepherd in their traditional society. On further inquiry during the interviews it emerged that, among the pastoral (or nomadic) Pökot the role of a shepherd is taken for granted and indeed people were very surprised when we asked this question. For them it is assumed that everybody (even a child) knows the role of a shepherd in the community. However, among those engaged in agriculture the omission was due

---

68. John 10:1–16.

69. John Gichuki is a retired teacher, who has worked in West Pökot all his life and has now settled in the county (at Keringet) upon his retirement. He has held various positions in the church leadership but is now a respected elder in his SCC.

to change in lifestyle and emphasis being made on crop production, seen as more profitable than animal husbandry.

People kept on talking of what the community expects of the shepherd, using the various terms attributed to the kind of shepherd in question. Componential analysis revealed the existence of various similarities (as well as contrasts) in the role of a shepherd as an acceptable reality in the community although many people, both the pastoralists and agriculturists, avoided using this term. Some of these similarities and dissimilarities lie in the following roles: taking the animals to the grazing field and safely back home, watering and protecting them from enemy attacks, ownership of the animals, permanence or temporality and percept-ion of their job in the community, and permission for ritual animals.

During rituals, it is the shepherd (*mösöwoon* or *kyakuyin*) who was asked for the permission to take away the animal prescribed by the seer (*werkoyon*). If he refused, he was enticed with some little gift(s) and even then, after the animal had been slaughtered there was always some special meat reserved for the shepherd. Also, when giving away or exchanging an animal with something else just as when selling it, the shepherd has, as a rule, to be given some token because it is his courage and hard work that has kept the animal alive thus far. Now for the shepherd to know for sure that it is the real owner of the animals that has sent the messenger to collect the animal from the grazing field, the latter had to bring with him the sitting stool (*kaideke*) from the former as proof of authenticity. However, not all shepherds enjoyed this privilege as the other three *(mötworin, ngorokö* and *ripin)* were excluded on various grounds.

Mötworin is seen as too low (a servant) to be given this honor, *ngorokö* is to head or clear the way for *mösöwoon,* while *ripin* stays at home and only takes over once the animals are back. Of the five terms, two (*ngorokö* and *mötworin*) have a negative connotation at different levels, while three (*mösöwoon, kyakuyin* and *ripin*) are always seen in a positive light. While the *ngorokö* are respected and praised as warriors in Karapökot, other tribes and the Pökot from other regions are wary and even afraid of them, because they regard them as thieves (*chori*) and robbers (*mosi*). While it is the proper job of a *mösöwoon* to look after animals, other kinds of shepherds would also be involved in other engagements that do not necessarily include shepherding.

For instance, *kyakuyin* is anybody who happens to be called upon to take care of the animals, say for a day a week, or a month. *Mötworin* is equated to a servant, who can be called upon to do any manual work at home that may include taking care of the animals. While the *ngorokö* protect or attack *mösöwoon* (as the case may be) *ripin* always protects, not only the animals at home, but also everything there is within the homestead, including *mösöwoon*. While *mösöwoon, kyakuyin* and *mötworin* have a duty to go and water the animals, *ngorokö* and *ripin* do not have such a duty, but they can do so when there is no one else to do the job. Ordinarily, *mösöwoon* and *ripin* own the animals they care for, but *mötworin* does not, while *ngorokö* and *kyakuyin* may or may not own the herd they care for.

The results of this analysis were summed up by one informant who told us that the main failures of workers (including Church workers) in West Pökot were lack of consultation with the people they work for. And he emphasized that these workers need to work with, rather than work for the Pökot. "Many things they think are of crucial importance to the people indeed do not matter at all; and yet many other things they take for granted are, in fact, what matters most to the people."[70] One of them is the role played by the community to appropriate the role of each person within the social structures and with it the punishment and reward that go with success or failure to live as one is expected.

The Place of a Shepherd in the Pökot Community

We have just discussed the role of a shepherd in the Pökot community, where we have established that a shepherd had many roles depending on the kind of a shepherd that he was, and that the fulfilment of his expected duties in the community earned him respect and recognition. We would now like to look at the place of Jesus, the shepherd, among the people of West Pökot. We had taken it for granted that being pastoralists, the Pökot would always find a place for Jesus the shepherd in their midst. However, we were, once again, proved wrong when only 22 people made this reference.

Our findings showed that it is not that they do not have a place for Jesus, the shepherd, amongst themselves but rather the cultural imagery of a shepherd is no longer appealing to them. They would have preferred a modern contemporary figure like an academician or an exemplary politician (as opposed to the current corrupt ones, as one informant intimated to us), rather than a shepherd, a job left (in some parts of Pökotland) to women and children from poor families that can-not afford going to school. The parents prefer a contemporary Jesus, a true model for their children and a symbol for development, in the modern sense of the word.

> The world is going on and moving at a supersonic speed, when you introduce your kids to the Pökot outdated cultures that are soon coming to an end they will find themselves left behind never to catch up with their peers, ever. Take circumcision as a practical example, boys go to this hut (*menchö*) and stay there for ages, by the time they come out the rest of the people are speaking a language they cannot and will never understand. This is why we lag behind in development and most of us still live below the poverty level. We want our children to get education and be informed in the current technology, like the computers, internet, name it; and open up our land to make it at par with the rest of the country. Pastoral communities live as though they do not live in the same country with the rest of Kenyans.[71]

---

70. Interview with Alexander Tulel, a 58-year-old businessman, who has also worked as a catechist for a long time and later on served as the chairman of the Parish Council in Chepareria.

71. Chelolombai, popularly known as Kama Kasilokot, is a 75-year-old lady, resident of Mnagei

This challenge to traditional wisdom is further manifestation of what Spradley calls cultural contradictions,[72] whereby at the surface it appears that a pastoral community would accommodate all images of a shepherd, while at the bottom of the cultural life, it is, in fact, the opposite. At first sight it can be assumed that it is another case of the influence of modernity from outside the community, but the sheer age of the informant in question and the time she made her decision to go against her culture in this regard challenges this assumption. In general terms, influence, no matter how slow and gradual, will finally catch up with even those communities thought of as the most closed. Another issue that cannot be ignored is that ambivalence to the figure of Jesus as a shepherd and people's failure to use the image of a cow puts the very efforts of inculturation to the test and raises the question whether it is, indeed, a people driven project.

A Fusion of Horizon

In the light of the discoveries above our earlier sensitizing concepts were nuanced by the fieldwork, which made us see the complexities and contradictions of the Pökot culture more clearly. This brought about what Gadamer calls a 'fusion of horizons'—*Horizontverschmelzung*[73] and change of thought on our part; leading to a new predisposition towards the Pökot, in the sense of Gadamer's new prejudgment (*Vorverständnis*).[74] We now think that there is no such thing as closed societies as Popper's two-volume book; *The Open Society and Its Enemies* (1966)[75] can easily be construed to allude.

This is, however, not to say that many of the aspects he regards as characteristic of his 'closed society' are lacking among the Pökot with the most obvious one being the nature of their unity, which is not cemented by "such abstract social relationships as division of labour and exchange of commodities, but by concrete physical relationships..."[76] What we do not buy, as our research has shown, is the notion that because of these characteristics they are, *ipso facto*, not responsible as individuals or that they have no room for new ideas. This discovery meant that we could not point out to what we can definitively call 'a Pökot worldview' because of the many meaning systems that interact between and within the people of different social standings.

Location in Kapenguria Division who refused to have her girls undergo female circumcision and now they are all educated and employed by the government.

72. Spradley (1980). Op. cit., 152.

73. Hans-Georg Gadamer (1975). *Truth and Method*. London: Sheed & Ward, 273.

74. Ibid.., 240.

75. Karl R. Popper (1966). *The Open Society and Its Enemies: The Spell of Plato*, Vol. 1. London: Routledge & Kegan Paul.

76. Karl R. Popper (1962). *The Logic of Scientific Discovery*, third impression. London: Hutchinson & Co., (Publishers) Ltd, 173.

Terrance Ranger shows the difficulty of finding 'pure' or 'authentic culture among the Africans, due to what he calls 'the invention of tradition in the colonial Africa' in the 1870s, 1880s and 1890s. He laments the consequences of this invention in the following words: "The invented traditions of African societies—whether invented by the Europeans or by Africans themselves in response—distorted the past but became in themselves realities through which a good deal of colonial encounter was expressed."[77] He, then, winds up his article with a stark warning to the historians:

> They have to free themselves from the illusion that the African custom recorded by officials or by many anthropologists is any sort of guide to the African past. But they also need to appreciate how much invented traditions of all kinds have to do with the history of Africa in the twentieth century and strive to produce better founded accounts of them than this preliminary sketch.[78]

Here again we encountered a concrete case that put to question our earlier assumption on the communitarian homogeneity of the Pökot people. This was a direct result of the Grounded Theory Approach, which tries to see how theory is changed by data gathered in the field. With this warning in mind, we shifted our attention from examining the difference between the Pökot tradition of communitarianism and what we had perceived as Western tradition of individualism, to examining the difference within Pökot communitarianism. We realized that there are many suppressed differences within the Pökot culture, that result from external influence by their neighbors, creating a false impression that it is fundamentally different from other cultures. We became interested in the nature of this influence, from the Pökot neighbors, and how it took place within the cultural set-up. So, we wanted to know how much the Pökot culture can indeed be said to be Pökot by tradition and set out to make the inquiry.

We noticed that much of what they do has always been borrowed from the Tugen, the Marakwet, the Turkana and the Karimojong in Uganda. As Visser had already discovered: "Their history shows that they adopted some customs and ceremonies from other people, for example, the *sapana* initiation from the neighboring Karimojong. The most popular dance—the *adonga*—is of Turkana origin."[79] The only difference is that while change in the traditional set-up was more systematic and gradual, current changes seem to be sudden and cataclysmic; hence traumatizing and unwelcome, especially by the elders. One such change is the sudden shift from the pastoral kind of economy that only stands short of being contemptuous of the cultural practice, to the arable and monetary economy that leaves many out of the economic reach: hence spiraling poverty even more among the ordinary people.

---

77. Terence Ranger (1983). The Invention of Tradition in Colonial Africa. In E. Hobsbawm and T. Ranger (eds). *The Invention of Tradition*. Cambridge: Cambridge University Press, 211.

78. Ibid., 262.

79. Visser (1983). Op. cit., 16.

Conclusion

In this chapter, we first tried to find out whether and, if yes, the extent to which the Pökot cultural meaning system is a communitarian one. We discovered that mundane cultural traits like, language, age-sets, clans, neighborhood and seasons depict a communal concern that encompasses, not just human beings but all other beings in existence. Spradley's social analysis method, which we used together with the Kwalitan computer method, helped us analyze the various social and religious domains or points of density in the Pökot culture. We tried to discover the underlying cognitive principle of the Pökot meaning system, which cuts a communitarian image to the effect that all of us belong to one large community. In it we have God, the deities, spirits, ancestors, human beings (both the living and those yet to be born), animate and inanimate beings Hence there is no life outside this community, and if there is, then it is not worth living.

In other words, life consists of a big set called community with many smaller interdependent subsets as already enumerated above. Of great import to our research is the discovery that the Pökot cultural scene is more complex than we had envisaged since communitarianism in the traditional community has never been a homogeneous reality; there have always been many cases of individualism that co-existed with it. Thus, we brought to the fore a hitherto suppressed difference within the Pökot culture that was used to create an illusion that it is different from other cultures, particularly the Western culture. Hence the need to proceed with caution and subject long held beliefs to a critical analysis before using them as if they are universal and self-evident truths.

Secondly, we tried to establish whether, and extent to which, the Pökot people use their cultural meaning system in the interpretation of the Gospel text of John 10: 1–16. This determination was gauged by the scope as well as the extension to which they referred to their cultural imagery in the sharing of the text in question. This helped us to determine if they had made the bible teaching their own, by domesticating it within their culture or not. Our impression was that cultural traits could always be detected in the religious sphere, sometimes for better, other times for worse, depending on how these are perceived by their Christian leaders. Of great importance in this chapter was that it served as a turning point to which our earlier sensitizing concepts were nuanced by the situation on the ground. It brought to the fore the complexity and contradictions of culture within the Pökot community, just as other scholars had witnessed elsewhere.[80] This brought with it an adoption of a different stance that looks at modern and post-modern understanding of culture, not as necessarily contradictory but rather as complementary to each other in certain ways.[81]

---

80. Spradley (1980). Op. cit., 152; Hannerz, op. cit., 8.
81. Tanner (1997). Op. cit., 56–57.

From this perspective, one understands culture as a 'consensus building', characterized by both 'agreement' and 'engagement'[82] because the two have different emphases. Thus, culture is at once an 'organization of diversity',[83] that is, a *process* that presupposes disagreements; as well as a 'shared meaning system',[84] a cultural *product* that presupposes the existence of a certain amount of consensus. Earlier on at the beginning of our research, we had formulated a number of questions on why the Gospel did not take root in West Pökot, and the extent to which the Pökot people interpret bible texts in an African (communitarian) way.

Other questions were the extent to which their pastors interpret the Gospel in a non-African (individualistic) way and how the interplay between popular and pastoral hermeneutics can be facilitated. Our conclusion is that the Gospel did not, in fact, take root among the Pökot because there has been no concerted effort on inculturation that takes their cultural motifs seriously. Moreover, complexity of culture makes it almost impossible to pin down specific cultural orientations for inculturation. As an aftermath to this, the Pökot are reluctant to accept the Gospel because they still regard it as a foreign imposition that is irrelevant to their life here and now. This notwithstanding, they still try to interpret the Bible in an African (predominantly communitarian) way. Now we move on to Chapter four and see how the pastors interpret the same Bible, in a bid to resonance with, and evangelize the Pökot.

---

82. Ibid., 57.
83. Hannerz, op. cit.
84. Spradley (1980). Op. cit.

CHAPTER 5

PASTORS' INTERPRETATION OF JOHN 10:1–16

Introduction

DURING OUR STAY IN West Pökot, we carried out three major activities with regard to the work of the pastors: first, we observed and analyzed their daily lives, then their Sunday homilies and then we analyzed the commentaries they use more often. In total, there were sixteen priests working in this region but we only got sermons from ten of them and nineteen catechists. We only managed to interview one sister who declined to have the interview recorded. Some priests respectfully declined to be interviewed; others kept on prevaricating or procrastinating over the issue, while others were openly hostile to our request for an interview. Just as we had done with 'ordinary' Christians, we observed the pastors' lives as participant observers and carried out inter-views wherever we deemed necessary.

Then we presented the Pökot version of the parable of the Good Shepherd[1] to them, but soon gave up when we realized that most of them could not read the Pökot language. We, therefore, presented an English version and asked them to prepare a Sunday homily or simply make a sermon at their own convenience. Some were kind enough to set aside a Sunday (not necessarily the Mission Sunday, which uses the above text as the Gospel reading) for this particular passage, while others simply wrote it down or chose to do it verbally outside the context of Mass celebration.

Just as we had done during the sharing of the Word of God, with the 'ordinary' Christians, we wanted to know if the pastors' way of relating to the Bible is, in fact, individualistic, and how their way of interpretation impacts on the people's lives in West Pökot. In short, the aims were two: firstly, to find out whether and, if yes, to what extent they understand and respond to bible texts in a way that is resonant to the Pökot worldview: that is, to what extent the pastors reach out to, and embrace, the Pökot cultural meaning system. Secondly, to find out whether and to what extent they use the Pökot meaning system in the interpretation of the above-mentioned bible passage.

1. John 10: 1–16.

This chapter, then, starts with a brief historical overview of the pastors' work, based on the personal testimony of two veteran pastors that witnessed the birth and growth of Christianity in West Pökot. They are, Leo Staples, a Catholic priest, who is still active in the ministry, outside West Pökot and Hans Visser, A Dutch Reformed Church Lay Missionary, who has been active in the Netherlands but has now retired.

Then the chapter examines the way the pastors interpret the Bible (by analyzing their homilies and/or sermons) and then tries to investigate the force behind their interpretation (by looking at the books they use as bible commentaries plus how their training influences their mode of preaching). Thus, the first aim is on the cognitive level, whereas the second one is on a practical level. As was the case in chapter three, we also use insights from Spradley's social research method for our analyses and the Kwalitan method for the organization of the research material in order to find the most commonly used words and recurrent themes.

A Brief Historical Overview of Evangelization in West Pökot

The people of West Pökot were first exposed to the missionary activities as early as 1931,[2] when the missionaries, Lawrence Totty and Cyril Punt, of the Bible Churchmen's Missionary Society (BCMS), a missionary branch of the Anglican Church, bought the old government buildings in Kacheliba[3] and started religious, health and educational activities there. In 1936 they moved to Nasokol, at the Mnagei highlands where the Catholics joined them in 1943 and established a station at Tartar,[4] about 10 kilometers away. According to Leo Staples, who has worked in West Pökot for over fifty years, the first missionary priests were Mill Hill Fathers, from Mukumu, (now in Kakamega Diocese) and they had approached Kenya from Uganda. They used to come to Tartar as an outstation under the then larger Kisumu Diocese, and the station was only upgraded to a parish status in 1946. The Mill Hill Fathers later gave way to the St. Patrick's Missionary priests (also known as Kiltegans) in 1953, with himself as one of the first priests, but their efforts to evangelize never succeeded until very recently. He explains:

> We have tried our best to evangelise the Pökot population but we have actually not achieved much so far. Out of an estimated 400,000 people, according to the 1989 census report, only about 10% of them are Christians. And the number of Muslims is even more negligible. Although there are no known official statistics, I do not think it goes beyond 1% of the total population. There were

---

2. Ken Shingledecker (1982). *Unreached Peoples of Kenya Project: Pokot Report.* Nairobi: Daystar Communications, 18.

3. Government Headquarters had been moved from Kacheliba to Kapenguria, on the Mnagei highlands, and this has now been transformed into the County Headquarters.

4. Dietz (1987). Op. cit., 204.

many stumbling blocks to the work of evangelisation, mainly owing to the fact that West Pökot was one of the then frontier districts closed to outsiders by the colonial government, ostensibly because of insecurity. This fact in itself means that Christianity reached Pökotland at the same time with colonialism, which turned out to be the most insurmountable obstacle. The people hated the colonialists because they saw them as mere tax gatherers, intruders and disturbers of justice, who were out to manipulate them and tamper with their traditions. Then we made the mistake of quoting the Bible to justify the colonial authority as being from God (Rom. 13:1–3).[5]

Challenges to Evangelization

Leo Staples told us that when he stepped into West Pökot his work of evangelization faced many challenges, which Schneider regarded later on as the crux of the 'Pakot resistance to change'.[6] These challenges were many and they came from the colonial administrators as well as from his would-be converts, but four of them stand out above all the rest. We divided them into cultural and functional problems. The main cultural problems were the following: cattle rustling, belief in witchcraft (consulting witchdoctors, diviners and medicine men and women, polygyny, clitoridectomy and property inheritance for women, and girls in particular.

We have already talked about the first two and cattle rustling is revisited later on in this study. Since the last three are so crucial and still a thorn in the flesh to most evangelizers, we will discuss them shortly at the end of this chapter. The practical or functional problems were as follows: coincidence of evangelization with colonialism, the Pökot religious affiliation, communication barrier and high mortality rate as a result of disease and poverty. The first obstacle had to do with the fact that the county was one of those regarded by the colonial government as 'closed frontiers' because of insecurity. So, he did not have free access to the people and had nearly always to be accompanied by a colonial administrator, on any visit to the people's homesteads, their attitude towards the administration notwithstanding. Due to this fact, it was extremely difficult for them to distinguish between the colonialists and the missionaries; they regarded all of them as European invaders, out to manipulate them and their land.

The second obstacle to evangelization was that, the Pökot people had no room for what they regarded as foreign doctrines that contravened and were set to destroy their cultural heritage in the name of God, a fact that led to further isolation and rejection of the missionaries. The basic question from the elders was: 'why should the Pökot people abandon their religious beliefs and their God (*Tororöt*), who has

---

5. Interview with Leo Staples, a 75-year-old Kiltegan (also known as St. Patrick) Missionary from Ireland. He was in-charge of Sigor Parish at the time, retired at Kibomet Parish, out of West Pökot, after serving in many other parishes. The interview was held in Sigor Parish on 26/05/2002.

6. Schneider (1959). Op. cit., 144–167.

been worshipped by their forefathers since time immemorial, in favor of a foreign god and religion'? What is more, the Pökot perceived Christianity in terms of disruption of their customary practices without offering any tangible advantage(s). Schneider captures this mood:

> Resistance to Christianity is also based in part on simple indifference. There seems to be nothing in Christianity to appeal to them, and their own beliefs seem to have been sufficient for their needs . . . .
>
> But reaction to missions is based on other things as well. In West Suk conversion means going to school, and the criticisms of education hold for both mission and government schools. Furthermore, to worship in a Christian manner, one must live a sedentary life, reside near other people and the church, recognize a religious leader with authority, abandon polygyny, and refrain from circumcising the young, all things held to be undesirable if not impossible.[7]

The third difficulty encountered by these missionaries was communication: both linguistic and physical. It was not possible to travel with ease since most places had no roads. The only available means of transport then was to carry one's luggage on the back while walking on foot or by riding donkeys. The other communication barrier was language. On the one hand, the Pökot people did not know either Kiswahili or English while, on the other hand, the missionaries did not speak the Pökot language. The only way out, for Staples, was to learn the Pökot language in order to communicate with the people directly. Before then he recruited the first catechists and worked with them to translate the catechism into Pökot, so as to start working.

Totty translated the Bible much later, in 1967, without much acceptance by the people, necessitating another bible translation in the 1970s.[8] Mojola elaborates on this initiative as follows: "The current ongoing Pokoot-language translation was initiated in the late 1970s when it was acknowledged that orthographical problems as well as those affecting naturalness and clarity meant that then existing Pokoot New Testament was neither fully accepted by the churches nor fully readable and intelligible in the Pokoot speaking area."[9] According to Tibaldo, the Combonis faced the same problems in West Pökot and employed the same pattern they had used in Karamoja. "Usually a multi-purpose building was used as church-school-catechumenate; the

---

7. Ibid., 159.

8. The first New Testament Pökot translation of the bible (*Kisilat Nyo Rel*) was done by Annette Totty of BCMS and published by the Trinitarian Bible Society, London, in 1967. This was followed by a newer version (*Lökoy cho Karamach cho pö Piich Lapoy*) that was translated by the Bible Soceity of Kenya (BSK) in 1988. In the meantime, the book of Ruth (translated by Tom Collins) had been published as early as 1936 by the AIM at Kijabe and the Gospel of Mark (translated by Lawrence and Annette) published in the same year by the BFBS (British and Foreign Bible Soceity). Matthew, Acts and Romans were published by the BFBS, Nairobi, in 1963. The work on the translation of the Old Testament has been completed, but the Deutero-Canonical books have, unfortunately, been left out.

9. Aloo Osotsi Mojola (1995). *150 Years of Bible Translation in Kenya 1844–1994: An Overview and Reappraisal*. Nairobi: Bible Societies of Kenya, 35.

most important centres could eventually become missions where missionaries could permanently live."[10]

Catechism had to be translated first because the starting point of first evangelization is catechetics and pedagogy. Staples would then read the Bible in English and translate it into Kiswahili for the catechists to translate the message into Pökot. This worked as a major breakthrough in evangelization and the catechists worked as a bridge to reach the people and share the Gospel with them. So, the bible message all the time reached the people through the perception and interpretation of the missionaries, with catechists' keen to ensure that this was translated word for word where possible. On the importance of the role played by the catechists, Staples had this to say, "Catechists were absolutely important, we could not move without them." The language problem reported by Staples in 1956 was also reported as late as 1979 by Tescaroli as a pastoral problem experienced by Verona Fathers (also called Combonis, after their founder, Daniel Comboni):

> In the Mission of Kaceliba, as elsewhere, there is a problem of language, or rather, of languages. Preaching and catechetical instruction is done in Kiswahili, the national language of Kenya, but there are very few Pokot who understand it. Father Pietro, with the help of some material left by a missionary linguist from Uganda, is preparing a grammar, a dictionary and catechetical texts in the Pokot language.[11]

This problem still remains a major obstacle to evangelization in West Pökot, even among the African priests and sisters. Apart from two Kiltegan missionaries and one Comboni missionary, we did not come across any other priest or sister who could speak fluent Pökot, let alone preach in the language. Leo Staples explains the reason for this: "People shy away from learning the Pökot language because it is difficult and yet they are afraid of making mistakes, yet I do not know of any other way to learn a language apart from listening to it being spoken and then making a genuine attempt to speak it."[12] With the passage of time he realized the importance of learning the Pökot language himself due to the handicap he sometimes faced when he wanted to communicate certain points of view to the people. Moreover, sometimes the catechists were not able to relay the exact message, as he wanted it done, although mostly the translation was acceptably good and reliable.

He then emphatically observes that it will never be possible to evangelize the people of West Pökot without learning their language, in spite of the fact that both the pastors speak good Kiswahili and so they communicate with Christians, even if not all of them, since the very old people can only speak Pökot. And yet, as Staples told us, the elderly, too, deserve to hear the Word of God in their own mother tongue

---

10. Tibaldo (2006). Op. cit., 174.
11. Tescaroli, op. cit., 33.
12. Interview with Leo Staples.

as observed by the Pontifical Council for Culture, with regard to the Pentecost event when people heard the apostles preach in their own tongues. "The nations gathered in the Upper Room at Pentecost did not hear in their respective tongues a discourse about their own human cultures, but they were amazed to hear, each in their own tongue, the Apostles proclaim the marvels of God."[13] While extensively quoting from the encyclical, *Evangelii Nuntiandi* (On Evangelization in the Modern World), Staples insisted that to know a culture of a people is to know their language and to understand them is to communicate with them in their mother tongue: any other vehicle for inculturation, according to him, amounts to self-deception and leads to failure.

> The split between the Gospel and culture is without a doubt the drama of our time, just as it was of other times. Therefore every effort must be made to ensure a full evangelization of culture, or more correctly of cultures. They have to be regenerated by an encounter with the Gospel. But this encounter will not take place if the Gospel is not proclaimed.[14]

The fourth obstacle to evangelization was disease in general and malaria in particular, due to the fact that the place is hot and favorable to the breeding of mosquitoes. Infant and maternal mortality rates were very high due to the prevalence of many other diseases and the fact that there was no hospital in the whole of West Pökot, except for a dispensary at Kapenguria. Together with this was the need for education so that people could learn the primary health care lessons and general hygiene. So, medical and educational, amenities had to go hand in hand with evangelization, heavily depending on the catechists without whom their efforts could have been rendered futile. Staples later on moved and opened another parish at Ortum (1956) as soon as another priest (Michael Dillon), joined him in Tartar. There were to be no new parishes until 16 years later when Dillon moved and opened another parish between Tartar and Ortum at Chepareria (1971) followed, a year later, by Staples who moved on to open another parish at Sigor (1972).

In the meantime, the entire Karapökot (the low-lying stretch of land on the Kenyan-Uganda border, which includes current administrative divisions of Alale, Kacheliba and parts of Kapenguria) was administratively under the Government of Uganda until 1970, when it was returned to the control of the government of Kenyan. Ecclesiastically the Verona Fathers living in Karamoja, Uganda, were serving this part. "The language used to evangelize the Pokot was Karimojong: prayers and the catechism were first taught in that language at least until the only mission among the pastoralist Pokot remained Amudat, on the Uganda side of the border"[15]. After the transfer of jurisdiction, they had either to move on to Kenya or give up their service

---

13. Pontifical Council for Culture (1999). *Towards A Pastoral Approach to Culture*. Vatican: Pontifical Council for Culture, no. 5.
14. Pope Paul VI (1977). Op. cit., no. 20.
15. Tibaldo (2006). Op. cit., 173.

to this part altogether, they opted for the former. After the dust of power transfer had settled (1973) the Veronas opened a parish at Kacheliba, which until then served as the headquarters of West Pökot County and major taxation center (hence the word 'Kacheliba', which means 'the home of payment', a corruption of the Swahili question, *umelipa*—have you paid (the tax)? "The mission of Santa Croce of Kaceliba was initiated in July 1972 by Father Pietro and a Verona Brother who is a builder and who came from Uganda for this purpose." [16]

The following year this center was moved to Kapenguria and the Veronas opened yet another parish at Bendera (1973). After twelve years, they opened two more parishes in quick succession, one at Amakuriat (1985) and another at Kabichbich (1986). Then Chepnyal was opened in 1992, with Michael Dillon as the Father-in-charge and Sinar was opened in 2004 with Cosmas Ngomba as the Father-in-Charge. Lastly, Makutano Parish was opened in 2006 with John Barasa as its first Parish Priest. At the moment, there is only one Kiltegan priest (Dillon), as Staples moved to Kipsaina Parish, in the neighboring Trans Nzoia County and as such four of the parishes they started (that is Tartar, Chepareria, Ortum and Sigor) have been handed over to the African clergy, diocesan and missionaries. The trend seems to be the same among the Combonis, who have handed over one of their four parishes (Kabichbich) to diocesan clergy.

The Mission of the Protestant Churches in West Pökot

Apart from the expansion of Catholic evangelization, the Protestants equally met with limited success in scope and extension. The Anglicans intensified their projects in the whole of West Pökot and they deepened the old ones, that is, education, women's projects, agricultural projects and, most importantly, bible translation, which they did (and continue doing) in conjunction with other Protestant churches. This last one cannot be equated to any other, in terms of evangelization, because it has exceptionally helped to bring the Bible closer to the people, even though most of them cannot read or write. Majority of the 'ordinary' Pökot Christians access the Bible only through the oral, aural and visual media, because theirs is an oral, not a written culture.

They, for instance, get their literate children to read bible stories, in the Pökot language, at home in the evening and then they discuss their lessons to the family within their social context. "At the same time, wherever the Bible is available in local languages, it becomes an integral part of local literature in the same way that it did in Europe during the Reformation."[17] And surely, this has proved to be a powerful tool for evangelization by keeping the fire of Christianity burning, even in times of crises. Hence the emphasis on education, which resulted in the building of both primary and secondary schools by missionaries of all Christian religions. Education

---

16. Tescaroli, op. cit., 31.
17. Mugambi (2003). Op. cit., 122.

is not only seen as a vehicle for spreading the Gospel but also as a means to uplift people's life standard.

Apart from the achievements of the Anglican Church, more Protestant Churches have been planted in the county as follows: The Seventh Day Adventist (SDA, with its headquarters at Chepareria), Evangelical Lutheran Church of Kenya (ELCK, also with headquarters in Chepareria), African Gospel Church (AGC, based in Sook, but with headquarters in Kericho), the Baptist Church (based at Konyao) and the Reformed Church of East Africa (RCEA, based at Amolem, with headquarters in Eldoret). We had regular meetings with Hans Visser, the first missionary of the latter in West Pökot, and he shared with us both his joys and anxiety about evangelization in the county. Hans Visser arrived in West Pökot in 1975 and started the church in three places—Sekerr, Masol and Tamkal. Like his Catholic and Anglican counterparts, he started projects on medical work and agriculture but added research, on Pökot religion and culture to his pastoral duties (1980–1981). During the research period, Visser[18] was replaced by Haanschoten, who took over all pastoral duties, due to the demanding nature of research.

Hans Visser was a teacher of history and civics by profession and had worked in Zambia (1971–1973), before going to West Pökot. His main question on evangelization is this: "How can you preach the Gospel when you do not know the people's language, culture and religion?" He speaks very good Pökot and says that he learned a lot during his research, which included undergoing the Pökot ritual of *sapana*, after which he was given the name Lopitakit. His admiration and vision for the Pökot people, is still as alive and fresh as it was in the 1980s. Among the issues he regards to be of main concern to evangelization is the fact of cattle raiding at Nasalot and Amolem that make people to be always on the move, which means that to reach them the missionary has also to be on the move.

The second important thing for him is the need for the people to be able to read the Word of God in their own language—which can express their life situation in a way they understand better. For these reasons, he joined hands with the Anglicans and the Catholics to initiate the bible translation project that sought to update the then existing New Testament edition that was done by Totty, in 1976. The members of the committee were himself, Leo Staples (for the Catholic Church), David Tumko, Joseph Murupus, Jackson Katina, James Korelach and Alston Toroitich (for the Anglican and Reformed Church), who were later joined by Gerrit van Steenbergen.

Commenting on the importance of the bible translation project in Africa, Mojola observes that it empowers the Christians so that they do not have to be totally dependent on the missionaries. "Translation of the bible into African languages," he says, "empowers African Christians to interpret the Bible texts into their own languages, for themselves, without missionary interventions—on the basis of mastery of their native

---

18. Visser later went back to the Netherlands and became the rector of Hendrik Kraemer Instituut; from where he retired in 2004.

idioms and native thought forms."[19] Part of these 'thought forms' in the Pökot thought pattern entail a communitarian, though complex, understanding and approach to the Word of God.

More than just being able to read the Word of God in their mother tongue, we think that bible translation into the Pökot language has had an effect of restoring their dignity and identity,[20] and also helped to decolonize their minds,[21] in the sense that they no longer need to rely on European or any other foreign categories to conceptualize or articulate their Christian religious experience. Visser's other major concern is the lack of sufficiently committed missionaries, leading to ways of preaching that hardly touch the people, mostly because of irrelevance. Finally, like Leo Staples, his counterpart in the Catholic Church, Visser advises all missionary workers in the region to learn the language, which is the key, not only to the people's hearts but also to their lifestyle that lays bare their joys and sorrows in a more articulate and natural way.

According to Visser the key issue at stake in evangelization "is how the Gospel should be proclaimed and transmitted into the world of the Pokot."[22] On the method of evangelization Hans Visser revealed that upon his arrival in West Pökot his first approach to the preaching of the Gospel was to start with the New Testament stories of Jesus Christ, as most missionaries do. But it did not take him long before he realized his mistake and soon made a personal decision to start with the story of creation in the Old Testament. The reasons for this, he says, are two—one theological, the other practical. First, he noticed that people did not easily get the concepts like, Jesus is the Messiah, or that he is the Son of the Father. Then he realized that preaching Jesus in isolation from the Old Testament turns him into kind of a super being that soon takes the place of God in people's minds. It is for these reasons that he thought it wise to go back to the beginning of the Scriptures and start there with the people, while at the same time drawing from the Pökot cosmogonic myths.

In his journal on the missionary approach among the Pökot, Visser points out at three key elements, necessary for the success of evangelization. These are: communication, identification and participation.[23] While commenting on the nature of communication, Kamma emphasizes on "Contact between people in whom the gap between person and person is bridged as much as possible. . . It is to penetrate behind the mask of the super-ego, that culture is putting on a person."[24] On the issue of identification, he calls upon missionaries and all other agents of the Gospel not to

---

19. Aloo Osotsi Mojola (2004). Foreword. In Ernst R. Wenland and Jean-Claude Loba-Mkole (eds). *Biblical Texts & African Audiences.* Nairobi: Acton Publishers, ii.

20. Mayor. Op. cit.

21. Ngugi Wa Thiong'o (1986). *Decolonising the Mind: The Politics of Language in African Literature.* Nairobi: East African Educational Publishers.

22. Visser (1982). Op. cit.

23. Ibid., 53.

24. F. C. Kamma (1976). *Dit Wonderlijke Werk.* Oegstgeest: Hendrik Kraemer Instituut, 805.

'feel good' about the 'top-position in their society' that they assume upon reaching the pastoral field and to undergo a change of attitude. He recommends Neill's understanding of mission, which he quotes as follows: "Mission is that one beggar tells the other beggar, where he can get bread." [25]

On the point of identification Visser notes with Kamma that the problem of mission is basically the missionaries themselves, and continues to say "One has to pray for wisdom for missionaries that they not alienate the people through their foolishness." [26] On this point, he insists that the missionary will get a shock if he really plunges into the Pökot culture (or any other culture for that matter). "His reaction will be to draw the people into his system and to teach his [own] values [rather than those of the gospel." [27] He, however, cautions against this temptation and suggests that pastoral agents accommodate themselves to the fact of learning to think in categories and concepts that people use in their culture and language.[28]

Analysis of the Homilies

Just as we had done with people's contributions in the SCCs (in chapter 3), we subjected the homilies on the parable of the Good Shepherd, by the ten priests working in West Pökot to a linguistic analysis. In general, they interpret this parable in a mainly eschatological and spiritual sense. Their preaching is based on the five concepts of shepherd, the gate, the thief, the gatekeeper and the sheep. Culpepper[29] and Bruce[30] see this parable as rooted in the book of Ezekiel (chapter 34) where the prophet castigates religious leaders in the Old Testament as being poor shepherds.

The God of Israel has appointed them as 'under-shepherds' to look after his people. "But those shepherds [like the 'worthless shepherd' of Zech. 11:17] are denounced for being more concerned to feed themselves than to feed the sheep entrusted to their care."[31] Culpepper admits that the parable is open to several other interpretations, namely historical—in the context of Jesus' ministry, ecclesiological—in the context of the Johannine community and cosmological—in the context of John's interpretation of Jesus as the Logos.[32] In most cases, none of these three concepts was used by the pastors in West Pökot, and if they did, it was only in passing. The spiritual sense of

25. Visser (1982). Op. cit., 65.
26. Kamma, op. cit., 184.
27. Visser (1982). Op. cit., 49.
28. Ibid., 50.
29. Alan R. Culpepper (1998). *The Gospel of John and Letters of John*. Nashville: Abingdon Press, 179.
30. Frederick F. Bruce (1983). *The Gospel of John: Introduction, Exposition and Notes*. Grand Rapids, Michigan: William B. Eerdmans Publishing Company, 223.
31. Ibid., 223.
32. Culpepper, op. cit., 180.

their interpretation saw Jesus as the spiritual gate to heaven,[33] for the righteous and so they appealed to the people to turn away from their evil ways in order not to give Satan, the thief and robber, a chance to snatch them away.

Our analysis of the homilies shows that the pastors start from the bible text and then try to apply it to the situation on the ground. Indeed, some saw the parable as an ideal challenge to the Pökot people to renounce their 'primitive cultural practices', like cattle rustling, and join the fold of 'the chosen ones', who are destined to heaven. In this regard Zinkuratire thinks that it would be more helpful to ask socially relevant questions of a bible text vis-à-vis its social context in Africa.[34] He leads the way by asking what the Bible means to Africans in the face of the post-independence dreams of political freedom, social stability and economic prosperity as opposed to the prevailing political chaos and economic collapse. We move on and analyze the homilies of pastors and see the extent to which they address the prevailing social circumstances.

Word-count

Once again, we used the Kwalitan word-count to check the recurrence of the pluralistic words versus the singular ones, in a bid to discover the cultural themes. The results were as follows: the word 'we' was used 93 times against the word 'I' which was used 151 times (a difference of 58 times), the word 'us' was used 23 times as opposed to the word 'me' which was used 49 times (a difference of 26 times). The word 'our' was used 35 times against the word, 'my' which was used 29 times (a difference of 6 times). The word 'they' appeared 88 times whereas the words 'he' and 'she' appeared 52 and 8 times respectively (a difference of 28 times). The word 'them' appeared 36 times whereas the words 'him' and 'her' were used 16 and 11 times (a difference of 5 times). The words 'you'/yourselves were used 16 times in contrast to the singular forms of 'you' and 'yourself, used 86 times.

Finally, the words 'mine', 'your(s)', 'his'/ 'hers'/ 'its', and 'their(s)' were used 0, 22, 25/0/0, 53 times respectively. The individualistic elements in these words seem to take preference over the pluralistic ones. The most divergent findings, however, were that the word community was used 77 times in its singular form and 4 times in its plural form by 6 out of 9 priests while 3 priests did not use it at all. We also noted that 3 priests had a dominant pluralistic orientation of using the word 'we' against the singular usage of the pronoun 'I', although the difference is marginal (Dillon 24 versus 17, Antonio 6 versus 2 and Siundu 12 versus 8).

---

33. Bruce, op. cit., 225–226.
34. Victor Zinkuratire (2004b). Life Context of the Interpretation. In Daniel Patte et al (eds). *Global Bible Commentary.* Nashville: Abingdon Press, 186.

Table 9. Pronoun Articles

Plural	Frequency	Singular	Frequency	Difference
We (*acha*)	93	I (*ani, ante*)	151	58
Us (*acha*)	23	Me (*ani, ante*)	49	26
Our(s) (*chicha*)	35	My/mine (*nyinyan*)	29	6
You/yourselves (*akwa/akwane*)	16	You/yourself (*nyi*)	86	70
Their(s) (*nyingwa*)	53	His/hers/its (*nyenyi*)	22/0/0	31
Them/they (*chane*)	36	Him/her (*nyinte*)	16/11/25	16
Your(s) (*nyinkwa/chikwa*)	10	Your(s) (*nyengu/cheku*)	22	12

The Understanding of the Concept 'Shepherd'

Our next interest was to know what the priests themselves understood with the term 'shepherd' or how they conceptualized it before passing this knowledge to the Pökot people. Not one of the nine priests made an attempt to define the term or give it some conceptual analysis. This is in spite of the fact that the Pökot have four different terms used to refer (although sometimes loosely) to a shepherd as mentioned earlier. We asked one priest what he thought of the wide difference in terminology between the two languages and why he did not bother to refer to it, but he said this does not bother him at all. This is because it does not have any negative consequences to the outcome of his pastoral ministry, and as such he sees it as irrelevant in the practical terms of the Pökot pastoral situation.

> I see no problem with the word *mösöwoon*, which is a general word that refers to all those caring for animals. When we speak of the Good Shepherd we might be talking about minding the sheep. Here in Pökot the sheep are not that important, the goats would be more important. I, however, see no problem since all is caring for the animals. In the Gospel Jesus talks about being the gateway to the fold this will not have much significance to our people because the fold is for the individual family and the animals are not mixed up. If we talk in a general way about caring of animals, we find that it is similar. In preaching, for instance, it does not matter to the people whether I talk about a *mösöwoon*, a *rïpin* or *kyakuyin*. The only word I know, for sure, they cannot

accept, and I too cannot use it, is *ngorokö*: and this is not because of its linguistic connotations or denotations but because of its social ramifications.[35]

The Problem of Translation

Upon going through the Pökot version of the parable of the Good Shepherd, it became clear to us that it was not a direct translation of the original Greek Bible, which means it is a translation of another (English or Kiswahili) translation. This is important because, as we have already seen, the Pökot culture is an oral one and people's relationship with the Bible is basically oral. This means that the text has to be translated, one way or another, in order for it to be understood. The problem of translation rests on two factors—translatability of one language to another and commensurability of cultures.[36]

Languages are usually not congruent in terms of words and idiomatic expressions. As a result, certain points cannot be transliterated and so one is forced to look for a word or words that only faintly or vaguely express the thought to be translated. This is particularly the case when the word to be translated has many equivalent words in the new language, and as such it is up to the translators to decide which word to use. Thus, "every translation of the Bible into an African language is an interpretative act."[37] If the translators are not careful or knowledgeable enough, this can end up dealing a devastating blow to people's understanding because translation is not just a matter of words, but carries many other societal aspects, which together make up people's 'frame of reference'. Mojola and Wendland captured this reality when they observed that "...the reading, interpretation and translation of texts are influenced by presuppositions and assumptions, prejudices and biases, value systems and believe systems, textual traditions and practices, worldviews, ideology and interests."[38]

When a Pöchon reads the original Greek text of John 10: 1–16,[39] he or she will not at once know what exactly the word ποιμίν means, because it has five almost related Pökot equivalents. The United Bible Societies (1989) translation has made a clarification to Modern Greek speakers by interchangeably using another word, βοσκός, which means the same as ποιμήν in order to distinguish between the narrow concept

---

35. Matthias Mulumba was the parish priest of Kabichbich. He is 40 years old and he has successfully worked with the Pökot people for the past 5 years. The interview was carried out on 14/04/2002. The 'social ramifications' that Mulumba is talking about is the hostility that we will talk about later in this book.

36. Mojola (2004). Op. cit., 5.

37. West (2005). Op. cit., 6.

38. A. O Mojola. and E. R. Wendland (2003). Scripture in the Era of Translation Studies. In T. Wilt (ed). *Bible Translation: Frames of Reference*. Manchester: St. Jerome, 8.

39. Barbara Aland and Kurt (eds) (1998). *Greek-English New Testament*. 8th edition. 2nd print. Stuttgart: Deutsche Bibelgesellschaft.

of a shepherd and the wider one of a herder.⁴⁰ However, the Pökot Bible just translates the word 'ποιμήν' as *mösöwoon*, at the expense of *kyakuyin*, *rïpin* and *mötworin*, needless to mention the more controversial term *ngoroköin*. Another problem we noticed is that the original Greek text shows the distinction between the owner of the sheep (ποιμήν) and a hireling (μισθωτός, verse 12). Despite the fact that there is an equivalent of this Greek term in the Pökot language (*mötworin*), the bible translation (1988) uses the negative explanation of "*chii nyo melö mösöwoon*—a person who is not a shepherd."⁴¹ Perhaps it would have been a lot clearer if the present Pökot Bible was a mirror of the original Greek Bible with clarifications (instead of omissions) as shown in the Modern Greek translation.

Mojola puts forward these problems in the form of questions. He asks whether complete translatability between two languages is possible, and whether two distinct socio-cultural and linguistic traditions can be completely commensurable. He wonders if one can completely and fully understand or represent one culture and language in terms of another, without a certain amount of distortion, incompleteness, betrayal and unnaturalness.⁴² Going by the earlier examples we have given with regard to the issue of words and translations, we think that answers to the questions above are in the negative. Thus, there is a real need for bible scholars to engage themselves more vigorously in the project of bible translation and intessfy the writing of African Bible commentaries that can properly help in contextualizing the biblical message.⁴³ Mojola acknowledges the existence of this problem but also recognizes the success of bible translation project, in spite of the constraint.

> But the ideal is a along [sic] way from being realised, at least in Bible translation. It is not therefore surprising that many Bible translations in the local languages of our continent (and probably elsewhere as well) were done by people who possessed much commitment and dedication but often lacked competence in the languages of the source-texts and the required related disciplines. Some of the translations were done (and in some cases are still being done) by people whose command of the receptor-language is secondary. Many translators in Africa do not possess first-language or native-language competence and proficiency. Despite this constraint, the current generation of Bible translations has had a huge and positive impact on the spread and growth of Christianity in our continent.⁴⁴

Related to the problem of translation is the perennial problem of the exact way to write the Pökot language. As we mentioned in chapter three, the language has not

---

40. United Bible Societies (1989). Op. cit.
41. John 10: 12.
42. Mojola (2004). Op. cit., 5.
43. SECAM (2005). Op. cit., no. 26.
44. Mojola (2004). Op. cit., ii.

existed in writing until the coming of the missionaries, and even then, as it is the case now, not many people could read and write it well. Many people do not know how to read and those who know rarely read well and even more seldom is their agreement on how particular words should be written or how they should be translated. For example, it is not clear whether the word age-set should be written as *pïn* or as *pën*, or whether the word thieves should be written as *chorï* or as *chorü*. The same problems are faced by the SCCs in West Pökot and we, too, had more than our fair share when we tried to put bible sharing in writing. The problems above still hamper the efforts to empower the 'ordinary' Pökot Christians to interpret the Bible in their native idioms and thought forms and in particular those of communitarianism.

Relevance of Jn. 10:1–16 to a Pastor's Life

To gauge whether, and to what extent, the priests tried to make the parable of the Good Shepherd sound relevant to the Christian life of the people in West Pökot, we counted how many of them gave concrete steps that people needed to take in order to experience conversion and how many used personal examples. The reason for doing this is that the cultural set-up of the Pökot community is such that imageries, examples and stories are powerful symbols that leave long lasting impression in people's minds. Three priests did not cite personal examples from their daily lives during the sermons, while three cited general examples that have nothing to do with their own lives or the Pökot people's daily activities. In contrast to the priests, nearly all catechists extensively quoted examples from their personal lives, and in particular how they had tried to shepherd the people of God, entrusted to them by their priest. This could easily lead to a conclusion that six priests have not internalized the reading in a way that can inspire a Pökot listener to follow and internalize the reading in his/her own life.

The people were also not happy with the performance of such priests, when they only talked of things in 'a general and disaffected way'. As mentioned elsewhere in this book, the Pökot people like stories (*lökoy*) and can listen to them for as long as the story is interesting and has something to do with their lifestyle. The same applies to the bible stories. Since many Pökot people cannot read and write, they pay keen attention to the bible narratives and always want to draw a connection between them and their own lives. If this connection is missing, then the story is judged as a failure. If it is there then the bible teaching is a success and that is what they regard as the day's preaching. Even when a new priest visits them and no one can remember his name, people will always refer to him in connection with the story he narrated. If he did not, then young people simply refer to him as 'that boring priest'.

We tried to find out why the priests did not, or only rarely used personal examples in their homilies. They explained that parables are a pointer to the kingdom of God, and Jn 10: 1–16 is no exception and it must be treated as such. Hence its message is eschatological in nature. Thus, it is their job to direct people to Jesus Christ and his kingdom rather than to themselves. But the catechists see it differently. In line with the Pökot cultural notion of God's transcendence they see themselves as a ladder through which the people can reach him. Moreover, the notion of a kingdom to come in some distant future is not very appealing to the people. "You know," one of them Catechists told us, "the Pökot eschatology is a realized one and people want something concrete and tangible that makes sense here and now, because our concept of the future does not extend too far away."[45]

The Place of a Shepherd Among the Pastors

On the place of Jesus, the shepherd, among the pastors in West Pökot, we expected that because they were working among a mainly pastoralist people, the pastors would try to locate the place of Jesus in the Pökot community and use this as the starting point of their homilies. However, none of them made this reference and so we wanted to know their reasons for the omission. Our findings showed that this omission is rooted in the pre-conceived ideas that each of the two parties has about the other on the question of animals and shepherding.

One diocesan, non-Pökot priest, who did not want to be named, said this to us: "You know the main problem we have about this bible text and the imagery of the shepherd has to do with the notion of a shepherd around here," he lamented. "A good shepherd is gauged in terms that are directly forbidden by the Bible, like cattle rustling, and yet if you speak up against the practice they claim that you are becoming partisan, mixing politics with religion and at the same time attacking their culture."[46]

Apart from the softly-softly approach to the cultural issues, which they regard as a raw nerve, the other problem the priest mentioned was the difficulty to distinguish what is truly Pökot from what is not, due to influence from outside the community. We became interested in knowing the exact nature of this influence and how it took place within the cultural set-up. So, we tried to know how much the Pökot culture, particularly cattle rustling, could indeed be said to be *Pökot* by tradition. We realized that although our informants agree that they have borrowed much from their neighbors—especially the Tugen, the Marakwet, the Turkana and the Karimojong in Uganda—nobody knows exactly when the borrowing took place and the extent to which they borrowed the custom(s) in question.

So, it is also not easy to say with any degree of certainty that cattle rustling is an originally Pökot practice as it, too, could have been borrowed from their neighbors. Change in the traditional set-up was more systematic and gradual, as opposed to the modern change, which seems to be sudden and cataclysmic; hence it is traumatizing

---

45. Interview with Simeon Kapeluk, a 30-year-old catechist, who has since joined politics and was elected the councillor of Krich Ward in Sook Location but lost in subsequent elections.

46. Patrick Njenga (not his real name) is a young priest, who was recently posted to a Parish in West Pökot but finds things to be very different from the rest of Kenya, as he puts it.

and unwelcome, especially by the elders. One such reality is the sudden change from the pastoral kind of economy, in which the pastoralists only stand short of being contemptuous of the agricultural practice, to the farming and salary economy that leaves many of them out of the economic reach. Hence lack of a coordinated approach to economic empowerment has resulted in spiraling poverty, especially, among the 'ordinary' people.

The Role of a Shepherd Among the Pastors

As mentioned already in this book, our choice of the parable of the Good Shepherd[47] was influenced by the fact that the Pökot are strongly influenced by pastoral orientation and that they have a very special relationship with animals; one that amazes every outsider, even those who have lived there for long. We wanted to know whether, and to what extent, the homilies presented by the priests make a deliberate effort to locate the role of a shepherd in the Pökot community and then build on this social reality to develop a parallelism with the parable's teaching on the same; and perhaps make a symbiosis of the two.

In their homilies, three out of nine priests did not talk of the traditional role of a shepherd or even compare it to the role of Jesus in the Christian setting. We also observed that this omission was confined to the diocesan priests and that four priests only cited a cultural example but did not compare it to the role of Jesus as a shepherd. This leaves us with two priests, which, warrants us to say that the priests did not approach the role of a shepherd from a cultural angle, even from their own cultures. On further inquiry during the interviews it emerged that they still look at the Bible, not as an African book, but as a foreign piece of literature that, in a sense, does not quite fit in people's way of life and this is why they must change their 'evil' ways if they are to be counted worthy of the heavenly kingdom. One priest candidly said this to us: "The saddest news we have here is that the Pökot have lapsed back to paganism and the Gospel will never take root in this place unless they abandon their evil traditions."[48] When we inquired about these 'evil' traditions we were given examples of traditional rituals, like the rites of passage; a manifestation of the negative influence seen earlier.

During interviews, however, the priests agreed that a shepherd had a host of roles in the traditional set-up in the Pökot community, though most of these have changed in many areas, but still in force in many others. Talking to a veteran scripture teacher, George Cheboryot (himself an African, but not Pökot) about this discrepancy, he admitted that much remains to be done with respect to helping catechists, seminarians and young priests to appreciate their own cultures and incorporate their cultural values to the Gospel teachings, but also said that he leaves this task to them.

---

47. John 10: 1–16.

48. Fr. Fintan McDonald (not his real name) is a missionary priest, who has worked in West Pökot for a relatively short period compared to his compatriots.

And that it requires a lot of ingenuity and hard work to come up with fitting examples and relevant imageries.

> In the course of scripture, I am not so much preoccupied with the African culture. I try to make them understand a bible passage and leave it to the Holy Spirit for them to discover how to apply and relate it to the situation in which they live, and their culture. I am conscious that the Jewish culture in the Bible has much in common with the African culture. I see inculturation as their task and I try to help with background understanding of the basic resources of scientific exegesis.[49]

Another Scripture teacher, in a catechetical center, said that he leaves that task to the teacher of homiletics and said that it is his main task to provide the students with the scientific tools of the Bible, and then someone else can help them put this into perspective within their social contexts. We asked him what he thinks about biblical hermeneutics and he said that this was never taught during his formative years and so it requires those studying now to take it up and introduce it in seminaries.

However, a professor of scripture at the Catholic University of Eastern Africa, Victor Zinkuratire, did not think this was a sufficient excuse not to introduce students to biblical hermeneutics. "This is a generally new subject, I admit," said he, "but the fact that it was not being taught in one's formative years is, in itself, not a justifiable reason not to indulge in serious reading about it and at least introduce students to the subject. If we are to make our faith African, it is the high time we confronted, head on, the two subjects of biblical exegesis and biblical hermeneutics and reviewed them to suit the African perspective."[50]

Cultural Traits in the Pericope

As we went through the homilies we were eager to know how much the priests interpreted the pericope of the Good Shepherd from a cultural perspective; that is, by quoting examples from their own cultures (or the Pökot culture) during the explanation of the pericope to the people of West Pökot. Two priests did not, the other seven quoted from their own cultures with one missionary and a diocesan priest quoting from the Pökot culture. We tried to find out the reason for this kind of divergence but we did not come to a clear understanding. Whereas some said they were at home with their own cultures, others said that they find the Pökot culture a bit too closed to serve as an ideal example of the Gospel teaching. Then there are those who simply think this cultural stuff would die off naturally, even if slowly, a

---

49. Fr. George Cheboryot is a priest in the Diocese of Eldoret and a long-serving teacher of the scriptures, who has taught in both Nairobi and Tindinyo theological seminaries and has immense wealth of biblical studies.

50. Fr. Victor Zinkuratire is a professor of scriptures at the Catholic University of Eastern Africa, and he has published a lot of articles and books on inculturaton and biblical hermeneutics in Africa.

fact, according will make evangelization easy and enjoyable. They may have an idea of what culture would say on particular issues but they deliberately chose to ignore them and, instead, drew examples from modern 'existential life situations' that are devoid of cultural complications.

Inculturation of the Pericope

In our effort to know if the priests had managed to penetrate the worldview of the Pökot people and hence the ability to present the text from the Pökot perspective, we tried to examine how often they appealed to the cultural imageries related to the whole phenomenon of shepherding in their homilies and to see how they would apply it to Jesus. In this regard, we captured and counted the most commonly used folk terms in relation to the parable and the results were as follows. The term 'cattle rustling', or 'cattle raiding', was used only once in spite of the fact that it is a very rampant practice in this community: 3 out of 9 priests used the word 'thief' 12 times, even though Jesus used it in an indicting way to those who are responsible.

We noticed that the priests were either evasive of this traditional practice or they did not exactly know what to say about it. When we put this question to one of them, he said that this is an area that is both delicate and sensitive due to its complexity. He said they have to maintain the balance between being for the people and also respect their culture, while at the same time they have to support government's effort to weed out most cultural practices, like FGM. The word 'culture' was used 36 times by 7 out of 9 priests with the majority explaining that the people have to let the Gospel sieve through their culture and let it take what is good in it. Although they did not say this to us, it sounded like the Gospel is the yardstick with which to measure, which cultural practices are good and which ones are bad. The word 'door' (or its equivalents of 'gate' and 'gateway') was used 113 times by 7 out of 9 priests despite the fact that traditionally there was no door to the sheep pen among the Pökot. This means that, in traditional terms the idea of a door to the sheepfold makes little or no sense at all.

The word 'goat' was used 18 times by 6 priests while the word 'sheep' was used 68 times by all 9 priests. Although the parable specifically uses the sheep as the object of teaching, we had thought that the geographical difference would tilt the interpretation of the text and reflect people's orientation. Those people who live in the cold high lands of Cherangani and Sondany hills can only rear sheep as their major source of 'livestock income' and as such it is easier for them to associate themselves with the Gospel reading than those in the low dry plains of Karapökot. However, this did not come out as a factor since some priests from the low areas could place emphases on the sheep while others in the high lands could emphasize the cow. Then the word 'water' was not used even once and yet much of the land is dry and so, water is part of the vital 'components' of life here. Finally, the word 'cow' was used 12 times by 7 out of 9 priests and yet a cow is, as it were, 'the blood line of the Pökot lifestyle'. Many clan and/

or tribal wars start at the watering point, particularly in the dry spell when everybody wants to water their animals. Going by this criterion, it can be concluded that the priests have not inculturated the Word of God and made it part of their parishioners' social and environmental reality.

Analysis of Commentaries

In general priests in West Pökot hardly use bible commentaries and dictionaries, and if they do, then it is the d*The New Jerome Biblical Commentary*[51] or *McKenzie Dictionary of the Bible*,[52] both of which are easily available at the Catholic bookshop in Nairobi. We mentioned the International Bible Commentary, which contains articles from African contributors and not one priest had an idea of it. To prepare the Sunday homily (normally on Saturday night) they use Sunday commentaries and two in particular: *Celebrating the Word—Commentary on the Readings* by Fernando Armellini, and *Africa: Our Way to Preach God's Word*, by Michael McGrath (SMA) and Grégoire Nicole (S.A., popularly known as White Sisters, even though many of them are no longer white). So, they tend to be more 'homiletical' than exegetical in their analysis of bible texts and preaching. The Sunday commentaries are divided into three volumes, years A, B, and C in accordance with the division of the liturgical years in the Catholic Church.

They seem to be the *de facto* officially sanctioned commentaries for Sunday readings because they are found in almost every diocesan and at the national Catholic bookshop; and as such nearly every diocesan priest has a set or at least one, if not two of the books. However, we only used years A and B of both series because our selected reading (John 10:1-16) is covered in the two volumes. We separately subjected the commentaries, together with the Sunday sermons to the same criteria as we did to the bible sharing with the Christians in SCCs. We aimed at determining two points as follows: one, whether the commentaries are communitarian or individualistic in orientation. And two, whether they help the reader internalize the reading in a way that is geared towards inculturation and further realization of the Pökot culture in the Word of God, lest they remain both superficial and ephemeral. Thus, it can be determined, with some degree of certainty, how the commentaries and pastors' preaching impact on people's Christian life by analyzing their own understanding of the same text.

Fernando Armellini is an Italian priest and member of the congregation of the Sacred Heart of Jesus, which was founded in France in 1878, by Jean Leon Dehon. He had his theological studies in Bologna and got a licentiate at the Urbaniana Pontifical University. He specialized in biblical studies and got another degree at the Pontifical Biblical Institute. He advanced this specialization at the University of Jerusalem, where he studied bible history and archaeology and the Hebrew language. He worked

---

51. Raymond E. Brown et al. (eds) (1990). *The New Jerome Biblical Commentary*. London: Geoffrey Chapman.

52. John L. McKenzie (1965). *Dictionary of the Bible*. New York: Macmillan Publishing Company.

for ten years in Mozambique and is now a professor of sacred Scriptures in the seminary of the Açores Islands and a visiting lecturer in many places in Italy and Mozambique. He is the author of numerous books apart from the Sunday commentaries for which we mention him here.

Michael McGrath is an SMA, Irish priest who has been engaged in the formation of catechists in Nigeria for some decades. Nicole Grégoire is a French Canadian and belongs to the religious congregation of Our Lady of Africa. She came to East Africa in 1969 and for some time she was directly engaged in the formation of catechists in Tanzania. McGrath and Grégoire met at the AMECEA Pastoral Institute—Gaba in Eldoret (Kenya) in the 1970s and have been producing catechetical materials ever since. API is the only institute of its kind in the region that provides ongoing formation and renewal in a supportive setting, enriched by dialogue between lay persons, religious men and women and the clergy.

Commentaries on the Good Shepherd

Just as we had done with the bible sharing in SCCs and priests' homilies, we subjected the two above-named commentaries, to word-count in search of their orientation, with some words being combined as one, due to the Pökot linguistic structure. Apart from this relational linguistic usage we also counted the pluralistic personal pronouns like us, we (*acha*), they, them (*chane*), you, yourselves (*akwa, akwane*), our/s (*chicha*) and theirs (*chikwa*) against individualistic ones like I, me, myself (*ani, ante*), he/she, him/her (*nyinte*), you, yourself (*nyi*) mine (*nyinyan*), my (*nyan*) your/yours (*nyengu*), and his/hers/its (*nyenyi*).

As we already mentioned elsewhere Spradley, considers the recurrence of a single idea or word in more than one domain as a suggestion for the possibility of a cultural theme.[53] We, again, employed the Kwalitan computer program in the word-count for the above-mentioned articles, but we also checked their spread within the said commentaries, hence showing the difference in their usage of the words. The results for the two Sunday commentaries were as follows: the word 'we' was used 69 times against the word 'I' which is used 26 times (a difference of 43 times), the word 'us' is used 57 times as opposed to the word 'me' which is used 14 times (a difference of 43 times). The word 'our/s' is used 37 times against the word, 'my' which is used 12 times (a difference of 25 times). The word 'they' appears 71 times, while the words 'he' and 'she' appear 118 and 2 times respectively (a difference of 49 times). The word 'them' appears 31 times whereas the words 'him' and 'her' are used 36 and 1 time (a difference of 6 times).

The plural form of the words 'you'/yourselves are used 12 times in contrast to the singular forms of 'you' and 'yourself', which were used 44 times (a difference of

---

53. Spradley (1980). Op. cit., 141.

32 times). Finally, the words 'mine', 'your'/ 'yours', 'his'/ 'hers'/ 'its', and 'their'/ 'theirs' were used 0, 10/1, 83/0/0, 18/0 times respectively. Clearly, the pluralistic elements in these articles seem to take preference over the singular ones. The word community is used only once in its plural form by Armellini,[54] and the concept of ownership does not come out clearly. There is, for instance, a clear discrepancy between the overriding majority of 'our' or 'ours' (used 37 times) against the word 'my' or 'mine' (used 12 time), on the one hand and the dominance of the word 'his' (used 83 times) against the word 'their' or 'theirs' (used 18 times), on the other hand. Below is a table of personal pronoun articles, their frequency and difference in usage.

Table 10. Pronoun Articles

Plural	Frequency	Singular	Frequency	Difference
We (*acha*)	69	I (*ani, ante*)	26	43
Us (*acha*)	57	Me (*ani, ante*)	14	43
Our(s) (*chicha*)	37	My/mine (*nyinyan*)	12/0	25
You/yourselves (*akwa/akwane*)	5	You/yourself (*nyi*)	44	39
Their(s) (*nyingwa*)	18	His/hers/its (*nyenyi*)	81/0/0	63
Them (*chane*)	31	Him/her (*nyinte*)	36/1	6
Your(s) (*chikwa*)	0	Your(s) (*nyengu*)	9	9
They (*chane*)	71	He/she (*nyinte*)	118/2	49

The Understanding of the Concept 'Shepherd'

We had a particular interest in knowing how these commentaries contextualize the concept 'shepherd' within the African set-up in order to create a powerful imagery that appeals to the reader and help him/her vivify the work of a shepherd. None of them made any attempt to define the term or give some conceptual analysis of it. Although it is really not imperative to start a homily with concept definition, it is of great help to do so in order to help capture people's imagination and let them know exactly what you are talking about. As already mentioned in the last chapter, the Pökot have four different terms that are used in connection with the work of shepherding:

---

54. Fernando Armellini (1992). *Celebrating the Word: Year A—Commentary on the Readings*. Nairobi: Paulines Publications, 125.

that is, *mösöwoon, kyakuyin, rïpin* and *mötworin*, all of which are, by far, wider than the English word 'shepherd'.

Then there is one more controversial term (*ngoroköin*) that only has a positive meaning, of a sentry, in Karapökot among the purely pastoral Pökot. In other parts of the county it is regarded as negative or even derogatory since it refers to armed cattle rustlers who are equated to brigands (*chelosëy*) or bandits (*chelolos*). Hermeneutics deals with the meaning of words, which is finally hoped to lead one to the truth, but once this meaning is obscured in the web of words then it distorts the very truth it is intended to communicate. For this reason, Staples and Visser have insisted on the importance of learning the Pökot language if missionaries are to understand the way of life and thought patterns of the Pökot people. In this light, it can be considered an omission that the commentaries did not account for such a linguistic analysis.

Cultural Traits in the Pericope

Going through the commentaries we were eager to know how much they interpret the pericope of the Good Shepherd[55] from a cultural perspective; that is, by quoting examples from the many cultures in Africa where the books are widely used, while explaining their understanding of the pericope. McGrath and Grégoire,[56] gave only one such example, of a film they watched in which a shepherd went looking for his lost sheep until he found it in a ditch after much hardship. And even this did not give any cultural dimension; say of pastoral communities and how such an action was celebrated or what it means in the communities concerned.

Moreover, it even looks odd and out of place in a social setting where it is not an ordinary thing for a shepherd to go looking for his lost sheep or cow alone. When, for example, an animal gets lost among the Pökot, it becomes a crisis in the entire home, and even neighbors will join in the search: after which they sit down to celebrate; more or less in the style of the prodigal son as depicted by Luke, or the lost sheep and the lost coin parables.[57] Elijah Lopuke explains his own observation with regard to the case of a lost animal among the Pökot:

> If one animal does not return home, heheee . . . it is a crisis in that home and no one will have peace until it is found. Everybody will have to go out and look for it. If it proves difficult to find, the neighbors will join in the search and finally it becomes a clan issue. If the remains of the animals are not found to prove that wild beasts ate it, then it becomes clear that someone helped

---

55. John 10: 1–16.

56. Michael McGrath and Grégoire Nicole (1988). *Africa: Our Way to Preach God's Word: Book 2—Year A*. Alton: Redemptorist Publication, 126.

57. Luke 13: 15–24; Luke 15: 1–10.

himself with it and if the thief does not own up then the council of elders is called in, to administer the traditional cursing ritual called *mutat*.[58]

What we realized is that the books are general in nature and are not, designed for specific situations like West Pökot; hence the need for the pastors to bridge the existing gaps, loopholes and hiatuses between generality and specificity. This, we believe, cannot be done in any other way but to learn the people's culture and the structure of their community life, which is first and foremost imbedded in their language. Any effective evangelization, then, hinges around language as the basic tool for communication and the doorway to the thought pattern of the Pökot; because it may, in turn, help the agents of evangelization to grasp the meaning system of their subjects.

Inculturation of the Pericope

We also tried to find out whether the commentaries presented the reading from an African point of view of the act of shepherding and to know the exact image they put in the mind of an African reader. We tried to examine how often they appealed to the cultural imageries related to the whole phenomenon of shepherding and to see how they would apply it to Jesus. In this regard, we captured and counted the most commonly used terms in relation to the parable.

The term 'cattle rustling', or 'cattle raiding', a common practice in all nomadic communities in Africa, is not used at all. Armellini uses the singular form of the word 'thief' twice, and uses its plural form, 'thieves', six times: and this is in spite of Jesus himself using it and in a forcefully indicting all those responsible. The word 'culture' is not used, but its derivative form 'cultural', is used once, again by Armellini.[59] The word 'door' is not used, while its synonym 'gate' is used once by McGrath and Grégoire,[60] in spite of Jesus referring to himself as the 'door' or gateway to the sheepfold and repeating it 4 times. The word 'goat' is not used at all while the word 'sheep' is used 45 times, while the word 'water' is used two times.

Finally, the word 'cow' is not used in total disregard of the fact that in Africa there is, generally speaking, no provision for a shepherd as such, that is, someone who specializes in looking after sheep. We asked Mulumba whether in his community it is usual to find a person who specializes in looking after sheep and he answered in the negative.

> In my Luhya community a sheep is normally used for witchcraft purposes, mainly as a protective measure against an evil eye, an envious neighbor and so

---

58. Elijah Lopuke is a 35-year-old teacher at Nasokol Secondary School, but he comes from Amakuriat Parish in Alale. He worked as a catechist for several years before going for higher education. The interview was carried out at Nasokol Secondary School on 18/06/2002.

59. Armellini, op.cit., 115.

60. McGrath and Grégoire, op. cit., 126.

on. For this reason, people, do not keep so many of them and most people do not keep them at all: much less keeping sheep only. If one decided to specialize in sheep keeping then stories would go around that he is, in fact a witch, just as it happens when a person keeps a lot of them: even if he has other animals like cows and goats.[61]

It is ordinarily presumed that one would have other animals apart from the sheep and when this did not happen, the person is said to be 'poor' and still lagging behind on his way to 'riches', that is, to acquiring some cattle. So, the word 'shepherd' is normally translated as 'one who looks after animals'—sheep, cows and goats included. Among the Pökot, for instance, it is almost anathema to talk about animals without mentioning a cow because it is, as it were, the blood-line of their lifestyle. The importance of the cow and the special role it plays in the daily life of a Pöchon cannot be gainsaid. The failure by the commentators to mention this important animal would seem to the Pökot to be a gross omission of a key concept for inculturating this pericope into their life situation.

Indeed, to translate the word 'shepherd' into Pökot, the more general term 'mösöwoon' is used, but it always has to be qualified as *mösöwonto kechir*, which in English would sound something like 'the shepherd of sheep'! Again, the general nature of the Sunday commentaries comes into the fore, and it is understandable because they were not written with the Pökot community in mind. What this does is to place a much heavier responsibility on the shoulders of the pastors to earth the Gospel in the Pökot social scene, by discovering and using the community's cultural themes. With regard to the issue of inculturation, we found the work of Galván and Resende,[62] to be more down to earth and particularly in addressing the cultural symbols, imageries and stories, among the people of East Pökot. They relate these to the bible pericopes and parables in such a simple and clear way that even the disinterested or lukewarm Christian would easily identify himself or herself with the biblical pericope.

Religious Practice Among the Pastors in West Pökot

Although the religious practices of the Pastors in West Pökot is, in many ways similar to those of the 'ordinary' Christians (or parishioners, as they call them), they are also dissimilar in many other ways, some of which are a stark contrast. We observed three main traits that we would like to mention here. One, there is a notion that the higher you are in rank within the church, the more knowledgeable you are, and as such the more respect you deserve: hence there is a lack of collegiality among pastoral workers. This complacency gives the pastors a know-it-all attitude in their dealings with the rest of

---

61. Fr. Matthias Mulumba, the parish priest of Kabichbich, is an African diocesan priest, who is a Luhya rather than Pökot, a factor that helps him a lot to make a comparison during his pastoral duties.

62. M. E. G. Galván and F. M. O. Resende (2000). *An African Journey Through Mark's Gospel: A Tool for Small Christian Communities*. Nairobi: Pauline Publications Africa.

the Christians and allows a form of discrimination, rather than distinction based on job description, between various cadres of the pastors (that is, catechists, sisters and priests). Then there is an implicit attitude of superiority among the pastors towards other Christians; whom they refer to as 'ordinary Christians' (*wakristo wa kawaida*), and yet the Christians seem to accept this as the *de facto* nature of events in the Catholic Church as ordained by God. In a fit of anger, one curate complained to us that the parish priest gone for a holiday and left the parish finances in the hands of 'a mere layman'.

Their behavior portrays them as a special breed of people, who are distinguished from the 'ordinary people' and they must always be treated differently. This mentality has also taken root among the 'ordinary' Christians, who are willing to turn a blind eye to the failings of a priest, instead of addressing them, simply on the grounds that he is a priest; and the same attitude is extended to the bishops and other church leaders. Even traffic policemen on the road, for instance, are willing to overlook traffic offences committed by the priest(s). One day we decided to test this theory by driving a priest's car that had smooth tires and an expired road license. When we came to a roadblock, there were two tough-looking policemen who stopped us and asked that we identify ourselves. When we said that we come from a Catholic Parish the reaction was surprising: "*Oh, pole Father, enda tu*" (Oh we are sorry Father, just go).

The Know-it-all Attitude

With the exception of the three elderly missionaries (Dillon, Staples and Antonio) other pastors and catechists in particular, approach the Gospel from the perspective that they know it all, while the Christians know nothing. This is despite the fact that Mwalye has warned against such an attitude because, as she says, it " . . . can lead to a strained relationship with the laity."[63] The attitude we observed among the pastors in West Pökot, however, is that they are there to teach, instruct and give advice on all sorts of things, while the Christians are there to listen, learn and execute what they are told. A case in point is when Christians were giving their contributions on the parable of the Good Shepherd.

If a Christian seemed to hesitate in giving an explanation, a catechist would nearly always interject and make suggestions on how to 'give an appropriate explanation' or try to complete sentences for the respondent. This was not an isolated case or typical to one catechist but was a common occurrence among all pastors, which only stopped when we expressly told them to let the respondents tell us what they actually thought. At one point, we felt that the pastors were in fact telling us what they think the respondents have in mind or what they would have said given the chance. In our discussion with, Terry Hanley, the then teacher of Bible and Catechetics at

---

63. Hellen Mwalye (1999). Formation of Women Religious. In *Africa Ecclesial Review* 141 (4, 5 & 6). Eldoret: AMECEA Gaba Publications, 267–281.

the Mitume Catechetical Institute, we asked what he thought was the reason for this attitude and he had the following to say:

> I think there are a number of points that may be relevant here. One is certain bossiness or sense of superiority that a catechist might feel because he has a little training and thinks he knows more than other Christians. This should be discouraged. The second point is that the traditional catechism emphasis was on question and answers and unfortunately this is still the case in many places. It is true that the Bible was not used in catechesis although I would think and hope that over the last twenty years with the emphasis on the small Christian community and the use of the Bible there, and the emphasis we have at Mitume training center on the importance of the Bible that this is changing slowly. The view of the catechist that 'ordinary' Christians do not understand the Bible could still be a hangover from the past way where many Christians were not much accustomed to using the Bible.[64]

Another extreme example, of the know-it-all attitude, was portrayed by a Comboni priest, who did not only refuse to co-operate with us, but also claimed to know that 'his' parish is not the right place to carry out an ethnographic research. The conversation went on like this:

> Priest: Well this is a wrong place for you to do an academic research.
>
> Researcher: Why is it a wrong place?
>
> Priest: Because there are no Christians here.
>
> Researcher: And what are you doing here without Christians?
>
> Priest: Just sitting.
>
> Researcher: Just sitting, doing nothing?
>
> Priest: Yes, doing nothing. I mean there are only five Christians here and only two of them are Pökot. Yet you want to interview the Pökot.
>
> Researcher: And where can I find these five?
>
> Priest: One of them is a nurse at the dispensary, the other three are teachers, one is the headmistress of the girls' boarding in primary, and the other two are teachers in the secondary school, while the last one is a cook for the sisters. Oh. . .there she is, you can talk to her. She is the chairman in the church. Go and knock the sisters' front door and say I have sent you to her.
>
> Researcher: Thank you very much.[65]

---

64. Terry Hanley is a 60-year-old lay missionary from Australia and has worked in Africa all his life. At the time of this interview, he was working at the Mitume Catechetical and Pastoral Centre. Now he has retired and opened an AIDS counselling house, where he also lives. The interview was carried out on 24-07-2002.

65. Fr. Francesco Pierli (not his real name) is a Comboni Missionary, who has worked in West

A Segregatory Exclusivistic Attitude

The other element we observed is that there is a form of exclusivism[66] among the pastoral workers. Priests tend to exclude catechists from their midst, while catechists tend to exclude sisters in their midst. Even priests tend to exclude each other by grouping themselves in accordance with whether they are religious or diocesan. Although we did not gather any evidence to show that this action is intentional, or that it is a result of malice, the overall picture that we got is that exclusivism is an accepted norm among the pastoral workers.

In general, missionaries, for instance, are faithful to the recitation of the breviary (or the Divine Office) while they seemingly do not invite their lay (catechist) co-workers to do the same. We asked one priest, who did not want to be named, the reason for this and he said it was not necessary to 'disturb' the lay people with this kind of prayers because 'they have many other things to do', and yet it was not mandatory for them to say them. One head catechist reported that they feel excluded in certain aspects of the pastoral work. "We only saw Father go to church with a black book, but we do not know the kind of prayer book it is."[67]

He further said that he once tried to peep into the book but did not grasp anything so he dropped his curiosity, thus expressing the feeling that catechists are like bats: sometimes they are treated as church ministers, but other times they are treated as, 'mere laymen'. A diocesan priest also complained that missionaries tend to see themselves as special, or as the true priests, compared to their diocesan counter-parts whom they regard as 'secular' priests, because they do not take the three evangelical vows, one of them told us on condition of anonymity. On their part, diocesan priests too think that missionaries do not give them their due respect and look down on them, chiefly because they are poor.

This tension manifested itself in one incident in which Christians of a certain out-station were supposed to move from Kabichbich Parish to Chepareria Parish because of distance and other logistic reasons but they refused, ostensibly, for the fear of losing the material support they were enjoying. These incidents go against Bellagamba's advocacy of the concept of a 'team ministry' where all ministers (ordained and non-ordained, religious or diocesan) are considered equal, share in the decision-making process and each minister is answerable to the whole team.[68] It also

---

Pökot for a long time. He is currently the Parish Priest of Kacheliba Parish.

66. Exclusivism here is not used in the sense of the various trends of mission, but the social act of excluding others. This practice is, however, not limited to the pastors because even the Christians exclude their pastors (mainly priests and sisters) from many of their own social activities, because they always regard them as outsiders. The victims of this state of affairs are the catechists who (do not seem to know where they belong and as such) always try to identify themselves with both groups, depending on the situation.

67. Interview with Matthew Kalele, who is a former head catechist, in Chepareria Parish and he has also worked in Sigor Parish. He now works for the Justice and Peace Office in Chepareria Division.

68. Bellagamba (1992). Op. cit., 74.

goes against the idea of communitarianism, where all members are treated the same and accorded their due respect.

The priests and sisters are not regular goers of the SCCs; they only go there occasionally when the priest has specific things to do. This, we observed, takes place when there is Mass in the SCCs, annual canonical visitation or some other celebration, like the Patron Saint's Day, *Mavuno* (harvest) Day and so on. For this reason, we were only able to gather two sharing sessions within SCC set-up, by the only (two) priests, who participated with us. One SCC leader in Chepareria, Pius Meriekeren, did not understand why we should take SCCs so seriously and decide to carry out a research there and yet ordained and consecrated church leaders never took them seriously. "Priests and Sisters do not attend the SCC prayers in this parish, we have never seen our bishop in the SCC here and we have never even heard that he ever attended in any one such prayer meeting,"[69] he regretted. One catechist in Kacheliba, Anna Teko, had similar complaints and felt that the clergy have abandoned the SCC leaders.

We used to receive letters from different places, that is Chepareria, Tartar, Eldoret, Matunda and we could share ideas from different parishes, which gathered together with men. This is a Christian way and it could spread in the village. Those from Matunda used to help us; however, from the year 2000 up to now, we have not received any letter. Therefore, we have not met with Christians from different parishes. I think this makes us regress in our community spirit. I also think, as Imelda said, if priests and sisters came with us to the Small Christian Community it could have helped, but I find there is a weakness in this. If men saw the priest attending, they would be encouraged. To the Pökot, a woman is a child and cannot say anything that will catch their attention. If a man spoke they would take it seriously. So, they see the small Christian Community as a childish thing.[70]

With regard to the question posed by Pius, we concurred that it would have been better if the priests were present during the sharing of the Word, but the fact that they were not around did not have to deter us from carrying out the research. We, later, put this question to Ben Chesoli, the person charged with the duty of instructing catechists and Christians in general at the Mitume Catechetical Centre, about SCCs and he had this to say:

> We can see priests or even bishops insisting on people to attend small Christian community yet they do not attend it themselves. Priests go to the small Christian community if there will be a regular or harvest Mass. Once the harvest is over they don't go to the small Christian community again until the next harvest. When the beans harvest is over they wait for maize. I do not want to say it is all priests who do not go to the small Christian community. There are some who try to go while others claim to be 'very busy' to attend

---

69. Pius Meriekeren is a 55-year-old catechist and committed leader of the SCC in his outstation. The interview was carried out in his home, at Chepareria on 15/04/2002.

70. Interview with Anna Teko.

the SCC prayer and yet this word 'very busy' has entered into the church and spoiled the good planning of the church they are supposed to attend like any other Christian but this word 'very busy' has oppressed us. We know there are important things that should be done like meetings and so on. If, therefore, a priest or the bishop failed to attend the SCC prayer meeting because he had gone for a meeting, that is okay. However, if he is in the office that is a Christian office he should close it and attend the small Christian community. Many people will go to the small Christian community if they see that a priest of the bishop has attended.[71]

Manifestation of Power and Control

During our stay in Kabichbich Parish, we had an opportunity to observe what the pastors do in the main parish and also to visit three outstations and observe what happens there, the relationship between the Christians themselves and their relationship with their pastors. In these occasions, we participated in a Sunday Service (without a priest), Mass and instructions on the SCCs respectively. In a break from the trend in which religious leaders act in a manner that suggests superiority over their parishioners Antonio (the parish priest of Kabichbich Parish at the time) with sister Elizabeth, who is in charge of pastoral work, had embarked on a program to personally work out the meaning, purpose and benefits of the SCCs with the people; and how they facilitate the general well-being of Christian living. This was a grand pastoral project, aimed at directly empowering the Christians, but even in this down-to-earth pastoral project, the sense of superiority, on the part of the religious leaders, was not lacking. One example of a visit to a sub-parish, called Kaptabuk, will suffice.

The four of us, set off on Thursday, morning at 10.00 o'clock, in a four-wheeled Land Cruiser pickup: the rest being Jonas Beka (assistant to the Parish Priest), Elizabeth (Sister in charge of pastoral work) and Mary, the parish social worker. It took us two long hours of negotiating through winding and climbing up and down dusty and narrow road, with truly magnificent landscapes and the good-looking ranching ridges. Due to the fact that the place is very cold, the inhabitants keep the Merino sheep, which were introduced by the British government during the colonial era, as well as growing pyrethrum as a cash crop. They also keep a limited number of exotic (referred to as 'grade') cows because, 'a Pöchon without cows is a dead one', but they do not do very well due to the harshly cold climate. On the way, we were stopped by so many hitchhikers, some of whom wanted to get to Kaptabuk center, while others only wanted a lift to some other smaller centers along the way.

---

71. Ben Chesoli is a pastoral instructor at Mitume Catechetical and Pastoral Centre, specialised on SCCs. He has worked there for 15 years and is 65 years old. The interview was carried out on 21/06/2002.

The first experience of the sense of superiority was on the way these people approached the driver to ask for a hike and the way some of them were treated in return: shouting, mocking or simply ignoring them. In this case, we attributed the feeling of superiority among the pastors on two major factors: one, the attitude that people do not know, and need to be taught how to live the Gospel and two, the sheer material benefit, like the car, the money and other minor privileges that the pastors enjoy in the face of badly disadvantaged people, due to the economic downturn. This experience reminded us of a strikingly similar observation made by Wijsen and Tanner, in Sukumaland in Tanzania. "Sitting in a car sets a priest apart, elevating him in eyes of his parishioners into the ranks of the oppressive bureaucratic bourgeoisie or as the possible provider of lifts, a sort of ordained taxi driver."[72]

General Observation on Preaching Practices

Our research showed that only those missionaries that have been in the field for many years have made a successful effort to interpret the Gospel from the perspective and culture of the people. Young priests (both missionaries and the local clergy) nurture a kind of enthusiasm that does not allow them an opportunity to learn. "They are in a hurry to teach and teach quickly before the Lord comes and takes away the righteous; leaving behind the condemned ones," quips Leo Staples.[73] They reproduce the same homiletics contents they acquired in their seminary training, either by teachers from the West or using books prepared in the West, leaving very little room, if any, for inculturation. Staples admitted that he too, had this kind of 'jumpy' attitude when he came to West Pökot 50 years ago, but he also concedes that life has humbled and taught him over the time. It is he, indeed, who was to learn from the people.

> When I came here fifty years ago, I understood salvation as just that; reading the Gospel, preaching and baptizing people: and I measured my success with the number of people that came to church, the number of Christian registers and physical amenities, like churches, dispensaries and schools. While all this is good in itself, the Pökot have taught me the actual meaning of salvation—to walk with the people through their hardships and to be there for them when they need you. Share in people's anguish and joy and the rest will slowly but surely follow. They have taught me to live the Gospel.[74]

He recalls that his method of evangelization through 'teaching' and 'trying to save souls' first hit a snag when he went to Ortum, as no one seemed interested in what he was doing with the few catechists he had managed to convert. So, for the first time, he asked them if it was a good idea that they attend the traditional ceremonies where

---

72. Wijsen and Tanner (2000). Op. cit., 18.
73. Interview with Leo Staples.
74. Idem.

they could meet and talk to the elders. To his surprise, he was told this is not possible since he does not qualify as an elder and so he has no moral authority to talk to elders and that they regarded all he was doing as only good for women and children! That is why no self-respecting elder would bother with what he was doing. He was told that to qualify as an elder he had to undergo the *sapana* rite of passage, which, he promptly did and was given the name Lokomol. From then on, he was able to freely mix with the elders and they were willing to learn from him and his religion of a 'white god'.[75]

Pastors' Interpretation of John 10:1–16

With regard to bible interpretation among the pastors, we established that their perspective is slightly different from the one taken by 'their' Christians. The process is pretty much the same as it was in the beginning of evangelization as reported earlier on by Leo Staples. The priests call a meeting of all catechists, they go through all Sunday readings of one month (or longer, depending on the local practice) and discuss the meaning of the texts with them. We attended three such meetings in different regions of the county and our impression was that the priests simply hand down their own interpretation to the catechists and sisters, who in turn hand it down to other Christians in a sanctimoniously. There are a few exceptions to this rule (actually two), but they can be treated as the exceptions that prove the rule. Although we observed many instances of what we deem to be proof of individualistic interpretation of the passage in question, nine of them caught were the best examples. We are going to discuss them briefly.

Individual Nature of Sin

The first element we noticed in the Sunday homilies of the pastors is that there was a deliberate emphasis on the individual nature of sin over its communal aspect. Seven priests used singular pronouns like 'my sin', 'your failure', 'I repent', 'God forgives me' and others, 60 times, while the pluralistic one like 'we sin', 'our responsibility', were used 10 times. Two priests exceeded plural pronouns, which they used 15 times over the singular ones, which they used 10 times. Verse ten of this pericope "…the thief comes in order to steal…" was interpreted to be a warning to individual Christians against sinful acts like stealing other people's property, destructive behavior and any other sin that injures a person's relationship with God. While this individualistic aspect of sin is recognized among the Pökot, there is another more important social aspect to theft.

---

75. Although Leo Staples says that he underwent this rite in Ortum, other sources, which did not want to be named, say that he did not actually go through it, but that people merely started talking about it and he chose not to question the rumours that ended up being accepted as the truth of what actually happened.

The cultural practice is that if a person steals a cow belonging to a fellow Pöchon there is a fixed fine of four cows (because they count the legs, 3.10.1). In the event that the thief does not have the said cows, then his parents, close relatives or even the clan members were liable to pay. The social ramification of this was that apart from making his family, or clan, poor materially, the thief also subjected them to public ridicule and this acted as a deterrent and cause for the parents to severely discipline their children at the earliest signs of kleptomania. Perhaps there was need for the pastors to discuss theft, as mentioned in the pericope, but also emphasize its two aspects as depicted in the Pökot culture. Then add the gospel contribution of universalizing theft as a sin, not only within the Pökot community but also between the Pökot and their neighbors. Thus, the maxim 'thou shall not steal from your fellow Pöchon' would also incorporate 'taking away' (actually, stealing) the cows that belong to the enemy.

Individual Accomplishments of the Shepherd

The second element that manifested an individualistic tendency was centered on personal accomplishments of the Good Shepherd. Verses two, three and eleven, of our text, enumerate the commendable deeds of the person considered to be a good shepherd. He enters by the door of the sheep's shed, leads them to the grazing field and ultimately lays down his own life for the sheep. The pastors concentrated on this great theme and identified Jesus with the Good Shepherd, just as he says, and points out the fact that he came so that sinners may have abundant life (Jn. 10:10). They, therefore, called upon every Christian, in return, to be ready to lay down his or her life for the sake of Jesus and the Gospel, even if it means abandoning one's parents and relatives, or even accepting martyrdom.

This interpretation resonates a powerful cultural theme among the Pökot—that of 'laying down one's life for the sake of the cow (rather than the sheep), owing to the fact that they are a pastoralist community. Indeed, there is no greater accomplishment that can bring honor to a shepherd than dying while defending his flock against intruders. The expression used is that 'the warrior died at the feet of cattle' (*kemeghchï muröno kelyo tich*) and as such people were not supposed to cry or mourn but admire him and young people always looked at him as a source of inspiration.

However, this honor and heroism did not lie in the fact that he had accomplished a heroic deed as an individual; it was tied to the benefits it brought to the community. The fact that his death was an inspiration to other warriors in the community when faced by impending threats from their enemies and the fact that he died protecting the single animal that determine the very survival of the Pökot as a people. Moreover, as one catechist explained to us, this 'protecting' goes beyond what a non-Pökot would imagine. It includes protecting the cows from their 'captors', who took them from the Pökot ancestors in the past, by bringing them back home, where they belong (a justification of cattle rustling. And yet the pastors did not seem to incorporate this aspect of the Pökot culture in their sharing sessions. A sharing from a catechist may clarify this point:

> My name is David Lonyangapuo and I am a catechist from Kewawa. I thank God. Jesus said he is the Good Shepherd who takes care of his sheep and he is also the door of the sheep and leads them to pasture. He was a shepherd of people and not of sheep but compared them to sheep. As a teacher, I know that I have sheep to guide i.e., the people at the station. Jesus said that a hired worker does not care about the sheep since he cares about his salary. Jesus gives his life for the sheep. As a teacher, I must take care of God's sheep. The reading is important to me because I resemble Christ since I guide the flock of God and I care for the sheep since God entrusted them to me. There was a man who tended cows and the cows knew him however when he died, the cows did not know the wife when she tried to milk them. The guard of the door is one who is known by the sheep since he is with the sheep all the time. Thieves are just young men who do not have something to do or they want to marry and do not have the bride price. They plan the theft with their friends. Some young men go to church not to hear the Word but to seduce girls. These young men are like the wolf and they spoil the girl then they run away from the church. Also, when people miss a place to graze the animals they resort to stealing. Corruption is on the increase because of poor governance. Both the Pökot and the Turkana people have a lacking in them. If Christians are not satisfied with the word and do not have faith, then it is easy for evil to enter the church.[76]

The contribution above gives examples that are not concrete in the sense that the catechist does not give practical solutions to the problems facing the people. He, for instance, says that 'Pökots and Turkanas have a lacking in them', but never says what this 'lacking' is or what can be done about it. He further says that as a teacher he must take care of God's sheep, but he never says how he has to do this in order to ensure that they live in accordance with the gospel values. He presumes that it is clear to the people what needs to be done and that everybody understands him, just as it is the case with tacit cultural themes.

To discover what these themes pertaining to the shepherd are, we asked descriptive questions with regard to the understanding of the concept 'shepherd'. We discovered that members simply transposed their tacit cultural understanding of the term shepherd to that of the sacred Scriptures without attempting to fill the existing hiatus between the two. Some of these themes exhort the shepherd to be brave in protecting his livestock and going to bring more from the community's enemies to prove his bravery.

---

76. This contribution was recorded during a SCC prayer meeting and was delivered by a catechist whose name and place of service have been altered to conceal his identity.

Preaching to Christians Individually

The other aspect we noticed in the Sunday preaching is that pastors, generally speaking, direct what they regard as the gospel teaching to individual Christians rather than to the community as a whole. Expressions like '*hebu jiulize*—just ask yourself (*tepekei lo*)', '*kila mtu ajiulize*—let everybody ask himself or herself (*tepekei chi lowïr*)' and '*imani yako*—your faith (*kighanatengu*)' were a common feature that clearly appealed to the Christians not to think in terms of a community of the faithful but as individuals. The final thrust of this kind of individualistic preaching was the oft quoted bible passage on the last judgement where every person will account for his deeds personally without recourse to his brother, sister, relatives or friends (Mt. 25: 31–46). This was summed up in a powerful question, *wewe utakuwa wapi atakapokuja mwana wa Mungu*—Where will you be when the Son of God comes (*mitenyi ono atoni ngunei wero Tororöt*)?

This widespread appeal to the individual's faith goes directly against the grain of the Pökot life in and within the community and in some cases, has served as the very reason for the rejection of Christianity in this region. Leo Staples narrated to us one incident during one of his many *safari* Masses into the interior of Mwino. One elder (Loitangura) asked him about his Christian message and its purpose and he thought he had found a good opportunity to catechize the old man. So, he said the purpose of the Christian message was to ensure that he knows Jesus Christ, so that he can go to heaven after his worldly life.

Then the man asked him what would happen to his own ancestors who had not heard about Christ and Staples, having been instructed in the pre-Vatican II theology of *extra ecclesiam nulla salus* (outside the Church there is not salvation), said they will all go to hell. And the man said in confidence that, in that case, he would not want to become a Christian because he wants to be with his ancestors in the afterlife. A similar sense of communitarian inclination was exhibited by SCC-goers, who argued that once in heaven God will ask them of the whereabouts of their neighbors.

Pastors as the Good Shepherd

Another element that is identifiable with individualistic bible interpretation is that many pastors (mainly the catechists) personally identified them-selves with the Good Shepherd and compared their individual achievements to those of Jesus Christ. They, for instance, told us how they had started and nurtured some local churches single-handedly exuding the confidence that they are not just shepherds but actually good shepherds in the footsteps of their master. When we asked how this concept worked in relation to the role of their own parish priests, they said that those too are good shepherds in their own right and so is the bishop, but the same cannot be said of the 'ordinary' Christians, ostensibly because they are not 'set aside' for the task. This, once again, goes against the grain of opportunism, fame and privileges, in the Pökot traditional sense of the words, since their leadership 'was neither authoritarian nor hierarchic'.[77]

What they had was *kokwö* (council of elders) where *kirwok* (the decision-making process) was reached through consensus. If any of the elders could be regarded as a leader, then it was only on informal rather than formal basis, and he was no more than the first among equals. This leadership, though, was different from the kind of leadership that involved a *kirwokïn* (chief), which was only introduced by the colonial government, where the leader had absolute authority over his subjects. This element of the Pökot notion of leadership was, however, lacking in the sermons. Below is a sermon by one respected catechist:

> Today I am very happy with the reading that talks about a Good Shepherd because I see myself in this category. Today as I was visiting the homes of Christians, I discovered many things and I knew that there is still more sheep that is not in the fold of the Good Shepherd. And as I went around looking for these sheep, I realized in my heart when I met others who have stayed for a long time without seeing this fold of the Good Shepherd. There and then I prayed to the Holy Spirit to enable me talk to them. I learned from them that as soon as I spoke to them, they realized where they stand . . . Thus I see that Jesus Christ has promised me a good life once I bring back those sheep to the fold he has prepared for them, then on the last day I will be counted as righteous. I will be counted as one who cared most for his sheep, more than the money that I may have seen in front of me. Let us praise Jesus Christ.[78]

Abstract Conceptualization in Preaching

The pastors generally gave abstract, incoherent and generalized preaching, based on one's own individual experience rather than the common experiences of the community of the faithful. For the purpose of illustrating our point we are going to reproduce part of one sermon that was delivered in a SCC without naming the priest in question.

> Jesus gives us an example of sheep but I am sure most of you do not eat mutton. How many among you, do not eat mutton? I am sure most of you, as you indicate with your hands up. Since mutton as we know has a bad smell. A sheep is also foolish even when they walk on the road they walk foolishly. There was a time I was driving then I saw sheep and gave them a chance to pass but they did not cross the road instead some of them went under my car and as I drove I crushed one and broke its legs. Sheep are very gentle animals

---

77 Dietz (1987). Op. cit., 179.

78. This Bible sharing was done by a 35-year-old catechist, Maurice Wanjala Nyongesa, from Mutua Outstation, in Tartar Parish.

and they expect life to be smooth. When Jesus was born some of the Jews were shepherds and were not held highly. Since they lived with sheep and smelt like sheep, even their brains were like that of sheep. If a person calls you sheep, he signifies that you are as foolish as the sheep. Although the shepherds were despised they were the first to hear the message of Christ's birth from the angels, saying that a king has been born, go and adore him and they left in a hurry to go and witness the birth of Jesus. Yet, these are people who were not held with high regard by the society. Why did God choose to reveal himself to the foolish? It is because Jesus was supposed to be like the Good Shepherd.[79]

In this example, the priest proceeded from his own individual experience and went on to relate it to the bible passage of our choice and then drew his message from the two. This was not an isolated case, and more often than not pastors used their own experiences, which no one could corroborate, either for the purpose of authentication or falsification. Then they went on to make an abstract connection with the Gospel, a connection that, in most cases, had nothing to do with people's actual lifestyle. This made the preaching dry and tasteless and we could observe kids start crying, Christians walking in and out of the church and others dozing off right in front of our eyes. But, whenever a pastor said something that touched on people's day-to-day life experiences (like the low prices of maize and livestock and the dry weather condition, and so forth) all those whose minds had started wandering off suddenly paid attention.

Individual Reward-centered Preaching

In what one priest characterized as 'positive theology', we noticed that pastors also centered their preaching on individual heavenly reward in the after-life. This became, according to the Christians, a kind of enticement to those who are backsliding and some sort of justification for the rest to 'hang on' to the faith, in spite of the many difficulties they endure. The Christian idea of some distant reward (or punishment) has contributed to the lack of enthusiasm in Christianity among the Pökot. This is because to them it looks like a child play that promises some distant non-existent goodies, something that does not amuse the adults. According to them, the situation is compounded by the fact that this distant (eschatological) reward is a preserve for individual believers.

What about the family, one's relatives, the clan and community in general? The Christian answer is not too appealing as it often falls back to the answer Jesus gave about the woman who had been married by seven brothers, that in heaven there is no marriage,[80] relations and so on. According to the Pökot culture, a reward or

---

79. Fr. Patrick Murunga (not his real name) is a diocesan priest from Kakamega Diocese, working in West Pökot. He holds an MA degree in biblical theology from the Catholic University of Eastern Africa.

80. Matthew 22: 23–30.

punishment is meted out there and then for all to see and know what awaits those who entertain the actions similar to those rewarded or punished, while if one merited some reward he (or she) always received it in the name of the community. This comes close to the concept of 'realized eschatology', which seems to be more 'at home' with the expression of Jesus that the kingdom of God is already within us.[81] And yet the concept (though difficult to translate) did not feature anywhere as we listened to all the sermons.

Individualistic Appeal of the Christian Faith

Then there was insistence by the pastors that faith is an individual matter between a person and his or her God. On the occasion of the parable of the Good Shepherd, the pastors challenged people individually to go through Jesus, who is the door to the Father, by everybody cultivating a personal relationship with Jesus. This was linked to the sacrament of confess-ion where a number of priests insisted on individual confession as opposed to the communal confession that most people are used to and seem to prefer. The argument here was that it is individuals who sin and not the community and as such the forgiveness of sin (*lastagh po ngoki*) depends on individual disposition. The main message here was that there is no 'blanket' forgiveness of sin and everybody has to work for his or her own salvation, without looking at what others are doing or not doing.

Here we see that faith and its nurturing are portrayed as an individual affair that has no communal orientation, or as if the latter does not really matter. This falls short of the expectation within the Pökot culture whereby everything one does has both an individual and a communal ramification, with the latter being given more prominence. In this regard we noticed a clear dichotomy between the sermons by the catechists, which strictly follow the deliberations by the priests, and their bible sharing sessions in the SCCs, which were more community centered. In this regard, they were caught up in the 'vicious circle' in which "interpreters produce and reproduce each other regardless of their ideological or socio-economic locations."[82]

Matters of Faith and Social Life

We noticed a clear distinction between 'the matters of faith' (*ngala kighanat*) and 'matters of the world' (*ngala nguny*) or dichotomy between the sacred and the secular, even though this is not the case in the Pökot culture. The pastors (mainly the catechists) were not comfortable to relate or even compare the work of Jesus as a shepherd with that of shepherds in their own midst. One catechist gave a good analysis of the work of

---

81. Luke 17:21.
82. Speckman, op. cit., 40.

Jesus as a shepherd and then said: "Well...we are the sheep..." We asked him how that reverberates to the people in the light of his culture and he was lost of words.

He admitted that culturally it would be abusive to regard people as sheep, even analogically, but added that it was okay for Jesus to regard us as his sheep, because he was God. This dichotomy seemed to lead to some kind of artificiality in religious matters and as such, people did not take their Christian obligation as seriously as they took their daily and cultural matters. A concrete example of this is when a young man in the parish youth group impregnated a girl (names withheld at their request) he did not really love. He was asked to have a church wedding as a commitment to the relationship and he had no problem with it; but when, after the church wedding, he was asked to perform the customary rites related to marital commitment he objected, particularly the girl being fitted with the traditional wedding ring called *tïrim*.

To find out the reason for the above-mentioned dichotomy we decided to participate in some of the pastoral meetings that catechists have with their priests in order to know what actually goes on during such meetings. Here we only report one of them that took place in Chepnyal Parish, within Sook location. The Priests invite catechists (and sometimes sisters as well) for the planning of the meetings (once a month or once in two or three months as the case may be) during which part of the proceedings include going through the Sunday readings and making a common interpretation.

Michael Dillon calls this 'an ongoing formation' which in his parish takes on a three-phase procedure, characterized by pastoral, social and spiritual activities. Catechists meet once every month during which time they report on the success and failure they have encountered in their outstations; they arrange the monthly Masses with the priest, discuss baptisms, weddings and all other sacraments that the priest might need to dispense during that month. This pastoral phase is followed by a social phase that deals with mundane issues like the work-for-food program run jointly with relief organizations (like World Vision and World Food Organization).

The meeting takes two to three days, depending on the number of issues that need to be discussed, but the final day is strictly set aside for the spiritual growth of the catechists. On this day, they have their monthly recollection and then go through all Sunday readings of the entire period before their next meeting. So, in essence, catechists do not preach their own reflections, but those given to them by the priest during their last meeting with him. For a few of them there is room for personal reflection and widening the scope of what the priest had shared with them, but for many the priest's words are final, and so they reproduce them sometimes word for word.

Communitarianism in Individualistic Interpretation

Our observation of the general lifestyle of the pastors and their way of interaction with other Christians suggested that there are a lot of communitarian elements in their lives as opposed to their preaching trend. It was clear that during their day-to-day interactions every priest addressed the Christians, not as individuals but as a community of the faithful (though not necessarily using the word 'community'), particularly when there were community affairs like, development meetings and SCC prayers (as opposed to Mass celebrations) and so on. We noticed the usage of expressions like, brethren (*tupchenichu*), dear friends (*wechara*) and beloved Christians (*wakristu chole chaman*). All priests, in general, led a community lifestyle with all those who live within the parish compound as well as in the neighborhood, and they participated in most social issues, like insecurity, impending drought and so on. However, catechists are the most entrenched in this kind of life.

Although their preaching is basically individualistic, most other aspects of their lives are communitarian, though interwoven with individualistic homily mindset. These include their way of life and how they carry out their day-to-day life activities like caring for their animals, tilling their land, solving disputes and partaking in the traditional ceremonies and rites of passage. Even when discussing the events of the bible passage we had chosen outside the formal interview setting or religious service, their approach was communitarian. It seems that the dual approach to the Bible and the ordinary life is further proof of the tension that exists due to different worldviews between the presenters of the Gospel and its recipients. Below is a sermon by one priest, Antonio Guirao that depicts this reality within the context of SCC prayers:

> What has really touched me is where Jesus says, "I am the door." If the sheep have to pass through that way they will get good food, repose and there will really be freedom without fear and one will truly be saved. In our lives, there are various doors and maybe some doors can call us more because of wealth, simple life and other reasons. Jesus Christ says I am the door and he is the only door that we need to pass: both when going out and when coming in. If we want to get to the Father, to the Kingdom of God, it is Jesus Christ alone. There is no other, there is no other way. He says he is also the way, the truth and the life, and if we would like to have all these things in our lives, in this world and in then in the kingdom of heaven. So, we see that Jesus is a good shepherd but also the door that we need to pass always. We need to pray to God to help him or her and other people to always know these things and follow them in order to get happiness, life and salvation. Thanks.[83]

Training in Seminaries and Catechetical Institutions

We discussed, with a number of pastors about their training in seminaries and catechetical institutes and asked them how much these had prepared (or failed to prepare) them for the work of evangelization in their current workstations. While they generally agreed

---

83. Fr. Antonio Guirao delivered this homily during a SCC Mass for Mavuno (yearly harvest) on 26/04/2002.

that their days in these training institutions were not 'a wasted time' they were unanimous that the institutions need to undergo a radical surgery; lest they are overtaken by events and become irrelevant in the face of a quickly changing world.

Seminary Formation

There is no doubt that the Kenya Episcopal Conference (KEC) makes a lot of efforts, as a body, to train quality priests, who are responsive to people's needs, and has gone to great lengths in creating a Seminary Commission to ensure this goal is realized. However, this goal is far from being realized for various reasons, all of which cannot be discussed here. We will just mention the key ones that need urgent attention. Kenyan national seminaries can easily be classified as a conservative and 'closed' system that continues to train priests similar to those trained in the inter-Vatican Europe, who find themselves short of social expectation in the contemporary society. Indeed, in one case, a seminary is surrounded by a perimeter stonewall, ostensibly to keep burglars at bay, yet in practice it is also serves to prevent seminarians from going out.

The training takes nine years—one spiritual year, three years of philosophy, one pastoral year and four years of theology. The spiritual year mainly consists of reading spiritual books and numerous other spiritual exercises like retreats and recollections. Philosophical training is mainly hinged on the neo-scholastic philosophy, with St. Thomas being regarded as *the* teacher; hence locking out any other kind of 'irrelevant' philosophy that is deemed dangerous and capable of 'corrupting' the minds of the young seminarians. Philosophical studies thus remain a theoretical and foreign enterprise that rarely prepares seminarians to deal with contextual social and philosophical issues.

Theology is equally a traditional and conservative enterprise that avoids other African theologies (like liberation theology, theology of reconstruction and feminine theology to mention but a few) that hardly feature the works of major African theologians. One bishop jokingly gave a reason for their exclusion and said: "The problem is that many of these people think that they are theologians, but the bishops do not think so!"[84] The dependence on traditional theologians, it is argued some, is a strategy designed so that the Propaganda Fide does not become suspicious of the goings-on in Kenyan seminaries. Indeed, as one priest put it, "the intention is not to train academic priests, but pastoral priests, who can celebrate Mass and dispense other vital sacraments to the people of God." The result is personnel that are ill prepared to handle and deal with concrete and current theological issues that affect the African Church and her people.

---

84. Bishop Collin Davies of Ngong Catholic Diocese made these remarks during one of the many pastoral visits to a major seminary in Kenya, on the occasion of the preparation for the papal visit that was just around the corner.

In Mariology, for instance, Mary is ordinarily understood and appraised only as the Mother of God (Θεοτοκος—Theotokos), but never as the mother of those women, in the streets, struggling to liberate themselves from the male yoke of domination and oppression (both inside and outside the church), while in dogmatics the liberation that Jesus talked about in the Gospel of Luke (4:18-22) is interpreted in a strictly spiritual sense, lest the Christians get incited and rise up against the powers that be. "Such alien discourse," as Manus,[85] has observed, "does not help us to address ourselves to the material, moral and spiritual problems that preoccupy Africans in their cultural settings." Apart from the irrelevance of the substance of the discourse itself, the language of instruction is a further barrier to the efficacy of the candidates.

> Theological training is still conducted in foreign languages—English, French, Portuguese and Arabic. Thus, the language of ministerial formation is different from the language of ecclesial life. This discrepancy causes much alienation on the part of pastors and theologians, because they have to continually translate their theological learning into the local language of the people they serve.[86]

In a word, the priestly training often leads to the separation of the candidate from the experience of the living communities.[87] Thus, a priest remains an 'alien', a 'stranger' or a 'sojourner' to the same people he is supposed to serve, even where one is posted to his own home parish,[88] All they share is a common childhood and the social delicacy that go with it, yet mentally he is nowhere close to their thought-pattern because he thinks Western thoughts and even dreams Western dreams. According to Bellagamba, priestly training in Africa seems to be leaning towards 'mass formation', which can be equated to the capitalistic system of mass production, with the end results of a business-like relationship where the priest is a trader while the Christian is the consumer.[89] Healey expresses such a feeling of inadequacy in his own ministry:

> In my own ministry I often felt that I was merely dispensing the sacraments, that I was a clerical attendant running an ecclesiastical service station. The Christians would come in, fill up their sacramental tanks, and then go off. An even deeper problem was that this service was limited to small segments of the lives of Christians, mostly on Sunday mornings. Ongoing Christian formation was very difficult.[90]

This problem was recently articulated by one lay Christian, while presenting a paper on the formation of priests, whereby he listed incompatibility and irrelevance

---

85. Chris Ukachukwu Manus (2003). *Intercultural Hermeneutics in Africa: Methods and Approaches*. Nairobi: Acton Publishers, 1.
86. Mugambi (2003). Op. cit.
87. Schreiter (1985). Op. cit., 18.
88. Wijsen and Tanner (2000). Op. cit.,17-18.
89. Bellagamba (1992). Op. cit.
90. Joseph G. Healey (1981). Op. cit., 40.

of the priestly training as part of its major weaknesses. He blames the irrelevance of many priests on the formation that embraces: "A theoretical approach based on Western Philosophy and theology, incompatible with the philosophies of the African cultural and traditional context...A pedagogical approach not based on live case studies..."[91] Hence, he says, priests in Africa (and everywhere else in the world) should be trained against the background of the people they are going to serve.

Verstraelen has warned against brainwashing the clergy in general. "Ministers in Africa should no longer be carbon copies of European or American clergy...It is especially important that ministers should not lose contact with, and feeling the popular mentality or world-view of those whom they serve..." On the issue of culture, he says, "In training for ministry, as in all other areas of church life, African cultural experiences must be taken far more seriously than hereto-fore, while recognizing after some time the varied and dynamic nature of this cultural experience."[92] K'Otienoh puts the requisites of contemporary priestly training more bluntly:

> Priestly formation today must be multi-dimensional because the priest whom it should produce is far from being a traditional cultic priest. A Priest for modern times must be a leader; an enlightened guide in spiritual and other matters. He has to be a man for people to be able to speak out on their behalf if need arises. As their spiritual leader, he has to live an exemplary life.[93]

Far from going back to the past and glorifying it, the past should inspire us where we are now with all the complexities of life, brought about by influence from outside. A traditional priest was in touch with his people but also limited to their world view, yet a modern priest should at once be close to the people but not limited to their world view.

Fear and Despondency

Our discussions with seminarians on the quality of the training revealed that nothing much is going on with regard to making their training relevant to their social context, at least not overtly. "You are taken from your village," lamented one distraught seminarian, "and introduced to a kind of lifestyle that systematically alienates you from your own people, and then after ordination you are sent to go back and work with the same people you have been alienated from for so long."[94] The most impor-

---

91. Benard C. Ojil (1999). Formation of Priests as Agents of Evangelization for the Church-As-Family of God (II). In *AFER*, Vol. l 41, Nos. 4, 5 & 6. Eldoret: Gaba Publications, 257–266.

92. Frans J. Verstraelen (1976). *Tradition and Reconstruction in Mission: A Report of IAMS Conference at San José, Cost Rica*. Leiden: Interuniversity Institute for Missiological and Ecumenical Research (IIME), 16.

93. Cosmas A. R. K'Otienoh (1999). Formation of Priests as Agents of Evangelization for the Church-As-Family of God (I). In *Africa Ecclesial Review* l 41 (4, 5 & 6). Eldoret: AMECEA Gaba Publications, 248.

94. George M. Iregi was a seminarian at the time we carried out this field research, but he has since

tant concern, though, was that many seminary staff members are not sufficiently qualified for their work, even though there are many other qualified people out there, who are not allowed to go and teach in seminaries because they might 'poison' the minds of the young seminarians.

The other major problem is to use seminaries as a sort of dumping ground for priests not wanted in their own dioceses anymore, irrespective of whether they are qualified to teach or not. When we asked the seminarians whether they had raised this issue with the relevant authorities they said they had not done so for the fear of reprisals. One ex-seminarian gave an emotive testimony of the goings-on in seminaries:

> You know, seminarians are given everything for free and authorities can do away with them at any time with impunity and they will never give any consideration for their future life. And what is worse is that they are a law unto themselves, answerable to no one, and yet Canon Law offers no guarantee or leeway for a seminarian to seek remedy for the damage caused by diocesan bishops and/or superiors of religious congregations and orders. They simply count on their goodwill.[95]

The seminarians gave a concrete example when a few years ago a seminarian stood up against the behavior of some priests, whose actions he did not consider to be in line with their position as priests in the church. In revenge, these priests fabricated some flimsy accusations (of arrogance and disobedience) against him, to the bishop who never consulted him to hear his side of the story. The seminarian never became a priest, and no reason was ever given for the decision and he never received an official letter of expulsion. So, over one decade down the line he is still a candidate to the priesthood in the records of his former diocese!

We traced down this seminarian in Nairobi where he is working as a lecturer of both philosophy and theology, and asked what exactly went on and he narrated an appalling story. He said the bishop did not give any reason for refusing to ordain him but only said: "No, no, no, there is nothing, it is only that me and Father thought it is better for you not to become a priest."[96] When he decided to go for further studies the bishop promised to help him meet half the cost of his tuition fee, which he did not. The irony of it all is that the same person judged as 'unworthy' of becoming a priest was now teaching candidates to the priesthood and professed religious sisters and brothers.

---

been ordained a priest in the Catholic Diocese of Eldoret.

95. Peter Mugeni was a Consolata seminarian who was thrown out of the institution without any explanation or recompense for the time spent or anything to go and start his new life with.

96. The late Bishop Cornelius Korir of the Catholic Diocese of Eldoret is said to have dismissed the seminarian without an expulsion letter or a stated reason for the refusal to ordain him. He was, however, buried in the church as a sign of being a man of God and eulogized as a peace maker during the burial ceremony.

Thus, priestly training is seen more as a way to realize personal ambition rather than a service to the people. Perhaps such excesses are made possible by the current individualistic church structures that are not answerable to the community of the faithful and could be avoided if the approach to the vocation office was bestowed on a community of upright clergy and the laity, rather than individuals who could easily be swayed against certain seminarians (or even priests) through self-aggrandizement, personal vendetta or outright survival instincts. In the same way, the more community-based Pökot (or African) culture can be used to transform other church organs from the more individual-centered and paternalistic Western structures to ensure an active participation of all members the church community, insofar as this does not contradict the Christian doctrine and the spirit of the Gospel. Indeed, such changes would help realize the empowerment of the laity, so zealously defended in the documents of Vatican II Council (*Gaudium et Spes*) and vividly stipulated in the Code of the Canon Law (canons 224–231).

Due to the prevalence of incidents like the ones mentioned above many young people do not dream of becoming priests anymore, leading to the belief among a section of the Kenyan society that seminaries are the breeding grounds for social rejects. "When one has no capacity to compete in the open world, the only way out is to seek shelter in the closed world of religious cocoons," said one young person who does not think much about the church.[97] A spot check that was not conclusively determined indicated that a majority of seminarians did not qualify to join public universities. It can, therefore, easily be argued that they opted to go to the seminary, not because they had a vocation to the priesthood but for lack of a better alternative. As a matter of fact, many people think that Africa will soon go the European way in matters of secularism.

A discussion with the rector of the minor seminary in Eldoret, revealed his disappointment with the many young people who all along prepare to join the major seminary, but once they qualified to join the university just changed their minds or postponed the decision indefinitely. "Most of these boys are just here to get a good education," he lamented, "while pretending to be genuinely called to the priesthood, but once they pass their grades, that is the last you will ever hear of them. We can hardly pride ourselves of many pupils who voluntarily decided to join the seminary and forgo a chance to the university. I hope they become good Christians out there"[98] And commenting on the problem facing the training of the church personnel in Africa, Magesa had this to say:

> In the Catholic denomination, for instance, there are few, if any, centres of learning that specialize in Scripture studies other than biblical theology. The situation is much the same in the Protestant Churches. This is bad enough

---

97. Bongani Nkomo was a religious brother of CMM, from Zimbabwe, but decided to leave after what he thought was a lot of hypocrisy in church circles.

98. Interiew with Fr. Daniel Nakameti, the then rector at Mother of Apostles Seminary, Eldoret.

where the training of students of the Bible is concerned. The situation becomes much worse, however, when not only the scholars (strictly speaking) but all the interpreters of the bible—ministers, priests, catechists—are schooled in the Northern social economic and theological framework. Such schooling cannot help but make them internationalize key ideological presuppositions and viewpoints of the same Northern hemisphere as the basis for hermeneutics. With very few exceptions, African biblical scholars operate on this basis as though by reflex. What this means is that they seldom subject dominant presuppositions to critical scrutiny. If they are conscious of their method of interpretation, they are rarely aware of the methodology behind it.[99]

Catechetical Training

The story is pretty much the same in the catechetical institutes. Catechists, generally speaking, do not have any say on the kind of training they think suits their local situations; even in cases where they have worked for long. The study program is prepared elsewhere and presented to them without consultation. Those who are not ready to co-operate are simply asked to quit the program. The other problem affecting a sound training of catechists is that the level of education of most trainees is low (the primary grade) and one can never hope to do much with them. After training, the situation is even compounded by the fact that the church does not remunerate the catechists as a matter of principle; the burden is left to the initiatives of individual priests which hardly come by.

And yet many of them do not do anything, thus seriously affecting the working morale and productivity of the catechists. For this reason, just as is the case with joining the seminary, to become a catechist is seen as an option for those who are desperate in life. The then director of Mitume Catechetical Institute explained:

> I cannot tell exactly why, however our people want their children, after finishing school, to be employed and get money. Maybe catechetics is taken as the work of rejects since our church does not employ catechists on a full-time basis. Most of them are just volunteers and whatever they are given is something very little, so this discourages people from becoming catechists. In this diocese, we try to encourage Christians to assist the catechists. Since in many parishes we do not have full time catechists so people see catechists as a job of volunteers.[100]

---

99. Magesa (1997). Op. cit.

100. Cosmas Ngomba is 45 years old. He was the Director of Mitume Catechetical Institute in Kitale Town, and later served as the father-in-charge of the newly started Sinar Parish, in West Pokot. The interview was carried out at the institute on 21/06/2002.

Tension Between People's and their Pastors' Religious Practices

Although both the pastors and the 'ordinary' Christians in West Pökot are working hard to live with their differences in the understanding and interpreting the Bible, there still are many unsorted areas that call for further proactive action from both sides. Here we will only mention the tensions, which Tanner and Wijsen, would rather call 'working misunderstanding',[101] or what Mall, prefers to call 'understanding misunderstanding' or misunder-standing understanding'[102] as we perceived them and then make recommendations, in the last chapter, as suggested by the people. The main ones that we would like to mention here are three: celebration of liturgy, the preaching method and cultural conflicts.

Sunday Celebration of the Liturgy

We begin with the Sunday celebration of the liturgy. There seems to be silent opposition between the presiding priest and the participating Christians. While the worshippers prefer it to be more of a coming together designed in the traditional manner, with song and dance, some priests sees it as 'a job'. They want Mass to end quickly so that they can go to another outstation, and then back home to take lunch and go out in the evening to some secluded place for relaxation.

On the prayers of the faithful, the people would like to express themselves in their mother tongue and address their personal needs to God in freedom and spontaneity. But many were the times when priests either pinpointed those who were to offer the prayers beforehand or simply cut short people while praying, when they felt the prayers of the faithful were taking too long. On the issue of songs, most people prefer religious Pökot songs, yet clearly more priests would rather they sing the songs in the official Catholic Church hymn book called *Tumshangilie Bwana* (Let us Praise the Lord). So, they reluctantly end up singing Kiswahili songs, but the somber mood changes when a Pökot song is intoned and women immediately stand up and start waving their hands with jubilation (*liliey*).

The Method of Preaching

The other element we noticed is that when preaching, the pastors normally do so in the second or third person pronouns; a kind of telling people what they should do or should not do, excluding themselves. These conflicting ideals were, however, never discussed as the people felt it is not right to criticize "our Father". So, they resorted to resentment and silent opposition. In some parishes people, did not offer the prayers

---

101. Tanner and Wijsen (1993). Op. cit., 177–193.
102. Runus A. Mall (1995). *Philosophie im Vergleich der Kulturen: Interkulturelle Philosophie, ein neue Orientierung.* Darmstadt: Wissenschaftliche Buchgesellschaft, 78.

of the faithful unless expressly asked to do so by the priest, the catechist or the parish council chairman (they are nearly always men here).

This is in stark contrast to the method used by Michael McGrath and Grégoire Nicole, in their work quoted earlier on. They use such inclusive expressions like "we find the word shepherd coming again and again", "And you and me today, there are many voices calling out to us,"[103] "They place before you and me, values, . . ."[104] "He tells us who He is, He accepts us the way we are. . .."[105] This you-should-do-this, or the-Bible-tells-you-this attitude, though it may not be deliberate, tends to antagonize the people against the preacher because they get the impression that the message is only meant for the listeners. Incidentally, majority of the pastors have been entangled in this web.

The feeling among most Christians was that the pastors show their Christians the way to heaven, but they are not part of the journey themselves. They seem to run what Anthony Bellagamba,[106] calls 'a one-man show' within their jurisdiction and anyone asking probing questions is perceived as a threat to be done away with. This seems to be part of the reason why the pastors do no regularly attend the SCC prayers, and when they attend they want to do the preaching and tell everybody else what the Bible says. Even where they allow free sharing, they still try to control what the Christians have to say and how to say it, by 'giving cues' in advance on the meaning of the bible text. One Christian, Luka Pkech, complains loudly:

> It is difficult to understand this kind of preaching. I think that the Word of God is meant for all of us and we are all learning from it, both the church leaders and the followers. In a way, we are all teachers to each other and students at the same time, the leaders give us theological expertise while we reify it with our experience of life, since most of them have not been exposed, due to the nature of their long training. The fact that we are all sojourners, travelling together on our way to heaven, needs to come out, particularly in a Sunday sermon.[107]

Conceptual and Cultural Conflicts

Although evangelization has been going on, in West Pökot, for almost a century now, we detected many conflicts between the pastors and their subjects, which we classified into conceptual and cultural differences. The mental differences have basically to do with the way the two groups read and interpret reality around them. The pastors'

---

103. McGrath and Nicole, op. cit., 22.
104. Ibid., 123.
105. Ibid., 127.
106. Bellagamba, op. cit.
107. Luka Pkech is a 55-year-old committed Christian, who also works for the County Government as the County Chief Executive in charge of environment.

way of thinking is predominantly, and in some cases, exclusively literary, linear and visual whereas that of the Christians is more formulaic, elaborate, and 'rhapsodic'; an important distinction between literate and non-literate cultures.[108]

In like manner, truth, among the people, lies more in common sense reference to experience, while among the pastors it resides in logical and coherent argument,[109] devoid of any form of fallacies. Finally, for the people, a textual meaning is negotiated during the discourse in the community context, while for the pastors the meaning is seen to exist either in the bible text itself, or somewhere in a Bible Commentary. While understanding among the people is more involved and subjective, thus achieved through a sense of identification with the speaker; for the pastors, it is more detached, objective, logical and analytical.

We noticed that the cultural conflicts cited by the missionaries at the beginning of this chapter are still a serious social problem that divides the people from their pastors, on the one hand and divides the pastors down the middle, on the other hand. These are: cattle rustling, belief in witchcraft (consulting witchdoctors, diviners and medicine men and women), polygyny, clitoridectomy and property inheritance for women, and girls in particular. We have already talked about the first two in the previous sections and cattle rustling is revisited in the following chapter. We would, therefore, like to briefly discuss the last three. These three issues fall under the Women Empowerment Act, introduced by the Kenya government after the Beijing Conference. They are sensitive because of the government efforts to sensitize the community about the educational rights of the girl child. Thus, many non-governmental organizations (NGOs) have sprung up in order to augment the government's efforts.

Our research showed that these cultural issues impact negatively on the process of evangelization in West Pökot due to compartmentalization and rigidity of thought process on the part of the pastors. They approach the issues in their own right, judging them from their individual merit or lack of it, as if they were not part and parcel of the Pökot culture. But the people look at them differently; they form part of their communal and cultural heritage, and an attack on them is also an attack on their culture and their dignity, as well as their very identity. This explains the resilience of many cultural elements, among the Christians, in spite of the campaign by government agents and the church to wipe them out in the name of Christianity and development.

Polygyny

According to Hillman, polygyny "…is a preferential form of marriage in areas where there is a relationship of mutual support and reinforcement between polygamy and

---

108. Walter J. Ong (1968). Knowledge in Time. In Walter J. Ong (ed). *Knowledge and the Future of Man.* New York: Holt, Rinehart & Winston, 25–29.

109. David R. Olson (1977). From Utterance to Text: The Bias of Language in Speech and Writing. In *Harvard Educational Review*, 47: 3, 277.

culture, polygamy and tradition, polygamy and public opinion, and where polygamy enjoys superior prestige, as compared with monogamy; so that respected males in the society will normally seek to acquire more than one wife."[110] As we have already noted, polygyny is part and parcel of the age-old traditions among the Pökot and it is not easy to do away with it overnight. The Catholic Church is firmly opposed to this practice and as such her adherents find themselves between a rock and a hard place when it comes to the question of loyalty.

Although Christians openly admit that polygyny is wrong because, as most people said, "God created only Eve for Adam and the two became one flesh"[111] and "what God has united no man should put asunder,"[112] actual life practice suggests otherwise. When it comes to the question of choosing between maintaining one's honor in the community as opposed to maintaining the same in the Church many choose the former. Many catechists and other church leaders have left the church or opted to become 'ordinary' Christians after taking another wife and resisting attempts to persuade them to change their minds. The most recent and 'disappointing' case is that of a hardworking and committed social worker in Chepnyal, who upon becoming an Assistant Chief decided to marry a second wife. Although we know this person very well, we did not succeed in arranging for an interview with him. However, we had a long discussion with other church elders on what could have led to this turn of events.

They told us that the main issue is that of social honor, status and prestige. It is not possible, they argued for the man to be a leader in the community when he had only one wife! No elder, most of whom have three to four wives, could listen to him. But we pointed out another case whereby a catechist had been also appointed to the same position in a neighboring sub-location and yet he had not married another wife. The answer they gave was that, the latter was only a boy and that it was only a matter of time before he, too, followed suit; because a one-eyed man cannot lord it over two or three eyed men, but can only do so among the blind. So, essentially, the problem of polygyny traces its roots to the issue of relationship between men and women and the entire societal fabric in relation to the division of labor as well as the hierarchy of values: all that is what needs to be addressed, rather than just asking men not to marry many wives. Hence, the need for an open and frank dialogue, where there is a give and take spirit rather than making apodictic and arbitrary declarations.

Clitoridectomy

The issue of women empowerment, as contained in the Affirmative Action of the Beijing Conference is mainly felt on the question of clitoridectomy in West Pökot. There have been a lot of campaigns against the practice from various quarters: the

---

110. Hillman, op. cit., 88.
111. Genesis 2: 22–24.
112. Matthew 19: 6.

government, the church and NGOs. We held a daylong discussion with the Tamugh Elite Group[113] on what they thought about this issue. While they generally agreed with the concept of women empowerment and its perceived benefits to the girl child, they at the same time argued that certain issues could not be looked at from the governmental, scientific or ecclesiastical perspectives only. For, instance, whereas they accepted the scientific reasons advanced against clitoridectomy as a way to boost women reproductive health, none of them was willing to marry a girl who had not undergone the rite. Tonyirwone explains the nature of the dilemma:

> Female circumcision is not just a medical issue; it is also as much cultural as it is a social issue. If you marry an uncircumcised girl your parents will never eat food cooked by her because they regard her as a child. She is discriminated against and segregated by other women of her age, because she is not yet a grown up. They will never associate with her in ordinary daily chores like going to the river and fetching firewood. When a quarrel arises between her and other women she is derogatorily referred to as *chawïr*—clitoris. And what is worse, *Chemeri* (recently initiated girls) compose songs to tease her and sing lyrics like "I have nothing hanging underneath me, I am a woman," just to mock her. I tell you it would be hell for her and she will finally give in to the ritual even though she may be an old woman.[114]

Another participant, Chelomut,[115] recounted the problems uninitiated girls went through in the hands of elderly men and women, and their own peers. The most recent example she gave was the African Gospel Church (AGC), in Sook location, which encouraged girls not to undergo the primitive ritual and instead go through an alternative, Christian rite. When the boys, in this church, finally decided to get married, they left behind their own uninitiated girlfriends and went for the initiated ones from other churches, or even nonbelievers. These poor ladies were, in the end, forced to undergo the ritual but by then they were too old to be approached by young men, so they ended up getting married as second and third wives. "Is the church, then, a unifying factor or is it a destructive force in the Pökot community?" she posed.

Inheritance for Girls

The Affirmative Action that resulted from the Beijing Conference instigated the adoption of another act in the Kenyan parliament called the Succession Act (1979), which decrees that women and girls can inherit their fathers' or their husbands' wealth. Although, again, the church supports this Act, it does not augur well with the Pökot

---

113. This group consists of all those people in Tamugh Area of West Pökot that have completed secondary, and in some cases, have had a tertiary, education.

114. Interview with Jackson Tonyirwone, a 25-year-old student nurse at Ortum Nursing Hospital.

115. Interview with Stella Chelomut, a 29-year-old nursery school teacher at Chepnyal, within Sook Location.

people, Christians included. In fact, much of its recommendations remain in paper, as very few women have directly benefitted from it. But its existence, according to some pastors, is a step towards the right direction and serves as a stepping-stone for better legislation in the future. It is, however, unheard of in the Pökot culture that women can inherit property; especially land, from their deceased relatives. They can be given land to till by their fathers, but as soon as they get married the whole equation changes and they become strangers to their own homes. They now belong to another clan and will have to learn to live in accordance with the rules of their new homes.

As Wachege has observed, inheritance for women and widows in particular, is a thorny issue in many African communities. "A thorn in the wounded flesh of our women is the succession and inheritance law. Justice is not seen to be done with regards to the specificity of the inalienable rights of a woman who has lost her husband in death with or without the legal document called marriage certificate."[116] We once again presented this issue to the group and discussed the merits and demerits of allowing girls to inherit property. Not one man in the group advocated the idea of allowing women to own property from their fathers or husbands.

They argued that if this happens, then, women would be advantaged over men because their husbands also give them property. "What will happen when my father gives land to my sister and she gets married, will she bring her husband to live on our clan land?" wondered Jasania.[117] All Participants were in agreement that the government was pushed to adopt irrelevant resolutions tailored by non-Africans for the Africans. They also lamented that instead of the church helping them fight such foreign ideologies; it joins hands with them to oppress people's cultural ideals. Mundane and irrelevant as these issues may appear to be, the truth of the matter is that they squarely affect the relationship between the church leaders and the Christians who feel that the leaders do not understand them. The leaders, on their part, feel that Christians are simply hard-headed, while catechists are caught in between without a clear knowledge of where they stand or who they are in the church.

In some cases, they are treated as esteemed pastors of the church while in other cases they are treated as 'mere lay people' who are seemingly not 'really' called because they are neither consecrated nor ordained. The people we talked to in West Pökot have the feelings that they are witnessing a continuation of missionary onslaught on the African traditional community, as it happened in other parts of Kenya, in particular and Africa in general. "Some of the traditional African practices that were disregarded were polygamy, the role of women, ancestral veneration, initiation rituals like female circumcision, ritual beer drinking, traditional dances and animal sacrifice."[118] The missionaries

---

116. Wachege (1992). Op. cit., 68.

117. Jacob Jansania is a 30-year-old resident of Tamugh Sub-location in Sook Location and a trained primary school teacher, who still waits to be deployed when the government starts employing teachers.

118. Philomena Mwaura (2004). African Independent Churches: Their Role and Contribution to

tried to fight the cultural heritage of the people and then sought the assistance of the colonial government when they failed. The people viewed this as an attempt to undermine their traditional education system and resented the attempt by the missionaries to impose their norms on their converts. The same attitude is manifested in West Pökot, where a government official said they are 1000 years behind the West![119]

Conclusion

In this chapter, we have basically surveyed the work of evangelization in West Pökot as done by the pastors of the Catholic Church. We have also briefly mentioned the work done by the pastors in the Protestant Churches, who were, in fact the first ones to reach this region. The main point that emerged is that, although there exist dominant traits in each group, it is still not easy to make a clear-cut distinction between the way the people and their pastors understand and interpret the Bible. Moreover, it would be simplistic to try and pit one against the other in absolutistic terms as some scholars have tried to do.[120] Once again, due to the concept of cultural complexity mentioned earlier on in this book; there are too many grey lines that need careful scrutiny. A critical analysis, however, shows there is a fundamental, though only apparent, difference in the way the two groups read, interpret and respond to the Scriptures, and it is not just an academic difference, but also one that stems from their basic cultural orientations.

We have established, in chapter four, that the Pökot way of interpreting the Bible is predominantly communitarian, although there exist many aspects of individualism in their understanding of the bible text in question. But, in this chapter, we have also established that the pastors' approach is primarily the opposite of the one used by the Christians. The pastors interpret the Bible from a more individualistic perspective, even as they try to give a communitarian angle to their preaching. Moreover, pastors approach issues from a compartmentalized position, whereas the people look at them as part of the cultural whole, a situation that creates a cultural tension that can be said to be a result of different worldviews. In the next chapter (five), therefore, we will look at what this tension portends for evangelization in West Pökot and its effects on inculturation in particular, and then suggest the way forward.

African Christianity. In Kwame Bediako et al (eds). *A New Day Dawning: African Christians Living the Gospel.* Zoetermeer: Uitgeverij Boekencentrum, 98–115.

119. Visser (1983), op.cit.
120. See for instance Walt (1997). Op. cit.

CHAPTER 6

TOWARDS A COMMUNITARIAN HERMENEUTICS

Introduction

IN THIS CHAPTER, WE will re-visit the consequences of the tension between the people's worldview and that of their pastors, and suggest a way forward. In chapter three, we analyzed the behavior, language and artefacts of the Pökot people and concluded that these depict them as more communitarian than individualistic in their social emphases, even though individualism was not missing. In chapter four, we showed that their pastors laid more emphasis on individualism, although there are genuine attempts, by some of them to incorporate communitarianism in their modes of preaching and lifestyle. If the practical way of bible interpretation among the people is predominantly communitarian, then there is a dire need to have an equally communitarian theory of bible interpretation. Through a componential analysis, we will endeavor to show the various components of meaning and the various dimensions of contrast that come into play in the making of a worldview.

As mentioned at the beginning of this book, we will consequently propose the development of a communitarian hermeneutics, one that is community-centered, with the community as its starting point (community-based) as well as its final point (community-oriented): a hermeneutics that hinges on the central issue of communitarianism versus individualism as the foundation for evangelization and inculturation in West Pökot. This is because the Pökot social situation, as our research revealed, is more inclined towards the community over and above, (and even sometimes against) the individual life (like in the case of human sacrifice). Then we will explore the advantages and disadvantages of communitarianism and show how a communitarian hermeneutics can correlate with, as well as confront, the culture by using the two key concepts, of *lük* (cattle rustling) and *kokwö* (the council of elders), which we have already observed among the Pökot people.

But in order to do this successfully, there is need to deconstruct these concepts, a fact that will also affect current evangelization method(s) in order to adopt a new disposition that takes into account the prevailing situation of the people on the ground, and accordingly re-evaluate the mission of the Church and its relevance to the new world order. Finally, we will show the place of a communitarian hermeneutics in the ever-growing field of inter-cultural hermeneutics, necessitated by the process of globalization, lest it is dismissed as yet another sectarian hermeneutics that seeks to alienate the Pökot from rest of the world.

This should, however, not be construed to mean that we are actually going to develop such hermeneutics in this chapter, which could be a life-long activity. We are only going to show the basis and justification of such an endeavor and argue that inter-cultural hermeneutics is a forum for the various 'localized' hermeneutics to learn from each other and hence augment the different worldviews, all of which have distorted reality in one way or another. In order to have a 'bargaining power' in such a world forum, it is of paramount that local hermeneutics be firmly rooted in their localities and worldviews before endeavoring to learn from the rest of the world.

Tension Between Two Worldviews

The traditional Pökot worldview can loosely be constructed from the people's meaning system, studied in chapter three and be demonstrated by a rectangle that represents the community, in which there are various ellipsoids representing different players. They have God (*Tororöt*), at the highest echelon; followed by the deities (*ilat, asis, kokel, arawa*), the spirits (*oy, onyötey*), ancestors (*kukötin nko kokötin*), the people (*pich*), living beings (*tikun cho sötote*) and non-living beings (*tikuk cho mosötotia*) at the lowest echelon; all of which are mutually dependent on each other, in a tightly bound relationship.

The only exception to this mutuality of dependence is God, whose dealings surpass human ken, whereas man is perceived as the center of the universe, because he not only mediates between the visible and the invisible, but he also has the capacity to engage his enemies into a dialogical relation-ship, which must, however, be sanctioned by the society. The other aspect that is worth mentioning in the Pökot worldview is the nature of the relationship between oneself and other people. It is characterized by the insider-outsider divide that we saw in the previous chapters.

The culturally sanctioned way of treating each other is that a Pöchon treats the other Pöchon as the self, because he or she is an insider. The insider 'other' is perceived as greater than, and as making part of the self, and also marks the boundary of human relationship. That is why when two Pökot people meet they try as much as possible to get to a point of commonality—village, clan, age-set (*pïn*), anything that will make them refer to each other as relatives (*kapor* or *tilyay*).

Relationship within the community is taken for granted and it is always presumed, but that is as far as it goes. The community must sanction any relationship with a non-Pökot, just because he or she is an outsider. Here, the other is treated as another, an alien or properly speaking, an enemy (*punyon*). An outsider's humanity is something the Pökot can easily dispense with, without any sense of guilt or remorse. That is why a warrior who kills an enemy is given special healing powers and becomes a *kölölyon*. There is no clear-cut distinction between the spiritual and the physical, although both realities are accepted and well revered. The distinction seems to depend on the issue at stake, sometimes the spiritual is emphasized, while other times the physical is emphasized. This worldview can be expressed as: "A relationship of being and of life of everyone with descendants, his family, his clan-brothers, his ascendants and with God, the ultimate source of all life; an analogical relation of everyone with his milieu, with his foundations, together with everything they contain and produce, with everything that grows and lives into it."[1]

Figure 1: The Pökot Worldview (Ndegwah 2006: 65)

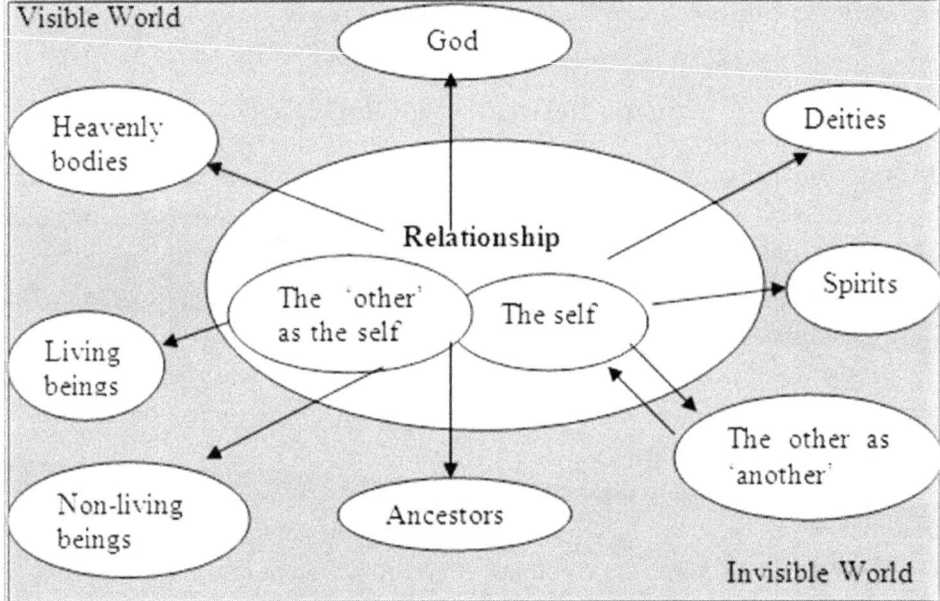

The pastors' worldview on the other hand, has God as the center of the universe; it has a clear-cut distinction between the things that are individual and those that are communal, on the one hand; and those that belong to God or the religious sphere and those that belong to the world, on the other hand. Although both worldviews contain both elements found in the individualism versus communitarianism divide, their emphases and priorities are different. This cultural difference shapes and determines a people's worldview and dictates their cosmology. Hence the physical differences are but the tip of an iceberg as Kirwen found out when he was posted to work in Tanzania.

---

1. Vincent Mulago (1962). *Un Visage Africaine du Christianisme: L'union vitale Bantu face à l'unité ecclésiale*. Paris: Presence Africaine, 117.

There was no electricity, no running water, no cars, no paved roads, no newspapers or telephones. It was a strange world to me. Neither my life at home nor education had prepared me to understand and live with this different way of life . . .

I soon found out that in Africa the real differences were not that the people didn't have electricity, but that their way of thinking about the world was so strange to me. Their *cosmology* baffled and challenged me. To talk with my African friends, I first had to understand the way they thought about the world.[2]

A componential table of some dimensions of contrast that make the differences between the Pökot worldview and that of their pastors can be drawn in terms of their components of meaning as shown below:

Table 12. Components of Meaning

Pökot Worldview	Pastors' Worldview
Popular outlook	Professional[3] outlook
Communitarian leaning	Individualistic leaning
Localized view of things	Globalized view of things
Bottom-up approach to issues	Top-down approach to issues
Emphasis on relationship	Emphasis on rationality
Concrete particularity	Abstract generalizations
Inductive reasoning	Deductive reasoning
Emphasis on mutuality	Emphasis on expertise
Liberative social structures	Oppressive protocol structures
Oral literature dominant	Written literature dominant
Meaning is negotiated and flexible	Meaning is in written texts and rigid
Holistic view of life	Compartmentalized view of life

As with all cases of componential analysis, the above table is more rigid and absolutist than is the actual case on the ground and as such these dimensions of contrast should only be regarded as pointers rather than an absolute representation of the relationship between the two groups. The cause of this, as we have already said elsewhere, is that the situation on the ground is more fluid and complex than the table shows. In

---

2. Michael C. Kirwen (1987). *African Widows: An Empirical Study of the Problems of Adapting Western Christian Teachings on Marriage to the Leviratic Custom for the Care of Widows in Four Rural African Societies.* Maryknoll, New York: Orbis Books, xi.

3. The word 'professional' here is not used in the same sense as Boff and Boff's (1983: 11–21) did in reference to theology as done by academicians. We use it as an emphasis on a skilled way of doing things and as an antithesis to the so-called unskilled way of doings.

general terms, the difference between different people and different regions of the world is mainly conceived in terms of material realities and physical infrastructure.

The essential difference, however, is in the mind and remains hidden in the most treasured part of people's hearts. The challenge then, seems to be, to persuade the Pökot people to open up their hearts so that outsiders can envisage their worldview, fit in their cosmology and look at the world through the glasses of their culture. Otherwise inculturation will remain both ephemeral and superficial. Training in seminaries, catechetical institutes or even convents hardly prepare candidates to deal with a reality like this one, leaving only one option—to learn it the hard way out in the field. And this is not only limited to missionaries who come to work in West Pökot; it equally applies to all non-Pökot clergy who come to work in the region.

As already noted in the previous chapters, when missionaries came to West Pökot, they brought with them not only the Word of God, but also the European social structures of governance and worldview, inherited from the medieval institutions. Following the footsteps of many philosophers and anthropologists, who openly spoke against anything non-European, they attributed the status of 'fallenness' and sought to destroy anything Pökot, just as they did with other African institutions, rather than allowing it to function as 'the other' and learn from it. These structures (like outstations, parishes and dioceses) contrasted sharply with the Pökot understanding of governance in which a council of elders makes decisions based on concession, rather than decrees from a one-man regime (where the parish priest is the king of the parish), which they saw as authoritarian.

Apart from other inconveniences to the Pökot social dispensation, the missionary style of worship, where they were forced to renounce their age-old traditions and accept a foreign spiritual leader with authority over them, was a key point of contention that made them drift further away from the mission centers. This meant that a fusion of horizon (*Horizontverschmelzung*) as advocated by Gadamer[4] was not possible, due to the irreconcilable differences in their worldviews, as observed by Kimmerle.[5] Of particular interest is the fact that Western worldview is predominantly individualistic yet the Pökot worldview is predominantly communitarian. Indeed, Mall dismisses Gadamer's concept of the 'fusion of horizons' as no more than 'something mystical'.[6]

Thus, Christianity and culture, in West Pökot, cannot simply agree on certain doctrinal issues creating an internal impasse. But pastors and their Christians sought the way forward and they have been involved in what Tanner and Wijsen regarded as a 'working misunderstanding',[7] or what Mall regards as 'understanding misunder-

---

4. Gadamer (1975). Op. cit., 273.

5. Heinz Kimmerle (1995). *Mazungumzo: Dialogen tussen Afrikaanse en Westerse filosofieën*. Amsterdam: Boom, 19–20.

6. Mall, op. cit., 90.

7. Tanner and Wijsen (1993). op. cit.

standing' or misunderstanding understanding'.[8] That is, they have been carrying on anyway, even if none actually understood the other's point of view. The aftermath is a damaged historical consciousness (or *wirkungsgeschichtliches Bewusstsein*, as claimed by Gadamer)[9] that resulted in perennial tension between the Pökot and the missionaries, which persists to this day in the form of tension between the people's worldview and that of their pastors.[10]

Missionaries take European superiority as a matter of course, at least in actions, which translates into economics or financial power. In many cases, they seem to identify the Gospel with development and progress, which is seen in terms of modernity, as understood in the West. So, they seek to 'modernize' the Pökot people in terms of their understanding of modernity, which is basically equated to economic growth, as envisaged in tall buildings, airplanes, tractors, computers, piped water and so on, yet the Pökot do not see it that way; hence their repulsion of Christianity.

But this is countered by the prolonged dialogue between culture and Gospel and the divide falls asunder in the face of the new power relations—the power of interpretation in the hands of Christian communities.[11] Evangelizers are afraid of such an eventuality and so they stick to their traditional methods, even when they do not seem to bear fruit, hence keeping the people at bay. Schneider has already outlined the cultural divide that is behind the Pökot lack of attraction to Christianity, even as Christianity promises 'development'.[12]

However, the Gospel cannot be identified with progress, development, civilization[13] or any other term one may prefer because it is none of those things, says Donovan. "The gospel is not progress or development. It is not nation building. It is not adult education. It is not school system. It is not a health campaign. . . It is not the civil rights movement. It is not violent revolution."[14] Hence the need for an alternative kind of theology that addresses Africa's damaged historical consciousness, mentioned above. We choose theology of reconstruction as the way forward.

---

8. Mall, op. cit., 78ff.

9. Gadamer (1975). Op. cit., 267ff.

10. This conclusion has been built on a mixture of personal observations and interviews that we carried out and conclusions from the broader research as found in the available literature.

11. Cochrane, op. cit., 9.

12. Schneider (1959). Op. cit., 159–160.

13. Although the gospel is not to be identified with development, progress or civilization, it is important to guard against the other extreme in which people expect free things or material recompense, as was the case with *Dini ya Msambwa*. One of their key teachings was that since they fought for independence, the adherents were entitled to free land, free education, free health care. . .everything for free, without paying tax, in spite of the costs involved in the attainment of these amenities. Pastors have a duty to encourage the 'ordinary' Christians to work for, and earn a just living, and at same time to admonish the idlers (1Thessalonians 5: 14), and in doing this they should lead by example since actions speak louder than words and sometimes they even speak without words.

14. Donovan, op. cit., 123.

Theology of Reconstruction

Theology of reconstruction is, according to its proponents Mugambi (of Kenya) and Villa-Vicencio (of South Africa),[15] a new paradigm for African Christian theology in the 'New World Order'. Its aim "...is to address the current religious, cultural, political and economic conditions facing the African continent. Conditions such as the prevailing refugee situation, lack of democracy, poverty, illiteracy, the AIDS pandemic, etc. Accordingly, reconstruction theology, talks of the renewal or renaissance of Africa from a theological perspective."[16] In showing the need for a paradigm shift in theological enterprise, Mugambi says that theological development cannot be divorced from socio-economic and political development in Africa. He, therefore, portrays the clamor for liberation theology as the direct result of oppression in Latin America, North America and Africa.[17]

He then shows the link between political and theological struggle as directly proportional, with Exodus 10: 1–6, as the main driving force. This starts with the dictatorial regimes in Latin America to the connection between civil rights groups in America and the religious consciousness of the black communities in United States of America to the struggle for liberation in Africa that culminated with the fall of apartheid in South Africa. With the coming of independence though, things have not been as expected and Mugambi cites political disappointment as the main reason for a theological shift from the 'Post-Exodus to Post-Exilic imagery'. In this light, then "Nehemiah becomes the central text of the new theological paradigm in African Christian theology, as a logical development from the Exodus motif."[18] This is necessitated by the very nature and obligation of any theological enterprise.

Theology, at best, must respond to the joys, sorrows, hopes and fears of the community of faith, which the theologian represents. "The theologian's primary audience, therefore, must be the community on whose behalf he or she engages in the theological quest."[19] However, Manus looks at Mugambi's work from a political perspective and says thus: "Reconstruction has recently become, in contemporary African Christian theological enterprise, a new language register to rationalize the

---

15. For details on their works, historical backgrounds and occupations see Wa Ngugi (2002). *Creation in "The Catechism of the Catholic Church": A Basis for Catechesis in Post-Colonial Africa.* Ph.D. Dissertation. Nairobi: Paulines Publications Africa, 63, 79), but he omits an equally important work on reconstructionism in the Francophone Africa, by Kä Mana (1993). *Théologie Africain Pour Temps de Crise: Christianisme et Reconstruction de l'Afrique.* Paris: Karthala).

16. Elelwani Farisani (2004). Transformation and Renewal in Contemporary Africa (Rom. 12:1–2). In J. N. K. Mugambi and Johannes A. Smit (eds). *Text and Context in New Testament Hermeneutics.* Nairobi: Acton Publishers, 63.

17. J. N. K. Mugambi (1995). *From Liberation to Reconstruction: African Christian Theology After the Cold War.* Nairobi: East African Educational Publishers Ltd., 2–13.

18. Ibid., 13.

19. Ibid., 11.

new African initiatives associated with the African leaders who lobbied for establishment of the African Union (AU)."[20]

He agrees that the concept of reconstruction is appropriate for describing our contextual effort to promote social transformation in contemporary Africa but accuses Mugambi of oversight in choosing Nehemiah as a role model for reconstruction in Africa.

> But Mugambi has failed to recognize the central figure in New Testament, Jesus of Nazareth, the Christ himself as the Master Reconstructor of both spiritual and the social wellbeing of the bnaiya Israel, the simple folk of his day in the first century Palestine. This class is the contemporary equivalent of the African Wananchi in Kenya, the talaka in southwetern Nigeria, the Ogbenye in eastern Nigeria, and so on.[21]

Following Hans Dieter Betz' suggestion, Manus recommends "the notion of reconstruction in the New Testament Studies."[22] In this regard, Betz sees reconstructionism as a theme that pervades the entire New Testament and insists on its adoption.

> Reconstruction is what the New Testament is all about. Indeed the New Testament itself is the result of reconstruction. The text of the Greek New Testament has been reconstructed from thousands of manuscripts and fragments of manuscripts, a process that still continues. The same is true of the Old Testament/Hebrew Bible. The history of early Christianity must be reconstructed from widely scattered pieces of information and tradition found in the sources. The theologies of Paul and the authors of the Gospels and Acts must be reconstructed by critical analysis of the sources.[23]

Consequently, Manus urges the use of the Bible, as an open-ended library of God's Word to provide us with eminent figures that can inspire African scholars in their efforts to engage contemporary African political culture with the Gospel. He suggests various approaches and methods, under the aegis of intercultural hermeneutics as his preferred methodology in endeavor to reconstruct the New Testament studies, "...in order to derive meaning suitable to one's contexts."[24]

On his part, Villa-Vicencio centers his work on the South African apartheid situation, and addresses the issues of social, political and economic transformation: human rights, racism and lack of equality in his country.[25] Applying the happenings

---

20. Manus (2003). Op. cit., 2.

21. Ibid., 2.

22. Ibid., 5.

23. Dieter H. Betz (2001). Remarks of the SNTS President. In Mary N. Getui, T. Maluleke and J. S. Ukpong (eds). *Interpreting the New Testament in Africa.* Nairobi: Acton Press, 6.

24. Manus (2003). Op. cit., 35.

25. Charles Villa-Vicencio (1992). (1992). *Theology of Reconstruction: Nation-Building and Human Rights.* Cambridge: Cambridge University Press, 1.

in South Africa to the global stage, he sees the 'winds of change' in other parts of the world, which present a challenge to theology. "The new situation offers the church new challenges; society now wants to know the church's position on issues of individual and social morality, politics, economics, ecology, culture, education, international relations, the rearing of children, and much more."[26]

He argues that institutional churches in South Africa have been trapped in apartheid due to their imperial dream and superiority complex, and as such they cannot attain their theological goals. He, therefore, looks forward for a new church, a church of the poor, one that identifies itself with those ensnared in the grinding wheels of poverty, whose personal and communal struggle for survival identifies personal and the social Gospel.[27] According to Wa Ngugi, Villa-Vicencio makes "...a shift from not only saying NO but also emphatically saying YES to the challenge of reconstruction and nation-building demanded by the structural transformation on all levels of society in the post-apartheid era."[28]

Other theologians, like Maluleke and Botman,[29] have criticized the reconstruction paradigm of Mugambi and Villa-Vicencio for various shortfalls, ranging from exclusivism to superficiality and short sightedness. The main criticism, however, comes from Wa Ngugi who thinks it does not represent an integrated theology because it fails to address "...the problem of the fragmentation of African cosmology as a result of increasing disintegration of the traditional social fabric of African communities through the impact of colonial rule and industrialization. Such fragmentation," he contends, "leaves us in Africa without a moral world to support the needed reconstruction."[30]

For this reason, Wa Ngugi sets forth to "...explore [the] doctrine of creation in the Catechism of the Catholic Church as a paradigm that can serve as a framework for catechesis in post-colonial Africa," and suggests "ways of adapting the CCC to Africa's pastoral needs with a focus on building a human community, and on human rights and caring for the environment as part of Christian catechesis."[31] The concern

26. Ibid., 81–82.

27. Villa-Vicencio, Charles (1986). *Between Christ and Caesar: Classic and Contemporary Texts on Church and State.* Grand Rapids, Michigan: William B. Eerdmans Publishing Company, 197.

28. Wa Ngugi, op. cit., 86.

29. Sam Tinyiko Maluleke (1997). Half A Century of African Christian Theologies: Elements of the Emerging Agenda for Twenty First Century. In *Journal of Theology for Southern Africa*, 99, 23; Russell Botman (1997). Who Is 'Jesus Christ as Community' for Us Today? The Quest for Community: A Challenge to Theology in SA. In *Journal of Theology in South Africa*, 97, 32.

30. Wa Ngugi, op. cit., 132.;

31. Ibid., 133. Although Wa Ngugi has opened a new window through which one can approach the teaching of catechism in Africa, that is, based on the doctrine of creation and its quest for the fullness of life (Mary N. Getui and Emmanuel A. Obeng (2003). *Theology of Reconstruction: Exploratory Essays.* Nairobi: Acton Publishers, 10–89), he conveniently avoids three key issues facing this doctrine in the African situation. The first one is its agricultural bias, of a garden, flowing rivers, fruit and so on (Gen. 2: 5–17) that seems to ignore pastoralist communities; the second one is the issue of the various forms

of reconstruction theologians is in line with Pope Paul VI, who addressed the need for the Church to constantly revise the methods of evangelization, in order to fine-tune them to the changing times. He said: "The conditions of society in which we live oblige all of us therefore to revise our methods, to seek by every means to study how we can bring the Christian message to modern man. For it is only in the Christian message that modern man can find the answer to his questions and the energy for his commitment to human solidarity."[32]

We agree with the goals of reconstruction theology, particularly the need for theology to 'respond to the joys and sorrows' of the people and the need for the church to 'constantly revise the method of evangelization'. However, we think that there can be no genuine or meaningful reconstruction without deconstruction. In order to reconstruct a social situation that has outlived its usefulness, or one that is simply misunderstood, there is a need 'to know the effects of differences already at work in it'.[33] Then we can proceed "by identifying and dismantling differences by means of other differences that cannot be fully identified or dismantled."[34]

We have done that by showing that the perceived difference between Pökot communitarianism and Western individualism is based on the suppressed differences within the Pökot culture, which is at once communitarian and individualistic.[35] We are also of the opinion that reconstruction of theology has to be done within the ranks of the communities of believers in conjunction with the 'ordinary' Christians, because it is they who know which aspects of theology need to be reconstructed. In this regard, we concur with Sarpong's views. "The role of a social scholar," he says, "is to analyse the situation and draw conclusions from it. The social scholar says nothing that people did not know before. He does not invent anything; he only draws attention to what is there which people may not have noticed."[36]

As we already stated elsewhere in this work, we are using the epistemological theory of 'constructivism' (which is philosophical) as a bridge between anthropology and theology. As 'constructivists' say (against 'objectivists'): knowledge is not a reflection

---

of marriage practiced in Africa, like polygyny (Hillman, op. cit., 87–127), while the third one is the question of the relations of power. Donders (1985). *Non-Bourgeois Theology: An African Experience of Jesus.* Maryknoll, New York: Orbis Books, 69–79) addresses this issue by contrasting the community power with the institutional impotence and calls for a non-bourgeois theology (Ibid., 151–158), while Schreiter (1985). Op. cit., 2–3) following the tradition of Schillebeeckx (1967). Naar een Katholiek Gebruik van de Hermeneutiek: Geloofsindentiteit in het Herinterpreteren van het Geloof. In H. van der Linde and H.A.M. Fiolet (eds). *Geloof bij Kenterend Getij.* Roermond, 95–96) frames it as the issue of 'new questions' arising in local situations against the (usually unsatisfactory) 'old answers' given by the official church.

32. Pope Paul VI (1973). *Address to the College of Cardinals.* Rome: AAS 65, 383.

33. Barbara Johnson (1982). *The Critical Difference: Essays in the Contemporary Rhetoric Reading.* Baltimore and London: The John Hopkins University Press, xi.

34. Ibid., x.

35. Van der Walt, op. cit., 46.

36. Sarpong (2002). Op. cit., 22.

of reality but constructed, through a power game, as Foucault would add. We would, therefore, like to revisit an important and relevant idea put forth by the hermeneutical philosophy trend, within African philosophy. It suggests, the deconstruction, not only of texts (both written and oral) and traditions, but also of mental categories that are not in conformity with people's needs and aspiration.[37] To do this, we use the concept of 'deconstruction' in a loose way, as was done by scholars like Johnson, Mudimbe, Chatelion-Counet and Stenger[38] as the way forward to reconstruct a new atmosphere for the Word of God to 'feel at home'[39] in the Pökot lifestyle and worldview.

The Concept of Deconstruction

We already said, in the general introduction, that deconstruction is a term that was coined by Jacques Derrida but it has since turned into an intellectual movement that permeates virtually all academic disciplines like philosophy, literary theory and criticism.[40] It enjoys the support of philosophers and theologians like Johnson, Mudimbe, Chatelion-Counet and Stenger already cited above and elsewhere in this study. Others who have explored this word include Gayatri Chakravorty Spivak, Hillis Miller, Paul de Man, Jean-Francois Lyotard, Jonathan Culler and Geoffrey Bennington; all of whom have resisted calls to give a succinct definition of the word. According to Derrida, deconstruction is neither a school of thought nor a method: rather, it is an occurrence within a text.

When asked what deconstruction is, Derrida once stated the following: "I have no simple and formalizable response to this question. All my essays are attempts to have it out with this formidable question."[41] Consequently, there is a great deal of confusion as to what exactly deconstruction can be said to bea school of thought, a method of reading, or merely a 'textual event'. Due to this controversy and the fluidity of its meaning, the term *deconstruction* is highly resistant to formal definition. The central concern of deconstruction is a radical critique of the enlightenment project of metaphysics, including in particular the founding texts by such philosophers as Plato, Rousseau and Husserl but also other sorts of texts in literature within Western philosophical tradition. It is mainly aimed at the 'metaphysics of presence' (also known as logocentrism or sometimes phallogocentrism), which holds that

---

37. Imbo, op, cit., 30.

38. Johnson (1982). Op. cit., Mudimbe (1988). Op. cit., Chatelion-Counet (2000). Op. cit., and Fritz Stenger (2001). *White Fathers in Colonial Africa—A Critical Examination of V. Y. Mudimbe's Theories on Missionary Discourse in Africa.* Hamburg: Lit.

39. Welbourn and Ogot, op. cit.

40. Odell-Scott, David W., (2000). Deconstruction. In A. K. M. Adam (ed). *Handbook of Postmodern Biblical Interpretation.* St. Louis, Missouri: Chalice Press, 55.

41. Derrida (1985). Op. cit., 4.

speech-thought (the *logos*) is a privileged, ideal, and self-present entity, through which all discourse and meaning are derived.

This logocentrism is the primary target of deconstruction. Perhaps Martin Heidegger was the first person to use this term (in its German form of *Destruktion*), in contrast to Nietzsche's concept of demolition, then Derrida 'Frenchnized' it into *déconstruction*. "Derrida says that he selected the term *deconstruction* to translate Heidegger's term *destruction* . . . because the French phonetic equivalent (*destruction*) implied annihilation, which Derrida judged to be more like Nietzschean 'demolition' than Heidegger's genealogical study of metaphysics."[42] It is a lot easier to give a negative definition of deconstruction by explaining what it is *not*. According to Derrida, deconstruction is not 'an analysis, a critique, a method, an act, or an operation'.[43] Johnson explains deconstruction in terms of what it does and what it does not do:

> *Deconstruction* is not synonymous with *destruction*, however. It is in fact much closer to the original meaning of the word *analysis*, which etymologically means "to undo"—a virtual synonym for "to de-construct." The de-construction of a text does not proceed by random doubt or arbitrary subversion, but by the careful teasing out of warring forces of signification within the text itself. If anything is destroyed in a deconstructive reading, it is not the text, but the claim to unequivocal domination of one mode of signifying over another. A deconstructive reading is a reading that analyzes the specificity of a text's critical difference from itself.[44]

In addition to the explanation above, deconstruction is *not* the same as nihilism or relativism, as some have already suggested. It is not an abandonment of meaning, but a demonstration that human thought has not satisfied its quest for a 'transcendental signifier' that will give unequivocal meaning to all other signs. In the process of interpreting a scriptural (or any other text) it focuses on the importance of the materiality of the signifier and how that materiality both plays a part in and disrupts the construction of meaning.[45] According to Smith and Kerrigan, "Deconstruction is not an enclosure in nothingness, but an openness to the other."[46] An attempt "to discover the non-place or non-lieu which would be [that] 'other' of philosophy."[47] Thus, meaning is 'out there', but it cannot be located by metaphysics, because the text gets in the way. Part of the difficulty in defining *deconstruction* arises from the fact that the act of defining *deconstruction* in the language of Western metaphysics requires

---

42. Odell-Scott, op. cit., 55.

43. Derrida (1985). Op. cit., 3.

44. Johnson, op. cit., 5.

45. Aichele, George (2016). *The Play of Signifiers: Poststructuralism and Study of the Bible*. Leiden: Brill.

46. Joseph H. Smith and William Kerrigan (eds) (1984). *Taking Chances: Derrida, Psychoanalysis and Literature*. Baltimore: John Hopkins University, 124.

47. Ibid., 112.

one to accept the very metaphysical ideas that are the subject of deconstruction. This notwithstanding, several writers have come up with a number of rough definitions. Allison, an early translator of Derrida, says that deconstruction

> ... signifies a project of critical thought whose task is to locate and 'take apart' those concepts which serve as the axioms or rules for a period of thought, those concepts which command the unfolding of an entire epoch of metaphysics. 'Deconstruction' is somewhat less negative than the Heideggerian or Nietzschean terms 'destruction' or 'reversal'; it suggests that certain foundational concepts of metaphysics will never be entirely eliminated...There is no simple 'overcoming' of metaphysics or the language of metaphysics.[48]

Moynihan quotes De Man as explaining deconstruction by what it does. "It's possible, within text, to frame a question or to undo assertions made in the text, by means of elements which are in the text, which frequently would be precisely structures that play off the rhetorical against grammatical elements."[49] Thus, viewed in this way, the term 'deconstruction', refers in the first instance to the way in which the 'accidental' features of a text can be seen as betraying, subverting, or contradicting its purportedly 'essential' message.[50]

The fact that deconstruction has turned into a movement that enjoys the support of scholars in various fields of scholarship it has, so to speak, gained a life of its own; one that even goes against the intention and desire of its founder. Against all Derrida's inclinations and passion, deconstruction is often perceived by many as a method that retrieves and describes the blurring ambiguities between what, in modern thought, are considered to be the structuralist inspired binary oppositions within a text (like, writing versus speech, center versus margin, self-versus other, insider versus outsider, signifier versus signified, good versus evil, male versus female and so on). Although we do not make such a claim here, we see deconstruction as an attempt to show that such would-be binary structures are never indeed so rigid as to withstand the rational implications of the other, often suppressed voices in the text.[51]

The key argument of deconstruction is that, in all these structuralist dualities, one term is often privileged or considered to be more important than the other, and as such it serves as the point of reference. For instance, when talking about the terms 'inside' and 'outside', the former is taken to be the criterion of determining who is an outsider and who is not; assuming an unnecessarily advantaged position over

---

48. David B. Allison (1973). Introduction. In Derrida, Jacques. *Speech and Phenomena and Other Essays on Husserl's Theory of Signs*. Trans. Allison. Evanston: Northwestern U.P., xxxii.

49. Robert Moynihan (1986). *Recent Imagining: Interviews with Harold Bloom, Geoffrey Hartmen, Paul DeMan, J. Hillis Miller.* New Haven: Shoe String Press,156.

50. Richard Rorty (1995). From Formalism to Poststructuralism. In *The Cambridge History of Literary Criticism*, Vol. 8. Cambridge: Cambridge University Press.

51. March C. Taylor (1982). *Deconstructing Theology.* New York: The Crossroad Publishing Company and Scholars Press, xx.

the latter. Hence deconstruction endeavors to develop concepts that are not vulnerable to either side of these oppositions. Among them are the following: *différance, trace, écriture, supplement, hymen, pharmakon, slippage, marge, entame, parergon, text*, and *same*.[52]

Deconstruction has important and far reaching consequences in a number of fields including our own fields of interest, religious and cultural studies. While directing our attention to critical problems that merit serious consideration, deconstruction also identifies questions that contemporary theology and philosophy can no longer avoid.[53] Deconstructive reading, in these disciplines, tries to show that texts are not univocal. They can be interpreted in different ways, hence standing on the way to clear and straightforward meaning.

That they are not innocent, and so they cannot simply be read as works by individual authors communicating distinct and clear messages. Instead, they must be read as sites of conflict within a given localized culture or worldview. As a result of deconstruction, texts reveal a multitude of mostly conflictual, if not contradictory, viewpoints existing side by side. A comparative deconstructive reading of a text with a more traditional one shows how many of these viewpoints are violently suppressed and ignored, to create an illusion of unity or systematization. Deconstruction can as well be extended beyond texts to other aspects of reality, like oral literature and mindsets where it would reveal similar conflicts.

Going back to its original German roots (*Destruktion*), as used by Heidegger, we get helpful insights, through analysis, 'freeing-up' and 'de-structuring' our thoughts about evangelization, as depicted in the preceding pages, where early missionaries looked down on the African culture and infused a sense of cultural inferiority among their Christian converts. Deconstruction does not mean to 'reverse' the trend of evangelization and now look at the Western worldview as inferior to the African worldview or to argue that one is ideal in its own right and that it has nothing to learn from the other.

We understand deconstruction as a philosophical concept that looks at texts and re-examines their weaknesses, reviews the systems and attitudes that have always straight jacketed people's thought-patterns. By way of deconstruction we revisit those little things that we have always taken for granted and again address their weakness. If this deconstructive trend is accepted in other academic disciplines, and especially in theology, then it would be easy to accept and correct prejudiced notions like, 'anything non-European is inferior' because it is that 'which is non-European' that helps to define and thus determine what is European. It is, therefore, a same-different relationship rather than an inferior-superior one. We also reject the equally misleading notion that idealizes the African culture and seeks to Africanize the so-called 'foreign' ideologies wholesale without first determining what is 'African'.

52. Jacques Derrida (1976). *Of Grammatology*. Baltimore, MD: Johns Hopkins University Press.
53. Taylor (1982). Op. cit., xix.

Nangoli gives an example of what we mean by 'idealizing' or 'romanticizing' the African culture. "Once upon a time in Africa, we paid no taxes, there was no crime, there was no police, there was no inflation, there was no unemployment, men did not beat or divorce their wives, then the white men came to improve things!"[54] The so-called good old days could have as well been the bad old days, but no one has the guts to acknowledge, let alone confront the latter. Wiredu, however, rejects this romanticized view of the traditional African society, accusing it of several vices like authoritarianism, supernaturalism and anachronism.[55]

Thus, our efforts to explore the difference, in worldview, between the communitarian Africans and the individualistic Europeans ended up exploring the differences within the African (and particularly, Pökot) culture, which is at once communitarian and also individualistic. So, these suppressed differences within the Pökot culture made it look like a unified whole that is diametrically opposed to another unified whole, that is, the European culture. Johnson paraphrases the workings of these two kinds of differences:

> Reading, here, proceeds by identifying and dismantling differences by means of other differences that cannot be fully identified or dismantled. The starting point is often a binary difference that is subsequently shown to be an illusion created by the workings of differences much harder to pin down. The differences *between* entities (prose and poetry, man and woman, literature and theory, guilt and innocence) are shown to be based on repression of differences *within* entities, ways in which an entity differs from itself.[56]

The term 'deconstruction' is used in a great many ways, or not used at all, whereas the process that the term refers to is still going on. Segovia gives an example of 'decolonizing theology'[57] as a form of deconstructionism that has been going on in the third world over the years. Early European explorers and missionaries in the turn of the 18th century came to Africa with the Word of God in what could be regarded as a theology of domination, aimed at 'civilizing and evangelizing'.[58]

This means that the religious factor cannot be wished away in the development of the modern history of the African continent. The missionaries were not only around during the great exploration epoch, but also during the slave trade and colonialism and in both cases, they were important allies to the powers that were. Hence Christianity played a significant role in the shaping of Africa's identity to the rest of the world. Mazrui points out that role as follows:

54. Musamaali Nangoli (1986). *No More Lies About Africa: Here's The Truth From An African*. East Orange, New Jersey: African Heritage Publishers, 18.

55. Kwasi Wiredu (1980). *Philosophy and an African Culture*. Cambridge: Cambridge University Press, 2–13.

56. Johnson, op. cit., x-xi.

57. Segovia (2000b). Op. cit.

58. Mudimbe (1988). Op. cit., 138.

Christianity in Africa played the dual and paradoxical role of being part of the vanguard of a new religion, on the one hand, and the vanguard of a secular Western civilization, on the other. The missionary schools in the African continent proclaimed the word of God, but they also came with the skills and normative orientations of a Europe which had already witnessed an industrial revolution. A related paradoxical role played by the missionary was that of being at once part of a new cultural conditioning in Africa based on European interpretations of Christianity, and part also of a new intellectual ferment which could generate potential innovative leaps.[59]

Accordingly, the missionaries made certain mental constructions of Africa and its people that influenced not only non-African readers of the history of Africa but also early African scholars, including theologians who "for a long time qualified African religious beliefs as superstition and lacking rationality."[60] It is these mental constructs that Mudimbe (of course with others) has worked so tirelessly to deconstruct and so present the true image of Africa and the African people. He laments the superficial and dismissive nature of the Western writers concerning the continent.

> They constitute a mosaic which, although bearing witness to an idea of Africa as expounded within the Western tradition, including, indeed, Africans' reactions to the idea, does not elaborate on ancient descriptive designations of the continent, but rather invites questions about their credibility, about the authenticity of African identities, geography and mythology presented in the literature.[61]

According to Stenger, Mudimbe does not intend to romanticize an African vision of the glorious past but, he makes a genuine "search for 'an idea' which is not defined and thereby dominated by the Western epistemological order, by exposing Western discourses on Africa for their conceptual disguises."[62] Thus, his line of thought lies in the epistemological order of knowledge from which he works to disentangle Africa from dependence on the West and he as such "destroys the bases of present discourse as part of Western epistemological assumptions about the standards of rationality."[63] He develops an 'archaeological deconstruction of African discourse'.[64]

Two criticisms, however, tend to eclipse Mudimbe's efforts. Firstly, Stenger observes that, Mudimbe "subversively employs Western philosophical tools. He bases his analysis on the post-structural approach of M. Foucault's methodology of analysing

---

59. Mazrui (1977). Op. cit., 89.

60. Stenger, op cit., 2.

61. V. Y. Mudimbe (1994). *The Idea of Africa.* Bloomington and Indianapolis: Indiana University Press, xi.

62. Stenger, op. cit., 2.

63. Dismas A. Masolo (1994). *African Philosophy in Search of Identity.* Edinburg: Edinburg University Press Ltd, 2.

64. Ibid., 189–190.

the rules that subjugate the discourse on Africa."[65] Secondly, Masolo calls us to the "realization that even Mudimbe's idea of an invented Africa is itself also a construct, an ideology which in turn requires deconstruction."[66] These criticisms notwithstanding, we think, and Masolo himself admits, that Mudimbe made a major contribution by pointing out the glaring discrepancy "...between facts representing African reality on the one hand, and a construct or an invention as the colonial discourse on the other."[67] For the purpose of carrying out the process of deconstruction, we resort to Mudimbe's implicit suggestion that we return to ethnography.[68]

To carry out a deconstruction exercise would mean that we start by destructuring our own learned or acquired thought pattern, and its inherent prejudices against those we perceive to be different from ourselves. This will ensure, as Mudimbe suggests, that we do not ignore the past, since we cannot reduce the slavery legacy and "the colonial experience to a sheer parenthesis in African histories...."[69] But we cannot also afford to dwell on the past at the expense of current development and plans for the future. Rather than continue to demonize slavery and colonialism or idealize either of the two, what we need at the moment is a 'wholly other' way with which to approach these marks and make them relevant to the needs of our time. In the religious sphere, for instance, there is need to accept a thinking that goes beyond the 'Eurocentric-Afrocentric' divide and deconstruct conventional images and stereotypes about Europe and Africa.[70]

This way we can see more clearly and address the patent issues of cultural complexity and its inherent contradictions, in order to have the possibility of inculturation based on genuine dialogue. This is founded on the recognition and acceptance of the principle that the Holy Spirit has over the ages manifested his presence in people's cultures and is still leading all people to the attainment of truth. If we admit that Europe does not have the monopoly of religious truth (or any other truth for that matter) and also that Christianity does not have the monopoly of the history of salvation, then we will understand that all of us have distorted the Truth in one way or another to suit our own blurred visions and short-term interests.

It is these interests, distortions, and shortcomings that need to be highlighted and given 'serious considerations'[71] in order to place the Word of God in its proper

65. Stenger, op. cit., 3.
66. Masolo, op. cit., 190.
67. Ibid., 190.
68. Mudimbe (1988). Op. cit., 166.
69. Mudimbe (1997) *Tales of Faith: Religion as Political Performance in Central Africa.* London: The Athlone Press, 199.
70. See Hofstede's (2001. *Culture's Consequences: Comparing Values, Behaviors, Institutions and Organizations Across Nations.* 2nd edit. Thousand Oaks, CA: Sage Publications, 25) divide of individualism between Kenya and The Netherlands, Sundermeier's (1998: 17) and Van der Walt's (1997: 171) clear-cut distinction of communitarianism versus individualism between Africa and the West.
71. Taylor (1982). Op. cit., xix.

perspective as dictated by the social conditions in which it finds itself. This attitude does not help in the efforts to initiate dialogue and the unity desired by many, since unity has to be radically distinguished from uniformity or conformity. It suggests that professional theologians look up to our communities to provide them with theological raw material and tools for theologizing in full partnership with them. Likewise, Christianity has a moral obligation to recognize, respect and approach the Pökot as human beings made in the image and likeness of God, which is the essence of the very concept of Christian love. This means giving due respect to their religion, an attitude that can ensure a genuine dialogue that would, in turn, ensure that Christianity is accepted among the Pökot as a partner and player in the dynamism of the Pökot cultural heritage.

Communitarianism Among the Pökot

As we have already observed above, the process of deconstruction started during our field research, through a personal 'fusion of horizons' (*Horizontverschmelzung*) in the sense that we modified our pre-understanding of communitarianism among the Pökot. We discovered that the Pökot are not a purely or cohesively communitarian people. Although (structural) communitarianism is a natural phenomenon, maintenance and nurturing of the *status quo* has acquired an economic (or functional) dimension. They remain communitarian as long as this practice guarantees some material or social benefits (like, say, during marriage or cattle raiding expeditions). But they are also individualistic if, and when, this brings with it some obvious advantages (like the scramble for the loot after a cattle raid).

Thus, the Pökot people always remain communitarian in a structural sense (i.e., 'natural' or 'biological' communitarianism based on blood relations) but in practice they can, and have often chosen to ignore it, if and when the situation dictates so. Below are some "components of meaning" of communitarianism.

Table 13. Forms of Communitarianism

	Structural communitarianism	Functional communitarianism
Communitarianism as a cognitive structure: worldview—concept in the mind—theory	"community" as something that is good in itself —what "ought to be"—a "moral obligation"—normative	"community" as an idea that it only accepted when it "works"—when it is "practical"—when it brings benefit to the individual and his or her family
Communitarianism as social structure: practice—reality	"natural community"— "biological"—based on kinship/blood relations—unavoidable — extended family—clan—ethnic groups	"willed community"— one can choose to be part of this community for strategic reasons—network

The table above might explain why many of them are running away from functional communitarianism and only lapse to it as a survival strategy. It would, therefore, be wrong to make a dichotomy and contrast the Pökot communitarianism with European individualism, since individualism also exists among the Pökot, even if in a milder form than among the Europeans. And this is the deconstructive effect we have talked about above and elsewhere in this study. Donders reports an old man explaining why individualism has taken toll among the Africans, which includes the Pökot.

> Our community spirit disappeared because we no longer need it. Formerly, in the olden days we had to do things together in order to survive. We needed each other to defend ourselves against wild animals and human enemies. We had to organize ourselves and to divide our workload in order to live. All those things are not necessary anymore. Everything has changed. Everything is organized in another way, and the whole of our community has collapsed.[72]

Although, as we have observed above, communitarianism has been a survival strategy that helped the Pökot to keep their enemies at bay as well as fend for the society, Ukpong's position on African identity still stands and it is equally true for the Pökot people. "The Africans," he says, "define themselves not in egoistic terms but rather in terms of their community and thus find identity there."[73] Due to their usage and emphasis over a long time, both the structural and functional aspects of communitarianism have become part of Pökot identity and they cannot but identify with the two as part of their cultural heritage that determines their worldview. As we have, however, established in the preceding chapters (three and four) there is tension between the official image that is portrayed and what exactly happens in the community.

72. Donders, op. cit., 70.
73. Justin S. Ukpong (1984). *African Theologies Now a Profile*, (Spearhead 80). Eldoret: Gaba Publications, 60.

While Spradley regards this as 'cultural contradictions',[74] Wiredu sees it as a crisis of identity, between tri-partite forces of 'what we used to be, what we are and what we ought to be'.[75] At the methodological and pedagogical level we can build on the dominant trait of communitarianism in the Pökot worldview and reconstruct[76] it into a communitarian hermeneutics, as a part of the 'contextual hermeneutics'.[77] This would be better placed to address the community's many religious problems and cultural tensions that result from the influence of the modern world surrounding its members.[78] Such hermeneutics would create "an awareness of the role that communities of faith play in bible interpretation, as well as for the transforming role of the Bible in the broader society."[79]

The Pökot people continue to live in a dangerous world characterized by lack of brotherly love, unemployment, constant famine and hunger, the ravage of AIDS, increased crime, including organized crime syndicates like cattle rustling and banditry that threaten to tear their community apart. In this regard, then, communitarianism is in itself not a once-for-all panacea to all their problems, including those of evangelization. However, we think that it is a good starting point to address them in a concrete, holistic and realistic way that leads to hermeneutics *of* and *for* the people. Donders sees the same traditional communitarian spirit as the force behind today's SCCs and commends them for one thing, approaching solutions to people's problems from a communitarian perspective.

> The old African community did not know of unemployment or marginal people. Everyone had a task, however humble. The African bishops spoke of the presence of the Holy Spirit as the go-between in a small Christian community. It is within such a community that God is Emmanuel, God with us. Within those communities individuals try to analyze their situations together with all those who suffer under similar conditions.[80]

In this light then, what Zvarevashe observed about the missionaries who are seriously out to evangelize is also true about the diocesan clergy who are seriously out to talk to the Pökot people in their own categories. He said thus: "The missionaries

---

74. Spradley (1980). Op. cit., 152.

75. Wiredu (1992). Op. cit., 60.

76. With the reconstruction of the Pökot communitarian worldview we move from structural and functional communitarianism to normative communitarianism, in a speculative activity that depicts the weak points of the community. It does this in the light of its ideals in comparison to the real situation on the ground, or what it ascribes to as it ought to be vis-à-vis what actually happens under the prevailing circumstances.

77. Ukpong (2004). Op. cit., 22.

78. Kwame Bediako (2000). A Half Century of African Christian Thought: Pointers to Theology and Theological Education for the Next Half Century. In *Journal of African Christian Thought*, 3, 34.

79. Louis Jonker (2001). Towards a "communal" Approach for Reading the Bible in Africa. In Mary N. Getui et al (eds). In *Interpreting Old Testament in Africa*. Nairobi: Acton Publishers, 84.

80. Donders (1985). Op. cit., 73.

undergo a cultural and personal keno-sis in order to communicate the Gospel in the best way possible; in the incarnation way."[81] What our research revealed in the Pökot situation is that bible interpretation lacks the major element of the community spirit because of many reasons of economic and sociological nature, but the most important one to us is the apparent fact that pastors app-roach the Bible from a more individualistic, rather than communitarian angle. And yet there is no meaningful discussion going on, at least not at the official level, between Christianity and the Pökot culture. Magesa reports Govender[82] as blaming this state of affairs in the church on what she terms as 'privatized bible interpretations'[83] that only caters for the needs of a small privileged class.

Privatized interpretations are usually the options of people with a reasonable amount of social security. They usually emanate from that class of people who had a reasonably well off life with or without middle class care. Thus, such an interpretation is more a revelation of the class positions of interpreters, than the understanding of the text from the social position determined by an option for the oppressed classes . . . Private interpretations usually rob the text of . . . [its] radical social protest character, render its message apolitical and avoid its revolutionary significance. Further they leave the true address[es] of the Gospel, viz. the marginalized of our world, without any comfort from God's Word and without a chance to turn the Gospel into an instrument of their liberation.[84]

The Strength of Communitarianism

Communitarian hermeneutics is not merely influenced by what happens within the community, in the light of cultural encounter with other communities, but rather, it is a conscious analysis of this context, which is itself an integral part of the hermeneutical process.[85] While it is possible to envisage many advantages that can be associated with a communitarian hermeneutics, three of them come out more strongly. Firstly, we already saw that the Pökot community was (and still is) egalitarian and did not recognize a single, authoritative religious leader. But Christianity has brought just that kind of hierarchical establishment that is seen in the government institutions where protocol is adhered to and followed to the letter.[86]

---

81. I. M. Zvarevashe (1993). Racist Missionaries: An Obstacle to Evangelization in Africa. In *AFER*, Vol. 35, No. 2. Eldoret: Gaba Publications, 123.

82. S. P. Govender (1987). In *Search of Tomorrow. The dialogue between black theology and Marxism in South Africa.* Kampen: Kok, 185.

83. Magesa (1997). Op. cit., 29.

84. Tihagale and Mosala (1986). Op. cit., 176–177.

85. Teresa Okure (2000). I Will Open my Mouth in Parables (Matt. 13: 35): A Case Study of a Gospel-based Biblical Hermeneutics. In *New Testament Studies*, Vol. 46, 445–455.

86. Schneider 1959: 159–160.

Through *kokwö* (the council of elders) that represented the wider community in a congregational way, the Pökot solved their social problems—be they administrative, judicial, moral or otherwise. They did not know and did not even trust a single religious leader with exclusive authority on religious matters, over and above the community. The same concept can be borrowed in the process of evangelization and bible interpretation, while taking seriously the counsel in the bible, where religious leaders are warned against acting like pagan leaders who 'load it over their subjects'.[87] Instead of depending on the current presbyter system in which one person's word is treated as the whole truth, there would be various communities of faith, whose work is to contextualize the Gospel by rooting it in the cultural and religious values of the whole community.[88]

If we deliberately adopt this Pökot congregational system, in which power, ultimately lies with the people,[89] and widen it to cover the entire communities of faith, then everyone will have a chance to air their opinion because they have a feeling of being a chosen people and responsible representatives of God's kingdom on earth; a truly holy (and universal) priesthood.[90] This stance parts way with the current practice in the SCCs, whereby people just come and sit in a circle and wait for the community leaders to 'feed' them with the word, as it is the case in Presbyterian systems where power ultimately lies with the leaders, not with their subjects.

Secondly, communitarian hermeneutics, rather than promoting uniformity, recognizes diversity in which various communities interpret the scriptures in the light of their prevailing social, economic and political situations, but also encourages the unity of sharing the same religious faith. This amounts to enrichment and widening the horizon of shared faith manifested in various cultural dressings. Thirdly, this kind of hermeneutics enables individual scholars, like sage philosophers have already done, to appreciate and take seriously the contribution of the interpretation by members of the small Christian communities (professional or otherwise), which can lead to a global community of bible interpreters.[91] This community spirit can be

---

87. Matthew 20: 25.

88. An example of a misunderstood cultural value is the meaning of the bride price in the Pökot community. Many outsiders see it as simply 'buying' and 'selling' of girls. But although the Pökot people use the same word roots—*ala* and *alta*—the meaning is different from say, buying a dress. Bride price is meant to legitimize the union of the spouses and the resultant offspring and also to act as a bond of economic relationship (3.5.1) between families, clans and neighbors. While the obligatory cows given to the relatives have special designations, like *tupa koyugh* or *kantin* (which are further divided into *tupa papo* (father's cattle), *tupa kapor* (father's younger brothers' cattle), *tupa chepkö* (father's sisters' cattle), *tupa kamama* (mother's brothers' cattle) and *tupa kökö* (grandmothers' (both maternal and paternal) cattle—Visser 1989: 67), those given out freely to neighbors and friends fall in the classification of *tilya* (3.5.2).

89. Bujo (1998). Op. cit., 27.

90. 1 Peter 2: 5.

91. Jonker (2001). Op. cit., 83.

an invaluable contribution of the African church to non-African churches, in form of intercultural hermeneutics.

In an experiment with intercultural reading of the Bible in the Netherlands, De Wit reports an impasse that different interpreters from different parts of the world reached for "the *lack of criteria* with which to determine the weight to be given to each of the mediating factors."[92] A solution was found at a new interaction, not between individuals, who could obviously not agree on various issues, but between the text and the group as a group. "We had to practice a 'communitarian' reading of the text, and, triggered by the text, also a critical interpretation of the cultural practices we were used to."[93] In this case, communitarianism served as a strategy that helped us realize what Schreiter calls *a new catholicity*.[94]

The Weakness of Communitarianism

Although, as mentioned above, communitarianism has many advantages appended to it in the African situation, we cannot close our eyes to the many weak points that are associated with it, among the Pökot in particular, and among other African communities in general. Two serious weaknesses that surfaced during our fieldwork are introspection and development. Introspection proved to be increasingly difficult among the Pökot because they rarely look inside themselves. They always look outside at someone else out there, even when a person makes a mistake, it is extremely difficult to turn to one's inner self and ask where he or she may have gone wrong—always somebody or something has to blame for a person's failures. Typical of our experience was the case of lateness or people's failure to turn up for interviews: not even one person, among the many potential interviewees took responsibility for their failures.

They blamed bad roads, weather, cows and even their spouses for not being time conscious! On the notion of development, communitarianism is to blame for the state of backwardness that many communities still endure. Individuals are afraid to make strides, even when they can, for fear of being bewitched by the less endowed members of the community or the notion that they ought to be like everyone else in the community. The other issue has to do with resistance to change that we already mentioned elsewhere in this research; when individuals (mainly those who went to school) embrace change (including Christianity or Islam) and try to prevail upon their communities to do the same, the main question they are asked is this: Who do you think you are? We have been doing things like this long before you were born! Plapan, who tries to introduce such change by campaigning against clitoridectomy had this to say:

---

92. De Wit (2003). Op. cit., 23.
93. Ibid., 24.
94. Robert J. Schreiter (1997). *The New Catholicity: Theology Between the Global and the Local.* Maryknoll, New York: Orbis Books.

> Change among our people is difficult because they see it as a personal endeavour that is both untested and has nothing to do with the community at large. On the issue of female genital mutilation, which I am campaigning against, I once brought some experts and called a meeting to explain its dangers to men and women so that they do not mete it out on their girls. Then we fielded questions to our audience and one elder asked me what I knew about the dangers of the cut (*mutat*) yet I was still a child, whereas they have been practising it since time immemorial and even our ancestors did it without any complaint. And this is despite the fact that I am in my mid 50s and had gone there with specialists in medical field![95]

Our own position on the way forward with regard to African communitarianism, once again, lies on the concept of deconstruction. Deconstruct-ion does not transform the concept of communitarianism, whether structural or functional, into yet another hermeneutical model or paradigm. Rather, deconstruction lays bare the hitherto un-identified, ignored, or unthought-of aspects of communitarianism in Africa, with the results that it helps in 'freeing-up' or 'de-structuring' our frame of reference.

Deconstruction concerns itself with the category of the 'wholly other' and here we are looking at the 'wholly other' side of the unexplored rhetoric of African communitarianism, that is, African individualism. "Deconstruction *is* the inadequacy of language. It remembers that something has been lost. Not what has been lost, but that something has been lost. That some-thing has been suppressed, has been pushed over the edge as being a useless instrument or garbage."[96]

Deconstruction thus seeks out those aspects within a system where it disguises the fact of its incompleteness, hence its failure to maintain itself as coherent self-contained whole. The art of locating these weak points and then applying a kind of leverage to them amounts to deconstructing the system rather than destroying or dismantling the entire system as such. It demonstrates how a system maintains the illusion of completeness through logical and rhetorical contradictions, thus calling for a fresh look at the way we interpret and respond to the fundamentals of our systems.[97] To some scholars, deconstructive criticismis a form of mischief because it spoils the party of status quo interpretation by reavealing the inherent instability in language.[98] In our case, we are introducing a 'mischief' by questioning the assumption of truth as a 'self-identical immediacy', which has been sustained by previous attempts to portray Africans as a communitarian people, *always* considerate of each other's welfare.

95. Interview with Lilian Plapan, the head of SETAT Women Group that promotes women's rights, by fighting against retrogressive cultural practices, particularly against clitoridectomy in West Pökot County.

96. Chatelion-Counet, op. cit., 3.

97. George Aichele (2004). *Poststructuralists*. http://www.yale.edu/yup/bible/poststructuralits.html, 1.

98. George Aichele et al (eds) (1995). *The Postmodern Bible: The Bible and Culture Collective*. New Haven: Yale University Press.

We postulate that such rhetoric feigns coherence by ignoring and finally excluding all that it cannot assimilate because it poses as the 'other' to it. The basic aim of this task is summed up in the fundamental question posed by Derrida: "what if what cannot be assimilated, the absolute indigestible, played a fundamental role in the system, an abysmal role rather?"[99] Deconstruction then, means maintaining a concept while shifting and moving aspects of its meaning.[100]

Van der Veen has given an insight into this kind of thinking on development in Africa. He explored the tribulations that Africa has faced right from the time of the Cold War; the economic decline the continent went through, to civil wars that amounted to genocide and finally the disintegration of some states.[101] Admittedly, he points out that the failure of Africa to develop can be blamed on internal as well as external factors, as most people have always done, but he insists that external factors could not have been the overriding cause.[102] He randomly compared African and Asian countries; most of which were at par during independence, with the latter coming out on top.

One specific example he used was of interest to us. "Or take Kenya and Singapore, which thirty years ago, were just about equally poor. Now Singaporeans earn an average of about 24,000 euros a year, while the average Kenyan earns about 340 euros a year, or one-seventieth of that amount."[103] And he blames this on misappropriation of funds from the donors, selfishness and greed. He further says: "The crucial factor, however, was what was done with the money, how profitably it was put to use. . .A case in point is Nigeria, which for decades had several billion US dollars a year of 'extra' income from oil. The Nigerian elite became both extremely rich and extremely large by African standards."[104] And all this happened in a supposedly communitarian society where the needs of community members are equitably attended to.

In the light of this weakness of communitarianism, and the fact that it is not a preserve of the Pökot people, it may appear as though we have put ourselves in a corner by killing the very notion that we set forth to investigate. What we, or rather the field research, has killed is the hitherto unexamined claim that Africans are communitarian, a claim that pits them against the individualistic Westerners. Moreover, it is not to say communitarianism, as a concept cannot be used for the purpose of inculturation. It can be used in a more careful and critical way.

Deconstruction can help us in our search for escapes and blind spots that lie behind these social phenomena. It is not a theory for creating rules or justifications

---

99. Derrida (1976). Op. cit., 120.

100. Chatelion-Counet, op. cit., 69.

101. Van der Veen, Roel (2004). *What Went Wrong with Africa: A Contemporary History*. Amsterdam: KIT Publishers, 2004.

102. Ibid., 356.

103. Ibid., 356–357.

104. Ibid., 257.

of a given form of communitarianism. Indeed, as Chatelion-Counet has already said, deconstruction belongs to the 'context of discovery'.[105] It is, therefore, not a once-for-all action, but rather an ongoing activity that keeps reviewing our understanding of communitarianism and its dynamics in Africa. Thus, we are trying to develop a different way of looking at African communitarianism, by showing that the binary difference, like the claim that Africans are communitarian while Europeans are individualistic, is an illusion created by 'the workings of differences much harder to pin down'[106] within African communities.

Inculturation Among the Pökot People

With the deconstruction of communitarianism in Africa, the question that we need to address now is whether this leads to some sort of biased hermeneutics that alienates the Pökot from other people. In the introduction, we referred to the problem of this kind of hermeneutics, as seen in both Latin America and South Africa, where the Bible was used to justify unjust and oppressive social systems. What we need to ask ourselves, at this juncture, is whether the said situation applies to West Pökot as well. The issue at stake is the engagement between the text and the context, that is, the "...explicit engagement of the bible *text* [of our choice, i.e., Jn. 10: 1–16] with a specific *context* [of West Pökot]."[107]

We try to answer this question by investigating whether the situation on the ground is characterized by the existence of harmony or conflict between these two sources, a continuity or discontinuity, correlation or confrontation. To do this, we opt for the method of both critical correlation and critical confrontation,[108] which embraces a discontinuous continuity or harmony as well as differentiation. This means that there are many Pökot cultural values that can be incorporated into the teaching of the Gospel, but there is a limit, or the extent to which this can go. And once this limit has been reached, a line of differentiation must be drawn.

Thus, pastors must genuinely be with the Pökot people but also not allow themselves to be 'swallowed' up by their culture; accept and incorporate everything that is in accordance with the teaching of the Gospel, but not be blinded by empathy to compromise it and accommodate cultural short-comings. As much as they ought to recognize the fact that God was already in West Pökot before them, as other authors

---

105. Chatelion-Counet, op. cit., 143.

106. Johnson, op. cit., x.

107. Ukpong (2004). Op. cit., 24. Brackets and italics are our addition.

108. Hans Küng (1987). *Theologie im Aufbruch: eine ökumenische Grundlegung*. München: Piper. It is, however, important to note that Edward Schillebeeckx first used the term 'critical correlation' in his quest to use the philosophical 'Critical Theory' in his hermeneutics, but not satisfied with his explanation, Hans Küng insisted that 'there is no critical correlation without critical confrontation'.

have recognized elsewhere;[109] missionaries also need to acknowledge an equally important fact, that like the Israelites in the Old Testament, God only revealed himself to the Pökot, through their culture, perhaps in an imperfect way.

Like marriage which, as the saying goes, is not a bed of roses, symbiosis between the Gospel and culture has not been a smooth and harmonious relationship in all its counts. It has been sustained by a simple, resolute co-existence that is sometimes characterized by rough edges of real agreements and disagreements. Hence there is a need to have a trained theologian within the community who must, however, work in partnership with the members. We clarify this option by focusing on *lük* or cattle rustling and the concept of *kokwö*, or council of elders, among the Pökot.

Communitarianism and Lük (Cattle Rustling)

In the Pökot and the weaknesses and challenges to communitarianism take on a specific nature in the form of *lük* (cattle rustling or raiding) and the dominance of the idea of *kokwö* (council of elders) over and above individual freedom. Our linguistic analysis of the number of times the words *lük* and *chorisyö* (theft) were used showed a very low contribution. The former was used six times by four people, while the latter was used 39 times by 20 people.

This is in spite of the fact that Jesus explicitly used the words thief, brigand and robber and indicted them for being the antitheses of the qualities of a good shepherd. In order for inculturation to be a successful reality, all positive values in the society need to be incorporated to the Word of God which has, in turn, to be used to identify and heal all negative values in the society.[110] Cattle rustling is one such negative value, among the Pökot, that must be tackled head on, if the Gospel is to retain its characteristic of being 'sharper than any double-edged sword'.[111]

As we have already observed in previous pages, cattle rustling or cattle raiding, is an age-old practice that even the staunchest Christians feel strained to talk about, and if they do, they feel obliged to defend or explain it away, even as their faith disapproves of the practice. Although we do not claim to have an instant solution to this problem, perhaps analysis of the elements involved in the practice can help us see the best way to bring it into terms with the Gospel. To begin with, we would like to clarify that contrary to many stereotype slogans, not every Pöchon (singular f Pökot) is involved in cattle rustling, particularly in the agricultural zones of the county. Indeed, many of them are as much victims of the practice as are their non-Pökot neighbors.

Many young Pökot men and women have gone to school and taken up income generating jobs that include, government employment, mining, business and farming

---

109. Leonardo Boff (1991). *Gott Kommt Früher als der Missionar: Neuevangeli-sierung für eine Kultur des Lebens und de Freiheit.* Düsseldorf: Patmos Verlag; Donovan, op. cit., 48.

110. John Paul II (1995). Op. cit., 37.

111. Hebrew 4: 12.

(both livestock rearing and crop production). They have done away with many traditional values that are regarded as retrogressive or incompatible with modern development, but this is not to say that cattle rustling is not a social problem. It is a serious obstacle that hinders social development and it needs to be addressed and sorted out in the light of the Gospel. Indeed, more problematic is the new form of banditry that many young people have taken upon themselves for the sheer purpose of selfish gain that disregards all traditional rules. Dillon talks about this form of theft hidden behind the traditional garb of culture.

> As Christians we cannot condone that, it is directly against the teaching of the Gospel. I think really it is just an abuse, especially in these days; it is becoming more and more an abuse, because they are just using cattle rustling as a form of *biashara* [trade]. They are just stealing cattle to take and sell them at the market, just for money. It could never be justified even in the past, but it was coming out of their limited vision of the world. They only saw themselves and their community as the only ones that should be cared for, that should be loved, protected and helped. They saw their neighbors as their enemies, and I suppose often their neighbors were enemies to them, because they were afraid maybe that they would come and steal their cattle. But, I think, in today's world those who are using the term *lük* [cattle rustling or cattle raiding] are only looking for an excuse to justify them to say, 'Oh, it is alright to steal from the neighboring tribe'. So, I think it has to be condemned . . . completely . . . [112]

Our research identified four basic points that can be regarded as the root cause of *lük* (or cattle rustling) in West Pökot. The first one is the sheer need for survival, owing to the fact that a cow is, for them, everything in life. So, should Tororöt get angry with them and bring forth an epidemic or unprecedented drought that kills most, if not all of their cattle, then they have to go and 'bring' a replacement, for the express purpose of re-stocking. The second reason has to do with revenge. Once the non-Pökot (for whatever reason) come and take away the cattle belonging to the Pökot, they inevitably meet and plan a counter-attack, 'in order to bring back our cattle home'.

The third reason has to do with sheer prestige, in the form of more animals with which they can use to pay dowry for more wives, in order to get more children and to provide for sacrifice, ritual or simply to be able to show their generosity by giving out an ox to the elders for slaughter, as a present. The fourth reason is lack of a viable economic alternative that is income gene-rating, on which young people can spend their energy. This is compounded with the traditional belief that all cows belong to the Pökot and only went to their neighbors by mistake. These two elements are, then, enforced by their under-standing of a person, which defines as a brother only a fellow Pöchon who lives in accordance with their common tradition.

---

112. Oral interview with Michael Dillon.

As we already mentioned a non-Pöchon is seen as another (an outsider, a stranger, an alien or an enemy—*punyon*), creating the mentality of insider versus outsider, us against them, the innocent versus the guilty and so on. This attitude regards the non-Pökot as lesser human beings who do not really matter, and it is okay to dispense with them, if need be. That is why a warrior who kills an enemy is decorated and given special powers to heal; an opposite of what happens when one kills a fellow Pöchon. The same is manifested when they refuse to agree that a fellow Pöchon can be bad, a trouble-maker or simply evil.

They will always look for some explanation in cases where people are caught doing weird things or in improper behavior, attributing their action(s) to some external influence, like bad spirits (oy). They claim that the offender is cursed by his/her ancestors or is bewitched, or some other cultural causes that will give them reason to perform a ritual to 'cleanse' the evildoer: yet, on the same token, they cannot believe that an outsider can be good at all, under any circumstances. Hence their notion of a community is exclusive rather than inclusive and anybody going against the communal wisdom and tenets is branded an outsider or an enemy within (a euphemism for a spy).

Although, as indicated above, *lük* (cattle raiding/rustling) is an age-old tradition, it is a communal practice directed to outsiders, who are not members of the Pökot community and there is always a meticulous arrangement between the raiders and the elders, who determine when, how and the means to execute it. There are strict rules to be followed, the failure of which invites a heavy penalty. Visser explains that youngsters take the initiative and request for the permission to go raiding from the elders using a secret language, they learn in seclusion:

> "Now father I have roamed and I saw a warthog sleeping. I have come to ask father. I want to go. It is still sleeping in my house."
>
> "Are there any other requests?"
>
> "My father this we heard only."
>
> The elders think it over among themselves for a while:
>
> "What should we do?"[113]

During the deliberations, the seer's advice is of paramount importance because it is believed that he or she has 'seen' all possible dangers that may befall the raiding party. The seer is then prevailed upon to give the go ahead or to refuse and should the former happen, then he or she gives exact directions, like the route to be followed, the do's and don'ts and might even choose the party's leader. Of greater importance is whether the captured enemies are to be killed. Visser further explains the exact words used when the seer finally accepts the request. "Open the door," he says, "who will

---

113. Visser (1989). Op. cit., 21–22.

stop these children from going?" And a messenger is sent to the young men with the words: "Come at dawn."[114]

Then preparations are done, which basically include "discussions of strategy, shield and spear practice, the putting on of colors, dances and blessings."[115] The blessing ritual includes the smearing of clay and milk on the faces, chests and the backs of the warriors. The prayers differ from one place to another, depending on their mode and vocabulary but the essence remains the same. It is a wish for the young men to travel safely and come back peacefully and for the enemies' eyes to be blinded.

The above explanation shows the extent to which the entire community is involved in the preparation for the raids and the blessing of the raiders, making it a communal rather than individual affair. The raids are never directed towards fellow Pökot because of natural affinity or a common genealogy, under the same progenitor, hence every Pöchon has some sort of 'natural right' to claim as his own a cow owned by a fellow Pöchon (as in the case of *tilya*. If *lük* (cattle raiding) is a communal affair and is directed to the *püng* (enemies) simply on account of their not being members of the Pökot community then the Gospel needs to understand this cultural concept, confront and *heal* its narrow vision of the human community, by giving it a *universalistic* character.[116] This is in accordance with the teaching of the Church that the Gospel is not subservient to any culture.

> The Gospel, and therefore evangelization, are certainly not identical with culture, and they are independent in regard to all cultures. Nevertheless, the kingdom which the Gospel proclaims is lived by men who are profoundly linked to a culture, and the building up of the kingdom cannot avoid borrowing the elements of human culture or cultures. Though independent of cultures, the Gospel and evangelization are not necessarily incompatible with them; rather they are capable of permeating them all without becoming subject to any one of them.
>
> The split between the Gospel and culture is without a doubt the drama of our time, just as it was of other times. Therefore every effort must be made to ensure a full evangelization of culture, or more correctly of cultures. They have to be regenerated by an encounter with the Gospel. But this encounter will not take place if the Gospel is not proclaimed.[117]

Here we use the words of Jesus in the same text of our choice to nuance the very ideals espoused by the Pökot tradition but go against the Christian teaching. Jesus said thus: "he who does not enter the sheepfold by the door but climbs in by another

---

114. Ibid., 22.
115. Ibid., 22.
116. Donders, op. cit., 114–117.
117. Pope Paul VI (1977). Op. cit., no. 20.

way, that man is a thief and a robber"[118] and again that "The thief comes only to steal and kill and destroy. . . ."[119] As Christians, the Pökot belong to a higher, more universal community tied together by their religious affinity, which embraces all human beings, with the same progenitor—God. Thus, Jesus surprised doctor of law saying that even the Samaritans are his neighbors, giving the concept a new dimension that included his enemies.[120]

After universalizing their concept of community then the words of Jesus "And I have other sheep, that are not of this fold; I must bring them also, and they will heed my voice. So, there shall be one flock, one shepherd,"[121] take on a new meaning that also includes those who are not Pökot. Otherwise the narrow understanding confines the 'other sheep' to those Pökot members who have not accepted Christianity as yet. Success in widening the traditional understanding of the community, in which human beings, like the Pökot, found themselves in the world, without any choice of their own, has another effect. The Christian commandment 'Thou shalt not steal', which is normally confined within the Pökot community, shades off its ethnic tag and takes on a wider dimension that includes all other human beings, including the communities surrounding the Pökot. Theft is an abominable crime, and if one is caught stealing a cow from a neighbor the punishment is to pay four cows, because they count the legs of the animal (the means by which it was taken away). For that reason, cattle rustling is given a different name (*lük*), to differentiate it from theft (*chorisyö*) or unsanctioned cattle raids for personal gain (*setat*).

In the same vein the Pökot religion sanctions against theft within the community for the reasons of common genealogy and the concept of common ownership of property, particularly land and cattle. Once Christianity comes into talking terms with the Pökot religion, the Gospel is likely to help raise these traditional values and give them a universal characteristic in which all of us share a wider, common genealogy that goes back to our Proto-Ancestor.[122] The concept of ownership too would be widened, in the sense that we are, after all, not the absolute owners of anything on earth, since all things belong to God, by the virtue of being the Creator. He has only bestowed on all human beings, the Pökot included, the responsibility of stewardship towards the created things, among them cattle.

Given that many of these raids are a result of the need to have (more) cattle, a mere conceptual understanding of the universality of Christian brotherhood is not enough. Something both concrete and practical needs to be done to help those who abandon *lük* (or cattle rustling) find an alternative way of survival and personal advancement. In short, evangelization has to go hand in hand with humanization,

118. John 10:1b.
119. John 10:10a.
120. Luke 10: 25–37.
121. John 10: 16.
122. Nyamiti (1989). Op. cit., 17–39; Bujo (1992). Op. cit., 77–91.

through poverty alleviation because poverty has a tendency to dehumanize people. Talking about the need for the Church to think and consider 'the development of peoples', Pope Paul VI had this to say:

> The progressive development of peoples is an object of deep interest and concern to the Church. This is particularly true in the case of those peoples who are trying to escape the ravages of hunger, poverty, endemic disease and ignorance; of those who are seeking a larger share in the benefits of civilization and a more active improvement of their human qualities; of those who are consciously striving for fuller growth.[123]

Indeed, Pope Paul VI later on put it more succinctly that development of the people is part and parcel of evangelization. He said thus:

> Between evangelization and human advancement—development and liberation—there are in fact profound links. These include links of an anthropological order, because the person who is to be evangelized is not an abstract being but is subject to social and economic questions. They also include links in the theological order, since one cannot dissociate the plan of creation from the plan of Redemption. The latter plan touches the very concrete situations of injustice to be combated and of justice to be restored.[124]

Our argument, however, is that the Gospel should not seek to impose foreign solutions to the people, a fact that reduces it to mere rhetoric, but to build on what the cultures it finds itself in have to offer. Here then, our suggestion is revisiting the traditional Pökot practice of *tilya*, mentioned earlier on in this book. We said that the key functions of this practice are two: first, to maintain a closer tie between neighbors or clans, since everyone is a debtor to everyone else and secondly, it functions as a form of livestock insurance against calamities like pestilence and theft. But *lük* has the same practical effects as *tilya*, with the only differences being the objects and methods of the two activities. The latter is directed to the non-Pökot, while the former is practiced among the Pökot themselves.

When going for *lük* (cattle rustling) they go as a group with spears, shields and arrows, and these days, with guns, but when going for *tilya* they go alone, as individuals, armed with confidence and goodwill. In both cases, they could get or fail to get the animals, except that in the former, they could also lose their lives. Hence the Gospel contribution would be to extend the *tilya* system to the Pökot neighbors (the Turkana, Karimojong and Sebei) who are, in the eyes of Christianity, no longer *püng* (enemies) but *werko* (brothers). This will maintain a closer tie between them as well as ensuring that all of them have the cattle, in spite of drought and other pestilences like epidemic.

---

123. Pope Paul VI (1967). *On the Development of Peoples.* Nairobi: Paulines Publications Africa, no. 1.

124. Pope Paul VI (1977). Op. cit., no. 3.

Although this is the crux of the matter, as far as contact between the Gospel and *lük* is concerned, it does not end here. This is because of the modern situation, whereby many young people go to school, get removed from their cultural lifestyle and yet do not get employment. They end up hanging around in shopping centers and eventually get into the new form of cattle rustling (*setat*) and other vices. There is, therefore, the need to come up with viable income-generating projects that target these young people. An environmentalist, Ton Dietz, from the University of Amsterdam (Universiteit van Amsterdam—UvA) the Netherlands, with a lot of experience in field research in Zambia and Kenya (West Pökot), has been trying to do this kind of thing by looking into ways and means of improving the Pökot economy[125] while preserving the environment, and still continues with the research on the economic situation among the pastoral Pökot. He does this by 'examining the interface between nature's capacity and human livelihood strategies', in what he refers to as 'development-oriented geography'.[126]

Dietz' work lacks the evangelization aspect and needs to be augmented with proactive and down-to-earth pastoral programs, like the DELTA (Development Education for Leadership Training in Action) method, which explicitly addresses the twin issues of poverty and evangelization.[127] Churches, in West Pökot, have a moral duty to engage in developmental issues and see to it that they address the twin issue of material well-being of their followers as well as the key issue of general human development, without making them charity-dependent.[128] Hence the need for churches to join hands with the government and NGOs, and work as a single entity, as opposed to the current bickering and division.

This will boost their efforts to help the people to become self-reliant by improving social amenities and other provisions like roads and schools, and also restore their self-worth that has been trampled upon for long. As things stand now, various

---

125. Dietz (1987). Op. cit., 193ff. Antonius Johannes (Ton) Dietz was a sitting board member of many scientific journals and internationally recognized committees on environmental issues, among them: NWO Steering Committee Climate Change, Adaptation and Mitigation (NWO-KAM) (October 2003 onwards); African Environmental Review, refereed journal of Moi University, School of Environmental Studies; and coordinator of NUFFIC-MHO Program for Moi University School of Environmental Studies, Eldoret, Kenya (until July 2004) among many others. In the West Pökot situation, he tries to give a theoretical framework of viable development projects, while many NGOs are practically implementing his ideas. For instance, the Netherlands Harambee Foundation, a development project supported by the ING bank of the Netherlands, has two branches. One looks at the provisions of clean water, while the other one looks at the question of human and animal health. At Nasukuta, there is a pilot project going on to try and crossbreed traditional animals with the exotic ones in order to come up with a better breed of animals that are both resistant to the harsh climatic conditions but are also more productive in terms of milk and meat.

126. Ton Dietz (1990). Development-oriented Geography: examining the interface between nature's capacity and human livelihood strategies. *IMWOO-bulletin* (17, 1989-4), 13–16.

127. Josephus B. M. Kronenburg (1986). *Empowerment of the Poor: A Comparative Analysis of two Development Endeavours in Kenya*. Amsterdam: Koninklijk Instituut voor de Tropen, 83–10.

128. Speckman, op. cit., 82–98.

churches do their own things; NGOs do their own things, while the government does its own things, and all this to the detriment of the people they are supposed to serve. We consider the role of churches to be crucial because of their proximity to the people and, therefore, concur with Sartorius that "...churches, because of their close contact with the people, can have a manifold influence on development and on the efforts to create among the people the will for development and an awareness of the possibilities for achieving it and can follow this up with advice and practical help..."[129]

Communitarianism and *Kokwö* (Council of Elders)

The other concept that needs to be closely looked at is that of *kokwö*, which means the council of elders itself or the meeting place from where the elders make social as well as juridical decisions. Although the system is seen and understood as egalitarian, a closer look at the goings-on in the everyday life suggests otherwise, a further manifestation of what Spradley regards as cultural contradiction between the official image that is portrayed and what actually happens.[130] The word of *mutinto ngal* (decision maker, or cutter of words literally) is final and nobody within the council dares to criticize him, much less outside the council by the uninitiated and junior elders, who do not take part in *kokwö*.

Although he ordinarily speaks after everyone else and simply summarizes the popular opinion or point of view, the same cannot be said of those outside this council of elders. The chain of command goes down the ladder, based on age and gender. Young men are regarded as the leaders of tomorrow (*kipöghtoghis cho pö asiyech werkö*), with women at the lowest rank whereby they are not allowed to raise a voice, either against their husbands or any other man in the community. Then children, as we have seen already, are almost regarded as non-human and their opinion, together with that of women, is never sought, in line with Pökot tradition.

Many African writers have praised this model of leadership, with Bujo calling upon African politicians to learn from it.[131] He further elaborates the palaver model, which he regards as 'an efficient institutionalization of communicative action'. "If an important decision is to be arrived at over matters that affect the people as a community," he says, "the wisest representatives of the people are called together for a

---

129. Peter Sartorius (1975). *Churches in Rural Development: Guidelines for Action*. Geneva: Commission on the Church's Participation in Development, WCC, 10. This stimulation for development among the people is not, *per se*, a biblical hermeneutical solution to the issue of poverty in West Pökot. It is necessary because Christianity is a supernatural or spiritual force that caters for the whole human being—body and soul. Moreover, the church does not operate in a vacuum, and as such Christianity is a strong force for social change. However, this view must not be confused with 'identifying the gospel with development or progress', which we already rejected on the grounds that it sometimes leads to a culture of dependency.

130. Spradley (1980). Op. cit., 152.

131. Bujo (1998). Op. cit., 20.

palaver."[132] Showing the dynamism of the palaver model, he gives an example of cross clan or cross-cultural marriage whereby "the eldest and wisest of both families or clan communities were called together for palaver (consultation), where the well-being of all would be taken into consideration. The concerned couple was also consulted, and only then was a valid decision made. Depending on the arguments, the old tradition would remain valid or be abolished."[133]

Consequently, he recommends this model as a good journey 'towards a communitarian-ecclesial model of conscience'.[134] We wish to deconstruct this grand narrative by pointing out that Bujo does not address the weak points associated with this palaver model, as many points of contention came to the fore during our field research. He does not, for instance, say who actually took part in this palaver and the role that women and children played in decision-making.

We once overheard a missionary discussing the possibility of creating a water reservoir in the form of a dam in Sincho area (within Sook location) with some women he had found drawing water in a drying up spring and they wondered. "Why do you tell us that?" They asked in a surprised tone. "We are just women; you better discuss such ideas with the elders," they said. Upon inquiring, as to whether they could not, on their own right, make the decision they responded in unison "*Aai, chicha monïng*—yes, we are children." This kind of authoritarianism by the elders and permissiveness on the part of women and children is not limited to the cultural sphere; it also permeates into the political arena, and the church ranks. For that reason, the faithful are very hesitant, for instance, to criticize a wayward priest or bishop, "because they are the spiritual fathers of all parishioners," said one informant who did not want to be named.

So, when the Christians are not happy with their parish priest, instead of talking to him they go and report him to the bishop and if they are not unhappy with the decision that the bishop takes, then they do not know where to go next. And so, the resentment continues as well as the problem, entangling the church in the same problem found in other social fields. Bujo rejects the notion that the absolutist ways of African politicians and the authoritarian behavior of some religious leaders are rooted in the traditional concept of a chief,[135] yet discussions in the SCCs revealed just that.

Several verses in the bible text of our choice directly contradict, or do not tally, with the traditional Pökot idea of a good shepherd, and yet people were not courageous enough to point out this fact. Traditionally, and even now, a good shepherd does not 'lead the sheep into the pasture' as the study text suggests.[136] He remains behind so that he can easily notice and help any particular sheep that may be having some difficulties, one informant told us. A good shepherd is not the gate of the sheep, because

132. Ibid., 36.
133. Ibid., 36–37.
134. Ibid., 79.
135. Ibid., 158.
136. John 10: 4.

then, when the raiders come, he will be the first one to be killed and then lose not only his animals, but his life as well.

A good shepherd spends the night outside the sheep pen in order to keep guard, just in case of an attack. Even where the shepherds are protected by the warriors, still they do not act as vanguards of the sheep. He does not merely lead the sheep out to the pasture, because that is not a test of his goodness and acumen; he succeeds in bringing them back into their fold. Of most importance is the way the Pökot people find their identity in the parable. Contrary to the traditional way in which many commentaries identify Christians with the sheep and Jesus with the shepherd, the Pökot agree that Jesus is, indeed a good shepherd, but that they too, are shepherds, although they sometimes fail to be as good shepherds as Jesus is. Thus, the sheep are anyone or anything entrusted to their care: for mothers, it is their children and all those things that pertain to them at home, for men it is members of their families and all their belonging, for the catechists it is the Christians who are entrusted to their care.

Although this is the understanding that emerged from the fieldwork, no one was ready or willing to 'criticize' the word of Jesus, even where it went directly against their traditions, 'because Jesus is God' as one catechist told us. "You know," said Simiyu (a convert from Islam and popularly still known by his earlier name, Rajabu), "Jesus is God and although it is an abuse to regard people as sheep in our tradition, God cannot err and so we just accept it that way."[137] This domineering top-down attitude was also manifested in the attitude of pastors (of all cadres) towards the 'ordinary' Christians as reported during our interviews but they never questioned it, even though they knew it was not right. So, the few who went against the *status quo* and dared to criticize or question those in higher ranks than themselves paid dearly for it.

Indeed, we reported a case of a seminarian who 'lost his vocation' and was declared 'unworthy to become a priest' because he had done the 'unimaginable' by questioning the uprightness of the actions by some ordained priests. This timidity to face issues and take them head-on as the situation may demand is an inheritance from the traditional sense of respect to the elders or leaders and has consequently robbed the church of its prophetic role of challenging the *status quo* and pointing out ills in the society, particularly where they are perpetrated by those in leadership. In short, the church has failed to observe the two principles of solidarity and subsidiarity, criticizing and energizing the community. Hence, as Brueggemann puts it, "The task of prophetic ministry is to nurture, nourish, and evoke a consciousness and perception alternative to the conscious-ness and perception of the dominant culture around us."[138] In order to realize the Church's prophetic role, there is need to borrow a leaf from Imbo and say with him that philosophy has the task to carefully deconstruct such traditions, and reject the mind-set steeped in categories that subject a group of

---

137. Interview with Rajab Simiyu, a 50-year-old catechist in Tartar Parish.
138. Walter Brueggemann (1989). *The Prophetic Imagination.* Minneapolis: Fortress Press, 13.

people to domination.[139] Even the seemingly inclusive expression of 'consulting the bed—*petoy kilap*', among the Pökot, is still subject to the goodwill as well as the whims of the elders; and this too should be deconstructed.

The same situation applied to the Pökot *kokwö*, nothing good or bad happened without the express permission of the elders until the coming of the colonizers, and even after that they still wielded a lot of power and influence. Whereas the idea of respect to the elders is in itself a noble one, the lack of a reciprocal gesture from the elders, and the apparent stifling of initiatives from the young people and women is something to be challenged by the Gospel. The fact that the elders agree on certain tenets to guide their community does not make them universally acceptable. Even the Afrikaner Bible readers in apartheid South Africa interpreted the Bible only to suit their small community, while at the same time they oppressed the black majority and colored South Africans.

However, we argue that it would be a good idea to use people's disposition to the council of elders but with bible teaching as the yardstick in making and promulgating community rules and by-laws. Thus, the suitability of the tenets of communitarianism (or lack of it) must be "judged by their faithfulness to the basic human and biblical values of love and respect for others, community building, justice, peace and inclusiveness."[140] That way, they uphold human dignity and treat all people as image and likeness of God, in line with the scriptures.[141]

A concrete example of the clash between the insistence, by the council of elders, on respect to the elders at any cost, to the detriment of the Gospel values was reported by one young priest, Godfrey Siundu (then Parish Priest of Tartar Parish), who worked among the Pökot for ten years. When he was newly posted to the county, he preached about the 'parable of the two sons'[142] and exulted the virtues of the first son (who had bluntly said to his father "I will not go" but later thought the better of it and went), over and against the second one (who said he would go but actually never went).

After the Mass, they had a small social gathering and two elders said him, "Father, you got it all wrong in today's Gospel reading." "About what did I go wrong?" The surprised priest asked. "You see Father," one of them started, "the first son invited a curse upon himself by directly opposing his father to the face. There is no way then, the change of mind can absolve him from the guilt without seeking forgiveness from his father. Better the one who, although he did not comply with his father's wish showed respect by not telling him so in the face."[143]

---

139. Imbo, op. cit., 30.
140. Ukpong (2001). Op. cit., 192.
141. Genesis 1: 27.
142. Matthew 21: 28–31.
143. The discussion was reported to have been held between Fr. Godfrey Siundu and two elderly members of the church—Mr Paraiywa and Mr. Domokwang. We were, however, not able to meet them to corroborate this story since they were out in search of pasture in the Republic of Uganda.

In the name of respect, the elders, and community at large are willing to forget all other misdeeds of a person and classify him as upright. But this is not the spirit of the Gospel where, as it were, a greater wrong is expected to cancel a lesser one. While it does not fault the first son for directly saying 'no' to his father, it abhors the second son's lackadaisical behavior of prevarication and beating around the bush and finally failing to do what his father had asked of him. The Gospel encourages Christians to speak out openly and courageously on all matters and particularly on matters religious. But we can also add that they need to do this in accordance with the local customs of showing respect to all strata of the society.

That way, the Gospel will have brought in something new but this will be tailored to suit the communal way of doing it. The benefit of such a working relationship rests on the fact that, while the converts are helped to mold their lives in accordance with the Gospel teaching, they do so within the framework of their tradition, which encompasses their thought patterns and mental categories. This resonates with Magesa's suggestion of community involvement in transforming biblical hermeneutics from 'privatized hermeneutics' to 'popular hermeneutics':

> Biblical interpretation informed by actual experiences of Africans in their socio-economic, political and religious environs is therefore what will move hermeneutics from its captivity of privatization. In other words, it will transform the exercise of interpretation away from the sphere of ideology towards the arena of truth. But this cannot be done if the people or the local community is not involved in the exercise. Somehow, the community itself and its struggles and its perception of the world must influence, if not determine, the orientation and the findings of biblical hermeneutics.[144]

Communitarianism and Intercultural Hermeneutics

Our suggestion for a communitarian hermeneutics, as a locally grounded way of evangelizing the Pökot people, does not in any way contradict the wider quest for an intercultural hermeneutics, necessitated by the process of globalization. We see the former as a necessary pre-requisite for the latter. "*Intercultural hermeneutics,*" asserts Manus, "is one way of describing the process of doing contextual exegesis and theology for contemporary culturally renaissant persons, such as those in Africa today."[145] We understand intercultural hermeneutics as a new way of interpreting the Bible in the context where people from different cultural backgrounds are in constant, if necessary, contact and yet still retain their differences.

Thus, it is an open forum, rather than open hermeneutics,[146] for diverse cultural and contextual interpretations to engage each other into a dialogue with a tenacity of

---

144. Magesa (1997). Op. cit., 36.
145. Manus (2003). Op. cit., 32.
146. Mall, op. cit., 68.

purpose; which is, to develop sensitivity for the blind spots in people's own interpretation processes, thus providing a perspective that exceeds the limits of one context or cultural circle. "This is possible as a result of globalisation, and is also urgent due to globalisation."[147] It is, therefore, a theoretical reflection on the way to interpret the Bible in an intercultural context. This way, it advocates the necessity of people to discover and celebrate their own spirituality, generated from their rich and diverse cultural heritages. It also expresses "a need to articulate a decolonizing mission to enable people to take pride in their own languages celebrate their ethnicity, faith, and otherwise acknowledge difference without closing the door on each other."[148]

Consequently, the starting points of intercultural hermeneutics are particular localities, where people (like the Pökot and their pastors) are influenced by their traditional customs that shape their worldviews into contact and enter into a dialogue. In the beginning of this study we presupposed that the Pökot worldview is a communitarian one. Yet, the form of hermeneutics they have so far been exposed to is based on a Western worldview, which is individualistic. This might have been the reason why the Word of God has not sufficiently taken root among the people of West Pökot.

As we have seen in our section on the history of inculturation in Kenya, the Word of God was brought by 'expatriate', missionaries coming from Europe, and they brought the Word of God unavoidably in a European fashion. And also, after the Kenyan church became more localized, the 'native' missionaries and other evangelizers continued to preach the Gospel in a European way trained, as they are, in European thought patterns in seminaries, convents and catechetical institutions. Hence the need to develop a communitarian hermeneutics, based on the people's world view.

This endeavor put our project in an intercultural perspective because, as we have already shown, in chapters three and four the encounter between the people and their pastors, in West Pökot, is mostly, though not always, an intercultural encounter between European and African cultures. The basic tenet of intercultural hermeneutics is that "there is no universal hermeneutics [in the sense of Western particularistic universalism][149] which is ready-made and applicable to every country or situation in the world. Instead every hermeneutics is concretely rooted in and influenced by the specific context out of which it arises and for which it is devised."[150]

It engages certain points of view and brings them into a confrontation. The most important of these that came into the fore during our fieldwork are: illiteracy versus literacy, orality versus writing, particularity versus universality, identity versus

---

147. De Wit (2004). Op. cit., 39.

148. Byamungu (2002). Op. cit., 149.

149. Parentheses are our addition. When examining the influence of the West, particularly the erosion of collectivism in other non-Western civilizations Van der Ven et al (2004. Op. cit., xi-xiii) contrast Western particularistic universalism to (a presumably non-Western) complex, polycentric universalism.

150. Manus (2003). Op. cit., 32.

difference and, yes, communitarianism versus individualism. And as we have already said, this dichotomy is exacerbated by the suppressed internal differences. Whereas the people have a more localized Afro-centric cultural orientation, their pastors, particularly the priests (both missionaries and local clergy) have a more Westernized, universalistic orientation.

This boils down to the battle of differentiation: the particular versus the universal, the communal versus the individual, identity versus difference, familiarity versus strangeness and so on, as each fears domination or subjugation by the other. Hence the key problem, as already observed, is that of power relations, that is, how power can be distributed and exercised. In this regard, then, the other must not only be allowed to be 'other', but there is need to celebrate the similarity with the 'self', and to strike the balance between the two because the situation on the ground is not that clear-cut. "If, however, the strange is to be hearable, if interpretation is to be both possible and necessary, otherness cannot be simply other, difference not merely different. . . . Hermeneutics, in other words presupposes an interplay of the familiar and the strange, a reciprocity of identity and difference in which each become itself through the dialectical relation to the other."[151]

During our fieldwork, we discovered that the Pökot were more individualistic than we thought, and that the form of hermeneutics they have so far been exposed to by their pastors is more communitarian than we had imagined. To a certain extent the older 'expatriate' priests tend to be more communitarian than their younger African colleagues. Thus, the form of hermeneutics that is needed in West Pökot must go beyond the superficial dichotomy between Africa and the West.

Unfortunately, scholars such as Hofstede, Sundermeier and Van der Walt still make the clear-cut distinction of communitarianism versus individualism.[152] This does not seem to be tenable anymore and the developing of a sound hermeneutic theory in Africa must of necessity demythologize and demystify this notion. Gyekye's reflection on 'moderate' communitarianism as opposed to 'radical' communitarianism seems to be more promising as a way forward in the field of hermeneutics.[153] However, we think that this can only be achieved as a deconstructive enterprise for both communitarian and intercultural hermeneutics, based on the empirical evidence we have exuded in this study.

Conclusion

In this chapter we have argued our case for a communitarian hermeneutics that is built on the Pökot concept of communitarianism, which is the dominant spirit underlying their traditional worldview. We were under no illusion as to try and romanticize that

---

151. Taylor (1982). Op. cit., 67.
152. Hofstede, op. cit., 25; Sundermeier (1998), op. cit., 17 and Van der Walt, op. cit., 171.
153. Gyekye (1992). Op. cit.

traditional worldview as a purely unified whole that is unique to the Pökot people, due to the many points of influence from their neighboring communities. We accepted both modern and post-modern positions on culture, as a product as well as an ongoing process. Of great importance is the understanding that cultures are not bounded wholes and so we settled for the notion of 'cultural orientations', which meant that even the Pökot, are not stable in their Pökotness, the strength of which varies from place to place and with one's companions.

This notwithstanding we contended that there is always a dominant cultural orientation and that no meaningful hermeneutics could take root if this reality is ignored. By the use of the philosophical concept of deconstruction, we showed the weaknesses of the Pökot worldview, by analyzing two cultural practices of *lük* (cattle rustling) and *kökwo* (the council of elders). Then we showed how these traditional concepts could be used as building stones, rather than allowing them to become stumbling blocks to inculturation, which we already argued is a necessary part of the mission of the church to evangelize the world, including the Pökotland. Hence it must be taken seriously by all those who are genuinely interested in evangelization. We have shown that communitarian hermeneutics is not opposed to intercultural hermeneutics and said that the former is a prelude to the latter.

We started by postulating that, the Word of God cannot take root among the Pökot (and this goes for all other people), if evangelizers ignore, or worse, neglect the cultures of the people they are out to evangelize. In this relation, we can make two conclusions: firstly, that inculturation does not amount to romanticizing the African culture and, therefore, taking it whole-sale. It means understanding the culture, through learning the language of the people and their customary practices in a way that is not judgmental. Secondly, inculturation is not just aimed at making local cultures more local, but also at universalizing them by the use of the Gospel values, even as cultures help to localize the Gospel; an achievement that is only possible through an honest commitment to the people as people.

GENERAL CONCLUSION

THIS GENERAL CONCLUSION BRINGS us to the end of our research project. It is time for us to take stock, in the light of the questions we set forth to answer and examine what we have achieved and what we have failed to achieve; and also, look again at the issues arising from our investigations. At the onset of this research we said that it is interdisciplinary in nature; it uses insights and instruments of three disciplines: philosophy, anthropology and theology. It set forth to examine the process of Evangelization and inculturation from a missiological perspective, which itself has had an interdisciplinary approach comprising the philosophy, science and theology of mission.[1] We explained that evangelization is the basic mission of the church and that inculturation is a method of accomplishing that mission, though by no means the only one.

We also said that inculturation is basically a dialogue between the Gospel and culture, represented by the main actors—the people, on the one hand, and their pastors, on the other hand, in a particular place. Through participant observation we observed the (mis-) communication between the people (at the popular level) and their pastors (at the pastoral level) due to their diverse ways of interpreting the bible passage of our choice,[2] which gave it a hermeneutic character. Then we suggested the way to make their communication more effective by engaging popular and pastoral hermeneutics. This would be possible by developing a communitarian hermeneutics as a deconstructive enterprise.

The first chapter is, thus, conceptual in nature, as it dwells on the philosophical-theological debate in Africa, particularly on the issues of inculturation, culture and the concept of communitarianism among the Africans, in relation to the development of an authentic African hermeneutics. Chapter two is mainly descriptive in nature and serves as the hinge that moves the reader from the abstract academic-speculative debate to the actual life on the ground, by introducing him or her to the realities of the Pökot social context in which the bible passage of John 10: 1–16 was read and interpreted by the people and their pastors. Chapters three and four

1. Jongeneel, op. cit.
2. John 10:1–16.

are anthropological in nature and they dwell on the methods of ethnography that helped us understand the Pökot people and the way they perceive and interpret the Bible vis-à-vis the interpretation methods of their pastors. Chapter five is a reflection on the correlation and interplay between the conceptual chapter one and the empirical chapters three and four.

Our research was triggered by several questions that lurk in our minds, key of which hinge on why the Gospel did not take root in West Pökot and the extent to which the Pökot people interpret the Gospel in an African (communitarian) way. The extent to which their pastors interpret the Gospel in a non-African (individualistic) way and how the interplay between popular and pastoral hermeneutics can be facilitated. We do not claim to have achieved once-for-all answer to all these questions or solutions to all other issues that come with the questions. But we have set forth an ethnographic path that we think is potentially beneficial in dealing with them effectively.

We were also aware that our very presence in the SCC prayers with research tools made people curious, and even made others shy away from the tape recorder. This could have had the effects of tilting their opinion and make them say what they thought we expected to hear. But we tried our level best to make them 'feel at home' and share their insights as they always did on their own. Thus, we indevoured to be what Gramsci called an 'organic intellectual' and saw to it that our job was to articulate 'grassroots' concerns.[3] We were able to come up with several insights, based on the observation and recommendation that were made by the 'ordinary' Pökot Christians, concerning the inception of the evangelization process in their land. Our fieldwork revealed that the Gospel did not actually take root among the people of West Pökot because it remained at the surface of their culture. The pastors, in spite of their efforts, did not succeed in penetrating the Pökot worldview or in interpreting their own religious experience from the perspective of the people.

This failure is mainly based on the fact that the first missionaries demonized all African cultures, leading to some Africans actually hating their own cultures. Other factors include social and economic changes that make people identify themselves with modernity rather than their traditional lifestyle. These pose a serious problem to the quest for inculturation, leading to critical questions like the following: 'Who is supposed to do the inculturation? Who needs it anyway, and to what extent can it go? Moreover, the people have been reluctant to accept the Gospel because they see it as a foreign imposition. For most of them, Christianity is just a religious dimension of the wider project of the colonial invasion that only came to disrupt their otherwise serene lifestyle. And yet it, according to them, has nothing to offer beyond what they already have in their traditional religion. We leave these issues as an open question that call for further research and theological reflections, outside the framework of a dissertation study.

---

3. Antonio Gramsci (1983). *Selection from Prison Notebooks of Antonio Gramsci*. London: Lawrence & Wishart, 5.

Then there is a minority that has either idealized the Christian faith and thus wants nothing to do with the Pökot customs and tradition, or has pledged loyalty to the two traditions—the Christian tradition and the Pökot tradition. For them, an appeal to either of the traditions depends on the seriousness of the matter at hand and the direct material benefits accrued to either of them. We have thus, established that the Pökot try, though not always successfully, to interpret biblical texts from their own African perspective. Despite the clash of cultures and difference in worldviews, the pastors also try to interpret the Bible from the perspective of the people, but they basically remain outsiders. They, for instance, interpret the Bible from a more individualistic than communitarian perspective. We have suggested the development of a communitarian hermeneutics, based on the fact that the Pökot are more inclined to community life than they are attracted to individualistic lifestyle. This means the preparedness to take the community values seriously; among which we included opinions and wisdom of the 'ordinary' Christians, even though they are not theologically trained.

We also noted that these issues are not as simple, or straightforward, as we have put them down in writing. We did not, therefore, suggest a return to the past but rather to build on the past while being focused on the future. Deep in the center of evangelization is the question of culture, which cannot be separated from theology. Culture helps shape us into who we are today. It determines, among other things, how we conceptualize religious matters and how we respond to religious experience. Theology, thus, is part of culture[4] and cannot be disentangled from all other cultural activities that pertain to mundane affairs, at least not in Africa.[5]

Thus, we realized that it is not possible to draw a clear line of demarcation between religion and culture, in order to come up with a pure 'Gospel message' to be infused into culture. In other words, the Gospel message does not exist 'somewhere out there'. It is the result of the interplay between the scripture and people's response to it, which they always do within the ambience of their culture.[6] Hence the Gospel message is always culture-specific. Thus, as Derrida said, "a text. . .is henceforth no longer a finished corpus of writing some content enclosed in a book, or its margins, but a differential networka fabric of traces referring endlessly to something other itself, to other differential traces . . . "[7] This, however, does not deny the universality of the Gospel values. What it means is that the way these values are perceived, articulated and actualized in one culture is different from another culture.

Whereas we started, in the philosophical-theological chapter (one), with apodictic, clear-cut, statements about what is African and what is not (communitarianism

---

4. Tanner (1997). Op. cit., 64.
5. Mbiti (1995). Op. cit., 1.
6. Ndegwah (2006). Op. cit., 85.
7. Jacques Derrida (1979). Living on: Border Lines. In Harold Bloom et al. (eds). *Deconstruction and Criticism*. New York: Seabury, 84.

versus individualism) the anthropological practical chapters (three and four) showed that cultural situation is a lot more complex than we thought. This complexity of culture was manifested in cultural contradictions, like the existence of communitarianism side by side with individualism, to mention only one example.

Based on the notion of the complexity of cultures[8] it became clear to us that a 'fusion of horizons'[9] is not possible due to irreconcilable differences in people's worldviews. Thus, we suggested a movement from the notion of going out to convert the people (e.g., by telling them what the Gospel says to them) to the notion of going out share one's own religious experience with the people of other cultures. This also marked a shift in the quest of our earlier search for a symbiosis between the Gospel and culture from a harmonious and smooth relationship to a simple co-existence that is sometimes characterized by rough edges of real disagreements.

To move on, we embraced the idea of 'a working misunderstanding', 'understanding misunderstanding' or even 'misunderstanding understanding', as espoused by Wijsen and Tanner, as well as Mall.[10] We realized that harmony is not always possible. In that case, the Gospel and culture have no choice but must agree to disagree and respect each other's position. We moved from examining the difference between African and non-African cultures to examining the differences within the African, and specifically Pökot, culture.

While we started with the presumption that the Pökot are a purely communitarian people the results of our fieldwork nuanced this position because their communitarianism exists side by side with individualism. Whereas structural communitarianism only depicts the normativity of communitarianism as a cognitive structure, functional communitarianism is more complex as a social structure because it is only accepted when it works, say, by bringing obvious material benefits. The former can, however, serve as a model of how a Christian community ought to operate, and how the relationship between a pastor and the 'ordinary' Christians ought to be for the benefit of the entire community.

We discovered that there are various tensions between the Pökot worldview and that of their pastors, which emanate from the predominantly individualistic worldview from the West, in spite of the pastors' genuine efforts to adopt a communitarian worldview that is predominantly manifested among the people they work with. Using the classification of Boff and Boff, who identify three levels of doing theology as popular, pastoral and professional,[11] we looked at the hermeneutic endeavor from the same perspective. Our interest was in the interplay between popular and pastoral hermeneutics and we tried to identify the weakness inherent in both, in the way of deconstruction. We, therefore, suggested that a possible way forward lies in a situation where pastoral

---

8. Hannerz, op. cit., 8.
9. Gadamer (1975). Op. cit., 273.
10. Tanner and Wijsen (1993). Op. cit., 177–193; Mall, op. cit., 78ff.
11. Boff and Boff, op. cit., 12–14.

hermeneutics becomes more popular, in its approach, and popular hermeneutics reciprocates this gesture by becoming more pastoral in orientation.

This means that, on the one hand, pastors should not be buried in the universal teaching of the church (magisterium and encyclicals) to the detriment of the actual problems of the people they are called to serve.[12] On the other hand, Christians should not act as though the entire church only consists of their SCCs, parishes, or dioceses. They should not be obsessed by their local needs and seek to satisfy them through purely cultural means or personal gains irrespective of what the universal church thinks about the morality and legitimacy of their actions.[13] This brought us to communitarian hermeneutics, which is an academic harmonization of the first two levels of the hermeneutic enterprise that is, popular and pastoral hermeneutics. Trained theologians are, therefore, important to the community, and the three (laity, pastors and theologians) are complementary to each other[14] in developing a realistic theology that addresses people's needs and aspirations in a more genuine and realistic way.[15]

We used philosophy as an interface between anthropology and theology. The philosophical concept of deconstruction served as a bridge between the anthropological modern and post-modern understanding of culture and theology of reconstruction. Thus, we argued in favor of deconstructing the African traditional concept of community, in order to identify its weaknesses and bring it in tune with the current social reality. Then one can go on and develop a communitarian hermeneutics, based on the predominant concept of communitarianism, among the Pökot, in order to make the Gospel 'feel at home'. Thus, the Pökot traditional practice of cattle rustling (which is based on communal loyalty) ought to be replaced with the more universal value of Christian brotherhood. But this, in itself, is not enough; there is a pastoral need for evangelization to go hand in hand with humanization. Hence the church has a duty to join forces with non-governmental organizations (NGOs) involved in the integral development of West Pökot County, which would make the church's approach to evangelization more comprehensive.

In order not to develop yet another biased hermeneutics that would isolate the Pökot from other people, we observed that there is a need to go beyond Eurocentric and Afrocentric stereotypes, and embrace unity in diversity, particularity and universality, and showed the place of communitarian hermeneutics in the larger enterprise of intercultural hermeneutics. Finally, we want to say that from this research, we have realized that there is an urgent need for further research within the communities of faith, who have for a long time been neglected where theological enterprise was concerned, on the grounds that lay people (even when theologically trained) cannot

---

12. Wijsen and Tanner (2000). Op. cit., 20.
13. Ibid., 16.
14. Schreiter (1985). Op. cit., 18.
15. Arbuckle (1991). Op. cit., 2–7.

theologies, simply because of their 'lay' status. And yet, as we have said earlier African biblical scholarship consists of scholars and non-scholars.[16]

Hence communities are important fora or occasions to theologies and have our ideas refined, enriched or even redefined by fellow community members. This is in contrast to what many theologians and other intellectuals do. They ordinarily carry out a desk research and top it up with personal reflections, then they go ahead to construct mental presentations of their own interpretation of reality; which, in some cases, has nothing to do with what is, in fact, the case on the ground. But lay people's theology is a practical one, devoid of academic decorations and colorful jargons, but firmly rooted on the ground, interpreting the Word of God in accordance with their true state of life. This is where biblical scholarship needs to direct its research attention, not only in Africa but, in the whole world.

---

16. Gerald O. West (2001). *Biblical Hermeneutics of Liberation: Modes of Reading the Bible in the South African Context.* Pietermaritzburg: Cluster Publications, 87; Okure (1993). Op. cit., 77.

GLOSSARY

Amat	reconciliation ritual between age-sets.
Amoros	sacrifice (pl. *amorostin*).
Anyïn	sweet or sweetness
Apoy	an elder (pl. *poy*).
Ara psör	the Milky Way
Ara tipïn	constellation.
Arawa	the moon (pl. *oroo*).
Aryon	ash.
Ateker	large wooden basin that is curved from a tree used by a group of young men for drinking blood during their graduation ceremony as warriors (pl. *atekertin*).
Chelolosion	a bandit (pl. *chelolos*).
Chelosëy	a brigand (pl. *chelosoytin*).
Chemeri	initiated girls, before they are healed (pl. *chemerion*).
Chemowos	diviner (pl. *chemowostin*).
Chemnyokoria	any coward whether a boy or `girl (pl. *chemnyokorien*).
Chepta	a name given to a girl who fears facing the knife (pl. *chepten*).
Chepelaleyo	dancing groups or a kind of dance.
Cheperow	a clan name given to an initiated girl, if she is the second-born in her family.
Chepsakeyon	a witchdoctor (pl. *chepsakeyis*).
Chepsakitian	an herbalist (pl. *chepsakitis*).
Chepto	a young girl, a daughter or daughter of (pl. *tipin*).

Cheptughmu	(lit. someone with a black stomach) a wickedness or malevolent person.
Chesortum	a visiting girl who 'jumps into' an initiation ceremony and gets initiated.
Chö	milk in general.
Chi	a person (pl. *piich*).
Chipöt	a curse or abuse.
Chorin	a thief (pl. *chori*).
Eghin	an ox (pl. *egh*).
Egyan	the entails or intestines of an animal.
Horizontverschmelzung	fusion of horizons.
Ighin	creator or molder.
Ilat	the god of rain.
Ipso facto	by that very fact.
Kacheripkö	this is a section of the Pökot people in one region (Karapökot) who are said to spend much of their time in the house, which they are said to watch over (*ripkö*).
Kaideke or ngachar	a hand stool used by elders to sit on, support the head and as a shield in case of an attack.
Kamar	a prized ox one is given after a major event, like circumcision (pl. *kamartin*).
Kamas	a hill.
Kanasyan	a homestead (pl. *kaneston*).
Koipa pagh	a common grinding stone, normally found at the river side.
Koipa koghin	a personal grinding stone, found at home.
Kapolok	traditional remote-control phenomenon in which you treat someone like a zombie or robot and make him or her do what you like, or simply overlook your own weakness or machinations to exploit him or her.
Kaporet	a clan name given to an initiated girl, if she is the first-born in her family.
Kapulokyon	magician (pl. *kapulokyontin*).
Karachïna	a youngster (sing. *karachinin*).

Karatapögh	(lit. tying water) untying ritual one by the elders to the people, if they think that they have been tied into barrenness by an enemy or some evil person in the comm.-unity.
Kasauria	these are the Pökot people in the same region (Karapökot) who are named after the famous cattle watering point called Sauriria, because men spend much of them time around it (sing. *kasaurin*).
Kaw	home (pl. *keston*).
Kech	sheep (*kechir*).
Kegha	fresh milk.
Keghot kelat	initiation ceremony in which two lower teeth are removed.
Kensyö	marriage.
Keporyak	camping groups.
Kighanat	faith, covenant or testament.
Kikatat	a ritual to ward off individual misfortune and disease.
Kirwokïn	a litigator or judge (pl. *kirwokïs*).
Kïmïr	a lighter, faster and vague shadow that only the spiritual beings or extraordinary people can communicate with.
Kiporcha asis	showing the child to the sun for the first time.
Kïpuno	the passing out ceremony for girls after initiation.
Kilokat	a ritual meant to treat the disease of *ilat*.
Kirial	lightning.
Kïtontögh	the human shadow, which cannot be grasped or touched that moves with a person where he or she goes and is believed to leave the body at the time of death.
Kokelion	a star (pl. *kokel*).
Kokö	grandmother (pl. *kokötin*).
Kokwö	council of elders, a meeting by such a council or even the venue of the meeting.
Kor	land.
Koretaran	the Orion.
Korka	a woman or wife (pl. *kor*).
Kot	injury.
Kö	house (pl. *korin*).

Kölölyon	a traditional cleansing ceremony for someone perceived to be unclean, also the one carrying out the cleansing.
Kömöy	hunger, famine or drought.
Konet	teacher/catechist (pl. *konetin*).
Kukötin nko kokötin	grandfathers and grandmothers or all ancestors combined.
Kukö	grandfather (pl. *kukötin*).
Kumïn	traditional beer.
Kunstlehre	technology.
Kuting	mountain (pl. *kutingkot*).
Kyak	livestock.
Kyakuyin	a person who happens to relieve the *mösöwoon*, for a given period.
Lapan	a ceremony carried out on female initiates a few days after initiation.
Lapay	a traditional ceremony to avenge the killing of a person and the resultant fixed fine of sixty heads of cattle for a man and thirty for a woman.
Lalwa	a river (pl. *lalwatin*).
Lastagh	simple forgiveness that is granted upon confession.
Lëkip	a walking, mainly used by elderly people (pl. *lëkiip*).
Lelut	a mistake that is not intentional.
Liliey	waving of hands, by women, at the time of singing.
Lökötyö	A belt of beads worn by women after delivery and also, when their children are in a perceived danger (pl. *lökötyin*).
Lökoy	stories/news/conversation.
Lölön/lölöte	sour milk.
Malal	the ritual of welcoming a newborn, twins, triplets or quadruplet into this world.
Mama	uncle (brother to one's mother, not one's Father, who is regarded one's father too).
Matai	finger millet (sing. *mötaiywo*).
Meghat	death, also rituals concerning death.
Menchö	a temporary house built in the bush for male initiates.
Mïkulow	heart or soul (pl. *mükulowis*).
Mis	a ritual to ensure the continuation of peace in the community.

Mïkö	calabash (pl. *mken*).
Mogh	a calf.
Monïng	child/children.
Mosïn	a robber (pl. *mosi*).
Mosong	sorghum.
Möngöt	a village or residence.
Möngöy	living, as in staying at a certain place.
Morï	past (unknown or 'unremembered') mistakes.
Mösör	a heifer (pl. *mosortin*).
Mösöwoon	a shepherd, that is, a person who takes care of his own animals (pl. *mosowü*).
Mötworin	a worker or servant who does all work at home, including shepherding (pl. *mötwor*).
Moy	a ritual meant to remedy any form of abnormality.
Mrön	a warrior (pl. *mrën*).
Misïk	a tree stump.
Muma	an oath.
Mutat	the cut, particularly for girls (clitoridectomy).
Mutin	sorcerer (pl. *mutï*).
Mutinto ngal	(lit. cutter of words), an arbitrator or juror.
Mwata	a cleansing ceremony for people caught in adultery. It includes the sinful partners, plus the children of the sinning woman.
Ngala Pökot	(lit. Pökot words) the Pökot language.
Ngaror/nekö	goats (sing. *aran*).
Ngisya	a small grinding stone, used to grind the grains against the bigger one.
Ngokï	sin in general.
Ngoroköin	(pl. *ngorokö*) a heavily armed youth, protecting those who mind the animals and homesteads.
Ngotinyön	proverbs or secret language learned during seclusion after initiation.
Nkuiyon	any kind of vegetables.
Nogsyö	wedding.
Omisyö	(pl. *omisyei*) food in general.

GLOSSARY

Onyöt	in Pökot religion it means a unifying spirit that pervades the entire creation—people, animals, plants, inanimate objects, and even the heavenly bodies. But evangelists today use to refer to spirit of a dead person (pl. *onyötey*).
Ortïn/lïlo	clan.
Orus	general ritual uncleanness that whether it results from a grave or light sin or evil.
Osïl	custom.
Otöp	custom, behavior or manners (pl. *otöptin*).
Otüpo	a small wooden dish used for drinking milk by groups of warriors out in the grazing field (pl. *otupoy*).
Oy	evil, destructive and uncreated spirits.
Pagh	cereals or grains.
Pan	(has many meanings but here used to mean) a common food among the Pökot, made by mixing boiling water with maize flour.
Papo	father (pl. *papotin*).
Parpara	a reconciliation ritual.
Peny	any kind of meat.
Pipö	the people of, the people that belong to a given place.
Pïn	age-group or age-set (pl. *pïnwey*).
Pöchon	a native of Pökotland (pl. *Pökot*).
Pögh	water.
Pöghin	a generous man.
Pöghisyö	greeting, harmony, milking, work or general social affairs/household chores.
Ponïn	a witch (pl. *ponü*).
Pororis	neighborhood, or several ridges together (sing. *poror*).
Ptengöwo	the vigil dance that precedes the ritual of clitoridectomy.
Ptakal	any extraordinary or unnatural sin, like bestiality.
Punyon	an enemy (pl. *püng*).
Rel	new or white.
Rïpin	a night watch, one who watches over the animals and the entire homestead (pl. *ripu*).
Riwoy	the ritual of welcoming a newborn baby into this world.

Rurwö	the static shadow that is projected by any object, animate or inanimate.
Sakit	medicine (sing. *sakitian*).
Sapana	an initiation ceremony between circumcision and (or in place of circumcision) leading to marriage.
Semeut	disease in general (pl. *semeu*).
Seretow	a clan name given to an initiated girl, if she is the third-born in her family.
Sïkïryö	a donkey (pl. *sïkïröy*).
Sikonöt	wealth, which in the traditionally meant a lot of livestock, wives and children.
Sirmyon	a neck chain (pl. *sirim*).
Sirrïp	a misunderstanding that results from a quarrel.
Sokoria	the leaves of the *tuyunwo* (*balanite aegyptica*) tree, used as vegetables.
Somchon	an uncircumcised boy (pl. *somchï*).
Söpon	life or being in good health.
Sorïn	an uninitiated girl (pl. *sori*).
Sorïm	body decorations.
Sörö	thank you, goodbye.
Sulputyon	general lack of self-respect, but mostly in connection with failure to observe dietary regulations.
Sus	grass.
Tamas	a camel (pl. *tamastin*).
Tany	a cow in general (pl. *tich*).
Telengan	tradition, (pl. *telenganen*).
Teta	a particular cow (pl. *tuka*).
Tyankoy	riddles.
Tilet	thunder.
Tilya	an economic relationship or a person with whom one has such a relationship.
Tilyatan (*tilya tany*)	a person helped to attain acceptable wealth status in the society by another.
Tïngän	an industrious woman.

Tïrïimyon	a leather band traditionally worn in the arm, as a wedding ring (pl. *tïrïm*).
Tisö	a ritual meant to cater for an individual's instant needs.
Tororöt	the high most being, God.
Töpogh	the positions of the Morning Star and the Evening Star vis-à-vis each other.
Tum	song, celebration or dance.
Tulwö	anthill (pl. *tulwoy*).
Tuyunwo	a deciduous tree with thin leaves, botanically called *balanite aegyptica*.
Tyos	male initiates (sing. *tyosion*).
Vorverständnis	prejudgment or bias.
Weltanschauung	worldview.
Weri	a young boy, a son or son of (pl. *werko*).
Werkoyon	a seer (pl. *werkoy*).
Wutin	sorcery.
Wutot	the evil eye phenomenon.
Yomöt	wind.
Yim	traditionally means the sky, but Christians also use it to mean heaven, a hitherto unknown concept among the Pökot people.
Yo	mother (pl. *yotin*).
Yïyï	parents (sing. *yïyïn*).

APPENDIX 1

MAPS

Map 1: Location of West Pökot County in Kenya (Hendrix et. al. 1985: 4)

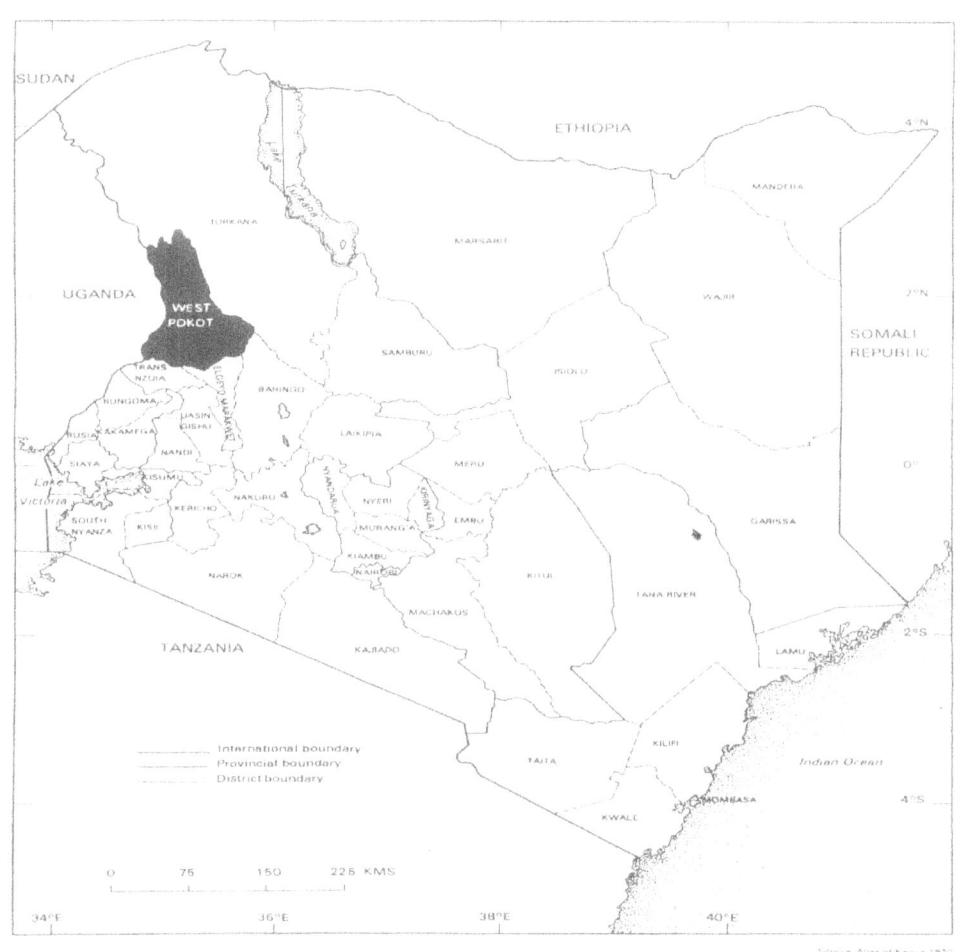

Map 2: Administrative Boundaries of West Pökot (Hendrix et. al. 1985: 5)

MAPS

Map 3: Topography of West Pökot County (Hendrix 1985: 7)

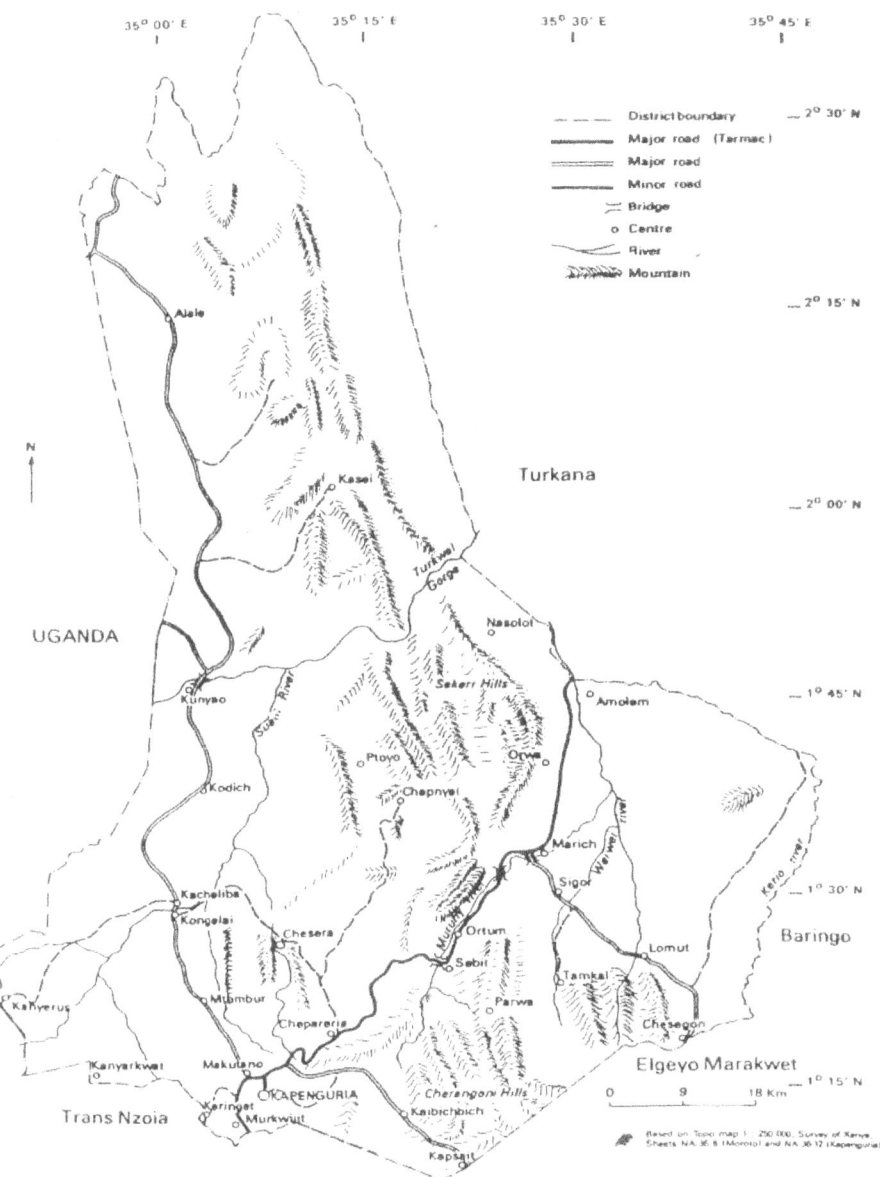

APPENDIX 2

SKETCHES

Sketch 1: Homestead of Pastoralist Pökot with Livestock Enclosure

Sketch 2: Pökot Ritual of Sapana (Visser 1989:181)

APPENDIX 3

PICTURES

Picture 1: Pastoral Pökot Homestead (Kasauria Region)

Picture 2: Pastoral Pökot Huts (Kasauria region)

APPENDIX 3: PICTURES

Picture 3: Agricultural Pökot Homestead (Lelan Region)

Picture 4: Agricultural Pökot Farms

APPENDIX 3: PICTURES

Picture 5: Agricultural Pökot Ranches

Picture 6: Pökot Cattle—*Tupa Pökot* (see *Consolata Fathers,* 11)

APPENDIX 3: PICTURES

Picture 7: Initiated Girls—Chemeri (see *Consolata Fathers*, 16)

Picture 8: Pökot Jewelry (see *Consolata Fathers*, 27)

APPENDIX 3: PICTURES

Picture 9: Pökot Boys Make Weapons (see *Consolata Fathers*, 19)

Picture 10: Traditional Pökot Weaponry

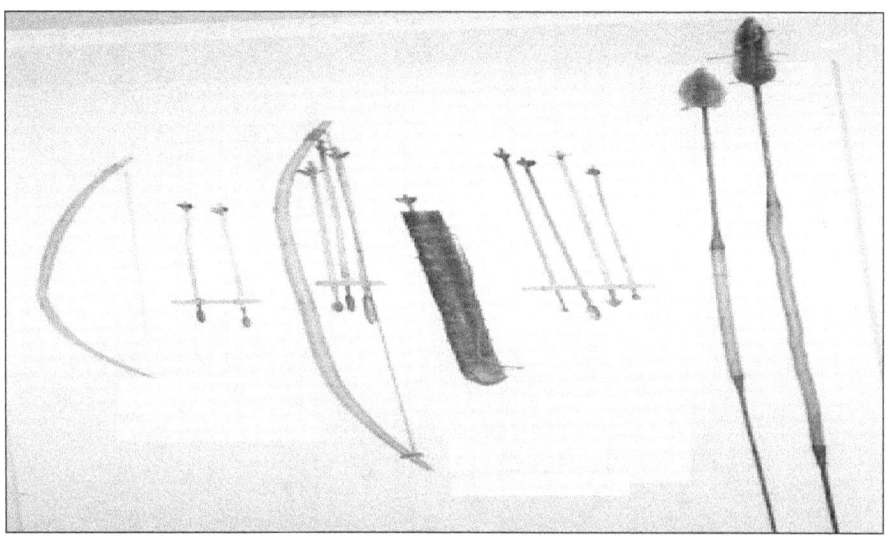

Picture 11: Pökot Mrën going for Lük (see *Consolata Fathers*, 19)

Picture 12: Pökot Mrën after Sapana (see *Consolata Fathers*, 5)

APPENDIX 3: PICTURES

Picture 13: Pökot *Adonga* Dance (see *Consolata Fathers*, 23)

Picture 14: Pökot War Dance (see *Consolata Fathers*, 23)

Picture 15: Pökot Sacrificial Dance (see *Consolata Fathers*, 23)

Picture 16: Reading Animal Entrails and Traditional Basins (*atekertin*) (see *Consolata Fathers*, 25)

APPENDIX 3: PICTURES

Picture 17: Communitarian and Individualistic Artefacts (*ateker nko otüpo*)

Picture 18: More Traditional Artefacts

APPENDIX 3: PICTURES

Picture 19: Traditional Gourds used for Drinking Milk
(see *Consolata Fathers*, 25)

BIBLIOGRAPHY

Aichele, George. *The Play of Signifiers: Poststructuralism and Study of the Bible.* Leiden: Brill, 2016.
Aichele, George, et al., eds. *The Postmodern Bible: The Bible and Culture Collective.* New Haven: Yale University Press, 1995.
Aland, Barbara, and Kurt Aland, eds. *Greek-English New Testament.* 8th edition. Stuttgart: Deutsche Bibelgesellschaft, 1998.
Allison, David B. "Introduction." In *Speech and Phenomena and Other Essays on Husserl's Theory of Signs,* by Jacques Derrida and translated by David B. Allison, 3–16. Evanston: Northwestern University Press, 1973.
Angele, Daniel P. *Pokot Proverbs, Sayings and Idiomatic Expressions.* Kapenguria: Arid and Semi-Arid Lands Development Programme, 1993.
Appiah, Simon K. *Africanness Inculturation Ethics: In Search of the Subject of an Inculturated Christian Ethics.* Frankfurt: Lang, 2000.
Appiah-Kubi, Kofi, and Sergio Torres, eds. *African Theology En Route.* Maryknoll: Orbis, 1979.
Arbuckle, Gerald A. "Inculturation, Not Adaptation: Time to Change Terminology." *Worship* no. 369, 511–52. Eldoret: GABA Publications, 1988.
———. *Earthing the Gospel: An Inculturation Handbook for Pastoral Workers.* London: Chapman, 1991.
Arinze, Francis Cardinal. "Pastoral Attention to Traditional Religions." http://www.vatican.va/roman_curia/pontifical_councils/interelg/documents/rc_pc_interelg_doc_21111993_trad-relig_en.html.
Armellini, Fernando. *Celebrating the Word, Year A: Commentary on the Readings.* Nairobi: Paulines, 1992.
Arrupe, Pedro. Letter to the Whole Society on Inculturation. In *Studies in the International Apostolate of Jesuits,* 7 (June 1978).
Assefa, Hezekias, and George Wachira. *Peacemaking and Democratisation in Africa: Theoretical Perspectives and Church Initiatives.* Nairobi: East African Educational, 1996.
Bahemuka, Judith Mbula. "Social Changes and Women's Attitudes Towards Marriage in East Africa." In *The Will to Arise: Women, Tradition, and the Church in Africa,* edited by Mercy Aamba Oduyoye and Musimbi R. A. Kanyoro, 119–35. New York: Orbis, 1992.
Banana, Canaan S. "The Case for a New Bible." In *"Rewriting" the Bible: The Real Issues: Perspectives from within Biblical and Religious Studies in Zimbabwe,* edited by Isabel Mukonyora et al., 17–32. Religious and Theological Studies 1. Gweru: Mambo, 1993.

Baroja, Tomás Herreros, et al. *Inside the Beehive of Life: A Descriptive Work of the Most Peculiar Traditions of the Pökot People.* Unpublished, 1991.

Barton, Juxton. "Notes on the Suk Tribe of the Kenya Colony." *The Journal of the Royal Anthropological Institute* 51 (1921) 82–89.

Baur, John. *Two Thousand Years of Christianity in Africa: An African History 62–1992.* Nairobi: Paulines, 1994.

Bediako, Kwame. "A Half Century of African Christian Thought: Pointers to Theology and Theological Education for the Next Half Century." *Journal of African Christian Thought* 3 (2000) 5–11.

Beech, Mervyn W. H. *The Suk: Their Language and Folklore.* Reprint. New York: Negro Universities Press, 1969.

Bellagamba, Anthony. "The Role of Cross-Cultural Ministers in Mission and their Formation." *African Christian Studies* 7.1 (1991) 1–28.

———. *Mission and Ministry in the Global Church.* Maryknoll: Orbis, 1992.

Beller, Remy. *Life, Person and Community in Africa: A Way Towards Inculturation With the Spirituality of the Focolare.* Nairobi: Paulines, 2001.

Bennet, John, and Melvin Tumin. *Social Life.* New York: Knopf, 1948.

Betz, Dieter H. "Remarks of the SNTS President." In *Interpreting the New Testament in Africa*, edited by Mary N. Getui et al., 5–8. African Christianity Series. Nairobi: Acton, 2001.

Bible Society of Kenya. *Lökoy cho Karamach cho pö Piich Lapoy.* Nairobi: Bible Society of Kenya, 1988.

Blomjous, Joseph. "Development in Mission Thinking and Practice 1959–1980: Inculturation and Interculturation." *AFER* 22.6 (1980) 393–98.

Boadt, Lawrence. *Reading the Old Testament: An Introduction.* New York: Paulist, 1984.

Boff, Leonardo. *Gott Kommt Früher als der Missionar: Neuevangeli-sierung für eine Kultur des Lebens und de Freiheit.* Düsseldorf: Patmos, 1991.

Boff, Leonardo, and Clodovis Boff. *Introducing Liberation Theology.* 9th ed. Maryknoll: Orbis, 1996.

Botman, Russell. "Who Is 'Jesus Christ as Community' for Us Today? The Quest for Community: A Challenge to Theology in SA." *Journal of Theology in South Africa* 97 (1997) 30–38.

Bowker, John, ed. *The Oxford Dictionary of World Religions.* Oxford: Oxford University Press, 1997.

Brown, Raymond E., et al., eds. *The New Jerome Biblical Commentary.* London: Geoffrey Chapman, 1990.

Bruce, Frederick F. *The Gospel of John: Introduction, Exposition and Notes.* Grand Rapids: Eerdmans, 1983.

Brueggemann, Walter. *The Prophetic Imagination.* Minneapolis: Fortress, 1989.

Bujo, Bénézet. *African Theology: In Its Social Context.* Translated by John O'Donohue. Nairobi: Orbis, 1992.

———. *The Ethical Dimension of Community: The African Model and the Dialogue Between North and South.* Nairobi: Paulines, 1998.

Bultmann, Rudolf. *Kerygma and Myth: A Theological Debate.* New York: Harper & Row, 1961.

Bunnin, Nicholas, and Eric Tsui-James, eds. *The Blackwell Companion to Philosophy.* 2nd ed. Oxford: Blackwell, 2003.

Burke, Joan F. *These Catholic Sisters are all Mamas! Towards the Inculturation of the Sisterhood in Africa, an Ethnographic Study.* Leiden: Brill, 2001.

Byamungu, Gosbert T. M. "Scripture, Tradition(s) and the Church(es): An Ecumenical Quo Vadis." In *Interkulturelle Hermeneutik und Lectura Popular: Neuere Konzepte in Theorie un Praxis*, edited by Silja Joneleit-Oesch and Miriam Neubert, 139–69. Beiheft zur Okumenischen Rundschau 72. Frankfurt an Main: Lembeck, 2002.

Campbell, D. J., and G. H. Axinn. "Pastoralism in Kenya: Obsolete Societies en route to Extinction, or Appropriate Technologies for a Fragile Environment?" http://www.icwa.org/wp-content/uploads/2015/09/DJC-1.pdf.

Caputo, John D. *Radical Hermeneutics: Repetition, Deconstruction and the Hermeneutics Project*. Indianapolis: Indiana University Press, 1987.

Castells, Manuel. *The Internet Gallaxy: Reflections on the Internet, Business, and Society*. Oxford: Oxford University Press, 2001.

Catholic Church. "Rite of Marriage During Mass." In *The Roman Missal*, ##–##. Rome: Libreria Editrice Vaticana, 1998.

Cazeneuve, Jean. *Lucien Lévy-Bruhl*. New York: Harper & Row, 1972.

Chatelion Counet, Patrick. *John, A Postmodern Gospel: Introduction to Deconstructive Exegesis Applied to the Fourth Gospel*. Leiden: Brill, 2000.

Chibuko, Patrick C. "Inculturation as a Method of Evangelization in the Light of the African Synod." *Journal of Inculturation Theology* 3.1 (1996) 31–44.

Cissé, Salmane. "Sedentarization of Nomadic Pastoralists and 'Pastoralization' of Cultivators in Mali." In *The Future of Pastoral Peoples: Proceedings of a Conference Held in Nairobi, Kenya, 4–8 August 1980*, edited by John G. Galaty et al., 318–24. Ottawa: International Development Research Centre, 1981.

Cochrane, James R. *Circles of Dignity: Community Wisdom and Theological Reflection*. Minneapolis: Fortress, 1999.

Conant, Francis P. "A Variable Unit of Physical and Social Space Among the Pokot of East Africa." *American Anthropologist* 67.2 (1965) 429–34.

Consolata Fathers. *Pokot*. Nairobi: Consolata Fathers, 1990.

Croatto, Severino J. *Biblical Hermeneutics: Towards a Theory of Reading as the Production of Meaning*. Translated by Robert R. Barr. Maryknoll: Orbis, 1987.

Culpepper, Alan R. *The Gospel of John and Letters of John*. Nashville: Abingdon, 1998.

DDC. *West Pökot: District Development Plan 1997–2001*. Nairobi: Office of the Vice-President and Ministry of Planning and National Development of the Republic of Kenya, 1997.

De Groot, A. "One Bible and Many Interpretive Contexts: Hermeneutics in Missiology." In *Missiology: An Ecumenical Introduction: Texts and Contexts of Global Christianity*, edited by F. J. Verstraelen et al., 144–56. Grand Rapids: Eerdmans, 1995.

De Jong, Albert. *Mission and Politics in Eastern Africa: Dutch Missionaries and African Nationalism in Kenya, Tanzania and Malawi 1945–1965*. Nairobi: Paulines, 2000.

Denzin, Norman K. *The Research Act in Sociology*. London: Butterworth, 1970.

Derrida, Jacques. *Of Grammatology*. Baltimore: Johns Hopkins University Press, 1976.

———. "Living On: Border Lines." In *Deconstruction and Criticism*, edited by Harold Bloom et al., 75–176. New York: Seabury, 1979.

———. "Letter to A Japanese Friend." In *Derrida and Différance*, edited by David Wood and Robert Bernasconi, ##–##. Warwick Studies in Continental Philosophy. Warwick: Parousia, 1985.

De Wit, Hans. "Through the Eyes of Another: Towards Intercultural Reading of the Bible." In *Interkulturelle Hermeneutik und lectura popular: Neuere Konzepte in Theorie und*

Praxis, edited by Silja Joneleit-Oesch and Miriam Neubert, 19–64. Frankfurt am Main: Lembeck, 2003.

———. "Through the Eyes of Another: Objectives and Back-grounds." In *Through the Eyes of Another: Intercultural Reading of the Bible*, edited by Hans de Wit et al., 3–53. Amsterdam: Institute of Mennonite Studies, 2004.

Dickson, John P. "Gospel as News: εὐαγγελ—from Aristophanes to the Apostle Paul." In *New Testament Studies* 51.2 (April 2005) 212–17.

Dickson, Kwesi A. *Aspects of Religion and Life in Africa*. Accra: Ghana Academy of Arts and Sciences, 1977.

Dietz, A. J. "Development-oriented Geography: Examining the Interface Between Nature's Capacity and Human Livelihood Strategies." *IMWOO Bulletin* 17 (1990) 13–16.

Dietz, Ton. *Pastoralists in Dire Straits: Survival Strategies and External Interventions in a Semi-arid Region at the Kenya/Uganda Border: Western Pokot, 1900–1986*. Nederlandse Geografische Studies 49. Amsterdam: Koninklijk Nederlands Aardrijkskundig Genootschap : Instituut voor Sociale Geografie, Universiteit van Amsterdam, 1987.

Dilthey, Wilhelm. *Selected Writings*. Edited by H. P. Rickman. Cambridge: Cambridge University Press, 1976.

Donders, Joseph G. *Non-Bourgeois Theology: An African Experience of Jesus*. Maryknoll: Orbis, 1985.

Donovan, Vincent J. *Christianity Rediscovered: Twenty-Fifth Anniversary Edition*. 2nd ed. Maryknoll: Orbis, 2004.

Dorr, Donal. *Mission in Today's World*. Maryknoll: Orbis, 2000.

Droogers, André F. "Syncretism: The Problem of Definition, the Definition of the Problem." In *Dialogue and Syncretism: An Interdisciplinary Approach*, edited by Jerald Gort et al., 7–25. Grand Rapids: Eerdmans, 1989.

———. "Changing Culture and The Missiological Mission." In *Fullness of Life for All: Challenges for Mission in Early 21st Century*, edited by Inus Daneel et al., 59–71. Amsterdam: Rodopi, 2003.

Dube, Musa W. "Rereading the Bible: Biblical Hermeneutics and Social Justice." In *African Theology Today*, edited by Emmanuel Katongole, 57–68. Scranton: University of Scranton Press, 2002.

Duraisingh, Christopher. "Syncretism." In *Dictionary of Third World Theologies*, edited by Virginia Fabella and R. S. Sugirtharajah, 192–94. Maryknoll: Orbis, 2000.

Dyson-Hudson, Neville, and Rada Dyson-Hudson. "The Structure of East African Herds and the Future of East African Herders." *Development and Change* 13 (1982) 213–38.

Eboh, Simeon Onyewueke. *African Communalism: The Way to Social Harmony and Peaceful Co-Existence*. Frankfurt: Interkulturelle Kommunikation, 2004.

Éla, Jean-Marc. *My Faith as an African*. Nairobi: Acton, 2001.

Farisani, Elelwani. "Transformation and Renewal in Contemporary Africa (Rom. 12:1–2)." In *Text and Context in New Testament Hermeneutics*, edited by J. N. K. Mugambi and Johannes A. Smit, ##–##. Nairobi: Acton, 2004.

Fasholé, Edward, et al., eds. *Christianity in Independent Africa*. London: Oxford University Press, 1978.

Faulkner, Mark R. J. *Overtly Muslim, Covertly Boni: Competing Calls of Religious Allegiance on the Kenya Coast*. Leiden: Brill, 2006.

Fedders, Andrew, and Cynthia Salvadori. *Peoples and Cultures of Kenya*. Reprint. Nairobi: Transafrica, 1998.

Fish, Stanley. "Literature in the Reader: Affective Stylistics." In *Reader-Response Criticism: From Formalism to Post-Structuralism*, edited by J. P. Tompkins, 70–100. Baltimore: Johns Hopkins University Press, 1980.

Flannery, Austin, ed. *Vatican II Council*. Northport, NY: Costello, 1975.

Gadamer, Hans-Georg. *Truth and Method*. London: Sheed & Ward, 1975.

Galaty, John G., and Dan R. Aronson. "Research Priorities and Pastoralist Development: What Needs to be Done?" In *The Future of Pastoral Peoples: Proceedings of a Conference Held in Nairobi, Kenya, 4–8 August 1980*, edited by John G. Galaty et al., ##–##. Ottawa: International Development Research Centre, 1981.

Galván, María Elena González, and Felipe Miguel Oliveira Resende. *An African Journey Through Mark's Gospel: A Tool for Small Christian Communities*. Nairobi: Pauline, 2000.

Getui, Mary. "Mission of the Church and Concern for the Environment." In *Mission in African Christianity: Critical Essays in Missiology*, edited by A. Nasimiyu-Wasike and D. W. Waruta, 40–58. Nairobi: Acton, 2000.

Getui, Mary N., and Emmanuel A. Obeng. *Theology of Reconstruction: Exploratory Essays*. Nairobi: Acton, 2003.

Goetz, Philip W. "Hermeneutics." In *Encyclopaedia Britannica* 8:###–###.

Goode, William J. *The Family*. Englewood Cliffs: Prentice Hall, 1964.

Goody, John R. *The Power of Written Tradition*. Washington, DC: Smithsonian, 2000.

Graham, Gordon. *The Internet: A Philosophical Inquiry*. London: Routledge, 1999.

Gramsci, Antonio. *Selection from Prison Notebooks of Antonio Gramsci*. London: Lawrence & Wishart, 1983.

Gritti, Jules. *L'expression de la foi dans les cultures humaines*. Paris: Centurion, 1975.

Gyekye, Kwame. "Person and Community in African Thought." In *Person and Community: Ghanaian Philosophical Studies*, edited by Kwasi Wiredu and Kwame Gyekye, 1:101–22. Washington, DC: Council for Research in Values and Philosophy, 1992.

———. *Tradition and Modernity: Philosophical Reflections on the African Experience*. New York: Oxford University Press, 1997.

Haaland, G. "Nomadism as an Economic Career Among the Sedentaries in the Sudan Savannah Belt." In *Essays in Sudan Ethnography: Presented to Sir Edward Evans-Pritchard*, edited by Ian Cunnison and Wendy James, 148–72. London: Hurst, 1972.

Habermas, Jürgen. *The Theory of Communicative Action: The Critique of Functionalist Reason*. Cambridge: Polity, 1981.

Hannerz, Ulf. *Cultural Complexity: Studies in the Social Organization of Meaning*. New York: Columbia University Press, 1992.

Hastings, Adrian. *Church and Mission in Modern Africa*. London: Burns & Oats, 1967.

Healey, Joseph G. *A Fifth Gospel: The Experience of Black Christian Values*. Maryknoll: Orbis, 1981.

Healey, Joseph, and Donald Sybertz. *Towards An African Narrative Theology*. Nairobi: Paulines, 1997.

Hegel, Georg Wilhelm Friedrich. *The Philosophy of History*. New York: Dover, 1956.

Heidegger, Martin. *Being and Time*. Translated by John Macquarrie and Edward Robinson. London: SCM, 1962.

Hendrix, Hubert, Michael S. Mwangi and Niiels de Vos. *District Atlas: West Pokot*. Kapenguria: Arid and Semi-Arid Lands Development Programme, 1985.

Hillman, Eugene. *Polygamy Reconsidered: African Plural Marriages and the Christian Churches*. Maryknoll: Orbis, 1975.

Hjort, Anders. "A Critique of 'Ecological' Models of Pastoral Land Use." *Nomadic Peoples* 10 (1982) 11–27.

Hoebel, Adamson E. *Anthropology: The Study of Man.* 4th ed. New York: McGraw-Hill, 1972.

Hofstede, Geert. *Culture's Consequences: Comparing Values, Behaviors, Institutions and Organizations Across Nations.* 2nd ed. Thousand Oaks: Sage, 2001.

Holy, L. "Property Differentiation and Pastoralism in an Agricultural Society: the Berti." In *Property, Poverty and People: Changing Rights in Property and Problems of Pastoral Development*, edited by P. T. W Baxter and Richard Hogg, 206–16. Manchester: University of Manchester, 1987.

Hopkins, Dwight N. *Introducing Black Theology of Liberation.* Maryknoll: Orbis, 1999.

Imbo, Samuel Oluoch. *An Introduction to African Philosophy.* Lanham: Rowman & Littlefield, 1998.

Jahnke, Hans E. *Livestock Production Systems and Livestock Development in Tropical Africa.* Vauk: Kieler Wissenschaftsverlag Vauk, 1982.

John Paul II, Pope. "The Gospel and African Cultures." *Africa Ecclesial Review* 22.4 (1980) 222–28.

———. "Letter to Cardinal Agostino Casaroli, Secretary of State, 20th, May." *L'Osservatore Romano*, June 28, 1982.

———. *Redemptoris Missio.* Nairobi: Paulines, 1991.

———. *Ecclesia in Africa.* Nairobi: Paulines, 1995.

———. "'Post-Synodal Apostolic Exhortation' in Africa Faith and Justice Network." In *The African Synod: Documents, Reflections, Perspectives.* Maryknoll: Orbis, 1996.

Johnson, Barbara. *The Critical Difference: Essays in the Contemporary Rhetoric Reading.* Baltimore: John Hopkins University Press, 1982.

Jongeneel, Jan. *Philosophy, Science and Theology of Mission in the 19th and 20th Centuries: A Missiological Encyclopedia, Parts I and II.* Frankfurt am Main: Lang, 1995.

Jonker, Louis. "Towards a 'Communal' Approach for Reading the Bible in Africa." In *Interpreting Old Testament in Africa*, edited by Mary N. Getui et al., 77–88. Nairobi: Acton, 2001.

Journal of African Marxists. *Independent Kenya.* London: Zed, 1982.

Kalilombe, Patrick A. "Preface." In *Bantu Wisdom: A Collection of Proverbs*, ##–##. Kachebere: Privately printed, 1969.

———. Spirituality in the African Perspective. In *Paths of African Theology*, edited by Rosino Gibellini, 115–35. Maryknoll: Orbis, 1994.

———. *Doing Theology at the Grassroots: Theological Essays from Malawi.* Gweru: Mambo, 1999.

———. "Praxis and Methods of Inculturation in Africa." In *Theology of Inculturation in Africa Today: Methods, Praxis and Mission*, edited by Patrick Ryan, 38–48. Nairobi: CUEA, 2004.

Kamma, F. C. *Dit Wonderlijke Werk.* Oegstgeest: Hendrik Kraemer Instituut, 1976.

Kapello, James P. W. *Keneta Kegh Ngala Pökot.* Nairobi: Regal, 1985.

Kaunda, Kenneth. *A Humanist in Africa.* New York: Nashville, 1966.

Kenyatta, Jomo. *Facing Mount Kenya.* Reprint. Nairobi: Kenway, 1999.

Kim, Caleb Chul-Soo. *Islam among the Swahili in East Africa.* Nairobi: Acton, 2004.

Kimmerle, Heinz. *Mazungumzo: Dialogen tussen Afrikaanse en Westerse filosofieën.* Amsterdam: Boom, 1995.

Kirwen, Michael C. *African Widows: An Empirical Study of the Problems of Adapting Western Christian Teachings on Marriage to the Leviratic Custom for the Care of Widows in Four Rural African Societies.* Maryknoll: Orbis, 1979.

———. *The Missionary and the Diviner.* Maryknoll: Orbis, 1987.

K'Otienoh, Cosmas A. R. "Formation of Priests as Agents of Evangelization for the Church-As-Family of God (I)." *Africa Ecclesial Review* 41.4–6 (1999) 248–57.

Kraft, Charles H. *Christianity in Culture: A Study in Dynamic Biblical Theologizing in Cross-Cultural Perspective.* Maryknoll: Orbis, 1979.

Kroeber, Alfred L., and Clyde Kluckhohn. *Culture: A Critical Review of Concepts and Definitions.* New York: Vintage, 1952.

Kronenburg, Josephus B. M. *Empowerment of the Poor: A Comparative Analysis of Two Development Endeavours in Kenya.* Amsterdam: Koninklijk Instituut voor de Tropen, 1986.

Kuhn, Thomas S. *The Structure of Scientific Revolution.* 2nd ed. Chicago: University of Chicago Press, 1970.

Küng, Hans. *Theologie im Aufbruch: eine ökumenische Grundlegung.* München: Piper, 1987.

Levoratti, Armando J. "How to Interpret the Bible." In *The International Bible Commentary*, edited by William R. Farmer et al., 9–35. Collegeville: Liturgical, 1998.

Loba-Mkole, Jean-Claude. "Bible Translation and Inculturation Hermeneutics." In *Biblical Texts & African Audiences*, edited by Ernst R. Wenland and Jean-Claude Loba-Mkole, 37–58. Nairobi: Acton, 2004.

Locheng, Callisto. "Praxis and Methods of Inculturation in Africa: A Response." In *Theology of Inculturation in Africa Today: Methods, Praxis and Mission*, edited by Patrick Ryan, 49–56. Nairobi: CUEA, 2004.

Lo Liyong, Taban. *Culture is Rutan.* Nairobi: Longman, 1991.

Lord, Albert B. *The Singer of Tales.* Cambridge: Harvard University Press, 1964.

Lumbala, Francoise Kabasele. "Africans Celebrate Jesus Christ." In *Paths of African Theology*, edited by Rosino Gibellini, 78–94. Maryknoll: Orbis, 1994.

Luzbetak, Louis J. *The Church and Cultures: New Perspectives in Missiological Anthropology.* 8th ed. Maryknoll: Orbis, 1998.

Magesa, Laurenti. "Overview of 100 Years of Catholicism in Kenya." *AFER* 32.1 (1990) 42–58.

———. "From Private to Popular Biblical Hermeneutics." In *The Bible in African Christianity*, edited by Hannah W. Kinoti and John M. Waliggo, Nairobi: Acton, 1997.

———. *African Religion: The Moral Traditions of Abundant Life.* Nairobi: Paulines, 1998.

———. "Reconstructing the African Family." In *Marriage and Family in African Christianity*, edited by Andrew A. Kyomo and Sahaya G. Selvan, Nairobi: Acton, 2004.

———. *Anatomy of Inculturation: Transforming the Church in Africa.* Nairobi: Paulines, 2004.

Mair, Lucy. *An Introduction to Social Anthropology.* Oxford: Clarendon, 1965.

Malinowski, Bronislaw. *Argonauts of the Western Pacific.* London: Routledge, 1922.

Mall, Runus, A. *Philosophie im Vergleich der Kulturen: Interkulturelle Philosophie, ein neue Orientierung.* Darmstadt: Wissenschaftliche Buchgesellschaft, 1995.

Maluleke, Sam Tinyiko. "Half A Century of African Christian Theologies: Elements of the Emerging Agenda for Twenty First Century." *Journal of Theology for Southern Africa* 99 (1997) 4–23.

Mana, Kä. *Théologie Africain Pour Temps de Crise: Christianisme et Reconstruction de l'Afrique.* Paris: Karthala, 1993.

Manus, Chris Ukachukwu. "Methodological Approaches in Contemporary African Biblical Scholarship: The Case of West Africa." In *African Theology Today*, edited by Emmanuel Katongole, 1–21. Scranton: University of Scranton Press, 2002.

———. *Intercultural Hermeneutics in Africa: Methods and Approaches*. Nairobi: Acton, 2003.

Marty, Martin E., and R. Scott Appleby. *The Glory and the Power: The Fundamentalist Challenge to the Modern World*. Boston: Beacon, 1992.

Masolo, Dismas A. *African Philosophy in Search of Identity*. Edinburgh: Edinburgh University Press, 1994.

Mayor, Frederico and Jérôme Bindé. *The World Ahead: Our Future in the Making*. London: Zed, 2001.

Mazrui, Ali A. *Africa's International Relations: The Diplomacy of Dependency and Change*. Boulder: Westview, 1977.

———. *The African Condition: A Political Diagnosis*. London: Heinemann, 1980.

———. *The Africans: A Triple Heritage*. London: BBC, 1986.

Mbiti, John S. *New Testament Eschatology in an African Background: A Study of the Encounter Between New Testament Theology and African Traditional Concepts*. Oxford: Oxford University Press, 1971.

———. "Theological Impotence and the Universality of the Church." In *Mission Trends No. 3: Third World Theologies*, edited by Gerald H. Anderson and Thomas F. Stransky, 6–18. New York: Paulist, 1986.

———. *African Religions and Philosophy*. Reprint. Nairobi: East African Educational, 1995.

McGarry, Cecil. "Preface." In *Inculturation: Its Meaning and Urgency*, 7–9. Nairobi: St. Paul, 1986.

McGrath, Michael. and Grégoire Nicole. *Africa: Our Way to Preach God's Word: Book 2 - Year A*. Alton: Redemptorist, 1988.

McKenzie, John L. *Dictionary of the Bible*. New York: Macmillan, 1965.

Menkiti, Ifeanyi A. "Person and Community in African Traditional Thought." In *African Philosophy, An Introduction*, edited by Richard A. Wright, 171–80. Lanham: University Press of America, 1984.

Meyerhoff, Elizabeth L. *The Socio-Economic and Ritual Roles of a Pokot Woman*. Cambridge: Lucy Cavendish College Press, 1981.

———. "The Threatened Way of Kenya's Pokot People." *National Geographic*, January 1982.

Míguez, Néstor. "Reading John 4 in the Interface Between Ordinary and Scholarly Interpretation." In *Through the Eyes of Another: Intercultural Reading of the Bible*, edited by Hans de Wit et al., 334–47. Amsterdam: Institute of Mennonite Studies, 2004.

Mojola, Aloo Osotsi. *150 Years of Bible Translation in Kenya 1844–1994: An Overview and Reappraisal*. Nairobi: Bible Societies of Kenya, 1995.

———. "Foreword." In *Biblical Texts & African Audiences*, edited by Ernst R. Wenland and Jean-Claude Loba-Mkole, i–iv. Nairobi: Acton, 2004.

Mojola, A. O. and E. R. Wendland (2003). Scripture in the Era of Translation Studies. In T. Wilt (ed). *Bible Translation: Frames of Reference*. Manchester: St. Jerome.

Mosala, Itumeleng J., (1989). *Biblical Hermeneutics and Black Theology of Liberation in South Africa*. Grand Rapids, Michigan: Eerdmans.

———. (1996). Race, Class, and Gender as Hermeneutical Factors in the African Independent Churches' Appropriation of the Bible, *Semeia*, 73, 43–57.

Moynihan, Robert (1986). *Recent Imagining: Interviews with Harold Bloom, Geoffrey Hartmen, Paul DeMan, J. Hillis Miller*. New Haven: Shoe String Press.

Mpagi, Peter Wassa (2002). *African Christian Theology: In the contemporary context.* Kisubi: Marianum Publishing Company Limited.

Mudimbe, V. Y., (1988). *The Invention of Africa: Gnosis, Philosophy, and the Order of Knowledge.* Bloomington and Indianapolis: Indiana University Press.

———. (1994). *The Idea of Africa.* Bloomington and Indianapolis: Indiana University Press.

———. (1997). *Tales of Faith: Religion as Political Performance in Central Africa.* London: The Athlone Press.

Mugambi, J. N. K., (1995). *From Liberation to Reconstruction: African Christian Theology After the Cold War.* Nairobi: East African Educational Publishers Ltd.

———. (2001). Foundations for an African Approach to Biblical Hermeneutics. In: Mary Getui et al (eds). *Interpreting the New Testament in Africa.* Nairobi: Acton Publishers, 9-29.

———. (2002). *Christianity and African Culture.* Nairobi: Acton Publishers.

———. (2003). *Christian Theology and Social Reconstruction.* Nairobi: Acton Publishers.

Mukonyora, Isabel et al (eds) (1993). Introduction. In I. Mukonyora et al (eds). *"Rewriting" the Bible: The Real Issues.* Gweru: Mambo Press, x-xii.

Mulago, Vincent., (1962). *Un Visage Africaine du Christianisme: L'union vitale Bantu face à l'unité ecclésiale.* Paris: Presence Africaine.

Museveni, Yoweri K., (1996). Science and Technology as a Solution to Africa's Underdevelopment. In T. Abdul-Raheem (ed). *Pan Africanism: Politics, Economy and Social Change in the Twenty-First Century.* London: Pluto Press. 193-197.

Mwalye, Hellen (1999). Formation of Women Religious. In *Africa Ecclesial Review* l 41 (4, 5 & 6). Eldoret: AMECEA Gaba Publications, 267-281.

Mwaura, Philomena (2004). African Independent Churches: Their Role and Contribution to African Christianity. In Kwame Bediako et al (eds). *A New Day Dawning: African Christians Living the Gospel.* Zoetermeer: Uitgeverij Boekencentrum, 98-115.

Nangoli, Musamaali (1986). *No More Lies About Africa: Here's The Truth From An African.* East Orange, New Jersey: African Heritage Publishers.

Nasaka, Olivia (1996). Women and Taboo: A Case Study in Buganda. In R. A. Musimbi et al (eds). *Groaning in Faith: African Women in the Household of God.* Nairobi: Acton Publisher, 163-167.

Nathanson, Stephen (2001). *An Eye for An Eye? The Immorality of Punishing by Death.* 2nd ed. New York: Rowman & Littlefied Publishers, Inc.

Ndegwah, David (2004). The Pökoot: Christianity and Cultural Heritage. In Kwame Bediako et al (eds). *A New Day Dawning: African Christians Living the Gospel; Essays in Honour of Dr. J.J. (Hans) Visser.* Zoetermeer: Uitgeverij Boekencentrum, 75-95.

———. (2006). Understanding the Nomads: The Role of Culture in Evangelisation. In Francesco Pierli et al (eds). *The Pastoralists: A Challenge to Churches, State, Civil Society.* Nairobi: Paulines Publications Africa.

Ndung'u, Nahashon (1997). The Bible in an African Independent Church. In Hannah W. Kinoti and John M. Waliggo (eds). *The Bible in African Christianity.* Nairobi: Acton Publishers.

Ngona, Dieudonné (2003). Inculturation as a Face of African Theology Today. In Patrick Ryan (ed). Faces of African Theology. Nairobi: CUEA Publications.

Njenga, John (1974). Customary African Marriage. In *AFFER*, Vol. XVI, Nos. 1&2. Eldoret: GABA Publications.

Nkemnkia, M., (1999). *African Vitalogy. Step Forward in African Thinking.* Nairobi: Paulines Publications.

Nkéramihigo, Théoneste (1986). Inculturation and the Specificity of the Christian Faith. In *Inculturation: Its Meaning and Urgency.* Nairobi: St. Paul Publications - Africa. 67–74.

Nthamburi, Zablon and Douglas Waruta (1997). Biblical Hermeneutics in African Instituted Churches. In Hannah W. Kinoti and John M. Waliggo (eds). *The Bible in African Christianity.* Nairobi: Acton Publishers.

Nyamiti, Charles (1989). African Christologies Today. In J.N.K. Mugambi and Laurenti Magesa (eds) *Jesus in African Christianity: Experimentation and Diversity in African Christology.* Nairobi: Initiatives Ltd, 17–39.

Nyasani, Joseph (1991). The Ontological Significance of 'I' and 'We' in African Philosophy. In *African Christian Studies* 7 (1). Nairobi: C.H.I.E.A., 52–62.

Nyerere, Julius K., (1967). *Freedom and unity.* Dar es Salaam: Oxford University Press.

———. (1968). *Freedom and socialism.* Dar es Salaam: Oxford University Press.

Obeng, Emmanuel Adow (1997). The use of Biblical Critical Methods in Rooting the Scriptures in Africa. In Hannah W. Kinoti and John M. Waliggo (eds). *The Bible in African Christianity.* Nairobi: Acton Publishers.

O'Brian, P. T., (1995). *Gospel and Mission in the Writings of Paul: An Exegetical and Theological Analysis.* Grand Rapids, MI: Baker Books.

Ochieng'-Odhiambo, F., (1997). *African Philosophy: An Introduction,* 2nd edit. Nairobi: Consolata Institute of Philosophy.

Odell-Scott, David W., (2000). Deconstruction. In A. K. M. Adam (ed). *Handbook of Postmodern Biblical Interpretation.* St. Louis, Missouri: Chalice Press, 55–61.

Oduyoye, Mercy A., (1998). Family: An African Perspective. In William R. Farmer et al (eds). *The International Bible Commentary.* Collegeville, Minnesota: The Liturgical Press, 289–292.

Oeming, Manfred (1998). *Biblische Hermeneutik: Eine Einführung.* Darmstadt: Wissenschaftliche Buchgesellschaft.

Ojil, Benard C., (1999). Formation of Priests as Agents of Evangelization for the Church-As-Family of God (II). In *AFER,* Vol. l 41, Nos. 4, 5 & 6. Eldoret: Gaba Publications, 257–266.

Okure, Teresa (1990). Inculturation: Biblical/Theological Bases. In Teresa Okure, Paul van Tiel et al (eds). *Inculturation of Christianity in Africa* (Spearhead, 111–114). Eldoret: Gaba Publications, 112–114.

———. (1993). Feminist Interpretations in Africa. In E. S Fiorenza (ed) *Searching the Scriptures: A Feminist Introduction.* New York: Crossroad, 76–85.

———. (2000). I Will Open my Mouth in Parables (Matt. 13: 35): A Case Study of a Gospel-based Biblical Hermeneutics. In *New Testament Studies,* Vol. 46, 445–463.

Olson, David R., (1977). From Utterance to Text: The Bias of Language in Speech and Writing. In *Harvard Educational Review,* 47: 3.

Ong, Walter J., (1968). Knowledge in Time. In Walter J. Ong (ed). *Knowledge and the Future of Man.* New York: Holt, Rinehart & Winston.

Onwubiko, Oliver A., (2000). *The Church as the Family of God (Ujamaa): In the Light of Ecclesia in Africa.* Nsukka: Fulladu Publishing Company.

Opler, Morris E., (1945). Themes as Dynamic Forces in Culture. In *American Journal of Sociology,* No. 53, 198–206.

Orobator, A. E., (2000). *The Church as Family: African Ecclesiology in Its Social Context.* Nairobi: Paulines Publications Africa.

Oruka, Odera H., (1991). *Sage Philosophy: Indigenous Thinkers and Modern Debate on African Philosophy.* Leiden: E. J. Brill.

Palmer, G. B., (1996). *Towards a Theory of Cultural Linguistics.* Austin: University of Texas Press.

Patterson, David (1969). The Pökot of Western Kenya 1910-1963: The Response of a Conservative People to a Colonial Rule. In *Syracuse Occasional Paper*, 53.

Paul VI, Pope (1967). *On the Development of Peoples.* Nairobi: Paulines Publications Africa.

———. (1969a). To the Inaugural 1969 SECAM, Kampala. In Teresa Okure, Paul van Tiel et al (eds). *Inculturation of Christianity in Africa* (Spearhead, 111-114). Eldoret: Gaba Publications, 33-34.

———. (1969b). Closing Discourse to All-Africa Symposium. In *Gaba Pastoral Paper,* 7. Kampala: Gaba Pastoral Institute, 50-51.

———. (1973). *Address to the College of Cardinals.* Rome: AAS 65.

———. (1977). *Evangelii Nuntiandi (On Evangelization in the Modern World).* New York: Liturgical Press.

p'Bitek, Okot (1970). *African Religions in Western Scholarship.* Kampala: East African Literature Bureau.

———. (1983). On Culture, Man and Freedom. In H. Odera Oruka and D. A. Masolo (eds). *Philosophy and Culture.* Nairobi: Bookwise Ltd.

Pearsall, Judy (ed.). (1999). *Concise Oxford Dictionary*, 10th ed. New York: Oxford University Press, Inc.

Perera, Rienzie (2000). Fundamentalism. In Virginia Fabella and R. S. Sugirtharajah (eds) *Dictionary of Third World Theologies.* Maryknoll, New York: Orbis Books, 90.

Plapan, Lilian J. C., (2000). *Secret Sweet: Female Genital Mutilation in West Pökot, Kenya.* MA Thesis. London: University of Reading.

Plato (1992). *Republic.* Trans by G.M.A. Grube. Indianapolis: Hacket Publishing Company, Inc.

Platvoet, Jan & Van Rinsum (2003). Is African Incurably Religious? Confessing and Contesting an Invention. In *Exchange* Vol 32:2, April.

Pontifical Biblical Commission (1993). *The Interpretation of the Bible in the Church.* Rome: Libreria Editrice Vaticana, 117-119.

Pontifical Council for Culture (1999). *Towards A Pastoral Approach to Culture.* Vatican: Pontifical Council for Culture.

Popper, Karl R., (1962). *The Logic of Scientific Discovery*, third impression. London: Hutchinson & Co., (Publishers) Ltd.

———. (1966). *The Open Society and Its Enemies: the Spell of Plato*, Vol. 1. London: Routledge & Kegan Paul.

Propaganda Fide (1907). *Collectanea S. Congregationis de Propaganda Fide seu Decreta, instructiones, rescripta, pro apostolicis missionibus.* Romae: Ex Typographia Polyglotta.

Pui-lan, Kwok (1999). Hearing and Talking: Oral Hermeneutics of Asian Women. In James A. Scherer and Stephen B. Bevans (eds). *New Directions in Mission and Evangelization.* Maryknoll, New York: Orbis Books, 76-90.

Rahner, Karl (ed). (1986). *Encyclopedia of Theology: A Concise Sacramentum Mundi,* reprint. London: burns & Oats.

Ranger, Terence (1983). The Invention of Tradition in Colonial Africa. In E. Hobsbawm and T. Ranger (eds). *The Invention of Tradition.* Cambridge: Cambridge University Press.

Ricoeur, Paul (1970). Qu' est-ce qu'un texte? Expliquer et Comprendre. In R. Bubner et al (eds). *Hermeneutik und Dialektik.* Tübingen: Mohr, 181–200.

———. (1983). *Hermeneutics and the Human Sciences.* Cambridge: Cambridge University Press.

Rippin, Andrew (1993). *Muslims: Their Religious Beliefs and Practices.* London and New York. Routledge.

Rorty, Richard (1995). From Formalism to Poststructuralism. In *The Cambridge History of Literary Criticism*, Vol.8. Cambridge: Cambridge University Press.

Russell, Letty M., (1985). *Feminist Interpretation of the Bible.* Oxford: Basil Blackwell.

Rutten, Marinus M. E. M., (1992). *Selling Wealth to Buy Poverty: the Process of the Individualization of Landownership Among the Maasai Pastoralists of Kajiado District, Kenya, 1890–1990.* Saarbrücken-Fort Lauderdale: Verlag Breitenbach Publishers.

Ryan, Patrick (2003). Seven Theses on Inculturation: A Response to "Inculturation as a Face of African Theology Today. In Patrick Ryan (ed). *Faces of African Theology.* Nairobi: CUEA Publications.

Ryle, Gilbert (1955). *The Concept of Mind*, reprint. London: Hutchinson & Co (Publishers) Ltd.

Saifulin, Murad and Richard R. Dixon (1984). *Dictionary of Philosophy.* New York: International Publishers.

Sandford, S., (1983). *Management of Pastoral Development in the Third World.* London: John Wiley & Sons, Overseas Development Institute.

Sarpong, Peter K., (1975). Christianity Should be Africanized not Africa Christianized. In *AFER*, Vol. 20. Eldoret: AMECEA Gaba Publications, 325.

———. (2002). *Peoples Differ: An Approach to Inculturation in Evangelisation.* Accra: Sub-Saharan Publishers.

Sartorius, Peter (1975). *Churches in Rural Development: Guidelines for Action.* Geneva: Commission on the Church's Participation in Development, WCC.

Schillebeeckx, Edward (1967). Naar een Katholiek Gebruik van de Hermeneutiek: Geloofsindentiteit in het Herinterpreteren van het Geloof. In H. van der Linde and H.A.M. Fiolet (eds). *Geloof bij Kenterend Getij.* Roermond, 78–116.

Schineller, Peter (1992). Inculturation and the Issue of Syncretism: What is the Real Issue? In Justin S. Ukpong et al (eds). *Evangelization in Africa in the Third Millenium: Challenges and Prospects.* Port Harcourt: CIWA Press.

Schleiermacher, F. D. E., (1977). *Hermeneutics: The Handwritten Manuscripts.* Ed. by H. Kimmerle. Missoula, MT: Scholars' Press.

Schneider, Harold K., (1955). The Moral System of the Pakot. In Vergilius Ferm (ed). *Encyclopedia of Morals.* New York: Philosophical Library. 403–409.

———. (1959). Pokot Resistance to Change. In W.R. Bascom and M.J. Herskovits (eds). *Continuity and Change in African Cultures.* Chicago. 144–167.

———. (1981). Livestock as Food and Money. In John G. Galaty et al (eds). *The Future of Pastoral Peoples: Proceedings of a Conference held in Nairobi, Kenya, 4–8 August 1980.* Ottawa: International Development Research Centre.

Schreiter, Robert J., (1985). *Constructing Local Theologies.* Maryknoll, New York: Orbis Books.

———. (1997). *The New Catholicity: Theology Between the Global and the Local.* Maryknoll, New York: Orbis Books.

Schwartz, S. & H. J. Schwartz (1985). Nomadic Pastoralism in Kenya – Still a Viable System of Production? In: *Quarterly Journal of International Agriculture*, Vol. 24, and No.1.

SECAM, (2005). *The Bible: Source of Christian Life and Vocation.* Takoradi: St. Francis Press Ltd.

Senghor, Leopold S. (1964). *On African Socialism.* Trans. Mercer Cook. New York: Praeger.

Segovia, Fernando F., (2000a). *Decolonizing Biblical Studies: A View from the Margins.* Maryknoll, New York: Orbis Books.

———. (2000b). Deconstruction. In Virginia Fabella and R. S. Sugirtharajah (eds). *Dictionary of Third World Theologies.* Maryknoll, New York: Orbis Books, 66–67.

Serequeberhan, Tsenay (ed). (1991). *African Philosophy: The Essential Readings.* New York: Paragon House.

———. (1994). *The Hermeneutics of African Philosophy: Horizon and Discourse.* New York: Routledge.

Shingledecker, Ken (1982). *Unreached Peoples of Kenya Project: Pokot Report.* Nairobi: Daystar Communications.

Shorter, Aylward (1977). *African Christian Theology: Adaptation or Incarnation?* Maryknoll, New York: Orbis Books.

———. (1987). New Attitudes to African Culture and African Religions. In *Towards African Christian Maturity.* Nairobi: St. Paul Publications – Africa, 15–28.

———. (1998). *African Culture: An Overview.* Nairobi: Paulines Publications Africa.

Sihna, C. and Jansen de López K., (2000). Language, Culture and the Embodiment of Spatial Cognition. In *Cognitive Linguistics* 11 (1/2), 17–41.

Silverman, David (2000). *Interpreting Qualitative Data: Methods for Analysing Talk, Text and Interaction*, 2nd ed. London: SAGE Publications.

Smith, Joseph H. and William Kerrigan (eds) (1984). *Taking Chances: Derrida, Psychoanalysis and Literature.* Baltimore: John Hopkins University.

Smith Nicolas H., (1997). *Strong Hermeneutics: Contingency and Moral Identity.* London: Routledge.

Smith, Simon E., (2002). Forward. In Fabien E. Bougala (2002). *Christianity Without Fetishes: An African Critique and Recapture of Christianity.* Hamburg, London: Lit Verlag Münster.

Speckman, M. T., (2001). *The Bible and Human Development in Africa.* Nairobi: Acton Publishers.

Spradley, James M., (1972). Foundations of Cultural Knowledge. In: J. M. Spradley, *Culture and Cognition.* New York: Chandler Publishing Company, 3–38.

Spradley, James P., (1980). *Participant Observation.* New York: Holt, Rinehart and Winston, Inc.

Stenger, Fritz (2001). *White Fathers in Colonial Africa – A Critical Examination of V. Y. Mudimbe's Theories on Missionary Discourse in Africa.* Hamburg: Lit.

Sterk, Jan P. and Margaret J. Muthwi (2004). The Publishing of Christian Scriptures in Africa: Sociolinguistic Challenges. In Ernst R. Wenland and Jean-Claude Loba-Mkole (eds). *Biblical Texts & African Audiences.* Nairobi: Acton Publishers, 150–170.

Sundermeier, Theo (1998). *The Individual and Community in African Traditional Religions.* Hamburg: LIT.

Tanner, Kathryn (1997). *Theories of Culture: A New Agenda for Theology.* Minneapolis: Fortress Press.

Tanner, Ralph and Frans Wijsen (1993). Christianity in Usukuma: A Working Misunderstanding. In *Neue Zeitschrift für Missionwissenschaft*, 49, 3, 177–193.

Taylor, John V., (1963). *The Primal Vision: Christian Presence Amid African Religion*. London: SCM Press Ltd.

Taylor, March C., (1982). *Deconstructing Theology*. New York: The Crossroad Publishing Company and Scholars Press.

Tempels, Placide (1969). *Bantu Philosophy*. Paris: Presence Africaine.

Tescaroli, Cirillo (1979). The Karapokot, A Waiting People. In *Worldvision*, Vol. 30. No. 3.

The Nation Media Group (2000). Editorial: Lessons Kenya can Learn from Ghana. *Daily Nation*, 8 December. Nairobi: The Nation Media Group.

Thiselton, Anthony C., (1993). *The Two Horizons: New Testament Hermeneutics and Philosophical Description*. Carlisle: Grand Rapids.

———. (1996). *Interpreting God and the Postmodern Self: On Meaning, Manipulation and Promise*. Edinburgh: T&T Clark Ltd.

———. (2002). *A Concise Encyclopedia of the Philosophy of Religion*. Oxford: Oneworld Publications.

Tibaldo, Mariano (2006). The Challenges to the Survival of Pastoral Peoples. In Francesco Pierli et al (eds). *The Pastoralists: A Challenge to Churches, State and Civil Society*. Nairobi: Paulines, 163–179.

Tihagale, B. and I. Mosala (eds) (1986). *Hammering Swords into Plough Shares: Essays in Honor of Desmond Tutu*. Johannesburg: Skotaville Publishers.

Tonnies, F., (1935). *Gemeinschaft und Gesellschaft*. Leipzig: Buske.

Torres, S. and V. Fabella (1976). *The Emergent Gospel: Theology From the Underside of History. Papers from the Ecumenical Dialogue of Third World Theologians*. Maryknoll, New York: Orbis Books.

Towa, Marcien (1971). *Essai sur la problematique philosophique dans l'Afrique actuelle*. Yaounde: Editions CLE.

Turnbull, Colin (1972). *The Mountain People*. London: Pimlico, Random House.

Turner, Victor W., (1969). *The Ritual Process, Structure and Anti-Structure*. Chicago: Chicago University Press

———. (1974). *Dramas, Fields and Metaphors*. Ithaca.

Ukpong, Justin S., (1984). *African Theologies Now a Profile*, (Spearhead 80). Eldoret: Gaba Publications.

———. (1995). Rereading the Bible with African eyes: Inculturation and Hermeneutics. In *Journal of Theology for Southern Africa*, 91, 3–14.

———. (1999). Developments in Biblical Interpretation in Modern Africa. In *Missionalia*, 27(3) (November), 313–329.

———. (2001). Bible Reading with a Community of Ordinary Readers. In Mary Getui et al (eds). *Interpreting the New Testament in Africa*. Nairobi: Acton Publishers, 188–212.

———. (2004). Contextual Hermeneutics: Challenges and Possibilities. In J. N. K. Mugambi and Johannes A. Smit (eds). *Text and Context in New Testament Hermeneutics*. Nairobi: Acton Publishers, 22–55.

UNESCO/UNEP/FAO (1979). *Tropical Grazing Land Ecosystems: A State-of-Knowledge Report*. Paris: Unesco Natural Resources Research no. XIV.

United Bible Societies (1989). *The New Testament in Today's Greek Version*. Athens: United Bible Societies.

Uzukwu, Elochukwu E., (1994). Inculturation and the Liturgy (Eucharist). In Rosino Gibellini (ed). *Paths of African Theology.* Maryknoll, New York: Orbis Books.

Van Binsbergen, Wim (1999a). 'Cultures do not exist': Exploding Self-evidences in the Investigation of Interculturality. In Wim van Binsbergen (2003). *Intercultural Encounters: African and Anthropological Lessons Towards a Philosophy of Interculturality.* Münster: Lit Verlag, 459–522.

———. (1999b). Some Philosophical Aspects of Cultural Globalisation: With Special Reference to Mall's Intercultural Hermeneutics. In Wim van Binsbergen (2003). *Intercultural Encounters: African and Anthropological Lessons Towards a Philosophy of Interculturality.* Münster: Lit Verlag, 375–394.

Van der Veen, Roel (2004). *What Went Wrong With Africa: A Contemporary History.* Amsterdam: KIT Publishers.

Van der Ven, Johannes A., (1993). *Practical Theology.* Kampen: Kok Pharos Publishing House.

Van der Ven, Johannes A. et al (2004). *Is there a God of Human Rights? The Complex Relationship Between Human Rights and Religion: A South African Case.* Leiden. Boston: Brill.

Van der Walt, B. J., (1997). *Afrocentric or Eurocentric? Our Task in a Multicultural South Africa.* Potchefstroom: Potchefstroom University of Christian Higher Education.

Van Sanders, E., (2001). *A Missiological Analysis of Traditional Religion Among the Pokot People of East Africa.* PhD Dissertation. Fort Worth: Southwestern Baptist Theological Seminary.

Vansina, J., (1961). *De la Tradition Orale. Essai de Méthode Historique.* Tervuren: Musée Royal de l'Afrique Centrale.

Van Steenbergen, Gerrit (1999). Translating "Sin" in Pökoot. In *The Bible Translator.* Vol. 42, No. 4, 431- 437.

Vähäkangas, Auli (2004). The Crisis of Christian Marriage. In Andrew A. Kyomo and Sahaya G. Selvan (eds). *Marriage and Family in African Christianity.* Nairobi: Acton Publishers.

Verstraelen, Frans J., (1976). *Tradition and Reconstruction in Mission: A Report of IAMS Conference at San José, Cost Rica.* Leiden: Interuniversity Institute for Missiological and Ecumenical Research (IIME).

———. (1993). The Real Issues Regarding the Bible: Summary, Findings and Conclusions. In I. Mukonyora et al (eds). *"Rewriting" the Bible the Real Issues.* Gweru: Mambo Press. 263–289.

Verstraelen, Frans J. et al (eds). (1995). *Missiology: An Ecumenical Introduction. Texts and Contexts of Global Christianity.* Grand Rapids, Michigan: William B. Eerdman Publishing Company.

Villa-Vicencio, Charles (1986). *Between Christ and Caesar: Classic and Contemporary Texts on Church and State.* Grand Rapids, Michigan: William B. Eerdmans Publishing Company.

———. (1992). *Theology of Reconstruction: Nation-Building and Human Rights.* Cambridge: Cambridge University Press.

Visser, Johannes Jacobus (1982). *Towards a Missionary Approach Among the Pökot.* Zaandijk: The Netherlands.

———. (1983). We Follow Someone who Speaks the Truth. In Wout van den Bor (ed). *The Art of the Beginning: First Experiences and Problems of Western Expatriates in Developing Countries with Special Emphasis on Rural Development and Rural Education.* Wageningen: PUDOC.

———. (1989). *Pökoot Religion*. Oegstgeest: Hendrik Kraemer Instituut.

Wachege, P. N., (1992). *African Women Liberation: A Man's Perspective*. Nairobi: Industrial Printing Works Ltd.

———. (2001). Inculturation and Salvation Within the African Context. In *AFER*, Vol. 43 Nos.1&3. Eldoret: Gaba Publications, 28–39.

Waliggo, John Mary (1986). Making a Church that is Truly African. In *Inculturation: Its Meaning and Urgency*. Nairobi: St. Paul Publications – Africa, 11–30.

———. (1990). The African Clan as the True Model of the African Church. In J. N. K. Mugambi and Laurenti Magesa (eds). *The Church in African Christianity: Innovative Essays in Ecclesiology*. Nairobi: Initiative Printers.

———. (1994). The Church as Family of God and Small Christian Communities. In *AMECEA Documentation Service*, No. 429, 1 December.

———. (1997). From Private to Popular Biblical Hermeneutics. In Hannah W. Kinoti and John Mary Waliggo (eds). *The Bible in African Christianity*. Nairobi: Acton Publishers.

Wa Ngugi, Njoroge J., (2002). *Creation in "The Catechism of the Catholic Church": A Basis for Catechesis in Post-Colonial Africa*. Ph.D. Dissertation. Nairobi: Paulines Publications Africa.

Warigi, Gitau (2000). Kenya: Tribalism Is Not High Art, It Is Bad Politics, *Daily Nation*, 24 December. Nairobi: The Nation Media Group.

Wa Thiong'o, Ngugi (1986). *Decolonising the Mind: The Politics of Language in African Literature*. Nairobi: East African Educational Publishers.

Welbourn, F. B. and B. A. Ogot (1966). *A Place to Feel at Home: A Study of Two Independent Churches in Western Kenya*. London: OUP.

West, Cornel (1988). *Prophetic Fragments*. Grand Rapids, Mich.: William B. Eerdmans.

West, Gerald O., (1997). On the eve of an African Biblical Studies: Trajectories and Trends. In Journal *of Theology for Southern Africa*, 99, 99–115.

———. (2001). *Biblical Hermeneutics of Liberation: Modes of Reading the Bible in the South African Context*. Pietermaritzburg: Cluster Publications.

———. (2002). Negotiating With the "White Man's Book": Early Foundations for Liberation Hermeneutics in Southern Africa. In Emmanuel Katongole (ed). *African Theology Today*. Scranton: The University of Scranton Press, 23–56.

———. (2005). African Biblical Hermeneutics and Bible Translation. In Jean-Claude Loba-Mkole and Ernst R. Wendland (eds). *Interacting With Scriptures in Africa*. Nairobi: Acton Publishers.

West, Gerald O. and Musa W. Dube (2000). *The Bible in Africa: Transactions, Trajections and Trends*. Leiden: Brill.

Whitaker, Philip (1964). *Political Theory and East African Problems*. London: Oxford University Press.

Wijsen, Frans (1993). *There is Only One God*. Ph.D. Dissertation. Kampen: Uitgeverij Kok.

Wijsen, Frans and Ralph Tanner (2000). *Seeking a Good Life*. Nairobi: Paulines Publications Africa.

———. (2002). *'I am Just a Sukuma': Globalization and Identity Reconstruction in Northwest Tanzania*. Amsterdam: Editions Rodopi, B.V.

Wilson, Monica (1951). *Good Company: A study of Nyakyusa Age-Villager*. London, New York, Toronto: Oxford University Press.

Wiredu, Kwasi (1980). *Philosophy and an African Culture*. Cambridge: Cambridge University Press.

———. (1992). Problems in Africa's Self-Definition n the Contemporary World. In Kwasi Wiredu and Kwame Gyekye (eds). *Person and Community: Ghanaian Philosophical Studies I,* Washington D.C.: The Council for Research in Value and Philosophy, 59–70.

———. (2005). African Philosophy, Anglophone. In Edward Craig (ed). *The Shorter Routledge Encyclopedia of Philosophy.* London and New York: Routledge, 8–9.

Zani, Agnes P., (1997). The Family in its African Socio-Cultural Context. In Patrick Ryan (ed). *The Model of "Church-as-Family": Meeting the African Challenge.* Nairobi: The Catholic University of Eastern Africa.

Zinkuratire, Victor (2001). Morphological and Syntactical Correspondences Between Hebrew and Bantu Languages. In Mary N. Getui et al (eds). In *Interpreting Old Testament in Africa.* Nairobi: Acton Publishers, 217–226.

———. (2004a). Inculturation the Biblical Message in Africa: Current Trends. In *African Christian Studies*, Vol. 20, No. 1. Nairobi: CUEA Publications, 41–70.

———. (2004b). Life Context of the Interpretation. In Daniel Patte et al (eds). *Global Bible Commentary.* Nashville: Abingdon Press, 186–194.

Zvarevashe, I. M., (1993). Racist Missionaries: An Obstacle to Evangelization in Africa. In *AFER,* Vol. 35, No. 2. Eldoret: Gaba Publications.

Internet Sources

Aichele, George (2004). *Poststructuralists.* http://www.yale.edu/yup/bible/poststructuralits.html Accessed on 04/04/2007.

Hayes, Nicky (2000). Psychology. http://www.canisius.edu/~gallaghr/her.html Accessed on 27/07/2018.

SECAM (2007). http://www.sceam-secam.org/english/documents/bicam.rtf Accessed on 02/04/2007.

Sovereign Order of Malta (1048). http://www.smom-za.org/cidsa.htm Accessed on 27/07/2018.

Oral Sources

Chebet, Imelda is a 33-year-old nurse at Kacheliba Health Centre and a committed leader in her SCC. The interview was held in Kacheliba Parish on 26/07/2002.

Cheboryot, George is a priest in the Diocese of Eldoret and a long-serving teacher of the scriptures, who has taught in both Nairobi and Tindinyo theological seminaries and has immense wealth of biblical studies. The interview was held in Eldoret on 16/08/2002.

Chelolombai, popularly known as Kama Kasilokot, is a 75-year-old lady, resident of Mnagei Location in Kapenguria Division who refused to have her girls undergo female circumcision and now they are all educated and employed by the government. The interview was held in Tartar Parish on 28/04/2002.

Chelomut, Stella is a 29-year-old nursery school teacher at Chepnyal, within Sook Location.

Chesoli, Ben is a pastoral instructor at Mitume Catechetical and Pastoral Centre, specialised on SCCs. He has worked there for 15 years and is aged 65 years old. The interview was carried out on 21/06/2002.

Davies, Collin was the Bishop of Ngong Catholic Diocese but retired after reaching the mandatory retirement age of 75 years, and has now retired at Asumbi Sisters Convent, where he also serves a chaplain. The remarks were made during a canonical visit to Tindinyo Theological Seminary on 22/04/1994.

Dillon, Michael is a 72-year-old Kiltegan missionary who has worked in West Pökot for forty-three years. He is currently the parish priest of Chepnyal Catholic Parish in Sook location. The interview was carried out on 16/06/2002.

Gichuki, John is a retired teacher, who has worked in West Pökot all his life and has now settled in the county (at Keringet) upon his retirement. He has held various positions in the church leadership but is now a respected elder in his SCC. The interview was held at Kirenget in Tartar Parish on 26/04/2002.

Guirao, Antonio is a 70-year-old Comboni Missionary Priest in Bendera Parish and delivered this homily during a SCC Mass for Mavuno (yearly harvest) on 26/04/2002.

Hanley, Terry is a 60-year-old lay missionary from Australia and has worked in Africa all his life. At the time of this interview, he was working at the Mitume Catechetical and Pastoral Centre. Now he has retired and opened an AIDS counselling house, where he also lives. The interview was carried out on 24–07–2002.

Iregi, George Mambura was a 25-year-old seminarian at the time we carried out this field research, but he has since been ordained a priest in the Catholic Diocese of Eldoret. The interview was carried out on 10/08/2002

Jansania, Jacob is a 30-year-old resident of Tamugh Sub-location in Sook Location and a trained primary school teacher, who still waits to be deployed when the government starts employing teachers. 26/06/2002

Kalele, Matthew is a former head catechist, in Chepareria Parish and he has also worked in Sigor Parish. He now works for the Justice and Peace Office in Chepareria Division. The interview was held on 20/05/2002.

Kapeluk, Simeon is a 30-year-old catechist, who has since joined politics and was elected the councillor of Krich Ward in Sook Location but lost in subsequent elections. 18/06/2002

Kirwa, Felistus (not her real name) is a 35-year-old member of one of the SCCs regarded as very progressive in West Pökot. The interview was held in Kacheliba Parish on 10/04/2002.

Korir, Cornelius was, until his death, the bishop of the Catholic Diocese of Eldoret, and is said to have dismissed the seminarian without an expulsion letter or a stated reason for the refusal to ordain him. He was, however, buried in the church as a sign of being a man of God and eulogized as a peace maker during the burial ceremony.

Kotomei, Albino is a 56-year-old resident of Kacheliba and active Church member. He is also involved in various research projects with different foundations from the Netherlands. The interview was held in Kacheliba Parish on 26/07/2002.

Lokeliman, Simeon is a teacher at Empokech Primary School and also the chairman of the Parish Council in Chepnyal Parish, within Sook Location. 17/06/2002

Lopuke, Elijah is a 35-year-old teacher at Nasokol Secondary School, but he comes from Amakuriat Parish in Alale. He worked as a catechist for several years before going for higher education. The interview was carried out at Nasokol Secondary School on 18/05/2002.

McDonald, Fintan (not his real name) is a missionary priest, who has worked in West Pökot for a relatively short period compared to his compatriots. The interview was held in Sigor Parish on 26/05/2002.

Meriekeren, Pius is a 55-year-old catechist and committed leader of the SCC in his outstation. The interview was carried out in his home, at Chepareria on 15/05/2002.

Mugeni, Peter was a 22-year-old Consolata seminarian who was thrown out of the institution, at the Novitiate stage, without any explanation or recompense for the time spent or anything to go and start his new life with. The interview was held on 15/08/2002.

Mulumba, Matthias was the priest in-charge of Kabichbich Parish. He is 40 years old and he has successfully worked with the Pökot people for the past 5 years. The interview was carried out on 14/04/2002. The 'social ramifications' that Mulumba is talking about is the hostility that we will talk about later in this book.

Murunga, Patrick (not his real name) is a diocesan priest from Kakamega Diocese, working in West Pökot. He holds an MA degree in biblical theology from the Catholic University of Eastern Africa. The interview was held in Sigor Parish on 16/05/2002

Nakameti, Daniel is 54 years old, ordained Catholic Priest in Kitale Diocese, who worked as the rector at Mother of Apostles Seminary, Eldoret. 30/04/2002

Nekesa, Teresa is a 51-year-old leader of the SCC in Kacheliba Parish and also works as a cook to the Sisters in their convent. The interview was held on 20/07/2002.

Ngomba, Cosmas is 52-year-old priest, who worked as the father-in-charge of Sinar Parish, in West Pökot, at the time of the research. He has since left West Pökot and taken up a new assignment as the Vicar General of Kitale Diocese. The interview was carried out at the institute on 21/05/2002.

Njenga, Patrick (not his real name) is a young priest, who was recently posted to Chepareria Parish in West Pökot but finds things to be very different from the rest of Kenya, as he puts it. The interview was held on 30/05/2002.

Nkomo, Bongani was a 36-year-old religious brother of CMM, from Zimbabwe, but decided to leave after what he thought was a lot of hypocrisy in the church. The interview was held in Nairobi on 14/08/2002

Pierli, Francesco (not his real name) is a Comboni Missionary, who has worked in West Pökot. He is currently the Parish Priest of Kacheliba Parish. The interview was held on 07/07/2002.

Pkech, Luka is a 55-year-old committed Christian, who also works for the County Government as the County Chief Executive in charge of environment. The interview was held in Chepnyal Parish on 05/06/2002

Plapan, Lilian is a 69-year-old head of SETAT Women Group that promotes women's rights, by fighting against retrogressive cultural practices, particularly against clitoridectomy in West Pökot County. The interview was held in Bendera Parish on 26/04/2002.

Samali, Jacob is a 32-year-old, successful educated farmer and businessman in Chepareria Division. He is one of the few committed Christian and regular churchgoers. The interview was held in Chepareria Parish on 15/05/2002.

Staples, Leo is a 75-year-old Kiltegan (also known as St. Patrick) Missionary from Ireland. He was in-charge of Sigor Parish at the time the interview was held, but has now retired at Kibomet Parish, out of West Pökot, after serving in many other parishes, for 40 years. The interview was held in Sigor Parish on 26/05/2002.

Teko, Anna is a 54-year-old chairperson of the Parish council at Kacheliba, is basically, who is a livestock farmer and only works part time as a catechist. The interview was held in Kacheliba Parish on 06/07/2002.

Tonyirwone, Jackson is a 25-year-old student nurse at Ortum Nursing Hospital. The interview was held in Sigor Parish on 27/05/2002.

Tulel, Alexander is a 58-year-old businessman, who has also worked as a catechist for a long time and later on served as the chairman of the Parish Council in Chepareria. The interview was held on 09/05/2002.

Ywalaita, Benedict is a school teacher and has served the Catholic Church in various capacities, particularly in Chepnyal Parish, where he hails from. The interview was held on 10/06/2002.

Zinkuratire, Victor is a professor of scriptures at the Catholic University of Eastern Africa (CUEA), and he has published a lot of articles and books on inculturation and biblical hermeneutics in Africa. The interview was held at CUEA on 26/08/2002.

Simiyu, Rajab a 50-year-old catechist in Tartar Parish. The interview was held on 10/04/2002.

Index

abnormal, 182
abominable crime, 139, 294
abominable sins, 182
abuse, 291, 299, 312
academic, 6, 11
academic circles, 17
academic decorations, 310
academic discipline, 17, 19
academic disciplines, 274, 277
academic function, 17
academic harmonisation, 309
academic hermeneutical debate, xiv
academic hermeneutics, 8
academic insight, 76
academic priests, 251
academic research, 237
academic type of theology, 22
adaptation, 13, 37, 60
adequate hermeneutical approach, 36, 100
adequate hermeneutics, 99
ad infinitum, 62
administration system, 123
adopt, xv, 53, 262, 264
adopted, 17, 111, 208
adoption, 155, 209, 261, 271
adultery, 98, 150, 156, 315
a fifth gospel, 43, 62
Africa-in-the-bible approach, 68
African, 2, 4, 7, 48, 58, 78, 82, 83, 90, 98, 99, 213, 253, 278, 280, 282, 288, 339, 340, 341, 342, 344, 346, 348, 349
African adherents, 93
African anthropology, 80
African aspirations, 39
African audiences, 43, 110, 219, 339, 340, 345
African behaviour, 82
African bible, 65
African bible commentary, 224
African biblical hermeneutics, xiv, 4, 33, 70, 348

African biblical scholars, 70, 256
African biblical scholarship, 67, 69, 310, 340
African biblical studies, 348
African biblical translation, 70
African bishops, 60, 283
African categories, 36
African Catholics, 52
African Christian, 2, 10, 270, 272, 283, 334, 339, 341
African Christian communities, 63
African Christianity, 1, 57, 60, 97, 100, 263, 337, 341, 347, 348
African Christians, 10, 42, 49, 50, 57, 61, 65, 73, 218, 341
African Christian studies, 41, 79, 334, 342
African Christian theology, 270
African Christian theology, 37, 53, 270, 341, 345
African Christian thought, 283, 334
African christologies, 2, 61, 342
African church, 36, 96, 99, 251, 286, 348
African clan system, 99
African clergy, 217
African colleagues, 303
African communalism, 2, 94, 336
African communal life, 85
African communitarianism, 287, 289
African (communitarian) way, 11, 306
African communities, 83, 262, 272, 286
African community, 283
African concept of a community, 100
African concept of communitarianism, 36
African condition, 78, 340
African context, 18, 36, 42, 67, 68, 69, 71, 72, 76, 97, 187, 310, 348
African continent, 36, 51, 60, 88, 270, 278, 279
African contributors, 230
African cosmology, 272
African countries, 25, 52, 68, 87, 88
African critique, 1, 38, 345

353

African cultural experiences, 253
African cultural expression, 54
African cultural values, 63
African cultural way of life, 70
African culture, xiv, 2, 33, 36, 39, 45, 53, 54, 55, 56, 57, 59, 61, 65, 68, 72, 78, 79, 85, 89, 90, 91, 100, 101, 177, 228, 277, 278, 304, 345
African cultures, 302, 306, 338
African customs, 51
African deities, 136
African discourse, 279
African ecclesiology, 95, 343
African environmental review, 296
African ethnic groups, 49
African experience, 2, 29, 273, 336, 337
African extended family system, 88
African families, 99
African family, 49, 95, 96, 97, 98, 99, 339
African frame of reference, 69
African friends, 267
African gnosis, 9
African gospel church, 218, 261
African hermeneutics, vii, 36, 63, 69, 70, 78, 100, 305
African hermeneutic theory, 4, 6, 14
African histories, 280
African history, 2, 334
African house, 61
African humanism, 84
African identity, 81, 282
African individualism, 287
African institutions, 268
African interpretation, 63
Africanization, 37
African language, 223
African languages, 80, 218
African liberation struggle, 3
African life, 245
African life and culture, 93
African men and women, 63
African mental categories, 100
African model, 2, 334
African modernity, 90
African names, 55
African narrative theology, 71, 95, 337
African nationalism, 56, 335
African nations, 86
African (or Pökot) culture, 278
African people, 48, 89, 93, 95, 157, 279
African peoples, 84, 93
African perspective, 2, 307, 338
African philosophers, 80

African philosophy, 3, 15, 33, 79, 80, 81, 82, 83, 91, 92, 93, 100, 274, 279, 338, 340, 342, 343, 345
African plural marriages, 99, 337
African point of view, 234
African politicians, 297, 298
African priests and sisters, 215
African problems, 84, 99, 348
African Protestants, 52
African reader, 2, 234
African reading of the Bible, 61
African religion, 40, 48, 49, 54, 68, 78, 79, 99, 339, 346
African religions, 2, 40, 78, 81, 340, 343, 345
African religious beliefs, 279
African religious experience, 68
African Renaissance, 37
African scholars, 29, 271, 279
African sense, 7
African sense of community, 94
African sense of family, 95
African setting, 12
African set-up, 232
African situation, 65, 67, 92, 93, 96, 97, 272, 286
African social context, 2
African socialism, 85
African societies, 87, 208
African society, 52, 80, 83, 85
African soil, 37, 61, 67, 72, 93, 94
African standards, 288
African studies, 22
African synod, 40, 94, 335, 338
African terms, 61
African theologians, 1, 33, 37, 59, 63, 251
African theological colleges and seminaries, 65
African theologies, 251
African theology, 2, 8, 37, 39, 45, 46, 61, 67, 68, 93, 94, 100, 333, 334, 336, 338, 339, 340, 341, 344, 347, 348
African theology today, 67, 340
African thought, 11, 12, 38, 82, 337
African thought patterns, 82
African thought system, 81
African traditional community, 262
African Traditional Concepts, 340
African traditional practices, 59
African traditional religions, 45, 48, 75, 345
African traditional religious practice, 59
African traditional societies, 86
African traditional values, 90
African traditional ways, 115
African traditions, 40, 68, 92
African views, 132
African vision, 279

African vitalogy, 83, 135, 342
African widows, 98, 267, 339
African women theologians, 69
African world-view, 70
African worldview, 79, 192, 277
African writers, 297
Africans, xv, 11, 39, 46, 49, 50, 53, 54, 56, 58, 63, 65, 67, 68, 71, 77, 78, 79, 80, 81, 83, 89, 92, 93, 94, 97, 148, 208, 221, 252, 282, 287, 300, 301, 306, 340
Africans are communitarian, 288, 289
Africans are notoriously religious, 132, 135
Africans are notoriously secular, 135
Africans in the Bible, 68
Africans' reactions, 279
against Africans, 55
against colonialism, 84
age, xvi, 140, 145, 147, 170, 173, 175, 181, 261, 316
age and gender, 297
age grade, 125, 129
age group, 192
age mate, 188
age mates, 129, 148, 151
age of the Reformation, 47
age-old practice, 142, 290
age-old tradition, 58, 292
age-old traditions, 42, 160, 260, 268
age-set, 80, 129, 140, 162, 170, 179, 180, 225, 265, 316
age-set members, 171
age-sets, 129, 167, 178, 179, 201, 209, 311
age-set system, 129
aggiornamento, 37, 45
agricultural Pökot, 135, 148, 152
AIDS, 159, 237, 270, 350
Akũrinũ, 57
alien concept, 5, 80
Allison, 276, 333
amat, 180, 181
AMECEA, 95, 236, 253, 341, 344, 348
amoros, 179, 181, 180, 311
anachronistic, 40, 93
ancestor, 196, 294
ancestors, 54, 79, 89, 114, 126, 132, 133, 134, 137, 138, 142, 143, 145, 149, 162, 169, 175, 196, 209, 245, 265, 287, 292, 314
Anglican Church, 212, 218
animal grazing, 118
animate, 317
annihilation, 275
anthill, 132, 146, 318
anthropological contempt, 56
anthropologists, 8, 56, 74, 82, 111, 208, 268

anthropology, 9, 56, 75, 79, 103, 273, 305
anthropology and theology, 21, 309
anthropou-logos, 9
anti-colonial struggle, 84
anyïn, 139, 150
anyïn sopon, 151
anyïn tany, 140
apartheid, 5, 270, 300
apologetic philosophy, 80
Appiah-Kubi, 42, 93, 333
approach to inculturation, 42, 49
appropriate cultural dress, 103
ara psör, 131, 311
ara tipïn, 131, 311
arawa, 131, 137, 169, 265, 311
Arbuckle, 37, 50, 309, 333
archaeological deconstruction, 279
Arinze, 48, 49, 333
Armellini, 230, 232, 333
Arrupe, 37, 333
asis, 131, 137, 169, 181, 265, 313
aspect of hermeneutics, 4
Assefa, 87, 333
assimilation, 39
ata popolos, 168
ata rop, 168
ateker, 171
authentically Africans, 39

balanite aegyptica, 125, 318
bandit, 199, 311
banditry, 283, 291
Baptist Church, 218
Baroja, 102, 147, 154, 334
Barton, 110, 334
basic community, 26
basic human values, 41
basic mission of the church, 16
Baur, 2, 5, 51, 52, 53, 57, 59, 334
Beech, 102, 103, 110, 111, 334
behavioural sources, 34, 165, 166
being, 60, 99, 110, 286
being sent, 20
belief system, 115, 136, 152
belong, 8, 170, 294
biased hermeneutics, 5, 289, 309
bible in Africa, 2, 33, 61, 63, 100, 283, 338, 348
bible in African Christianity, 2, 10, 342
bible interpretation in Africa, 67, 69
bible interpreters, 5
bible scholars, 45, 224
bible sharing, 27, 28, 31, 71, 197, 198, 200, 202, 204, 225, 230, 231
bible sharing experience, 28

bible sharing sessions, 10, 34, 65, 102, 164, 248
bible text, xiv, xv, 9, 22, 34, 44, 165, 193, 197, 221, 226, 258, 259, 263, 289, 298
bible translation, 65, 70, 214, 217, 218, 219, 224
bible translation project, 218, 224
biblical apostolate, 64
biblical apostolate movement, 65
biblical hermeneutical solution, 297
biblical hermeneutics, xiii, xiv, 2, 3, 4, 5, 6, 7, 10, 17, 34, 62, 63, 65, 67, 68, 70, 99, 165, 228, 284, 301, 310, 335, 336, 339, 340, 341, 342, 348
biblical hermeneutics in Africa, 62
biblical history of salvation, 68
biblical inculturation, 63
biblical interpretation, 4, 17, 63, 68, 69, 301, 346
biblical interpretations, 17
biblical pericope, 235
biblical scholarship, 310
biblical texts, xiii, 20, 176
biblical theology, 255
biblical understanding, 134
biblical values, 10, 300
biblische hermeneutik, 4, 17, 342
Binsbergen, 74, 76, 347
birth of hermeneutics, 7
birth of Jesus, 247
bishop, 239, 240, 245, 251, 254, 298
bishop of Rome, 46
black-belly, 56
black communities, 270
black stomach, 157
black theology, 68
black theology, 5, 37, 69, 338, 340
blessing ritual, 293
Blomjous, 2, 37, 334
Boff, 8, 267, 290, 308, 334
bottom-up, 21
bounded wholes, 304
bride price, 123
brigand, 199, 290, 311
British colonialists, 146
brotherhood of humankind, 57
Bultmann, 17, 334

calabash, 111, 315
calf, 119, 121, 122, 315
capitalistic system, 252
Caputo, 16, 335
casual relationship, 160
catechist, 27, 114, 143, 146, 161, 189, 200, 206, 226, 234, 236, 237, 238, 239, 243, 244, 246, 248, 256, 258, 260, 299, 314, 350, 351, 352

catechists, 25, 27, 30, 50, 164, 168, 193, 211, 214, 215, 216, 225, 226, 231, 236, 238, 239, 241, 242, 245, 248, 249, 256, 260, 262, 299
categories, 4, 16, 31, 32, 62, 75, 83, 85, 104, 112, 136, 155, 156, 166, 167, 170, 283, 299
categories and concepts, 220
category-mistake, 85, 136
Catholic Church, 12, 37, 44, 52, 56, 59, 98, 218, 219, 230, 236, 257, 260, 263, 270, 272, 348
Catholic evangelisation, 217
cattle ear marks, 127
cattle ownership, 118
cattle raiding, 113, 114, 119, 131, 139, 143, 199, 218, 229, 234, 281, 290, 291, 292, 293
cattle raids, 145, 155, 294
cattle rustling, xvi, 29, 40, 104, 106, 129, 139, 142, 168, 175, 176, 191, 199, 213, 221, 226, 229, 234, 243, 259, 264, 283, 290, 291, 294, 296, 304, 309
ceremony, 112, 127, 148, 152, 155, 156, 191, 311, 312, 313, 314, 315, 317
challenge of modernity, 157
challenge to theology, 272, 334
changing African context, 64
chaos, 14
charity-dependency, 108
Chatelion-Counet, 7, 274, 287, 288, 289, 335
chawïr, 152, 261
chelolos, 233, 311
chelolosion, 311
chemnyokoria, 127
chemowos, 311
chepelaleyo, 311
chepsakitian, 135, 137, 311
chepsakitis, 134, 168, 311
chi, 132, 312
child of nature, 56
chi nyo oror, 123
chipöt, 154, 312
chö, 312
chorin, 312
Christian brotherhood, 294, 309
Christian communities, 47, 96, 269
Christian community, 9, 95, 237, 239, 283, 308
Christian community leaders, 64
Christian evangelisation, 61
Christian experience, 40
Christian faith, 5, 39, 43, 54, 62, 78, 307
Christian family, 96
Christian fundamentalists, 44
Christianity, xiv, xvi, 1, 2, 7, 10, 19, 29, 38, 39, 43, 44, 45, 48, 49, 53, 54, 58, 59, 60, 61,

62, 77, 78, 97, 99, 104, 105, 135, 174, 176,
  197, 198, 201, 212, 213, 214, 217, 224,
  245, 247, 259, 268, 269, 271, 277, 278,
  279, 280, 281, 284, 286, 294, 295, 297,
  306, 334, 335, 336, 339, 341, 342, 343,
  344, 345, 346, 347, 348
Christianity and culture, 78
Christianity and humanism, 47
Christianity in Africa, 56
Christianity Rediscovered, 4, 336
Christian life, 50, 60, 165, 199, 203, 225, 230
Christian love, 57
Christian mission, 51
Christian Pöchon, 135
Christian religion, 44, 72
Christian religious experience, 219
Christians, xv, 27, 29, 31, 33, 34, 40, 45, 53, 58,
  62, 104, 108, 135, 138, 142, 147, 160, 167,
  174, 191, 196, 197, 198, 212, 215, 218,
  230, 236, 237, 238, 239, 240, 242, 244,
  245, 246, 247, 249, 252, 255, 256, 257,
  258, 259, 260, 262, 263, 268, 290, 291,
  294, 298, 299, 301, 309, 341
Christian scriptures, 43, 110, 345
Christian setting, 204, 227
Christian theology, 61, 196, 217, 341
Christian thought, 40
Christian tradition, 307
Christian worldview, 104
church as communion, 95
church as family, 94, 95
church-as-family, 34, 94, 95, 96, 97, 98, 349
church-as-family model, 100
church communities, 95
church community, 255
church elder, 146
church hierarchy, 46, 62
church in Africa, xiv, 39, 45, 95, 99
circumcise, 59
circumcision, 54, 59, 124, 127, 136, 145, 148,
  151, 155, 162, 191, 206, 207, 312, 317,
  349
circumcision controversy, 59
clan, 49, 71, 114, 122, 123, 124, 125, 126, 127,
  129, 140, 151, 155, 163, 167, 172, 173,
  177, 178, 184, 192, 200, 229, 233, 243,
  247, 262, 265, 282, 298, 311, 312, 316,
  317
clan-brothers, 266
clans, 109, 118, 119, 126, 148, 172, 179, 209, 285,
  295
cleansing, 155, 179, 182, 314, 315
cleansing ceremonies, 150, 156
cleansing ceremony, 142, 145, 155, 156

cleansing ritual, 124, 155, 191
clear-cut distinction, 167, 263, 266, 280, 303
climatical conditions, 167
clitoridectomy, 124, 127, 148, 152, 158, 213, 259,
  260, 286, 315, 316
closed frontiers, 213
closed system, 251
close relationship, 119, 204
cognitive structure, 282, 308
cohabitation, 98
coherent group work., 30
colonial, 54, 213, 280
colonial administrator, 213
colonial Africa, 208
colonial authority, 213
colonial chiefs, 52
colonial counterpart, 51
colonial counterparts, 53
colonial encounter, 208
colonial endeavour, 53
colonial enterprise, 51
colonial era, 110, 240
colonial experience, 280
colonial government, 54, 124, 133, 213, 263
colonial heritage, 53
colonial hosts, 53
colonial invasion, 306
colonialism, xiv, 36, 51, 55, 92, 100, 213, 278, 280
colonialists, 52, 77, 110, 213
colonial masters, 246
colonial occupation, xiv
colonial past, 93
colonial readings/interpretations, 65
colonial rule, 146, 272
colonial settlers, 100
colonial yoke, 68, 83
colonisation, 51, 55
colonisers, 36, 52, 300
committed interpretation, 69
common, 44, 113
common aspect, 167
common beliefs, 75
common cultural values, 115
common enemy, 12
common experiences, 246
common focus, 74, 75
common food, 316
common genealogy, 293, 294
common goal, 12, 129
common good, 134
common grinding place, 173
common grinding stone, 171
common interests, 166
common neighbourhood, 7

357

common ornamental design, 129
common ownership, 294
common practice, 168, 234
common property, 85
common sense truths, 91
common tradition, 291
common use, 171
common weal, 189
communal, 209, 266, 293
communal affair, 142, 293
communal amulets, 171
communal Approach, 2, 283, 338
communal approval, 191
communal aspect, 242
communal aspirations, xiv
communal confession, 248
communal democracy, 90
communal enterprise, 201
communal evolution, 12
communal harmony, 189
communal identity, 86
communalism, 11, 79
communality, 7, 148
communal life, 7, 80
communal loyalty, 309
communal marriages, 40
communal maxims, 91
communal orientation, 248
communal ownership, 30
communal philosophy, 83
communal practice, 292
communal ramification, 248
communal religious activities, 136
communal social activities, 172
communal struggle, 272
communal way, 173, 301
communal wisdom, 292
communal world, 94
Communal worship, 137
communication barrier, 213, 214
communicative action, 297
communitarian, xv, xvi, 11, 78, 79, 80, 82, 104,
    157, 165, 166, 169, 174, 176, 180, 188,
    193, 197, 208, 209, 219, 230, 245, 250,
    263, 264, 265, 268, 273, 281, 284, 303
communitarian Africans, 278
communitarian angle, 263
communitarian claim, 191
communitarian-ecclesial model, 298
communitarian elements, 249
communitarian hermeneutic model, 6
communitarian hermeneutics, xiv, xvi, 7, 33, 34,
    264, 283, 284, 285, 301, 302, 303, 304,
    305, 307, 309

communitarian hermeneutics, 284, 302
communitarianism, xiii, xv, xvi, 11, 12, 20, 30,
    36, 78, 79, 80, 81, 84, 89, 90, 93, 100, 101,
    162, 166, 169, 178, 182, 183, 187, 192,
    193, 208, 209, 225, 239, 249, 264, 281,
    282, 283, 284, 286, 290, 297, 300, 308
communitarianism in Africa, 33, 287, 289
communitarianism versus individualism, 33, 36,
    81, 89, 100, 187, 188, 264, 303, 308
communitarian nature, 96
communitarian people, 191, 192, 281, 287, 308
communitarian perspective, 307
communitarian problem, 89
communitarian reading of the text, 286
communitarian society, 288
communitarian values, 89
communitarian way, 12
communitarian way of bible interpretation, xv
communitarian way of life, 161
communitarian worldview, 21, 177, 308
communities, 10, 11, 12, 77, 83, 109, 113, 129,
    143, 166, 188, 192, 207, 233, 273, 281,
    283, 284, 285, 286, 294, 298, 304, 309,
    310
communities of faith, 283, 285
communities of hackers, 12
community, xiv, xv, 5, 6, 10, 11, 12, 14, 18, 29, 30,
    43, 47, 49, 61, 62, 76, 78, 79, 80, 81, 82,
    83, 89, 91, 110, 114, 117, 118, 120, 122,
    123, 124, 125, 129, 132, 134, 135, 139,
    140, 141, 143, 144, 145, 146, 147, 148,
    150, 151, 152, 153, 154, 155, 156, 157,
    158, 160, 162, 163, 165, 166, 167, 172,
    175, 176, 177, 178, 179, 180, 181, 182,
    184, 185, 186, 187, 189, 190, 191, 192,
    193, 197, 199, 200, 201, 202, 204, 205,
    206, 209, 220, 221, 225, 226, 229, 232,
    234, 239, 243, 244, 245, 247, 248, 255,
    259, 260, 265, 273, 282, 283, 284, 285,
    286, 287, 290, 291, 292, 293, 294, 297,
    300, 301, 309, 313, 314
community affair, 191
community-based, 6, 7, 11, 255, 264
community-centeredness, 11
community-centred, 6, 7, 33, 79, 80, 264
community-centred hermeneutics, 100
community context, 259
community leaders, 168, 285
community level, 10
community life, 94, 126, 129, 156, 166, 175, 177,
    178, 182, 234, 307
community lifestyle, 157, 166, 250
community members, 28, 175, 288, 310
community of faith, 270

community of interpreters, 7
community of the faithful, 246, 250
community of the oppressed, 93
community-oriented, 6, 7, 11, 264
community rituals, 190
community setting, 8
community spirit, 239, 282, 284, 285
comparative religion, 65
compartmentalized position, 263
complexity and contradictions of culture, 209
complex relationship, 97
componential analysis, 29, 30, 31, 32, 178, 179, 186, 202, 205, 264, 267
components of meaning, 267
Conant, 126, 335
concept, viii, ix, x, xi, xiv, xvi, 5, 9, 34, 35, 36, 38, 41, 48, 49, 66, 80, 85, 94, 95, 97, 98, 99, 100, 105, 117, 119, 120, 132, 133, 134, 136, 149, 155, 159, 162, 165, 168, 178, 186, 198, 201, 222, 223, 226, 232, 235, 238, 244, 245, 248, 261, 263, 268, 271, 274, 275, 277, 281, 282, 285, 287, 288, 290, 293, 294, 297, 298, 303, 304, 305, 309, 318, 344,
concept 'écriture', 66
concept of Christian love, 281
concept of communitarianism, xvi, 34, 287, 305, 309
concept of community, 309
concept of deconstruction, 9, 35, 304, 309
concept of evil, xiv
concept of family, 100
concept of ownership, 117, 119, 162, 232, 294
concept of relationship, 119, 120
concept of ritual, 178
conceptual analysis, 232
conceptual mistake, 104
conceptual system, 176
conceptual understanding, 294
confession, 121, 155, 248, 314
consciencism, 81
conservative Protestants, 44
constellation, 38, 131, 311
constructivism, 21, 73, 273
contemporary context, 2, 341
contemporary situation, 67
contemporary theology, 277
contemporary theology and philosophy, 15
context, 13, 16, 25, 61, 93, 134, 135, 164, 166, 181, 211, 220, 250, 284, 289, 301, 302
context of a cow, 140
context of discovery, 289
context of inculturation, 42
context of the reading community, 70

context of the text, 70
contextual, 8, 34, 37, 251
contextual effort, 271
contextual exegesis, 301
contextual frame of reference, 70
contextual hermeneutics, 5, 283, 346
contextual interpretation, 69
contextual orientation, 19
contextualisation, 11, 13, 70
contextualisation of the Gospel, 6
contextualise, xiii, 45, 232
contextualise the Gospel, 285
contextualizing the Gospel, 68
conventional tilya, 121, 122
cosmology, 266, 267
council, 313
council of elders, xvi, 52, 118, 122, 123, 124, 126, 153, 157, 161, 168, 172, 189, 190, 234, 246, 264, 268, 285, 290, 297, 300, 304, 313
counselling, 237, 350
coups d'état, 86
covenant, 313
cow, 83, 112, 119, 120, 121, 122, 123, 126, 138, 139, 140, 141, 145, 146, 147, 153, 154, 157, 160, 162, 163, 166, 189, 192, 198, 200, 202, 207, 229, 233, 234, 235, 243, 291, 293, 294, 317
cow relative, 119
cradle of evangelisation, 39
creatio ex nihilo, 132
creator, 154, 294
crisis of identity, 283
crisis of pastoralism, 107, 116
critical analysis, 209, 263, 271
critical theory, 289
criticism and historical criticism, 66
crossbreed traditional animals, 296
cross-cultural, 103
cross-cultural marriage, 298
cross-cultural Ministers, 41, 334
cross-cultural missionaries, 104
Culpepper, 220, 335
cultural, 176, 339
cultural analysis, 74
cultural and contextual interpretations, 301
cultural and religious heritage, 53
cultural artefacts, 183
cultural artifacts, 23
cultural behavior, 23
cultural behaviour, 183
cultural bias, 55
cultural circle, 302
cultural complexity, 180, 192, 263, 280

cultural complexity, 14, 72, 337
cultural conflicts, 257
cultural conflicts, 258
cultural context, 102, 196
cultural depersonalization, 58
cultural development, 58
cultural differences, 73, 126, 258
cultural dispositions, 49
cultural domains, 29, 31, 166, 167, 171
cultural encounter, 284
cultural experience, 69
cultural expertise, 40
cultural heritage, 6, 8, 53, 68, 72, 76, 101, 191, 213, 259, 263, 282
cultural Heritage, 10, 73, 341
cultural identity, 113
cultural institutions, 53
cultural knowledge, 23, 32
cultural knowledge, 14, 345
cultural linguistics, 20, 343
cultural matrix, 6
cultural meanings, 167
cultural meaning system, 34, 177, 209
cultural orientations, xvi, 10, 74, 76, 164, 210, 263, 304
cultural overlaps, 77
cultural points of contact, 104
cultural points of density, 30, 168, 171
cultural practices, 39, 40, 54, 58, 62, 113, 157, 158, 221, 229, 286, 304
cultural product, 74, 210
cultural recognition, 37
cultural relationship, 138
cultural-religious domains, 168
cultural roots, 72, 101
cultural scene, 10, 20, 23, 186
cultural schizophrenia, xiv, 36, 57, 58, 100
cultural self-awareness, 50
cultural settings, 252
cultural speech, 23, 183
cultural theme, 145, 162, 173, 183, 231, 243
cultural themes, 20, 28, 29, 30, 31, 33, 177, 183, 186, 198, 199, 221, 235, 244
cultural traditions, 65, 68
cultural traits, 197, 228, 233
cultural value, 146, 285
cultural values, xvi, 33, 34, 38, 41, 51, 77, 102, 114, 138, 162, 227
culture and context-bound, 55
culture and Gospel, 269
culture and language, 220, 224
culture and non-culture, 76
culture and religion, 218
culture and social structure, 74, 75, 76

culture as something shared, 75, 164
culture-conditioned, 6
culture-friendly hermeneutics, 33
cultures are group-specific, 73
culture shock of villagization, 86
current political situation, 167
current understanding, 66, 72
current understanding of culture, 72
curse, 121, 133, 137, 153, 300, 312
cursing ceremony, 154
cursing ritual, 234
customary African marriage, 99, 341
cut off, xvi, 128, 153, 176, 178
cutter of words, 123, 315
cutting off evil, 179
cutting the linkage, 121

damaged historical consciousness, 269
dance, 71, 124, 148, 152, 257, 311, 316, 318
dancing, 46, 54, 311
danger, 48, 78, 90, 131, 136, 202, 314
daughter, 122, 311
daughters, 144
death, 243
death of a language, 110
deciduous, 318
deciduous tree, 125
decision-making process, 123, 238, 246, 298
decolonizing theology, 278
deconstructing theology, 6, 15, 276, 346
deconstruction, xvi, 11, 14, 15, 16, 33, 66, 70, 72, 100, 273, 274, 275, 276, 277, 278, 280, 287, 288, 289, 308, 335, 342, 345
deconstructionism, 278
deconstructive enterprise, 14, 303, 305
deconstructive reading, 15, 277
deconstructive way, 8
deeper understanding, 50
delivery, 120, 182, 314
demythologise the New Testament, 17
Derrida, 15, 35, 66, 274, 275, 276, 277, 288, 333, 335, 345
destroy, 53, 55, 135, 189, 195, 294
destruction, 51, 52, 57, 275, 276
de-structuring, 277, 287
destructuring, 280
destruktion, 275, 277
deutero-canonical books, 214
dialectical relationship, 21, 33
dialogical relationship, 265
dialogue, 39, 43, 48, 54, 64, 94, 231, 260, 280, 281, 301, 302, 305
dialogue with modernity, 89
diametrically opposed, 57, 278

dichotomized life, 42, 50
different interpreters, 286
dignity and identity, 219
dignity as pastoralists, 196
Dilthey, 17, 336
dimensions of contrast, 267
dini ya msambwa, 57, 133, 269
diocesan priests, 25, 215, 227, 238
disarm the community, 176
discipleship, 1
discipline of hermeneutics, 28, 29, 30, 33
discrimination against women, 49
disharmony, 154
dismantling differences, 273, 278
distributive understanding of culture, 75
district atlas, 103, 337
district commissioner, 52
district officer, 52
disturbing phenomenon, 59
divine inspiration, 50
diviner, 132, 137, 311
doing philosophy, 83, 92
domain, 32, 166, 167, 170, 231
domain analysis, 29, 30, 34, 169, 186
dominant spirit, 303
domineering top-down attitude, 299
donkey, 198, 317
double-faceted, 33, 58
double-faceted problem, 93
double identity, 42, 50, 58
down-to-earth pastoral programmes, 296
drought, 46, 80, 117, 132, 135, 137, 138, 144, 153, 250, 291, 295, 314
drumming, 46
dual religious systems, 58

earthing the gospel, 50, 333
east African community, 11
ecclesial communion, 95
ecclesiastical power, 41
ecclesiology, 52, 61, 95
ecological deterioration, 107
economic arrangement, 120
economic collapse, 221
economic communities, 11
economic relationship, 119, 120, 121, 123, 285, 317
economic relationship, 118
economic relatives, 121, 126, 168
economic system, 119, 120
écriture, 67, 277
effective African hermeneutics, 78
eghin, 121
egyam, 156

elder, 139, 155, 158, 172, 187, 204, 242, 245, 260, 287, 311, 350
elements of communitarianism, 165, 169, 183
elements of individualism, 165, 183
elusive process of differentiations, 66
emergence of African theology, 93
empowerment of the oppressed, 92
encounter, xiii, 50, 187, 216, 293, 302
encounter God, 25
end of colonialism, 87
enemy, 32, 40, 114, 125, 129, 139, 140, 142, 143, 152, 154, 155, 180, 181, 185, 188, 191, 192, 205, 243, 266, 292, 313, 316
enemy's secrets, 175
eschatological community, 198
ethnographical fieldwork, 8
ethnographic field research, 21
ethnographic research, 23
ethnophilosophy, 81, 82, 83, 91
Euro-American values, 49
Eurocentric concepts and categories, 92
European and African culture, 302
European and North American Christianity, 19
European canons, 93
European categories, 15, 93
European Christianity, 52
European colonisation of Africa, 84
European culture, 100, 278
European economic community, 11
European hegemony, 92
European individualism, 282
European invaders, 213
European philosophers, 55
Europeans, 83, 101, 208, 282
Europeans are individualistic, 289
European superiority, 269
evaluative method, 68, 69
evangelical Lutheran church of Kenya, 218
evangelii nuntiandi, 216
evangelisation, xvi, 1, 5, 11, 15, 18, 20, 30, 34, 36, 42, 43, 45, 51, 53, 57, 59, 60, 64, 77, 78, 161, 202, 213, 215, 216, 217, 218, 219, 229, 234, 241, 242, 250, 258, 259, 263, 264, 273, 277, 283, 294, 295, 296, 304, 305, 306, 307, 309
evangelisation in Africa, 58
evangelization in Africa, 95
evangelizers, 50, 304
evening star, 131, 318
every Pöchon is extremely religious, 136
evil, 45, 54, 55, 65, 133, 136, 137, 151, 152, 154, 156, 171, 176, 187, 221, 234, 244, 292, 313, 316, 318
evil acts, 157

evil eye, 168
evil forces, 162
evil spell, 155
evil spirits, 138
evil ways, 227
exclusive religious system, 44
exegesis and hermeneutics, xiv, 62
exegetical-hermeneutical debate, 165
existential attitude, 9
existential hermeneutics, 17
exotic, 65, 240, 296
exotic animals, 161
exotic cows, 24
exotic faith, 135
expatriate, missionaries, 302
experience, 10, 22, 40, 65, 77, 87, 104, 203, 225, 241, 252, 253, 258, 259, 286, 296
exploit, 168, 312
extended African family, 96
extended family relationship, 94
external interventions, 103, 336
extra ecclesiam, 55, 245
extraordinary, 169, 189, 313, 316
extra-ordinary people, 134, 168
extraordinary people, 134
extraordinary sin, 154
extraordinary synod of bishops, 37
extreme danger, 144

faith and culture, 60
faith communities, xvi
faith experience, 26
familiarity versus strangeness, 303
family, 71, 85, 90, 95, 96, 97, 98, 99, 120, 121, 122, 129, 138, 140, 141, 147, 149, 151, 152, 155, 156, 159, 167, 172, 173, 177, 180, 184, 202, 217, 222, 243, 247, 266, 282, 311, 312, 317
family life, 166, 167, 203
family model, 36, 95, 96
family set-up, 96
famine, 46, 144, 283, 314
feel at home, xv, xvi, 18, 39, 63, 77, 163, 274, 306, 309
female circumcision, 261, 262
female genital mutilation, 103, 343
feminine artefacts, 171
feminine theology, 251
feminist hermeneutics, 69
feminist theology, 37
field of hermeneutics, 303
field research, 25, 288, 296
fieldwork, xv, 22, 28, 29, 33, 34, 140, 207, 286, 299, 302, 303, 306, 308

final ceremony, 124
first-born, 127, 312
folk terms, 29, 32, 167, 169, 199, 229
food, 98
food-for-work programmes, 27
food production, 115
foreign categories, 219
foreign spiritual leader, 268
forgiveness, 155, 172, 248, 300, 314
formal theological work, 9
form of communitarianism, 289
form of hermeneutics, 21, 302, 303
fornication, 98
Francophone Africa, 270
freeing-up, 277, 287
friend, 32
fruitful inculturation, 72
functional communitarianism, 12, 283, 308
functional communitarians, 12
functional communities, 12
fundamentalism, 43, 44, 343
fundamentalists, 43
fundamental truths, 44
fusion of horizons, xv, 207, 268, 281, 308, 312

Gadamer, xv, 8, 17, 207, 268, 269, 308, 337
gaudium et spes, 40, 60, 255
gemeinschaft, 12, 346
gender equality, 37
general hermeneutics, 6, 17
general interpretation, 17
genuine dialogue, 78, 281
geographical difference, 200, 201, 229
geographical place, 76
gesellschaft, 12, 346
Gĩkũyũ, 52
Gĩkũyũ people, 59
girl, 312, 317
global Christian, 43
global community of bible interpreters, 285
globalisation, xvi, 10, 64, 96, 97, 265, 301, 302
global rejection, 39
global stage, 272
god of rain, 144, 312
God of the bible, 105
golden age, 40
good news, 16, 38, 51, 69, 78, 100
good shepherd, 21, 28, 30, 34, 163, 165, 193, 194, 196, 197, 199, 201, 203, 204, 211, 220, 222, 223, 225, 227, 228, 231, 233, 236, 243, 244, 245, 246, 247, 248
good versus evil, 276
goodwill tilya, 121
gospel and African cultures, 39, 338

gospel and culture, 37, 48, 78, 216, 290, 293, 305, 308
gospel groups, 25
gospel of Mark, 214
government chief, 52
grazing, 131, 172
grazing field, 171, 204, 205, 243, 316
grinding stone, 171, 312, 315

happy symbiosis, 48
harambee, 81, 86
hardships of life, 168
harmonious relationship, 290
harmonizing culture, 40
harmony, 14, 41, 89, 129, 141, 146, 149, 154, 162, 289, 308, 316
having a philosophy, 83
head tax, 52
healthy dialogue, 43
heathen practices, 57
heaven, 136, 175, 221, 245, 247, 258, 318
Heidegger, 8, 17, 275, 277, 337
hermeneusis, xiv, 16, 17, 21, 102
hermeneutical approach, 90
hermeneutical character, 305
hermeneutical debate, 4
hermeneutical methods, 62
hermeneutical model or paradigm, 287
hermeneutical orientations, 92
hermeneutical philosophy, 33, 93, 274
hermeneutical principles, 68
hermeneutical process, 284
hermeneutical questions, 6
hermeneutical response, 3
hermeneutical theory, 8
hermeneutic endeavor, 308
hermeneutic model, 22
hermeneutic practice, 102
hermeneutics, xiii, xvi, 5, 6, 7, 8, 11, 16, 17, 36, 67, 99, 256, 265, 289, 301, 305
hermeneutics, xiv, 2, 3, 6, 8, 10, 16, 17, 43, 67, 71, 233, 252, 270, 303, 335, 336, 339, 340, 343, 344, 345, 346
hermeneutics of and for the people, 283
hermeneutics of production, 66
hermeneutics of reception, 66
hermeneutics of sache, 66
hermeneutics of suspicion, 68
hermeneutic theories, 21
hermeneutic theory, 17, 22
hermeneutic thought, 16
historical context, 36, 100
historical process of evangelisation, 100
history of inculturation, 302

history of salvation, 280
history of theology, xiv
holistic inculturation, 69
holy ghost fathers, 51
holy spirit, 39, 44, 94, 228, 246, 280, 283
homestead, 141, 149, 150, 163, 168, 171, 173, 179, 192, 201, 205, 312, 316
homogeneously communitarian, 192
horizons and worldview, 93
horizontverschmelzung, xv, 207, 268, 281, 312
human being, 9, 83, 134, 144, 297
human beings, 16, 73, 132, 145, 149, 161, 177, 209, 281, 292, 294
human community, 272, 293
human conditions, 47
human diversity, 73
human gathering, 42
humanism, 81, 90
humanity and humanism, 89
human relationship, 79, 169
human sacrifice, 49, 144, 264
human understanding, 17
human universal, 73
hunger, 115, 138, 283, 295, 314
hunter-gatherer populations, 116
husband and wife, 172

ideal challenge, 221
identity, 4, 10, 42, 80, 81, 110, 113, 150, 162, 167, 244, 259, 278, 299, 303
identity versus difference, 303
idiomatic expressions, 25, 62, 146, 153, 177, 187, 223
Ilat, 104, 137, 144, 180, 312
illiteracy versus literacy, 302
immediate dialogue, 99
inanimate beings, 209
incompatible religions, 48
inculturation, xiii, xvi, 1, 4, 6, 11, 13, 15, 18, 19, 20, 33, 34, 36, 37, 38, 41, 43, 44, 45, 47, 48, 49, 50, 61, 65, 68, 69, 77, 78, 100, 207, 210, 216, 228, 230, 235, 241, 263, 264, 268, 280, 288, 290, 304, 305, 306
inculturational orientations, 19
inculturation biblical hermeneutics, 69
inculturation from the bottom up, 42
inculturation hermeneutics, 69
inculturation in Africa, 41
inculturation, in Kenya, 51
inculturation of the Gospel, 6, 165
inculturation theology, 42, 40, 335
indicators of communitarianism, 171
indicators of individualism, 187
indigenization, 37

indigenized context, 92
indigenous belief system, 135
individual affair, 122, 172, 248, 293
individual-centred, 7, 255
individual experience, 246, 247
individual family lives, 166
individualism, xv, xvi, 11, 18, 20, 89, 93, 166, 177, 178, 184, 186, 187, 189, 190, 191, 192, 193, 197, 209, 263, 264, 280, 308
individualism versus communitarianism, 266
individualistic communities, 188
individualistic Europeans, 278
individualistic interpretation, 249
individualistic lifestyle, 78, 307
individualistic perspective, 263
individualistic westerners, 288
individualistic worldview, 308
industrialisation, 90
industrious woman, 151
influence of modernity, 102, 110, 187, 198, 207
inheritance for women, 213, 259, 262
initiated, 114, 129, 148, 159, 182, 214, 217, 311, 312, 317
initiated girl, 311
initiating dialogue, 41
initiation rite, 152
institutional church, 45
integrated system, 13
integrated theology, 272
intercultural encounter, xvi
intercultural hermeneutics, xvi, 76, 265, 271, 286, 301, 302, 303, 304, 309, 347
interdisciplinary, 34, 100, 305
interdisciplinary approach, 20, 305
international community, 37
interpretation, 136
interpretation of texts, 7, 17
interpretation of the gospel, 9, 31, 209
interpreters, 248
interpreters of the bible, 256
interpret experience, 14
interpreting the bible, xvi, 17, 33, 63, 65, 212, 257, 301
interpreting the scriptures, 197
interpretive approach, 69
interpret the bible, xiv, xv, 5, 21, 25, 210, 218, 225, 263, 302, 306, 307
invariable religious beliefs, 167
invented traditions, 208
invention of tradition, 208
inyorï takat, 153
ipso facto, 123, 148, 207, 312
iraite nko asis, 153
is African incurably religious? 135, 343

Islam, 32, 286, 299, 338
Islamic control, 51
Islamic presence, 51

Javanese culture, 73
Johnson, 273, 274, 275, 278, 289, 338
junior elder, 148

kacheripkö, 111, 312
kaideke, 187, 188, 312
Kalenjin communities, 113
Kalenjin ethnic group, 32
Kalenjin speaking communities, 24
kalya, 149
kamar, 143
kamar, 312
kanasyan, 312
kapolok, 312
kaporet, 312
kasauria, 111, 137, 313
kechir, 168, 313
kedonga, 125, 168
keghot kelat, 114, 147, 181
kensyö, 148, 155, 168, 181
kensyö, 313
Kenya mpya, 111
Kenyan national seminaries, 251
kepa rotwo, 152
keporyak, 313
ketarta kyak, 168
keyakuy, 168
kikatat, 180, 313
Kikuyu culture, 73
killing of twins, 40
kïmïr, 313
kind of food, 102
kinds of evil, 178
kinds of tilya, 120
kinetic orality, 71
kingdom of heaven, 84
kirwok, 123, 168, 246
kirwokïn, 124, 168, 246, 313
knocking out of teeth, 147, 148
koipa koghin, 312
köipa pagh, 171
kokwö, xvi, 123, 124, 148, 161, 165, 189, 246, 264, 285, 290, 297, 300
kokwö, 297, 313
kölölyon, 142, 143, 152, 266
kölölyon, 314
kömöy, 314
konget, 32
ko pö chemeri, 127
koretaran, 131

INDEX

kunstlehre, 7
kuting, 314
kyak, 132, 168, 314
kyakuyin, 201, 202, 205, 222, 224, 233
kyakuyin, 201, 314

lack of criteria, 286
lapan, 314
lapay, 180, 181, 314
lastagh, 314
level of identity, 170
liberation, 19
liberation hermeneutics, 68, 69, 348
liberation in Africa, 270
liberation theology, 8, 37, 251, 270, 334
life experience, 202, 247
life experiences, 42, 50, 136, 140, 196
life of a Pöchon, 203
lifestyle of the pastors, 249
lightning, 135, 136, 137, 144, 313
linguistic analysis tools, 66
literary theory and criticism, 274
liturgical renewal, 60
lived experience, 7
livestock, 106, 108, 115, 116, 131, 132, 143, 150, 162, 166, 168, 174, 198, 200, 244, 247, 291, 314, 317, 351
livestock farmer, 122
livestock herders, 107
livestock insurance, 295
livestock wars, 109
living Christian communities, 95
living communities, 10
living sacrifice, 144
local community, 22, 190, 192
local culture, 13, 50
local cultures, 51, 60, 304
localised culture, 15, 277
local languages, 48, 64, 217, 224
local literature, 217
lökötyö, 142, 182, 314
lökoy, 195, 214, 314, 334
lopitakit, 218
love and marriage, 49
Luhya community, 234
lük, xvi, 139, 168, 199, 264, 290, 291, 292, 293, 294, 295, 296, 304
lumen gentium, 59, 94

Maasai pastoralists, 115, 344
Magesa, 2, 7, 48, 49, 51, 57, 61, 63, 96, 97, 99, 100, 255, 256, 284, 301, 339, 342, 348
magical view of the bible, 44
magician, 191, 312

major categories, 19
male-female relationship, 149
malevolence, 157
mama, 314
marital relationship, 98
marriage, 27, 49, 54, 97, 119, 121, 122, 124, 140, 144, 148, 155, 159, 168, 172, 175, 247, 273, 281, 290, 313, 317
marriage certificate, 262
masankwï, 133
matai, 314
material sources, 34, 165, 166, 187
matrilineal communities, 98
matrimonial ritual, 49
meaningful dialogue, 18
meaningful hermeneutics, 304
meaningful relationship, 70
meaning of community life, 94
meaning producing force, 66
meaning system, 20, 22, 23, 165, 166, 176, 177, 192, 193, 201, 234
meat, 316
medicine, 51, 127, 168, 213, 317
medicine man, 58, 191
medicine men and women, 259
medicine woman, 135, 137
medicine women, 134
mediocrity, 43, 45, 87
meeting place, 173, 297
meghat, 148
member of the community, 182
members of the community, 142, 158
menchö, 206, 314
mental categories, 37, 38, 274, 301
mental disposition, 28
mental frameworks, 21
mental life, 59, 85
message of Christianity, 100
message of salvation, 18, 61
metaphysical fear, 148
metaphysical ideas, 15, 276
methodical biblical hermeneutics, 69
Methodists, 51
method of evangelisation, 77, 219
methods of bible interpretation, 4, 65, 67
methods of ethnography, 306
mïkulow, 134, 141, 169, 314
milk, 316
milky way, 131
millet, 314
mïrön, 315
mis, 179, 181, 305
misfortune, 113, 134, 138, 190, 192, 313
missiological perspective, 20, 305

mission, 1, 5, 11, 18, 19, 21, 41, 53, 55, 64, 65, 77, 78, 139, 214, 216, 217, 220, 238, 265, 268, 302, 304, 305, 338
missionaries, xvi, 19, 25, 33, 34, 36, 51, 52, 53, 54, 55, 57, 59, 60, 63, 65, 77, 100, 103, 138, 212, 213, 214, 215, 217, 218, 219, 220, 225, 233, 236, 238, 241, 259, 262, 268, 269, 277, 278, 279, 283, 303, 306
missionary, 10, 20, 53, 54, 56, 57, 61, 212, 215, 218, 219, 220, 228, 237, 279, 298, 350
missionary enterprise, 61
missionary movement, 19
missionary onslaught, 262
missionary priest, 183, 350
missionary reading of the Bible, 22
missionary seminary, 56
missionary style of worship, 268
mission of the church, 20, 34, 95, 305
mistake, 181, 213, 219, 286, 291
misunderstanding, 317
misunderstanding understanding, 269, 308
misuse of concepts, 136
Mitume catechetical Centre, 239
mixed domain, 178
mixed economy, 112, 116
mix pastoralism with agriculture, 112, 201
mkö, 154
moderate communitarianism, 90
modern community, 89
modern education, 158
modernity and globalisation, 115
modern medicine, 137
modern methods of exegesis, 66
modern understanding, 131
modern understanding of culture, 72, 73, 76, 209
modern world, 40, 60, 78, 216, 283
modus essendi, 61
modus operandi, 61
mogh, 315
monïng, 117, 132, 146, 158, 168, 298, 315
monogamy, 98, 99, 104, 260
moon, 131, 136, 181, 311
moral system, 151
morï, 169
morning star, 131
mosïn, 315
mosong, 315
mösör, 315
mösöwonto kechir, 235
mösöwoon, 165, 194, 195, 201, 202, 205, 222, 224, 233, 235, 314
mösöwoon, 165, 201, 315
mötworin, 201, 202, 205, 224, 233
mötworin, 205, 315

moy, 180, 315
mrön, 199
msango, 133
mūbīa, 53
Mudimbe, 274
Mugambi, 2, 5, 53, 61, 68, 100, 196, 217, 252, 270, 271, 272, 336, 341, 342, 346, 348
muma, 315
mutat, 315
mūthūngū, 53
mutin, 315
mutinto ngal, 123, 168, 297
mutinto ngal, 315
mutual relationship, 52
my faith as an African, 9, 47, 336

name of the community, 87, 134, 182, 248
national communal identity, 81
nationalist-ideological philosophy, 81, 83
national liturgical rite, 38
native, 52, 56, 57, 316
native idioms, 219
native idioms and thought forms, 225
native-language, 224
native missionaries, 302
native's point of view, 31, 165
native thought forms, 219
natural groups, 167
natural phenomenon, 281
nature of being, 82
nature of communitarianism, 35
nature of sin, 242
nature of the sacrifice, 137
Ndembu culture, 73
neighbourhood, 25, 26, 167, 171, 174, 192, 209, 250
neighbouring communities, 106, 113
neighbouring community, 181, 199
neo-colonialism, 92
neo-colonial present, 93
network of individuals, 12
newborn, 314, 316
new creation, 41
new meaning, 26, 294
new paradigm, 270
new power relations, 269
new questions, 273
new religion, 58, 279
New Testament, 5, 8, 16, 25, 68, 96, 195, 214, 218, 219, 223, 224, 270, 271, 284, 333, 336, 340, 341, 342, 346
New Testament hermeneutics, 5, 346, 270, 336
New Testament studies, 271, 284, 342
new theological category, 95

new world order, 270
ngala Pökot, 25, 110, 114, 338
ngaror, 315
ngaror/nekö, 168
ngokï, 315
ngorokö, 201, 202, 205, 223, 315
ngoroköin, 224, 233
ngoroköin, 315
ngotinyön, 114
ngotinyön, 315
nguiyon, 168
nogsyö, 315
nomadic communities, 234
non-African culture, 308
non-African (individualistic) way, 11
non-African readers, 279
non-African values, 39
non-bourgeois theology, 273, 336
non-Pökot, 265
non-Pökot clergy, 268
non-scholars, 61, 100
normative communitarianism, 283
normativity of communitarianism, 308
not being religious, 136
notion of communitarianism, 102
notoriously irreligious, 136
notoriously religious, 135, 136
nuclear family members, 97
nuclear family system, 97
number of the livestock, 112
nyalat, 168, 173

oath, 123
obstacle to evangelisation, 216
obstetricians, 8
official declaration, 57
of human relationship, 265
of world religions, 44, 334
old age, 146
old answers, 273
Old Testament, 2, 47, 52, 68, 134, 214, 219, 220, 271, 290, 349
omisyö, 188
one man with one wife, 99
onyöt, 136, 148, 156, 189
onyötey, 156, 169, 265
open hermeneutics, 301
opposite of dialogue, 48
oppressed, 240
oppression of women, 69
option for the poor, 1, 19
oral culture, 70, 71
oral history, 53
orality, 70, 100

orality versus writing, 302
oral literature, 71, 267
oral transmission, 71
ordinary, 123, 155, 187
ordinary African 'readers', 69
ordinary Africans, 67
ordinary believers, 9
ordinary bible interpreters, 71
ordinary, chairs, 188
ordinary Christians, 8, 9, 22, 34, 44, 164, 211, 236, 237, 245, 257, 260, 269, 273, 299, 307, 308
ordinary circumstances, 27
ordinary daily talks, 167
ordinary form of prayer, 138
ordinary life, 250
ordinary people, 8, 21, 168, 208, 227, 236
ordinary Pöchon, 165
ordinary Pökot Christians, 25, 217, 225, 306
ordinary reader, 8, 69, 346
ordinary thing, 233
organization of diversity, 74, 210
original meaning, 66, 67, 185, 275
ortïn, 316
orus, 316
osïl, 316
otöp, 316
otüpo, 316
ownership, xiv, 30, 90, 178, 188, 205
ox, 119, 121, 122, 140, 143, 156, 173, 188, 191, 291, 312
oy, 138, 156, 162, 169, 179, 180, 181, 265, 316

pagan customs, 56
pagh, 316
pagha koghin, 171
Pakot moral system, 135
Pakot religious life, 135
palaver, 297
pan, 316
pan Africanism, 90, 341
papal encyclical, 216
papo, 316
paradigm shift, 270
parameters of the community, 144, 173
parish, 298
parish council, 196, 200, 206, 350, 258, 351, 352
parish priest, 27, 183, 240, 350
parpara, 32, 113, 125, 134, 143, 148, 168, 169, 178, 179, 180, 181, 182, 316
parparin, 179
particular communities, 7
particularity versus universality, 302
particular place, 305, 315

passbook, 52
passing out ceremony, 171
pastoral communities, 206
pastoral community, 207
pastoral experience, 228, 349
pastoral hermeneutics, 11, 308
pastoralism, 24, 107, 112, 115, 116
pastoralist communities, 193, 272
pastoralist community, 191, 243
pastoralists, 28, 103, 106, 107, 109, 112, 115, 124, 125, 139, 152, 205, 206, 215, 227, 336, 346
pastoral Pökot, 24, 125, 138, 201, 296
pastoral priests, 251
pastoral theology, 43
pastoral work, 238, 240
pastors, xv, xvi, 5, 6, 10, 11, 21, 24, 27, 28, 29, 30, 31, 33, 34, 62, 164, 167, 193, 210, 211, 220, 221, 226, 234, 235, 236, 238, 240, 241, 242, 243, 245, 246, 247, 248, 250, 252, 257, 258, 259, 262, 263, 264, 267, 268, 284, 289, 299, 302, 303, 305, 306, 307, 308, 309
pastors' worldview, 266
past (unknown or 'unremembered') mistakes, 169
patriarchal and polygynous, 98
peace, 300
peaceful co-existence, 94
pedagogical approach, 253
peny, 316
people of Africa, 3
people of the book, 71
people of the word, 71
people's religion, 40
people's understanding, 223
people's world view, 302
people's worldviews, 308
permanent relationship, 120
personal experience, 7, 21, 144
personal relationship, 248
personal well-being, 105
person and community, 11, 12, 337
pervade, 142
phenomenon, 45, 88, 94, 96, 133, 156, 168, 181, 182, 189, 198, 199, 229, 234, 312, 318
philosophers and theologians, 15, 100, 274
philosophical conceptions, 113
philosophic sagacity, 90
philosophy, xiv, 14, 20, 33, 81, 82, 83, 85, 89, 91, 251, 274, 275, 277, 299, 305, 309
philosophy and culture, 38, 343
philosophy and theology, 36, 79, 254
philosophy of sociality, 89

pich chole koot, 111
piich, 194, 195, 214, 334
pïn, 129, 179, 188, 225, 265
pïn, 316
pïnwöy, 129, 167, 170
piped water, 269
pipö, 316
pipö mïkö, 111
pipö pagh, 24, 112, 125
pipö tich, 24, 112
place, 137, 265, 275, 317
place of orality, 71
plants, 316
Plapan, 103, 120, 123, 126, 286, 343
plural marriage, 98
Pöchon, 109, 113, 114, 118, 124, 125, 131, 138, 139, 147, 149, 150, 151, 152, 154, 162, 163, 170, 173, 176, 181, 199, 200, 223, 235, 240, 243, 265, 290, 291, 292, 293, 316
pögh, 316
pöghisyö, 141, 146, 149, 154, 156, 162, 168, 179, 181, 189
pöghisyö, 149, 180, 316
pökoot religion, 57, 103, 113, 135, 161, 190, 348
Pökot, xv, xvi, 110, 129, 142, 146, 202, 265, 267, 292, 313, 315, 316
pökot ancestors, 243
pökot anthropology, 133
pökot artefacts, 171
pökot astronomy, 131, 162
pökot beliefs and values, 157
pökot belief system, 135, 162
pökot Christians, 29
pökot clan system, 29
pökot communitarianism, 273, 282
pökot communitarian spirit, 170
pökot communitarian worldview, 283
pökot community, xv, 5, 119, 125, 141, 143, 146, 149, 150, 154, 156, 160, 161, 165, 176, 184, 187, 191, 193, 200, 204, 206, 209, 226, 227, 235, 243, 261, 284, 285, 292, 293, 294
pökot concept, 134
pökot concept of a person, 132
pökot concept of communitarianism, 303
pökot concept of ownership, 117
pokot concept of tororot, 105
pökot congregational system, 285
pökot context, 202
pökot cosmology, 153
pökot county, 23, 111
pökot cultural heritage, 281
pökot cultural meaning system, 209, 211

pökot cultural norms, 121
pökot cultural notion, 226
pökot cultural scene, 202, 209
pökot cultural themes, 31, 199
pökot cultural values, 138, 289
pökot cultural wisdom, 146
pökot culture, xv, 10, 29, 32, 36, 105, 115, 122, 132, 155, 157, 160, 165, 178, 183, 198, 199, 208, 209, 220, 223, 226, 228, 230, 243, 244, 247, 248, 255, 259, 262, 273, 278, 284, 308
pökot customs and tradition, 307
pökot elder, 131
pökot equivalents, 223
pökot eschatology, 226
pökot family, 115
pökot form of communitarianism, 182
pökot girl, 114
pökot identity, 113, 282
pökot informants, 29
pökotland, 111, 114, 124, 126, 137, 157, 161, 182, 206, 213, 304, 316
pökot language, xv, 24, 110, 114, 123, 150, 169, 197, 199, 211, 214, 215, 217, 219, 224, 233
pökot language and culture, 102
pökot leadership, 123, 124
pökot life, 104, 155
pökot lifestyle, 29, 103, 109, 140, 153, 200, 229, 274
pökot linguistic structure, 231
pökot meaning system, 165, 209, 211
pökot moral system, 162
pökot neighbours, 208
pökotness, 113, 304
pökot notion of leadership, 246
pökot notion of witchcraft, 104
pokot people, 103, 113, 340, 347
pökot people, xv, xvi, 4, 10, 11, 21, 22, 23, 28, 29, 30, 31, 33, 36, 102, 103, 104, 105, 109, 110, 111, 112, 113, 114, 117, 122, 124, 132, 137, 145, 151, 161, 162, 163, 164, 166, 167, 184, 185, 188, 192, 196, 201, 208, 210, 213, 214, 218, 222, 223, 225, 229, 233, 262, 264, 265, 267, 268, 269, 281, 282, 283, 285, 288, 299, 301, 304, 306, 318, 334, 351
pökot population, 108, 212
pökot practice, 186, 226
pökot predisposition, 166
pökot priest, 25
pökot religion, 103, 104, 105, 135, 136, 218, 294, 316
pökot religious affiliation, 213

pökot ritual, 218
pökot rituals, 178
pökot ritual system, 178
pökot scriptures, 43
pökot situation, 284, 290
pökot social and cultural context, 102
pökot social behaviour, 190
pökot social context, 149, 305
pökot social dispensation, 268
pökot social experience, 164
pökot social life, 189
pökot social situation, 28, 113, 264
pökot thought pattern, 219
pökot tradition, 154, 208, 307
pokot traditional belief system, 104
pökot traditional community, 187
pökot traditional sense, 246
pökot translation, 136, 224
pökot translation of the bible, 214
pökot understanding, 159, 165, 177
pökot understanding of governance, 268
pökot version, 193, 211, 223
pökot way of interpreting the bible, 263
pökot way of life, 34, 104, 115, 182, 198
pökot women, 140
pökot world-view, 63, 70, 253
pökot worldview, xiv, 166, 176, 183, 193, 211, 265, 266, 268, 283, 302, 304, 306
political chaos, 221
political development, 270
political frivolity, 86
political hegemony, 51
political liberation, 37, 84, 93
political philosophy, 84
polygamy, 40, 49, 98, 99, 262
polygamy and culture, 260
polygamy and public opinion, 260
polygamy and tradition, 260
polygamy reconsidered, 99, 337
polygyny, 98, 99, 104, 213, 214, 259, 260, 273
ponïn, 316
pontifical council, 48
pontifical council for culture, 216, 343
poor shepherds, 220
popular and pastoral hermeneutics, 8, 210, 306, 309
popular Catholicism, 56
popular dance, 208
popular hermeneutics, 7, 301, 309
population growth, 107
pororis, 316
Portuguese, 252
Portuguese presence, 51
positions of interpreters, 284

positive theology, 247
post-colonial Africa, 272
post-colonial context, 3
post-colonial encounter, 2
post-colonial period, 3
post-colonial state, 87
post-colonial subject, 61
post-modern, 13, 72, 76, 209, 304
postmodern biblical interpretation, 274, 342
post-modern position, 74
post-modern understanding, 100
post-modern understanding of culture, 14, 72, 309
post-modern view, 74
post-modern view of culture, 73
poststructuralism, 66, 275, 276, 333, 344
poststructural criticism, 66
power of written tradition, 71, 337
poy, 146, 147, 175, 311
preferential form of marriage, 259
pre-modern times, 12
preparatio evangelica, 105
presbyter system, 285
pre-understanding of communitarianism, 281
priest, 27, 42, 52, 53, 150, 174, 175, 212, 215, 216, 217, 222, 223, 225, 226, 227, 228, 230, 231, 235, 236, 237, 238, 239, 240, 241, 246, 247, 249, 250, 251, 252, 253, 254, 257, 258, 268, 298, 299, 300, 349, 351
priests, 25, 30, 47, 98, 137, 150, 164, 168, 193, 211, 212, 220, 221, 222, 225, 227, 228, 229, 230, 231, 236, 238, 239, 241, 242, 245, 248, 249, 250, 252, 254, 255, 256, 257, 299, 303
priests and sisters, 239
primitive mentality, 56
primitive people, 82
principles of hermeneutics, 21
privatized hermeneutics, 301
prize-ox, 140, 143
problem of polygyny, 260
problem of translation, 223, 224
process of a community, 70
process of being defined, 67
process of deconstruction, 14, 280, 281
process of evangelisation, 285
process of inculturation, 4, 13, 41, 63
process of judgement, 168
proclaim salvation, 20
production of meaning, 3
professional African philosophers, 91
professional philosophers, 86, 91, 92
professional philosophy, 81, 88
professional theologians, 281

promulgating community rules, 300
propaganda, 55
Propaganda Fide, 54, 251, 343
proper context, 95
prophetic criticism, 50
protest, 284
Protestant, 217, 255
Protestant and Catholic churches, 47
Protestant churches, 217, 218, 263
Protestant fundamentalism, 45
Protestants, 217
proverb, 140, 185, 186
proverb analysis, 183
proverbs, 25, 140, 146, 164, 177, 184, 186, 187, 315
provisions of clean water, 296
ptakal, 154, 316
ptengöwo, 316
püng, 32, 139, 159, 316
punyon, 32, 125, 143, 266, 292
pure Pökot, 24

qualitative research, 29, 31
qualitative research method, 22
quality priests, 251
quarrel, 169, 317
quasi families, 97

rain, 138
raisons d'être, 13
ravage of AIDS, 283
reactive-proactive, 68
reader-focused exegesis, 66
reader-focused criticism, 66
reader-oriented, 66
reader-response criticism, 7, 337
reading community, 70
reading of the bible, 2, 70, 101, 286
recently initiated girls, 261
receptor-oriented approach, 104
receptor-oriented evangelisation, 104
reconciliation, 1, 19, 125, 148, 168, 178, 179, 311, 316
reconciliation ceremony, 32, 147
reconciliation ritual, 113, 179
reconstructionism, 270, 271
reconstruction of theology, 273
reconstruction paradigm, 272
reconstruction theologians, 273
reconstruction theology, 270
Reformation, 217
Reformed Church of East Africa, 218
regional hermeneutics, 17
reinterpretation of culture, 74

rejected Christianity, 57
rejection of twins, 49
relationship, xiv, xvi, 7, 32, 33, 49, 60, 74, 75, 76,
    79, 82, 83, 85, 113, 114, 122, 134, 140,
    150, 152, 162, 169, 170, 177, 182, 198,
    223, 227, 240, 242, 249, 252, 259, 262,
    265, 267, 277, 308, 317
relationship between men and women, 260
relationship cattle, 119
relationship with women, 147
relevant hermeneutics, 5, 9
relief food, 108
religion, 5, 84, 103, 133, 135, 153, 158, 160, 162,
    173, 214, 226, 242, 281
religion and culture, 307
religion and life, 79, 336
religion of the people, 56
religious beliefs, 167, 213
religious brothers and sisters, xiii
religious consciousness, 270
religious experience, 41, 164, 306, 307, 308
religious experiences, 77
religious hegemony, 51
religious Pökot songs, 257
religious practice, 135, 235
religious practices, xiv, 135, 162, 235
religious practices, 257
religious sphere, 266
religious studies, 62
religious traditions, 68
remedial rituals, 179
remedy, 169, 315
requirements for inculturation, 50
research, xiii, xiv, 6, 9, 10, 18, 22, 23, 24, 28, 31,
    48, 49, 65, 103, 106, 111, 113, 121, 138,
    155, 165, 176, 193, 197, 198, 207, 209,
    210, 218, 237, 239, 241, 259, 264, 269,
    281, 284, 286, 291, 298, 305, 306, 309,
    310, 350
research activities, 10, 165
research method, 21, 27, 30, 165
research methods, 28
research project, 193
research questions, 21, 31
Resende, 235
resistance to change, 213, 286
resistance to Christianity, 214
responsible community members, 124
revised theology, 55
Rewriting the Bible, 61, 341
Ricoeur, 6, 8, 9, 17, 344
riddle, 146
ridge, 124
rïpin, 201, 202, 205, 222, 224, 233

rite, 114, 124, 147, 242, 261
rite of passage, 121, 173, 242
rites of passage, xiv, 82, 124, 131, 132, 138, 145,
    146, 147, 148, 155, 158, 160, 162, 168,
    172, 173, 178, 227, 250
ritual, 60, 120, 121, 123, 135, 140, 143, 145, 148,
    150, 153, 162, 174, 178, 179, 181, 182,
    188, 192, 205, 261, 262, 291, 292, 311,
    313, 314, 315, 316, 318
ritual activities, 162
ritual impurity, 155
ritualistic tilya, 121
ritual offering, 138
ritual purification, 154
ritual purity, xiv, 148, 152, 162
ritual system, 34
ritual uncleanness, 162
ritual visits, 49
robber, 194, 221, 290, 294, 315
role of women, 262
Roman Catholic Church, 106
root paradigms, 10
rural African village, 79
rurwö, 317

sacramental, 52
sacramental tanks, 252
sacred domain, 131
sacred place, 96
sacrifice, 121, 135, 179, 180, 262, 291, 311
sacrificial, 121
sacrificial tilya, 121, 122
safe delivery, 147, 179
sage philosophy, 81, 90, 91, 343
salvation, 18, 20, 36, 38, 42, 50, 52, 55, 61, 62, 68,
    241, 245, 248, 250, 280, 348
Sandford, 116, 344
sapana, 121, 125, 148, 155, 178, 181, 208, 218,
    242
sayings, 25, 140, 146, 177, 183, 186, 187
SCC context, 71
SCC prayers, 25, 27, 193, 196, 239, 250, 258, 306
schisms, 5
Schleiermacher, 6, 17, 344
Schneider, 108, 112, 145, 213, 344
scholars, xv, xvi, 7, 31, 56, 58, 61, 65, 76, 99, 100,
    135, 142, 183, 256, 263, 276, 285, 303
scholars and non-scholars, 310
scholarship, 276
schooling system, 101
Schreiter, 10, 58, 252, 273, 286, 309, 344
science and theology, 21
scientific, 2, 8, 45, 67, 89, 90, 261
scientific community, 11

scientific exegesis, 228
scientific journals, 296
scientific theory, 8
scientific tools, 228
scientific worth, 5
seclusion period, 136
second-born, 311
secrets of life, 146
secrets of the community, 159
secular domain, 131
secular themes, 167
self-criticism, 74
self-sacrifice, 56
semantic relationship, 169
semantic relationships, 167
semeut, 168, 317
sense of communitarianism, 198
sensitising concepts, 21
sensitising concepts of communitarianism, 92
Serequeberhan, 3, 4, 92, 93, 345
seretow, 317
serious mistakes, 169
seriousness of sin, 45
servant, 205
sets of categories, 86
Seventh Day Adventist, 218
shared elements, viii, 113, 162, 164
shared meaning-system, 74, 210
sheep, 220
sheepfold, 94, 194
shepherd, 222
Shorter, 2, 37, 54, 58, 177, 345, 349
sikiröy, 168
sikïryö, 317
sikonöt, 167
sikonöt, 185
sin, 132, 155, 168, 181, 198, 248, 315, 316
sinful partners, 156, 315
single mothers and mistresses, 159
single parent families, 97
single semantic relationship, 32, 170, 202
sirmyon, 317
sirrïp, 154, 317
sisters, 9, 25, 30, 147, 150, 236, 237, 238, 239, 242, 249, 254
sïta, 131
Sizt-im-Leben, 45
slavery, 280
small Christian communities, 12, 22, 23, 28, 50, 95, 235, 285, 337, 348
small Christian community, 239
social being, 82
social ceremony, 121
social communities, 12

social context, 4, 25, 101, 217, 221, 253
social-cultural context, 70
social harmony, 94
social-historical context, 70
social reconstruction, 61, 196, 217, 341
social research method, 212
social sciences method, 167
social situation, 22, 23, 145, 167, 171, 273
social structure, 20, 34, 74, 75, 76, 192, 282, 308
social system, 23, 80
social wisdom, 146
socio-communal event, 120
socio-cultural situations, 69
sociology, 12, 75
sokoria, 125, 168
somchon, 317
something mystical, 268
something new, 41, 49, 301
son and the spirit, 19
song, 124, 147, 148, 173, 257, 318
sons and daughters, 51
sopon, 139
sorcery, 152, 157, 318
sorghum, 112, 125, 188, 315
sorïm, 317
sorïn, 152
sorïn, 317
sörö, 138, 317
soul, 134, 314
sous rature, 67
South Africa, 5, 11, 18, 25, 63, 65, 69, 88, 197, 270, 272, 289, 300, 334, 340, 347
South African apartheid situation, 271
south of the Sahara, 52
special relationship, 141, 204
specific context, 289, 302
specific relationship, 60
spirit, 11, 85, 89, 136, 148, 189, 260, 316
spirit of inculturation, 43
spirit of reconciliation, 172
spirit of the Gospel, 255, 301
spiritual beings, 134, 313
spirituality, 302
spoken Pökot, 24
stages of understanding, 22
star, 131, 318
starvation-prone, 109
state of economy, 167
status ad quem, 6
status a quo, 6
status quo, 5, 89, 281, 299
stepping-stone, 262
stock association system, 119
stomach, 133, 312

stone, 312
strained relationship, 236
structural communitarianism, 12, 80, 308
structural communitarians, 12
structural communities, 13
structural method, 31
structural questions, 29
sub-clan, 120, 127, 128
sub clans, 126
sub-clans, 127
subject of deconstruction, 15, 276
subjects rather than objects, 109
suffering misfortune, 58
sun, 131, 136, 138, 153, 181, 182, 185, 200, 313
supportive community, 90
survival strategies, 103, 336
sweet, 139, 140, 151, 311
symbiosis, 10, 48, 82, 105, 227, 290, 308
syncretism, 47, 48, 336, 344
syncretistic Christianity, 39
system, 87, 119, 156, 190, 220, 265, 287, 288, 297
system of political governance, 162
system 'out there', 73

tany, 138, 141, 153, 200, 317
taxonomic analysis, 29, 170
taxonomies, 31
taxonomy, 32, 170
tendency to individualism, 96
tender age, 139
terms of wealth, 167
testament, 2, 5, 271, 283, 334, 338, 340, 346
text and context, 3
text-oriented, 66
thanksgiving ceremony, 137
the communal versus the individual, 303
the cut, 124, 148, 287, 315
theme analysis, 186
theologians, 36, 37, 38, 44, 47, 50, 59, 61, 62, 70, 93, 94, 99, 251, 252, 272, 279, 310
theological development, 270
theological enterprise, 270, 309
theological paradigm, 94, 270
theological perspective, 270
theology, xiii, xv, 2, 8, 9, 12, 14, 21, 22, 33, 94, 100, 245, 251, 253, 267, 269, 270, 272, 273, 277, 283, 286, 301, 305, 307, 308, 309, 310, 334, 338, 339, 340, 341, 343, 345, 346, 348
theology of Church-as-family, 98
theology of hell, 52
theology of inculturation, 37, 45, 63, 71, 338, 339
theology of reconstruction, 251, 269, 270, 271, 272, 309, 337, 347

theology under the tree, 9
theoretical approach, 253
theoretical framework, 296
theories of culture, 14, 345
theories of hermeneutics, 21
theory of communicative action, 17, 337
the particular versus the universal, 303
the people of cows, 24
the people of grains, 24, 112
the spirit world, 105
thief, 189, 194, 195, 199, 220, 221, 229, 234, 242, 243, 290, 294, 312
third wife, 160
third world theologians, 22, 346
third world theologies, 14, 48, 336
threat of excommunication, 52
thumb-print promise, 59
tiatiy, 126, 235
tich, 132, 138, 168, 204, 243, 317
tightly bound relationship, 265
tilya, 170, 317
tilya economic system, 123
tilya system, 118, 119, 295
tilya tany, 119, 120
tilyay quarrel, 121
tïngän, 150
tïrim, 249
tisö, 168, 179, 180, 181, 190
top-down, 21
töpogh, 131, 318
Tororöt, 104, 124, 132, 136, 137, 138, 144, 147, 155, 157, 160, 167, 169, 173, 213, 245, 265, 291, 318
Töroröt, 149
totems, 127
totem system, 140
traditional African belief system, 90
traditional African community, 80
traditional African community spirit, 85
traditional African practices, 49, 262
traditional Africans, 71, 82
traditional African society, 85, 278
traditional African structures, 96
traditional African system, 86
traditional African understanding, 96
traditional authority, 52
traditional birth attendant, 159
traditional clan system, 201
traditional communitarian spirit, 283
traditional concept, 98
traditional education system, 263
traditional food, 112
traditionalists, 44, 45
traditional legal system, 190

traditional pastoralism, 116
traditional pastoralists, 116
traditional Pökot community, 156, 158
traditional Pökot idea, 298
traditional Pökot lifestyle, 189
traditional Pökot practice, 295
traditional Pökot worldview, 265
traditional practices, 39, 156, 160
traditional priest, 253
traditional religion, 48, 57, 103, 306, 347
traditional systems, 50
traditional understanding, 78, 294
traditional values, xiv, 157, 291, 294
traditional way of life, 158, 161, 196
traditional wedding ring, 249
traditional worldview, 304
tradition and modernity, 2, 29, 337
trained theologians, 309
traits of individualism, 192
triple heritage, 58
true religion, 55
truly African, 39, 1, 348
truly Christians, 39
truly Pökot, 226
tulwö, 132, 146
tum, 124, 148, 152, 181
tupa Pökot, 119, 122
tupa tilya, 119
tuyunwo, 125, 317
twins, 157, 314
two biblical sciences, xiv
types of categories, 85

uhuru, 84, 87
ujamaa, 81, 85, 86, 88, 94
Ukpong, 2, 4, 5, 8, 47, 63, 68, 69, 271, 282, 283, 289, 300, 334, 344, 346
uncircumcised girl, 159
uncivilised negro, 56
uncleanness, 151, 152, 153, 154, 155, 156, 162, 169, 182, 316
underlying danger, 41
understanding, xiv, xv, 4, 12, 20, 22, 33, 34, 35, 40, 42, 48, 72, 75, 89, 95, 134, 148, 149, 158, 162, 166, 177, 187, 197, 209, 219, 220, 228, 230, 233, 244, 257, 259, 263, 284, 294, 299, 304
understanding and assimilation, 103
understanding misunderstanding, 257, 269, 308
understanding of a person, 291
understanding of communitarianism, 289
understanding of culture, 70, 72, 75, 77
understanding of the 'church', 95
understanding of the Gospel, xv

unifying principle, 14
unintentional mistake, 154, 314
unintentional mistakes, 169
universal, 62, 209
universal characteristic, 294
universal church, 42, 48, 77, 309
universal Church, 40
universal community, 294
universal concern, 92
universal hermeneutics, 302
universalising theft as a sin, 243
universalistic character, 293
universal plane, 43
universal priesthood, 285
universal teaching, 309
universal value, 309
unremembered, 315
unsatisfied ancestors, 168
untying, 179, 180, 313

vague, 313
values of a community, 86
values of tradition, 46
value system, 176
Vatican II Council, 40, 59, 94, 255, 337
verbal sources, 34, 165, 166, 166, 183
view of culture, 38, 76
vigil dance, 124
village, 70, 71, 124, 125, 127, 167, 239, 253, 265, 315
village elders, 52
Villa-Vicencio, 270, 271, 272, 347
virtual communities, 11
visible, 265
visit, 155, 174
Visser, 57, 103, 109, 111, 112, 114, 123, 124, 126, 132, 133, 135, 137, 140, 149, 150, 161, 176, 187, 190, 191, 192, 208, 212, 218, 219, 220, 233, 263, 292, 347
voluntary association, 12
Vorverständnis, xv, 207, 318

wakristo wa kawaida, 236
ward off, 12, 35, 109, 131, 155, 156, 162, 190, 313
warrior, 139, 143, 144, 155, 199, 243, 266, 292, 315
warriors, 125, 139, 142, 143, 145, 171, 191, 199, 205, 243, 293, 299, 311, 316
water, 234, 313, 316
water points, 24
weakness of communitarianism, 288
wealth, 138, 317
wedding, 49, 156, 168, 249, 315
wedding ring, 318

well-being, 40, 134, 201, 240, 296
Weltanschauung, 83, 318
werkoy, 134, 146, 168, 180, 318
werkoyon, 132, 142, 181, 191, 205, 318
West, xv, 2, 4, 7, 63, 67, 69, 70, 71, 93, 196, 223, 280, 310, 348
western culture, 209
western epistemological order, 279
western individualism, 273
western metaphysics, 15, 275
western philosophy, 253
western scholarship, 78, 343
western spectacles, 91
western structures, 255
western theology, 93
western tradition of individualism, 208
western world, 12, 98
western worldview, 192
West Pokot, 103, 337
West Pökot, xiv, 5, 6, 9, 10, 21, 23, 25, 28, 30, 33, 34, 42, 44, 50, 101, 103, 104, 105, 106, 107, 108, 109, 111, 119, 122, 123, 126, 138, 146, 149, 157, 160, 162, 165, 167, 174, 176, 182, 183, 192, 197, 201, 203, 204, 206, 210, 211, 212, 213, 214, 215, 216, 217, 218, 219, 220, 225, 226, 230, 234, 235, 236, 241, 257, 258, 259, 260, 263, 264, 268, 287, 289, 291, 296, 297, 302, 303, 306, 335, 343, 350, 351
West Pokot County, 23, 105, 106, 107, 109, 160, 164, 189, 217, 287, 309, 319, 321, 351
West Pökot District, 105
West Pökot situation, 296
West Suk, 214
white man's religion, 57, 58
wickedness, 155, 312
widow, 98
widow inheritance, 98
wife, 49, 143, 144, 148, 151, 172, 244, 260, 313
willed community, 12
willed phenomenon, 12
will of God, 51
wirkungsgeschichtliches Bewusstsein, 269

wise sayings, 91
witch, 153, 189, 235, 316
witchcraft, 40, 150, 189, 190, 213, 234, 259
witchdoctor, 138, 311
woman, 144, 313, 314, 315, 317
women, 297, 298, 314
women empowerment, 260
women's movements, 99
word analysis, 275
word-context, 31
word-count, 31, 183, 221
word-counting, 31, 169
word in context, 167
Word of God, xiv, xvi, 2, 4, 5, 21, 23, 34, 43, 59, 62, 63, 71, 102, 196, 200, 211, 215, 218, 219, 230, 258, 268, 274, 278, 280, 290, 302, 304, 310
word-search, 31
working misunderstanding, 257, 268, 308
working relationship, 105, 301
workings of differences, 289
world, 16, 60, 343
worldview, xiii, 3, 5, 8, 11, 15, 20, 33, 34, 69, 76, 82, 86, 103, 104, 115, 159, 176, 177, 184, 207, 229, 264, 266, 267, 268, 269, 274, 277, 278, 282, 303, 318
worldviews, 3, 34, 41, 82, 177, 223, 250, 263, 265, 266, 268, 307
worst enemy, 132
wutin, 318
wutot, 168

yim, 124, 136, 137
yiyï, 118
yomöt, 136, 137
young girl, 311
young missionaries, 56

Zebra, 130
Zinkuratire, 2, 4, 61, 63, 65, 67, 68, 69, 70, 221, 228, 349
zombie, 168, 312

www.ingramcontent.com/pod-product-compliance
Lightning Source LLC
Chambersburg PA
CBHW060505300426
44112CB00017B/2557